NEW 전공영어

중등교원 임용고시 시험대비

김수아 영미문학

영미문학 최고의 선택

명/쾌/한 설명으로 영미문학이 쉬워진다!

Reading for Literature II

김수아

전공영어 영미문학

Reading for Literature II

PREFACE

김수아 영미문학
Reading for Literature II

MY DEVOTION

If I Can . . .

If I can stop one heart from breaking,

I shall live in joy;

If I can ease one life the uncertainty,

Or cool one pain,

Or help one fainting mind

Unto her position again,

I shall live in joy for life.

* Edited from Sua's favorite poem
"If I Can Stop One Heart from Breaking" by Emily Dickinson

김수아 영미문학 학습 가이드

임용시험의 특성에 맞게 학습 내용·범위·방향·전략 설정
→ 자신의 학습 스타일에 맞는 학습 방법·계획 설정
→ 출제 경향 파악 → 문제 풀이 전략과 스킬 연습
"단단한 마음가짐으로 꾸준히 학습하기!"

1. 임용시험의 특성 알기

- **시험에서 요구되는 학습 수준을 파악해야 합니다.**
  영미문학은 영역이 특정화되지 않으므로 시험에 맞는 영역과 난이도, 지문의 분량 등 학습 대상을 최대한 좁혀서 시작하지 않으면 아주 방대한 양으로 다가와 학습 방향을 잃고 포기하거나 일반영어 실력에만 의존하는 학습이 되기 쉽습니다.

- **문제를 효과적·효율적으로 풀 수 있는 전략과 스킬을 길러야 합니다.**
  시험을 위한 학습이므로 철저하게 문제를 파악하고 답을 도출해서 쓰는 응용 전략이 연계되는 학습이어야 합니다. 열심히 내용을 공부하다보면 문제도 잘 풀 것이라는 생각으로는 빠른 시간 안에 점수를 올릴 수가 없습니다.

2. 김수아 영미문학 수업 특징

임용 시험에서 영미문학 문제는 문제마다 평가하고자 하는 문학 개념이 있습니다. 또한 지문을 읽을 때는 장르적 특성에 맞게 읽어야 빠른 독해가 가능합니다. 이를 위해, 핵심 **문학 개념 이해**와 장르적 특성에 맞는 전략적 작품 읽기 (focused-reading)를 먼저 학습하도록 안내합니다.

- **영미문학 기본학습 Ⅰ : Reading For Literature Ⅰ (Poetry) (1~2월)**
  - 영문으로 된 기본서를 읽으면서 문학 이해에 필요한 주요 **개념**과 **키워드**를 학습합니다.
  - 임용시험에서 자주 다루는 **주제 중심**으로 작품을 보면서 **내용 스키마**를 형성합니다.
  - 시는 **분석**을 스스로 할 수 있도록 **분석표**(Poetry Analysis Worksheet)로 연습합니다.

김수아 영미문학
Reading for Literature II

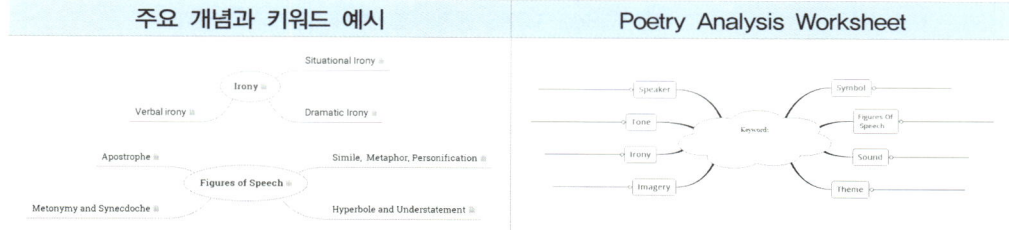

- **영미문학 기본학습 II : Reading For Literature II (Novels & Dramas) (3~4월)**
  - 영문으로 된 기본서를 읽으면서 소설과 드라마 장르적 특성 이해해 필요한 주요 **개념과 키워드**를 학습합니다.

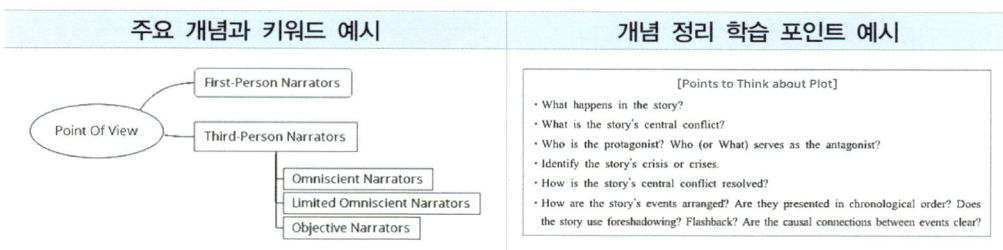

- **기출 메타 분석 및 TOKS 학습 (5~6월)**
  - 기출 문제를 과제(Task) 유형으로 분류하고 각 과제의 특징과 평가 요소를 확인하여 향후 문제풀이 학습의 범위와 방향을 제시합니다.
  - 기출 작품에서 빈번하게 다루는 주제를 파악하여 내용 스키마를 형성합니다.
  - 기출문항의 과제(Task) 유형과 각 유형에 따른 답안 구조(Organization)를 확인하여, 임용시험에서 요구하는 독해와 쓰기 수준을 확인하고 효과적인 문제풀이 전략을 도출합니다.

- **TOKS 문제풀이 (7~11월)**
  - 기출 문제와 유사한 문항 과제(Task)에 따른 답안 구성구조(Organization)와 필요한 키워드(Keyword), 대체 단어(Synonym)를 준비하는 연습으로 효율적이고 효과적인 문제풀이 전략을 내제화해 나갑니다.

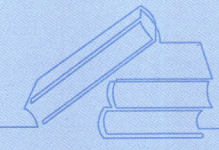

INFOMATION

- **첨삭 및 Writing Seminar**
  - 답안 첨삭을 통해 공통된 오류 유형을 분석해 수업을 통해 수정 방법을 제시합니다.
  - 효율적으로 답안을 작성할 수 있는 틀을 형성하도록 안내합니다. 풍부한 수험생 답안 예시를 통해 각 개인의 수준에 적합하고 수월한 답안 작성 방법을 개발할 수 있는 방안을 제시합니다.

3. 김수아 수업 내 것 만들기

- **기본개념부터, 기출문제, 응용문제까지 학습합니다.**
  교재에는 해당 장르에 대한 충분한 학습을 할 수 있도록 순차적으로 기본 개념학습, 형성평가, 기출문제 및 모의고사 문제 순으로 구성하였습니다. 예습, 강의, 복습, 문제 연습까지 종합적인 학습 계획을 가지고 학습하시기 바랍니다.

- **영미문학 학습 과정은 작품을 이해하는 방법론을 배우는 것입니다.**
  - 수업에서 배운 내용을 직접 적용하는 **과제를 성실히** 해야 자기 것으로 확실히 습득할 수 있습니다.
  - **상반기 첨삭 과제에는** 자신의 상태를 정확하게 처방받고 학습할 수 있도록 **적극적으로 참여**하시기 바랍니다. 내 실력을 드러내고 처방받아 고쳐보는 것이, 필요한 쓰기 수준에 도달할 수 있는 가장 빠른 방법입니다.

김수아 영미문학
Reading for Literature II

— **하반기에는 복습과제**를 활용하여 작품과 지문을 새롭게 보면서 강의에서 학습한 내용을 이해하고 다시 한 번 문제를 풀어봅니다. 복습은 학습의 정확성을 담보해줍니다.

하반기 모의고사 복습과제 예시

CONTENTS

PART 01 READING FOR NOVELS

Chapter 01 Fiction Analysis — 14

- 01 Understanding Fiction — 14
- 02 Plot — 15
- 03 Character — 18
- 04 Setting — 21
- 05 Point of View — 25
- 06 Style, Tone, Language — 34
- 07 Symbol and Allegory — 37
- 08 Theme — 42
- 09 Practices — 48

Chapter 02 Novels to Read — 57

- 01 Summary of Novels To Read — 57
- 02 Analysis of Novels To Read — 58
- 03 Novels To Read — 74
- 04 Translated Novels To Read — 160

Chapter 03 Novels in the Exam — 233

Chapter 04 Novels in the Mock-Exam by Task — 247

김수아 영미문학
Reading for Literature II

PART 02 READING FOR DRAMAS

Chapter 01 Drama Analysis ─ 300
    01 Plot ─ 301
    02 Character ─ 305
    03 Staging ─ 312
    04 Theme ─ 313

Chapter 02 Dramas to Read ─ 319
    01 Summary of Dramas To Read ─ 319
    02 Analysis of Dramas To Read ─ 320
    03 Dramas To Read ─ 332
    04 Translated Dramas To Read ─ 369

Chapter 03 Dramas in the Exam ─ 402

Chapter 04 Dramas in the Mock-Exam by Task ─ 414

PART 03 LITERARY TERMS

Chapter 01 Literary Terms ─ 444

READING FOR LITERATURE II

1. READING FOR NOVELS

1. Fiction Analysis

- Understanding Fiction
  - Narrative and Fiction
  - Kinds of Fiction
- Plot
  - Conflict
  - Stages of Plot
  - Order and Sequence
- Character
  - Round and Flat Characters
  - Dynamic and Static Characters
  - Motivation
- Setting
  - Historical Setting
  - Geographical Setting
  - Physical Setting
- Style, Tone, Language
  - Style and Tone
  - The Uses of Language
  - Formal and Informal Diction
  - Imagery
  - Figure of Speech
- Symbol, Allegory
  - Symbol
    - Literary Symbols
    - Recognizing Symbols
  - Allegory
  - Myth
- Theme
  - Interpreting Themes
  - Indentifying Themes
- Practices

2. Novels to Read
- Summary of Novels to Read
- Novels to Read
- Analysis of Novels to Read
- Translated Novels To Read

3. Novels in the Exam (2021-2014)

4. Poems in the Mock-Exam by Task
- Theme
- plot
- Figures of Speech

2. READING FOR DRAMAS

1. Drama Anlaysis

- Plot
  - Plot Structure
  - Plot and Subplot
  - Plot Developmnet
  - Foreshadowing
  - Flashbacks
- Character
  - Character's Words
  - Monologuy, Soliloquy
  - Formal and Informal Language
  - Plain and Elaborate Language
  - Tone
  - Irony
  - Character's Actions
  - Actors' Interpretation
- Staging
  - Stage Directions
  - The Uses of Staging
- Theme
  - Conficts
  - Dialogue
  - Characters
  - Staging

2. Dramas to Read
- Summary of Dramas to Read
- Dramas to Read
- Analysis of Dramas to Read
- Translated Dramas To Read

3. Dramas in the Exam

4. Poems in the Mock-Exam by Task
- Theme
- Plot

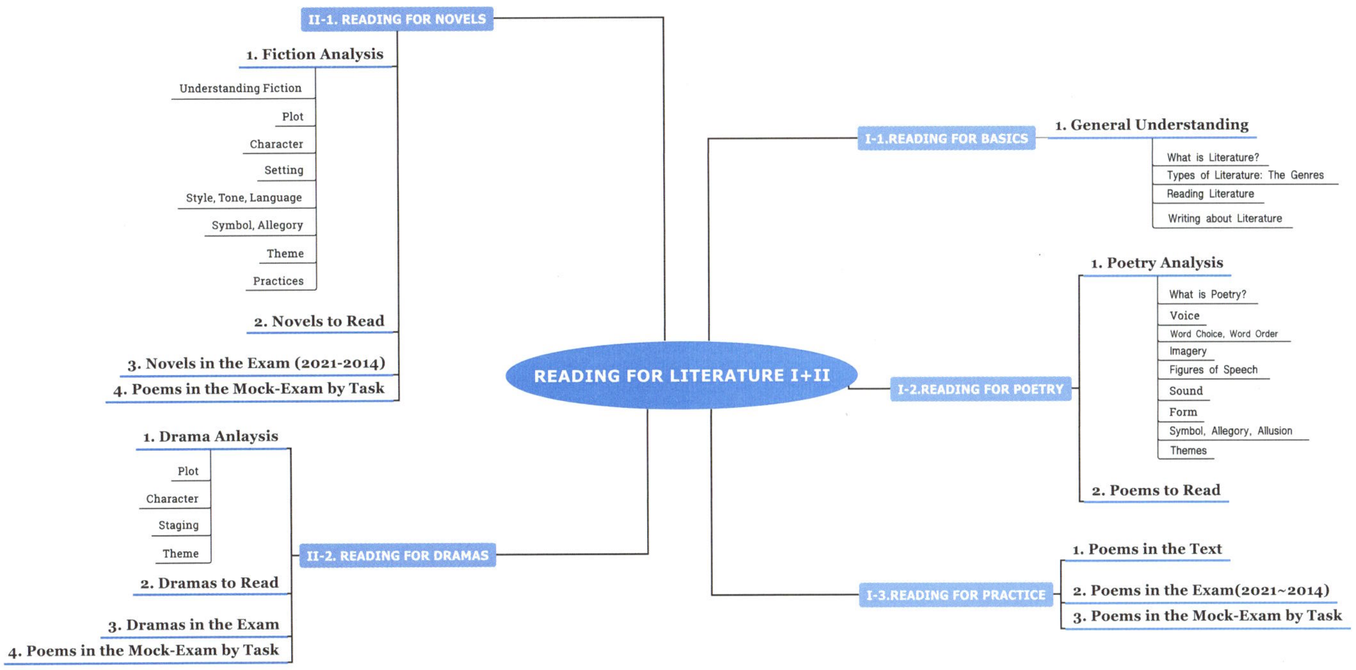

김수아 영미문학
Reading for Literature II

READING FOR LITERATURE I+II

I-1. READING FOR BASICS
- **1. General Understanding**
  - What is Literature?
  - Types of Literature: The Genres
  - Reading Literature
  - Writing about Literature

I-2. READING FOR POETRY
- **1. Poetry Analysis**
  - What is Poetry?
  - Voice
  - Word Choice, Word Order
  - Imagery
  - Figures of Speech
  - Sound
  - Form
  - Symbol, Allegory, Allusion
  - Themes
- **2. Poems to Read**

I-3. READING FOR PRACTICE
- **1. Poems in the Text**
- **2. Poems in the Exam (2021~2014)**
- **3. Poems in the Mock-Exam by Task**

II-1. READING FOR NOVELS
- **1. Fiction Analysis**
  - Understanding Fiction
  - Plot
  - Character
  - Setting
  - Style, Tone, Language
  - Symbol, Allegory
  - Theme
  - Practices
- **2. Novels to Read**
- **3. Novels in the Exam (2021-2014)**
- **4. Poems in the Mock-Exam by Task**

II-2. READING FOR DRAMAS
- **1. Drama Anlaysis**
  - Plot
  - Character
  - Staging
  - Theme
- **2. Dramas to Read**
- **3. Dramas in the Exam**
- **4. Poems in the Mock-Exam by Task**

김수아 전공영어 **영미문학**

Reading for Literature II

PART
01

Reading for Novels

Chapter 01	Fiction Analysis
Chapter 02	Novels to Read
Chapter 03	Novels in the Exam
Chapter 04	Novels in the Mock-Exam by Task

Chapter 01 Fiction Analysis

김수아 전공영어 | 영미문학 Reading for Literature II

01 Understanding Fiction

1. Narrative and Fiction

A **narrative** tells a story by presenting events in some logical or orderly way. A work of **fiction** is a narrative that originates in the imagination of the author rather than in history of fact. Certainly some fiction — historical or autobiographical fiction, for example — focuses on real people and is grounded in actual events, but the way the characters interact, what they say, and how the plot unfolds are largely the author's invention.

Even before they know how to read, most people have learned how narratives are structured. As children learn how to tell a story, they start to experiment with its form, learning the value of exaggerating, adding or deleting details, rearranging events, and bending facts. In other words, they learn how to fictionalize a narrative to achieve a desired effect. This kind of informal, personal narrative is similar to more structured literary narratives.

2. Kinds of Fiction

A **novel**, as a genre of fiction, is an invented prose narrative of considerable length and a certain complexity that deals imaginatively with human experience, usually through a connected sequence of events involving a group of persons in a specific setting. Within its broad framework, the genre of the novel has encompassed an extensive range of types and styles: picaresque, epistolary, Gothic, romantic, realist, historical — to name only some of the more important ones. A **novella** is an extended short story that shares some characteristics (for example, concentrated action) with a short story while retaining some qualities of a novel, including greater character development.

A **short story** is a work of fiction that is marked by its brevity, its relatively limited scope of temporal and character development, and its ability to achieve thematic significance in a relatively short space. While the novel is an extended piece of narrative fiction, the short story is distinguished by its relative brevity, which creates a specific set of expectations and possibilities. Unlike the novelist, the short story writer cannot devote a great deal of space to developing a highly complex plot or a large number of characters. As a result, the short story often begins close to or at the height of action and its more limited in the number of characters it can develop. Usually focusing on a single incident, the writer develops one or more characters by showing their reactions to events.

In many contemporary short stories, a character experience an epiphany, a moment of illumination in which something hidden or not understood becomes immediately clear. In other short stories, the thematic significance, or meaning, is communicated through the way in which the characters develop, or react, over time. Regardless of the specifics of its format or its theme, a short story offers readers an open window to a world that they can enter — if only briefly.

The short story "Hills Like White Elephants[1]" by Earnest Hemingway illustrates many of the characteristics of the modern short story. Although it is so brief that it might be more accurately called a short-short story, it uses its limited space to establish a setting and develop two characters.

02 Plot

Plot is more than "what happens"; it is how what happens is revealed, the way in which a story's events are arranged. Plot is shaped by causal connections — historical, social, and personal — by the interaction between characters, and by the juxtaposition of events.

1. Conflict

Reader's interest and involvement are heightened by a story's conflict, the struggle between opposing forces that emerges as the action develops. This conflict is a clash between the protagonist, a story's principal character, and an antagonist, someone or something presented in opposition to the protagonist. Sometimes the antagonist is easily identified as a villain; more often, he or she simply represents a conflicting point of view or advocates a course of action different from the one the protagonist chooses to follow. Sometimes the antagonist is not a character at all but a situation (war, poverty) or an event (a natural disaster, such as a flood or a storm) that challenges the protagonist. In other stories, the protagonist may struggle against a supernatural force, or the conflict may be internal, occurring within a character's mind. It may, for example, be a struggle between two moral choices, such as whether to stay at home and care for an aging parent or leave to make a new life. In such a case, the parent is not the antagonist; rather, the conflict occurs within the protagonist's mind.

2. Stages of Plot

A work's plot explores one or more conflicts, moving from exposition through a series of complications to a climax, and finally, to a resolution.

During a story's exposition the writer presents the basic information readers need to understand the events that follow. Typically, the exposition sets the story in motion: it establishes the scene, introduces the major characters, and perhaps suggests the major events or conflicts to come.

As the plot progresses, the story's conflict unfolds through a series of complications that eventually lead readers to the story's climax. As it develops, the story may include several crises. A crisis is a peak in the story's action, a moment of considerable tension or importance. The climax is the point of greatest tension or importance, the scheme that presents a story's decisive action or event.

The final stage of plot, the resolution, or denouement (French for "untying of the knot"), draws the action to a close and accounts for all remaining loose ends. Sometimes this resolution is achieved with the help of an intervention of some force or agent previously extraneous to the story — for example, the sudden arrival of a long-lost relative or a fortuitous inheritance, the discovery of a character's true identity, or a last-minute rescue by a character not previously introduced. Usually, however, the resolution is more plausible: all the events lead logically and convincingly (though not necessarily predictably) to the resolution. Sometimes the ending of a story is indefinite — that is, readers are not quite sure what the protagonist will do or what will happen next. This kind of resolution, although it may leave some readers feeling cheated, its advantages: it mirrors the complexity of life, where closure rarely occurs, and it can keep readers involved in the action as they try to understand the significance of the story's ending or to decide how conflicts should have been resolved.

3. Order and Sequence

A writer may present a story's events in strict chronological order, presenting each event in the sequence in which it actually takes place. More often, however, especially in relatively modern fiction, writers do not present events chronologically. Instead, they present incidents out of expected order, or in no apparent order. For example, a writer may choose to begin in the midst of things, starting with a key event and later going back in time to explain events that preceded it. Or, a writer can decide to begin a work of fiction at the end and then move back to reconstruct events that led up to the final outcome, as William Faulkner does in "A Rose for Emily[3]." Many sequences are possible as the writer manipulates events to create interest, suspense, confusion, wonder, or some other effect.

Writers who wish to depart from strict chronological order use flashbacks and foreshadowing. A flashback moves out of sequence to examine an event or situation that occurred before the time in which the story's action takes place. A character can remember an earlier event, or a story's narrator can re-create an earlier situation. For example, in Edgar Allan Poe's "The Cask of Amontillado[2]," the entire story is told as a flashback. Flashbacks are valuable because they can substitute for or supplement formal exposition by presenting background readers need to understand a story's events. One disadvantage of flashbacks is that, because they interrupt the natural flow of events, they may be intrusive or distracting. Such distractions, however, can be an advantage if the writer wishes to reveal events gradually and subtly or to obscure causal links.

Foreshadowing is the introduction early in a story of situation, events, characters, or objects that hint at things to come. Typically, a seemingly simple element—a chance remark, a natural occurrence, a trivial event—is eventually revealed to have great significance. For example, a dark cloud passing across the sky during a wedding can foreshadow future problems for the marriage. Foreshadowing allows a writer to hint provocatively at what is to come, so that readers gradually become aware of a particular detail's role in a story. Thus, foreshadowing helps readers sense what will occur and grow increasingly involved as they see the likelihood (or even the inevitability) of a particular outcome.

In addition to using conventional techniques like flashbacks and foreshadowing, writers may experiment with sequence by substantially tamper with — or even dispensing with — chronological order. (An example is the scrambled chronology of "A Rose for Emily[3]") In such instances, the experimental form enhances interest and encourages readers to become involved with the story as they work to untangle or reorder the events and determine their logical and causal connections.

Points to Think about Plot

- What happens in the story?
- What is the story's central conflict?
- Who is the protagonist? Who (or What) serves as the antagonist?
- Identify the story's crisis or crises.
- How is the story's central conflict resolved?
- How are the story's events arranged? Are they presented in chronological order? Does the story use foreshadowing? Flashback? Are the causal connections between events clear?

---

03 Character

A character is a fictional representation of a person usually (but not necessarily) a psychologically realistic depiction. Writers may develop characters through their actions, through their reactions to situations or to other characters, through their physical appearance, through their speech and gestures and expressions, and even through their names.

Generally speaking, characters' physical traits, as well as their feelings and beliefs, are communicated to readers in two ways. First, readers can be told about characters. Third-person narrators can provide information about what characters are doing, saying, and thinking; what experiences they have had; what they look like; how they are dressed; and so on. Sometimes they also offer analysis of and judgments about a character's behavior or motivation. Similarly, first-person narrators can tell us about themselves or about other characters. Thus, Sammy in John Updike's "A&P[4]" tells readers what he thinks about his job and about the girls who come into the supermarket where he works. He also tells us what various characters look like and describes their actions, attitudes, speech, and gestures.

Alternatively, a character's personality traits and motivation may be revealed through actions, dialogue, or thoughts. For instance, Sammy's vivid fantasies and his disapproval of his customers' lives suggest to readers that he is something of a nonconformist; however, Sammy himself does not actually tell us this.

1. Round and Flat Characters

English novelist E. M. Forster classifies characters as either **round** (well developed, closely involved in and responsive to the action) or **flat** (barely developed or stereotypical). To a large extent, these categories are still useful. In an effective story, the major characters are usually complex and fully developed; if they are not, readers do not care what happens to them. Sometimes, readers are encouraged to become involved with the characters, even to identify with them, and this empathy is possible only when we know something about the characters — their strengths and weakness, their likes and dislikes.

Unlike major characters, minor characters are frequently not well developed. Often they are flat, perhaps acting as *foils* for the protagonist. A **foil** is a supporting character whose role in the story is to highlight a major character by presenting a contrast with him or her. For instance, in "A&P[4]," Stokesie, another young checkout clerk, is a foil for Sammy. Because he is a little older than Sammy and seems to have none of Sammy's imagination, restlessness, or nonconformity, Stokesie suggests what Sammy might become if he were to continue to work at the A&P. Some **flat characters** are stock characters, easily identifiable types who behave so predictably that readers can readily recognize them. The kindly old priest, the tough young bully, the ruthless business executive, and the reckless adventurer are all stock characters. Some flat characters can even be **caricatures**, characterized by a single dominant trait, such as miserliness, or even by one physical trait, such as nearsightedness.

2. Dynamic and Static Characters

Characters may also be classified as either *dynamic* or *static*. A **dynamic character** grows and changes in the course of a story, developing as he or she reacts to events and to other characters. In "A&P[4]," for instance, Sammy's decision to speak out in defense of the girls — as well as the events that lead him to do so — changes him. His view of the world has changed at the end of the story, and as a result his position in the world will change too. A static character may face the same challenges a dynamic character might face but will remain essentially unchanged: a regardless of the nature of the story's conflict. In the fairy tale "Cinderella", for example, the title character is as sweet and good-natured at the end of the story — despite her mistreatment by her family — as she is at the beginning. Her situation may have changed, but her character has not.

Whereas round characters tend to be dynamic, flat characters tend to be static. But even a very complex, well-developed major character may be static; sometimes, in fact, the point of a story may hinge on a character's inability to change. A familiar example is the title character in William Faulkner's "A Rose for Emily[3]," who lives a wasted, empty life, at least in part because she is unwilling or unable to accept that the world around her and the people in it have changed.

A story's minor characters are often static; their growth is not usually relevant to the story's development. Moreover, we usually do not learn enough about a minor character's traits, thoughts, actions, or motivation to determine whether the character changes significantly.

3. Motivation

Because round characters are complex, they are not always easy to understand. They may act unpredictably, just as real people do. They wrestle with decisions, resist or succumb to temptation, make mistakes, ask questions, search for answers, hope and dream, rejoice and despair. What is important is not whether we approve of a character's actions but whether those actions are *plausible* — whether the actions make sense in light of what we know about the character. We need to see a character's **motivation** — the reasons behind his or her behavior — we will not believe or accept that behavior. For instance, given Sammy's age, his dissatisfaction with his job, and his desire to impress the young woman he calls Queenie, the decision he makes at the end of the story is perfectly plausible. Without having established his motivation, Updike could not have expected readers to accept Sammy's actions.

Of course, even when readers get to know a character, they still are not able to predict how a complex, round character will behave in given situation; only a flat character is predictable. The tension that develops as readers wait to see how a character will act or react, and thus how a story's conflict will be resolved, is what holds readers' interest and keeps them involved as a story's action unfolds.

> **Points to Think about Character**
>
> - Who is the protagonist? Who (or What) is the antagonist? Who are the other major characters?
> - Who are the minor characters? What roles do they play in the story?
> - What do the major characters look like? Is their physical appearance important?
> - What are the major characters' most noticeable personality traits?
> - What are the major characters' likes and dislikes? Their strengths and weaknesses?
> - What are we told about the major characters' backgrounds and prior experiences? What can we infer?
> - Are the characters round or flat? Are the characters dynamic or static?
> - Do the characters act in a way that is consistent with how readers expect them to act?

04 Setting

The **setting** of a work of fiction establishes its historical, geographical, and physical context. *Where* a work is set — on a tropical island, in a dungeon, at a crowded part, in the woods — influences our reactions to the story's events and characters. *When* a work takes place — during the French Revolution, during the Vietnam War, today, or in the future — is equally important. Setting, however, is more than just the approximate time and place in which a work is set; setting also encompasses a wide variety of physical and cultural elements.

Clearly, setting is more important in some works than in others. In some stories, no particular time or place is specified or even suggested, perhaps because the writer does not consider a specific setting to be important or because the writer wishes the story's events to seem timeless and universal. This is the case in Nathaniel Hawthorne's "Young Goodman Brown[13]", which is set in a forest in an unidentified location. In other stories, a writer may provide only minimal information about setting, telling readers little more than where and when the action takes place. Sometimes, however, a particular setting may be vital to the story, perhaps influencing characters' behavior.

1. Historical Setting

A particular historical period, and the events and customs associated with it, can be vital to a story; therefore, some knowledge of the period is useful (or even essential) to readers who wish to understand the story fully. The historical context establishes a story's social, cultural, economic, and political environment. Knowing, for instance, that Charlotte Perkins Gilman's "The Yellow Wallpaper[5]" was written in the late nineteenth century, when doctors treated women as delicate and dependent creatures, helps to explain the narrator's emotional state. Likewise, it may be important to know that a story is set during a particularly volatile (or static) political era, during a time of permissive (or repressive attitudes toward sex, during a war, or during a period of economic prosperity or recession. Any one of these factors may help to explain characters' actions and motivation. Historical events or cultural norms may, for instance, limit or expand a character's options, and our knowledge of history may reveal to us a character's incompatibility with his or her milieu.

2. Geographical Setting

In addition to knowing *when* a work takes place, readers need to know *where* it takes place. Knowing whether a story is set in can help to explain anything from why language and customs are unfamiliar to us to why characters act in ways we find improbable. For example, knowing that William Faulkner's "A Rose for Emily[3]" is set in the post-Civil War American South helps to explain why the townspeople are so chivalrously protective of Miss Emily.

The size of the town or city in which a story takes place may also be important. In a small town, for example, a character's problems are more likely to be subject to intense scrutiny by other characters, as they are in stories of small-town life such as those in Sherwood Anderson's *Winesburg, Ohio*. In a large city, characters may be more likely to be isolated and anonymous. Of course, a story may not have a recognizable geographical setting: its location may not be specified, or it may be set in a fantasy world. Choosing unusual settings may free writers from the constraints placed on them by familiar environments, allowing them to experiment with situations and characters, unaffected by readers' expectations or associations with familiar settings.

3. Physical Setting

Physical setting can clearly influences a story's mood as well as its development. For example, *time of day* can be important. The gruesome murder described in Edgar Allan Poe's "The Cask of Amontillado[2]" takes place in an appropriate setting: not just underground but in the darkness of night. Conversely, the horrifying events of Shirley Jackson's "The Lottery[12]" takes place in broad daylight, contrasting dramatically with the darkness of the society that permits — and even participates in — such events. Many stories, of course, move through several time periods as the action unfolds, and changes in time may also be important. For instance, the approach of evening, or of dawn, can signal the end of a crisis in the plot.

Whether a story is set primarily inside or out-of-doors may also be significant. The characters may be physically constrained by a closed-in setting or liberated by an expansive landscape. Some interior settings may be psychologically limiting. For instance, the narrator in "The Yellow Wallpaper[5]" feels suffocated by her room, whose ugly wallpaper comes to haunt her. In many of Poe's stories, the central character is trapped, physically or psychologically, in a confined, suffocating space. In other stories, an interior setting may have a symbolic function. For instance, in "A Rose for Emily[3]," the house is for Miss Emily a symbol of the South's past glory as well as a refuge, a fortress, and a hiding place. Similarly, a building or house may represent society, with its rules, norms, and limitations. In John Updike's "A&P[4]," for instance, the supermarket establishes social as well as physical limits.

Conversely, an outdoor setting can free a character from social norms of behavior, as it does for Ernest Hemingway's Nick Adams, a war veteran who, in "Big Tow-Hearted River (1925)," finds order, comfort, and peace only when he is away from civilization. An outdoor setting can also expose characters to physical dangers, such as untamed wilderness, uncharted seas, and frighteningly empty open spaces.

Weather can be another important aspect of setting. A storm can threaten a character's life or just make the character — and readers — *think* danger is present, distracting us from other, more subtle threats. Extreme weather conditions can make characters act irrationally or uncharacteristically, as in Kate Chopin's "The Storm[10]", where a storm provides the story's complication and determines the character's actions. In numerous stories set in hostile landscapes, where extremes of heat and cold influence the action, weather may serve as a test for characters, as it does in Jack London's "To Build a Fire (1908)," in which the main character struggles unsuccessfully against the brutally cold, hostile environment of the Yukon.

Points to Think about Setting

- Is the setting specified or unidentified? Is it fully described or only suggested?
- Is the setting just background, or is it a key force in the story?
- In what time period does the story take place? How can you tell? What social, political, or economic characteristics of the historical period might influence the story?
- At what time of day is the story set? Is time important to the development of the story?
- What role do weather conditions play in the story?
- What kind of atmosphere or mood does the setting create?
- How does the setting influence the characters? Does it affect (or reflect) their emotional state?
- How does the setting influence the story's plot? Does it cause characters to act?

05 Point of View

All stories are told by a **narrator**, and one of the first choices writers make is who tells the story. This choice determines the story's **point of view** — the vantage point from which events are presented. The implications of this choice are far-reaching. The perspective from which a story is told determines what details are included in the story and how they are arranged — in short, the plot. In addition, the perspective of the narrator affects the story's style, language, and themes.

The narrator of a work of fiction is not the same as the writer — even when a writer uses the first-person I. Writers create narrators to tell their stories. Often the personalities and opinions of narrators are far different from those of the author. The term **persona** — which literally means "mask" — is used for such narrators. By assuming this mask, a writer expands the creative possibilities of a work.

When deciding on a point of view for a work of fiction, a writer can choose to tell the story either in the *first person* or in the *third person*.

1. First-Person Narrators

Sometimes the narrator is a character who uses the first person (*I* or sometimes *we*) to tell the story. Often this narrator is a major character — Sammy in John Updike's "A&P"[4] and the boy in James Joyce's "Araby"[6], for example — who tells his or her own story and is the focus of that story. Sometimes, however, a first-person narrator tells a story that is primarily about someone else. Such a narrator may be a **minor character** who plays a relatively small part in the story or simply an **observer** who reports events experienced or related by others. The narrator of William Faulkner's "A Rose for Emily"[3], for example, is an unidentified witness to the story's events. By using *we* instead of *I*, this narrator speaks on behalf of all the town's residents, expressing their shared views of their neighbor, Emily Grierson.

Writers gain a number of advantages when they use first-person narrators. First, they are able to present incidents convincingly. Readers are more willing to accept a statement like "My sister changed a lot after that day" than they are to accept the impersonal observations of a third-person narrator. The first-person narrator also simplifies a writer's task of selecting details. Only the events and details that the narrator could actually have seen or experienced can be introduced into the story.

Another major advantage of first-person narrators is that their restricted view can create **irony** — a discrepancy between what is said and what readers believe to be true. Irony may be dramatic, situational, or verbal. **Dramatic irony** occurs when a narrator (or character) perceives less than readers do; **situational irony** occurs when what happens is at odds with what readers are led to expect; **verbal irony** occurs when the narrator says one thing but actually means another.

"Gryphon[7]," by Charles Baxter, illustrates all three kinds of irony. Baxter creates **dramatic irony** when he has his main character see less than readers do. For example, at the end of the story, the young boy does not yet realize what readers already know — that he has learned more from Miss Ferenczi's way of teaching than from Mr. Hibler's. The setting of the story — a conventional school — create **situational irony** because it contrasts with the unexpected events that unfold there. In addition, many of the narrator's comments create **verbal irony** because they mean something different from what they seem to mean. At the end of the story, for example, after the substitute, Miss Ferenczi, has been fired, the narrator relates another teacher's comment that life will now return to "normal" and that their regular teacher will soon return to test them on their "knowledge." This comment is ironic in light of all Miss Ferenczi has done to redefine the narrator's ideas about "normal" education and about "knowledge."

(1) Unreliable Narrators

Sometimes first-person narrators are self-serving, mistaken, confused, unstable, or even insane. These **unreliable narrators**, whether intentionally or unintentionally, misrepresent events and misdirect readers. In Edgar Allan Poe's "The Cask of Amontillado[2]," for example, the narrator, Montresor, tells his story to justify a crime he committed fifty years before. Montresor's version of what happened is not accurate, and perceptive readers know it: his obvious self-deception, his sadistic manipulation of Fortunato, his detached description of the cold-blooded murder, and his lack of remorse lead readers to question his sanity and, therefore, to distrust his version of events. This distrust creates an ironic distance between readers and narrator.

The narrator of Charlotte Perkins Gilman's "The Yellow Wallpaper[5]" is also an unreliable narrator. Suffering from "nervous depression," she unintentionally distorts the facts when she says that the shapes in the wallpaper of her bedroom are changing and moving. Moreover, she does not realize what is wrong with her or why, or how her husband's "good intentions" are hurting her. Readers, however, see the disparity between the narrator's interpretation of events and their own, and this irony enriches their understanding of the story.

Keep in mind that all first-person narrators are, in a sense, unreliable because they present a situation as only one person sees it. When you read, you should look for discrepancies between a narrator's view of events and your own. Discovering that a story has an unreliable narrator enables you not only to question the accuracy of the narrative but also to recognize the irony in the narrator's version of events. By doing so, you gain insight into the story and learn something about the writer's purpose.

2. Third-Person Narrators

Sometimes a writer uses the **third person** (*he*, *she*, *they*) to tell the story from the point of view of a narrator who is not also a character. Third-person narrators fall in three categories: **omniscient, limited omniscient**, and **objective**.

(1) Omniscient Narrators

Some third-person narrators are **omniscient** (all-knowing) narrators, moving at will from one character's mind to another. One advantage of omniscient narrators is that they have none of the naïveté, dishonesty, gullibility, or mental instability that can characterize first-person narrators. In addition, because omniscient narrators are not characters in the story, their perception is not limited to what any one character can observe or comprehend. As a result, they can present a more inclusive view of events and characters than first-person narrators can. Omniscient narrators can also convey their attitude toward their subject matter.

Occasionally, omniscient narrators move not only in and out of the minds of the characters but also in and out of a **persona** (representing the voice of the author) that speaks directly to readers. It permitted writers to present themselves as masters of artifice, able to know and control all aspects of experience.

(2) Limited Omniscient Narrators

Third-person narrators can have **limited omniscience**, focusing on only what a single character experiences. In other words, events are limited to one character's perspective, and nothing is revealed that the character does not see, hear, feel, or think. Limited omniscient narrators, like all third-person narrators, have certain advantages over first-person narrators. When a writer uses a first-person narrator, the narrator's personality and speech color the story, creating a personal or even an idiosyncratic narrative. Also, the first-person narrator's character flaws or lack of knowledge may limit his or her awareness of the significance of events. Limited omniscient narrators are more flexible: they take readers into a particular character's mind just as a first-person narrator does, but without the first-person narrator's subjectivity, self-deception, or naïveté.

In the following example from Ann Tyler's 1984 story "Teenage Wasteland[8]," the limited omniscient narrator presents the story from the point of view of a single character, Daisy:

> Daisy and Matt sat silent, shocked. Matt rubbed his forehead with his fingertips. Imagine, Daisy thought, how they must look to Mr. Lanham: an overweight housewife in a cotton dress and too-tall, too-thin insurance agent in a baggy, frayed suit. Failures, both of them — the kind of people who are always hurrying to catch up, missing the point of things that everyone else grasps at once. She wished she'd worn nylons instead of knee socks.
>
> (데이지와 매트는 충격으로 조용히 앉아있었다. 매트는 손가락으로 이마를 문질렀다. 데이지는 생각했다. 상상해보시라, 란햄씨한테 그들이 어떻게 보이겠는지. 면 옷을 입은 뚱뚱한 아줌마와 아주 크고 마른 체격에 늘어지고 헤어진 양복을 입은 보험판매원이라. 둘 다 다른 사람들은 다 알아듣는 이야기도 초점을 못잡고 이해하려고 허덕되는 그런 사람들이다. 데이지는 무릎까지 오는 양말 대신 나일론 스타킹을 신었으면 좋았을 걸 했다.)

Here the point of view gives readers the impression that they are standing off the side watching Daisy and her husband Matt. However, at the same time we have the advantage of this objective view, we are also able to see into the mind of one character.

(3) Objective Narrators

Third-person narrators who tell a story from an *objective* (or *dramatic*) point of view remain entirely outside the characters' mind. With **objective narrators**, events unfold the way they would in a play or a movie: narrators tell the story only by presenting dialogue and recounting events; they do not reveal he characters' (or their own) thoughts or attitudes. Thus, they allow readers to interpret the actions of the characters without any inference. Earnest Hemingway uses the objective point of view in his short story "A Clean, Well-Lighted Place" (1933):

> The waiter took the brandy bottle and another saucer from the counter inside the café and marched out to the old man's table. He put down the saucer and poured the glass full of brandy.
>
> "You should have killed yourself last week," he said to the deaf man. The old man motioned with his finger. "A little more," he said. The waiter poured on into the glass so that the brandy slopped over and ran down the stem into the top saucer of the pile. "Thank you," the old man said. The waiter took the bottle back inside the café. He sat down at the table with his colleague again.
>
> (그 웨이터가 카페 안 카운터에서 브랜디 한 병과 브랜디 잔을 가지고 노인의 테이블로 척척 걸어갔다. 그는 잔을 내려놓고 브랜디를 잔에 꽉 채우며 따랐다.
> "당신은 저번 주에 죽었어야 했어요." 웨이터는 귀머거리 노인에게 말했다. 노인은 손가락을 까딱했다. "조금만 더." 노인이 말했다. 웨이터는 브랜디가 넘쳐서 잔 기둥까지 흘러내리도록 계속해서 술을 따랐다. "고맙소." 노인이 말했다. 웨이터는 병을 들고 카페 안으로 들어갔다. 그 웨이터는 다른 웨이터와 다시 테이블에 앉았다.)

The story's narrator is distant, seemingly emotionless, and this perspective is consistent with the author's purpose: for Hemingway, the attitude of the narrator reflects the stunned, almost anesthetized condition of people in the post — World War I world.

3. Selecting an Appropriate Point of View

Writers of short stories often maintain a consistent point of view. The main criterion writers use when they decide on a point of view is how the distance they maintain from their material will affect their narrative. The passages that follow illustrate the options writers have.

(1) Limited Omniscient Point of View

In the following passage from the short story "Doe Season[14]," David Michael Kaplan uses a third-person limited omniscient narrator to tell the story of Andy, a nine-year-old girl who is going hunting with her father for the first time.

They were always the same woods, she thought sleepily as they drove through the early morning darkness — deep and immense, covered with yesterday's snowfall, which had frozen overnight. They were the same woods that lay behind her house, *and they stretch all the way to here, she thought, for miles and miles, longer than I could walk in a day, or a week even, but they are still the same woods.* The thought made her feel good: it was like thinking of God; it was like thinking of the space between here and the moon; it was like thinking of all the foreign countries from here geography book where even now, Andy knew, people were going to bed, while they — she and her father and Charlie Spoon and Mac, Charlie's eleven-year-old son — were driving deeper into the Pennsylvania countryside, to go hunting.

(그녀는 어둑한 이른 아침 달리는 차 안에서 졸며 생각했다. 언제나 똑같은 숲들이었다. — 깊고 웅장하며 어제 내린 눈이 밤새 얼어 덮인. 집 뒤로도 똑같은 숲들이었다. *그 숲들이 여기까지 뻗어 있는 거야. 그녀는 생각했다. 내가 하루나, 일주일 내에 걸어서 갈 수 없는 수 마일을 왔는데도 여전히 똑같은 숲이네.* 그 생각을 하니 기분이 좋았다. 하나님을 생각할 때처럼, 여기서부터 달까지의 공간을 생각할 때처럼, 여기 지도에 있는 외국의 다른 나라들, 앤디가 알기로는 이렇게 그녀나 그녀의 아빠, 찰리 스푼이나 맥과 찰리의 11살된 아들이 펜실베니아 외곽으로 사냥을 위해 차를 타고 더 깊이 들어가고 있는 동안에 거기는 잠자고 있을 시간인 그런 나라들을 생각하는 것처럼 그랬다.)

They had risen long before dawn. Her mother, yawing and not trying to hide her sleepiness, cooked them eggs and French toast. Her father smoked a cigarette and flicked ashes into his saucer while Andy listened, wondering *Why doesn't he come?* and *Won't he ever come?* until at last a car pulled into the graveled drive and honked. "That will be Charlie Spoon," her father said; he always said "Charlie Spoon," even though his real name was Spreun, because Charlie was, in a sense, shaped like a spoon, with a large head and a narrow waist and chest.

(동이 트기 훨씬 전에 그들은 일어났다. 그녀의 엄마는 졸음을 전혀 감출 기색 없이 하품을 하면서 달걀 요리를 하고 토스트를 구웠다. 그녀의 아빠는 담배를 비우고는 재를 자기 컵받침에 털었다. 앤디는 들으면서 의구심이 나, *그가 왜 안오지? 그리고 "그가 안오려나?"* 하고 있는데, 차가 한 대 자갈길로 들어와 서더니 경적을 울렸다. "찰리 스푼일 게야." 아빠가 말했다. 그의 이름이 스프런인데도 아빠는 항상 "찰리 스푼"이라고 말했다. 왜냐하면 찰리는 머리가 크고 허리와 가슴이 좁아 어떻게 보면 꼭 스푼처럼 생겼기 때문이었다.)

Here the limited omniscient point of view has the advantage of allowing the narrator to focus on the thoughts, fears, and reactions of the child while at the same time giving readers information about Andy that she herself is too immature or unsophisticated to know. Rather than simply presenting the thoughts of the child (represented in the story by italics), the third-person narrator makes connections between ideas and displays a level of language and a degree of insight that readers would not accept from Andy as a first-person narrator. In addition, the limited omniscient perspective enables the narrator to maintain some distance.

(2) First-Person Point of View (Child)

Consider how different the passage would be if it were narrated by nine-year-old Andy.

"I like the woods," I thought. "They're big and scary. I wonder if they're the same woods that are behind my house. They go on for miles. They're bigger than I could walk in a day, or a week even." It was neat to think that while we were driving into the woods people were going to bed in other countries.

When I woke up this morning, I couldn't wait to go hunting. My mother was cooking breakfast, but all I could think of was, "When will he come?" and "Won't he ever come?" Finally, I heard a car honk. "That will be Charlie Spoon," my father said. I think he called him "Charlie Spoon" because he thought Charlie was shaped like a big spoon.

As a first-person narrator, nine-year-old Andy must have the voice of a child; moreover, she is restricted to only those observations that a nine-year-old could reasonably make. Because of these limitations, the passage lacks the level of vocabulary, syntax, and insight necessary to develop the central character and the themes of the story. This point of view could succeed only if Andy's words established an ironic contrast between her naïve sensibility and the reality of the situation.

(3) Omniscient Point of View

Kaplan could also have used an omniscient narrator to tell his story. In this case, the narrator would be free to reveal and comment not only on Andy's thoughts but also on those of her father, and possibly even on the thoughts of her mother and Charlie Spoon.

In the following passage, the omniscient narrator interprets the behavior of the characters and tells what each one is thinking.

> They were always the same woods, she thought sleepily as they drove through the early morning darkness — deep and immense, covered with yesterday's snowfall, which had frozen overnight. They were the same woods that lay behind her house, and they stretch all the way to here, she thought, for miles and miles, longer than I could walk in a day, or a week even, but they are still the same woods.
>
> They had risen before dawn. Her mother, yawing and not trying to hide her sleepiness, cooked them eggs and French toast. She looked at her husband and her daughter and wondered if she was doing the right thing by allowing them to go hunting together. "After all," she thoughts, "he's not the most careful person. Will he watch her? Make sure that no harm comes to her?"
>
> The father smoked a cigarette and flicked ashes into his saucer. He was listening to the sounds of the early morning. "I know everything will be all right," he thought. "It's about time Andy went hunting. When I was her age. . . ." Andy listened, wondering Why doesn't he come? and Won't he ever come? until at last a car pulled into the graveled drive and honked. Suddenly the father cocked his head and said, "That will be Charlie Spoon."
>
> Andy thought it was funny that her father called "Charlie Spoon" even though his real name was Spreun, because Charlie was, in a sense, shaped like a spoon, with a large head and a narrow waist and chest.

Certainly this point of view has its advantages; for example, the wide scope of this perspective provides a great deal of information about the characters. However, the use of an omniscient point of view deprives the story of its focus on Andy.

(4) Objective Point of View

Finally, Kaplan could have used an objective narrator. This point of view would eliminate all interpretation by the narrator and force readers to make judgments solely on the basis of what the characters say and do.

> Andy sat sleepily staring into her cereal. She played with the dry flakes of bran as

they floated in the surface of the milk.

Andy's mother, yawning, cooked them eggs and French toast. She looked at her husband and her daughter, paused for a second, and then went about what she was doing.

Andy's father smoked a cigarette and flicked ashes into his saucer. He looked out the window and said, "I wonder where Charlie Spoon is?"

Andy squirmed restlessly and repeatedly looked up at the clock that hung above the stove.

The disadvantage of this point of view is that it creates a great deal of distance between the characters and the readers. Instead of gaining the intimate knowledge of Andy that the limited omniscient point of view provides — knowledge even greater than she herself has — readers must infer what she thinks and feels without any help from the narrator.

Summary about an Appropriate Point of View

First-Person Narrators (use I or WE)

- *Major character telling his or her own story*

   "Every morning I lay on the floor in the front parlour watching her door." (James Joyce, "Araby[6]")

- *Minor character as witness*

   "And so she died. . . . We did not even know she was sick; we had long since given up trying to get information. . . ." (William Faulkner, "A Rose for Emily[3].")

Third-Person Narrators (use HE, SHE and THEY)

- *Omniscient — able to move at will from character to character and comment about them*

   "Although they lived in style, they felt always an anxiety in the house. There was never enough money." (D.H. Lawrence, "The Rocking-Horse Winner[15]")

- *Limited Omniscient — restricts focus to a single character*

   "The wagon went on. He did not know where they were going." (William Faulkner, "Barn Burning[11]")

- *Objective (Dramatic) — simply reports the dialogue and the actions of characters*

   "You'll be drunk,' the waiter said. The old man looked at him. The waiter went away." (Earnest Hemingway, "A Clean, Well-Lighted Place")

06 Style, Tone, Language

One of the qualities that gives a work of literature its individuality is its **style**, the way in which a writer uses language, selecting and arranging words to say what he or she wants to say. Style encompasses elements such as word choice; syntax; sentence length and structure; and the presence, frequency, and prominence of imagery and figures of speech.

Closely related to style is **tone**, the attitude of the narrator or author of a work toward the subject matter, characters, or audience. Word choice and sentence structure help to create a work's tone, which may be intimate or distant, bitter or affectionate, straightforward or cautious, supportive or critical, respectful or condescending. Also, tone may also be ironic.

1. The Uses of Language

Language offers almost limitless possibilities to a writer. Creative use of language (such as unusual word choice, word order, or sentence structure) can enrich a story and add to its overall effect. Sometimes, in fact, a writer's use of language can expand a story's possibilities through its very inventiveness. For example, James Joyce's innovative **stream-of-consciousness** style mimics thought, allowing ideas to run into one another as random associations are made so that readers may follow and participate in the thought processes of the narrator. When used as a term in literature, stream of consciousness is a narrative form in which the author writes in a way that mimics or parallels a character's internal thoughts. Sometimes this device is also called "internal monologue," and often the style incorporates the natural chaos of thoughts and feelings that occur in any of our minds at any given time. Just as happens in real life, stream-of-consciousness narratives often lack associative leaps and are characterized by an absence of regular punctuation. Here is a stream-of-consciousness passage from Joyce's experimental 1922 novel *Ulysses*.

> Gibraltar as a girl where I was a Flower of the mountain yes when I put the rose in my hair like the Andalusian girls used *or shall I wear a red* yes and how he kissed me under the Moorish wall and I thought well as well him as another and then I asked him with my eyes to ask again yes and then he asked me would I yes to say

yes my mountain flower and first I put my arms around him yes and drew him down to me so he could feel my breasts all perfume yes and his heart was going like mad and yes I said yes I will Yes.

(내가 소녀로서 야산의 꽃이었던 지브롤터 그렇지 내가 저 안달루시아 소녀들이 항상 그러하듯 머리에다 장미를 꽂았을 때 혹은 *난 붉은 걸로 달까봐* 그렇지 그리고 그이는 내게 무어의 성벽 밑에서 어떻게 키스했던가 그리고 나는 그이를 당연 다른 사람만큼 훌륭하다고 생각했지 그런 다음 나는 그이에게로 눈으로 요구했지 다시 한 번 내게 요구하도록 말이야 그래 그러자 그이는 내게 요구했어 내가 그러세요 라고 말하겠는가고 그래요 나의 야산의 꽃이여 그리고 처음으로 나는 나의 팔로 그이의 몸을 감았지 그렇지 그리고 그이를 나에게 끌어당겼어 그이가 온갖 향내를 풍기는 나의 앞가슴을 감촉 할 수 있도록 그래 그러자 그이의 심장이 미칠 듯이 팔딱거렸어 그리하여 그렇지 나는 그러세요 하고 말했어 그렇게 하겠어요 네.)

In it, the character Molly is seemingly reflecting on accepting a marriage proposal from Bloom, her husband. The lack of punctuation or stops and starts is characteristic both of Joyce's writing style and stream of consciousness in general. The **repetition** of the word "yes" is the connective tissue between all of Molly's disparate thoughts.

2. Figure of Speech

Figures of speech — such as *similes*, *metaphors*, and *personifications* — can enrich a story, subtly revealing information about characters and themes.

By using **metaphors** and **similes** — figures of speech that compare two dissimilar items — writers can indicate a particular attitude toward characters and events. Thus, Flannery O'Connor's many grotesque similes in "A Good Man Is Hard to Find" help to dehumanize her characters; the children's mother, for instance, has a face "as broad and innocent as a cabbage." In Tillie Olsen's "I Stand Here Ironing[9]", an extended metaphor in which a mother compares her daughter to a dress waiting to be ironed expresses the mother's attitude toward her child, effectively suggesting to readers the daughter's vulnerability. Similes and metaphors are used throughout in Kate Chopin's "The Storm[10]." In a scene of sexual awakening, Calixta's skin is "like a cream lily," her passion is "like a white flame," and her mouth is a "fountain of delight"; these figures of speech add a lushness and sensuality to the story.

Personification — a figure of speech, closely related to metaphor, that endows inanimate objects or abstract ideas with life or with human characteristics — is used in "Araby[6]," where houses, "conscious of decent lives within them, gazed at one another with brown imperturbable faces." This use of figurative language expands readers' vision of the story's setting and gives a dreamlike quality to the passage. (Other figures of speech, such as **hyperbole** and **understatement**, can also enrich works of fiction.)

Allusions — references to familiar historical, cultural, literary, or biblical texts, figures, or events — may also expand readers' understanding and appreciation of a work. An allusion widens a work's context by bringing it into the context of a related subject or idea. For instance, in Charles Baxter's short story "Gryphon[7]," the narrator's allusions to Pinocchio and Betty Crocker enable readers who recognize the references to gain a deeper understanding of what a central character is really like.

> "Hi, Mom," I said, hopping around the playpen to kiss her. "Guess what?"
>
> "I have no idea."
>
> "We had this substitute today, Miss Ferenczi, and I'd never seen her before, and she had all these stories and ideas and stuff."
>
> "Well. That's good." My mother looked out the window in front of the sink, her eyes on the pine woods west of our houses. That time of the afternoon her skin always looked so white to me. Strangers always said my mother looked like Betty Crocker, framed by the giant spoon on the side of the Bisquick box. "Listen, Tommy," she said. "Would you please go upstairs and pick your clothes off the floor in the bathroom, and then go outside to the shed and put the shovel and ax away that your father left outside this morning?
>
> "She said that six times eleven was sometimes sixty-eight!" I said. "And she said she once saw a monster that was half lion and half bird." I waited. "In Egypt."

Points to Think about Style, Tone, and Language

- Does the writer make any unusual creative use of word choice, word order, or sentence structure?
- Is the story's tone intimate? Distant? Ironic? How does the tone advance the writer's purpose?
- Does the story use simile and metaphor? Personification? What is the effect of these figures of speech?
- Do figures of speech reinforce the story's theme? Reveal information about characters?
- Does the story make any historical, literary, or biblical allusions? What do these allusions contribute to the story?

07 Symbol and Allegory

1. Symbol

A **symbol** is a person, object, action, place, or event that, in addition to its literal meaning, suggests a more complex meaning or range of meanings. **Universal** or **archetypal symbols**, such as the Old Man, the Mother, or the Grim Reaper, are so much a part of human experience that they suggest the same thing to most people. **Conventional symbols** are also likely to suggest the same thing to most people (a rose suggests love, a skull and crossbones denotes poison), provided the people have common cultural and social assumptions. Such symbols are often used as a kind of shorthand in films, popular literature, and advertising, where they encourage predictable responses.

A conventional symbol such as the stars and stripes of the American flags can evoke powerful feelings of pride and patriotism in a group of people who share a culture, just as the maple leaf (Canada) and the Union Jack (England) can. Symbols used in works of literature can function in much the same way, enabling writers to convey particular emotions or messages with a high degree of predictability. Thus, spring can be expected to suggest rebirth and promise; autumn, declining years and powers; summer, youth and beauty. Because a writer expects a dark forest to evoke fear, or a rainbow to communicate hope, he or she can be quite confident in using such images to convey a particular idea or mood (provided the audience shares the writer's frame of reference).

Many symbols, however, suggest different things to different people, and different cultures may react differently to the same symbols. (In the United States, for example, an owl suggests wisdom; in India it suggests the opposite.) Thus, symbols enrich meaning, expanding the possibilities for interpretation and for readers' interaction with the text. Because they are so potentially rich, symbols have the power to open up a work of literature.

(1) Literary Symbols

Both universal and conventional symbols can function as **literary symbols** that take on additional meanings in particular works. For instance, a watch or clock denotes time; as a conventional symbol, it suggests the passing of time; as a literary symbol in a particular work, it might also convey anything from a character's inability to recapture the past to the idea of time running out — or it might suggest something else.

Considering an object's possible symbolic significance can suggest a variety of ways to interpret a text. For instance, William Faulkner focuses attention on an unseen watch in a pivotal scene in "A Rose for Emily[3]." The narrator first describes Emily Grierson as "a small, fat woman in black, with a thin gold chain descending to her waist and vanishing into her belt." Several sentences later, the narrator returns to the watch, noting that Emily's visitors "could hear the invisible watch ticking at the end of the gold chain." Like these visitors, readers are drawn to the unseen watch as it ticks away. Because Emily is portrayed as a woman living in the past, readers can assume that the watch is intended to reinforce the impression that she cannot see that time (the watch) has moved on. The vivid picture of the pale, plump woman in the musty room with the watch invisibly ticking does indeed suggest both that she has been left back in time and that she remains unaware of the progress around her. Thus, the symbol enriches both the depiction of character and the story's theme.

In "Barn Burning[11]," another Faulkner story, the clock is a more complex symbol. The itinerant Snopes family is without financial security and apparently without a future. The clock the mother carries from shack to shack — "The clock inlaid with mother-of-pearl, which would not run, stopped at some fourteen minutes past two o'clock of a dead and forgotten day and time, which had been [Sarty's] mother's dowry" — is their only possession of value. The fact that the clock no longer works seems at first to suggest that time has run out for the family. On another level, the clock stands in stark contrast to Major de Spain's grand home, with its gold and glitter and Oriental rugs. Knowing that the clock was part of the mother's dowry, and that a dowry suggests a promise, readers may decide that the broken clock symbolizes lost hope. The fact that the mother still clings to the clock, however, could suggest just the opposite: here refusal to give up.

As you read, you should not try to find one exact equivalent for each symbol; that kind of search is limiting and unproductive. Instead, consider the different meanings a symbol might suggest. Then, consider how these various interpretations enrich other elements of the story and the work as a whole.

(2) Recognizing Symbols

When is a clock just a clock, and when is it also a symbol with a meaning (or meanings) beyond its literal significance? If a character waiting for a friend glances once at a watch to verify the time, there is probably nothing symbolic about the watch or about the act of looking at it. If, however, the watch keeps appearing again and again in the story, at key moments; if the narrator devotes a good deal of time to describing it; if it is placed in a conspicuous physical location; if characters keep noticing it and commenting on its presence; if it is lost (or found) at a critical moment; if its function in some way parallels the development of plot or character (for instance, if it stops as a relationship ends or when a character dies); if the story's opening or closing paragraph focuses on the timepiece; or if the story is called "The Watch" — the watch most likely has symbolic significance. In other words, considering how an image is used, how often it is used, and when it appears will help you to determine whether or not it functions as a symbol.

Symbols expand the possible meanings of a story, thereby heightening interest and actively involving readers in the text. In "The Lottery[12]," for example, the mysterious black box has symbolic significance. It is mentioned prominently and repeatedly, and it plays a pivotal role in the story's action. Of course, the black box is important on a purely literal level: it functions as a key component of the lottery. But the box has other associations as well, and it is these associations that suggest what its symbolic significance might be.

The black wooden box is very old, a relic of many past lotteries; the narrator observes that it represents tradition. It is also closed and closely guarded, suggesting mystery and uncertainty. It is shabby, "splintered badly along one side . . . and in places faded or stained," and this state of disrepair could suggest that the ritual it is part of has also deteriorated or that tradition itself has deteriorated. The box is also simple in construction and design, suggesting the primitive (and therefore perhaps outdated) nature of the ritual. Thus, this symbol encourages readers to probe the story for value and ideas, to consider and weigh the suitability of a variety of interpretations. It serves as a "hot spot" that invites questions, and the answers to these questions reinforce and enrich the story's theme.

2. Allegory

An **allegory** communicates a doctrine, message, or moral principle by making it into a narrative in which the characters personify ideas, concepts, qualities, or other abstractions. Thus, an allegory is a story with two parallel and consistent levels of meaning — one literal and one figurative. The figurative level, which offers some moral or political lesson, is the story's main concern. The allegorical figures are significant only because they represent something beyond their literal meaning in a fixed system.

Whereas a symbol has multiple symbolic associations as well as a literal meaning, an allegorical figure — a character, object, place, or event in the allegory — has just one meaning within an allegorical framework, the set of ideas that conveys the allegory's message. (As the simplest level, for instance, one character can stand for good and another can stand for evil.) For this reason, allegorical figures do not open up a text to various interpretations the way symbols do. Because the purpose of allegory is to communicate a particular lesson, readers are not encouraged to speculate about the allegory's possible meanings; each element has only one equivalent, which readers must discover if they are to make sense of the story.

Naturally, the better a reader understands the political, religious, and literary assumptions of a writer, the easier it will be to recognize the allegorical significance of his or her work. John Bunyan's *The Pilgrims' Progress,* for example, is a famous seventeenth-century allegory based on the Christian doctrine of salvation. In order to appreciate the complexity of Bunyan's work, you would have to familiarize yourself with this doctrine — possibly by consulting an encyclopedia or a reference work such as *The Oxford Companion to English Literature*.

One type of allegory, called a beast fable, is a short tale, usually including amoral, which animals assume human characteristics. Aesop's fables are the best-known examples of beast fables. More recently, contemporary writers have used beast fables to satirize the political and social conditions of our time. In one such tale, "The Gentlemen of the Jungle" by the Kenyan writer Jomo Kenyatta, an elephant is allowed to put his trunk inside a man's hut during a rainstorm. Not content with keeping his trunk dry, the elephant pushes his entire body inside the hut, displacing the man. When the man protests, the elephant takes the matter to the lion, who appoints a Commission of Enquiry to settle the matter.

Eventually, the man is forced not only to abandon his hut to the elephant, but also to build new huts for all the animals on the Commission. Even so, the jealous animals occupy the man's new hut and begin fighting for space; while they are arguing, the man burns down the hut, animals and all. Like the tales told by Aesop, "The Gentlemen of the Jungle" has a moral: "Peace is costly," says the man as he walks away happily, "but it's worth the expense."

Some works contain both symbolic elements and allegorical elements, as Nathaniel Hawthorne's "Young Goodman Brown[13]" does. The names of the story's two main characters, "Goodman" and "Faith," suggest that they fit within an allegorical system of some sort: Young Goodman Brown represents a good person who, despite his best efforts, strays from the path of righteousness; his wife, Faith, represents the quality he must hold on to in order to avoid temptation. As characters, they have no significance outside of their allegorical functions. Other elements of the story, however, are not so clear-cut. The older man whom Young Goodman Brown meets in the woods carries a staff that has carved on it "the likeness of a great back snake, so curiously wrought, that it might almost be seen to twist and wriggle itself like a living serpent." This staff, carried by a Satanic figure who represents evil and temptation, suggests the snake in the Garden of Eden, an association that neatly fits into the allegorical framework of the story. Alternately, however, the staff could suggest the "slippery," ever-changing nature of sin, the difficulty people have in perceiving sin, or even sexuality (which may explain Young Goodman Brown's susceptibility to temptation). This range of possible meanings suggests that the staff functions as a symbol (not an allegorical figure) that enriches Hawthorne's allegory.

Other stories work entirely on a symbolic level and contain no allegorical figures. "The Lottery[12]," despite its moral overtones, is not an allegory because its characters, events, and objects are not arranged to serve one rigid, didactic purpose. In fact, many different interpretations have been suggested for this story. When it was first published in June 1948 in the New Yorker, some readers believed it to be a story about an actual custom or ritual. As Shirley Jackson reports in her essay "Biography of a Story," even those who recognized it as fiction speculated about its meaning, seeing it as (among other things) an attack on prejudice, a criticism of society's need for a scapegoat, or a treatise on witchcraft, Christian martyrdom, or village gossip. The fact is that no single allegorical interpretation will account for every major character, object, and event in the story.

> **Points to Think about Symbol and Allegory**
>
> - Are any universal symbols used in the work? Any conventional symbols? What is their function?
> - Is any character, place, action, event, or object given unusual prominence or emphasis in the story? If so, does this element seem to have symbolic as well as literal significance?
> - What possible meanings does each symbol suggest?
> - How symbols help to depict the story's characters?
> - How symbols help to characterize the story's setting?
> - Does the story have a moral or didactic purpose? What is the message, idea, or moral principle the story seeks to convey? Is the story an allegory?

08 Theme

The **theme** of a work of literature is its central or dominant idea. *Theme* is not the same as *plot* or *subject*, two terms with which it is sometimes confused. A summary of the plot of Tadeusz Borowski's "Silence," a story about survivors of the Holocaust, could be, "Prisoners are liberated from a concentration camp, and, despite the warnings of the American officer, they kill a captured German guard." The statement "'Silence' is about freed prisoners and a guard" could define the *subject* of the story. A statement of the *theme* of "Silence," however, has to do more than summarize its plot or define its subject; it has to convey the values and ideas expressed by the story.

Many effective stories are complex, expressing more than one theme, and "Silence" is no exception. You could say that "Silence" suggests that human beings have a need for vengeance. You could also say the story demonstrates that silence is sometimes the only response possible when people confront unspeakable horrors. Both these themes — and others — are expressed in the story, yet one theme seems to dominate: the idea that under extreme conditions the oppressed can have the same capacity for evil as their oppressors.

When you write about theme, you need to do more than tell what happens in the story. The theme you identify should be a general idea that extends beyond the story and applies to the world outside fiction. Compare these two statements about Edgar Allan Poe's "The

Cask of Amontillado[2]":

1. Poe's "The Cask of Amontillado" is about a man who has an obsessive desire for revenge.
2. Poe's "The Cask of Amontillado" suggests that when the desire for revenge becomes obsessive, it can deprive individuals of all that makes them human.

The first merely tells what the story is about; the second statement identifies the story's theme, a general observation about humanity.

Granted, some short words (fairy tales or fables, for example) have themes that can only be expressed as **clichés** — overused phrases or expressions — or as **morals** — lessons dramatized by the work. The fairy tale "Cinderella," for example, expresses the clichéd theme that a virtuous girl who endures misfortune will eventually achieve her just reward; the fable "The Tortoise and the Hare" illustrates the moral "Slow and steady wins the race." Like "The Cask of Amontillado[2]," however, the stories in this anthology have themes that are more complex than clichés or morals.

1. Interpreting Themes

Contemporary critical theory holds that the theme of a work of fiction is as much the creation of readers as of the writer. Readers' backgrounds, knowledge, values, and beliefs all play a part in determining the theme or themes they will identify in a work. Most readers, for example, will realize that David Michael Kaplan's story "Doe Season[14]" — in which the main character goes hunting, kills her first deer, and is forced to confront suffering and death — expresses a conventional initiation theme, revealing growing up to be a disillusioning and painful process. Still, different readers bring different perspectives to the story and, in some cases, see different themes.

One student familiar with hunting saw more than others did in the story's conventional initiation theme. He knew that in many states there really is a doe season, which lasts approximately three days. Shorter than the ten-day buck season, it allows hunters to control the size of the deer herd by killing females. This knowledge enabled the student to conclude that by the end of the story the female child's innocence is destroyed, just as the doe is.

Another student pointed out that the participation of Andy — a female who uses a male name — in hunting, a traditional male rite of passage, leads to her killing the deer and to her subsequent disillusionment. It also leads to her decision to abandon her nickname. By contrasting "Andrea" with "Andy," the story reveals the conflict between her "female" nature (illustrated by her compassion) and her desire to emulate the men to whom killing is a sport. This interpretation led the student to conclude that the theme of "Doe Season[14]" is that males and females have very different outlooks on life.

Other students did not accept the negative characterization of the story's male characters that the preceding interpretation implies. They pointed out that the father is a sympathetic figure who is extremely supportive; he encourages and defends his daughter. He takes her hunting because he loves her, not because he wants to initiate her into life or to hurt her. One student mentioned that Andy's reaction (called buck fever) when she sees the doe is common in children who kill their first deer. In light of this information, several students concluded that far from being about irreconcilable male and female perspectives, "Doe Season[14]" makes a statement about a young girl who is hunting for her own identity and who in the process discovers her own mortality. Her father is therefore the agent who enables her to confront the inevitability of death, a fact she must accept if she is going to take her place in the adult world. In this sense, the theme of the story is the idea that in order to mature, a child must come to terms with the reality of death.

Different readers may see different themes in a story, but any interpretation of a theme must make sense in light of what is actually in the story. Evidence from the work, not just your feelings or assumptions, must support your interpretation, and a single symbol or one statement by a character is not enough in itself to reveal a story's theme. Therefore, you must present a cross-section of examples from the text to support your interpretation of the story's theme. If you say that the theme of James Joyce's "Araby[6]" is that an innocent idealist is inevitably doomed to disillusionment, you have to find examples from the text to support this statement. You could begin with the title, concluding the word *Araby* suggests idealistic dreams of exotic beauty that the boy tries to find when he goes to the bazaar. You could reinforce your interpretation by pointing out that Mangan's unattainable sister is a symbol of all that the boy wants to desperately to find. Finally, you could show how idealism is ultimately crushed by society: at the end of the story, the boy stands alone in the darkness and realizes that his dreams are childish fantasies.

Although other readers may have different responses to "Araby[6]," they should find your interpretation reasonable if you support it with enough examples.

2. Identifying Themes

Every element of a story can shed light on its themes. As you analyze a short story, you should look for features that reveal and reinforce what you perceive to be the story's most important ideas.

- *A **narrator's or character's** statement can reveal a theme.* For example, at the beginning of Alberto Alvaro Rios's "The Secret Lion," the first-person narrator says, "I was twelve and in junior high school and something happened that we didn't have a name for, but it was there nonetheless like a lion, and roaring, roaring that way the biggest things do. Everything changed." Although the narrator does not directly announce the story's theme, he does suggest that the story will convey the idea that the price children pay for growing up is realizing that everything changes, that nothing stays the way it is.

- *The **arrangement of events** can suggest a story's theme, as it does in an Ernest Hemingway's story, "The Short Happy Life of Francis Macomber."* At the beginning of the story, the title character is a coward who is struck in an unhappy marriage. As the story progresses, he gradually learns the nature of courage and, finally, finds it in himself. At the moment of his triumph, however, Francis is shot by his wife; his "happy life" is short indeed. The way the events of the story are presented, through foreshadowing and flashbacks, reveals the connection between Macomber's marriage and his behavior as a hunter, and this connection in turn helps to reveal a possible theme: that sometimes courage can be more important than life itself.

- *A **story's conflict** can offer clues to its theme.* In "Araby[6]," the young boy believes that his society neglects art and beauty and glorifies the mundane. This conflict between the boy's idealism and his world can help readers understand why the boy isolates himself in his room reading books and why he retreats into dreams of idealized love. A major theme of the story — that growing up leads to the loss of youthful idealism — is revealed by this central conflict.

  Similarly, the main character in "The Yellow Wallpaper[5]," a woman who has recently had a baby, is in conflict with the nineteenth-century society in which she lives. She is suffering from "temporary nervous depression," what doctors today recognize as postpartum depression. Following the practice of the time, her physician has ordered complete bed rest and has instructed her husband to deprive her of all mental and physical stimulation. This harsh treatment leads the narrator to lose her grasp on reality; eventually, she begins to hallucinate. The central conflict of the story is clearly between the woman and her society, controlled by men. This conflict communicates the theme: that in nineteenth-century America, women are controlled not just by their husbands and the male medical establishment, but also by the society they have created.

- *The **point of view** of a story can also help shed light on theme.* For instance, a writer's use of an unreliable first-person narrator can help to communicate the theme of a story. Thus, Montresor's self-serving first-person account of his crime in "The Cask of Amontillado[2]" — along with his attempts to justify these actions — enables readers to understand the dangers of irrational anger and misplaced ideas about honor. The voice of a third-person narrator can also help to convey a story's theme. For example, the detachment of the narrator in Stephen Crane's Civil War novel *The Red Badge of Courage* reinforces the theme of the novel: that bravery, cowardice, war, and even life itself are insignificant when set beside the indifference of the universe.

- *A story may give names, places, and objects **symbolic significance**.* These symbols can not only enrich the story but also help to convey a central theme. For example, the rocking horse in D. H. Lawrence's "The Rocking-Horse Winner[15]" can be seen as a symbol of the boy's desperate desire to remain a child. Interpreted in this way, it reinforces the theme that innocence cannot survive when it confronts adult greed and selfishness. Similarly, Hawthorne's "Young Goodman Brown[13]" uses symbols such as the walking stick, the woods, sunset and night, and the vague shadows to develop one of its central themes: that once a person strays from the path of faith, evil is everywhere.

- ***Changes in a character*** *can shed light on the theme or themes of the story.* The main character in Charles Baxter's "Gryphon[7]," for example, eventually comes to realize that the "lies" Miss Ferenczi tells may be closer to the truth than the "facts" his teachers present, and his changing attitude toward Miss Ferenczi helps to communicate the story's central theme about the nature of truth.

Points to Think about Theme

- What is the central theme of the story?
- What other themes can you identify?
- Does the narrator, or any character, make statements that express or imply a theme?
- In what way does the arrangement of events in the story suggest a theme?
- In what way does the central conflict of the story suggest a theme?
- How does the point of view shed light on the story's central theme?
- Do any symbols suggest a theme?
- Do any characters in the story change in any significant way? Do these changes convey a particular theme?
- Does your statement of the story's central theme make a general observation that has an application beyond the story itself?

09 Practices

01 Read the passage and follow the directions.

> "Did you say something, Sammy?" "I said I quit." "I thought you did." "You didn't have to embarrass them." "It was they who were embarrassing us." I started to say something that came out "Fiddle-de-doo." It's a saying of my grand-mother's, and I know she would have been pleased. "I don't think you know what you're saying," Lengel said. "I know you don't," I said. "But I do." I pull the bow at the back of my apron and start shrugging it off my shoulders. A couple customers that had been heading for my slot begin to knock against each other, like scared pigs in a chute.
>
> Lengel sighs and begins to look very patient and old and gray. He's been a friend of my parents for years. "Sammy, you don't want to do this to your Mom and Dad," he tells me. It's true, I don't. But it seems to me that <u>once you begin a gesture it's fatal not to go through with it</u>. I fold the apron, "Sammy" stitched in red on the pocket, and put it on the counter, and drop the bow tie on top of it. The bow tie is theirs, if you've ever wondered. "You'll feel this for the rest of your life," Lengel says, and I know that's true, too, but remembering how he made that pretty girl blush makes me so scrunchy inside I punch the No Sale tab and the machine whirs "pee-pul" and the drawer splats out. One advantage to this scene taking place in summer, I can follow this up with a clean exit, there's no fumbling around getting your coat and galoshes, I just saunter into the electric eye in my white shirt that my mother ironed the night before, and the door heaves itself open, and outside the sunshine is skating around on the asphalt.

English novelist E. M. Forster classifies characters as either **round** (well developed, closely involved in and responsive to the action) or flat (barely developed or stereotypical). **Characters** may also be classified as either *dynamic or static. A dynamic character* grows and changes in the course of a story, developing as he or she reacts to events. *A static character* may face the same challenges a dynamic character might face but will remain essentially unchanged: a regardless of the nature of the story's conflict. Whereas **round** characters tend to be *dynamic*, **flat** characters tend to be static. But even a very complex, well-developed major character may be static; sometimes, in fact, the point of a story may hinge on a character's inability to change.

Identify the character type of Sammy in the passage below. Then explain the figurative meaning of the underlined part. Support your explanation with ONE example in the passage.

02 Read the passage and follow the directions.

> WHEN Miss Emily Grierson died, our whole town went to her funeral: the men through a sort of respectful affection for a fallen monument, the women mostly out of curiosity to see the inside of her house, which no one save an old man-servant — a combined gardener and cook — had seen in at least ten years.
>
> It was a big, squarish frame house that had once been white, decorated with cupolas and spires and scrolled balconies in the heavily lightsome style of the seventies, set on what had once been our most select street. But garages and cotton gins had encroached and obliterated even the august names of that neighborhood; only Miss Emily's house was left, lifting its stubborn and coquettish decay above the cotton wagons and the gasoline pumps — an eyesore among eyesores. And now Miss Emily had gone to join the representatives of those august names where they lay in the cedar-bemused cemetery among the ranked and anonymous graves of Union and Confederate soldiers who fell at the battle of Jefferson.
>
> Alive, Miss Emily had been a tradition, a duty, and a care; a sort of hereditary obligation upon the town, dating from that day in 1894 when Colonel Sartoris, the mayor — he who fathered the edict that no Negro woman should appear on the streets without an apron — remitted her taxes, the dispensation dating from the death of her father on into perpetuity. Not that Miss Emily would have accepted charity. Colonel Sartoris invented an involved tale to the effect that Miss Emily's father had loaned money to the town, which the town, as a matter of business, preferred this way of repaying. Only a man of Colonel Sartoris' generation and thought could have invented it, and only a woman could have believed it.

The **setting** of a work of fiction establishes its historical, geographical, and physical context. Physical setting can clearly influences a story's mood as well as its development. For example, whether a story is set primarily inside or out-of-doors may be significant. The characters may be physically constrained by a closed-in setting or liberated by an expansive landscape. Some interior settings may be psychologically limiting.

Locate the important physical setting in the passage. Then explain its figurative meaning in the story.

03 Read the passage and follow the directions.

> They were always the same woods, she thought sleepily as they drove through the early morning darkness — deep and immense, covered with yesterday's snowfall, which had frozen overnight. They were the same woods that lay behind her house, *and they stretch all the way to here, she thought, for miles and miles, longer than I could walk in a day, or a week even, but they are still the same woods*. The thought made her feel good: it was like thinking of God; it was like thinking of the space between here and the moon; it was like thinking of all the foreign countries from here geography book where even now, Andy knew, people were going to bed, while they — she and her father and Charlie Spoon and Mac, Charlie's eleven-year-old son — were driving deeper into the Pennsylvania countryside, to go hunting.
>
> They had risen long before dawn. Her mother, yawing and not trying to hide her sleepiness, cooked them eggs and French toast. Her father smoked a cigarette and flicked ashes into his saucer while Andy listened, wondering <u>*Why doesn't he come? and Won't he ever come?*</u> until at last a car pulled into the graveled drive and honked. "That will be Charlie Spoon," her father said; he always said "Charlie Spoon," even though his real name was Spreun, because Charlie was, in a sense, shaped like a spoon, with a large head and a narrow waist and chest.

Sometimes a writer uses the **third person** (*he, she, they*) to tell the story from the point of view of a narrator who is not also a character. Third-person narrators fall in three categories: **omniscient, limited omniscient,** and **objective**.

Identify the point of view for the work in the above passage and identify the protagonist. Then describe Andy's emotion suggested by the underlined part.

04 Read the passage and follow the directions.

> Every morning I lay on the floor in the front parlor watching her door. The blind was pulled down within an inch of the sash so that I could not be seen. In the classroom her image came between me and the page I strove to read, and yet her name was like a summons to all my foolish blood.
>
> On Saturday evenings when my aunt went marketing I had to go to carry some of the parcels. We walked through the flaring streets, jostled by drunken men and bargaining women, the shrill litanies of shopboys, and the nasal chanting of street singers. These noises converged in a single sensation of life for me: I imagined that I bore <u>my chalice</u> safely through the throngs of foes. Her name sprang to my lips at moments in strange prayers and praises which I myself did not understand. My eyes were often full of tears and at times a flood from my heart seemed to pour itself out into my bosom. I did not know whether I would ever speak to her or not or, if I spoke to her, how I could tell her of my confused adoration. But my body was like a harp and her words were like fingers running upon the wires.
>
> One evening I went into the back drawing-room. It was a dark rainy evening and there was no sound in the house. Through one of the broken panes I heard the rain impinge upon the earth, the fine incessant needles of water playing in the sodden beds. Some distant lighted window gleamed below me. I was thankful that I could see so little. All my senses seemed to desire to veil themselves and, feeling that I was about to slip from them, I pressed the palms of my hands together until they trembled, murmuring: *O love! O love!* many times.

The perspective from which a story is told determines what details are included in the story and how they are arranged — in short, the plot. In addition, the perspective of the narrator affects the story's style, language, and themes. When deciding on a point of view for a work of fiction, a writer can choose to tell the story either in the *first person* or in the *third person*.

Identify the point of view for the work in the above passage and identify the protagonist. Then write the figurative meaning of the underlined part.

05 Read the passage and follow the directions.

[1] The water of the Gulf stretched out before her, gleaming with the million lights of the sun. The voice of the sea is seductive, never ceasing, whispering, clamoring, murmuring, inviting the soul to wander in abysses of solitude. All along the white beach, up and down, there was no living thing in sight. A bird with a broken wing was beating the air above, reeling, fluttering, circling disabled down, down to the water.

[2] Edna had found her old bathing suit still hanging, faded, upon its accustomed peg.

[3] She put it on, leaving her clothing in the bath-house. But when she was there beside the sea, absolutely alone, she cast the unpleasant, pricking garments from her, and for the first time in her life she stood naked in the open air, at the mercy of the sun, the breeze that beat upon her, and the waves that invited her.

[4] How strange and awful it seemed to stand naked under the sky! how delicious! She felt like some new-born creature, opening its eyes in a familiar world that it had never known.

[5] The foamy wavelets curled up to her white feet, and coiled like serpents about her ankles. She walked out. The water was chill, but she walked on. The water was deep, but she lifted her white body and reached out with a long, sweeping stroke. The touch of the sea is sensuous, enfolding the body in its soft, close embrace.

[6] She went on and on. She remembered the night she swam far out, and recalled the terror that seized her at the fear of being unable to regain the shore. She did not look back now, but went on and on, thinking of the blue-grass meadow that she had traversed when a little child, believing that it had no beginning and no end.

Simile is a comparison between two unlike items that uses *like* or *as; metaphor* is an imaginative comparison between two unlike items that do not use *like* or *as* — that is, when it says "a *is* b" rather than "a *is like* b" — it is a metaphor.)

Write the six-word phrase from **Paragraph [1]** that refers to an object which implies the fate of Edna. Then find a simile in **Paragraph [5]** and explain it in relation to the fate of Edna.

06 Read the passage and follow the directions.

> They rose when she entered — a small, fat woman in black, with a thin gold chain descending to her waist and vanishing into her belt, leaning on an ebony cane with a tarnished gold head. Her skeleton was small and spare; perhaps that was why what would have been merely plumpness in another was obesity in her. She looked bloated, like a body long submerged in motionless water, and of that pallid hue. Her eyes, lost in the fatty ridges of her face, looked like two small pieces of coal pressed into a lump of dough as they moved from one face to another while the visitors stated their errand.
>
> She did not ask them to sit. She just stood in the door and listened quietly until the spokesman came to a stumbling halt. Then they could hear the invisible watch ticking at the end of the gold chain.
>
> Her voice was dry and cold. "I have no taxes in Jefferson. Colonel Sartoris explained it to me. Perhaps one of you can gain access to the city records and satisfy yourselves."
>
> "But we have. We are the city authorities, Miss Emily. Didn't you get a notice from the sheriff, signed by him?"
>
> "I received a paper, yes," Miss Emily said. "Perhaps he considers himself the sheriff . . . I have no taxes in Jefferson."
>
> "But there is nothing on the books to show that, you see We must go by the —"
>
> "See Colonel Sartoris. I have no taxes in Jefferson."
>
> "But, Miss Emily —"
>
> "See Colonel Sartoris." (Colonel Sartoris had been dead almost ten years.) "I have no taxes in Jefferson. Tobe!" The Negro appeared. "Show these gentlemen out."

A **symbol** is a person, object, action, place, or event that, in addition to its literal meaning, suggests a more complex meaning or range of meanings.

01 Recognize a symbol considering how an image is used, how often it is used, and when it appears will help you to determine whether or not it functions as a symbol.

02 Write the important symbol in the passage. Then explain its figurative meaning in the story.

07 Read the passage and follow the directions.

A colonial mansion, a hereditary estate, I would say a haunted house, and reach the height of romantic felicity — but that would be asking too much of fate!

Still I will proudly declare that there is something queer about it.

Else, why should it be let so cheaply? and why have stood so long untenanted?

There were greenhouses, too, but they are all broken now.

There was some legal trouble, I believe, something about the heirs and coheirs; anyhow, the place has been empty for years.

That spoils my ghostliness, I am afraid, but I don't care — there is something strange about the house — I can feel it.

I even said so to John one moonlight evening, but he said what I felt was a *draught*, and shut the window.

I get unreasonably angry with John sometimes. I'm sure I never used to be so sensitive. I think it is due to this nervous condition.

But John says if I feel so, I shall neglect proper self-control; so I take pains to control myself — before him, at least, and that makes me very tired.

I don't like our room a bit. I wanted one downstairs that opened onto the piazza and had roses all over the window, and such pretty old-fashioned chintz hangings! But John would not hear of it.

He said there was only one window and not room for two beds, and no near room for him if he took another.

He is very careful and loving, and hardly lets me stir without special direction.

I have a schedule pres

cription for each hour in the day; he takes all care from me, and so I feel basely ungrateful not to value it.

He said we came here solely on my account, that I was to have perfect rest and all the air I could get. "Your exercise depends on your strength, my dear," said he, "and your food somewhat on your appetite; but air you can absorb all the time." So we took the nursery at the top of the house.

A story's conflict can offer clues to its theme. Fill in the blank below with ONE word from the passage. You can change the word form if necessary.

> The central conflict of the story is clearly between the narrator "I," a woman, and her husband. This conflict communicates the theme: that in nineteenth-century America, women are _____ not just by their husbands and the male medical establishment, but also by the society they have created.

Answer Keys for Chapter 01 — Fiction Analysis

1. Sammy is a round and dynamic character. The underlined part means that since he chose to quit the job, he should experience any difficulties from that change afterward, taking responsibilities for his choice. This is suggested by Lengel's saying "You'll feel this for the rest of your life" and Sammy's acceptance.

2. Emily's house is the important physical setting in the passage. It is a symbol of the decaying glory of tradition, and it's a hiding place where past duty is reserved lonely from outside changes.

3. A third-person limited omniscient narrator is used in the above passage to tell the story of Andy, who is the protagonist. The underlined part implies that Andy is so excited expecting to go hunting and impatient at waiting for Charlie's family.

4. The first person narrator is used in the above passage, and the narrator as a shy boy is the protagonist. The meaning of the underlined part means "I"'s love for "her."

5. A bird with a broken wing. In Paragraph [5], a simile is employed to compare the sea waves to 'serpents,' which means death suggesting that Edna will be drown into the water just as a bird with a broken wing can not survive.

6. The invisible watch is the important symbol in the passage. The watch is intended to reinforce the impression that Emily cannot see that time (the watch) has moved on, which suggests both that she has been left back in time and that she remains unaware of the progress around her.

7. controlled

Chapter 02 Novels to Read

김수아 전공영어 | 영미문학 Reading for Literature II

01 Summary of Novels To Read

Novels in the Text

01. **Hills Like White Elephants** (1927) – *Ernest Hemingway
02. **The Cask of Amontillado** (1846) – Edgar Allan Poe
03. **A Rose for Emily** (1930) – William Faulkner
04. **A&P** (1961) – John Updike
05. ***The Yellow Wallpaper** (1892) – Charlotte Perkins Gilman
06. ***Araby** (1914) – James Joyce
07. **Gryphon** (1985) - Charles Baxter
08. **Teenage Wasteland** (1984) - Ann Tyler
09. **I Stand Here Ironing** (1961) - Tillie Olsen
10. **The Storm** (1899) - *Kate Chopin
11. **Barn Burning** (1939) - William Faulkner
12. **The Lottery** (1948) - Shirley Jackson
13. **Young Goodman Brown** (1835) - *Nathaniel Hawthorne
14. **Doe Season** (1985) - David Michael Kaplan
15. ***The Rocking-Horse Winner** (1920) - *D. H. Lawrence

• Novels or writers referenced in the teacher certification exam.

02 Analysis of Novels To Read

1. Hills Like White Elephants (1927) • Ernest Hemingway

An unnamed American man and a woman named Jig are waiting for the train to Barcelona. While drinking, the two talk obliquely about getting an abortion. Jig has reservations, but the man convinces her that it's simple: they just "let the air in." Jig and the American man wait forty-five minutes for a train. Jig looks out at the hills of Erbo, which she describes as white elephants. The American man more or less convinces Jig to get the abortion. They board the train, and the story ends.

Themes:

- Hemingway's characters seem to live in a world without a God, without traditions or clear and established values; they are, in Jean-Paul Sartre's words, "condemned to be free" and consequently are responsible for their own meaning. The man here is unequal to the challenge; he is a bored and listless fragment of a human being. He resolutely refuses to speak truthfully, to acknowledge his own hypocrisy. His unwillingness to be honest — and, by extension, modern humanity's refusal to live honestly — is a consistent motif of this sketch. The girl is, at least, profoundly distressed by the aimless and sterile nature of their existence and does not give in to vacuity without a struggle.

- One particularly interesting aspect of Hemingway's uncompromising dissection of the poverty of the modern world in this story is the juxtaposition of reason and emotion or imagination. The man is perfectly reasonable. He lives in a senseless and violent world; he has the financial resources to do as he pleases; he reasonably concludes that he should enjoy his life, not encumber himself with unnecessary conflicts or responsibilities, certainly not trouble himself with relationships that are demanding or in the least unpleasant. He is quite literal-minded, quite pragmatic, quite unemotional: an admirable fellow by modern patriarchal standards. The woman, on the other hand, is unreasonable enough to imagine that hills look like white elephants and that there might be some virtue to having a child who would surely be like a "white elephant," a sacred beast in some cultures, but in Europe and America something that is only apparently valuable and is in actuality more trouble than it is worth. Reason here is associated with dissimulation, death, nonmeaning; emotion with life, imagination, growth. Hemingway suggests that reason (the God of modern humanity) is an insufficient standard by which to live. The reasonable male here is a cipher, a man of straw who declines to acknowledge the necessity of making his every moment intense, honest, full.

- Hemingway's brief and seemingly objective story is a powerful condemnation of the aimlessness, hypocrisy, and moral and spiritual poverty of the modern world.

2. The Cask of Amontillado (1846) • Edgar Allan Poe

In "The Cask of Amontillado," Montresor describes how he took revenge on Fortunato during a carnival in Venice. Montresor lures Fortunato into the catacombs with a cask of amontillado, and then proceeds to bury him alive.

- Montresor tells Fortunato he has obtained some rare Amontillado wine and lures him into his cellar.
- Montresor leads the way into his family catacombs, with the drunk Fortunato following.
- Montresor chains Fortunato to a wall deep in the catacombs, then bricks up the opening. Fortunato screams for release, but Montresor only mocks him.
- Fortunato's body remains undiscovered for fifty years.

Themes:

- In "The Cask of Amontillado," though Montresor gets away with his crime, his soul is devoured by hate.
- Montresor is motivated by revenge to punish Fortunato for his insult. Fortunato's initial insult and Montresor's reflections on his act of revenge are not revealed to the reader.
- There is no indication in the story that Montresor is remorseful, and the reader is left to wonder why Montresor is confessing his crime and whether he is sorry for what he did.

Characters:

- In "The Cask of Amontillado," Montresor is the immoral narrator who tells the story of his revenge against Fortunato. Montresor lures Fortunato into his catacombs, chains him to a wall, and buries him alive.
- Fortunato is a friend of Montresor's who is unaware that Montresor is plotting to kill him. He is a connoisseur of wine who is enticed by Montresor to sample some rare Amontillado and lured into his trap.
- Luchesi is another wine connoisseur and an acquaintance of Montresor and Fortunato; Montresor urges Fortunato to sample his wine by threatening to allow Luchesi to try it first if Fortunato does not comply.

3. A Rose for Emily (1930)

• William Faulkner

Miss Emily Grierson was born into an aristocratic family. Isolated at an early age by her father, Emily is placed on a pedestal by the townspeople, who like to think of her as "a tradition, a duty," even though they find her haughty and scornful.

- Emily appears to have a mental breakdown following the death of her father. She initially refuses to acknowledge his death, then retreats into her house with a mysterious illness.
- One day, Homer Barron and his crew of laborers come to town to build sidewalks. Emily takes an interest in Homer in spite of the disapproval of the townspeople, who argue that he is too low class for Emily.
- Emily buys some arsenic, but refuses to explain why. Years later, when Emily dies, the townspeople find a man's skeleton in her bed. It's strongly implied that this skeleton is Homer Barron.

Themes:

- Major themes in "A Rose for Emily" include death, isolation, and the decline of the Old South. Of these, death takes center stage, with the skeleton in Emily's bed thematically reflecting the decay of the Old South.
- Emily's isolation fuels the curiosity of the townspeople, who paradoxically become more interested in her as she becomes more and more withdrawn.
- Generational divisions arise when Homer arrives in town. The older generation disapproves of his relationship with Emily, a woman of a much higher social station than him. The younger generation doesn't have a problem with it.

Characters:

- Miss Emily Grierson, a reclusive Southern Belle harboring a gruesome secret.
- Emily's father, a proud, aristocratic man who chases away his daughter's suitors because they aren't good enough for her.
- Homer Barron, a foreman, who has a brief relationship with Emily before mysteriously disappearing.
- Colonel Sartoris, who exempts Emily from paying taxes.

4. A&P (1961)
• **John Updike**

Three teenage girls walk into an A & P wearing nothing but bathing suits. Sammy, the young cashier, watches them closely. He names their leader "Queenie" because of her regal, disdainful manner.

- Queenie and the other two girls want to buy Kingfish Fancy Herring Snacks in Pure Sour Cream. When the girls approach the register, Sammy's manager, Lengel, reprimands them for not covering up before coming into the store.
- Seeing Queenie and the girls upset, Sammy tells Lengel that he didn't need to embarrass them like that. Lengel retorts that the girls embarrassed him and the town by flaunting their bodies.
- Sammy gallantly quits on the spot to defend Queenie's honor. She takes no notice. Sammy realizes that no one appreciates his gesture and that his romantic, chivalrous ideas will make life hard for him.

Themes:

- John Updike's "A&P" is a story about consequences. Each character in the story makes a choice that results in a negative consequence. Queenie and the other girls, for instance, choose to enter the A&P wearing nothing but their bathing suits. Sammy then decides to quit his job to defend their honor.
- Another important theme in "A&P" is power. There are many different kinds of power in the story: Lengel's power as the A&P's manager, Queenie's power as the perceived leader of her group, and the girls' power to inspire desire in the men around them.

5. *The Yellow Wallpaper (1892)
• **Charlotte Perkins Gilman**

In "The Yellow Wallpaper," the unnamed narrator (often identified as Jane) suffers from depression following the birth of her baby. Her husband misdiagnoses her with hysteria and prescribes "the rest cure." Trapped in bed, Jane grows bored. She's isolated from everyone but her husband and nurse, and she's not allowed to write, though this makes her feel better. Her condition quickly deteriorates. She starts to see a woman inside her yellow wallpaper. She thinks the woman is struggling to break free. Jane tears down the wallpaper in order to free the woman. Jane's husband comes to take her home, but faints when he realizes that she has gone mad.

Themes:

- "The Yellow Wallpaper" examines the stifling roles that denied women freedom of expression. The narrator (often identified as Jane) is driven mad by her inability to write or assert her independence.
- The story details Jane's mental and emotional decline.
- Gilman struggled to change the nineteenth-century view that serious mental illness like depression could be cured by limiting women's activity.

Characters:

- In "The Yellow Wallpaper," the narrator (who many believe is Jane) suffers from what is now called postpartum depression. The rest cure prescribed by her husband leads to her madness.
- John is Jane's husband and a physician who treats his wife in a paternalistic way. He exerts ultimate control over all the decisions affecting his wife's freedom.
- Jennie is John's sister who helps her brother control and observe Jane. She peers into the wallpaper and shows an interest in understanding Jane's point of view.
- Weir Mitchell popularized the rest cure and was a real figure who treated Gilman unsuccessfully in his sanatorium.

6. *Araby (1914)   • James Joyce

In "Araby," the story's narrator is infatuated with a girl known only as "Mangan's sister." The narrator promises to buy her a present from the titular bazaar, but leaves without one, disappointed with the idle chatter of a saleswoman he meets.

- The narrator lives with his aunt and uncle. The former tenant of his house died and left behind a library that intrigues the narrator.
- Mangan's sister asks the narrator if he plans on attending a bazaar called Araby, and he promises to get her something from the fair as a gift.
- The narrator is delayed in leaving to go to the fair as his uncle returns late from work with the money.

Themes:

- In "Araby," the narrator's immaturity is evident in both his inflated expectations concerning

the girl's love and his dashed hopes at the bazaar.
- The boy makes a transition in the story from his childish ideals to the realities of adult life.
- The narrator experiences isolation from his family, his friends, the object of his affection, and the larger society.

Characters:

- In "Araby," the narrator is a young boy who undergoes a transformation from an idealistic child to an adult dealing with realistic problems.
- Mangan's sister is the object of the narrator's schoolboy crush. She is unaware of the narrator's feelings for her.
- The narrator's aunt is a maternal figure who empathizes with the narrator.
- The narrator's uncle is an unreliable, self-centered man who forgets about the bazaar and almost causes the narrator to miss the event.

7. Gryphon (1985)
• Charles Baxter

To the narrator, Tommy, a normal fourth-grade boy, and other pupils at Garfield-Murray School in rural Five Oaks, Michigan, each day is much like another. As their teachers lecture to them about predictable subjects in predictable ways, they memorize facts and repeat them back. Occasionally, the routine is disrupted by a substitute teacher, but with only four substitutes in all of Five Oaks, the students know exactly what to expect from each of them. Oblivious to the dullness of their routine, the students do not know that there are other possibilities, other ways to learn, and other ways to look or think, so they do not feel a lack. Into their mundane world Miss Ferenczi, a new substitute teacher, suddenly arrives.

The students are mesmerized by her stories and her manner. When the regular teacher returns, they are careful not to reveal what's been going on in his absence. A few weeks later, Ms. Ferenczi reappears in the classroom. She shows up with a box of Tarot cards and begins to tell the students' futures. When a boy named Wayne Razmer pulls the Death card and asks what it means, she breezily tells him, "It means, my sweet, that you will die soon." The boy reports the incident to the principal, and by lunchtime, Ms. Ferenczi has left the school for good. Tommy, the narrator, confronts Wayne for reporting the incident and getting Ms. Ferenczi dismissed, and they end up in a fistfight. By the afternoon, all the students have been doubled up in other classrooms and are back to memorizing facts about the world.

Themes:

- Many of Charles Baxter's stories feature ordinary people encountering extraordinary strangers who disrupt their normal lives: A woman who visits a psychic and hears of great danger; a man who tries to help a homeless man, only to hurt his own family; a new substitute teacher who turns out to be crazy. In each case, the central character's life is orderly, even dull. However, unchanging day-to-day routines are no protection against peril. Just under the surface of the most orderly existence, disorder always lurks.

- Baxter has said that the idea for "Gryphon" came out of his own early experience as an elementary school teacher. One day as he presented a lesson about Egypt, he found his "facts" becoming increasingly fanciful. The experience made him realize that a teacher can enter a classroom and teach anything — facts or substitute facts — without anyone knowing the difference. As is the case with any good writer, this realization led Baxter to more questions than answers. For example, is it necessarily all bad to offer substitute facts occasionally in an educational setting? His fictional Miss Ferenczi is more creative, more engaging, than the "regular" teachers. Is not it important for children to dream and wonder, instead of merely memorizing?

- By the end of the story, Miss Ferenczi is a puzzle. She demonstrates less control each time that she teaches Tommy's class, until the final day, on which there is a subtle hint of real danger. Very likely, she should not be in a classroom. However, the reader cannot help regretting this when presented with the dreary alternative implied in the story's last line: "Mrs. Mantei said that our assignment would be to memorize these lists for the next day, when Mr. Hibler would certainly return and test us on our knowledge."

- Although Tommy's life has been ordered into careful dullness — predictable routines at school, simple chores at home after school — chaos appears suddenly and unexpectedly. For him, the days with Miss Ferenczi are confusing, even upsetting, but they also are freeing, expanding. His brief encounter with danger is also his first encounter with the wider world.

8. Teenage Wasteland (1984) • Ann Tyler

Daisy Coble meets with the principal of the private high school that her son, Donny, attends, and the principal tells her that Donny is disruptive and not responsive in class. At the principal's suggestion, Daisy supervises Donny's homework. His grades improve slightly, but the school reports new behavior problems, including smoking and possibly drinking. A psychologist recommends a tutor, Cal Beadle, whom Donny meets with three times a week and grows to like.

Cal says that Daisy and Matt, Donny's parents, are too controlling and accusatory. Although Daisy tries to be positive with Donny, his behavior continues to deteriorate, and eventually he is expelled from school. Cal calls the expulsion unjust, but Daisy no longer trusts Cal. She enrolls Donny in a public school and stops the tutoring sessions. One day Donny runs away from home, and he does not return. His parents search everywhere. They even question his favorite tutor, Cal, and his strange girlfriend, Miriam. Surprisingly, they have no idea where he may be. Donny is never heard from again. His parents are left to wonder what happened to Donny.

Themes:

- Anne Tyler's focus in this story is the gradual disintegration of the relationship between a teenage boy and his parents. The title of the story, taken from the lyrics of "Baba O'Riley," a song popularized by The Who in the early 1970's, clearly suggests Tyler's theme, although in an oblique way. "Teenage Wasteland" is a metaphor for the place where Donny's parents see him when they pick him up at Cal's: Students there are idly shooting baskets; loud music pours out through the windows; and Donny, "spiky and excited," looks like someone they do not know. To Daisy and Matt, all the students look like hoodlums. When Daisy murmurs, "Teenage Wasteland," recognizing the song, Matt, misunderstanding, replies, "It certainly is." Thus in only a few lines, Tyler encapsulates the enormous distance between them and the youngsters playing in Cal's backyard. The distance increases as Donny moves further from them, until communication between them nearly ceases. When Donny is expelled, the fact that he heads for Cal's house instead of home signifies both his preference for his tutor and his inability to make his mother accept his lame explanation of the incident that precipitated the expulsion.

- The image with which Tyler closes the story is subtle and moving. Lying awake at night, Daisy tries to understand what has happened and has a vision of Cal's yard, where a neighbor's fence casts narrow shadow bars across the spring grass. As she drifts off to sleep, she recalls that scene, the stripes of sunlight "as white as bones, bleached and parched and cleanly picked." It is a fearful image, one that Tyler does not explain, leaving it to the reader to interpret as an expression of Daisy's defeat and despair.

9. I Stand Here Ironing (1961)   • Tillie Olsen

In "I Stand Here Ironing," a mother stands at her ironing board ruminates on the life of her eldest daughter, Emily. The narrator was just nineteen when she has Emily, and she wasn't able to spend much time with Emily while she was growing up. She wants Emily to build a life for herself.

- The narrator receives a letter from Emily's school. It says that she needs help and that the narrator has to do something.
- The narrator reveals that she was just nineteen when she has Emily. She couldn't support her child, so she often sent her away. Now, Emily's nineteen, and their situations are very different.
- Emily has a talent for mimicry and wants to explore this. Her mother knows that she most likely won't reach her full potential, because few people do. Even so, the narrator doesn't want Emily to feel defeated.

Themes:
- The mother-child relationship is the focus of "I Stand Here Ironing." The close bond created in the days of infancy is threatened as soon as the mother must consign the child to a sitter. Both the mother and the child regret and resist the absences that weaken the bond and make it difficult for the mother to express her love for the little girl, but poverty and the demands of other family members prevail, so that by the time the story takes place, the mother believes that she can be of no help to the girl's further development.
- The daughter's view of the relationship is expressed only as it is perceived by the mother. However, the mother's memories of the infant crying, the small child finding reasons not to be separated from the mother, but never rebelling or begging, the stiffness and silence of the bigger child when her mother tried to hold or comfort her, the help in mothering and in cheering up her mother when the stepfather was away all suggest that the complexity of the relationship has been developing for a long time. Hurt and deprivation and anger have not severed the bond of love, but they have created barriers so that the mother and daughter are very separate people now.
- The mother's confidence that the daughter's common sense will prevail if only she can be persuaded that life is not futile is an acknowledgment of the daughter's maturity. The mother was persuaded against her own common sense to feed the child only at set intervals, to send the child to nursery school, and finally to place her in the convalescent home. In acquiescing to the advice of others instead of following her own instincts, she realizes now, she hurt the child emotionally; she will not make the same mistake again.

10. The Storm (1899)

• Kate Chopin

In "The Storm," Alcée stops at Calixta's house to get out of the rain. Alcée and Calixta were in love once, and the storm reignites their passion. Both of them, however, are married to different people, and they know that when the storm ends they must part forever.

- Bobinôt and his son, Bibi, are at the market when the storm comes. Bobinôt's wife, Calixta, is at home, where Alcée seeks shelter from the storm.

- Six years prior to this storm, Calixta and Alcée ran away together to have an affair. A year later, they intended to run away together again, but their plans were ruined when Clarisse convinced Alcée to marry her. Calixta married Bobinôt.

- During the storm, Calixta and Alcée reignite their passion. However, both know that their relationship cannot continue, and Alcée leaves before Bobinôt returns.

Themes:

- Chopin depicts sex as liberating and enjoyable. Indeed, for Calixta, adultery with Alcée is more satisfying than sex with her husband; it is with Alcée that "her firm, elastic flesh knew for the first time its birthright." Lovemaking with Alcée touches "depths . . . that had never yet been reached."

- Nor does this adultery end in tragedy — quite the reverse. Calixta, who would normally be upset with her husband and child for bringing dirt into the house, welcomes them warmly. She is truly happy to be reunited with her family. Because her physical needs have been met, she can share her newfound joy with others.

- Alcée's marriage also benefits. He may be telling Clarisse to stay in Biloxi so he can pursue his affair with Calixta — though there is no evidence in the story that the two continue their liaison — but his letter is nevertheless filled with love and regard for his wife and children. Like Calixta, he is physically satisfied and so can be emotionally generous.

- Clarisse eagerly snatches at Alcée's offer. For her, as, apparently, for Calixta, marriage is confining. Calixta escapes by having sex with Alcée; Clarisse escapes by forgoing "intimate conjugal life" with him for a while. She will return to her husband, just as Calixta will remain with Bobinôt, yet this innocent adultery has given everyone a breath of freedom, cleansing them as a summer storm freshens and purifies the air.

- Chopin's characters here do not rebel against the institution of marriage; they object only to being confined by traditional roles. Given the freedom to satisfy their physical or spiritual needs, they are content with their spouses. In fact, for marriage to succeed, Chopin argues, such freedom is crucial. Far from threatening marriage, this liberty is its only means of salvation.

11. Barn Burning (1939)   • William Faulkner

Ten-year-old Colonel Satoris "Sarty" Snopes lives with his father, a nasty drunk who relishes burning down the barns of employers who have crossed him.

- When the story opens, Sarty Snopes is sitting in a makeshift courtroom, where his father is being tried for burning down yet another barn. Sarty testifies against his father, for which he's later beaten.
- Sarty's father goes to work for Major de Spain, a rich, landed gentleman. Sarty's father resents de Spain for his high social standing. One day, he deliberately tracks dung onto one of the Major's carpets. When a judge orders him to pay a fine, Sarty's father takes action.
- Sarty attempts to warn Major de Spain about his father's plans to burn down the Major's barn. The Major is a step ahead of him, however, and shoots Sarty's father before he can burn down the barn.

Themes:

- Young Sarty Snopes describes his own inner conflict as "the being pulled two ways like between two teams of horses." On one side is "the old fierce pull of blood" — family loyalty. On the other are truth and justice. The pull of family ties is strong, but Sarty is old enough to have started to realize that what his father does is wrong.
- In the first courtroom scene, Sarty finds himself thinking of the plaintiff as his father's enemy and consciously has to correct himself: "Ourn! mine and hisn both! He's my father!" Leaving the courtroom, he attacks a boy half again his size who calls Snopes a barn burner. Throughout the story, a pattern is established. Sarty keeps trying to defend, through his speech and actions, the father to whom he knows he owes his life and his loyalty. His thoughts, however, and what Faulkner projects will be his future thoughts once he has reached manhood, reveal the ultimately stronger pull of truth and justice. When, after the first trial, his father strikes him and tries to convince him that the men who bring him to trial are only after revenge because they know that ultimately Snopes is in the right, Sarty says nothing, but Faulkner knows that twenty years later, Sarty will tell himself, "If I had said they wanted only truth, justice, he would have hit me again." The de Spain mansion immediately appears to Sarty as a symbol of hope that perhaps here is a power too great

—a power with which his father cannot even hope to contend. What he cannot yet comprehend, in his childish innocence, is that the greater the wealth, the greater the gulf between the landowner and the landless Snopes, and thus the greater his father's jealous rage —a rage that Snopes keeps tightly in check until it bursts out in the flames of the fires he sets.

- The battle goes on as Sarty continues outwardly to defend his father while inwardly his doubts grow stronger and stronger. When de Spain imposes the fine, Sarty protests to his father that de Spain should have told them how to clean the rug, that the fine is too high, that they will hide the corn from de Spain. When the fine is lowered, he still protests that the major will not get a single bushel. His outbursts in his father's behalf almost cause more trouble for Snopes when Sarty loudly protests, "He ain't done it! He ain't burnt." when the issue at hand this time is the damaged rug, not a burned barn.

- Sarty still seems to be supporting his father when he runs to get the oil to burn de Spain's barn. During the short trip, however, he decides that he can neither simply run away nor stand by idly as his father burns the barn. He returns with the oil to defy his father openly for the first time, and he takes his stand firmly on the side of truth and justice when he runs to warn the major. By the end, he has turned his back both literally and symbolically on his home and on what remains of his family. His turning away from his family, however, is presented as a sign of hope as he walks off into the woods as dawn breaks and morning birds' calls replace those of the birds of night.

12. The Lottery (1948)

• **Shirley Jackson**

In "The Lottery," the inhabitants of a New England town gather in the town square to draw lots. Whoever draws a slip of paper with a black dot on it will be killed. After two drawings, a woman named Tessie is stoned to death in the town square.

- A ritual begins: Mr. Summers brings forth a box with hundreds of slips of paper inside.
- The names of all the family members in the town are collected.
- Bill draws a slip of paper with a dark splotch and Tessie voices the concern that his selection was unfair.
- The slips are retrieved and the drawing continues. Tessie takes a slip with a black spot and is stoned to death by the other townspeople.

Themes:

- In "The Lottery," Shirley Jackson represents the notion of the scapegoat as someone who is blamed for the evils of a society and banished in order to expel sin and allow for renewal.
- The townspeople are governed by mob psychology and abandon their reason to act with great cruelty.
- The violence of the townspeople who initially seem civilized and genteel reflects the possibility of violent acts taking place in any context.
- The refusal of the townspeople to abandon tradition and question the lottery ritual suggests the negative consequences of blindly following tradition.
- The female identity of the victim suggests the violence committed against women in a patriarchal society.

Characters:

- In "The Lottery," Tessie Hutchinson is a middle-aged housewife who wins the lottery and is stoned to death. She voices protest against the ritual.
- Old Man Warner is the oldest man in the village and a staunch defender of the lottery tradition.
- Joe Summers is a wealthy businessman who administrates the lottery.
- Bill Hutchinson is Tessie's husband; he obeys the rules of the lottery and quickly brings his wife forth for stoning once she draws the spotted card.
- Mrs. Janey Dunbar draws the lottery tickets for her family in the absence of her husband. She throws only small stones and seems reluctant to participate.

13. Young Goodman Brown (1835)   • Nathaniel Hawthorne

In "Young Goodman Brown," Brown walks into the forest to meet with the Devil. There, he stumbles upon a debauched Walpurgis Night celebration in which his wife participates. Appalled, Brown becomes suspicious of everyone and dies a hopeless man.

- Young Goodman Brown goes into the forest to meet with a character who resembles both Brown and the Devil.
- He meets a pious member of the village on the way to meet this sinister character, and is surprised that someone so good would be undertaking the same errand.

- He discovers a witches' Sabbath where the minister, the deacon, and even his wife are in attendance.
- Brown calls out to his wife and the scene dissolves. He turns back and returns to the village.
- Brown is forever changed by the incident and suspicious of others. He dies a hopeless man.

Themes:

- Young Goodman Brown's guilty conscience is evident in his wavering between whether to turn back home or join the perverted communion service in the forest.
- Though Brown triumphs in resisting evil, he develops an inability to trust others.
- It is unclear whether Brown dreamed the entire incident in the woods or whether any part of it actually occurred.
- Goodman Brown uncovers evil in everyone he knows, but Hawthorne suggests that Brown is merely confirming his suspicions without sufficient proof and demonstrating his arrogance.
- Hawthorne critiques the Puritan belief in good and evil by portraying Brown as an absolutist. His wife Faith, on the other hand, manages to accept Brown despite his trip into the forest.

Characters:

- Young Goodman Brown is a pious, devoted member of the community until he becomes convinced that the outward goodness of those he knows is merely a sham.
- Faith is Goodman Brown's wife who represents goodness and devotion. Goodman comes to distrust her after he sees her at the witches' Sabbath.
- The Devil may represent the darker side of Goodman Brown's nature as well as the evil acts of his ancestors.
- Goody Cloyse, the Minister, and Deacon Gookin represent the hypocrisy that Goodman Brown sees in the village.

14. Doe Season (1985)

• David Michael Kaplan

This story is about a girl named Andrea who goes by the name Andy. Andy goes hunting with her father, his friend and son. In this story Andy is scared of the changes that she will going through as she becomes a woman. Andy is a girl who masks the fact that by doing manly activity's with her father she maybe would not have to go through the change to womanhood. Andy has a hidden girly side and she also masks that in the story as you can see throughout the story when

Mac makes fun of her and teases her. The sea symbolizes womanhood and the forest symbolizes manhood. Andy wants to please her father in this story. At the end of the story when they cut the doe open, Andy runs in to the woods. Andy at that point realizes that she will maybe never be a part of the manly group and activity's with acceptance. Andy will be a woman someday soon as suggested in the story when she and her mother were at the beach and her mother lost her top, Andy appeared to be embarrassed however Andy realized she also would have breast sometime in the future. Andy struggles with some self identity in this story and at the end maybe realizes that she can do manly sports however she will always be a female.

Themes:

- David Michael Kaplan introduces two children who, although certainly not typical nine-and eleven-year-olds, are nevertheless believable, and their contrasting reactions to the hunt are striking. The younger Andy, although hoydenlike, successfully fights off Mac's and his father's baiting even as, despite her dislike of the pair, she tries to prove herself a worthy companion. Eventually, she seems to overcome her ambivalence about being a girl and no longer responds to her boyish nickname because it is not her real name.

- As in several other stories, Kaplan illustrates, implicitly if not directly, the familiar theme of parent-offspring relationships. He does so not only with reference to the two parent-child pairs on the hunt but also with reference to Andy and her mother. Except for waving them good-bye after the breakfast she prepares on their departure day, the mother does not appear in the story. Indeed, mothers are generally unimportant in Kaplan's tales; they are often dead, gone, or insane.

- During the trip, each father shares confidences with his child, trivial secrets to which the mother at home would not be a party. Andy's father offers her otherwise forbidden coffee; Mac's father tells him it is good to get away from the house "and the old lady." The mother becomes a reality to Andy most dramatically in the flashback of the beach episode. On that occasion the woman, gone for a swim, momentarily lost the top of her bathing suit because of the waves and Andy, embarrassed by the event, ran away from her, just as she is now running away from her father and his friends butchering the doe.

- In the last analysis, this is a story about how Andy is initiated into the adult world of sexuality and death. At its conclusion, the ambivalent Andy is maturing into the woman, Andrea. The fact that no analogous development occurs in Mac, who is two years her senior, makes her metamorphosis even more striking.

15. *The Rocking-Horse Winner (1920)   • D. H. Lawrence

In "The Rocking-Horse Winner," Hester is an unhappy woman who feels her family does not have enough money. Her son Paul wins a large sum on a bet, but dies after falling off of his rocking-horse.

- Paul becomes determined to allay his mother's discontent by betting on horses to earn money.
- Paul believes that when he rides his rocking-horse, he obtains knowledge of the winning horse in the race.
- Paul makes a winning bet on a horse that earns his family a handsome sum of money, but he falls off his rocking horse and descends into a semiconscious state. He eventually dies.

Themes:

- In "The Rocking-Horse Winner," D.H. Lawrence suggests that materialism and love are incompatible.
- Hester's pressure on Paul to satisfy her needs arrests his own maturation and self-realization.
- D.H. Lawrence suggests that happiness comes from the inside rather than external sources like luck or money.
- Paul's generosity in giving Hester all his money contrasts with her insatiable greed.
- Paul's supplanting of his father as the family's breadwinner suggests a manifestation of the Oedipal complex.

Characters:

- In "The Rocking-Horse Winner," Paul is a young boy who fulfills his mother's desire for more luck and money by betting on horses. He plays the role of an adult, but his sacrifices for his family are not appreciated.
- Hester is greedy and irresponsible, unable to love others because she is obsessed with acquiring material wealth.
- Bassett is the family gardener who helps Paul carry out his money-making endeavor by placing his bets on horses.
- Oscar Cresswell is Paul's uncle, who uses Paul's gift to further his own wealth and does little to help Hester and her family.

03 Novels To Read

> 01. **Hills Like White Elephants** (1927) – *Ernest Hemingway
> 02. **The Cask of Amontillado** (1846) – Edgar Allan Poe
> 03. **A Rose for Emily** (1930) – William Faulkner
> 04. **A&P** (1961) – John Updike
> 05. ***The Yellow Wallpapaer** (1892) – Charlotte Perkins Gilman
> 06. ***Araby** (1914) – James Joyce
> 09. **I Stand Here Ironing** (1961) - Tillie Olsen
> 11. **Barn Burning** (1939) - William Faulkner
> 12. **The Lottery** (1948) - Shirley Jackson
> 15. ***The Rocking-Horse Winner** (1920) – *D. H. Lawrence
>
> • Novels or writers referenced in the teacher certification exam.

1. Hills Like White Elephants (1927) • Ernest Hemingway

The hills across the valley of the Ebro were long and white. On this side there was no shade and no trees and the station was between two lines of rails in the sun. Close against the side of the station there was the warm shadow of the building and a curtain, made of strings of bamboo beads, hung across the open door into the bar, to keep out flies. The American and the girl with him sat at a table in the shade, outside the building. It was very hot and the express from Barcelona would come in forty minutes. It stopped at this junction for two minutes and went to Madrid.

"What should we drink?" the girl asked. She had taken off her hat and put it on the table.

"It's pretty hot," the man said.

"Let's drink beer."

"Dos cervezas," the man said into the curtain.

"Big ones?" a woman asked from the doorway.

"Yes. Two big ones."

The woman brought two glasses of beer and two felt pads. She put the felt pads and the beer glass on the table and looked at the man and the girl. The girl was looking off at the line of hills. They were white in the sun and the country was brown and dry.

"They look like white elephants," she said.

"I've never seen one," the man drank his beer.

"No, you wouldn't have."

"I might have," the man said. "Just because you say I wouldn't have doesn't prove anything."

The girl looked at the bead curtain. "They've painted something on it," she said. "What does it say?"

"Anis del Toro. It's a drink."

"Could we try it?"

The man called "Listen" through the curtain. The woman came out from the bar.

"Four reales." "We want two Anis del Toro."

"With water?"

"Do you want it with water?"

"I don't know," the girl said. "Is it good with water?"

"It's all right."

"You want them with water?" asked the woman.

"Yes, with water."

"It tastes like liquorice," the girl said and put the glass down.

"That's the way with everything."

"Yes," said the girl. "Everything tastes of liquorice. Especially all the things you've waited so long for, like absinthe."

"Oh, cut it out."

"You started it," the girl said. "I was being amused. I was having a fine time."

"Well, let's try and have a fine time."

"All right. I was trying. I said the mountains looked like white elephants. Wasn't that bright?"

"That was bright."

"I wanted to try this new drink. That's all we do, isn't it — look at things and try new drinks?"

"I guess so."

The girl looked across at the hills.

"They're lovely hills," she said. "They don't really look like white elephants. I just meant the colouring of their skin through the trees."

"Should we have another drink?"

"All right."

The warm wind blew the bead curtain against the table.

"The beer's nice and cool," the man said.

"It's lovely," the girl said.

"It's really an awfully simple operation, Jig," the man said. "It's not really an operation at all."

The girl looked at the ground the table legs rested on.

"I know you wouldn't mind it, Jig. It's really not anything. It's just to let the air in."

The girl did not say anything.

"I'll go with you and I'll stay with you all the time. They just let the air in and then it's all perfectly natural."

"Then what will we do afterwards?"

"We'll be fine afterwards. Just like we were before."

"What makes you think so?"

"That's the only thing that bothers us. It's the only thing that's made us unhappy."

The girl looked at the bead curtain, put her hand out and took hold of two of the strings of beads.

"And you think then we'll be all right and be happy."

"I know we will. Yon don't have to be afraid. I've known lots of people that have done it."

"So have I," said the girl. "And afterwards they were all so happy."

"Well," the man said, "if you don't want to you don't have to. I wouldn't have you do it if you didn't want to. But I know it's perfectly simple."

"And you really want to?"

"I think it's the best thing to do. But I don't want you to do it if you don't really want to."

"And if I do it you'll be happy and things will be like they were and you'll love me?"

"I love you now. You know I love you."

"I know. But if I do it, then it will be nice again if I say things are like white elephants, and you'll like it?"

"I'll love it. I love it now but I just can't think about it. You know how I get when I worry."

"If I do it you won't ever worry?"

"I won't worry about that because it's perfectly simple."

"Then I'll do it. Because I don't care about me."

"What do you mean?"

"I don't care about me."

"Well, I care about you."

"Oh, yes. But I don't care about me. And I'll do it and then everything will be fine."

"I don't want you to do it if you feel that way."

The girl stood up and walked to the end of the station. Across, on the other side, were fields of grain and trees along the banks of the Ebro. Far away, beyond the river, were mountains. The shadow of a cloud moved across the field of grain and she saw the river through the trees.

"And we could have all this," she said. "And we could have everything and every day we make it more impossible."

"What did you say?"

"I said we could have everything."

"We can have everything."

"No, we can't."

"We can have the whole world."

"No, we can't."

"We can go everywhere."

"No, we can't. It isn't ours any more."

"It's ours."

"No, it isn't. And once they take it away, you never get it back."

"But they haven't taken it away."

"We'll wait and see."

"Come on back in the shade," he said. "You mustn't feel that way."

"I don't feel any way," the girl said. "I just know things."

"I don't want you to do anything that you don't want to do —"

"Nor that isn't good for me," she said. "I know. Could we have another beer?"

"All right. But you've got to realize —"

"I realize," the girl said. "Can't we maybe stop talking?"

They sat down at the table and the girl looked across at the hills on the dry side of the valley and the man looked at her and at the table.

"You've got to realize," he said, "that I don't want you to do it if you don't want to. I'm perfectly willing to go through with it if it means anything to you."

"Doesn't it mean anything to you? We could get along."

"Of course it does. But I don't want anybody but you. I don't want anyone else. And I know it's perfectly simple."

"Yes, you know it's perfectly simple."

"It's all right for you to say that, but I do know it."

"Would you do something for me now?"

"I'd do anything for you."

"Would you please please please please please please please stop talking?"

He did not say anything but looked at the bags against the wall of the station. There were labels on them from all the hotels where they had spent nights.

"But I don't want you to," he said, "I don't care anything about it."

"I'll scream," the girl said.

The woman came out through the curtains with two glasses of beer and put them down on the damp felt pads. "The train comes in five minutes," she said.

"What did she say?" asked the girl.

"That the train is coming in five minutes."

The girl smiled brightly at the woman, to thank her.

"I'd better take the bags over to the other side of the station," the man said. She smiled at him.

"All right. Then come back and we'll finish the beer."

He picked up the two heavy bags and carried them around the station to the other tracks. He looked up the tracks but could not see the train. Coming back, he walked through the bar-room, where people waiting for the train were drinking. He drank an Anis at the bar and looked at the people. They were all waiting reasonably for the train. He went out through the bead curtain. She was sitting at the table and smiled at him.

"Do you feel better?" he asked.

"I feel fine," she said. "There's nothing wrong with me. I feel fine.

2. The Cask of Amontillado (1846) • Edgar Allan Poe

THE thousand injuries of Fortunato I had borne as I best could, but when he ventured upon insult, I vowed revenge. You, who so well know the nature of my soul, will not suppose, however, that I gave utterance to a threat. AT LENGTH I would be avenged; this was a point definitively settled — but the very definitiveness with which it was resolved precluded the idea of risk. I must not only punish, but punish with impunity. A wrong is unredressed when retribution overtakes its redresser. It is equally unredressed when the avenger fails to make himself felt as such to him who has done the wrong. It must be understood that neither by word nor deed had I given Fortunato cause to doubt my good will. I continued as was my wont, to smile in his face, and he did not perceive that my smile NOW was at the thought of his immolation.

He had a weak point — this Fortunato — although in other regards he was a man to be respected and even feared. He prided himself on his connoisseurship in wine. Few Italians have the true virtuoso spirit. For the most part their enthusiasm is adopted to suit the time and opportunity to practise imposture upon the British and Austrian MILLIONAIRES. In painting and gemmary, Fortunato, like his countrymen , was a quack, but in the matter of old wines he was sincere. In this respect I did not differ from him materially; I was skillful in the Italian vintages myself, and bought largely whenever I could.

It was about dusk, one evening during the supreme madness of the carnival season, that I encountered my friend. He accosted me with excessive warmth, for he had been drinking much. The man wore motley. He had on a tight-fitting parti-striped dress and his head was surmounted by the conical cap and bells. I was so pleased to see him that I thought I should never have done wringing his hand.

I said to him — "My dear Fortunato, you are luckily met. How remarkably well you are looking to-day! But I have received a pipe of what passes for Amontillado, and I have my doubts."

"How?" said he, "Amontillado? A pipe? Impossible? And in the middle of the carnival?"

"I have my doubts," I replied; "and I was silly enough to pay the full Amontillado price without consulting you in the matter. You were not to be found, and I was fearful of losing a bargain."

"Amontillado!"

"I have my doubts."

"Amontillado!"

"And I must satisfy them." "Amontillado!"

"As you are engaged, I am on my way to Luchesi. If any one has a critical turn, it is he. He will tell me" —

"Luchesi cannot tell Amontillado from Sherry."

"And yet some fools will have it that his taste is a match for your own."

"Come let us go."

"Whither?"

"To your vaults."

"My friend, no; I will not impose upon your good nature. I perceive you have an engagement Luchesi" —

"I have no engagement; come."

"My friend, no. It is not the engagement, but the severe cold with which I perceive you are afflicted. The vaults are insufferably damp. They are encrusted with nitre."

"Let us go, nevertheless. The cold is merely nothing. Amontillado! You have been imposed upon; and as for Luchesi, he cannot distinguish Sherry from Amontillado."

Thus speaking, Fortunato possessed himself of my arm. Putting on a mask of black silk and drawing a roquelaire closely about my person, I suffered him to hurry me to my palazzo.

There were no attendants at home; they had absconded to make merry in honour of the time. I had told them that I should not return until the morning and had given them explicit orders not to stir from the house. These orders were sufficient, I well knew, to insure their immediate disappearance, one and all, as soon as my back was turned.

I took from their sconces two flambeaux, and giving one to Fortunato bowed him through several suites of rooms to the archway that led into the vaults. I passed down a long and winding staircase, requesting him to be cautious as he followed. We came at length to the foot of the descent, and stood together on the damp ground of the catacombs of the Montresors.

The gait of my friend was unsteady, and the bells upon his cap jingled as he strode.

"The pipe," said he.

"It is farther on," said I; "but observe the white webwork which gleams from these cavern walls."

He turned towards me and looked into my eyes with two filmy orbs that distilled the rheum of intoxication.

"Nitre?" he asked, at length

"Nitre," I replied. "How long have you had that cough!"

"Ugh! ugh! ugh! — ugh! ugh! ugh! — ugh! ugh! ugh! — ugh! ugh! ugh! — ugh! ugh! ugh!"

My poor friend found it impossible to reply for many minutes.

"It is nothing," he said, at last.

"Come," I said, with decision, "we will go back; your health is precious. You are rich, respected, admired, beloved; you are happy as once I was. You are a man to be missed. For me it is no matter. We will go back; you will be ill and I cannot be responsible. Besides, there is Luchesi" —

"Enough," he said; "the cough is a mere nothing; it will not kill me. I shall not die of a cough."

"True — true," I replied; "and, indeed, I had no intention of alarming you unnecessarily — but you should use all proper caution. A draught of this Medoc will defend us from the damps."

Here I knocked off the neck of a bottle which I drew from a long row of its fellows that lay upon the mould.

"Drink," I said, presenting him the wine.

He raised it to his lips with a leer. He paused and nodded to me familiarly, while his bells jingled.

"I drink," he said, "to the buried that repose around us."

"And I to your long life."

He again took my arm and we proceeded.

"These vaults," he said, "are extensive."

"The Montresors," I replied, "were a great numerous family."

"I forget your arms."

"A huge human foot d'or, in a field azure; the foot crushes a serpent rampant whose fangs are imbedded in the heel."

"And the motto?"

"Nemo me impune lacessit."

"Good!" he said.

The wine sparkled in his eyes and the bells jingled. My own fancy grew warm with the Medoc. We had passed through walls of piled bones, with casks and puncheons intermingling, into the inmost recesses of the catacombs. I paused again, and this time I made bold to seize Fortunato by an arm above the elbow.

"The nitre!" I said: "see, it increases. It hangs like moss upon the vaults. We are below the river's bed. The drops of moisture trickle among the bones. Come, we will go back ere it is too late. Your cough" —

"It is nothing" he said; "let us go on. But first, another draught of the Medoc."

I broke and reached him a flagon of De Grave. He emptied it at a breath. His eyes flashed with a fierce light. He laughed and threw the bottle upwards with a gesticulation I did not understand.

I looked at him in surprise. He repeated the movement — a grotesque one.

"You do not comprehend?" he said.

"Not I," I replied.

"Then you are not of the brotherhood."

"How?"

"You are not of the masons."

"Yes, yes," I said "yes! yes."

"You? Impossible! A mason?"

"A mason," I replied.

"A sign," he said.

"It is this," I answered, producing a trowel from beneath the folds of my roquelaire.

"You jest," he exclaimed, recoiling a few paces. "But let us proceed to the Amontillado."

"Be it so," I said, replacing the tool beneath the cloak, and again offering him my arm. He leaned upon it heavily. We continued our route in search of the Amontillado. We passed through a range of low arches, descended, passed on, and descending again, arrived at a deep crypt, in which the foulness of the air caused our flambeaux rather to glow than flame.

At the most remote end of the crypt there appeared another less spacious. Its walls had been lined with human remains piled to the vault overhead, in the fashion of the great catacombs of Paris. Three sides of this interior crypt were still ornamented in this manner. From the fourth the bones had been thrown down, and lay promiscuously upon the earth, forming at one point a mound of some size. Within the wall thus exposed by the displacing of the bones, we perceived a still interior recess, in depth about four feet, in width three, in height six or seven. It seemed to have been constructed for no especial use in itself, but formed merely the interval between two of the colossal supports of the roof of the catacombs, and was backed by one of their circumscribing walls of solid granite.

It was in vain that Fortunato, uplifting his dull torch, endeavoured to pry into the depths of the recess. Its termination the feeble light did not enable us to see.

"Proceed," I said; "herein is the Amontillado. As for Luchesi" —

"He is an ignoramus," interrupted my friend, as he stepped unsteadily forward, while I followed immediately at his heels. In an instant he had reached the extremity of the niche, and finding his progress arrested by the rock, stood stupidly bewildered. A moment more and I had fettered him to the granite. In its surface were two iron staples, distant from each other about two feet, horizontally. From one of these depended a short chain, from the other a padlock. Throwing the links about his waist, it was but the work of a few seconds to secure it. He was too much astounded to resist. Withdrawing the key I stepped back from the recess.

"Pass your hand," I said, "over the wall; you cannot help feeling the nitre. Indeed it is VERY damp. Once more let me IMPLORE you to return. No? Then I must positively leave you. But I must first render you all the little attentions in my power."

"The Amontillado!" ejaculated my friend, not yet recovered from his astonishment.

"True," I replied; "the Amontillado."

As I said these words I busied myself among the pile of bones of which I have before spoken. Throwing them aside, I soon uncovered a quantity of building stone and mortar. With these materials and with the aid of my trowel, I began vigorously to wall up the entrance of the niche.

I had scarcely laid the first tier of my masonry when I discovered that the intoxication of Fortunato had in a great measure worn off. The earliest indication I had of this was a low moaning cry from the depth of the recess. It was NOT the cry of a drunken man. There was then a long and obstinate silence. I laid the second tier, and the third, and the fourth; and then I heard the furious vibrations of the chain. The noise lasted for several minutes, during which, that I might hearken to it with the more satisfaction, I ceased my labours and sat down upon the bones. When at last the clanking subsided, I resumed the trowel, and finished without interruption the fifth, the sixth, and the seventh tier. The wall was now nearly upon a level with my breast. I again paused, and holding the flambeaux over the mason-work, threw a few feeble rays upon the figure within.

A succession of loud and shrill screams, bursting suddenly from the throat of the chained form, seemed to thrust me violently back. For a brief moment I hesitated — I trembled. Unsheathing my rapier, I began to grope with it about the recess; but the thought of an instant reassured me. I placed my hand upon the solid fabric of the catacombs, and felt satisfied. I reapproached the wall. I replied to the yells of him who clamoured. I reechoed — I aided — I surpassed them in volume and in strength. I did this, and the clamourer grew still.

It was now midnight, and my task was drawing to a close. I had completed the eighth, the ninth, and the tenth tier. I had finished a portion of the last and the eleventh; there remained but a single stone to be fitted and plastered in. I struggled with its weight; I placed it partially in its destined position. But now there came from out the niche a low laugh that erected the hairs upon my head. It was succeeded by a sad voice, which I had difficulty in recognising as that of the noble Fortunato. The voice said —

"Ha! ha! ha! — he! he! — a very good joke indeed — an excellent jest. We will have many a rich laugh about it at the palazzo — he! he! he! — over our wine — he! he! he!"

"The Amontillado!" I said.

"He! he! he! — he! he! he! — yes, the Amontillado. But is it not getting late? Will not they be awaiting us at the palazzo, the Lady Fortunato and the rest? Let us be gone."

"Yes," I said "let us be gone."

"FOR THE LOVE OF GOD, MONTRESOR!"

"Yes," I said, "for the love of God!"

But to these words I hearkened in vain for a reply. I grew impatient. I called aloud —

"Fortunato!"

No answer. I called again —

"Fortunato!"

No answer still. I thrust a torch through the remaining aperture and let it fall within. There came forth in return only a jingling of the bells. My heart grew sick — on account of the dampness of the catacombs. I hastened to make an end of my labour. I forced the last stone into its position; I plastered it up. Against the new masonry I re-erected the old rampart of bones. For the half of a century no mortal has disturbed them. In pace requiescat!

3. A Rose for Emily (1930)

• William Faulkner

I

WHEN Miss Emily Grierson died, our whole town went to her funeral: the men through a sort of respectful affection for a fallen monument, the women mostly out of curiosity to see the inside of her house, which no one save an old man-servant — a combined gardener and cook — had seen in at least ten years.

It was a big, squarish frame house that had once been white, decorated with cupolas and spires and scrolled balconies in the heavily lightsome style of the seventies, set on what had once been our most select street. But garages and cotton gins had encroached and obliterated even the august names of that neighborhood; only Miss Emily's house was left, lifting its stubborn and coquettish decay above the cotton wagons and the gasoline pumps — an eyesore among eyesores. And now Miss Emily had gone to join the representatives of those august names where they lay in the cedar-bemused cemetery among the ranked and anonymous graves of Union and Confederate soldiers who fell at the battle of Jefferson.

Alive, Miss Emily had been a tradition, a duty, and a care; a sort of hereditary obligation upon the town, dating from that day in 1894 when Colonel Sartoris, the mayor — he who fathered the edict that no Negro woman should appear on the streets without an apron — remitted her taxes, the dispensation dating from the death of her father on into perpetuity. Not that Miss Emily would have accepted charity. Colonel Sartoris invented an involved tale to the effect that Miss Emily's father had loaned money to the town, which the town, as a matter of business, preferred this way of repaying. Only a man of Colonel Sartoris' generation and thought could have invented it, and only a woman could have believed it.

When the next generation, with its more modern ideas, became mayors and aldermen, this arrangement created some little dissatisfaction. On the first of the year they mailed her a tax notice. February came, and there was no reply. They wrote her a formal letter, asking her to call at the sheriff's office at her convenience. A week later the mayor wrote her himself, offering to call or to send his car for her, and received in reply a note on paper of an archaic shape, in a thin, flowing calligraphy in faded ink, to the effect that she no longer went out at all. The tax notice was also enclosed, without comment.

They called a special meeting of the Board of Aldermen. A deputation waited upon her, knocked at the door through which no visitor had passed since she ceased giving china-painting lessons eight or ten years earlier. They were admitted by the old Negro into a dim hall from which a stairway mounted into still more shadow. It smelled of dust and disuse — a close, dank smell. The Negro led them into the parlor. It was furnished in heavy, leather-covered furniture. When the Negro opened the blinds of one window, they could see that the leather was cracked; and when they sat down, a faint dust rose sluggishly about their thighs, spinning with slow motes in the single sun-ray. On a tarnished gilt easel before the fireplace stood a crayon portrait of Miss Emily's father.

They rose when she entered — a small, fat woman in black, with a thin gold chain descending to her waist and vanishing into her belt, leaning on an ebony cane with a tarnished gold head. Her skeleton was small and spare; perhaps that was why what would have been merely plumpness in another was obesity in her. She looked bloated, like a body long submerged in motionless water, and of that pallid hue. Her eyes, lost in the fatty ridges of her face, looked like two small pieces of coal pressed into a lump of dough as they moved from one face to another while the visitors stated their errand.

She did not ask them to sit. She just stood in the door and listened quietly until the spokesman came to a stumbling halt. Then they could hear the invisible watch ticking at the end of the gold chain.

Her voice was dry and cold. "I have no taxes in Jefferson. Colonel Sartoris explained it to me. Perhaps one of you can gain access to the city records and satisfy yourselves."

"But we have. We are the city authorities, Miss Emily. Didn't you get a notice from the sheriff, signed by him?"

"I received a paper, yes," Miss Emily said. "Perhaps he considers himself the sheriff . . . I have no taxes in Jefferson."

"But there is nothing on the books to show that, you see We must go by the — "

"See Colonel Sartoris. I have no taxes in Jefferson."

"But, Miss Emily — "

"See Colonel Sartoris." (Colonel Sartoris had been dead almost ten years.) "I have no taxes in Jefferson. Tobe!" The Negro appeared. "Show these gentlemen out."

II

So SHE vanquished them, horse and foot, just as she had vanquished their fathers thirty years before about the smell.

That was two years after her father's death and a short time after her sweetheart — the one we believed would marry her — had deserted her. After her father's death she went out very little; after her sweetheart went away, people hardly saw her at all. A few of the ladies had the temerity to call, but were not received, and the only sign of life about the place was the Negro man — a young man then — going in and out with a market basket.

"Just as if a man — any man — could keep a kitchen properly," the ladies said; so they were not surprised when the smell developed. It was another link between the gross, teeming world and the high and mighty Griersons.

A neighbor, a woman, complained to the mayor, Judge Stevens, eighty years old.

"But what will you have me do about it, madam?" he said.

"Why, send her word to stop it," the woman said. "Isn't there a law?"

"I'm sure that won't be necessary," Judge Stevens said. "It's probably just a snake or a rat that nigger of hers killed in the yard. I'll speak to him about it."

The next day he received two more complaints, one from a man who came in diffident deprecation. "We really must do something about it, Judge. I'd be the last one in the world to bother Miss Emily, but we've got to do something." That night the Board of Aldermen met — three graybeards and one younger man, a member of the rising generation.

"It's simple enough," he said. "Send her word to have her place cleaned up. Give her a certain time to do it in, and if she don't . . ."

"Dammit, sir," Judge Stevens said, "will you accuse a lady to her face of smelling bad?"

So the next night, after midnight, four men crossed Miss Emily's lawn and slunk about the house like burglars, sniffing along the base of the brickwork and at the cellar openings while one of them performed a regular sowing motion with his hand out of a sack slung from his shoulder. They broke open the cellar door and sprinkled lime there, and in all the outbuildings. As they recrossed the lawn, a window that had been dark was lighted and Miss Emily sat in it, the light behind her, and her upright torso motionless as that of an idol. They crept quietly across the lawn and into the shadow of the locusts that lined the street. After a week or two the smell went away.

That was when people had begun to feel really sorry for her. People in our town, remembering how old lady Wyatt, her great-aunt, had gone completely crazy at last, believed that the Griersons held themselves a little too high for what they really were. None of the young men were quite good enough for Miss Emily and such. We had long thought of them as a tableau, Miss Emily a slender figure in white in the background, her father a spraddled silhouette in the foreground, his back to her and clutching a horsewhip, the two of them framed by the back-flung front door. So when she got to be thirty and was still single, we were not pleased exactly, but vindicated; even with insanity in the family she wouldn't have turned down all of her chances if they had really materialized.

When her father died, it got about that the house was all that was left to her; and in a way, people were glad. At last they could pity Miss Emily. Being left alone, and a pauper, she had become humanized. Now she too would know the old thrill and the old despair of a penny more or less.

The day after his death all the ladies prepared to call at the house and offer condolence and aid, as is our custom Miss Emily met them at the door, dressed as usual and with no trace of grief on her face. She told them that her father was not dead. She did that for three days, with the ministers calling on her, and the doctors, trying to persuade her to let them dispose of the body. Just as they were about to resort to law and force, she broke down, and they buried her father quickly.

We did not say she was crazy then. We believed she had to do that. We remembered all the young men her father had driven away, and we knew that with nothing left, she would have to cling to that which had robbed her, as people will.

III

SHE WAS SICK for a long time. When we saw her again, her hair was cut short, making her look like a girl, with a vague resemblance to those angels in colored church windows — sort of tragic and serene.

The town had just let the contracts for paving the sidewalks, and in the summer after her father's death they began the work. The construction company came with niggers and mules and machinery, and a foreman named Homer Barron, a Yankee — a big, dark, ready man, with a big voice and eyes lighter than his face. The little boys would follow in groups to hear him cuss the niggers, and the niggers singing in time to the rise and fall of picks. Pretty soon he knew everybody in town. Whenever you heard a lot of laughing anywhere about the square, Homer Barron would be in the center of the group. Presently we began to see him and Miss Emily on Sunday afternoons driving in the yellow-wheeled buggy and the matched team of bays from the livery stable.

At first we were glad that Miss Emily would have an interest, because the ladies all said, "Of course a Grierson would not think seriously of a Northerner, a day laborer." But there were still others, older people, who said that even grief could not cause a real lady to forget noblesse oblige — without calling it noblesse oblige. They just said, "Poor Emily. Her kinsfolk should come to her." She had some kin in Alabama; but years ago her father had fallen out with them over the estate of old lady Wyatt, the crazy woman, and there was no communication between the two families. They had not even been represented at the funeral.

And as soon as the old people said, "Poor Emily," the whispering began. "Do you suppose it's really so?" they said to one another. "Of course it is. What else could . . ." This behind their hands; rustling of craned silk and satin behind jalousies closed upon the sun of Sunday afternoon as the thin, swift clop-clop-clop of the matched team passed: "Poor Emily."

She carried her head high enough — even when we believed that she was fallen. It was as if she demanded more than ever the recognition of her dignity as the last Grierson; as if it had wanted that touch of earthiness to reaffirm her imperviousness. Like when she bought the rat poison, the arsenic. That was over a year after they had begun to say "Poor Emily," and while the two female cousins were visiting her.

"I want some poison," she said to the druggist. She was over thirty then, still a slight woman, though thinner than usual, with cold, haughty black eyes in a face the flesh of which was strained across the temples and about the eyesockets as you imagine a lighthouse-keeper's face ought to look. "I want some poison," she said.

"Yes, Miss Emily. What kind? For rats and such? I'd recom — "

"I want the best you have. I don't care what kind."

The druggist named several. "They'll kill anything up to an elephant. But what you want is — "

"Arsenic," Miss Emily said. "Is that a good one?"

"Is . . . arsenic? Yes, ma'am. But what you want — "

"I want arsenic."

The druggist looked down at her. She looked back at him, erect, her face like a strained flag. "Why, of course," the druggist said. "If that's what you want. But the law requires you to tell what you are going to use it for."

Miss Emily just stared at him, her head tilted back in order to look him eye for eye, until he looked away and went and got the arsenic and wrapped it up. The Negro delivery boy brought her the package; the druggist didn't come back. When she opened the package at home there was written on the box, under the skull and bones: "For rats."

IV

So THE NEXT day we all said, "She will kill herself"; and we said it would be the best thing. When she had first begun to be seen with Homer Barron, we had said, "She will marry him." Then we said, "She will persuade him yet," because Homer himself had remarked — he liked men, and it was known that he drank with the younger men in the Elks' Club — that he was not a marrying man. Later we said, "Poor Emily" behind the jalousies as they passed on Sunday afternoon in the glittering buggy, Miss Emily with her head high and Homer Barron with his hat cocked and a cigar in his teeth, reins and whip in a yellow glove.

Then some of the ladies began to say that it was a disgrace to the town and a bad example to the young people. The men did not want to interfere, but at last the ladies forced the Baptist minister — Miss Emily's people were Episcopal — to call upon her. He would never divulge what happened during that interview, but he refused to go back again. The next Sunday they again drove about the streets, and the following day the minister's wife wrote to Miss Emily's relations in Alabama.

So she had blood-kin under her roof again and we sat back to watch developments. At first nothing happened. Then we were sure that they were to be married. We learned that Miss Emily had been to the jeweler's and ordered a man's toilet set in silver, with the letters H. B. on each piece. Two days later we learned that she had bought a complete outfit of men's clothing, including a nightshirt, and we said, "They are married." We were really glad. We were glad because the two female cousins were even more Grierson than Miss Emily had ever been.

So we were not surprised when Homer Barron — the streets had been finished some time since — was gone. We were a little disappointed that there was not a public blowing-off, but we believed that he had gone on to prepare for Miss Emily's coming, or to give her a chance to get rid of the cousins. (By that time it was a cabal, and we were all Miss Emily's allies to help circumvent the cousins.) Sure enough, after another week they departed. And, as we had expected all along, within three days Homer Barron was back in town. A neighbor saw the Negro man admit him at the kitchen door at dusk one evening.

And that was the last we saw of Homer Barron. And of Miss Emily for some time. The Negro man went in and out with the market basket, but the front door remained closed. Now and then we would see her at a window for a moment, as the men did that night when they sprinkled the lime, but for almost six months she did not appear on the streets. Then we knew that this was to be expected too; as if that quality of her father which had thwarted her woman's life so many times had been too virulent and too furious to die.

When we next saw Miss Emily, she had grown fat and her hair was turning gray. During the next few years it grew grayer and grayer until it attained an even pepper-and-salt iron-gray, when it ceased turning. Up to the day of her death at seventy-four it was still that vigorous iron-gray, like the hair of an active man.

From that time on her front door remained closed, save for a period of six or seven years, when she was about forty, during which she gave lessons in china-painting. She fitted up a studio in one of the downstairs rooms, where the daughters and granddaughters of Colonel Sartoris' contemporaries were sent to her with the same regularity and in the same spirit that they were sent to church on Sundays with a twenty-five-cent piece for the collection plate. Meanwhile her taxes had been remitted.

Then the newer generation became the backbone and the spirit of the town, and the painting pupils grew up and fell away and did not send their children to her with boxes of color and tedious brushes and pictures cut from the ladies' magazines. The front door closed upon the last one and remained closed for good. When the town got free postal delivery, Miss Emily alone refused to let them fasten the metal numbers above her door and attach a mailbox to it. She would not listen to them.

Daily, monthly, yearly we watched the Negro grow grayer and more stooped, going in and out with the market basket. Each December we sent her a tax notice, which would be returned by the post office a week later, unclaimed. Now and then we would see her in one of the downstairs windows — she had evidently shut up the top floor of the house — like the carven torso of an idol in a niche, looking or not looking at us, we could never tell which. Thus she passed from generation to generation — dear, inescapable, impervious, tranquil, and perverse.

And so she died. Fell ill in the house filled with dust and shadows, with only a doddering Negro man to wait on her. We did not even know she was sick; we had long since given up trying to get any information from the Negro.

He talked to no one, probably not even to her, for his voice had grown harsh and rusty, as if from disuse.

She died in one of the downstairs rooms, in a heavy walnut bed with a curtain, her gray head propped on a pillow yellow and moldy with age and lack of sunlight.

V

THE NEGRO met the first of the ladies at the front door and let them in, with their hushed, sibilant voices and their quick, curious glances, and then he disappeared. He walked right through the house and out the back and was not seen again.

The two female cousins came at once. They held the funeral on the second day, with the town coming to look at Miss Emily beneath a mass of bought flowers, with the crayon face of her father musing profoundly above the bier and the ladies sibilant and macabre; and the very old men — some in their brushed Confederate uniforms — on the porch and the lawn, talking of Miss Emily as if she had been a contemporary of theirs, believing that they had danced with her and courted her perhaps, confusing time with its mathematical progression, as the old do, to whom all the past is not a diminishing road but, instead, a huge meadow which no winter ever quite touches, divided from them now by the narrow bottle-neck of the most recent decade of years.

Already we knew that there was one room in that region above stairs which no one had seen in forty years, and which would have to be forced. They waited until Miss Emily was decently in the ground before they opened it.

The violence of breaking down the door seemed to fill this room with pervading dust. A thin, acrid pall as of the tomb seemed to lie everywhere upon this room decked and furnished as for a bridal: upon the valance curtains of faded rose color, upon the rose-shaded lights, upon the dressing table, upon the delicate array of crystal and the man's toilet things backed with tarnished silver, silver so tarnished that the monogram was obscured. Among them lay a collar and tie, as if they had just been removed, which, lifted, left upon the surface a pale crescent in the dust. Upon a chair hung the suit, carefully folded; beneath it the two mute shoes and the discarded socks.

The man himself lay in the bed.

For a long while we just stood there, looking down at the profound and fleshless grin. The body had apparently once lain in the attitude of an embrace, but now the long sleep that outlasts love, that conquers even the grimace of love, had cuckolded him. What was left of him, rotted beneath what was left of the nightshirt, had become inextricable from the bed in which he lay; and upon him and upon the pillow beside him lay that even coating of the patient and biding dust.

Then we noticed that in the second pillow was the indentation of a head. One of us lifted something from it, and leaning forward, that faint and invisible dust dry and acrid in the nostrils, we saw a long strand of iron-gray hair.

4. A&P (1961)
• John Updike

In walks these three girls in nothing but bathing suits. I'm in the third check-out slot, with my back to the door, so I don't see them until they're over by the bread. The one that caught my eye first was the one in the plaid green two-piece. She was a chunky kid, with a good tan and a sweet broad soft-looking can with those two crescents of white just under it, where the sun never seems to hit, at the top of the backs of her legs. I stood there with my hand on a box of HiHo crackers trying to remember if I rang it up or not. I ring it up again and the customer starts giving me hell. She's one of these cash-register-watchers, a witch about fifty with rouge on her cheekbones and no eyebrows, and I know it made her day to trip me up. She'd been watching cash registers forty years and probably never seen a mistake before.

By the time I got her feathers smoothed and her goodies into a bag — she gives me alittle snort in passing, if she'd been born at the right time they would have burned her over in Salem — by the time I get her on her way the girls had circled around the bread and were coming back, without a pushcart, back my way along the counters, in the aisle between the check-outs and the Special bins. They didn't even have shoes on. There was this chunky one, with the two-piece — it was bright green and the seams on the bra were still sharp and her belly was still pretty pale so I guessed she just got it (the suit) — there was this one, with one of those chubby berry-faces, the lips all bunched together under her nose, this one, and a tall one, with black hair that hadn't quite frizzed right, and one of these sunburns right across under the eyes, and a chin that was too long — you know, the kind of girl other girls think is very "striking" and "attractive" but never quite makes it, as they very well know, which is why they like her so much — and then the third one, that wasn't quite so tall. She was the queen. She kind of led them, the other two peeking around and making their shoulders round. She didn't look around, not this queen, she just walked straight on slowly, on these long white prima donna legs. She came down a little hard on her heels, as if she didn't walk in her bare feet that much, putting down her heels and then letting the weight move along to her toes as if she was testing the floor with every step, putting a little deliberate extra action into it. You never know for sure how girls' minds work (do you really think it's a mind in there or just a little buzz like a bee in a glassjar?) but you got the idea she had talked the other two into coming in here with her, and now she was showing them how to do it, walk slow and hold yourself straight.

She had on a kind of dirty-pink — beige maybe, I don't know — bathing suit with a little nubble all over it and, what got me, the straps were down. They were off her shoulders looped loose around the cool tops of her arms, and I guess as a result the suit had slipped a little on her, so all around the top of the cloth there was this shining rim. If it hadn't been there you wouldn't have known there could have been anything whiter than those shoulders. With the straps pushed off, there was nothing between the top of the suit and the top of her head except just her, this clean bare plane of the top of her chest down from the shoulder bones like a dented sheet of metal tilted in the light. I mean, it was more than pretty.

She had sort of oaky hair that the sun and salt had bleached, done up in a bun that was unravelling, and a kind of prim face. Walking into the A&P with your straps down, I suppose it's the only kind of face you can have. She held her head so high her neck, coming up out of those white shoulders, looked kind of stretched, but I didn't mind. The longer her neck was, the more of her there was.

She must have felt in the corner of her eye me and over my shoulder Stokesie in the second slot watching, but she didn't tip. Not this queen. She kept her eyes moving across the racks, and stopped, and turned so slow it made my stomach rub the inside of my apron, and buzzed to the other two, who kind of huddled against her for relief, and they all three of them went up the cat-and-dog-food-breakfast-cereal-macaroni-rice -raisins-seasonings-spreads-spaghetti-soft drinks-rackers-and-cookies aisle. From the third slot I look straight up this aisle to the meat counter, and I watched them all the way. The fat one with the tan sort of fumbled with the cookies, but on second thought she put the packages back. The sheep pushing their carts down the aisle — the girls were walking against the usual traffic (not that we have one-way signs or anything) — were pretty hilarious. You could see them, when Queenie's white shoulders dawned on them, kind of jerk, or hop, or hiccup, but their eyes snapped back to their own baskets and on they pushed. I bet you could set off dynamite in an A&P and the people would by and large keep reaching and checking oatmeal off their lists and muttering "Let me see, there was a third thing, began with A, asparagus, no, ah, yes, applesauce!" or whatever it is they do mutter. But there was no doubt, this jiggled them. A few house-slaves in pin curlers even looked around after pushing their carts past to make sure what they had seen was correct.

You know, it's one thing to have a girl in a bathing suit down on the beach, where what with the glare nobody can look at each other much anyway, and another thing in the cool of the A&P, under the fluorescent lights, against all those stacked packages, with her feet paddling along naked over our checkerboard green-and-cream rubber-tile floor.

"Oh Daddy," Stokesie said beside me. "I feel so faint."

"Darling," I said. "Hold me tight." Stokesie's married, with two babies chalked up on his fuselage already, but as far as I can tell that's the only difference. He's twenty-two, and I was nineteen this April.

"Is it done?" he asks, the responsible married man finding his voice. I forgot to say he thinks he's going to be manager some sunny day, maybe in 1990 when it's called the Great Alexandrov and Petrooshki Tea Company or something.

What he meant was, our town is five miles from a beach, with a big summer colony out on the Point, but we're right in the middle of town, and the women generally put on a shirt or shorts or something before they get out of the car into the street. And anyway these are usually women with six children and varicose veins mapping their legs and nobody, including them, could care less. As I say, we're right in the middle of town, and if you stand at our front doors you can see two banks and the Congregational church and the newspaper store and three real-estate offices and about twenty-seven old free-loaders tearing up Central Street because the sewer broke again. It's not as if we're on the Cape; we're north of Boston and there's people in this town haven't seen the ocean for twenty years.

The girls had reached the meat counter and were asking McMahon something. He pointed, they pointed, and they shuffled out of sight behind a pyramid of Diet Delight peaches. All that was left for us to see was old McMahon patting his mouth and looking after them sizing up their joints. Poor kids, I began to feel sorry for them, they couldn't help it.

Now here comes the sad part of the story, at least my family says it's sad but I don't think it's sad myself. The store's pretty empty, it being Thursday afternoon, so there was nothing much to do except lean on the register and wait for the girls to show up again. The whole store was like a pinball machine and I didn't know which tunnel they'd come out of. After a while they come around out of the far aisle, around the light bulbs, records at discount of the Caribbean Six or Tony Martin Sings or some such gunk you wonder they waste the wax on, sixpacks of candy bars, and plastic toys done up in cellophane that fall apart when a kid looks at them anyway. Around they come, Queenie still leading the way, and holding a little gray jar in her hand. Slots Three through Seven are unmanned and I could see her wondering between Stokes and me, but Stokesie with his usual luck draws an old party in baggy gray pants who stumbles up with four giant cans of pineapple juice (what do these bums do with all that pineapple juice' I've often asked myself) so the girls come to me. Queenie puts down the jar and I take it into my fingers icy cold. Kingfish Fancy Herring Snacks in Pure Sour Cream: 49¢. Now her hands are empty, not a ring or a bracelet, bare as God made them, and I wonder where the money's coming from. Still with that prim look she lifts a folded dollar bill out of the hollow at the center of her nubbled pink top. The jar went heavy in my hand. Really, I thought that was so cute.

Then everybody's luck begins to run out. Lengel comes in from haggling with a truck full of cabbages on the lot and is about to scuttle into that door marked MANAGER behind which he hides all day when the girls touch his eye. Lengel's pretty dreary, teaches Sunday school and the rest, but he doesn't miss that much. He comes over and says, "Girls, this isn't the beach."

Queenie blushes, though maybe it's just a brush of sunburn I was noticing for the first time, now that she was so close. "My mother asked me to pick up a jar of herring snacks." Her voice kind of startled me, the way voices do when you see the people first, coming out so flat and dumb yet kind of tony, too, the way it ticked over "pick up" and "snacks." All of a sudden I slid right down her voice into her living room. Her father and the other men were standing around in ice-cream coats and bow ties and the women were in sandals picking up herring snacks on toothpicks off a big plate and they were all holding drinks the color of water with olives and sprigs of mint in them. When my parents have somebody over they get lemonade and if it's a real racy affair Schlitz in tall glasses with "They'll Do It Every Time" cartoons stencilled on.

"That's all right," Lengel said. "But this isn't the beach." His repeating this struck me as funny, as if it had just occurred to him, and he had been thinking all these years the A&P was a great big dune and he was the head lifeguard. He didn't like my smiling — as I say he doesn't miss much — but he concentrates on giving the girls that sad Sunday-school-superintendent stare.

Queenie's blush is no sunburn now, and the plump one in plaid, that I liked better from the back — a really sweet can — pipes up, "We weren't doing any shopping. We just came in for the one thing."

"That makes no difference," Lengel tells her, and I could see from the way his eyes went that he hadn't noticed she was wearing a two-piece before. "We want you decently dressed when you come in here."

"We are decent," Queenie says suddenly, her lower lip pushing, getting sore now that she remembers her place, a place from which the crowd that runs the A&P must look pretty crummy. Fancy Herring Snacks flashed in her very blue eyes.

"Girls, I don't want to argue with you. After this come in here with your shoulders covered. It's our policy." He turns his back. That's policy for you. Policy is what the kingpins want. What the others want is juvenile delinquency.

All this while, the customers had been showing up with their carts but, you know, sheep, seeing a scene, they had all bunched up on Stokesie, who shook open a paper bag as gently as peeling a peach, not wanting to miss a word. I could feel in the silence everybody getting nervous, most of all Lengel, who asks me, "Sammy, have you rung up this purchase?"

I thought and said "No" but it wasn't about that I was thinking. I go through the punches, 4, 9, GROC, TOT — it's more complicated than you think, and after you do it often enough, it begins to make a lttle song, that you hear words to, in my case "Hello (*bing*) there, you (*gung*) hap-py pee-pul (*splat*)" — the *splat* being the drawer flying out. I uncrease the bill, tenderly as you may imagine, it just having come from between the two smoothest scoops of vanilla I had ever known were there, and pass a half and a penny into her narrow pink palm, and nestle the herrings in a bag and twist its neck and hand it over, all the time thinking.

The girls, and who'd blame them, are in a hurry to get out, so I say "I quit" to Lengel quick enough for them to hear, hoping they'll stop and watch me, their unsuspected hero. They keep right on going, into the electric eye; the door flies open and they flicker across the lot to their car, Queenie and Plaid and Big Tall Goony-Goony (not that as raw material she was so bad), leaving me with Lengel and a kink in his eyebrow.

"Did you say something, Sammy?"

"I said I quit."

"I thought you did."

"You didn't have to embarrass them."

"It was they who were embarrassing us."

I started to say something that came out "Fiddle-de-doo." It's a saying of my grand-mother's, and I know she would have been pleased.

"I don't think you know what you're saying," Lengel said.

"I know you don't," I said. "But I do." I pull the bow at the back of my apron and start shrugging it off my shoulders. A couple customers that had been heading for my slot begin to knock against each other, like scared pigs in a chute.

Lengel sighs and begins to look very patient and old and gray. He's been a friend of my parents for years. "Sammy, you don't want to do this to your Mom and Dad," he tells me. It's true, I don't. But it seems to me that once you begin a gesture it's fatal not to go through with it. I fold the apron, "Sammy" stitched in red on the pocket, and put it on the counter, and drop the bow tie on top of it. The bow tie is theirs, if you've ever wondered. "You'll feel this for the rest of your life," Lengel says, and I know that's true, too, but remembering how he made that pretty girl blush makes me so scrunchy inside I punch the No Sale tab and the machine whirs "pee-pul" and the drawer splats out. One advantage to this scene taking place in summer, I can follow this up with a clean exit, there's no fumbling around getting your coat and galoshes, I just saunter into the electric eye in my white shirt that my mother ironed the night before, and the door heaves itself open, and outside the sunshine is skating around on the asphalt.

I look around for my girls, but they're gone, of course. There wasn't anybody but some young married screaming with her children about some candy they didn't get by the door of a powder-blue Falcon station wagon. Looking back in the big windows, over the bags of peat moss and aluminum lawn furniture stacked on the pavement, I could see Lengel in my place in the slot, checking the sheep through. His face was dark gray and his back stiff, as if he'd just had an injection of iron, and my stomach kind of fell as I felt how hard the world was going to be to me hereafter.

5. The Yellow Wallpaper (1892)

• Charlotte Perkins Gilman

It is very seldom that mere ordinary people like John and myself secure ancestral halls for the summer.

A colonial mansion, a hereditary estate, I would say a haunted house, and reach the height of romantic felicity—but that would be asking too much of fate!

Still I will proudly declare that there is something queer about it.

Else, why should it be let so cheaply? And why have stood so long untenanted?

John laughs at me, of course, but one expects that in marriage.

John is practical in the extreme. He has no patience with faith, an intense horror of superstition, and he scoffs openly at any talk of things not to be felt and seen and put down in figures.

John is a physician, and PERHAPS—(I would not say it to a living soul, of course, but this is dead paper and a great relief to my mind)—PERHAPS that is one reason I do not get well faster.

You see he does not believe I am sick!

And what can one do?

If a physician of high standing, and one's own husband, assures friends and relatives that there is really nothing the matter with one but temporary nervous depression—a slight hysterical tendency—what is one to do?

My brother is also a physician, and also of high standing, and he says the same thing.

So I take phosphates or phosphites—whichever it is, and tonics, and journeys, and air, and exercise, and am absolutely forbidden to "work" until I am well again.

Personally, I disagree with their ideas.

Personally, I believe that congenial work, with excitement and change, would do me good.

But what is one to do?

I did write for a while in spite of them; but it DOES exhaust me a good deal—having to be so sly about it, or else meet with heavy opposition.

I sometimes fancy that in my condition if I had less opposition and more society and stimulus—but John says the very worst thing I can do is to think about my condition, and I confess it always makes me feel bad.

So I will let it alone and talk about the house.

The most beautiful place! It is quite alone, standing well back from the road, quite three miles from the village. It makes me think of English places that you read about, for there are hedges and walls and gates that lock, and lots of separate little houses for the gardeners and people.

There is a DELICIOUS garden! I never saw such a garden—large and shady, full of box-bordered paths, and lined with long grape-covered arbors with seats under them.

There were greenhouses, too, but they are all broken now.

There was some legal trouble, I believe, something about the heirs and coheirs; anyhow, the place has been empty for years.

That spoils my ghostliness, I am afraid, but I don't care—there is something strange about the house—I can feel it.

I even said so to John one moonlight evening, but he said what I felt was a DRAUGHT, and shut the window.

I get unreasonably angry with John sometimes. I'm sure I never used to be so sensitive. I think it is due to this nervous condition.

But John says if I feel so, I shall neglect proper self-control; so I take pains to control myself—before him, at least, and that makes me very tired.

I don't like our room a bit. I wanted one downstairs that opened on the piazza and had roses all over the window, and such pretty old-fashioned chintz hangings! but John would not hear of it.

He said there was only one window and not room for two beds, and no near room for him if he took another.

He is very careful and loving, and hardly lets me stir without special direction.

I have a schedule prescription for each hour in the day; he takes all care from me, and so I feel basely ungrateful not to value it more.

He said we came here solely on my account, that I was to have perfect rest and all the air I could get. "Your exercise depends on your strength, my dear," said he, "and your food somewhat on your appetite; but air you can absorb all the time." So we took the nursery at the top of the house.

It is a big, airy room, the whole floor nearly, with windows that look all ways, and air and sunshine galore. It was nursery first and then playroom and gymnasium, I should judge; for the windows are barred for little children, and there are rings and things in the walls.

The paint and paper look as if a boys' school had used it. It is stripped off—the paper—in great patches all around the head of my bed, about as far as I can reach, and in a great place on the other side of the room low down. I never saw a worse paper in my life.

One of those sprawling flamboyant patterns committing every artistic sin.

It is dull enough to confuse the eye in following, pronounced enough to constantly irritate and provoke study, and when you follow the lame uncertain curves for a little distance they suddenly commit suicide—plunge off at outrageous angles, destroy themselves in unheard of contradictions.

The color is repellent, almost revolting; a smouldering unclean yellow, strangely faded by the slow-turning sunlight.

It is a dull yet lurid orange in some places, a sickly sulphur tint in others.

No wonder the children hated it! I should hate it myself if I had to live in this room long.

There comes John, and I must put this away,—he hates to have me write a word.

We have been here two weeks, and I haven't felt like writing before, since that first day.

I am sitting by the window now, up in this atrocious nursery, and there is nothing to hinder my writing as much as I please, save lack of strength.

John is away all day, and even some nights when his cases are serious.

I am glad my case is not serious!

But these nervous troubles are dreadfully depressing.

John does not know how much I really suffer. He knows there is no REASON to suffer, and that satisfies him.

Of course it is only nervousness. It does weigh on me so not to do my duty in any way!

I meant to be such a help to John, such a real rest and comfort, and here I am a comparative burden already!

Nobody would believe what an effort it is to do what little I am able,—to dress and entertain, and order things.

It is fortunate Mary is so good with the baby. Such a dear baby!

And yet I CANNOT be with him, it makes me so nervous.

I suppose John never was nervous in his life. He laughs at me so about this wall-paper!

At first he meant to repaper the room, but afterwards he said that I was letting it get the better of me, and that nothing was worse for a nervous patient than to give way to such fancies.

He said that after the wall-paper was changed it would be the heavy bedstead, and then the barred windows, and then that gate at the head of the stairs, and so on.

"You know the place is doing you good," he said, "and really, dear, I don't care to renovate the house just for a three months' rental."

"Then do let us go downstairs," I said, "there are such pretty rooms there."

Then he took me in his arms and called me a blessed little goose, and said he would go down to the cellar, if I wished, and have it whitewashed into the bargain.

But he is right enough about the beds and windows and things.

It is an airy and comfortable room as any one need wish, and, of course, I would not be so silly as to make him uncomfortable just for a whim.

I'm really getting quite fond of the big room, all but that horrid paper.

Out of one window I can see the garden, those mysterious deepshaded arbors, the riotous old-fashioned flowers, and bushes and gnarly trees.

Out of another I get a lovely view of the bay and a little private wharf belonging to the estate. There is a beautiful shaded lane that runs down there from the house. I always fancy I see people walking in these numerous paths and arbors, but John has cautioned me not to give way to fancy in the least. He says that with my imaginative power and habit of story-making, a nervous weakness like mine is sure to lead to all manner of excited fancies, and that I ought to use my will and good sense to check the tendency. So I try.

I think sometimes that if I were only well enough to write a little it would relieve the press of ideas and rest me.

But I find I get pretty tired when I try.

It is so discouraging not to have any advice and companionship about my work. When I get really well, John says we will ask Cousin Henry and Julia down for a long visit; but he says he would as soon put fireworks in my pillow-case as to let me have those stimulating people about now.

I wish I could get well faster.

But I must not think about that. This paper looks to me as if it KNEW what a vicious influence it had!

There is a recurrent spot where the pattern lolls like a broken neck and two bulbous eyes stare at you upside down.

I get positively angry with the impertinence of it and the everlastingness. Up and down and sideways they crawl, and those absurd, unblinking eyes are everywhere. There is one place where two breadths didn't match, and the eyes go all up and down the line, one a little higher than the other.

I never saw so much expression in an inanimate thing before, and we all know how much expression they have! I used to lie awake as a child and get more entertainment and terror out of blank walls and plain furniture than most children could find in a toy store.

I remember what a kindly wink the knobs of our big, old bureau used to have, and there was one chair that always seemed like a strong friend.

I used to feel that if any of the other things looked too fierce I could always hop into that chair and be safe.

The furniture in this room is no worse than inharmonious, however, for we had to bring it all from downstairs. I suppose when this was used as a playroom they had to take the nursery things out, and no wonder! I never saw such ravages as the children have made here.

The wall-paper, as I said before, is torn off in spots, and it sticketh closer than a brother—they must have had perseverance as well as hatred.

Then the floor is scratched and gouged and splintered, the plaster itself is dug out here and there, and this great heavy bed which is all we found in the room, looks as if it had been through the wars.

But I don't mind it a bit—only the paper.

There comes John's sister. Such a dear girl as she is, and so careful of me! I must not let her find me writing.

She is a perfect and enthusiastic housekeeper, and hopes for no better profession. I verily believe she thinks it is the writing which made me sick!

But I can write when she is out, and see her a long way off from these windows.

There is one that commands the road, a lovely shaded winding road, and one that just looks off over the country. A lovely country, too, full of great elms and velvet meadows.

This wall-paper has a kind of sub-pattern in a different shade, a particularly irritating one, for you can only see it in certain lights, and not clearly then.

But in the places where it isn't faded and where the sun is just so—I can see a strange, provoking, formless sort of figure, that seems to skulk about behind that silly and conspicuous front design.

There's sister on the stairs!

Well, the Fourth of July is over! The people are gone and I am tired out. John thought it might do me good to see a little company, so we just had mother and Nellie and the children down for a week.

Of course I didn't do a thing. Jennie sees to everything now.

But it tired me all the same.

John says if I don't pick up faster he shall send me to Weir Mitchell in the fall.

But I don't want to go there at all. I had a friend who was in his hands once, and she says he is just like John and my brother, only more so!

Besides, it is such an undertaking to go so far.

I don't feel as if it was worth while to turn my hand over for anything, and I'm getting dreadfully fretful and querulous.

I cry at nothing, and cry most of the time.

Of course I don't when John is here, or anybody else, but when I am alone.

And I am alone a good deal just now. John is kept in town very often by serious cases, and Jennie is good and lets me alone when I want her to.

So I walk a little in the garden or down that lovely lane, sit on the porch under the roses, and lie down up here a good deal.

I'm getting really fond of the room in spite of the wall-paper. Perhaps BECAUSE of the wall-paper.

It dwells in my mind so!

I lie here on this great immovable bed—it is nailed down, I believe—and follow that pattern about by the hour. It is as good as gymnastics, I assure you. I start, we'll say, at the bottom, down in the corner over there where it has not been touched, and I determine for the thousandth time that I WILL follow that pointless pattern to some sort of a conclusion.

I know a little of the principle of design, and I know this thing was not arranged on any laws of radiation, or alternation, or repetition, or symmetry, or anything else that I ever heard of.

It is repeated, of course, by the breadths, but not otherwise.

Looked at in one way each breadth stands alone, the bloated curves and flourishes—a kind of "debased Romanesque" with delirium tremens—go waddling up and down in isolated columns of fatuity.

But, on the other hand, they connect diagonally, and the sprawling outlines run off in great slanting waves of optic horror, like a lot of wallowing seaweeds in full chase.

The whole thing goes horizontally, too, at least it seems so, and I exhaust myself in trying to distinguish the order of its going in that direction.

They have used a horizontal breadth for a frieze, and that adds wonderfully to the confusion.

There is one end of the room where it is almost intact, and there, when the crosslights fade and the low sun shines directly upon it, I can almost fancy radiation after all,—the interminable grotesques seem to form around a common centre and rush off in headlong plunges of equal distraction.

It makes me tired to follow it. I will take a nap I guess.

I don't know why I should write this.

I don't want to.

I don't feel able.

And I know John would think it absurd. But I MUST say what I feel and think in some way—it is such a relief!

But the effort is getting to be greater than the relief.

Half the time now I am awfully lazy, and lie down ever so much.

John says I musn't lose my strength, and has me take cod liver oil and lots of tonics and things, to say nothing of ale and wine and rare meat.

Dear John! He loves me very dearly, and hates to have me sick. I tried to have a real earnest reasonable talk with him the other day, and tell him how I wish he would let me go and make a visit to Cousin Henry and Julia.

But he said I wasn't able to go, nor able to stand it after I got there; and I did not make out a very good case for myself, for I was crying before I had finished.

It is getting to be a great effort for me to think straight. Just this nervous weakness I suppose.

And dear John gathered me up in his arms, and just carried me upstairs and laid me on the bed, and sat by me and read to me till it tired my head.

He said I was his darling and his comfort and all he had, and that I must take care of myself for his sake, and keep well.

He says no one but myself can help me out of it, that I must use my will and self-control and not let any silly fancies run away with me.

There's one comfort, the baby is well and happy, and does not have to occupy this nursery with the horrid wall-paper.

If we had not used it, that blessed child would have! What a fortunate escape! Why, I wouldn't have a child of mine, an impressionable little thing, live in such a room for worlds.

I never thought of it before, but it is lucky that John kept me here after all, I can stand it so much easier than a baby, you see.

Of course I never mention it to them any more—I am too wise,—but I keep watch of it all the same.

There are things in that paper that nobody knows but me, or ever will.

Behind that outside pattern the dim shapes get clearer every day.

It is always the same shape, only very numerous.

And it is like a woman stooping down and creeping about behind that pattern. I don't like it a bit. I wonder—I begin to think—I wish John would take me away from here!

It is so hard to talk with John about my case, because he is so wise, and because he loves me so.

But I tried it last night.

It was moonlight. The moon shines in all around just as the sun does.

I hate to see it sometimes, it creeps so slowly, and always comes in by one window or another.

John was asleep and I hated to waken him, so I kept still and watched the moonlight on that undulating wall-paper till I felt creepy.

The faint figure behind seemed to shake the pattern, just as if she wanted to get out.

I got up softly and went to feel and see if the paper DID move, and when I came back John was awake.

"What is it, little girl?" he said. "Don't go walking about like that—you'll get cold."

I though it was a good time to talk, so I told him that I really was not gaining here, and that I wished he would take me away.

"Why darling!" said he, "our lease will be up in three weeks, and I can't see how to leave before.

"The repairs are not done at home, and I cannot possibly leave town just now. Of course if you were in any danger, I could and would, but you really are better, dear, whether you can see it or not. I am a doctor, dear, and I know. You are gaining flesh and color, your appetite is better, I feel really much easier about you."

"I don't weigh a bit more," said I, "nor as much; and my appetite may be better in the evening when you are here, but it is worse in the morning when you are away!"

"Bless her little heart!" said he with a big hug, "she shall be as sick as she pleases! But now let's improve the shining hours by going to sleep, and talk about it in the morning!"

"And you won't go away?" I asked gloomily.

"Why, how can I, dear? It is only three weeks more and then we will take a nice little trip of a few days while Jennie is getting the house ready. Really dear you are better!"

"Better in body perhaps—" I began, and stopped short, for he sat up straight and looked at me with such a stern, reproachful look that I could not say another word.

"My darling," said he, "I beg of you, for my sake and for our child's sake, as well as for your own, that you will never for one instant let that idea enter your mind! There is nothing so dangerous, so fascinating, to a temperament like yours. It is a false and foolish fancy. Can you not trust me as a physician when I tell you so?"

So of course I said no more on that score, and we went to sleep before long. He thought I was asleep first, but I wasn't, and lay there for hours trying to decide whether that front pattern and the back pattern really did move together or separately.

On a pattern like this, by daylight, there is a lack of sequence, a defiance of law, that is a constant irritant to a normal mind.

The color is hideous enough, and unreliable enough, and infuriating enough, but the pattern is torturing.

You think you have mastered it, but just as you get well underway in following, it turns a back-somersault and there you are. It slaps you in the face, knocks you down, and tramples upon you. It is like a bad dream.

The outside pattern is a florid arabesque, reminding one of a fungus. If you can imagine a toadstool in joints, an interminable string of toadstools, budding and sprouting in endless convolutions—why, that is something like it.

That is, sometimes!

There is one marked peculiarity about this paper, a thing nobody seems to notice but myself, and that is that it changes as the light changes.

When the sun shoots in through the east window—I always watch for that first long, straight ray—it changes so quickly that I never can quite believe it.

That is why I watch it always.

By moonlight—the moon shines in all night when there is a moon—I wouldn't know it was the same paper.

At night in any kind of light, in twilight, candle light, lamplight, and worst of all by moonlight, it becomes bars! The outside pattern I mean, and the woman behind it is as plain as can be.

I didn't realize for a long time what the thing was that showed behind, that dim sub-pattern, but now I am quite sure it is a woman.

By daylight she is subdued, quiet. I fancy it is the pattern that keeps her so still. It is so puzzling. It keeps me quiet by the hour.

I lie down ever so much now. John says it is good for me, and to sleep all I can.

Indeed he started the habit by making me lie down for an hour after each meal.

It is a very bad habit I am convinced, for you see I don't sleep.

And that cultivates deceit, for I don't tell them I'm awake—O no!

The fact is I am getting a little afraid of John.

He seems very queer sometimes, and even Jennie has an inexplicable look.

It strikes me occasionally, just as a scientific hypothesis,—that perhaps it is the paper!

I have watched John when he did not know I was looking, and come into the room suddenly on the most innocent excuses, and I've caught him several times LOOKING AT THE PAPER! And Jennie too. I caught Jennie with her hand on it once.

She didn't know I was in the room, and when I asked her in a quiet, a very quiet voice, with the most restrained manner possible, what she was doing with the paper—she turned around as if she had been caught stealing, and looked quite angry—asked me why I should frighten her so!

Then she said that the paper stained everything it touched, that she had found yellow smooches on all my clothes and John's, and she wished we would be more careful!

Did not that sound innocent? But I know she was studying that pattern, and I am determined that nobody shall find it out but myself!

Life is very much more exciting now than it used to be. You see I have something more to expect, to look forward to, to watch. I really do eat better, and am more quiet than I was.

John is so pleased to see me improve! He laughed a little the other day, and said I seemed to be flourishing in spite of my wall-paper.

I turned it off with a laugh. I had no intention of telling him it was BECAUSE of the wall-paper—he would make fun of me. He might even want to take me away.

I don't want to leave now until I have found it out. There is a week more, and I think that will be enough.

I'm feeling ever so much better! I don't sleep much at night, for it is so interesting to watch developments; but I sleep a good deal in the daytime.

In the daytime it is tiresome and perplexing.

There are always new shoots on the fungus, and new shades of yellow all over it. I cannot keep count of them, though I have tried conscientiously.

It is the strangest yellow, that wall-paper! It makes me think of all the yellow things I ever saw—not beautiful ones like buttercups, but old foul, bad yellow things.

But there is something else about that paper—the smell! I noticed it the moment we came into the room, but with so much air and sun it was not bad. Now we have had a week of fog and rain, and whether the windows are open or not, the smell is here.

It creeps all over the house.

I find it hovering in the dining-room, skulking in the parlor, hiding in the hall, lying in wait for me on the stairs.

It gets into my hair.

Even when I go to ride, if I turn my head suddenly and surprise it—there is that smell!

Such a peculiar odor, too! I have spent hours in trying to analyze it, to find what it smelled like.

It is not bad—at first, and very gentle, but quite the subtlest, most enduring odor I ever met.

In this damp weather it is awful, I wake up in the night and find it hanging over me.

It used to disturb me at first. I thought seriously of burning the house—to reach the smell.

But now I am used to it. The only thing I can think of that it is like is the COLOR of the paper! A yellow smell.

There is a very funny mark on this wall, low down, near the mopboard. A streak that runs round the room. It goes behind every piece of furniture, except the bed, a long, straight, even SMOOCH, as if it had been rubbed over and over.

I wonder how it was done and who did it, and what they did it for. Round and round and round—round and round and round—it makes me dizzy!

I really have discovered something at last.

Through watching so much at night, when it changes so, I have finally found out.

The front pattern DOES move—and no wonder! The woman behind shakes it!

Sometimes I think there are a great many women behind, and sometimes only one, and she crawls around fast, and her crawling shakes it all over.

Then in the very bright spots she keeps still, and in the very shady spots she just takes hold of the bars and shakes them hard.

And she is all the time trying to climb through. But nobody could climb through that pattern—it strangles so; I think that is why it has so many heads.

They get through, and then the pattern strangles them off and turns them upside down, and makes their eyes white!

If those heads were covered or taken off it would not be half so bad.

I think that woman gets out in the daytime!

And I'll tell you why—privately—I've seen her!

I can see her out of every one of my windows!

It is the same woman, I know, for she is always creeping, and most women do not creep by daylight.

I see her on that long road under the trees, creeping along, and when a carriage comes she hides under the blackberry vines.

I don't blame her a bit. It must be very humiliating to be caught creeping by daylight!

I always lock the door when I creep by daylight. I can't do it at night, for I know John would suspect something at once.

And John is so queer now, that I don't want to irritate him. I wish he would take another room! Besides, I don't want anybody to get that woman out at night but myself.

I often wonder if I could see her out of all the windows at once.

But, turn as fast as I can, I can only see out of one at one time.

And though I always see her, she MAY be able to creep faster than I can turn!

I have watched her sometimes away off in the open country, creeping as fast as a cloud shadow in a high wind.

If only that top pattern could be gotten off from the under one! I mean to try it, little by little.

I have found out another funny thing, but I shan't tell it this time! It does not do to trust people too much.

There are only two more days to get this paper off, and I believe John is beginning to notice. I don't like the look in his eyes.

And I heard him ask Jennie a lot of professional questions about me. She had a very good report to give.

She said I slept a good deal in the daytime.

John knows I don't sleep very well at night, for all I'm so quiet!

He asked me all sorts of questions, too, and pretended to be very loving and kind.

As if I couldn't see through him!

Still, I don't wonder he acts so, sleeping under this paper for three months.

It only interests me, but I feel sure John and Jennie are secretly affected by it.

Hurrah! This is the last day, but it is enough. John is to stay in town over night, and won't be out until this evening.

Jennie wanted to sleep with me—the sly thing! but I told her I should undoubtedly rest better for a night all alone.

That was clever, for really I wasn't alone a bit! As soon as it was moonlight and that poor thing began to crawl and shake the pattern, I got up and ran to help her.

I pulled and she shook, I shook and she pulled, and before morning we had peeled off yards of that paper.

A strip about as high as my head and half around the room.

And then when the sun came and that awful pattern began to laugh at me, I declared I would finish it to-day!

We go away to-morrow, and they are moving all my furniture down again to leave things as they were before.

Jennie looked at the wall in amazement, but I told her merrily that I did it out of pure spite at the vicious thing.

She laughed and said she wouldn't mind doing it herself, but I must not get tired.

How she betrayed herself that time!

But I am here, and no person touches this paper but me—not ALIVE!

She tried to get me out of the room—it was too patent! But I said it was so quiet and empty and clean now that I believed I would lie down again and sleep all I could; and not to wake me even for dinner—I would call when I woke.

So now she is gone, and the servants are gone, and the things are gone, and there is nothing left but that great bedstead nailed down, with the canvas mattress we found on it.

We shall sleep downstairs to-night, and take the boat home to-morrow.

I quite enjoy the room, now it is bare again.

How those children did tear about here!

This bedstead is fairly gnawed!

But I must get to work.

I have locked the door and thrown the key down into the front path.

I don't want to go out, and I don't want to have anybody come in, till John comes.

I want to astonish him.

I've got a rope up here that even Jennie did not find. If that woman does get out, and tries to get away, I can tie her!

But I forgot I could not reach far without anything to stand on!

This bed will NOT move!

I tried to lift and push it until I was lame, and then I got so angry I bit off a little piece at one corner—but it hurt my teeth.

Then I peeled off all the paper I could reach standing on the floor. It sticks horribly and the pattern just enjoys it! All those strangled heads and bulbous eyes and waddling fungus growths just shriek with derision!

I am getting angry enough to do something desperate. To jump out of the window would be admirable exercise, but the bars are too strong even to try.

Besides I wouldn't do it. Of course not. I know well enough that a step like that is improper and might be misconstrued.

I don't like to LOOK out of the windows even—there are so many of those creeping women, and they creep so fast.

I wonder if they all come out of that wall-paper as I did?

But I am securely fastened now by my well-hidden rope—you don't get ME out in the road there!

I suppose I shall have to get back behind the pattern when it comes night, and that is hard!

It is so pleasant to be out in this great room and creep around as I please!

I don't want to go outside. I won't, even if Jennie asks me to.

For outside you have to creep on the ground, and everything is green instead of yellow.

But here I can creep smoothly on the floor, and my shoulder just fits in that long smooch around the wall, so I cannot lose my way.

Why there's John at the door!

It is no use, young man, you can't open it!

How he does call and pound!

Now he's crying for an axe.

It would be a shame to break down that beautiful door!

"John dear!" said I in the gentlest voice, "the key is down by the front steps, under a plantain leaf!"

That silenced him for a few moments.

Then he said—very quietly indeed, "Open the door, my darling!"

"I can't," said I. "The key is down by the front door under a plantain leaf!"

And then I said it again, several times, very gently and slowly, and said it so often that he had to go and see, and he got it of course, and came in. He stopped short by the door.

"What is the matter?" he cried. "For God's sake, what are you doing!"

I kept on creeping just the same, but I looked at him over my shoulder.

"I've got out at last," said I, "in spite of you and Jane. And I've pulled off most of the paper, so you can't put me back!"

Now why should that man have fainted? But he did, and right across my path by the wall, so that I had to creep over him every time!

6. Araby (1914)

• James Joyce

North Richmond Street, being blind, was a quiet street except at the hour when the Christian Brothers' School set the boys free. An uninhabited house of two storeys stood at the blind end, detached from its neighbours in a square ground. The other houses of the street, conscious of decent lives within them, gazed at one another with brown imperturbable faces.

The former tenant of our house, a priest, had died in the back drawing-room. Air, musty from having been long enclosed, hung in all the rooms, and the waste room behind the kitchen was littered with old useless papers. Among these I found a few paper-covered books, the pages of which were curled and damp: The Abbot, by Walter Scott, The Devout Communicant, and The Memoirs of Vidocq. I liked the last best because its leaves were yellow. The wild garden behind the house contained a central apple-tree and a few straggling bushes, under one of which I found the late tenant's rusty bicycle-pump. He had been a very charitable priest; in his will he had left all his money to institutions and the furniture of his house to his sister.

When the short days of winter came, dusk fell before we had well eaten our dinners. When we met in the street the houses had grown sombre. The space of sky above us was the colour of ever-changing violet and towards it the lamps of the street lifted their feeble lanterns. The cold air stung us and we played till our bodies glowed. Our shouts echoed in the silent street. The career of our play brought us through the dark muddy lanes behind the houses, where we ran the gauntlet of the rough tribes from the cottages, to the back doors of the dark dripping gardens where odours arose from the ashpits, to the dark odorous stables where a coachman smoothed and combed the horse or shook music from the buckled harness. When we returned to the street, light from the kitchen windows had filled the areas. If my uncle was seen turning the corner, we hid in the shadow until we had seen him safely housed. Or if Mangan's sister came out on the doorstep to call her brother in to his tea, we watched her from our shadow peer up and down the street. We waited to see whether she would remain or go in and, if she remained, we left our shadow and walked up to Mangan's steps resignedly. She was waiting for us, her figure defined by the light from the half-opened door. Her brother always teased her before he obeyed, and I stood by the railings looking at her. Her dress swung as she moved her body, and the soft rope of her hair tossed from side to side.

Every morning I lay on the floor in the front parlour watching her door. The blind was pulled down to within an inch of the sash so that I could not be seen. When she came out on the doorstep my heart leaped. I ran to the hall, seized my books and followed her. I kept her brown figure always in my eye and, when we came near the point at which our ways diverged, I quickened my pace and passed her. This happened morning after morning. I had never spoken to her, except for a few casual words, and yet her name was like a summons to all my foolish blood.

Her image accompanied me even in places the most hostile to romance. On Saturday evenings when my aunt went marketing I had to go to carry some of the parcels. We walked through the flaring streets, jostled by drunken men and bargaining women, amid the curses of labourers, the shrill litanies of shop-boys who stood on guard by the barrels of pigs' cheeks, the nasal chanting of street-singers, who sang a come-all-you about O'Donovan Rossa, or a ballad about the troubles in our native land. These noises converged in a single sensation of life for me: I imagined that I bore my chalice safely through a throng of foes. Her name sprang to my lips at moments in strange prayers and praises which I myself did not understand. My eyes were often full of tears (I could not tell why) and at times a flood from my heart seemed to pour itself out into my bosom. I thought little of the future. I did not know whether I would ever speak to her or not or, if I spoke to her, how I could tell her of my confused adoration. But my body was like a harp and her words and gestures were like fingers running upon the wires.

One evening I went into the back drawing-room in which the priest had died. It was a dark rainy evening and there was no sound in the house. Through one of the broken panes I heard the rain impinge upon the earth, the fine incessant needles of water playing in the sodden beds. Some distant lamp or lighted window gleamed below me. I was thankful that I could see so little. All my senses seemed to desire to veil themselves and, feeling that I was about to slip from them, I pressed the palms of my hands together until they trembled, murmuring: 'O love! O love!' many times.

At last she spoke to me. When she addressed the first words to me I was so confused that I did not know what to answer. She asked me was I going to Araby. I forgot whether I answered yes or no. It would be a splendid bazaar; she said she would love to go.

'And why can't you?' I asked.

While she spoke she turned a silver bracelet round and round her wrist. She could not go, she said, because there would be a retreat that week in her convent. Her brother and two other boys were fighting for their caps, and I was alone at the railings. She held one of the spikes, bowing her head towards me. The light from the lamp opposite our door caught the white curve of her neck, lit up her hair that rested there and, falling, lit up the hand upon the railing. It fell over one side of her dress and caught the white border of a petticoat, just visible as she stood at ease.

'It's well for you,' she said.

'If I go,' I said, 'I will bring you something.'

What innumerable follies laid waste my waking and sleeping thoughts after that evening! I wished to annihilate the tedious intervening days. I chafed against the work of school. At night in my bedroom and by day in the classroom her image came between me and the page I strove to read. The syllables of the word Araby were called to me through the silence in which my soul luxuriated and cast an Eastern enchantment over me. I asked for leave to go to the bazaar on Saturday night. My aunt was surprised, and hoped it was not some Freemason affair. I answered few questions in class. I watched my master's face pass from amiability to sternness; he hoped I was not beginning to idle. I could not call my wandering thoughts together. I had hardly any patience with the serious work of life which, now that it stood between me and my desire, seemed to me child's play, ugly monotonous child's play.

On Saturday morning I reminded my uncle that I wished to go to the bazaar in the evening. He was fussing at the hallstand, looking for the hat-brush, and answered me curtly:

'Yes, boy, I know.'

As he was in the hall I could not go into the front parlour and lie at the window. I felt the house in bad humour and walked slowly towards the school. The air was pitilessly raw and already my heart misgave me.

When I came home to dinner my uncle had not yet been home. Still it was early. I sat staring at the clock for some time and, when its ticking began to irritate me, I left the room. I mounted the staircase and gained the upper part of the house. The high, cold, empty, gloomy rooms liberated me and I went from room to room singing. From the front window I saw my companions playing below in the street. Their cries reached me weakened and indistinct and, leaning my forehead against the cool glass, I looked over at the dark house where she lived. I may have stood there for an hour, seeing nothing but the brown-clad figure cast by my imagination, touched discreetly by the lamplight at the curved neck, at the hand upon the railings and at the border below the dress.

When I came downstairs again I found Mrs Mercer sitting at the fire. She was an old, garrulous woman, a pawnbroker's widow, who collected used stamps for some pious purpose. I had to endure the gossip of the tea-table. The meal was prolonged beyond an hour and still my uncle did not come. Mrs Mercer stood up to go: she was sorry she couldn't wait any longer, but it was after eight o'clock and she did not like to be out late, as the night air was bad for her. When she had gone I began to walk up and down the room, clenching my fists. My aunt said:

'I'm afraid you may put off your bazaar for this night of Our Lord.'

At nine o'clock I heard my uncle's latchkey in the hall door. I heard him talking to himself and heard the hallstand rocking when it had received the weight of his overcoat. I could interpret these signs. When he was midway through his dinner I asked him to give me the money to go to the bazaar. He had forgotten.

'The people are in bed and after their first sleep now,' he said.

I did not smile. My aunt said to him energetically:

'Can't you give him the money and let him go? You've kept him late enough as it is.'

My uncle said he was very sorry he had forgotten. He said he believed in the old saying: 'All work and no play makes Jack a dull boy.' He asked me where I was going and, when I told him a second time, he asked me did I know The Arab's Farewell to his Steed. When I left the kitchen he was about to recite the opening lines of the piece to my aunt.

I held a florin tightly in my hand as I strode down Buckingham Street towards the station. The sight of the streets thronged with buyers and glaring with gas recalled to me the purpose of my journey. I took my seat in a third-class carriage of a deserted train. After an intolerable delay the train moved out of the station slowly. It crept onward among ruinous houses and over the twinkling river. At Westland Row Station a crowd of people pressed to the carriage doors; but the porters moved them back, saying that it was a special train for the bazaar. I remained alone in the bare carriage. In a few minutes the train drew up beside an improvised wooden platform. I passed out on to the road and saw by the lighted dial of a clock that it was ten minutes to ten. In front of me was a large building which displayed the magical name.

I could not find any sixpenny entrance and, fearing that the bazaar would be closed, I passed in quickly through a turnstile, handing a shilling to a weary-looking man. I found myself in a big hall girded at half its height by a gallery. Nearly all the stalls were closed and the greater part of the hall was in darkness. I recognized a silence like that which pervades a church after a service. I walked into the centre of the bazaar timidly. A few people were gathered about the stalls which were still open. Before a curtain, over which the words Café Chantant were written in coloured lamps, two men were counting money on a salver. I listened to the fall of the coins.

Remembering with difficulty why I had come, I went over to one of the stalls and examined porcelain vases and flowered tea-sets. At the door of the stall a young lady was talking and laughing with two young gentlemen. I remarked their English accents and listened vaguely to their conversation.

'O, I never said such a thing!'

'O, but you did!'

'O, but I didn't!'

'Didn't she say that?'

'Yes. I heard her.'

'O, there's a... fib!'

Observing me, the young lady came over and asked me did I wish to buy anything. The tone of her voice was not encouraging; she seemed to have spoken to me out of a sense of duty. I looked humbly at the great jars that stood like eastern guards at either side of the dark entrance to the stall and murmured:

'No, thank you.'

The young lady changed the position of one of the vases and went back to the two young men. They began to talk of the same subject. Once or twice the young lady glanced at me over her shoulder.

I lingered before her stall, though I knew my stay was useless, to make my interest in her wares seem the more real. Then I turned away slowly and walked down the middle of the bazaar. I allowed the two pennies to fall against the sixpence in my pocket. I heard a voice call from one end of the gallery that the light was out. The upper part of the hall was now completely dark.

Gazing up into the darkness I saw myself as a creature driven and derided by vanity; and my eyes burned with anguish and anger.

9. I Stand Here Ironing (1961)
• Tillie Olsen

I stand here ironing, and what you asked me moves tormented back and forth with the iron. "I wish you would manage the time to come in and talk with me about your daughter. I'm sure you can help me understand her. She's a youngster who needs help and whom I'm deeply interested in helping."

"Who needs help." — Even if I came, what good would it do? You think because I am her mother I have a key, or that in some way you could use me as a key? She has lived for nineteen years. There is all that life that has happened outside of me, beyond me.

And when is there time to remember, to sift, to weigh, to estimate, to total? I will start and there will be an interruption and I will have to gather it all together again. Or I will become engulfed with all I did or did not do, with what should have been and what cannot be helped.

She was a beautiful baby. The first and only one of our five that was beautiful at birth. You do not guess how new and uneasy her tenancy in her now — loveliness. You did not know her all those years she was thought homely, or see her poring over her baby pictures, making me tell her over and over how beautiful she had been — and would be, I would tell her — and was now, to the seeing eye. But the seeing eyes were few or non-existent. Including mine.

I nursed her. They feel that's important nowadays. I nursed all the children, but with her, with all the fierce rigidity of first motherhood, I did like the books then said. Though her cries battered me to trembling and my breasts ached with swollenness, I waited till the clock decreed.

Why do I put that first? I do not even know if it matters, or if it explains anything.

She was a beautiful baby. She blew shining bubbles of sound. She loved motion, loved light, loved color and music and textures. She would lie on the floor in her blue overalls patting the surface so hard in ecstasy her hands and feet would blur. She was a miracle to me, but when she was eight months old I had to leave her daytimes with the woman downstairs to whom she was no miracle at all, for I worked or looked for work and for Emily's father, who "could no longer endure" (he wrote in his goodbye note) "sharing want with us."

I was nineteen. It was the pre-relief, pre-WPA world of the depression. I would start running as soon as I got off the streetcar, running up the stairs, the place smelling sour, and awake or asleep to startle awake, when she saw me she would break into a clogged weeping that could not be comforted, a weeping I can hear yet.

After a while I found a job hashing at night so I could be with her days, and it was better. But it came to where I had to bring her to his family and leave her.

It took a long time to raise the money for her fare back. Then she got chicken pox and I had to wait longer. When she finally came, I hardly knew her, walking quick and nervous like her father, looking like her father, thin, and dressed in a shoddy red that yellowed her skin and glared at the pockmarks. All the baby loveliness gone.

She was two. Old enough for nursery school they said, and I did not know then what I know now — the fatigue of the long day, and the lacerations of group life in the kinds of nurseries that are only parking places for children.

Except that it would have made no difference if I had known. It was the only place there was. It was the only way we could be together, the only way I could hold a job.

And even without knowing, I knew. I knew the teacher that was evil because all these years it has curdled into my memory, the little boy hunched in the corner, her rasp, "why aren't you outside, because Alvin hits you? that's no reason, go out, scaredy." I knew Emily hated it even if she did not clutch and implore "don't go Mommy" like the other children, mornings.

She always had a reason why we should stay home. Momma, you look sick, Momma, I feel sick. Momma, the teachers aren't there today, they're sick. Momma, we can't go, there was a fire there last night. Momma, it's a holiday today, no school, they told me.

But never a direct protest, never rebellion. I think of our others in their three, four -yearoldness — the explosions, the tempers, the denunciations, the demands — and I feel suddenly ill. I put the iron down. What in me demanded that goodness in her? And what was the cost, the cost to her of such goodness?

The old man living in the back once said in his gentle way: "You should smile at Emily more when you look at her." What was in my face when I looked at her? I loved her. There were all the acts of love.

It was only with the others I remembered what he said, and it was the face of joy, and not of care or tightness or worry I turned to them — too late for Emily. She does not smile easily, let alone almost always as her brothers and sisters do. Her face is closed and sombre, but when she wants, how fluid. You must have seen it in her pantomimes, you spoke of her rare gift for comedy on the stage that rouses a laughter out of the audience so dear they applaud and applaud and do not want to let her go.

Where does it come from, that comedy? There was none of it in her when she came back to me that second time, after I had had to send her away again. She had a new daddy now to learn to love, and I think perhaps it was a better time.

Except when we left her alone nights, telling ourselves she was old enough.

"Can't you go some other time, Mommy, like tomorrow?" she would ask. "Will it be just a little while you'll be gone? Do you promise?"

The time we came back, the front door open, the clock on the floor in the hall. She rigid awake. "It wasn't just a little while. I didn't cry. Three times I called you, just three times, and then I ran downstairs to open the door so you could come faster. The clock talked loud. I threw it away, it scared me — what it talked."

She said the clock talked loud again that night I went to the hospital to have Susan. She was delirious with the fever that comes before red measles, but she was fully conscious all the week I was gone and the week after we were home when she could not come near the new baby or me.

She did not get well. She stayed skeleton thin, not wanting to eat, and night after night she had nightmares. She would call for me, and I would rouse from exhaustion to sleepily call back: "You're all right, darling, go to sleep, it's just a dream," and if she still called, in a sterner voice, "now go to sleep, Emily, there's nothing to hurt you." Twice, only twice, when I had to get up for Susan anyhow, I went in to sit with her.

Now when it is too late (as if she would let me hold and comfort her like I do the others) I get up and go to her at once at her moan or restless stirring. "Are you awake, Emily? Can I get you something?" And the answer is always the same: "No, I'm all right, go back to sleep, Mother."

They persuaded me at the clinic to send her away to a convalescent home in the country where "she can have the kind of food and care you can't manage for her, and you'll be free to concentrate on the new baby." They still send children to that place. I see pictures on the society page of sleek young women planning affairs to raise money for it, or dancing at the affairs, or decorating Easter eggs or filling Christmas stockings for the children.

They never have a picture of the children so I do not know if the girls still wear those gigantic red bows and the ravaged looks on the every other Sunday when parents can come to visit "unless otherwise notified" — as we were notified the first six weeks.

Oh it is a handsome place, green lawns and tall trees and fluted flower beds. High up on the balconies of each cottage the children stand, the girls in their red bows and white dresses, the boys in white suits and giant red ties. The parents stand below shrieking up to be heard and the children shriek down to be heard, and between them the invisible wall "Not To Be Contaminated by Parental Germs or Physical Affection."

There was a tiny girl who always stood hand in hand with Emily. Her parents never came. One visit she was gone. "They moved her to Rose Cottage," Emily shouted in explanation. "They don't like you to love anybody here."

She wrote once a week, the labored writing of a seven-year-old. "I am fine. How is the baby.

If I write my leter nicly I will have a star. Love." There never was a star. We wrote every other day, letters she could never hold or keep but only hear read — once. "We simply do not have room for children to keep any personal possessions," they patiently explained when we pieced one Sunday's shrieking together to plead how much it would mean to Emily, who loved so to keep things, to be allowed to keep her letters and cards.

Each visit she looked frailer. "She isn't eating," they told us.

(They had runny eggs for breakfast or mush with lumps, Emily said later, I'd hold it in my mouth and not swallow. Nothing ever tasted good, just when they had chicken.)

It took us eight months to get her released home, and only the fact that she gained back so little of her seven lost pounds convinced the social worker.

I used to try to hold and love her after she came back, but her body would stay stiff, and after a while she'd push away. She ate little. Food sickened her, and I think much of life too. Oh she had physical lightness and brightness, twinkling by on skates, bouncing like a ball up and down up and down over the jump rope, skimming over the hill; but these were momentary.

She fretted about her appearance, thin and dark and foreign-looking at a time when every little girl was supposed to look or thought she should look a chubby blonde replica of Shirley Temple. The doorbell sometimes rang for her, but no one seemed to come and play in the house or be a best friend. Maybe because we moved so much.

There was a boy she loved painfully through two school semesters. Months later she told me how she had taken pennies from my purse to buy him candy. "Licorice was his favorite and I brought him some every day, but he still liked Jennifer better'n me. Why, Mommy?" The kind of question for which there is no answer.

School was a worry to her. She was not glib or quick in a world where glibness and quickness were easily confused with ability to learn. To her overworked and exasperated teachers she was an over-conscientious "slow learner" who kept trying to catch up and was absent entirely too often.

I let her be absent, though sometimes the illness was imaginary. How different from my now — strictness about attendance with the others. I wasn't working. We had a new baby, I was home anyhow. Sometimes, after Susan grew old enough. I would keep her home from school, too, to have them all together. Mostly Emily had asthma, and her breathing, harsh and labored, would fill the house with a curiously tranquil sound. I would bring the two old dresser mirrors and her boxes of collections to her bed. She would select beads and single earrings, bottle tops and shells, dried flowers and pebbles, old postcards and scraps, all sorts of oddments; then she and Susan would play Kingdom, setting up landscapes and furniture, peopling them with action.

Those were the only times of peaceful companionship between her and Susan. I have edged away from it, that poisonous feeling between them, that terrible balancing of hurts and needs I had to do between the two, and did so badly, those earlier years.

Oh there are conflicts between the others too, each one human, needing, demanding, hurting, taking — but only between Emily and Susan, no, Emily toward Susan that corroding resentment. It seems so obvious on the surface, yet it is not obvious. Susan, the second child, Susan, golden — and curly-haired and chubby, quick and articulate and assured, everything in appearance and manner Emily was not; Susan, not able to resist Emily's precious things, losing or sometimes clumsily breaking them; Susan telling jokes and riddles to company for applause while Emily sat silent (to say to me later: that was my riddle, Mother, I told it to Susan); Susan, who for all the five years' difference in age was just a year behind Emily in developing physically.

I am glad for that slow physical development that widened the difference between her and her contemporaries, though she suffered over it. She was too vulnerable for that terrible world of youthful competition, of preening and parading, of constant measuring of yourself against every other, of envy, "If I had that copper hair," "If I had that skin..." She tormented herself enough about not looking like the others, there was enough of the unsureness, the having to be conscious of words before you speak, the constant caring — what are they thinking of me? without having it all magnified by the merciless physical drives.

Ronnie is calling. He is wet and I change him. It is rare there is such a cry now. That time of motherhood is almost behind me when the ear is not one's own but must always be racked and listening for the child cry, the child call. We sit for a while and I hold him, looking out over the city spread in charcoal with its soft aisles of light. "Shoogily," he breathes and curls closer. I carry him back to bed, asleep. Shoogily. A funny word, a family word, inherited from Emily, Shoogily, invented by her to say: comfort.

In this and other ways she leaves her seal, I say aloud. And startle at my saying it. What do I mean? What did I start to gather together, to try and make coherent? I was at the terrible, growing years. War years. I do not remember them well. I was working, there were four smaller ones now, there was not time for her. She had to help be a mother, and housekeeper, and shopper. She had to set her seal. Mornings of crisis and near hysteria trying to get lunches packed, hair combed, coats and shoes found, everyone to school or Child Care on time, the baby ready for transportation. And always the paper scribbled on by a smaller one, the book looked at by Susan then mislaid, the homework not done. Running out to that huge school where she was one, she was lost, she was a drop; suffering over the unpreparedness, stammering and unsure in her classes.

There was so little time left at night after the kids were bedded down. She would struggle over books, always eating (it was in those years she developed her enormous appetite that is legendary in our family) and I would be ironing, or preparing food for the next day, or writing

V-mail to Bill, or tending the baby. Sometimes, to make me laugh, or out of her despair, she would imitate happenings or types at school.

I think I said once: "Why don't you do something like this in the school amateur show?" One morning she phoned me at work, hardly understandable through the weeping: "Mother, I did it. I won, I won; they gave me first prize; they clapped and clapped and wouldn't let me go."

Now suddenly she was Somebody, and as imprisoned in her difference as she had been in anonymity.

She began to be asked to perform at other high schools, even in colleges, then at city and statewide affairs. The first one we went to, I only recognized her that first moment when thin, shy, she almost drowned herself into the curtains. Then: Was this Emily? The control, the command, the convulsing and deadly clowning, the spell, then the roaring, stamping audience, unwilling to let this rare and precious laughter out of their lives.

Afterwards: You ought to do something about her with a gift like that — but without money or knowing how, what does one do? We have left it all to her, and the gift has as often eddied inside, clogged and clotted, as been used and growing. She is coming. She runs up the stairs two at a time with her light graceful step, and I know she is happy tonight. Whatever it was that occasioned your call did not happen today.

"Aren't you ever going to finish the ironing, Mother? Whistler painted his mother in a rocker. I'd have to paint mine standing over an ironing board." This is one of her communicative nights and she tells me everything and nothing as she fixes herself a plate of food out of the icebox.

She is so lovely. Why did you want me to come in at all? Why were you concerned? She will find her way.

She starts up the stairs to bed. "Don't get me up with the rest in the morning." "But I thought you were having midterms." "Oh, those," she comes back in, kisses me, and says quite lightly, "in a couple of years when we'll all be atom — dead they won't matter a bit."

She has said it before. She believes it. But because I have been dredging the past, and all that compounds a human being is so heavy and meaningful in me, I cannot endure it tonight.

I will never total it all. I will never come in to say: She was a child seldom smiled at. Her father left me before she was a year old. I had to work her first six years when there was work, or I sent her home and to his relatives. There were years she had care she hated. She was dark and thin and foreign-looking in a world where the prestige went to blondeness and curly hair and dimples, she was slow where glibness was prized. She was a child of anxious, not proud, love. We were poor and could not afford for her the soil of easy growth. I was a young mother, I was a distracted mother. There were the other children pushing up, demanding. Her younger sister seemed all that she was not. There were years she did not want me to touch her. She kept too much in herself, her life was such she had to keep too much in herself. My wisdom came too late. She has much to her and probably little will come of it. She is a child of her age, of depression, of war, of fear.

　Let her be. So all that is in her will not bloom — but in how many does it? There is still enough left to live by. Only help her to know-help make it so there is cause for her to know — that she is more than this dress on the ironing board, helpless before the iron.

11. Barn Burning (1939)

• William Faulkner

The store in which the justice of the Peace's court was sitting smelled of cheese. The boy, crouched on his nail keg at the back of the crowded room, knew he smelled cheese, and more: from where he sat he could see the ranked shelves close-packed with the solid, squat, dynamic shapes of tin cans whose labels his stomach read, not from the lettering which meant nothing to his mind but from the scarlet devils and the silver curve of fish-this, the cheese which he knew he smelled and the hermetic meat which his intestines believed he smelled coming in intermittent gusts momentary and brief between the other constant one, the smell and sense just a little of fear because mostly of despair and grief, the old fierce pull of blood. He could not see the table where the Justice sat and before which his father and his father's enemy (our enemy he thought in that despair; ourn! mine and hisn both! He's my father!) stood, but he could hear them, the two of them that is, because his father had said no word yet:

"But what proof have you, Mr. Harris?"

"I told you. The hog got into my corn. I caught it up and sent it back to him. He had no fence that would hold it. I told him so, warned him. The next time I put the hog in my pen. When he came to get it I gave him enough wire to patch up his pen. The next time I put the hog up and kept it. I rode down to his house and saw the wire I gave him still rolled on to the spool in his yard. I told him he could have the hog when he paid me a dollar pound fee. That evening a nigger came with the dollar and got the hog. He was a strange nigger. He said, 'He say to tell you wood and hay kin burn.' I said, 'What?' 'That whut he say to tell you,' the nigger said. 'Wood and hay kin burn.' That night my barn burned. I got the stock out but I lost the barn."

"Where is the nigger? Have you got him?"

"He was a strange nigger, I tell you. I don't know what became of him."

"But that's not proof. Don't you see that's not proof?"

"Get that boy up here. He knows." For a moment the boy thought too that the man meant his older brother until Harris said, "Not him. The little one. The boy," and, crouching, small for his age, small and wiry like his father, in patched and faded jeans even too small for him, with straight, uncombed, brown hair and eyes gray and wild as storm scud, he saw the men between himself and the table part and become a lane of grim faces, at the end of which he saw the justice, a shabby, collarless, graying man in spectacles, beckoning him. He felt no floor under his bare feet; he seemed to walk beneath the palpable weight of the grim turning faces. His father, stiff in his black Sunday coat donned not for the trial but for the moving, did not even look at him. He aims for me to lie, he thought, again with that frantic grief and despair. And I will have to do hit.

"What's your name, boy?" the justice said.

"Colonel Sartoris Snopes," the boy whispered.

"Hey?" the Justice said. "Talk louder. Colonel Sartoris? I reckon anybody named for Colonel Sartoris in this country can't help but tell the truth, can they?" The boy said nothing. Enemy! Enemy! he thought; for a moment he could not even see, could not see that the justice's face was kindly nor discern that his voice was troubled when he spoke to the man named Harris: "Do you want me to question this boy?" But he could hear, and during those subsequent long seconds while there was absolutely no sound in the crowded little room save that of quiet and intent breathing it was as if he had swung outward at the end of a grape vine, over a ravine, and at the top of the swing had been caught in a prolonged instant of mesmerized gravity, weightless in time.

"No!" Harris said violently, explosively. "Damnation! Send him out of here!" Now time, the fluid world, rushed beneath him again, the voices coming to him again through the smell of cheese and sealed meat, the fear and despair and the old grief of blood:

"This case is closed. I can't find against you, Snopes, but I can give you advice. Leave this country and don't come back to it."

His father spoke for the first time, his voice cold and harsh, level, without emphasis: "I aim to. I don't figure to stay in a country among people who…" he said something unprintable and vile, addressed to no one.

"That'll do," the Justice said. "Take your wagon and get out of this country before dark. Case dismissed."

His father turned, and he followed the stiff black coat, the wiry figure walking a little stiffly from where a Confederate provost's man's musket ball had taken him in the heel on a stolen horse thirty years ago, followed the two backs now, since between the two lines of grim-faced men and out of the store and across the worn gallery and down the sagging steps and among the dogs and half-grown boys in the mild May dust, where as he passed a voice hissed:

"Barn burner!"

Again he could not see, whirling; there was a face in a red haze, moonlike, bigger than the full moon, the owner of it half again his size, he leaping in the red haze toward the face, feeling no blow, feeling no shock when his head struck the earth, scrabbling up and leaping again, feeling no blow this time either and tasting no blood, scrabbling up to see the other boy in full flight and himself already leaping into pursuit as his father's hand jerked him back, the harsh, cold voice speaking above him: "Go get in the wagon."

It stood in a grove of locusts and mulberries across the road. His two hulking sisters in their Sunday dresses and his mother and her sister in calico and sunbonnets were already in it, sitting on and among the sorry residue of the dozen and more movings which even the boy could remember the battered stove, the broken beds and chairs, the clock inlaid with mother-of-pearl, which would not run, stopped at some fourteen minutes past two o'clock of a dead and forgotten day and time, which had been his mother's dowry. She was crying, though when she saw him she drew her sleeve across her face and began to descend from the wagon. "Get back," the father said.

"He's hurt. I got to get some water and wash his…"

His older brother had appeared from somewhere in the crowd, no taller than the father but thicker, chewing tobacco steadily,

"Get back in the wagon," his father said. He got in too, over the tail-gate. His father mounted to the seat where the older brother already sat and struck the gaunt mules two savage blows with the peeled willow, but without heat. It was not even sadistic; it was exactly that same quality which in later years would cause his descendants to over-run the engine before putting a motor car into motion, striking and reining back in the same movement. The wagon went on, the store with its quiet crowd of grimly watching men dropped behind; a curve in the road hid it. *Forever* he thought. *Maybe he's done satisfied now, now that he has …* stopping himself, not to say it aloud even to himself. His mother's hand touched his shoulder.

"Does hit hurt?" she said.

"Naw," he said. "Hit don't hurt. Lemme be."

"Can't you wipe some of the blood off before hit dries?"

"I'll wash to-night," he said. "Lemme be, I tell you."

The wagon went on. He did not know where they were going. None of them ever did or ever asked, because it was always somewhere, always a house of sorts waiting for them a day or two days or even three days away. Likely his father had already arranged to make a crop on another farm before he… Again he had to stop himself. He (the father) always did. There was something about his wolflike independence and even courage when the advantage was at least neutral which impressed strangers, as if they got from his latent ravening ferocity not so much a sense of dependability as a feeling that his ferocious conviction in the rightness of his own actions would be of advantage to all whose interest lay with his.

That night they camped in a grove of oaks and beeches where a spring ran. The nights were still cool and they had a fire against it, of a rail lifted from a nearby fence and cut into lengths — a small fire, neat, niggard almost, a shrewd fire; such fires were his father's habit and custom always, even in freezing weather. Older, the boy might have remarked this and wondered why not a big one; why should not a man who had not only seen the waste and extravagance of war, but who had in his blood an inherent voracious prodigality with material not his own, have burned everything in sight? Then he might have gone a step farther and thought that that was the reason: that niggard blaze was the living fruit of nights passed during those four years in the woods hiding from all men, blue or gray, with his strings of horses (captured horses, he called them). And older still, he might have divined the true reason: that the element of fire spoke to some deep mainspring of his father's being, as the element of steel or of powder spoke to other men, as the one weapon for the preservation of integrity, else breath were not worth the breathing, and hence to be regarded with respect and used with discretion.

But he did not think this now and he had seen those same niggard blazes all his life. He merely ate his supper beside it and was already half asleep over his iron plate when his father called him, and once more he followed the stiff back, the stiff and ruthless limp, up the slope and on to the starlit road where, turning, he could see his father against the stars but without face or depth — a shape black, flat, and bloodless as though cut from tin in the iron folds of the frockcoat which had not been made for him, the voice harsh like tin and without heat like tin:

"You were fixing to tell them. You would have told him."

He didn't answer. His father struck him with the flat of his hand on the side of the head, hard but without heat, exactly as he had struck the two mules at the store, exactly as he would strike either of them with any stick in order to kill a horse fly, his voice still without heat or anger: "You're getting to be a man. You got to learn. You got to learn to stick to your own blood or you ain't going to have any blood to stick to you. Do you think either of them, any man there this morning would? Don't you know all they wanted was a chance to get at me because they knew I had them beat? Eh?" Later, twenty years later, he was to tell himself, "If I had said they wanted only truth, justice, he would have hit me again." But now he said nothing. He was not crying. He just stood there. "Answer me," his father said.

"Yes," he whispered. His father turned.

"Get on to bed. We'll be there to-morrow."

To-morrow they were there. In the early afternoon the wagon stopped before a paintless two-room house identical almost with the dozen others it had stopped before even in the boy's ten years, and again, as on the other dozen occasions, his mother and aunt got down and began to unload the wagon, although his two sisters and his father and brother had not moved.

"Likely hit ain't fitten for hawgs," one of the sisters said.

"Nevertheless, fit it will and you'll hog it and like it," his father said. "Get out of them chairs and help your Ma unload."

The two sisters got down, big, bovine, in a flutter of cheap ribbons; one of them drew from the jumbled wagon bed a battered lantern, the other a worn broom. His father handed the reins to the older son and began to climb stiffly over the wheel. "When they get unloaded, take the team to the barn and feed them." Then he said, and at first the boy thought he was still speaking to his brother: "Come with me."

"Me?" he said.

"Yes," his father said. "You."

"Abner," his mother said. His father paused and looked back — the harsh level stare beneath the shaggy, graying, irascible brows.

"I reckon I'll have a word with the man that aims to begin to-morrow owning me body and soul for the next eight months."

They went back up the road. A week ago — or before last night, that is — he would have asked where they were going, but not now. His father had struck him before last night but never before had he paused afterward to explain why; it was as if the blow and the following calm, outrageous voice still rang, repercussed, divulging nothing to him save the terrible handicap of being young, the light weight of his few years, just heavy enough to prevent his soaring free of the world as it seemed to be ordered but not heavy enough to keep him footed solid in it, to resist it and try to change the course of its events.

Presently he could see the grove of oaks and cedars and the other flowering trees and shrubs where the house would be, though not the house yet. They walked beside a fence massed with honeysuckle and Cherokee roses and came to a gate swinging open between two brick pillars, and now, beyond a sweep of drive, he saw the house for the first time and at that instant he forgot his father and the terror and despair both, and even when he remembered his father again (who had not stopped) the terror and despair did not return. Because, for all the twelve movings, they had sojourned until now in a poor country, a land of small farms and fields and houses, and he had never seen a house like this before. Hit's big as a courthouse he thought quietly, with a surge of peace and joy whose reason he could not have thought into words, being too young for that: They are safe from him. People whose lives are a part of this peace and dignity are beyond his touch, he no more to them than a buzzing wasp: capable of stinging for a little moment but that's all; the spell of this peace and dignity rendering even the barns and stable and cribs which belong to it impervious to the puny flames he might contrive ... this, the peace and joy, ebbing for an instant as he looked again at the stiff black back, the stiff and implacable limp of the figure which was not dwarfed by the house, for the reason that it had never looked big anywhere and which now, against the serene columned backdrop, had more than ever that impervious quality of something cut ruthlessly from tin, depthless, as though, sidewise to the sun, it would cast no shadow. Watching him, the boy remarked the absolutely undeviating course which his father held and saw the stiff foot come squarely down in a pile of fresh droppings where a horse had stood in the drive and which his father could have avoided by a simple change of stride. But it ebbed only for a moment, though he could not have thought this into words either, walking on in the spell of the house, which he could even want but without envy, without sorrow, certainly never with that ravening and jealous rage which unknown to him walked in the iron like black coat before him: Maybe he will feel it too. Maybe it will even change him now from what maybe he couldn't help but be.

They crossed the portico. Now he could hear his father's stiff foot as it came down on the boards with clocklike finality, a sound out of all proportion to the displacement of the body it bore and which was not dwarfed either by the white door before it, as though it had attained to a sort of vicious and ravening minimum not to be dwarfed by anything — the flat, wide, black hat, the formal coat of broadcloth which had once been black but which had now the friction-glazed greenish cast of the bodies of old house flies, the lifted sleeve which was too large, the lifted hand like a curled claw. The door opened so promptly that the boy knew the Negro must have been watching them all the time, an old man with neat grizzled hair, in a linen jacket, who stood barring the door with his body, saying, "Wipe yo foots, white man, of you come in here. Major ain't home nohow."

"Get out of my way, nigger," his father said, without heat too, flinging the door back and the Negro also and entering, his hat still on his head. And now the boy saw the prints of the stiff foot on the doorjamb and saw them appear on the pale rug behind the machinelike deliberation of the foot which seemed to bear (or transmit) twice the weight which the body compassed. The Negro was shouting "Miss Lula! Miss Lula!" somewhere behind them, then the boy, deluged as though by a warm wave by a suave turn of carpeted stair and a pendant glitter of chandeliers and a mute gleam of gold frames, heard the swift feet and saw her too, a lady — perhaps he had never seen her like before either — in a gray, smooth gown with lace at the throat and an apron tied at the waist and the sleeves turned back, wiping cake or biscuit dough from her hands with a towel as she came up the hall, looking not at his father at all but at the tracks on the blond rug with an expression of incredulous amazement.

"I tried," the Negro cried. "I tole him to…"

"Will you please go away?" she said in a shaking voice. "Major de Spain is not at home. Will you please go away?"

His father had not spoken again. He did not speak again. He did not even look at her. He just stood stiff in the center of the rug, in his hat, the shaggy iron-gray brows twitching slightly above the pebble-colored eyes as he appeared to examine the house with brief deliberation. Then with the same deliberation he turned; the boy watched him pivot on the good leg and saw the stiff foot drag round the arc of the turning, leaving a final long and fading smear. His father never looked at it, he never once looked down at the rug. The Negro held the door. It closed behind them, upon the hysteric and indistinguishable woman-wail. His father stopped at the top of the steps and scraped his boot clean on the edge of it. At the gate he stopped again. He stood for a moment, planted stiffly on the stiff foot, looking back at the house. "Pretty and white, ain't it?" he said. "That's sweat. Nigger sweat. Maybe it ain't white enough yet to suit him. Maybe he wants to mix some white sweat with it."

Two hours later the boy was chopping wood behind the house within which his mother and aunt and the two sisters (the mother and aunt, not the two girls, he knew that; even at this distance and muffled by walls the flat loud voices of the two girls emanated an incorrigible idle inertia) were setting up the stove to prepare a meal, when he heard the hooves and saw the linen-clad man on a fine sorrel mare, whom he recognized even before he saw the rolled rug in front of the Negro youth following on a fat bay carriage horse — a suffused, angry face vanishing, still at full gallop, beyond the corner of the house where his father and brother were sitting in the two tilted chairs; and a moment later, almost before he could have put the axe down, he heard the hooves again and watched the sorrel mare go back out of the yard, already galloping again.

Then his father began to shout one of the sisters' names, who presently emerged backward from the kitchen door dragging the rolled rug along the ground by one end while the other sister walked behind it.

"If you ain't going to tote, go on and set up the wash pot," the first said.

"You, Sarty!" the second shouted, "Set up the wash pot!" His father appeared at the door, framed against that shabbiness, as he had been against that other bland perfection, impervious to either, the mother's anxious face at his shoulder.

"Go on," the father said. "Pick it up." The two sisters stooped, broad, lethargic; stooping, they presented an incredible expanse of pale cloth and a flutter of tawdry ribbons.

"If I thought enough of a rug to have to git hit all the way from France I wouldn't keep hit where folks coming in would have to tromp on hit," the first said. They raised the rug.

"Abner," the mother said. "Let me do it."

"You go back and git dinner," his father said. "I'll tend to this."

From the woodpile through the rest of the afternoon the boy watched them, the rug spread flat in the dust beside the bubbling wash-pot, the two sisters stooping over it with that profound and lethargic reluctance, while the father stood over them in turn, implacable and grim, driving them though never raising his voice again. He could smell the harsh homemade lye they were using; he saw his mother come to the door once and look toward them with an expression not anxious now but very like despair; he saw his father turn, and he fell to with the axe and saw from the corner of his eye his father raise from the ground a flattish fragment of field stone and examine it and return to the pot, and this time his mother actually spoke: "Abner. Abner. Please don't. Please, Abner."

Then he was done too. It was dusk; the whippoorwills had already begun. He could smell coffee from the room where they would presently eat the cold food remaining from the mid-afternoon meal, though when he entered the house he realized they were having coffee again probably because there was a fire on the hearth, before which the rug now lay spread over the backs of the two chairs. The tracks of his father's foot were gone. Where they had been were now long, water-cloudy scoriations resembling the sporadic course of a lilliputian mowing machine.

It still hung there while they ate the cold food and then went to bed, scattered without order or claim up and down the two rooms, his mother in one bed, where his father would later lie, the older brother in the other, himself, the aunt, and the two sisters on pallets on the floor. But his father was not in bed yet. The last thing the boy remembered was the depthless, harsh silhouette of the hat and coat bending over the rug and it seemed to him that he had not even closed his eyes when the silhouette was standing over him, the fire almost dead behind it, the stiff foot prodding him awake. "Catch up the mule," his father said.

When he returned with the mule his father was standing in the black door, the rolled rug over his shoulder. "Ain't you going to ride?" he said.

"No. Give me your foot."

He bent his knee into his father's hand, the wiry, surprising power flowed smoothly, rising, he rising with it, on to the mule's bare back (they had owned a saddle once; the boy could remember it though not when or where) and with the same effortlessness his father swung the rug up in front of him. Now in the starlight they retraced the afternoon's path, up the dusty road rife with honeysuckle, through the gate and up the black tunnel of the drive to the lightless house, where he sat on the mule and felt the rough warp of the rug drag across his thighs and vanish.

"Don't you want me to help?" he whispered. His father did not answer and now he heard again that stiff foot striking the hollow portico with that wooden and clocklike deliberation, that outrageous overstatement of the weight it carried. The rug, hunched, not flung (the boy could tell that even in the darkness) from his father's shoulder struck the angle of wall and floor with a sound unbelievably loud, thunderous, then the foot again, unhurried and enormous; a light came on in the house and the boy sat, tense, breathing steadily and quietly and just a little fast, though the foot itself did not increase its beat at all, descending the steps now; now the boy could see him.

"Don't you want to ride now?" he whispered. "We kin both ride now," the light within the house altering now, flaring up and sinking, He's coming down the stairs now, he thought. He had already ridden the mule up beside the horse block; presently his father was up behind him and he doubled the reins over and slashed the mule across the neck, but before the animal could begin to trot the hard, thin arm came round him, the hard, knotted hand jerking the mule back to a walk.

In the first red rays of the sun they were in the lot, putting plow gear on the mules. This time the sorrel mare was in the lot before he heard it at all, the rider collarless and even bareheaded, trembling, speaking in a shaking voice as the woman in the house had done, his father merely looking up once before stooping again to the hame he was buckling, so that the man on the mare spoke to his stooping back:

"You must realize you have ruined that rug. Wasn't there anybody here, any of your women…" he ceased, shaking, the boy watching him, the older brother leaning now in the stable door, chewing, blinking slowly and steadily at nothing apparently. "It cost a hundred dollars. But you never had a hundred dollars. You never will. So I'm going to charge you twenty bushels of corn against your crop. I'll add it in your contract and when you come to the commissary you can sign it. That won't keep Mrs. de Spain quiet but maybe it will teach you to wipe your feet off before you enter her house again."

Then he was gone. The boy looked at his father, who still had not spoken or even looked up again, who was now adjusting the logger-head in the hame.

"Pap," he said. His father looked at him — the inscrutable face, the shaggy brows beneath which the gray eyes glinted coldly. Suddenly the boy went toward him, fast, stopping as suddenly. "You done the best you could!" he cried. "If he wanted hit done different why didn't he wait and tell you how? He won't git no twenty bushels! He won't git none! We'll gether hit and hide hit! I kin watch…"

"Did you put the cutter back in that straight stock like I told you?"

"No sir," he said.

"Then go do it."

That was Wednesday. During the rest of that week he worked steadily, at what was within his scope and some which was beyond it, with an industry that did not need to be driven nor even commanded twice; he had this from his mother, with the difference that some at least of what he did he liked to do, such as splitting wood with the half-size axe which his mother and aunt had earned, or saved money somehow, to present him with at Christmas. In company with the two older women (and on one afternoon, even one of the sisters), he built pens for the shoat and the cow which were a part of his father's contract with the landlord, and one afternoon, his father being absent, gone somewhere on one of the mules, he went to the field,

They were running a middle buster now, his brother holding the plow straight while he handled the reins, and walking beside the straining mule, the rich black soil shearing cool and damp against his bare ankles, he thought Maybe this is the end of it. Maybe even that twenty bushels that seems hard to have to pay for just a rug will be a cheap price for him to stop forever and always from being what he used to be; thinking, dreaming now, so that his brother had to speak sharply to him to mind the mule: Maybe he even won't collect the twenty bushels. Maybe it will all add up and balance and vanish — corn, rug, fire; the terror and grief, the being pulled two ways like between two teams of horses — gone, done with for ever and ever.

Then it was Saturday; he looked up from beneath the mule he was harnessing and saw his father in the black coat and hat. "Not that," his father said. "The wagon gear." And then, two hours later, sitting in the wagon bed behind his father and brother on the seat, the wagon accomplished a final curve, and he saw the weathered paintless store with its tattered tobacco and patent-medicine posters and the tethered wagons and saddle animals below the gallery. He mounted the gnawed steps behind his father and brother, and there again was the lane of quiet, watching faces for the three of them to walk through. He saw the man in spectacles sitting at the plank table and he did not need to be told this was a Justice of the Peace; he sent one glare of fierce, exultant, partisan defiance at the man in collar and cravat now, whom he had seen but twice before in his life, and that on a galloping horse, who now wore on his face an expression not of rage but of amazed unbelief which the boy could not have known was at the incredible circumstance of being sued by one of his own tenants, and came and stood against his father and cried at the justice: "He ain't done it! He ain't burnt…"

"Go back to the wagon," his father said.

"Burnt?" the Justice said. "Do I understand this rug was burned too?"

"Does anybody here claim it was?" his father said. "Go back to the wagon."

But he did not, he merely retreated to the rear of the room, crowded as that other had been, but not to sit down this time, instead, to stand pressing among the motionless bodies, listening to the voices:

"And you claim twenty bushels of corn is too high for the damage you did to the rug?"

"He brought the rug to me and said he wanted the tracks washed out of it. I washed the tracks out and took the rug back to him."

"But you didn't carry the rug back to him in the same condition it was in before you made the tracks on it."

His father did not answer, and now for perhaps half a minute there was no sound at all save that of breathing, the faint, steady suspiration of complete and intent listening.

"You decline to answer that, Mr. Snopes?" Again his father did not answer. "I'm going to find against you, Mr. Snopes, I'm going to find that you were responsible for the injury to Major de Spain's rug and hold you liable for it. But twenty bushels of corn seems a little high for a man in your circumstances to have to pay. Major de Spain claims it cost a hundred dollars. October corn will be worth about fifty cents. I figure that if Major de Spain can stand a ninety-five dollar loss on something he paid cash for, you can stand a five-dollar loss you haven't earned yet. I hold you in damages to Major de Spain to the amount of ten bushels of corn over and above your contract with him, to be paid to him out of your crop at gathering time. Court adjourned."

It had taken no time hardly, the morning was but half begun. He thought they would return home and perhaps back to the field, since they were late, far behind all other farmers. But instead his father passed on behind the wagon, merely indicating with his hand for the older brother to follow with it, and he crossed the road toward the blacksmith shop opposite, pressing on after his father, overtaking him, speaking, whispering up at the harsh, calm face beneath the weathered hat: "He won't git no ten bushels neither. He won't git one. We'll⋯" until his father glanced for an instant down at him, the face absolutely calm, the grizzled eyebrows tangled above the cold eyes, the voice almost pleasant, almost gentle:

"You think so? Well, we'll wait till October anyway."

The matter of the wagon — the setting of a spoke or two and the tightening of the tires — did not take long either, the business of the tires accomplished by driving the wagon into the spring branch behind the shop and letting it stand there, the mules nuzzling into the water from time to time, and the boy on the seat with the idle reins, looking up the slope and through the sooty tunnel of the shed where the slow hammer rang and where his father sat on an upended cypress bolt, easily, either talking or listening, still sitting there when the boy brought the dripping wagon up out of the branch and halted it before the door.

"Take them on to the shade and hitch," his father said. He did so and returned. His father and the smith and a third man squatting on his heels inside the door were talking, about crops and animals; the boy, squatting too in the ammoniac dust and hoof-parings and scales of rust, heard his father tell a long and unhurried story out of the time before the birth of the older brother even when he had been a professional horse trader. And then his father came up beside him where he stood before a tattered last year's circus poster on the other side of the store, gazing rapt and quiet at the scarlet horses, the incredible poisings and convolutions of tulle and tights and the painted leer of comedians, and said, "It's time to eat."

But not at home. Squatting beside his brother against the front wall, he watched his father emerge from the store and produce from a paper sack a segment of cheese and divide it carefully and deliberately into three with his pocket knife and produce crackers from the same sack. They all three squatted on the gallery and ate, slowly, without talking; then in the store again, they drank from a tin dipper tepid water smelling of the cedar bucket and of living beech trees. And still they did not go home. It was a horse lot this time, a tall rail fence upon and along which men stood and sat and out of which one by one horses were led, to be walked and trotted and then cantered back and forth along the road while the slow swapping and buying went on and the sun began to slant westward, they — the three of them — watching and listening, the older brother with his muddy eyes and his steady, inevitable tobacco, the father commenting now and then on certain of the animals, to no one in particular.

It was after sundown when they reached home. They ate supper by lamplight, then, sitting on the doorstep, the boy watched the night fully accomplished, listening to the whippoorwills and the frogs, when he heard his mother's voice: "Abner! No! No! Oh, God. Oh, God. Abner!" and he rose, whirled, and saw the altered light through the door where a candle stub now burned in a bottle neck on the table and his father, still in the hat and coat, at once formal and burlesque as though dressed carefully for some shabby and ceremonial violence, emptying the reservoir of the lamp back into the five-gallon kerosene can from which it had been filled, while the mother tugged at his arm until he shifted the lamp to the other hand and flung her back, not savagely or viciously, just hard, into the wall, her hands flung out against the wall for balance, her mouth open and in her face the same quality of hopeless despair as had been in her voice. Then his father saw him standing in the door.

"Go to the barn and get that can of oil we were oiling the wagon with," he said. The boy did not move. Then he could speak.

"What⋯" he cried "What are you⋯"

"Go get that oil," his father said. "Go."

Then he was moving, running outside the house, toward the stable: this the old habit, the old blood which he had not been permitted to choose for himself, which had been bequeathed him willy nilly and which had run for so long (and who knew where, battening on what of outrage and savagery and lust) before it came to him. I could keep on, he thought. I could run on and on and never look back, never need to see his face again. Only I can't. I can't, the rusted can in his hand now, the liquid sploshing in it as he ran back to the house and into it, into the sound of his mother's weeping in the next room, and handed the can to his father.

"Ain't you going to even send a nigger?" he cried. "At least you sent a nigger before!"

This time his father didn't strike him. The hand came even faster than the blow had, the same hand which had set the can on the table with almost excruciating care flashing from the can toward him too quick for him to follow it, gripping him by the back of the shirt and on to tiptoe before he had seen it quit the can, the face stooping at him in breathless and frozen ferocity, the cold, dead voice speaking over him to the older brother who leaned against the table, chewing with that steady, curious, sidewise motion of cows:

"Empty the can into the big one and go on. I'll ketch up with you."

"Better tie him to the bedpost," the brother said.

"Do like I told you," the father said. Then the boy was moving, his bunched shirt and the hard, bony hand between his shoulder-blades, his toes just touching the floor, across the room and into the other one, past the sisters sitting with spread heavy thighs in the two chairs over the cold hearth, and to where his mother and aunt sat side by side on the bed, the aunt's arms about his mother's shoulders.

"Hold him," the father said. The aunt made a startled movement. "Not you," the father said. "Lennie. Take hold of him. I want to see you do it." His mother took him by the wrist. "You'll hold him better than that. If he gets loose don't you know what he is going to do? He will go up yonder." He jerked his head toward the road. "Maybe I'd better tie him."

"I'll hold him," his mother whispered.

"See you do then." Then his father was gone, the stiff foot heavy and measured upon the boards, ceasing at last.

Then he began to struggle. His mother caught him in both arms, he jerking and wrenching at them. He would be stronger in the end, he knew that. But he had no time to wait for it. "Lemme go!" he cried. "I don't want to have to hit you!"

"Let him go!" the aunt said. "If he don't go, before God, I am going up there myself!"

"Don't you see I can't?" his mother cried. "Sarty! Sarty! No! No! Help me, Lizzie!"

Then he was free. His aunt grasped at him but was too late. He whirled, running, his mother stumbled forward on to her knees behind him, crying to the nearer sister: "Catch him, Net! Catch him!" But that was too late too, the sister (the sisters were twins, born at the same time, yet either of them now gave the impression of being, encompassing as much living meat and volume and weight as any other two of the family) not yet having begun to rise from the chair, her head, face, alone merely turned, presenting to him in the flying instant an astonishing expanse of young female features untroubled by any surprise even, wearing only an expression of bovine interest. Then he was out of the room, out of the house, in the mild dust of the starlit road and the heavy rifeness of honeysuckle, the pale ribbon unspooling with terrific slowness under his running feet, reaching the gate at last and turning in, running, his heart and lungs drumming, on up the drive toward the lighted house, the lighted door. He did not knock, he burst in, sobbing for breath, incapable for the moment of speech; he saw the astonished face of the Negro in the linen jacket without knowing when the Negro had appeared.

"De Spain!" he cried, panted. "Where's…" then he saw the white man too emerging from a white door down the hall. "Barn!" he cried. "Barn!"

"What?" the white man said. "Barn?"

"Yes!" the boy cried. "Barn!"

"Catch him!" the white man shouted.

But it was too late this time too. The Negro grasped his shirt, but the entire sleeve, rotten with washing, carried away, and he was out that door too and in the drive again, and had actually never ceased to run even while he was screaming into the white man's face.

Behind him the white man was shouting, "My horse! Fetch my horse!" and he thought for an instant of cutting across the park and climbing the fence into the road, but he did not know the park nor how high the vine-massed fence might be and he dared not risk it. So he ran on down the drive, blood and breath roaring; presently he was in the road again though he could not see it. He could not hear either: the galloping mare was almost upon him before he heard her, and even then he held his course, as if the urgency of his wild grief and need must in a moment more find him wings, waiting until the ultimate instant to hurl himself aside and into the weed-choked roadside ditch as the horse thundered past and on, for an instant in furious silhouette against the stars, the tranquil early summer night sky which, even before the shape of the horse and rider vanished, strained abruptly and violently upward: a long, swirling roar incredible and soundless, blotting the stars, and he springing up and into the road again, running again, knowing it was too late yet still running even after he heard the shot and, an instant later, two shots, pausing now without knowing he had ceased to run, crying "Pap! Pap!," running again before he knew he had begun to run, stumbling, tripping over something and scrabbling up again without ceasing to run, looking backward over his shoulder at the glare as he got up, running on among the invisible trees, panting, sobbing, "Father! Father!"

At midnight he was sitting on the crest of a hill. He did not know it was midnight and he did not know how far he had come. But there was no glare behind him now and he sat now, his back toward what he had called home for four days anyhow, his face toward the dark woods which he would enter when breath was strong again, small, shaking steadily in the chill darkness, hugging himself into the remainder of his thin, rotten shirt, the grief and despair now no longer terror and fear but just grief and despair. Father. My father, he thought. "He was brave!" he cried suddenly, aloud but not loud, no more than a whisper: "He was! He was in the war! He was in Colonel Sartoris' cav'ry!" not knowing that his father had gone to that war a private in the fine old European sense, wearing no uniform, admitting the authority of and giving fidelity to no man or army or flag, going to war as Malbrouck himself did: for booty — it meant nothing and less than nothing to him if it were enemy booty or his own.

The slow constellations wheeled on. It would be dawn and then sun-up after a while and he would be hungry. But that would be to-morrow and now he was only cold, and walking would cure that. His breathing was easier now and he decided to get up and go on, and then he found that he had been asleep because he knew it was almost dawn, the night almost over. He could tell that from the whippoorwills. They were everywhere now among the dark trees below him, constant and inflectioned and ceaseless, so that, as the instant for giving over to the day birds drew nearer and nearer, there was no interval at all between them. He got up. He was a little stiff, but walking would cure that too as it would the cold, and soon there would be the sun. He went on down the hill, toward the dark woods within which the liquid silver voices of the birds called unceasing — the rapid and urgent beating of the urgent and quiring heart of the late spring night. He did not look back.

12. The Lottery (1948)
• Shirley Jackson

The morning of June 27th was clear and sunny, with the fresh warmth of a full-summer day; the flowers were blossoming profusely and the grass was richly green. The people of the village began to gather in the square, between the post office and the bank, around ten o'clock; in some towns there were so many people that the lottery took two days and had to be started on June 2th. but in this village, where there were only about three hundred people, the whole lottery took less than two hours, so it could begin at ten o'clock in the morning and still be through in time to allow the villagers to get home for noon dinner.

The children assembled first, of course. School was recently over for the summer, and the feeling of liberty sat uneasily on most of them; they tended to gather together quietly for a while before they broke into boisterous play. and their talk was still of the classroom and the teacher, of books and reprimands. Bobby Martin had already stuffed his pockets full of stones, and the other boys soon followed his example, selecting the smoothest and roundest stones; Bobby and Harry Jones and Dickie Delacroix — the villagers pronounced this name "Dellacroy" — eventually made a great pile of stones in one corner of the square and guarded it against the raids of the other boys. The girls stood aside, talking among themselves, looking over their shoulders at rolled in the dust or clung to the hands of their older brothers or sisters.

Soon the men began to gather. surveying their own children, speaking of planting and rain, tractors and taxes. They stood together, away from the pile of stones in the corner, and their jokes were quiet and they smiled rather than laughed. The women, wearing faded house dresses and sweaters, came shortly after their menfolk. They greeted one another and exchanged bits of gossip as they went to join their husbands. Soon the women, standing by their husbands, began to call to their children, and the children came reluctantly, having to be called four or five times. Bobby Martin ducked under his mother's grasping hand and ran, laughing, back to the pile of stones. His father spoke up sharply, and Bobby came quickly and took his place between his father and his oldest brother.

The lottery was conducted — as were the square dances, the teen club, the Halloween program — by Mr. Summers. who had time and energy to devote to civic activities. He was a round-faced, jovial man and he ran the coal business, and people were sorry for him. because he had no children and his wife was a scold. When he arrived in the square, carrying the black wooden box, there was a murmur of conversation among the villagers, and he waved and called. "Little late today, folks." The postmaster, Mr. Graves, followed him, carrying a three-legged stool, and the stool was put in the center of the square and Mr. Summers set the black box down on it. The villagers kept their distance, leaving a space between themselves and the stool. and when Mr. Summers said, "Some of you fellows want to give me a hand?" there was a hesitation before two men.

Mr. Martin and his oldest son, Baxter. came forward to hold the box steady on the stool while Mr. Summers stirred up the papers inside it.

The original paraphernalia for the lottery had been lost long ago, and the black box now resting on the stool had been put into use even before Old Man Warner, the oldest man in town, was born. Mr. Summers spoke frequently to the villagers about making a new box, but no one liked to upset even as much tradition as was represented by the black box. There was a story that the present box had been made with some pieces of the box that had preceded it, the one that had been constructed when the first people settled down to make a village here. Every year, after the lottery, Mr. Summers began talking again about a new box, but every year the subject was allowed to fade off without anything's being done. The black box grew shabbier each year: by now it was no longer completely black but splintered badly along one side to show the original wood color, and in some places faded or stained.

Mr. Martin and his oldest son, Baxter, held the black box securely on the stool until Mr. Summers had stirred the papers thoroughly with his hand. Because so much of the ritual had been forgotten or discarded, Mr. Summers had been successful in having slips of paper substituted for the chips of wood that had been used for generations. Chips of wood, Mr. Summers had argued. had been all very well when the village was tiny, but now that the population was more than three hundred and likely to keep on growing, it was necessary to use something that would fit more easily into he black box. The night before the lottery, Mr. Summers and Mr. Graves made up the slips of paper and put them in the box, and it was then taken to the safe of Mr. Summers' coal company and locked up until Mr. Summers was ready to take it to the square next morning. The rest of the year, the box was put way, sometimes one place, sometimes another; it had spent one year in Mr. Graves's barn and another year underfoot in the post office. and sometimes it was set on a shelf in the Martin grocery and left there.

There was a great deal of fussing to be done before Mr. Summers declared the lottery open. There were the lists to make up — of heads of families. heads of households in each family. members of each household in each family. There was the proper swearing-in of Mr. Summers by the postmaster, as the official of the lottery; at one time, some people remembered, there had been a recital of some sort, performed by the official of the lottery, a perfunctory. tuneless chant that had been rattled off duly each year; some people believed that the official of the lottery used to stand just so when he said or sang it, others believed that he was supposed to walk among the people, but years and years ago this part of the ritual had been allowed to lapse. There had been, also, a ritual salute, which the official of the lottery had had to use in addressing each person who came up to draw from the box, but this also had changed with time, until now it was felt necessary only for the official to speak to each person approaching. Mr. Summers was very good at all this; in his clean white shirt and blue jeans. with one hand resting carelessly on the black box. he seemed very proper and important as he talked interminably to Mr. Graves and the Martins.

Just as Mr. Summers finally left off talking and turned to the assembled villagers, Mrs. Hutchinson came hurriedly along the path to the square, her sweater thrown over her shoulders, and slid into place in the back of the crowd. "Clean forgot what day it was," she said to Mrs. Delacroix, who stood next to her, and they both laughed softly. "Thought my old man was out back stacking wood," Mrs. Hutchinson went on. "and then I looked out the window and the kids was gone, and then I remembered it was the twentyseventh and came a-running." She dried her hands on her apron, and Mrs. Delacroix said, "You're in time, though. They're still talking away up there."

Mrs. Hutchinson craned her neck to see through the crowd and found her husband and children standing near the front. She tapped Mrs. Delacroix on the arm as a farewell and began to make her way through the crowd. The people separated good-humoredly to let her through: two or three people said. in voices just loud enough to be heard across the crowd, "Here comes your, Missus, Hutchinson," and "Bill, she made it after all." Mrs. Hutchinson reached her husband, and Mr. Summers, who had been waiting, said cheerfully. "Thought we were going to have to get on without you, Tessie." Mrs. Hutchinson said. grinning, "Wouldn't have me leave m'dishes in the sink, now, would you. Joe?," and soft laughter ran through the crowd as the people stirred back into position after Mrs. Hutchinson's arrival.

"Well, now." Mr. Summers said soberly, "guess we better get started, get this over with, so's we can go back to work. Anybody ain't here?"

"Dunbar." several people said. "Dunbar. Dunbar."

Mr. Summers consulted his list. "Clyde Dunbar." he said. "That's right. He's broke his leg, hasn't he? Who's drawing for him?"

"Me. I guess," a woman said. and Mr. Summers turned to look at her. "Wife draws for her husband." Mr. Summers said. "Don't you have a grown boy to do it for you, Janey?" Although Mr. Summers and everyone else in the village knew the answer perfectly well, it was the business of the official of the lottery to ask such questions formally. Mr. Summers waited with an expression of polite interest while Mrs. Dunbar answered.

"Horace's not but sixteen yet." Mrs. Dunbar said regretfully. "Guess I gotta fill in for the old man this year."

"Right." Sr. Summers said. He made a note on the list he was holding. Then he asked, "Watson boy drawing this year?"

A tall boy in the crowd raised his hand. "Here," he said. "I'm drawing for my mother and me." He blinked his eyes nervously and ducked his head as several voices in the crowd said things like "Good fellow, lack." and "Glad to see your mother's got a man to do it."

"Well," Mr. Summers said, "guess that's everyone. Old Man Warner make it?"

"Here," a voice said. and Mr. Summers nodded.

A sudden hush fell on the crowd as Mr. Summers cleared his throat and looked at the list. "All ready?" he called. "Now, I'll read the names — heads of families first — and the men come up and take a paper out of the box. Keep the paper folded in your hand without looking at it until everyone has had a turn. Everything clear?"

The people had done it so many times that they only half listened to the directions: most of them were quiet. wetting their lips. not looking around. Then Mr. Summers raised one hand high and said, "Adams." A man disengaged himself from the crowd and came forward. "Hi. Steve." Mr. Summers said. and Mr. Adams said. "Hi. Joe." They grinned at one another humorlessly and nervously. Then Mr. Adams reached into the black box and took out a folded paper. He held it firmly by one corner as he turned and went hastily back to his place in the crowd. where he stood a little apart from his family. not looking down at his hand.

"Allen." Mr. Summers said. "Anderson.... Bentham."

"Seems like there's no time at all between lotteries any more." Mrs. Delacroix said to Mrs. Graves in the back row.

"Seems like we got through with the last one only last week."

"Time sure goes fast." — Mrs. Graves said.

"Clark.... Delacroix"

"There goes my old man." Mrs. Delacroix said. She held her breath while her husband went forward.

"Dunbar," Mr. Summers said, and Mrs. Dunbar went steadily to the box while one of the women said. "Go on. Janey," and another said, "There she goes."

"We're next." Mrs. Graves said. She watched while Mr. Graves came around from the side of the box, greeted Mr. Summers gravely and selected a slip of paper from the box. By now, all through the crowd there were men holding the small folded papers in their large hand. turning them over and over nervously. Mrs. Dunbar and her two sons stood together, Mrs. Dunbar holding the slip of paper.

"Harburt.... Hutchinson."

"Get up there, Bill," Mrs. Hutchinson said, and the people near her laughed.

"Jones."

"They do say," Mr. Adams said to Old Man Warner, who stood next to him, "that over in the north village they're talking of giving up the lottery."

Old Man Warner snorted. "Pack of crazy fools," he said. "Listening to the young folks, nothing's good enough for them. Next thing you know, they'll be wanting to go back to living in caves, nobody work any more, live hat way for a while. Used to be a saying about 'Lottery in June, corn be heavy soon.' First thing you know, we'd all be eating stewed chickweed and acorns. There's always been a lottery," he added petulantly. "Bad enough to see young Joe Summers up there joking with everybody."

"Some places have already quit lotteries." Mrs. Adams said.

"Nothing but trouble in that," Old Man Warner said stoutly. "Pack of young fools."

"Martin." And Bobby Martin watched his father go forward. "Overdyke.... Percy."

"I wish they'd hurry," Mrs. Dunbar said to her older son. "I wish they'd hurry."

"They're almost through," her son said.

"You get ready to run tell Dad," Mrs. Dunbar said.

Mr. Summers called his own name and then stepped forward precisely and selected a slip from the box. Then he called, "Warner."

"Seventy-seventh year I been in the lottery," Old Man Warner said as he went through the crowd. "Seventy-seventh time."

"Watson" The tall boy came awkwardly through the crowd. Someone said, "Don't be nervous, Jack," and Mr. Summers said, "Take your time, son."

"Zanini."

After that, there was a long pause, a breathless pause, until Mr. Summers. holding his slip of paper in the air, said, "All right, fellows." For a minute, no one moved, and then all the slips of paper were opened. Suddenly, all the women began to speak at once, saving. "Who is it?," "Who's got it?," "Is it the Dunbars?," "Is it the Watsons?" Then the voices began to say, "It's Hutchinson. It's Bill," "Bill Hutchinson's got it."

"Go tell your father," Mrs. Dunbar said to her older son.

People began to look around to see the Hutchinsons. Bill Hutchinson was standing quiet, staring down at the paper in his hand. Suddenly. Tessie Hutchinson shouted to Mr. Summers. "You didn't give him time enough to take any paper he wanted. I saw you. It wasn't fair!"

"Be a good sport, Tessie." Mrs. Delacroix called, and Mrs. Graves said, "All of us took the same chance."

"Shut up, Tessie," Bill Hutchinson said.

"Well, everyone," Mr. Summers said, "that was done pretty fast, and now we've got to be hurrying a little more to get done in time." He consulted his next list. "Bill," he said, "you draw for the Hutchinson family. You got any other households in the Hutchinsons?"

"There's Don and Eva," Mrs. Hutchinson yelled. "Make them take their chance!"

"Daughters draw with their husbands' families, Tessie," Mr. Summers said gently. "You know that as well as anyone else."

"It wasn't fair," Tessie said.

"I guess not, Joe." Bill Hutchinson said regretfully. "My daughter draws with her husband's family; that's only fair. And I've got no other family except the kids."

"Then, as far as drawing for families is concerned, it's you," Mr. Summers said in explanation, "and as far as drawing for households is concerned, that's you, too. Right?"

"Right," Bill Hutchinson said.

"How many kids, Bill?" Mr. Summers asked formally.

"Three," Bill Hutchinson said.

"There's Bill, Jr., and Nancy, and little Dave. And Tessie and me."

"All right, then," Mr. Summers said. "Harry, you got their tickets back?"

Mr. Graves nodded and held up the slips of paper. "Put them in the box, then," Mr. Summers directed. "Take Bill's and put it in."

"I think we ought to start over," Mrs. Hutchinson said, as quietly as she could. "I tell you it wasn't fair. You didn't give him time enough to choose. Everybody saw that."

Mr. Graves had selected the five slips and put them in the box. and he dropped all the papers but those onto the ground. where the breeze caught them and lifted them off.

"Listen, everybody," Mrs. Hutchinson was saying to the people around her.

"Ready, Bill?" Mr. Summers asked. and Bill Hutchinson, with one quick glance around at his wife and children. nodded.

"Remember," Mr. Summers said. "take the slips and keep them folded until each person has taken one. Harry, you help little Dave." Mr. Graves took the hand of the little boy, who came willingly with him up to the box. "Take a paper out of the box, Davy." Mr. Summers said. Davy put his hand into the box and laughed. "Take just one paper." Mr. Summers said. "Harry, you hold it for him." Mr. Graves took the child's hand and removed the folded paper from the tight fist and held it while little Dave stood next to him and looked up at him wonderingly.

"Nancy next," Mr. Summers said. Nancy was twelve, and her school friends breathed heavily as she went forward switching her skirt, and took a slip daintily from the box "Bill, Jr.," Mr.

Summers said, and Billy, his face red and his feet overlarge, near knocked the box over as he got a paper out. "Tessie," Mr. Summers said. She hesitated for a minute, looking around defiantly. and then set her lips and went up to the box. She snatched a paper out and held it behind her.

"Bill," Mr. Summers said, and Bill Hutchinson reached into the box and felt around, bringing his hand out at last with the slip of paper in it.

The crowd was quiet. A girl whispered, "I hope it's not Nancy," and the sound of the whisper reached the edges of the crowd.

"It's not the way it used to be." Old Man Warner said clearly. "People ain't the way they used to be."

"All right," Mr. Summers said. "Open the papers. Harry, you open little Dave's."

Mr. Graves opened the slip of paper and there was a general sigh through the crowd as he held it up and everyone could see that it was blank. Nancy and Bill. Jr.. opened theirs at the same time. and both beamed and laughed. turning around to the crowd and holding their slips of paper above their heads.

"Tessie," Mr. Summers said. There was a pause, and then Mr. Summers looked at Bill Hutchinson, and Bill unfolded his paper and showed it. It was blank.

"It's Tessie," Mr. Summers said, and his voice was hushed. "Show us her paper. Bill."

Bill Hutchinson went over to his wife and forced the slip of paper out of her hand. It had a black spot on it, the black spot Mr. Summers had made the night before with the heavy pencil in the coal company office. Bill Hutchinson held it up, and there was a stir in the crowd.

"All right, folks." Mr. Summers said. "Let's finish quickly."

Although the villagers had forgotten the ritual and lost the original black box, they still remembered to use stones. The pile of stones the boys had made earlier was ready; there were stones on the ground with the blowing scraps of paper that had come out of the box. Delacroix selected a stone so large she had to pick it up with both hands and turned to Mrs. Dunbar. "Come on," she said. "Hurry up."

Mr. Dunbar had small stones in both hands, and she said. gasping for breath. "I can't run at all. You'll have to go ahead and I'll catch up with you."

The children had stones already. And someone gave little Davy Hutchinson few pebbles.

Tessie Hutchinson was in the center of a cleared space by now, and she held her hands out desperately as the villagers moved in on her. "It isn't fair," she said. A stone hit her on the side of the head. Old Man Warner was saying, "Come on, come on, everyone." Steve Adams was in the front of the crowd of villagers, with Mrs. Graves beside him.

"It isn't fair, it isn't right," Mrs. Hutchinson screamed, and then they were upon her.

15. The Rocking-Horse Winner (1920)
• D. H. Lawrence

There was a woman who was beautiful, who started with all the advantages, yet she had no luck. She married for love, and the love turned to dust. She had bonny children, yet she felt they had been thrust upon her, and she could not love them. They looked at her coldly, as if they were finding fault with her. And hurriedly she felt she must cover up some fault in herself. Yet what it was that she must cover up she never knew. Nevertheless, when her children were present, she always felt the centre of her heart go hard. This troubled her, and in her manner she was all the more gentle and anxious for her children, as if she loved them very much. Only she herself knew that at the centre of her heart was a hard little place that could not feel love, no, not for anybody. Everybody else said of her: "She is such a good mother. She adores her children." Only she herself, and her children themselves, knew it was not so. They read it in each other's eyes.

There were a boy and two little girls. They lived in a pleasant house, with a garden, and they had discreet servants, and felt themselves superior to anyone in the neighbourhood.

Although they lived in style, they felt always an anxiety in the house. There was never enough money. The mother had a small income, and the father had a small income, but not nearly enough for the social position which they had to keep up. The father went into town to some office. But though he had good prospects, these prospects never materialised. There was always the grinding sense of the shortage of money, though the style was always kept up.

At last the mother said: "I will see if I can't make something." But she did not know where to begin. She racked her brains, and tried this thing and the other, but could not find anything successful. The failure made deep lines come into her face. Her children were growing up, they would have to go to school. There must be more money, there must be more money. The father, who was always very handsome and expensive in his tastes, seemed as if he never would be able to do anything worth doing. And the mother, who had a great belief in herself, did not succeed any better, and her tastes were just as expensive.

And so the house came to be haunted by the unspoken phrase: There must be more money! There must be more money! The children could hear it all the time though nobody said it aloud. They heard it at Christmas, when the expensive and splendid toys filled the nursery. Behind the shining modern rocking-horse, behind the smart doll's house, a voice would start whispering: "There must be more money! There must be more money!" And the children would stop playing, to listen for a moment. They would look into each other's eyes, to see if they had all heard. And each one saw in the eyes of the other two that they too had heard. "There must be more money! There must be more money!"

It came whispering from the springs of the still-swaying rocking-horse, and even the horse, bending his wooden, champing head, heard it. The big doll, sitting so pink and smirking in her new pram, could hear it quite plainly, and seemed to be smirking all the more self-consciously because of it. The foolish puppy, too, that took the place of the teddy-bear, he was looking so extraordinarily foolish for no other reason but that he heard the secret whisper all over the house: "There must be more money!"

Yet nobody ever said it aloud. The whisper was everywhere, and therefore no one spoke it. Just as no one ever says: "We are breathing!" in spite of the fact that breath is coming and going all the time.

"Mother," said the boy Paul one day, "why don't we keep a car of our own? Why do we always use uncle's, or else a taxi?"

"Because we're the poor members of the family," said the mother.

"But why are we, mother?"

"Well—I suppose," she said slowly and bitterly, "it's because your father has no luck."

The boy was silent for some time.

"Is luck money, mother?" he asked, rather timidly.

"No, Paul. Not quite. It's what causes you to have money."

"Oh!" said Paul vaguely. "I thought when Uncle Oscar said filthy lucker, it meant money."

"Filthy lucre does mean money," said the mother. "But it's lucre, not luck."

"Oh!" said the boy. "Then what is luck, mother?"

"It's what causes you to have money. If you're lucky you have money. That's why it's better to be born lucky than rich. If you're rich, you may lose your money. But if you're lucky, you will always get more money."

"Oh! Will you? And is father not lucky?"

"Very unlucky, I should say," she said bitterly.

The boy watched her with unsure eyes.

"Why?" he asked.

"I don't know. Nobody ever knows why one person is lucky and another unlucky."

"Don't they? Nobody at all? Does nobody know?"

"Perhaps God. But He never tells."

"He ought to, then. And are'nt you lucky either, mother?"

"I can't be, it I married an unlucky husband."

"But by yourself, aren't you?"

"I used to think I was, before I married. Now I think I am very unlucky indeed."

"Why?"

"Well-never mind! Perhaps I'm not really," she said.

The child looked at her to see if she meant it. But he saw, by the lines of her mouth, that she was only trying to hide something from him.

"Well, anyhow," he said stoutly, "I'm a lucky person."

"Why?" said his mother, with a sudden laugh.

He stared at her. He didn't even know why he had said it.

"God told me," he asserted, brazening it out.

"I hope He did, dear!", she said, again with a laugh, but rather bitter.

"He did, mother!"

"Excellent!" said the mother, using one of her husband's exclamations.

The boy saw she did not believe him; or rather, that she paid no attention to his assertion. This angered him somewhere, and made him want to compel her attention.

He went off by himself, vaguely, in a childish way, seeking for the clue to 'luck'. Absorbed, taking no heed of other people, he went about with a sort of stealth, seeking inwardly for luck. He wanted luck, he wanted it, he wanted it. When the two girls were playing dolls in the nursery, he would sit on his big rocking-horse, charging madly into space, with a frenzy that made the little girls peer at him uneasily. Wildly the horse careered, the waving dark hair of the boy tossed, his eyes had a strange glare in them. The little girls dared not speak to him.

When he had ridden to the end of his mad little journey, he climbed down and stood in front of his rocking-horse, staring fixedly into its lowered face. Its red mouth was slightly open, its big eye was wide and glassy-bright.

"Now!" he would silently command the snorting steed. "Now take me to where there is luck! Now take me!"

And he would slash the horse on the neck with the little whip he had asked Uncle Oscar for. He knew the horse could take him to where there was luck, if only he forced it. So he would mount again and start on his furious ride, hoping at last to get there.

"You'll break your horse, Paul!" said the nurse.

"He's always riding like that! I wish he'd leave off!" said his elder sister Joan.

But he only glared down on them in silence. Nurse gave him up. She could make nothing of him. Anyhow, he was growing beyond her.

One day his mother and his Uncle Oscar came in when he was on one of his furious rides. He did not speak to them.

"Hallo, you young jockey! Riding a winner?" said his uncle.

"Aren't you growing too big for a rocking-horse? You're not a very little boy any longer, you know," said his mother.

But Paul only gave a blue glare from his big, rather close-set eyes. He would speak to nobody when he was in full tilt. His mother watched him with an anxious expression on her face.

At last he suddenly stopped forcing his horse into the mechanical gallop and slid down.

"Well, I got there!" he announced fiercely, his blue eyes still flaring, and his sturdy long legs straddling apart.

"Where did you get to?" asked his mother.

"Where I wanted to go," he flared back at her.

"That's right, son!" said Uncle Oscar. "Don't you stop till you get there. What's the horse's name?"

"He doesn't have a name," said the boy.

"Get's on without all right?" asked the uncle.

"Well, he has different names. He was called Sansovino last week."

"Sansovino, eh? Won the Ascot. How did you know this name?"

"He always talks about horse-races with Bassett," said Joan.

The uncle was delighted to find that his small nephew was posted with all the racing news. Bassett, the young gardener, who had been wounded in the left foot in the war and had got his present job through Oscar Cresswell, whose batman he had been, was a perfect blade of the 'turf'. He lived in the racing events, and the small boy lived with him.

Oscar Cresswell got it all from Bassett.

"Master Paul comes and asks me, so I can't do more than tell him, sir," said Bassett, his face terribly serious, as if he were speaking of religious matters.

"And does he ever put anything on a horse he fancies?"

"Well — I don't want to give him away — he's a young sport, a fine sport, sir. Would you mind asking him himself? He sort of takes a pleasure in it, and perhaps he'd feel I was giving him away, sir, if you don't mind.

Bassett was serious as a church.

The uncle went back to his nephew and took him off for a ride in the car.

"Say, Paul, old man, do you ever put anything on a horse?" the uncle asked.

The boy watched the handsome man closely.

"Why, do you think I oughtn't to?" he parried.

"Not a bit of it! I thought perhaps you might give me a tip for the Lincoln."

The car sped on into the country, going down to Uncle Oscar's place in Hampshire.

"Honour bright?" said the nephew.

"Honour bright, son!" said the uncle.

"Well, then, Daffodil."

"Daffodil! I doubt it, sonny. What about Mirza?"

"I only know the winner," said the boy. "That's Daffodil."

"Daffodil, eh?"

There was a pause. Daffodil was an obscure horse comparatively.

"Uncle!"

"Yes, son?"

"You won't let it go any further, will you? I promised Bassett."

"Bassett be damned, old man! What's he got to do with it?"

"We're partners. We've been partners from the first. Uncle, he lent me my first five shillings, which I lost. I promised him, honour bright, it was only between me and him; only you gave me that ten-shilling note I started winning with, so I thought you were lucky. You won't let it go any further, will you?"

The boy gazed at his uncle from those big, hot, blue eyes, set rather close together. The uncle stirred and laughed uneasily.

"Right you are, son! I'll keep your tip private. How much are you putting on him?"

"All except twenty pounds," said the boy. "I keep that in reserve."

The uncle thought it a good joke.

"You keep twenty pounds in reserve, do you, you young romancer? What are you betting, then?"

"I'm betting three hundred," said the boy gravely. "But it's between you and me, Uncle Oscar! Honour bright?"

"It's between you and me all right, you young Nat Gould," he said, laughing. "But where's your three hundred?"

"Bassett keeps it for me. We're partner's."

"You are, are you! And what is Bassett putting on Daffodil?"

"He won't go quite as high as I do, I expect. Perhaps he'll go a hundred and fifty."

"What, pennies?" laughed the uncle.

"Pounds," said the child, with a surprised look at his uncle. "Bassett keeps a bigger reserve than I do."

Between wonder and amusement Uncle Oscar was silent. He pursued the matter no further, but he determined to take his nephew with him to the Lincoln races.

"Now, son," he said, "I'm putting twenty on Mirza, and I'll put five on for you on any horse you fancy. What's your pick?"

"Daffodil, uncle."

"No, not the fiver on Daffodil!"

"I should if it was my own fiver," said the child.

"Good! Good! Right you are! A fiver for me and a fiver for you on Daffodil."

The child had never been to a race-meeting before, and his eyes were blue fire. He pursed his mouth tight and watched. A Frenchman just in front had put his money on Lancelot. Wild with excitement, he flayed his arms up and down, yelling "Lancelot!, Lancelot!" in his French accent.

Daffodil came in first, Lancelot second, Mirza third. The child, flushed and with eyes blazing, was curiously serene. His uncle brought him four five-pound notes, four to one.

"What am I to do with these?" he cried, waving them before the boys eyes.

"I suppose we'll talk to Bassett," said the boy. "I expect I have fifteen hundred now; and twenty in reserve; and this twenty."

His uncle studied him for some moments.

"Look here, son!" he said. "You're not serious about Bassett and that fifteen hundred, are you?"

"Yes, I am. But it's between you and me, uncle. Honour bright?"

"Honour bright all right, son! But I must talk to Bassett."

"If you'd like to be a partner, uncle, with Bassett and me, we could all be partners. Only, you'd have to promise, honour bright, uncle, not to let it go beyond us three. Bassett and I are lucky, and you must be lucky, because it was your ten shillings I started winning with ..."

Uncle Oscar took both Bassett and Paul into Richmond Park for an afternoon, and there they talked.

"It's like this, you see, sir," Bassett said. "Master Paul would get me talking about racing events, spinning yarns, you know, sir. And he was always keen on knowing if I'd made or if I'd lost. It's about a year since, now, that I put five shillings on Blush of Dawn for him: and we lost. Then the luck turned, with that ten shillings he had from you: that we put on Singhalese. And since that time, it's been pretty steady, all things considering. What do you say, Master Paul?"

"We're all right when we're sure," said Paul. "It's when we're not quite sure that we go down."

"Oh, but we're careful then," said Bassett.

"But when are you sure?" smiled Uncle Oscar.

"It's Master Paul, sir," said Bassett in a secret, religious voice. "It's as if he had it from heaven. Like Daffodil, now, for the Lincoln. That was as sure as eggs."

"Did you put anything on Daffodil?" asked Oscar Cresswell.

"Yes, sir, I made my bit."

"And my nephew?"

Bassett was obstinately silent, looking at Paul.

"I made twelve hundred, didn't I, Bassett? I told uncle I was putting three hundred on Daffodil."

"That's right," said Bassett, nodding.

"But where's the money?" asked the uncle.

"I keep it safe locked up, sir. Master Paul he can have it any minute he likes to ask for it."

"What, fifteen hundred pounds?"

"And twenty! And forty, that is, with the twenty he made on the course."

"It's amazing!" said the uncle.

"If Master Paul offers you to be partners, sir, I would, if I were you: if you'll excuse me," said Bassett.

Oscar Cresswell thought about it.

"I'll see the money," he said.

They drove home again, and, sure enough, Bassett came round to the garden-house with fifteen hundred pounds in notes. The twenty pounds reserve was left with Joe Glee, in the Turf Commission deposit.

"You see, it's all right, uncle, when I'm sure! Then we go strong, for all we're worth, don't we, Bassett?"

"We do that, Master Paul."

"And when are you sure?" said the uncle, laughing.

"Oh, well, sometimes I'm absolutely sure, like about Daffodil," said the boy; "and sometimes I have an idea; and sometimes I haven't even an idea, have I, Bassett? Then we're careful, because we mostly go down."

"You do, do you! And when you're sure, like about Daffodil, what makes you sure, sonny?"

"Oh, well, I don't know," said the boy uneasily. "I'm sure, you know, uncle; that's all."

"It's as if he had it from heaven, sir," Bassett reiterated.

"I should say so!" said the uncle.

But he became a partner. And when the Leger was coming on Paul was 'sure' about Lively Spark, which was a quite inconsiderable horse. The boy insisted on putting a thousand on the horse, Bassett went for five hundred, and Oscar Cresswell two hundred. Lively Spark came in first, and the betting had been ten to one against him. Paul had made ten thousand.

"You see," he said. "I was absolutely sure of him."

Even Oscar Cresswell had cleared two thousand.

"Look here, son," he said, "this sort of thing makes me nervous."

"It needn't, uncle! Perhaps I shan't be sure again for a long time."

"But what are you going to do with your money?" asked the uncle.

"Of course," said the boy, "I started it for mother. She said she had no luck, because father is unlucky, so I thought if I was lucky, it might stop whispering."

"What might stop whispering?"

"Our house. I hate our house for whispering."

"What does it whisper?"

"Why - why" — the boy fidgeted — "why, I don't know. But it's always short of money, you know, uncle."

"I know it, son, I know it."

"You know people send mother writs, don't you, uncle?"

"I'm afraid I do," said the uncle.

"And then the house whispers, like people laughing at you behind your back. It's awful, that is! I thought if I was lucky -"

"You might stop it," added the uncle.

The boy watched him with big blue eyes, that had an uncanny cold fire in them, and he said never a word.

"Well, then!" said the uncle. "What are we doing?"

"I shouldn't like mother to know I was lucky," said the boy.

"Why not, son?"

"She'd stop me."

"I don't think she would."

"Oh!" — and the boy writhed in an odd way — "I don't want her to know, uncle."

"All right, son! We'll manage it without her knowing."

They managed it very easily. Paul, at the other's suggestion, handed over five thousand pounds to his uncle, who deposited it with the family lawyer, who was then to inform Paul's mother that a relative had put five thousand pounds into his hands, which sum was to be paid out a thousand pounds at a time, on the mother's birthday, for the next five years.

"So she'll have a birthday present of a thousand pounds for five successive years," said Uncle Oscar. "I hope it won't make it all the harder for her later."

Paul's mother had her birthday in November. The house had been 'whispering' worse than ever lately, and, even in spite of his luck, Paul could not bear up against it. He was very anxious to see the effect of the birthday letter, telling his mother about the thousand pounds.

When there were no visitors, Paul now took his meals with his parents, as he was beyond the nursery control. His mother went into town nearly every day. She had discovered that she had an odd knack of sketching furs and dress materials, so she worked secretly in the studio of a friend who was the chief 'artist' for the leading drapers. She drew the figures of ladies in furs and ladies in silk and sequins for the newspaper advertisements. This young woman artist earned several thousand pounds a year, but Paul's mother only made several hundreds, and she was again dissatisfied. She so wanted to be first in something, and she did not succeed, even in making sketches for drapery advertisements.

She was down to breakfast on the morning of her birthday. Paul watched her face as she read her letters. He knew the lawyer's letter. As his mother read it, her face hardened and became more expressionless. Then a cold, determined look came on her mouth. She hid the letter under the pile of others, and said not a word about it.

"Didn't you have anything nice in the post for your birthday, mother?" said Paul.

"Quite moderately nice," she said, her voice cold and hard and absent.

She went away to town without saying more.

But in the afternoon Uncle Oscar appeared. He said Paul's mother had had a long interview with the lawyer, asking if the whole five thousand could not be advanced at once, as she was in debt.

"What do you think, uncle?" said the boy.

"I leave it to you, son."

"Oh, let her have it, then! We can get some more with the other," said the boy.

"A bird in the hand is worth two in the bush, laddie!" said Uncle Oscar.

"But I'm sure to know for the Grand National; or the Lincolnshire; or else the Derby. I'm sure to know for one of them," said Paul.

So Uncle Oscar signed the agreement, and Paul's mother touched the whole five thousand. Then something very curious happened. The voices in the house suddenly went mad, like a chorus of frogs on a spring evening. There were certain new furnishings, and Paul had a tutor. He was really going to Eton, his father's school, in the following autumn. There were flowers in the winter, and a blossoming of the luxury Paul's mother had been used to. And yet the voices in the house, behind the sprays of mimosa and almond-blossom, and from under the piles of iridescent cushions, simply trilled and screamed in a sort of ecstasy: "There must be more money! Oh-h-h; there must be more money. Oh, now, now-w! Now-w-w - there must be more money! - more than ever! More than ever!"

It frightened Paul terribly. He studied away at his Latin and Greek with his tutor. But his intense hours were spent with Bassett. The Grand National had gone by: he had not 'known', and had lost a hundred pounds. Summer was at hand. He was in agony for the Lincoln. But even for the Lincoln he didn't 'know', and he lost fifty pounds. He became wild-eyed and strange, as if something were going to explode in him.

"Let it alone, son! Don't you bother about it!" urged Uncle Oscar. But it was as if the boy couldn't really hear what his uncle was saying.

"I've got to know for the Derby! I've got to know for the Derby!" the child reiterated, his big blue eyes blazing with a sort of madness.

His mother noticed how overwrought he was.

"You'd better go to the seaside. Wouldn't you like to go now to the seaside, instead of waiting? I think you'd better," she said, looking down at him anxiously, her heart curiously heavy because of him.

But the child lifted his uncanny blue eyes.

"I couldn't possibly go before the Derby, mother!" he said. "I couldn't possibly!"

"Why not?" she said, her voice becoming heavy when she was opposed. "Why not? You can still go from the seaside to see the Derby with your Uncle Oscar, if that that's what you wish. No need for you to wait here. Besides, I think you care too much about these races. It's a bad sign. My family has been a gambling family, and you won't know till you grow up how much damage it has done. But it has done damage. I shall have to send Bassett away, and ask Uncle Oscar not to talk racing to you, unless you promise to be reasonable about it: go away to the seaside and forget it. You're all nerves!"

"I'll do what you like, mother, so long as you don't send me away till after the Derby," the boy said.

"Send you away from where? Just from this house?"

"Yes," he said, gazing at her.

"Why, you curious child, what makes you care about this house so much, suddenly? I never knew you loved it."

He gazed at her without speaking. He had a secret within a secret, something he had not divulged, even to Bassett or to his Uncle Oscar.

But his mother, after standing undecided and a little bit sullen for some moments, said: "Very well, then! Don't go to the seaside till after the Derby, if you don't wish it. But promise me you won't think so much about horse-racing and events as you call them!"

"Oh no," said the boy casually. "I won't think much about them, mother. You needn't worry. I wouldn't worry, mother, if I were you."

"If you were me and I were you," said his mother, "I wonder what we should do!"

"But you know you needn't worry, mother, don't you?" the boy repeated.

"I should be awfully glad to know it," she said wearily.

"Oh, well, you can, you know. I mean, you ought to know you needn't worry," he insisted.

"Ought I? Then I'll see about it," she said.

Paul's secret of secrets was his wooden horse, that which had no name. Since he was emancipated from a nurse and a nursery-governess, he had had his rocking-horse removed to his own bedroom at the top of the house.

"Surely you're too big for a rocking-horse!" his mother had remonstrated.

"Well, you see, mother, till I can have a real horse, I like to have some sort of animal about," had been his quaint answer.

"Do you feel he keeps you company?" she laughed.

"Oh yes! He's very good, he always keeps me company, when I'm there," said Paul.

So the horse, rather shabby, stood in an arrested prance in the boy's bedroom.

The Derby was drawing near, and the boy grew more and more tense. He hardly heard what was spoken to him, he was very frail, and his eyes were really uncanny. His mother had sudden strange seizures of uneasiness about him. Sometimes, for half an hour, she would feel a sudden anxiety about him that was almost anguish. She wanted to rush to him at once, and know he was safe.

Two nights before the Derby, she was at a big party in town, when one of her rushes of anxiety about her boy, her first-born, gripped her heart till she could hardly speak. She fought with the feeling, might and main, for she believed in common sense. But it was too strong. She had to leave the dance and go downstairs to telephone to the country. The children's nursery-governess was terribly surprised and startled at being rung up in the night.

"Are the children all right, Miss Wilmot?"

"Oh yes, they are quite all right."

"Master Paul? Is he all right?"

"He went to bed as right as a trivet. Shall I run up and look at him?"

"No," said Paul's mother reluctantly. "No! Don't trouble. It's all right. Don't sit up. We shall be home fairly soon." She did not want her son's privacy intruded upon.

"Very good," said the governess.

It was about one o'clock when Paul's mother and father drove up to their house. All was still. Paul's mother went to her room and slipped off her white fur cloak. She had told her maid not to wait up for her. She heard her husband downstairs, mixing a whisky and soda.

And then, because of the strange anxiety at her heart, she stole upstairs to her son's room. Noiselessly she went along the upper corridor. Was there a faint noise? What was it?

She stood, with arrested muscles, outside his door, listening. There was a strange, heavy, and yet not loud noise. Her heart stood still. It was a soundless noise, yet rushing and powerful. Something huge, in violent, hushed motion. What was it? What in God's name was it? She ought to know. She felt that she knew the noise. She knew what it was.

Yet she could not place it. She couldn't say what it was. And on and on it went, like a madness.

Softly, frozen with anxiety and fear, she turned the door-handle.

The room was dark. Yet in the space near the window, she heard and saw something plunging to and fro. She gazed in fear and amazement.

Then suddenly she switched on the light, and saw her son, in his green pyjamas, madly surging on the rocking-horse. The blaze of light suddenly lit him up, as he urged the wooden horse, and lit her up, as she stood, blonde, in her dress of pale green and crystal, in the doorway.

"Paul!" she cried. "Whatever are you doing?"

"It's Malabar!" he screamed in a powerful, strange voice. "It's Malabar!"

His eyes blazed at her for one strange and senseless second, as he ceased urging his wooden horse. Then he fell with a crash to the ground, and she, all her tormented motherhood flooding upon her, rushed to gather him up.

But he was unconscious, and unconscious he remained, with some brain-fever. He talked and tossed, and his mother sat stonily by his side.

"Malabar! It's Malabar! Bassett, Bassett, I know! It's Malabar!"

So the child cried, trying to get up and urge the rocking-horse that gave him his inspiration.

"What does he mean by Malabar?" asked the heart-frozen mother.

"I don't know," said the father stonily.

"What does he mean by Malabar?" she asked her brother Oscar.

"It's one of the horses running for the Derby," was the answer.

And, in spite of himself, Oscar Cresswell spoke to Bassett, and himself put a thousand on Malabar: at fourteen to one.

The third day of the illness was critical: they were waiting for a change. The boy, with his rather long, curly hair, was tossing ceaselessly on the pillow. He neither slept nor regained consciousness, and his eyes were like blue stones. His mother sat, feeling her heart had gone, turned actually into a stone.

In the evening Oscar Cresswell did not come, but Bassett sent a message, saying could he come up for one moment, just one moment? Paul's mother was very angry at the intrusion, but on second thoughts she agreed. The boy was the same. Perhaps Bassett might bring him to consciousness.

The gardener, a shortish fellow with a little brown moustache and sharp little brown eyes, tiptoed into the room, touched his imaginary cap to Paul's mother, and stole to the bedside, staring with glittering, smallish eyes at the tossing, dying child.

"Master Paul!" he whispered. "Master Paul! Malabar came in first all right, a clean win. I did as you told me. You've made over seventy thousand pounds, you have; you've got over eighty thousand. Malabar came in all right, Master Paul."

"Malabar! Malabar! Did I say Malabar, mother? Did I say Malabar? Do you think I'm lucky, mother? I knew Malabar, didn't I? Over eighty thousand pounds! I call that lucky, don't you, mother? Over eighty thousand pounds! I knew, didn't I know I knew? Malabar came in all right. If I ride my horse till I'm sure, then I tell you, Bassett, you can go as high as you like. Did you go for all you were worth, Bassett?"

"I went a thousand on it, Master Paul."

"I never told you, mother, that if I can ride my horse, and get there, then I'm absolutely sure - oh, absolutely! Mother, did I ever tell you? I am lucky!"

"No, you never did," said his mother.

But the boy died in the night.

And even as he lay dead, his mother heard her brother's voice saying to her, "My God, Hester, you're eighty-odd thousand to the good, and a poor devil of a son to the bad. But, poor devil, poor devil, he's best gone out of a life where he rides his rocking-horse to find a winner."

04 Translated Novels To Read

01. 흰 코끼리같은 언덕(Hills Like White Elephants)
02. 아몬틸라도의 술통(The Cask of Amontillado)
03. 에밀리에게 장미를(A Rose for Emily)
04. A&P
05. 누런 벽지(The Yellow Wallpaper)
06. 애러비(Araby)
09. 나는 다림질을 하며 여기 서 있다(I Stand Here Ironing)
11. 헛간 방화(Barn Burning)
12. 제비뽑기(The Lottery)
15. 흔들 목마(The Rocking-Horse Winner)

| Interpretation of the original | 원문해석 |

1. 흰 코끼리같은 언덕(Hills Like White Elephants)

• 어니스트 헤밍웨이(Ernest Miller Hemingway)

　에브로 계곡 건너의 언덕은 하얗고 길었다. 언덕의 한쪽은 그림자도 나무도 없었고, 햇빛 속의 두 철로 사이에 역이 있었다. 역의 측면 가까이에 건물의 따뜻한 그림자와 바 안의 출입문을 가로질러 파리를 쫓기 위해 대나무 구슬로 엮은 발이 걸려 있었다. 건물 바깥의 그늘에 있는 테이블에 미국남자와 소녀가 앉아있었다. 밖은 매우 더웠고 바르셀로나 발 급행열차는 40분 만에 왔다. 그 열차는 정거장에서 2분간 멈췄고 마드리드를 향해 떠났다.

　"우리 무엇을 마실까?" 소녀가 물었다. 그녀는 모자를 벗어서 테이블 위에 올려놓았다.

　"꽤 덥군." 남자가 말했다.

　"맥주 마시자."

　"맥주 두 병(Dos cervezas)." 그 남자는 발 안쪽을 향해 말했다.

　"큰 걸로요?" 부인이 출입구에서 물었다.

　"예. 큰 거 2개요."

부인은 2개의 컵 받침에 맥주 2잔을 가지고 왔다. 그녀는 컵 받침을 놓고 맥주를 테이블 위에 올려놓았다. 그리고 그 남자와 소녀를 바라보았다. 소녀는 언덕의 능선을 바라보다가 멈췄다. 언덕은 햇볕을 받아 하얗고, 군데군데 얼룩져 있었다.

　"언덕이 흰 코끼리 같아." 소녀가 말했다.

　"난 전혀 그렇게 보이지 않는데." 남자는 맥주를 마셨다.

　"아니. 넌 못 봤을 걸."

　"나도 봤을지 몰라." 남자가 말했다. "네가 내게 보지 않았을 거라고 말한다고 해서 그게 뭔가를 나타내는 건 아냐."

　그 소녀는 발을 바라보았다.

　"발에 뭔가 그려져 있어." 소녀가 말했다.

　"뭐라고 쓰여 있어?"

　"Anis del Toro(Anis; aniseed로 맛을 낸 스페인·라틴 아메리카의 독한 술). 술이야."

　"우리 마셔볼까?"

　그러자 남자는 "여기요" 라고 발 안쪽을 향해 불렀다. 부인이 바에서 나왔다.

　"4 realres(옛 스페인의 화폐단위)."

　"아니스 델 토로 2잔 주세요."

　"물과 함께요?"

　"물이랑 같이 마셔볼래?"

　"잘 모르겠어." 소녀가 말했다. "물이랑 잘 어울려?"

　"괜찮아."

"물이랑 같이 가져다 드릴까요?" 부인이 물었다.

"네. 물이랑 주세요."

"이거 감초 맛이 나네." 소녀가 말하며 잔을 내려놓았다.

"항상 그런 식이네."

"그래." 소녀가 말했다. "모든 게 감초 맛 같아. 특히 네가 오랫동안 기다려 왔던 모든 것이 다 감초 맛이야. 마치 압생트(프랑스산의 독주)처럼."

"관두자."

"먼저 시작한 건 너야." 소녀가 말했다. "나는 아주 기분 좋았는데. 좋은 시간을 갖고 있었다고."

"좋은 시간을 갖도록 노력하자."

"좋아. 나는 노력 중이었어. 난 그 언덕이 흰 코끼리처럼 보인다고 말했어. 빛나지 않아?"

"빛나."

"나 새로운 술을 마시고 싶어. 그게 우리가 하는 전부야. 그렇지 않아? 그저 뭔가를 보며 다른 술을 마시는 것?"

"동감이야."

소녀는 언덕 건너를 바라보았다.

"너무나 사랑스러운 언덕이야." 소녀가 말했다. "전혀 흰 코끼리처럼 보이지 않아. 난 나무를 통해 언덕의 색이 뭘 뜻하는지 알아."

"우리 다른 것 마실까?"

"좋아." 따듯한 바람이 테이블을 향해 발을 흔들었다.

"맥주가 시원하고 좋아." 남자가 말했다.

"너무 멋져." 소녀가 말했다.

"무척이나 간단한 수술이야. 지그(Jig)." 남자가 말했다. "그런 건 수술도 아니라고."

소녀는 그저 테이블 다리가 서있는 바닥을 보고 있었다.

"네가 신경 쓰지 않는걸 알아. 지그(Jig). 아무것도 아냐. 단지 공기가 들어갈 뿐이라고."

소녀는 아무 말도 하지 않았다.

"내가 너와 함께 갈게. 그리고 항상 같이 있어줄게. 그들은 공기만 집어넣을 것이고 그러고 나면 모든 게 완벽히 자연스러워지는 거야."

"그리고 나서 우리는 어떻게 되는 건데?"

"우리는 그 뒤로 잘 될 거야. 전에 우리가 그랬던 것처럼."

"뭐가 널 그렇게 생각하게 하는데?"

"그건 단지 우리를 괴롭힐 뿐이야. 단지 우리를 불행하게 만든다고."

소녀는 발을 바라보았고, 손을 내밀어 발의 두 줄을 잡았다.

"그리고 넌 그리고 나선 우리가 잘 되고 행복할 거라고 생각하겠지."

"난 우리가 괜찮을 거란 걸 알아. 넌 두려워할 필요 없어. 난 많은 사람들이 그걸 해온걸 알고 있어."

"나도 알아." 소녀가 말했다. "그리고 그 후에 그들은 모두 행복했겠지."

"글쎄." 남자는 말했다. "만약 네가 원하지 않으면 하지 않아도 돼. 네가 싫다면 강요하지 않을 거야. 하지만 그건 정말 간단한 거야."

"넌 정말 원하는 거야?"

"내 생각엔 그게 최선이라고 생각해. 하지만 네가 정말로 원하지 않으면 난 더 이상 너에게 강요하지 않을 거야."

"만약 내가 그걸 한다면 넌 행복할 거고 모든 게 전 같아지겠지? 그리고 넌 날 다시 사랑할 테고."

"난 지금도 널 사랑해. 너도 내가 널 사랑하는걸 알잖아."

"나도 알아. 하지만 만약 내가 수술을 한다면 다시 좋아지겠지. 만약 내가 모든 게 하얀 코끼리 같아, 라고 말하면 넌 그걸 좋아할까?"

"난 좋아할 거야. 난 지금도 그걸 좋아하지만 그걸 생각할 수 없어. 너도 알잖아. 내가 걱정할 땐 어떻게 되는지."

"만약 내가 그 수술을 한대도 넌 걱정 안 하지?"

"그건 아주 간단한 거니까 난 걱정 안 해."

"그럼 나 할게. 난 내가 어떻게 돼도 상관없으니까."

"무슨 의미야?"

"난 어떻게 돼도 상관없다고."

"난 상관있어."

"아. 그래. 하지만 난 상관없어. 그리고 난 그걸 할 것이고 다시 모든 게 괜찮아 지겠지."

"네가 그런 식으로 생각한다면 난 네가 하지 않았으면 좋겠어."

소녀는 일어나 역 끝으로 걸어갔다. 맞은 편 에브로 강둑을 따라 곡식과 나무의 들판이 있었다. 멀리 강 건너 산이 있었다. 곡식의 들판을 가로질러 구름의 그림자가 움직였다. 그녀는 그 나무들 너머의 강을 보았다.

"우린 모두 가질 수 있었어." 소녀가 말했다. "그리고 그 모든 걸 다 가질 수 있었는데, 매일 우리는 점점 실현할 수 없는 것으로 만들고 있어."

"무슨 뜻이야?"

"난 우리가 뭐든지 모두 가질 수 있었다고 말했어."

"우린 뭐든지 모두 가질 수 있어."

"아니. 우린 할 수 없어."

"우린 어디든 갈 수 있어."

"아냐. 우린 못해. 그건 더 이상 우리 것이 아닌걸."

"그건 우리 것이야."

"아냐. 그렇지 않아. 그리고 그들이 그걸 가져가면 넌 절대로 되찾을 수 없어."

"하지만 아직 그들은 그걸 가져가지 않았잖아."

"우린 기다려 볼 수 있어."

"그늘로 다시 돌아와." 남자가 말했다. "항상 그런 식으로 생각하지 말아줘."

"하여튼 난 어떤 생각도 하지 않아." 소녀가 말했다. "난 그냥 알고 있을 뿐이야."

"난 네가 원하지 않는 건 무엇도 하길 원치 않아."

"내 몸에 좋지 않은 것도 안 돼." 소녀가 말했다. "알아. 우리 다른 맥주 마셔볼까?"

"좋아. 하지만 네가 알았으면 좋겠어."

"나도 알고 있어." 소녀가 말했다. "우리 그만 얘기하는 게 어때?"

그들은 테이블에 앉았다. 그리고 소녀는 계곡의 마른 언덕을 가로질러 바라보았다. 남자는 소녀를 바라보고 테이블을 바라보았다.

"넌 이해해야 해." 남자가 말했다. "네가 하고 싶지 않다면 나도 원하지 않아."

"그게 너에게 어떤 의미가 있는 거라면 난 기꺼이 너와 함께 할 거야."

"너에겐 아무런 의미가 없니? 우린 잘 해낼 수 있어."

"물론 그래. 하지만 난 네가 아니면 원치 않아. 난 아무도 원치 않아. 그리고 난 그게 아주 간단하다는 것도 알아."

"그래. 넌 그게 매우 간단하다는 걸 알지."

"네가 그런 식으로 얘기하는 것은 괜찮아. 그러나 난 알아."

"지금 나를 위해 뭐든지 해줄 수 있니?"

"널 위해서라면 뭐든지 할게."

"제발 제발 제발 제발 제발 제발 제발 말 좀 그만하면 안 될까?"

그는 아무 말도 하지 않았다. 그리고 역의 벽에 기대어 있는 가방들을 보았다. 가방에는 그들이 밤을 보냈던 호텔의 라벨이 붙어 있었다.

"하지만 난 네가 하는 걸 원치 않아." 남자가 말했다. "난 그 수술에 대해 아무 걱정도 하지 않아."

"내가 소리치겠지." 소녀가 말했다.

부인은 젖은 받침대 위에 맥주잔 2개를 올려놓고 발을 통해 나갔다.

"5분 안에 기차가 올 거예요." 부인이 말했다.

"그녀가 뭐래?" 소녀가 물었다.

"기차가 5분 안에 온대."

소녀는 부인에게 감사의 뜻으로 환하게 미소 지었다.

"다른 곳에 가방을 가져다 놓는 게 좋겠어." 남자가 말했다. 소녀는 남자를 향해 미소 지었다.

"좋아. 그리곤 돌아와서 마시던 맥주를 마저 마시자."

그는 무거운 가방 2개를 들어서 역의 다른 통로의 근처로 옮겼다. 그가 통로를 바라보았지만 기차는 보이지 않았다.

그는 기차를 기다리면서 술을 마시고 있는 사람들이 있는 술집을 지나서 걸었다. 그는 바에서 아니스(Anis)를 마시며 사람들을 바라보았다. 그들은 모두 나름대로 기차를 기다리고 있었다. 그는 발을 지나 밖으로 나갔다. 그녀는 테이블에 앉아서 남자를 향해 미소를 지었다.

"좀 나아졌어?" 그가 물었다.

"난 괜찮아." 소녀가 말했다. "내게 잘못된 것은 아무것도 없는걸. 난 괜찮아."

2. 아몬틸라도의 술통(The Cask of Amontillado)

• 에드거 앨런 포우(Edgar Allan Poe)

포르투나토의 수많은 못된 처사에도 될 수 있는 대로 참아왔으나 또다시 모욕을 가하려고 하니까 나는 복수할 것을 결심했다. 그러나 내 성격을 잘 알고 있는 자네라면, 말을 꺼내서 내가 상대방을 협박하지는 않았음을 상상할 수 있을 것이다. 결과적으로 꼭 원한을 풀어 보겠다는 것만은 분명히 다짐했다. 그러나 그렇게 단단히 마음 먹었지만 마음 한편 구석에는 위험한 짓은 저지르지 않아야 되겠다는 속셈이었다. 벌은 안겨 주지 않더라도, 이쪽이 해를 입지 않도록 하지 않으면 안되었던 것이다. 악을 응징한 것이 오히려 다시 보복을 받는다고 하면 무의미한 노릇이다. 악을 행한 상대방에게 자기가 보복을 당하고 있다는 것을 느끼지 못하게 한다고 해도 그것 또한 무의미한 노릇이다. 알아 두라고 하고 싶은 것은, 포르투나토에게 나의 호의를 의심받을 만한 말이나 행동을 절대로 나타내지는 않았던 것이다. 나는 여태까지와 마찬가지로 그의 앞에서 웃는 얼굴을 보였다. 그러나 그 웃는 얼굴로 내가 자기를 사로잡기 위하여 웃고 있다는 것을 전혀 그가 깨닫지 못했다.

이 작자 — 이 포르투나토에게는 한 가지 약점이 있었지만, 다른 점에서는 얕잡아볼 수 없는 두려운 존재였다. 그는 포도주를 감정하는 일을 자신만만하게 생각했다. 이탈리아 사람 쳐놓고 진정한 명수의 기질을 가진 사람은 별로 없다. 대개 그네들이 설치는 짓이란 때와 장소에 따라서 — 영국이나 오스트리아의 부자들을 속이는 것이 고작이다. 그림이나 보석 같은 것을 감정하는 데는 포르투나토도 자기 나라 사람들처럼 사기꾼이었다 — 그렇지만 묵은 술을 감정하는 데 있어서 만은 진지했다. 이 점에 대해서는 나나 그 사람이나 다를 것이 없었다. 나 자신도 이탈리아 포도주에 대해서는 환히 알고 있었고, 언제나 가능한 한 많이 사들였었다.

내가 이 친구를 만나게 된 것은 카니발의 열광이 절정에 달했던 어느날 저녁 해질 무렵이었다. 그는 얼근히 취해 있었으므로 매우 유쾌하게 나를 불렀다. 그는 광대 차림새였다. 몸에 착 달라붙는 얼룩덜룩한 옷에다가 머리에는 방울을 단 원추형의 뾰족한 고깔을 쓰고 있었다. 이 작자를 만나게 된 것이 매우 기뻐서 나는 그의 손을 꽉 쥐고 좀처럼 놓아주지 않았다.

나는 말했다. "이봐, 포르투나토 군, 참 잘 만났군. 오늘의 자네야말로 정말 멋쟁이군 그래! 그런데 말이야, 나는 아몬틸라도 주를 커다란 통으로 한 통 사들였다네. 그러나 좀 수상하단 말이야."

"뭐라고?" 그는 말했다. "아몬틸라도? 큰 것을 한 통이라고? 하필 카니발이 절정에 달한 이런 판에!"

"나도 수상쩍게는 생각하지. 그런 걸 자네와 의논도 하지 않고, 서슴없이 아몬틸라도 값어치의 값을 치르다니, 나도 제정신이 아닌 모양이지. 그렇지만 자네를 좀처럼 만날 수도 없고, 그런 좋은 물건을 놓칠 수야 없지 않았겠느냐 말이야."

"아몬틸라도!"

"좀 수상하다고는 생각하지만."

"아몬틸라도!"

"좀 잘 알아보긴 알아봐야겠는데."

"아몬틸라도!"

"자네는 일이 있나 보군. 그러면 나는 루체시한테 가봐야겠네. 그 사람은 가르쳐 줄 거야……"

"루체시 따위는 아몬틸라도와 셰리 주도 가려내지 못한단 말이야."

"그러나 감정하는 데는 그가 자네에게 지지 않을 거라고 말하는 멍청이도 있단 말이야."

"자아, 가보자구."

"어디로?"

"자네 집 술 창고로."

"아니야, 친구. 자네한테 폐를 끼치다니 될 말인가. 자네는 약속이 있는가 본데. 루체시라면……"

"약속 같은 건 없네…… 자아, 가기로 하세."

"그렇지만 자네는 안되겠네. 약속 같은 건 없는지 모르지만, 내가 보기엔 악성 감기에 걸려 있는 듯한데. 술 창고 속은 습기가 차 있다네. 초석도 사방에 널려 있고."

"아랑곳할 것 없네. 가세. 감기 따위가 다 뭐야. 아몬틸라도라고! 자넨 속은 거야. 더욱이 루체시 따위 녀석은 셰리 주와 아몬틸라도를 구분하지 못하지."

이렇게 말하면서 포르투나토는 내 팔을 잡았다. 나는 까만 비단의 가면을 쓰고 외투로 몸을 꼭 감싸고는 그가 말한 대로 나의 저택으로 걸음을 재촉했다.

집에는 하인들이 없었다. 마음껏 기분에 들떠서 돌아다니느라고 모두 자취를 감춘 것이다. 나는 아침까지는 돌아오지 않을 테니 모두 다 집에서 나가서는 안 된다고 일러두었던 것이다. 이렇게 일러두면 그 작자들은 내가 밖으로 나가기가 무섭게 한 놈도 빠짐 없이 즉시 뛰쳐나간다는 것은 의심할 나위도 없다는 것을 알고 있었다.

나는 하인 방의 벽에 있는 촛대에서 등화용 횃불 두 자루를 꺼내서 한 자루를 포르투나토에게 건네주고, 방들을 지나쳐서 지하의 술 창고로 통하는 복도로 안내했다. 뒤에서 따라오는 포르투나토에게는 조심을 하라고 주의를 시키면서 나는 길게 구부러진 계단을 내려갔다. 이윽고 계단 아래까지 내려와서, 우리는 전에 몬트레소르 가문의 지하 납골소였던 축축한 바닥 위에 내려섰다.

친구의 걸음걸이는 뒤뚱거렸고, 모자의 방울이 달랑 달랑 소리를 냈다.

"큰 술통이 어디 있나?" 하고 그가 물었다.

"더 앞쪽이야. 그런데 벽 쪽에 번쩍이고 있는 하얀 거미줄 같은 것을 잘 보게나."

"그는 이쪽을 돌아보더니, 자극을 받아서 눈물이 핀, 흐릿하고 움푹한 두 눈으로 내 눈을 바라보았다.

"초석이야?" 이윽고 그가 물었다.

"그렇지." 하고 나는 대답했다. "그런데 자네 기침은 언제부터 하게 되었나?"

"컥! 컥! 컥!…… 윽! 컥! 컥! 컥…… 컥! 컥! 컥!…… 컥! 컥! 컥!"

나의 가엾은 친구는 한참동안 대답조차 하지 못했다.

"아무것도 아니야." 하고 그가 겨우 대답했다.

"자아, 돌아가지." 이렇게 나는 결심한 듯이 말했다. "자네 몸이 더 중하네. 자네는 돈도 있고, 남에게 존경도 받으며, 사랑도 받고 있네. 옛날의 나처럼 자네는 행복하기도 하고 말이야. 자네는 남에게 사랑을 받지. 나야 그까짓 아무래도 상관없지만. 그러니까 어서 돌아가세. 자네가 병이라도 난다면 나는 책임을 질 수 없으니까. 더욱이 루체시도 있는데 뭐……"

"상관 없다니까." 그는 말했다. "이 기침은 아무것도 아니야. 그까짓 게 생명과 무슨 상관이 있다고. 기침 때문에 죽지는 않네."

"그건… 그렇지." 나는 대답했다. "그러나, 또다시 시시한 소리로 겁을 줄 생각은 없네…… 그러나 될 수 있는 대로 조심해야 한다네. 이 메독 주를 쭈욱 단숨에 마셔 버리게. 습기 따위는 문제없을 테니까."

그러고는 나는 바닥에 죽 놓여 있는 술병들 가운데서 하나를 집어 마개를 뽑았다.

"마시게." 나는 그에게 술병을 내밀면서 말했다.

그는 곁눈질을 하면서 그것을 들어 입술에 갖다댔다. 그러나 대뜸 마시지 않고 나를 보고 다정하게 끄덕일 때 모자의 방울이 울렸다.

"우리 주위의 잠자는 사자(死者)들을 위하여 건배하네." 하고 그는 말했다.

"그리고 나는 자네의 만수무강을 위하여."

그는 다시 내 팔을 잡았고 우리는 앞으로 걸어나갔다.

"이 지하 묘지는 상당히 크군." 그가 말했다.

"몬트레소르 가문은 대가족이었기 때문이야."

"자네 가문의 문장은 어떤 것이었나?"

"푸른 바탕에다 금빛의 커다란 사람의 다리가 그려져 있지. 그 다리는 뱀이 일어서려고 하는 것을 짓누르고 있고 뱀은 발뒤꿈치를 이빨로 물고 있다네."

"그럼 가훈은?"

"나를 해치는 자에게 벌을 주고 말리라(Nemo me impune lacessit)."

"좋군!" 그는 말했다.

술기운은 그의 눈을 빛나게 했고, 모자의 방울은 달랑거렸다. 나의 공상도 역시 메독 주 탓으로 열이 올랐다. 우리는 뼈가 쌓이고 크고 작은 술통이 뒹굴고 있는 사이를 빠져나가서 광 속의 제일 구석진 곳으로 들어섰다. 거기서 나는 우뚝 선 채, 이번에는 와락 포르투나토의 팔을 잡았다.

"초석이야!" 하고 내가 외쳤다. "보게나, 더 많아지지. 벽에 이끼처럼 매달렸군, 우리는 강 밑바닥까지 내려왔다네. 해골 속에 습기가 들어찼군 그래. 자아, 늦기 전에 돌아가세. 자네의 기침이……."

"아무것도 아니야. 그보다 더 가보자구. 참, 그보다 먼저 메독 주를 한 잔 더 마시세."

나는 드 그라브 술 한 병을 들어서 마개를 뽑고는 그에게 내밀었다. 그는 단숨에 그것을 마셔 버렸다. 그의 눈은 거칠게 번쩍였다. 그는 웃어대면서 무슨 뜻인지 알지도 못할 몸짓을 하더니 병을 위쪽으로 동댕이쳤다.

나는 놀라서 그를 바라보았다. 그는 괴상한 몸짓을 다시 한 번 되풀이 해 보였다.

"무언지 알아차리지 못하겠나?" 하고 그가 말했다.

"도저히 모르겠군." 이것은 내가 한 대답이었다.

"그렇다면 자네는 회원이 아니군 그래."

"무엇 말인가?"

"자네 석수조합원이 아니지."

"조합원이야." 나는 말했다. "틀림없이 그렇다네."

"자네가? 어림도 없는 소리! 석수조합원이라고?"

"석수조합원이지." 하고 내가 대답했다.

"그러면 표지를 보여주게나."

"이거야." 하고 나는 대답하고, 내가 입고 있던 외투 속에서 흙손을 꺼내 보였다.

"실없는 소리!" 그는 이렇게 소리치면서 몇 발짝 뒤로 물러섰다. "아무튼 아몬틸라도 술통이 있는 데까지만 가세나."

"그렇게 하지." 나는 대답하고 내 흙손을 외투 속에 넣고는 다시금 그의 팔짱을 꼈다. 그는 내 팔에 묵직하게 매달리는 것이었다. 우리는 아몬틸라도 술통을 찾으며 앞으로 나갔다. 우리는 여러 군데의 나지막한 구부러진 천장의 통로를 빠져나가 밑으로 내려가서는 다시 나아갔고, 또다시 밑으로 내려가서 깊은 광 속으로 들어갔는데, 그곳은 공기가 너무 축축하여 햇불의 불꽃이 타오르지 못하고 깜박거렸다.

그 광 속의 저쪽 끝에는 이쪽보다 좁은 광이 하나 보였다. 그 벽에 잇대어 사람의 뼈가 천장에까지 잔뜩 쌓여 있는 광경은 바로 저 파리의 커다란 지하 납골소를 연상시켰다. 이 구석진 광 속의 3면의 벽은 아직까지도 이렇게 사람의 뼈로 가려져 있었다. 그러나 나머지 한쪽의 벽만은 뼈가 무너져 땅바닥에 아무렇게나 너절하게 뒹굴고 있어서 그것이 조그만 무덤을 이루고 있는 곳도 있었다. 이렇듯이 뼈가 무너져 내려서 노출된 벽면에는 다시 구석 쪽으로 약 4피트, 너비 3피트, 높이 6,7피트의 움이 보였다. 이런 것은 그 자체가 특별한 목적이 있어서 만들어진 것 같지는 않고, 지하 납골소의 천장을 받치는 두 개의 커다란 지주와 지주 사이의 틈서리가 되어 있는 것이었다. 그리고 그 구석 쪽은 이 지하도의 단단한 화강석으로 된 벽으로 둘러싸여 있었다.

포르투나토는 불빛이 흐린 햇불을 들고 움 속의 구석을 들여다보려고 했지만 헛일이었다. 이렇게 흐릿한 불빛으로는 구석까지 도저히 볼 수가 없었다.

"그 속에 들어가란 말이야." 내가 말했다. "그 속에 아몬틸라도가 있다네. 저 루체시는……"

"그 따위가 무엇을 안다고 그래." 하고 내 말을 가로막더니 친구는 뒤뚱거리며 앞으로 발을 내디디며 나아갔고 나는 그 뒤를 따라섰다. 금방 그는 움 속의 끝에 이르러 바위가 막혀서 앞으로 나아갈 수 없자 바보처럼 어물거렸다. 그 순간 나는 날쌔게 그를 바위에다 비끄러맨 것이다. 바위의 표면에는 좌우 2피트의 간격으로 두 개의 꺾쇠가 박혀 있었다. 한쪽의 꺾쇠에는 짧은 쇠사슬이 매달려 있었고, 또 한쪽에는 자물쇠가 달려 있었다. 그의 허리에다가 쇠사슬을 감아서 눈 깜짝할 동안에 그것을 자물쇠로 잠가버린 것이다. 그는 어이가 없어서 저항조차 하지 않았다. 자물쇠의 열쇠를 뽑아들고 나는 움 속에서 바깥으로 나왔다.

"벽을 손으로 훑어보지." 하고 내가 말했다. "초석이 닿지 않을 수가 없겠지. 굉장히 지독한 습기. 다시 한번 부탁인데 어때 돌아가지 않겠나? 뭐야, 틀렸다고? 그렇다면 결국 자네를 여기에 두고 갈 도리밖에 없는데. 그러나 우선 가능한 주의는 해두지 않으면 안되겠네."

"아몬틸라도는 어떻게 되었어?" 하고 아직 놀라움에 휩싸인 채 포르투나토는 버럭 소리를 질렀다.

"사실이지, 그 아몬틸라도 말이야." 하고 내가 대답했다.

그렇게 말하면서 나는 먼저 말한 뼈의 무덤을 뭉개내렸다. 그 뼈들을 헤치고 나자 이윽고 그 속에서 적재며 모르타르가 나타났다. 흙손을 써서 나는 움 구멍에다 이 재료로 열심히 벽을 쌓기 시작했다.

돌을 한 층 쌓은 다음인지, 쌓기 전인지, 나는 포르투나토의 술기가 싹 가신 것을 알았다. 처음에 그것을 안 것은 움 구멍의 구석에서 낮은 신음소리를 들었기 때문이다. 그것은 틀림없이 취한 사람의 신음소리가 아니었다. 그 다음에는 상당히 오랫동안 답답한 침묵이 흘렀다. 나는 다시 두 번째 층을 쌓았고, 세 번째, 네 번째의 층도 쌓았다. 그러자 그 때 쇠사슬을 요란하게 흔드는 소리가 들려왔다. 그 소리는 몇 분 동안 계속 되었는데 그동안 나는 그 소리를 들으며 만족감을 한 층 더 맛보기 위하여 일손을 멈추고 뼈 위에 앉아 있었다. 이윽고 쇠사슬 소리가 멎게 되자, 다시 흙손을 잡고 도중에 쉬지도 않은 채 다섯째, 여섯째, 일곱째 층도 해냈다. 입구 쪽의 벽은 거의 내 가슴 높이가 되었다. 거기서 다시 한번 쉬고 돌을 쌓은 위쪽으로 햇불을 들어 구석에 있는 포르투나토에게 흐릿한 불빛을 비추었다.

그때 갑자기, 쇠사슬에 묶인 그의 목구멍에서 계속 하여 크고 날카로운 고함소리가 터져나와 나는 세차게 뒤로 떠밀리는 듯한 느낌이 들었다. 잠깐 동안, 나는 소스라치면서 — 부르르 몸이 떨렸다. 허리의 긴 칼을 뽑아들고 그 칼끝으로 구멍의 둘레를 쿡쿡 쑤셔 보았다. 그러나 곧 안도감을 느꼈다. 튼튼하게 쌓아올린 광 속의 벽을 만져보자 불안이 사라졌다. 거기서 다시 구멍 입구의 벽으로 돌아왔다. 나는 그곳에서 죽겠다고 떠들어대는 사나이의 소리에 응답했다. 상대방이 지르는 고함소리에 따라 — 악을 쓰면서 — 상대방보다 더 큰 소리를 질러 주었다. 내가 그렇게 해주자 상대도 드디어 외치기를 그쳤다.

한밤중이 되자 내 일도 끝나게 되었다. 여덟 층째, 아홉 층째, 열 층째도 끝났다. 마지막 열한 층도 대강 다 끝나게 되어 나머지 돌 하나만 얹고 모르타르를 바르기만 하면 되게끔 되었다. 나는 무거운 돌을 힘껏 들어서 그 위치에다 얹었다. 그러나 그 때 구멍 속에서 낮은 웃음소리가 흘러나왔는데 나는 머리끝이 곤두서는 것 같은 느낌이 들었다. 그러고는 계속해서 슬픔에 찬 소리가 들려왔는데, 그것이 그 기품이 당당한 포르투나토의 소리라고는 생각할 수 없을 정도였다……

"하! 하! 하!…… 히! 히! 히! 참 멋들어진 농담이군…… 훌륭한 농담이야. 나중에 집으로 돌아가서 둘이서 실컷 웃어보지 않겠나…… 히! 히! 히! …… 한 잔 들이켜면서 말야…… 히! 히! 히!"

"아몬틸라도 말이지!" 하고 내가 말했다.

"히! 히! 히!……히! 히! 히!…… 그렇지, 그래, 그 아몬틸라도 말이야. 그렇지만 늦은 건 아닌가? 집에서는 우리를 기다리고 있지 않겠나…… 포르투나토 부인과 다른 사람들이, 자아, 어서 가세!"

"좋아, 자아, 가세." 하고 내가 대답했다.

"제발 그렇게 해주게, 몬트레소르 군!"

"아암, 그렇게 해주고말고!" 내가 말했다.

그러나 귀를 기울여도, 내가 그렇게 말한 데에 대한 대답은 끝내 없었다. 나는 참을 수 없어서 큰 소리로 불렀다 — "포르투나토!"

역시 대답은 없었다. 나는 아직 마지막 손질을 남겨둔 틈으로 햇불을 밀어 넣어 안쪽으로 떨어뜨렸다. 그러나 그것에 응하여 들려온 것은 모자의 방울이 울리는 소리뿐이었다. 나는 숨이 차 가슴이 답답해 왔다 — 광 속의 습기 때문이었다. 서둘러서 일을 끝내려고 달려들었다. 최후의 돌을 그 장소에다 밀어넣었다. 그러고는 모르타르로 발라 버렸다. 이윽고 완성된 그 벽에 잇대어 나는 아까와 같이 사람의 뼈를 보루처럼 높이 쌓아올렸다. 그로부터 반 세기, 아무도 여기에 손을 댄 사람은 없다. 떠난 자에게 명복 있기를!

3. 에밀리에게 장미를(A Rose for Emily)

• 윌리엄 포크너(William Faulkner)

1장

　미스 에밀리 그리어슨이 죽었을 때 우리 읍내 사람들은 한 사람도 빠짐없이 그녀 장례식에 참석했다. 남자들은 이른바 쓰러진 기념비에 일종의 경의를 표하기 위해서였고, 아낙네들은 거의 대부분 그녀의 집안을 보고 싶은 호기심에서였다. 그녀의 집 내부는 과거 10년 동안 정원사 겸 요리사로 있는 늙은 하인을 제외하고는 아무도 본 사람이 없었다.

　이 집은 한때 흰 칠을 한, 크고 네모진 목조건물이었다. 1870년대 특유의 매우 우아한 양식을 본받은 둥근 지붕이며 뾰족한 탑이며 소용돌이 모양의 발코니 따위로 장식되어 있었다. 게다가 한때 우리 읍에서는 가장 세련된 거리였던 곳에 면하고 있었다. 그런데 그 뒤 차고라든지 목화씨 뽑는 기계 따위가 우리 읍내에 침입해 오자 그 부근의 위엄 있는 이름들마저 싹 지워버리고 말았다. 다만 미스 에밀리의 집만이 홀로 남아서 면화 마차와 가솔린 펌프 위에 우뚝 솟아 그 고집 세고 교태에 찬 한 때의 영화로운 모습을 드러내고 있었는데 그 모습이란 더할 나위 없이 눈에 거슬렸다. 그런데 그 미스 에밀리마저 이젠 고인이 되어 장병들이 잠들어 있는 그 으리으리한 묘지의 한구석을 차지하게 되었다. 그들은 제퍼슨의 전투에서 쓰러진 남군, 북군의 장병들로서 그녀 또한 유명 무명의 무덤 사이에 섞여 오리나무가 우거진 묘지에 누워 있었던 것이다.

　미스 에밀리가 살아있을 땐, 그녀는 하나의 전통이었고 하나의 의무였을 뿐더러 하나의 귀찮은 존재의 화신이기도 했다. 그것은 말하자면 이 마을에 부과된 일종의 세습적인 의무였는데, 읍장인 사토리스 대령이 — 그는 흑인 여자가 거리에 나올 땐 반드시 앞치마를 둘러야 한다는 포고령을 처음으로 내린 장본인이었다 — 그녀의 세금을 면제해 주었다. 1894년의 어느 날, 즉 그녀의 부친이 죽은 날부터 시작하여 영구히 계속되는 특별 면세였다. 그러나 미스 에밀리는 그런 자선을 받아들일 것 같지 않았다. 그래서 사토리스 대령은 한가지 임시방편의 구실을 만들어 냈던 것이다. 즉 미스 에밀리의 부친이 읍 당국에 돈을 꾸어 줬으니 읍으로서는 사무 절차상 의당 이런 방법으로 갚는 것이 좋겠다는 그럴싸한 구실을 날조했던 것이다. 이런 구실은 사토리스 대령의 세대나 그 세대의 사고방식을 가진 남자들만이 만들어 낼 법한 구실이요, 여자들만이 그런 이야기를 곧이들을 만한 그런 구실이었다.

　보다 현대적인 사고방식을 가진 다음 세대의 사람이 읍장이니 평의원 자리에 앉게 되자, 이와 같은 면세조처에 대해서 차츰 불만의 소리를 일으켰다. 그래서 정월 초하룻날 읍 당국은 에밀리에게 납세고지서를 보냈다. 2월말이 되어도 아무 반응이 없었다 그래서 이번에는 공문 서한을 띄워 언제든지 좋으니까 편리할 때 읍사무소로 나와달라고 부탁했다. 그런 일이 있은 1주일 뒤 읍장은 스스로 펜을 들어, 자기가 방문하거나 아니면 차를 보내도 좋은가 하고 물어 보았다. 그러자 이제는 외출을 전연 않게 되었다는 사연을, 구식 편지지에다 퇴색한 잉크로 가느다랗게 휘갈겨 쓴 한 통의 답장을 받았다. 세금 통지서도 그 안에 동봉되어 있었지만 세금에 대해선 일언반구도 없었다.

　읍 위원회에서는 특별소집을 했다. 그 결과, 대표가 선출되어 그녀의 집을 방문하기로 했다. 그들은 벌써 8년인지 10년 전에 그녀가 도자기 그림 공부를 제자들에게 가르치던 일을 그만두고 나서부터 방문객이 다녀간 적이라곤 한 번도 없었던 그녀의 집 문을 두드렸다. 일행은 늙은 흑인의 안내로 침침한 현관에 들어갔는데 거기에는 더욱 어두컴컴한 층계가 2층으로 통해 있었다. 오랫동안 쓰지 않았던 탓인지 위층 방에서 풍겨 오는 습기차고 퀴퀴한 냄새는 숨막힐 것 같았다. 흑인은 찾아온 사람들을 응접실로 안내했다. 응접실에는 가죽으로 만든 묵직한 가구들이 비치되어 있었다. 흑인이 들창문 휘장을 걷어 치웠을 때 가죽에 금이 가 있는 것이 눈에 띄었다. 그들이 의자에 앉았을 때 넓적다리 언저리에서 희미한 먼지가 슬슬 피어 올라와서, 외줄기 햇살 속에 느릿느릿 소용돌이쳤다. 벽난로 앞에 세워 둔, 변색된 금색의 화가(畵架) 위에는 크레용으로 그린 에밀리의 아버지 초상화가 세워져 있었다.

　그들은 에밀리가 응접실에 들어오자 일제히 일어섰다 — 검은 옷을 입은 작고 살찐 여자이며, 변색한 금색 꼭지가 달린 금줄을 허리까지 늘어뜨려 그 끝이 허리띠 아래로 감추어져 있었다. 몸집은 작은 데다 빈약했다. 딴 여자라면 그저 통통한 체구의 소유자라는 말을 듣겠지만 이 여자의 경우, 비만해 보이는 것은 그 때문이었으리라. 그녀는 괸 물에 오랫동안 잠가 놓았던 것처럼 부풀어 있고 피부색도 창백하게 보였다. 방문객들이 그들의 용건을 말하고 있는 동안 굴곡이 심한 우중충한 얼굴 속에 파묻힌 그녀의 두 눈은 이 사람의 얼굴에서 저 사람의 얼굴로 옮아가고 있었는데, 그것은 마치 밀가루 반죽 속에 파묻힌 두 개의 조그만 석탄 조각처럼 보였다.

그녀는 손님들에게 앉으라고 권하지도 않았다. 다만 문간에 선 채로, 대변자가 머뭇거리며 말문이 막힐 때까지 묵묵히 귀를 기울이고 있을 뿐이었다. 그때 일행은 금줄 끝에 매달린, 눈에 보이지 않는 시계의 재깍거리는 소리를 들을 수 있었다.

그녀의 목소리는 메마르고 싸늘했다. "저는 제퍼슨 읍에선 납세의 의무가 없단 말예요. 사토리스 대령이 그 이유를 설명해 주었어요. 당신들 중에서 누구든지 읍 당국에 비치된 문서를 대조하여 보면 잘 알 거예요."

"그러나 이미 대조해 봤는걸요. 미스 에밀리, 저희들이 바로 읍 당사자니 말이에요. 읍장이 서명한 납세 통지서를 받지 않으셨는지요?"

"네, 무슨 종이는 받긴 했어요" 하고 미스 에밀리는 말했다. "아마 그 친구가 읍장으로 자인하는 모양인데...... 하여간 나는 제퍼슨에선 세금을 내지 않아도 돼요."

"헌데 그런 것을 증명할 만한 근거가 장부에는 보이지 않던데요. 저희들은 기록문서가 없으면 부득이......"

"사토리스 대령을 만나 봐요. 난 제퍼슨에선 납세 의무가 없어요."

"그렇지만, 미스 에밀리, 저......"

"사토리스 대령을 만나 보라니까요." —사토리스 대령은 죽은 지 거의 10년이 되었다— "나도 제퍼슨에선 세금을 내지 않아도 된단 말이에요. 토오브!"

흑인 하인이 나타났다. "이 손님들을 돌아가게 해드려요!"

2장

이렇게 그녀는 그들 일행을 서슴지 않고 물리쳐 버렸던 것이다. —마치 그녀가 30년 전에, 그들의 부모들을 집안의 악취로 멋지게 무찔러 버린 것처럼. 그것은 그녀의 부친이 죽기 2년 전 그녀의 애인—그녀와 결혼하리라고 우리들이 믿고 있었던 사나이—이 그녀를 저버린 직후의 일이었다. 부친이 죽은 뒤 그녀는 외출하는 일이 아주 적어졌다. 그리고 애인한테 버림을 받은 뒤로는 읍 사람들은 그녀의 모습을 거의 볼 수 없었다. 몇몇 여인들은 대담하게도 그녀를 방문했지만 면회가 거절되었다. 그리고 이 집에 사람이 살고 있다는 유일한 표시로는 장바구니를 들고 시장에 드나드는 흑인 하인—그 당시엔 아직 젊었지만—뿐이었다. "마치 사내들은—어떤 사내이건—부엌일을 말끔히 알 수 있다고 생각하나봐" 그렇게 여인들은 숙덕거렸다. 그래서 그 집에서 악취가 풍겨 나와도 여인들은 당연히 일이라고 생각하여 수상히 여기지 않았다. 이거야말로 조잡하고 혼잡하며 뒤숭숭한 외계와 의젓하고 당당한 그리어슨 가(家)를 맺는 또 하나의 고리였다.

이웃에 사는 어느 여자가 여든 살 난 읍장인 스티븐스 판사에게 푸념을 늘어놓았다.

"그러면 부인, 그 일을 어떻게 처리했으면 좋겠습니까?"

"아 그거요, 악취가 나지 않도록 명령을 내려 주세요. 그러한 법은 없을까요?"

"그럴 필요까지는 없을 것 같군요." 하고 스티븐스 판사는 대답했다. "아마 그 집 검둥이 녀석이 마당에서 죽인 쥐나 뱀 때문이겠죠. 그 녀석에게 따끔히 일러두겠어요."

그 이튿날 읍장은 또 두 건이나 항의를 받았다. 그중 하나는 은근한 어조로 비난해 온 한 사나이의 불평이었다. "판사님, 정말이지 이건 어떻게 처리해야겠어요. 저도 미스 에밀리를 괴롭힐 생각은 추호도 없는 사람입니다만, 무슨 대책을 세우지 않으면 안되겠어요." 그날 밤, 읍 위원회가 열렸다 – 잿빛의 수염을 한 노인 네 명과 그보다 한결 젊은 청년위원 한 사람이 참석했다.

"지극히 간단한 문제지요." 하고 청년위원은 말했다. "울 안 청소를 깨끗이 하라고 명령하란 말입니다. 언제까지 하라는 기한을 주자고요. 만일 말을 듣지 않을 땐…."

"여보, 그걸 말이라고 하시오?" 하고 스티븐스 판사는 말했다. "그래 악취가 난다고 점잖은 부인을 어떻게 면박한단 말이오?"

그리하여 이틀날 밤 자정이 넘은 뒤 네 사람이 미스 에밀리 집의 잔디밭을 지나 도둑처럼 집 주위를 살금살금 돌아다니며 벽돌 틈새기와 지하실 입구의 냄새를 맡았다. 그러는 동안, 그들 중 한 사람은 어깨에 부대를 메고 꼭 씨앗 뿌리는 식으로 소독약을 뿌리고 다녔다. 그들은 지하실 문을 열어 젖히고 그 안에다 석회를 뿌렸다. 그리고 바깥 채에도 똑같이 석회를 뿌렸다. 일행이 잔디밭을 다시 가로질러 나갈 때, 이제까지 어두웠던 들창문에 불이 켜졌으며 불빛을 등지고 앉은 미스 에밀리의 모습이 눈에 띄었다. 그녀의 꼿꼿한 상체는 우상(偶像)의 그것처럼 부동의 자세였다. 일행은 가만가만히 잔디밭을 기어 나와 가로에 즐비한 아카시아 나무 그늘로 몸을 감추었다. 그후 한 두 주일이 지나자 그 악취는 사라졌다.

읍 사람들이 정말로 그녀를 불쌍히 여기기 시작한 것은 바로 그 무렵이었다. 우리 읍에 사는 사람들은 그녀의 고모 할머니가 되는 와이어트 부인이 마침내 완전히 미쳐 버리고 만 것을 회상하고는 그리어슨 가(家) 사람들이 자기네 분수도 잊어버리고 지나치게 거만을 부린다고 믿었던 것이다. 마을 청년들 가운데는 어느 누구도 미스 에밀리의 배필로 알맞게 보이지 않았다. 우리는 오랫동안 이 일족을 한 폭의 활인화(活人畵) – 예전에, 배경을 적당하게 꾸미고 분장한 사람이 그림 속의 사람처럼 보이게 만든 구경거리 〈역자 주〉 – 로 여기고 있었다. – 미스 에밀리는 흰옷차림의 날씬한 모습으로 뒤에 서고, 그녀의 부친은 그녀에게 등을 돌린 채 말채찍을 손에 쥐고 양다리를 버티고 선 실루엣의 모습으로 전면을 가리우고 있다 – 그들 두 사람 뒤에 활짝 열린 현관문이 사진틀의 구실을 하는 것이었다. 이리하여 에밀리의 나이가 서른이 되도록 독신으로 지낼 때 우리들은 반드시 기분이 좋았다고 까지는 못해도 속으로 고소함을 금치 못했다. 아무리 집안 혈통에 유전적으로 미친 사람이 있었다 하더라도, 정말 결혼할 기회가 나타나기만 했더라면 그 기회를 모조리 거절하지는 않았을 것이라고 생각되었기 때문이다.

에밀리의 부친이 죽었을 때 그녀가 이어받은 것은 집 한 채밖에 없었다는 소문이 나돌았다. 그리고 어느 의미에서 사람들은 좋아하였다. 이로써 미스 에밀리를 동정할 수 있으리라고 생각했기 때문이다. 거지꼴이나 다름없이 외톨이로 남게 됐으니 그녀도 인간미를 보이게 될 것이라고 생각했던 것이다. 이제는 그녀도 돈이 한 푼이라도 더 많으냐 적으냐에 따라서 전율을 느끼기도 하고 절망에 빠지기도 하고 예부터의 인간의 속성을 알게 되리라고 생각했기 때문이다.

부친이 죽은 다음 날 읍내 부인네들은 관습에 따라 그녀의 집을 방문하여 조의를 표하고 도와줄 채비를 갖추기로 했다. 그런데 미스 에밀리는 여느 때나 다름없는 복장에다 얼굴에도 슬픔의 기색 하나 나타내지 않고, 그들을 맞이하러 문간에 나와서는, 아버지가 죽지 않았다고 그들에게 말하였다. 목사들이 찾아오고 의사들이 그녀에게 장사를 지내라고 설득했지만 에밀리는 사흘 동안이나 꼭 같은 말을 되풀이하면서 고집을 부렸다. 사람들이 법에 호소하거나 실력행사를 하겠노라고 위협조로 나오자 그녀는 마침내 굴복했다. 그래서 읍 사람들이 서둘러 장사를 지냈던 것이다.

그때 우리들은 아무도 그녀가 미쳤다고는 말하지 않았다. 오히려 그렇게 하지 않으면 않되는 사정이 틀림없이 있으리라고 생각했다. 우리들은 그녀의 부친이 쫓아버린 수많은 청년들을 회상했다. 그리고 무엇 하나 뒤에 남은 것이 없다는 것을 알았을 때, 모든 사람들이 그렇게 했듯이, 그녀로서도 자기에게서 모든 것을 빼앗아 간 것에 매달리지 않으면 안될 것이라고 생각했던 것이다.

3장

그녀가 병석에 누운 지 오래 되었다. 우리가 그녀와 다시 만났을 때 머리가 짧게 잘려져 그녀의 모습은 마치 소녀와도 같았다. 교회 색유리에 그려진 천사와 닮은 데가 있어 약간 비극적이고 조용한 느낌마저 들었다. 읍 당국이 도로포장 계약을 막 끝맺은 후의 얘기이다. 그녀의 부친이 세상을 뜨고 난 여름, 읍 당국은 공사를 시작했다. 청부회사에서는 흑인 노동자와 공사에 필요한 여러 가지 기계를 가지고 왔다. 십장은 북부 출신의 호머 베론이라는 사람이었다. 그는 몸집이 큰데다 얼굴이 거무테테하고 날렵해 보이는 친구로 목소리가 우람하고 눈빛은 얼굴보다 좀 밝아 보였다. 어린애들이 떼를 지어 그의 뒤를 마냥 따라다녔다. 그가 흑인들을 야단치는 것을 구경하기가 무척이나 재미있었던 모양이다. 그리고 괭이가 오르내리는 데 따라 박자를 맞추어 노래부르는 것이 무척 신기해 보였던 것이다. 얼마 안되어 그도 읍내 사람들을 모두 알게 되었다. 광장의 어느 곳에서든 너털웃음이 터져나올 때면 언제나 그 무리 한가운데서 호머 베론의 모습을 볼 수 있었다. 얼마 후 그는 미스 에밀리와 함께 어울려 다니기 시작했다. 일요일날 오후면 마차 집에서 세낸, 노란 수레가 달린 이륜마차를 밤 색 말에 매달아 의좋게 어울려 지내는 모습이 번번이 눈에 띄었다.

처음에 우리들은, 미스 에밀리가 이제부터 살 재미를 붙이게 될 거라고 생각하며 기뻐했다. 아낙네들은 입을 모아 이렇게 수군거렸다. "가문이 좋은 그리어슨 집 규수가 북부 출신 날품팔이꾼 녀석을 진정으로 상대할려구" 그런데 나이가 든 다른 여자들 중에는 아무리 깊은 슬픔에 빠졌더라도 참된 숙녀라면 양반의 체통을 ― 바로 이런 표현을 사용한 것은 아니지만 ― 잊을 리가 있겠는가, 하고 말하는 이도 더러 있었다. 그리고 다들 "가엾은 에밀리! 친척이라도 와 주는 게 좋겠구면." 하고 말할 뿐이었다. 그녀에게는 앨라배마 주에 사는 친척이 있었다. 그러나 몇 해 전에 실성한 노파 와이어트 부인의 토지 문제로 에밀리의 부친과 언쟁이 있은 후로는 양가 사이엔 대화가 끊겨 버린 지 오래였다. 그들은 에밀리의 부친 초상 때에도 얼굴조차 내밀지 않았던 것이다.

노인들의 입에서 "에밀리는 불쌍도 하지!" 하는 말이 나오자 마자, 여기저기서 사람들이 수군거리기 시작했다. "정말 그렇다고 생각해?" 하고 사람들은 서로 주고받았다. "물론 그렇지, 그럴 수밖에 없겠지……"

사람들은 남들이 들을세라 입을 손으로 가리고 말했다. 일요일 오후 햇볕을 가리기 위해 들창 위에 쳐 놓은 발 뒤에서 목을 길게 내민 사람들의 입에 "가엾은 에밀리!" 하고 속삭이는 소리가 새어 나올 때면, 밖에서 비단 옷자락 스치는 소리에 섞여 말 두 필이 달리는 경쾌한 발굽 소리가 울려오는 것이었다.

그녀는 거만스럽게 고개를 높이 쳐들고 다녔다 ― 그녀가 이미 몰락했다고 우리들이 믿었을 때는 더욱 그러했다. 그것은 그리어슨 가(家)의 마지막 사람으로서 자기의 위엄을 이전보다 더욱 사람들에게 과시하려는 것 같았다. 그리고 또 자기의 고집을 세상 사람에게 확인시키기 위해서도 그런 속된 짓을 필요로 하고 있는 것 같았다. 그것은 그가 비소라는 쥐약을 살 때의 태도에도 잘 나타나 있었다. 그런 일이 있었던 것은 읍내 사람들 입에서 "불쌍한 에밀리!" 라는 말이 나오기 시작하고 나서 한 해가 넘은 뒤였으며, 두 명의 사촌 언니들이 그녀의 집을 방문하여 묵고 있는 동안의 일이었다.

"독약을 좀 주세요" 하고 그녀는 약제사에게 말했다. 그 때 에밀리는 이미 서른이 넘었는데, 몸매는 아직도 날씬했다. ― 여느 때보다 다소 말라보이긴 했지만, 관자놀이와 안공(眼孔) 사이의 살이 팽팽한 얼굴에 싸늘하고 거만해 보이는 검은 눈을 하고 있었다. 생각건대 등대지기의 얼굴 표정이 그렇지 않을런지 모르겠다. "독약을 좀 주세요" 하고 그녀는 말했다.

"아, 네, 에밀리양, 어떤 종류를 원하시죠? 쥐라도 잡으시려구요? 그렇다면 권하고 싶은 게……"

"제일 좋은 걸로 주세요, 종류 같은 건 상관없어요."

약제사는 대여섯 가지 약 이름을 댔다. "이것을 쓰면 코끼리라도 잡을 수 있죠. 헌데 댁이 원하시는 게……"

"비소요." 하고 미스 에밀리는 말했다. "그게 좋은 약인가요?"

"비소 말인가요? 물론입죠. 그런데 원하시는 것이……"

"비소를 달라니까요."

약제사는 그녀를 내려다보았다. 그녀는 꼿꼿하게 서서 그를 마주 보았는데 그 얼굴은 마치 팽팽한 깃발과도 같았다.

"네, 물론 드리죠. 그런데 꼭 그 약을 사시겠다면요. 그게 법률상으로는 그 약의 용도가 무엇인지 밝히도록 되어 있습니다."

미스 에밀리는 약제사의 눈을 마주 보기 위해 고개를 뒤로 젖힌 채로 그를 뚫어질 듯이 쳐다볼 뿐이었다. 마침내 약제사는 시선을 돌린 뒤 안에 들어가 비소를 꺼내어 종이에 쌌다. 흑인 사환이 종이에 싼 약을 그녀에게 갖다 주었다. 약제사는 밖으로 나오지 않았다. 에밀리가 집에 가서 포장을 풀어보니 약봉지 위엔 해골에 두 개의 대각선으로 엇갈린 뼈가 그려진 그림에 〈쥐약〉이라고 적혀 있었다.

4장

그리하여 이튿날 "그 여자는 자살할 거야" 하고 모두들 말했다. 그렇게 하는 것이 최상의 길일 거라고 말했다. 처음에 그녀가 호머 베론과 나란히 다니는 것을 보기 시작했을 때 누구나 "그 여자는 그 사나이와 결혼하게 될거야." 라고 말했던 것이다. 얼마 후 "그 사나이와 결혼하려면 그녀는 계속 그를 설득해야 할거야." 하고 우리들은 말했다. 호머 자신이 자기는 결혼할 사람이 아니라고 말했기 때문이다. 그가 젊은 남자들과 함께 엘크스 클럽에서 술을 자주 마시고 있다는 것은 잘 알려진 사실이었다. 그 후 일요일 오후가 되면 두 사람은 번쩍이는 마차를 타고 – 에밀리는 고개를 거만스럽게 쳐들고, 호머 베론은 모자를 비스듬히 쓰고 이빨 사이에 여송연을 물고 노란 장갑을 낀 한쪽 손에는 고삐와 채찍을 쥐고 거리를 지나갔다. 그럴 때면 읍내 사람들은 들창문을 가린 발 뒤에서 "에밀리는 가엾기도 하지" 하고 속삭였던 것이다.

바로 그때 몇몇 여자들은 에밀리가 그런 짓을 하는 것은 읍 전체에 대한 불명예이며 젊은이들에게 좋지 못한 본보기라고 비난하기 시작했다. 남자들은 그런 일에 간섭하지 않으려고 했지만, 마침내 여자들은 그 이상 참지 못하겠다는 듯이 침례교(浸禮敎) 목사 – 에밀리의 집안 사람들은 성공회(聖公會)에 속하고 있었다. – 에게 강요하다시피 해서 그 여자 집을 방문했다. 그녀와의 면담 중에 어떠한 일이 일어났는지에 관해서, 목사는 절대로 입밖에 내려고 하지 않았으나, 두 번 다시 그녀를 방문하기를 거절했다. 다음 일요일 그들이 마차를 타고 거리를 쏘다니는 모습이 눈에 띄었다. 그 이튿날 목사 부인이 앨라배마에 살고 있는 에밀리의 친척에게 편지를 보냈다.

이리하여 그녀도 한번 더 같은 지붕 밑에 친척을 맞이하게 되었는데 우리는 뒤로 물러서서 사태를 관망하였다. 처음에는 아무 일도 일어나지 않았다. 그 다음에 우리들은 그들이 머지않아 결혼할 것이라고 확신하였다. 미스 에밀리가 보석상에 가서 남자용 은(銀)제 화장도구를 한 세트 주문하고 그 하나 하나에 H. B라는 머릿글자를 새겨 넣도록 한 사실을 알았다. 그리고 이틀 후 그녀는 잠옷과 함께 남자용 의류를 한 벌 사들였다는 사실도 알았다. "이제는 결혼을 하겠구먼." 하고 우리는 말하면서 정말 기뻐했다. 우리들이 기뻐한 것은, 같이 살라고 온 에밀리의 두 종형제가 에밀리보다 더 그리어슨 가문을 자랑하는 듯 양반 티를 냈기 때문이다.

그래서 호머 베론이 읍을 떠났을 때에도 우리들은 그다지 놀라지 않았다 – 도로의 포장공사도 얼마 전에 끝났던 것이다. 우리들로서는 그들 사이에 감정의 폭발 같은 것이 없어서 다소 실망했다. 그렇지만 베론이 떠난 것은 에밀리를 맞이할 준비를 하기 위한 것이거나 혹은 에밀리의 종형제들을 쫓아보낼 기회를 만들어 주기 위한 것이라고 믿었다. (그때까지만 해도 그 일이 일종의 음모 같은 것으로 여겨졌는데 우리들은 모두 그녀 편에 서서 종형제들을 함정에 몰아넣으려는 일에 은근히 마음속으로 찬성하고 있었다) 아니나 다를까, 1주일 후 그들은 에밀리의 집을 떠나고 말았다. 그리고 우리들이 처음부터 예상한 그대로 그로부터 사흘 안에 호머 베론이 읍에 되돌아왔다. 어느 날 땅거미가 내릴 무렵, 흑인 하인이 부엌문으로 그를 맞아들이는 것을 이웃 사람이 보았다는 것이다.

그런데 우리가 호머 베론의 모습을 본 것은 그것이 마지막이었다. 게다가 미스 에밀리의 모습도 그후 당분간은 아무도 보지 못했다. 흑인 하인만은 장바구니를 들고 드나들었지만 앞문은 여전히 굳게 닫힌 채 열릴 줄 몰랐다. 이따금, 잠깐 동안 그녀의 모습이 들창문 가에 비치곤 했지만 — 마치 그날 밤, 석회를 뿌린 사람들이 본 것처럼 — 거의 여섯 달 동안이나 그녀는 일체 거리에 나타나지 않았다. 그때 우리들은 그럴 수도 있으려니 생각했다 — 그것은 여자로서의 그녀의 생활을 무참히 꺾어 놓고만 그녀 부친의 그 성품이 너무 지독하여 쉽사리 지워 버릴 수 없다는 데 그 원인이 있다고 생각했다.

그 다음에 우리들이 미스 에밀리를 만났을 땐 그녀의 몸은 뚱뚱해졌고, 머리칼은 반백이었다. 다음 2, 3년 동안 그녀의 머리는 점점 회색으로 바뀌었다가 마침내는 변색의 극한에 다다라 마치 후춧가루에 소금을 섞은 것 같은 철회색(鐵灰色)을 띠기에 이르렀다. 일흔 넷이라는 나이로 죽을 때까지 그녀의 머리 빛깔은 활동적인 남자의 머리칼과 같은 정력적인 철회색을 끝내 간직하고 있었다.

그때부터 줄곧 그녀의 집 앞문은 굳게 닫혀 있었다. 하기야 그녀의 나이가 마흔 전후였던 무렵, 즉 그녀가 도자기 그림 레슨을 해주던 7, 8년 동안만은 예외였다. 그때 그녀는 아래층 방에다 화실을 하나 꾸며 놓고, 사토리스 대령과 동년배 사람들의 딸이나 손녀들을 가르쳤다. 애들은 마치 헌금함에 넣을 25센트 짜리 은화를 갖고 교회로 보내질 때와 꼭같은 규칙성과 정신에서 그 화실로 보내졌던 것이다. 이때에도 에밀리는 세금면제의 혜택을 받고 있었다.

이윽고 새 세대 사람들이 읍의 중추를 이루고 이곳의 중심인물로 등장하면서부터 그림 배우는 제자들도 다 성장하여 하나 둘 빠져나갔고, 몇몇 사람들의 아이들도 물감 상자와 지저분한 화필이니 부인잡지에서 오려낸 그림 따위를 가지고 에밀리의 화실로 보내지는 일이 차츰 줄어들고 말았다. 그리고 에밀리의 집 앞문은 마지막 빠져나가는 제자와 더불어 영영 닫혀 버리고 말았다. 읍에서 무료우편제도가 실시되었을 때 에밀리만은 현관 위에 금속 번호표를 붙이거나 우편함을 다는 일을 한사코 마다했다. 그녀는 읍내 사람들의 말은 아예 귀담아 들으려고도 하지 않았다.

날이 가고 달이 가고 해가 바뀌어도 변함없이 흑인 하인은 장바구니를 들고 드나들었지만 그도 이제는 머리칼이 잿빛으로 변하고 허리도 마냥 굽어만 가는 것을 우리는 한눈에 알아볼 수 있었다. 3월이 되면 읍 당국은 납세고지서를 그녀에게 보냈지만 1주일 후에는 〈받는이 없음〉이라는 이유서가 붙여져 되돌아오곤 했다. 이따금 그녀의 모습이 아래층 들창문 안에 보이곤 하였다 — 그녀는 분명히 위층 방을 폐쇄하고 아래층 방을 쓰고 있는 모양이었다 — 창문 안에 마치 벽감(壁龕) — 장식을 위하여 벽면을 오목하게 파서 만든 공간. 등잔이나 조각품 따위를 세워 둔다 〈역자주〉 — 에 장식된 조각 흉상(胸像)과도 같은 그녀의 모습이 어른거리는 것을 보기도 했는데 그녀가 우리들을 보고 있는지 안 보고 있는지는 분간하기 힘들었다. 이리하여 그녀는 한 세대에서 다음 세대로 옮아갔다 — 다정하고 숙명적이며 무감각하고 침착하며 고집센 여인으로……

마침내 그녀는 그렇게 죽어갔다. 먼지와 그늘에 가득 찬 집안에서 병이 든 것이다. 임종할 사람이라곤 연로하여 비틀거리는 흑인 한 사람뿐이었다. 우리들은 그녀가 병석에 누운 사실조차 몰랐다. 우리들은 흑인으로부터 에밀리의 사정을 캐내려 애쓰던 옛버릇을 포기한 지도 이미 오래되고 말았다. 흑인은 아무에게도, 아마 그의 주인에게도 말을 안 했을지도 모른다.

그녀는 아래층 방안 커튼이 쳐진 묵직한 밤나무 침대 위에서 마지막 숨을 거두었다 — 오랜 세월 동안 햇빛을 받지 않은 탓인지 누렇게 곰팡이 핀 베개 위에 그녀의 회색 머리를 얹혀 놓은 채로……

5장

흑인은 문상 온 첫 손님들을 현관에서 맞아들이고 안으로 안내한 다음 사라져 버렸다. 손님들은 귓속말로 자기네들끼리 수군거렸고 호기심에 찬 민첩한 눈초리를 여기저기에 분주히 옮기고 있었다. 흑인은 집안으로 곧장 걸어가서 뒷문으로 빠져나간 뒤로는 두 번 다시 모습을 나타내지 않았다.

에밀리의 두 사촌들도 곧바로 찾아왔다. 죽은지 이틀 후에 그들은 장례식을 치렀다.

읍 사람들은 꽃더미 밑에 조용히 안치된 미스 에밀리에게 마지막 고별을 하기 위해 몰려왔다. 관 위에는 그녀의 부친의 초상화가 명상에 잠긴 듯 심각한 표정으로 내려다보고 있었다. 아낙네들은 음산한 표정으로 수군댔다. 아주 나이든 할아버지들 중엔 말끔히 손질한 남군(南軍) 제복을 단정히 차려입고 온 사람도 있었는데 – 베란다와 잔디밭 위에 자리잡고 서로 에밀리의 추억담을 한창 늘어놓고 있었다. 마치 미스 에밀리가 자기들과 같은 세대에 속하고, 그녀와 같이 춤을 추기도 했고, 어쩌면 그녀에게 구혼이라도 한 것처럼 믿고 있는 듯한 어조였다. 그들도 노인의 경우에 흔히 볼 수 있듯이 수학적으로 진행하는 시간관념에 혼란을 일으켰다. 그들은 모든 과거는 과거로 거슬러 올라갈수록 점점 좁아지는 것이 아니라, 겨울철도 감히 침범하지 못하는 광막한 초원과 같이 최근 10년간이라도 좁다란 병목에 의해 현재의 글로부터 격리되어 있다고 생각했다.

과거 40년 동안 누구 하나 본 일이 없는 방이 하나 계단 뒤에 있다는 사실을 우리는 벌써부터 알고 있었다. 그 방문을 억지로 부수고서라도 열지 않을 수 없었다. 그러나 열기 전에 미스 에밀리의 망령을 공손히 지하에 매장하지 않으면 안되었다.

그 문을 부술 때 자연히 거칠게 다루지 않을 수 없어서 온 방안에 먼지가 뿌옇게 피어올랐다. 무덤의 포장을 연상케 하는, 코를 찌르는 듯한 엷은 먼지의 장막이 신방으로 꾸며 놓은 이 방의 모든 것들 뒤덮고 있는 느낌이었다. 바랜 장미 빛의 침대 커튼 위에도, 장미빛 전등갓 위에도, 화장대 위에도, 우아하게 늘어선 유리 그릇 위에도, 그리고 호머 베론의 머릿글자가 잘 보이지 않을 정도로 퇴색한, 은으로 안을 입힌 남자용 화장도구 위에도 – 이 물건들 사이에 금방 풀어놓은 듯한 칼라와 넥타이가 놓여 있었는데 그것들을 집어들자, 먼지로 덮인 표면에 희미한 초생달 모양의 자국이 생겼다. 한 의자 위에는 단정히 개어 놓은 옷이 한 벌 걸려 있었다. 그리고 그 밑에는 구두 한 켤레와 벗어 던진 양말 두 짝이 놓여 있었다.

사나이는 침대 위에 눕혀 있었다.

오랫동안 우리들은 그 자리에 우두커니 선채로 살이 다 허물어져 나간 해골의 깊은 쓴웃음을 내려다 봤다. 사나이의 몸은, 한때는 포옹의 자세로 누워 있었던 모양인데, 지금은 사랑보다 더 영원한 쓴웃음마저 정복하고만 저 죽음이라는 긴 잠이 이 사나이를 간부(姦婦)의 남편으로 만들어 버렸다. 삭다 남은 희미한 잠옷의 흔적 밑에 엉겨붙은 사나이의 썩다 남은 유해는 이제 그가 누웠던 침대에서 뗄 수 없는 것이 되고 말았다. 그리고 사나이 위에도, 그 옆에 놓인 베개 위에도 참을성 있고 끈질긴 먼지가 덮개를 이루어 고루 뒤덮어 있었다.

그런 다음 우리들은 두 번째 베개 위에 사람의 머리 자국을 보았다. 우리들 중 한 사람이 그 베개 위에서 무엇인가를 집어올렸다. 희미하고 눈에 안 보이는 메마른 먼지가 코를 툭 쏘는 것을 느끼면서 몸을 앞으로 기울였을 때 한 가닥의 기다란 철회색 머리칼을 보았던 것이다.

4. A&P

• 존 업다이크(John Updike)

보도에는 세 명의 소녀가 수영복만을 입은 채 있었다. 나는 세 번째 계산대에 있었는데 문이 내 등 뒤에 있어서 그들을 보지는 않았다. 그녀들이 빵 코너에 오기 전까지는 말이다. 첫 번째로 내 시선을 사로잡은 것은 격자무늬의 녹색 투피스를 입고 있는 소녀였다. 그녀는 땅딸막한 키에 햇볕에 적당히 탄 살결을 가졌으며 엉덩이는 감미롭고 부드럽게 보이는 넓은 모습이었는데 바로 아래에 두 개의 새하얀 초승달 모양이 새겨져 있었다. 그곳은 그녀 뒷다리의 윗부분까지 햇빛이 결코 닿지 않을 것 같아 보였다(그만큼 키가 작고 땅딸막했다는 뜻). 나는 HiHo 크래커 박스 위에 손을 올려놓은 채로 (금전 등록기의 키를 눌러) 돈이 나오게 했는지 안 나오게 했는지 (계산을 했는지 안했는지)를 기억 하려 애쓰며 서 있었다. 그러다 나는 결국 다시 키를 눌러 돈이 나오게 했는데 (중복 계산을 했다는 말) 고객은 내게 욕을 하기 시작했다. 그 고객은 금전 등록기를 뚫어지게 쳐다보는 종류의 사람 중 하나였다. 나이 50이 넘어서는 광대뼈에 연지를 발랐는데 눈썹도 제대로 없는 추한 노파였다. 점원의 실수를 잡아내는 것이 노파를 매우 행복하게 만든다는 것을 나는 잘 알고 있었다.

그녀는 금전 등록기를 50년 동안이나 지켜봐왔을 것이고 아마도 이전에도 실수를 한 적은 없었을 것이다. (점원이 계산 실수를 하는지 안하는지 늘 살펴보고 잡아냈다는 뜻)

나는 노파의 마음을 좀 가라앉게 한 후에 그녀가 골라온 과자를 가방 안에 넣어주었다. 노파는 지나가면서 내게 '흥' 하고 콧김을 내뱉었다. 만약 그녀가 제 때에 태어났다면 사람들은 그녀를 예배당에서 불로 태워 죽였을 텐데. (중세시대 마녀 사냥을 얘기하는 것 같음. 노파의 고약한 성미로 보아 중세에 태어났으면 마녀로 몰렸을 거라는 뜻) 나는 노파가 가도록 그냥 내버려 두었고 세 명의 소녀들은 빵 코너 주변을 맴돌고 있었다. 소녀들은 쇼핑 카트 없이 계산대를 따라 걸어와 특별 할인 판매 코너 통로에 있는 내 계산대 구역으로 들어왔다. 그녀들은 심지어 신발도 신지 않은 상태였다. 그들 중 땅딸막한 소녀는 녹색 투피스를 입고 있었다.(주인공이 처음에 본 그 소녀) 투피스는 밝은 녹색이었고 브래지어 부분이 정교하게 잘 붙여져 있었으며 배 부분이 파리한 것으로 보아 나는 그녀의 녹색 투피스 수영복이 방금 산 것임을 추측할 수 있었다. 소녀들 가운데 또 한 명은 통통한 딸기 모양의 얼굴이었는데 입술이 코 아래에 오밀조밀하니 모여 있었고 키가 크며 검은 머리를 가졌는데 그다지 곱슬은 아니였다. 햇볕에 태운 선탠 자국 가운데 하나가 눈 아래 드리워져 있었고 턱은 너무 길었다. 당신도 알다시피, 그러한 종류의 소녀들에 대하여서 다른 소녀들의 반응은 '놀라워!' 내지는 '매력적이야!' 였지만 그대로 따라하지는 않았다. 그들도 매우 잘 알다시피 그대로 따라하지 않는다는 것이야말로 그녀들을 좋아하는 이유였다.

소녀들 가운데 마지막 세 번째 소녀는 키가 그리 크지 않았다. 그녀는 여왕이었다. 그녀는 거느리는 쪽이었다. 나머지 두 소녀는 주위를 두리번거리며 어깨를 구부린 채 돌아다녔다.

하지만 그녀는 주위를 두리번거리지 않았다. 딱히 여왕이기 때문에 그런게 아니라, 단지 하얀 프리마돈나의 다리처럼 천천히 똑바로 걸었을 뿐이었다. 그녀는 자신의 발뒤꿈치에 약간의 무게를 주면서 내려왔고 마치 맨발로는 그리 많이 걷지 않는 사람마냥 발뒤꿈치를 먼저 내려놓고 나서 발가락으로 무게를 옮겨 놓는 것이었다. 모든 스텝으로 바닥을 시험해보는 것 같이 신중하면서도 특이한 행동을 하고 있는 것이었다. 당신은 그 소녀들이 어떠한 생각을 하고 있는지 결코 모를 것이다. ─당신은 그녀의 머리속에 생각이라는 것이 정말 있다고 생각하는가? 아니면 유리잔에 든 벌이 윙윙거리는 것 같다고 생각하는가?─ 그러나 당신은 그러한 질문에 대한 답을 그녀가 나머지 둘에게 이 안으로 들어오라 말한 데서 얻을 수 있다. 그리고 이제는 그녀가 그들에게 그것을 어떻게 하는가 ─그것이라 함은 천천히 그리고 자신을 꼿꼿이 세운 채 걷는 방법을 말하는 것인데─에서 얻을 수 있는 것이다.

그녀는 다소 우중충한 분홍색─어쩌면 베이지색일지도 모르겠다─ 수영복을 입었는데 여기저기 조그만 마디가 있었다. 날 사로잡은 것은, 그녀의 수영복 어깨끈이 조금 흘러내리고 있다는 것이었다. 끈들이 그녀의 어깨로부터 벗어나 그녀 양팔의 시원한 꼭대기 부근에서 헐거워져서, 수영복이 조금 미끄러져 내려갔는데 그 때문에 수영복의 모든 가장자리 부분이 반짝여 보였다. 만약 그것이 거기에 없었다면(옷이 그렇게 흘러내리지 않았더라면) 당신은 그녀의 어깨보다 더 하얀 것은 없을 것이라 생각하지 못했을 것이다. (그녀의 어깨가 제일 하얗다는 말) 끈이 흘러내려져 수영복 위와 그녀의 머리 사이에는 그녀 자체(알몸)를 제외하곤 아무것도 없었다. 빛에 의해 기울어지고 움푹 패인 금속 판처럼, 어깨뼈에서부터 완전 그녀 가슴 위의 평평하고 반듯한 곳 – 완전히 발가벗겨진 – 사이에는 아무 것도 없었다(알몸). 나는 그것이 아름다움 그 이상이라고 생각했다.

그녀는 태양과 소금이 바래게 한 듯한 오크색의 머리를 가지고 있었고 곱슬머리로 된 부푼 모양의 머리로 손질되어 있었다. 그리고 새침한 얼굴을 하고 있었다. 만약 당신이 A&P에 갈 때 어깨끈을 흘러내린 채 하고 간다면 당신 역시 그런 새침한 얼굴을 할 수 있으리라. 그녀는 고개를 꼿꼿이 들고 있었다. 자신의 흰 어깨서부터 벗어나려는 듯 쭈욱 뻗는 것 같아 보였다. 그러나 나는 거기에 별로 신경 쓰지 않았다. 그녀의 목이 길면 길수록 그녀의 매력 자체가 더 많아지기 때문이었다.

그녀는 눈 양쪽 끝에서 나를 느꼈음이 틀림없다. 그리고 나의 어깨너머로 두 번째 계산대에 있는 스토케이지 역시 그녀를 보고 있는 것을 느꼈음에 틀림없다. 그러나 그녀는 알아차린 듯한 기색을 전혀 보이지 않았다. 이 여왕은 전혀 암시를 주지 않았다. 그녀는 선반을 가로질러 시선을 옮겼다. 그리고는 잠시 멈춰서 천천히 눈을 돌렸다. 그것은 앞치마를 두른 내 배 안쪽을 흥분으로 문질러 놓았다. 그리고는 몸을 웅크리고 있는 다른 두 소녀에게 소곤거렸다. 그리고 그들 셋 모두 고양이와 개 음식 – 아침 시리얼 – 마카로니 – 쌀 – 건포도 – 조미료 – 스프레드 – 스파게티 – 음료 – 크래커 – 그리고 쿠키가 있는 통로로 향해갔다. (내가 있는)세 번째 계산대에서는 고기 가판대까지 이어진 이 통로가 잘 보였기 때문에 나는 계속 그녀들을 주시할 수 있었다. 햇볕에 탄 뚱뚱한 소녀는 쿠키를 만지작거리다 다시 제자리에 돌려놓았다. 양들은(슈퍼마켓의 고객) 그들의 쇼핑 카트를 밀고 다녔고 – 소녀들은 보통 손님들이 다니는 길에 역행하여 둘러보고 있었다. 우리가 한 가지 길로 된 표시나 혹은 그 무엇을 가지고 있지 않았기 때문이었다. – 그들은(양들은) 매우 명랑해 보였다. 그리고 그 때 여왕의 하얀 어깨가 양들 가운데서 또렷한 모습으로 나타나자 양들은 약간 비틀거리고 뛰어 오르고 딸꾹질을 했다. 그러나 그들의 눈은 그들의 쇼핑 카트로 급속히 되돌아갔고 계속하여 밀고 나갔다. 나는 당신이 A&P를 다이너마이트로 폭파시킬 수 있다는 데에 내기를 걸고 싶다.(주인공은 자신이 일하고 있는 A&P를 싫어하는 듯함) 사람들은 대체로 오트밀에 손을 뻗쳐 그들의 리스트를(구입 해야 할 목록) 확인해 본다. 그리고는 중얼거린다. "어디 보자, 세 번째 것인데, A로 시작하는 거였는데... 아스파라거스... 아니야, 아 맞다! 사과소스였지!" 또는 그것이 무엇이든 간에 그들은 대체로 중얼거리는 것이었다. 그러나 그것들이 그들을 기진맥진하게 만든다는 데에는 의심할 여지가 없다. 머리에 컬러핀을 꽂은 몇몇 주부들은 심지어 쇼핑카트를 밀면서 자신이 산 것이 맞는 것인지 아닌지 지나가면서 다시 확인하고 둘러보곤 했다.

당신도 알다시피, 그것은 수영복을 입은 소녀들이 해변에 있는 것과 같은 맥락이다. 이 말인즉슨, 그곳에서는 번쩍이는 태양빛으로 인하여 어느 누구도 서로를 그다지 많이 쳐다보지 않는다는 것이다. 그런데 A&P에서의 상황을 들자면 형광등 불빛 아래에서, 그것도 꽉 찬 상자들에 대하여서, 거의 벗은 몸으로 녹색과 크림색의 고무 타일로 바닥이 된 흡사 장기판 같은 곳을 터벅터벅 걸어가는 상황은 별개의 문제이다.

"맙소사" 스토케이지가 내 옆에서 말했다. "나 기절할 것 같아"

"녀석" 내가 말했다. "나를 꼭 붙잡고 있으렴." 스토케이지는 두 아이를 둔 유부남이었다. 그러나 그것밖엔 내가 말할 수 있는 차이점이 없었다. 그는 22살이었고 나는 이번 4월에 19살이 되었다.

"저래도 되는 거야?" 그가 물었다. 결혼한 책임감 있는 남성들이 하는 물음처럼. 나는 그가 행운이 찾아 올 미래에 언젠가, 아마 저 위대한 알렉산드로프와 페트루스키 차 회사(A&P) 또는 그 이외 다른 이름으로 불리게 될 1990년쯤에 매니저가 되려고 생각한다는 말을 당신에게 해준다는 것을 잊어버렸다.

그가 의미한 바는("저래도 되는 거야?" 라는 말은), 우리 마을이 해변에서 5마일 정도 떨어져 있다는 것이다.

김수아 **전공영어** 영미문학 Reading for Literature Ⅱ

이는 마치 해변이 거느리고 있는 거대한 식민지와 같은 구실을 하고 있었다. 그러나 우리는 바로 마을의 중심에 있었다. 그리고 일반적으로 여자들은 거리로 나오기 전에 차 안에서 셔츠와 반바지 또는 그 무엇인가를 걸쳤다. 그리고 어쨌든 이들은 보통 6명의 아이를 둔 그리고 그들의 다리에 정맥이 튀어나와 지도와 같이 구불구불한 여자들이었고 어느 누구도 그들을 포함하여 아무도 전혀 개의치 않았다. 내가 말하고자 하는 것은, 우리는 바로 마을의 한 가운데에 있다는 것이고 그리고 만약 당신이 우리 상점 현관에 서있는다면 두 개의 은행과 교회와 신문 가판대와 3개의 부동산 사무소, 그리고 배설구가 다시 망가져서 약 27명의 공짜 술을 마시는 자들이 중심가에 오줌 자국을 내는 것을 볼 수 있다는 것이다. 그것은 마치 우리가 곶에 위치해 있는 것이 아니라 실은 보스턴의 북쪽에 있기 때문에 이 마을 사람들은 20년 동안이나 바다를 보지 못했다는 것 같았다.

　소녀들은 고기 가판대로 다가갔고 맥마흔에게 무엇인가를 물어보고 있었다. 그는 가리켰고, 그들도 가리켰다. 그리고 소녀들은 발을 질질 끌며 피라미드 모양의 "기쁨의 다이어트 복숭아"라고 쓰여진 통로 뒤로 사라졌다. 우리 눈에 보이는 것은 늙은 맥마흔이 그의 입술을 두드리며 소녀들의 몸매를 눈으로 좇아 평가하는 모습 뿐이었다. 불쌍한 아가씨들! 나는 그들에게 미안함을 느꼈다. 그렇게 하지 않을 수가 없었다.

　이제 이 이야기의 슬픈 부분이다. 적어도 우리 가족은 이 부분을 슬프다고 여긴다. 그러나 나는 그것이 나 자신에게 있어서는 결코 슬픈 것이라 생각하지 않는다. 가게는 텅비어 있었고 목요일 오후였다. 금전 등록기에 기댄채 서 있는 것을 제외하고는 아무런 할 짓이 없었다. 나는 그 소녀들이 다시 나타나기를 기다렸다. 전체 매장은 마치 핀볼 기계와 같았고 나는 어느 터널에서 그들이 나올지 몰랐다. 잠시 후 그들은 먼 통로를 돌아다니거나, 전구 주위를 서성거렸고, '캐리비안 식스'나 '토니 마틴 노래하다' 또는 왜 그러한 음반을 만드는지 궁금한 잡동사니를 할인 판매하는 음반들, 여섯 팩의 막대 사탕, 어린 아이가 보기만 해도 부서져 버리는, 셀로판으로 포장된 플라스틱 장난감 주위를 서성거렸다. 그들이 다가오자, 여왕은 여전히 길을 이끌고 있었고 그녀의 손에 갈색의 작은 항아리가 들려 있었다. 3번부터 7번 창구에는 사람이 배치되지 않았고 그래서 나는 그녀가 스토케이지와 나 사이를 배회하는 것을 볼 수 있었다. 그러나 스토케이지에게는 주로 나이 들어 헐렁하고 회색 바지를 입고 4개의 거대한 파인애플 쥬스캔을 든 채 비틀거리는 부류들이 몰렸다. — 이러한 부랑자들이 모두 파인애플 쥬스와 무슨 관련이 있는 건지 나는 늘 궁금했다 — 그리하여 소녀들은 내 계산대로 왔다. 여왕은 항아리를 내려놓았고 나는 그것을 얼음처럼 차가운 손으로 가져갔다. 순수 사워 크림으로 된 Kingfish Fancy Herring Snack(환상적인 킹 피쉬 청어 스넥)은 49센트였다. 이제 그녀의 손은 반지와 팔찌 없이 비어 있었고, 마치 신이 그들을 그렇게 만든 상태와 같이 발가벗은 모습이었다. 그리고 나는 어디서 돈이 나올지 궁금해졌다. 그녀는 여전히 새침한 표정을 유지한 채 접혀진 1달러 지폐를 그녀의 핑크 수영복 가운데에서 꺼내들었다. 그 항아리는 들어보니 무거웠고 정말로 사랑스러웠다.

　그러나 모두의 행운이 바닥나기 시작했는데, 렌젤이 주차장에 있는 양배추 트럭과 옥신각신 거리며 가게 안으로 들어왔기 때문이었다. 그는 Manager라고 쓰여진 문 뒤로 급히 가려 했다. 그 문은 아가씨들과 눈이 마주쳤을 때 그가 종일 숨어있는 곳이었다. 렌젤은 아주 따분한 사람으로, 주일 학교 학생들을 가르치거나 그 밖의 흥미 없는 일들을 하는 자이지만 그렇다고 작은 것을 놓치진 않았다. 그는 소녀들에게 가서 말했다. "아가씨들. 이곳은 해변이 아니란다."

　여왕은 얼굴을 붉혔고, 그것이 단지 햇볕에 그을린 탓이 아님을 나는 처음으로 알아차릴 수 있었지만, 이미 그녀는 너무 가까이 있었다. "엄마가 청어 스넥을 사오라고 말했어요." 그녀의 목소리는 나를 깜짝 놀라게 했는데, 그 놀라움은 어조가 외모와는 달리 예상 외로 아주 무미건조한 탓이었다. 그녀는 "Pick up"과 "Snack"을 느리게 발음하였다. 갑자기 나는 그녀의 목소리를 타고 그녀의 거실로 들어가 보았다. 그녀의 아버지와 다른 남자들은 아이스크림같은 코트를 입고 서 있었고 타이를 매고 있었다. 여자들은 샌들을 신은 채 큰 접시에서 이쑤시개로 집은 청어 스넥을 들고 있었고 그들은 모두 올리브와 민트 가지로 색을 낸 음료를 들고 있었다. 나의 부모님들이 누군가를 초대한다면 그들은 레모네이드를 마실 것이고, 그것이 만일 신선한 일로 여겨진다면 "그들은 그것을 매번 해요" 라는 제목의 선전문구가 인쇄된 긴 유리잔의 Schlitz(싸구려 상점) 맥주를 마신다.

"물론 그렇겠지" 렌젤이 말했다. "그러나 이곳은 해변이 아니란다." 그가 이렇게 반복적으로 말한 것이 마치 그 생각이 막 떠오르기라도 했던 것처럼 재미있다는 생각을 했다. 그리고 그는 이 모든 세월동안 A&P는 거대한 모래언덕이었고 그가 구조대 우두머리였다고 상상하고 있었다. 그는 내가 웃는 것을 그리 좋아하지 않았다. – 내가 말했던 것처럼 그는 많은 것을 놓치지 않았다 – 그러나 그는 소녀들에게 우울한 주일 학교 교장의 노려보는 표정을 지어보이는 것에 열중했다.

여왕의 홍조는 더 이상 태양에 그을린 자국이 아니었다. 그리고 격자무늬의 뚱뚱한 아가씨는 뒷모습이 더 좋아보였는데 – 정말로 매력적인 엉덩이였다 – "우리는 쇼핑하는 것은 아니에요. 우리는 단지 하나만 사러 왔단 말이에요."

"그게 무슨 차이가 있다는 거지" 렌젤이 그녀에게 말했다. 그리고 나는 그의 눈길이 가는 방향으로 보아 그녀가 투피스 수영복(비키니)을 입고 있다는 것을 렌젤이 이전까지 알아차리지 못하고 있음을 알았다. "우리는 말이지, 너희들이 이곳에 올 때는 좀 정중하게 입고 오기를 바란단다."

"우리는 알맞게 입었어요" 여왕이 갑자기 말했다. 그녀는 아랫입술을 삐쭉 내밀며 화를 냈다. 그녀의 입장에서 바라보면 A&P 슈퍼마켓을 경영하는 무리들은 매우 초라해 보였을 것이다. 그녀의 푸른 두 눈 안에서 Fancy Herring Snack(환상의 청어 스넥)이 빛이 났다.

"얘들아, 나는 너희들과 논쟁하고 싶지 않거든. 이 이후로부터는 너희들의 어깨 좀 가리고 여기 오렴. 그것이 우리의 정책이야." 그는 돌아섰다. 그것은 당신을 위한 정책이다. 정책은 간부들이 원하는 것이다. 다른 사람들이 원하는 것은 어린 소녀의 비행과 같은 것이었다.

이러는 동안(매니저와 소녀가 말다툼 하는 사이), 고객들은 그들의 쇼핑 카트를 몰고 나타났지만, 당신도 알다시피, 양들은 (싸우는)장면을 보러 종이 한 장을 부드럽게 마치 복숭아를 벗기듯이 쌓아 올리고 있는 스토케이지에게로 모여 들었다.(스토케이지의 계산대에 줄을 섬으로써 그 옆에서 벌어지는 매니저와 소녀의 말다툼을 빠짐없이 듣기 위함인 듯) 나는 한마디도 놓치지 않으려 침묵 속에서 모두들 초조해하고 있는 것을 느낄 수 있었고, 그 중에서도 특히 렌젤이 그러했다. 그는 내게 물었다. "쌔미, 이 상품 계산한 거야?"

나는 생각한 뒤 "아니요"라고 말했다. 그러나 그것이 내가 정말로 생각하던 것은 아니었다. 나는 그렇게 하기 (상품을 찍기) 위해서 4, 9, CROC, TOT(금전 등록기에서 계산하는 과정) 하는 과정을 거쳐야 했다. – 당신이 생각하는 것보다 훨씬 복잡한 일이다. 만약 당신이 그것을(계산하는 과정을) 제대로 했을 경우엔 조그만 노래 소리를 들을 수 있다. 그것은 마치 단어로 말하는 것 같이 들리는 데 나의 경우에는 "안녕(Bing~) 거기에 당신은 (Gung~) 행복한 사람(Splat~)"으로 들린다 – (Splat는 금전 등록기의 서랍이 열릴 때 나는 소리) – 나는 당신이 상상할 수 있을 정도로 부드럽게 지폐를 폈고, 그 지폐는 세상에서 내가 지금까지 보았던 가장 부드러운 두 젖가슴 사이에서 방금 나온 것이었다. 절반의 페니를 그녀의 작고 연분홍색인 손바닥에 건네고 봉투에 청어 스넥을 주의 깊게 넣어주고서 봉투 입구를 비틀어 그녀에게 넘겨주면서도 나는 내내 생각에 빠져 있었다.

소녀들, 그런데 누가 그들을 탓할 수 있을까 싶지만, 그들은 서둘러 밖으로 나갔다. 그래서 나는 "그만 두겠어요" 라고 렌젤에게 그들이 들을 수 있을 정도로 충분히 빠르게 말했다. 소녀들이 멈춰서 나를 갑작스레 나타나 자신들을 구원해준 영웅처럼 봐주길 희망했던 것이다. 그러나 그들은 멈추지 않고 전자동 센서를 향하여 계속해서 나아갔고, 문은 날 듯이 열려 그들은 주차장을 가로질러 차가 있는 곳으로 어느새 걸어 갔다. 여왕과, 격자무늬의 소녀와, 거대하고 키 큰 Goony-Goony는 몸매로 말할 것 같으면 그다지 나쁜 편은 아니었다. 나에게는 렌젤만이 남았고 그의 눈썹은 경련으로 파르르 떨렸다.

"쌔미, 뭐라고?"

"그만둔다고요."

"나는 네가 그런 말을 했다고는 생각지 않는다."

"당신은 그녀들을 당황하게 만들지 않았어도 됐어요."

"우리를 당황시킨 것은 바로 그 여자애들이야."

나는 "Fiddle-de-doo(얼간이)"라 말했다. 그것은 내 할머니가 종종 쓰던 말투였다. 그리고 나는 그녀가 이에 대해 틀림없이 기뻐했을 것이라 생각했다.

"나는 네가 뭐라 말하는 지 모르겠다." 렌젤이 말했다.

"나는 당신이 모를 거라는 것을 알아요." 내가 말했다. "그러나 나는 알지요." 나는 나의 앞치마의 뒤 끈을 당겼고 어깨를 으쓱해 그것을 벗어버렸다. 내 계산대로 향하고 있던 커플 고객은 서로를 쳐다보았고, 마치 비탈진 도랑의 겁먹은 돼지들 같았다.

렌젤은 한숨을 쉬었고 이 상황을 인내하는 듯 보였지만 늙고 창백했다. 그는 몇 년 전부터 나의 부모님의 친구였다. "쌔미, 너희 부모님은 그만두는 짓 따위 원치 않으실 텐데" 그가 나에게 말했다. 그래 사실이다. 그렇게 하질 원치 않으실 것이다. 그러나 나에게 있어 일단 행동을 시작한 이상은 겪어봐야 되지, 그렇지 않는다면 그것이 더 치명적인 일이었다. 나는 주머니가 있고 빨간색으로 된 앞치마를 접었다. 그리고는 카운터 위에 놓았다. 그리고 나비넥타이를 그 위에다 놓았다. 당신이 궁금할 수도 있는데, 나비넥타이는 그들의 것이었다. "너는 이제 남은 인생에서 이 사건이 얼마나 큰 타격을 주는 것인지 절실히 느낄 거다." 렌젤이 말했다. 나는 그것이 또한 사실임을 안다. 그러나 그가 그 귀여운 소녀들을 어떻게 붉히게 만들었는지를 생각하면 아직도 내 안에서 분노가 끓어오른다. 나는 "No Sale" 탭을 두드렸고 기계는 "Pee-Pul" 소리를 내었고 서랍은 철썩 튀어 나왔다. 이 일들이 여름에 일어났다는 사실에 대해 참 다행인 것은 코트와 덧신을 찾을 필요 없이 곧장 출구로 그들을 쫓아갈 수 있었다는 데에 있다. 나는 어제 밤에 어머니가 다려준 하얀 셔츠를 입고 자동문 센서를 향해 뛰어갔다. 문이 열려졌고 바깥에는 햇볕이 아스팔트 위를 스케이트 타는 듯 미끄러지며 비추고 있었다.

나는 나의 소녀들을 찾기 위해 둘러보았지만 그들은 가고 없었다. 거기에는 아무도 없었고 단지 젊은 유부녀와 함께 사탕으로 인해 울고 있는 그녀의 아이들만 있을 뿐이었다. 그들은 엷은 청색의 Falcon 역 짐마차의 문 옆에 있었다. 거대한 유리창을 뒤돌아보자, 포장도로 위에 쌓여 있는 토탄 이끼로 채워진 가방들과 알루미늄 잔디 관리 기구 너머로 렌젤이 양들이 지나가는 것을 체크하며 내가 담당했던 계산대에 서 있는 것이 보였다. 그의 얼굴은 어둡고 늙어보였고 그의 뒤는 마치 받침대를 꽂아놓은 것처럼 매우 뻣뻣해 보였으며, 그리고 험한 세상이 어떻게 장차 내게 닥쳐 올런지 생각하자 배가 힘없이 덜컹 내려앉는 느낌을 받았다.

5. 누런 벽지(The Yellow Wallpaper)

• 샬롯 퍼킨스 길먼(Charlotte Perkins Gilman)

존과 나처럼 평범한 사람들이 여름을 나기 위해 고풍스러운 저택을 구하는 건 매우 드문 일이다.

식민지 시대에 지어져 대대로 상속되어온 이 집에서—솔직히 내 생각엔 금방이라도 유령이 튀어나올 것 같다—낭만적인 행복에 젖을 수도 있겠으나, 그건 운명론적인 생각에 부로가할 것이다.

어쨌든 이곳에 뭔가 기묘한 구석이 있는 건 확실하다.

그렇지 않고서야 왜 이렇게 싸게 세를 놓았겠는가? 그리고 그렇게 오랫동안 비어 있었겠는가?

내가 이런 점들을 말했더니 존은 결혼한 남자들이 으레 그러듯이 코웃음을 쳤다.

존은 더할 나위 없이 실용적인 사람이다. 그는 신앙과 미신이라면 질색을 하고, 보거나 만질 수 없고 숫자로 표현되지 않는 것들을 이야기하면 대놓고 비웃는다.

그는 의사이면, 아마도—물론 나는 살아있는 사람에게는 이런 말을 하 ㅇ낳을 텐데 종이는 생명체가 아니라 정말 다행이다—그것이 내가 빨리 낫지 않는 한 가지 이유일 듯하다.

그는 내가 아프다는 사실을 믿지 않는다.

이런 상황에서 내가 무엇을 할 수 있단 말인가?

명망 높은 의사 남편이 단지 일시적인 신경쇠약—경미한 히스테리 기질—외에는 아무 문제도 없다고 친구들과 친척들을 안심시키는 상황에서 내가 무엇을 할 수 있을까?

역시 명망 높은 의사인 내 오빠 또한 똑같은 말을 할 뿐이다.

그래서 나는 인산염인가 아인산염인가 하는 약과 강장제를 먹고, 여행을 하고, 바람을 쐬고, 운동을 한다. 건강이 다시 좋아지기 전에는 일하는 것은 절대 금지되어 있다.

개인적으로 나는 그들의 의견에 동의하지 않는다.

나는 신나고, 변화가 있고, 내 성격에 맞는 일을 하는 것이 나한테 이로울 거라고 생각한다.

그러나 내가 무얼 어찌할 수 있단 말인가?

나는 그들의 만류에도 불구하고 한동안 글을 썼다. 강한 반대에 부딪히지 않으려면 완벽한 비밀리에 글을 써야 했으므로 글쓰기는 정말로 나를 녹초로 만들었다.

반대에 덜 부딪히며서 사람들과 더 많이 어울리고 더 많은 자극을 받는다면 내 건강 상태가 어떨지 가끔 상상해 본다. 그러나 존은 내 건강 상태를 생각하는 것이 내가 가장 해서는 안될 나쁜 일이라고 말한다. 솔직히 내 상태를 생각하면 늘 속이 상하기는 한다.

그러니 내 몸 상태에 대해서는 이쯤에서 접어두고 집에 대해 이야기하겠다.

저택은 너무나 아름답다! 도로에서 한참 뒤에, 마을에서는 거의 5킬로미터 정도 떨어진 곳에 외따로이 위치하고 있다. 울타리들과 담장들, 빗장 달린 문들이 있고, 정원사와 일꾼들이 거주하는 아담한 별채들이 있어 책에 나오는 영국 저택들이 떠오른다.

이렇게 멋진 정원은 처음 본다. 넓은 정원에 그늘이 드리워져있고, 가장자리로는 무수히 오솔길들이 나 있으며, 포도 덩굴로 덮인 나무 응달이 길게 뻗어 있고, 나무 아래에는 의자들이 놓여 있다.

비닐하우스도 있었지만 지금은 모두 망가진 상태다.

수년간 비어 있었던 이곳은 상속인, 공동 상속인과 관련된 어떤 법적 실랑이가 있었던 것 같다.

안타깝게도 그로써 내가 생각했던 유령 출몰설은 근거 없는 것이 되어버렸지만 상관없다. 어쨌든 나는 이 집에 뭔가 기괴한 게 존재하는 걸 느낄 수 있다.

어느 달밤에 존에게 이 말을 했더니 존은 내가 외풍을 느낀 것뿐이라며 창문을 닫아버렸다.

나는 때때로 이유 없이 존에게 성질을 부린다. 옛날에는 절대 이렇게 예민하지 않았는데 아마도 신경쇠약 때문인 듯하다.

그러나 존은 내가 그런 식으로 생각하면 자신을 절제하려는 노력을 덜 하게 될 거라고 말한다. 그래서 나는 남편 앞에서만이라도 감정을 자제하려고 무척 노력하는데, 그것 때문에 몹시 피곤하다.

나는 우리가 쓰는 방이 조금도 마음에 들지 않는다. 밖으로 연결되어 있고, 창가에 장미가 가득하며, 너무나도 예쁘고 고풍스러운 친츠(여러 빛깔의 작은 꽃무늬로 뒤덮인 면직물-옮긴이) 커튼이 달린 아래층 방이 마음에 들었지만 존은 내 말을 귓등으로도 듣지 않았다.

그는 아래층 방에 창문이 한 개밖에 없고, 침대 두 개를 놓을 공간이 없으며, 그가 필요할 때 쓸 만한 방이 가까이에 없다고 했다.

그는 매우 세심하고 다정해서, 내가 특별한 이유 없이 움직이게 내버려두지 않는다.

나는 매일 매 시간마다 정해진 일과를 따라야 한다. 이렇게 존은 내가 신경 쓸 모든 일을 도맡아 하고 있으니 더욱 고마움을 느끼지 않는다면 나는 배은망덕한 사람일 것이다.

그는 우리가 여기 온 이유가 전적으로 나 때문이라고, 내가 완벽하게 휴식을 취하고, 맑은 공기를 많이 마실 수 있게 하기 위해서라고 말했다. "여보, 운동을 얼마나 하는가는 당신 체력에 달려 있고, 음식을 먹는 것도 당신 식욕에 달려 있어. 하지만 신선한 공기를 들이마시는 건 얼마든지 할 수 있잖아." 그래서 우리는 집 꼭대기에 있는 육아실을 쓰기로 했다.

거의 한 층을 다 차지하는 육아실은 크고, 통풍이 잘 되며, 사방이 내다보이는 창문들이 있고, 공기와 햇빛이 듬뿍 들어온다. 어린아이들을 위해 창문에는 창살이 쳐져 있고, 벽에는 고리와 잡다한 것들이 걸려 있었다. 그것으로 보아, 이 방이 처음에는 육아실로 사용되다가 나중에는 놀이방과 체육관으로 쓰였을 거라는 생각이 든다.

벽에 칠한 페인트와 벽지를 보니 남자아이들이 이 방을 썼던 것 같다. 침대 머리맡을 빙 둘러 내 손이 닿는 높이까지 벽지가 여기 저기 벗겨져 있고, 맞은편 벽 아래쪽에는 벽지가 큰 부분 통째로 벗겨져 있다. 이보다 더 끔찍한 벽지를 내 생에 본 적이 없다.

벽지 무늬는 모든 예술성을 저버린 채 제멋대로 현란하게 뻗어 있다.

무늬는 무늬를 좇던 눈에 혼란을 줄 만큼 단조로웠지만 계속 신경을 거스르고 관찰을 유발할 만큼 도드라졌다. 조금 거리를 두고 변변찮고 모호한 곡선들을 따라가면 곡선들이 불쑥 자살을 하듯 엄청난 각도에서 뛰어내려 들어본 적 없는 모순 속에서 자멸한다.

벽지의 색깔은 혐오스럽고, 역겨우며, 서서히 바뀌는 햇빛에 이상하게 바래서 타다 만 듯 한 지저분한 누런색이다.

어떤 곳은 우중충하지만 야한 주황빛을 띠고, 어느 곳은 역겨운 유황 빛이 어려 있다.

당연히 아이들은 이 방을 싫어했을 것이다. 나 또한 이 방에서 오래 살아야 한다면 정말 싫을 것이다.

존이 오고 있다. 그는 내가 글 쓰는 것을 지독하게 싫어하니 당장 이걸 치워야 한다.

이곳에서 지낸 지 2주가 지났다. 첫날 이후로 그다지 글 쓸 마음이 생기지 않았다.

나는 지금 흉측한 육아실의 창가에 앉아 있고, 체력이 달리는 점 외에는 아무것도 내가 내키는 대로 글 쓰는 것을 막지 않는다.

존은 낮에는 늘 나가 있고, 밤에도 위중한 혼자가 있을 때면 집을 비운다.

내 건강 상태가 심각하지 않아서 다행이다.

그러나 신경과민 증상 때문에 몹시 우울하다.

존은 내가 얼마나 고통스러워하고 있는지 모른다. 그는 내가 고통스러울 이유가 전혀 없다고 생각하며 그에 흡족해 한다.

단지 신경과민일 뿐이지만 이런 상태가 나를 무겁게 짓눌러 아무 일도 하지 못하게 만든다.

나는 존에게 진정한 안식과 편안함을 주는, 그에게 도움이 되는 사람이 되고 싶었다. 그러나 이미 무거운 짐만 되고 말았다.

내가 할 수 있는 것은 고작 옷 입기, 손님 접대하기, 일 시키기 정도지만, 이런 일들을 하는 것조차 얼마나 힘이 드는지 아무도 믿지 못할 것이다.

메리가 아기를 잘 돌보아서 다행이다. 너무나도 사랑스러운 내 아들!

그런데 나는 아기와 함께 있으면 온통 신경이 곤두서기 때문에 아기와 같이 있을 수가 없다.

존은 살면서 신경과민이었던 적이 전혀 없었던 것 같다. 그는 내가 벽지에 대해 이야기하면 코웃음을 친다.

처음에 그는 새 벽지로 도배를 할 생각이었다. 하지만 나중에는 내가 벽지에 끌려 다니게 내버려 두고 있다면서 신경쇠약 환자는 그런 공상에 무너지는 것이 가장 나쁜 일이라고 말했다. 벽지를 바꾸면 그 뒤에는 육중한 침대, 창살이 쳐진 창문들, 그 다음은 계단 위 문 등을 내가 계속 문제 삼게 되리라는 것이 그의 생각이었다.

존이 말했다. "이곳이 당신 건강에 좋다는 거 알잖소. 게다가 고작 석 달 빌린 집을 수리할 생각은 추호도 없다오."

내가 말했다. "그럼 제발 아래층에서 지내요. 아래층에 예쁜 방들 있잖아요."

그러자 그는 나를 끌어안으며 귀여운 복덩어리라고 부르고는 내가 원한다면 지하실로 방을 옮기겠으며 벽에 하얀 페인트 칠을 하겠다고 말했다.

그러나 침대, 창문 등에 대해서는 그의 생각이 옳다.

이 방은 누구라도 만족할 만큼 통풍이 잘 되고 편안하다. 또한 나는 단지 일시적인 기분으로 남편을 불편하게 할 만큼 멍청하지 않다.

이 큰 방이 점차 좋아진다. 저 끔찍한 벽지만 빼면·······

정원이 내다보이는 창문을 통해 신비스럽고 깊게 드리워진 나무 그늘, 다양하고 고풍스러운 꽃들, 관목들과 울퉁불퉁 옹이진 나무들을 볼 수 있다.

다른 쪽 창문으로는 이 저택에 딸린 작은 개인용 부두와 아름다운 만의 전망이 눈에 들어온다. 이 집에서부터 그곳까지는 녹음이 우거진 예쁜 오솔길이 나 있다. 나는 사람들이 이 수많은 길과 나무 그늘을 거니는 모습을 늘 상상한다. 하지만 존은 절대 공상에 빠지지 말라고 주의를 주었다. 그는 나처럼 신경이 쇠약한 사람이 풍부한 상상력과 이야기를 지어내는 습관을 갖게 되면 온갖 쓸데없는 공상에 빠지게 되는 거라며, 이를 억제하기 위해 강한 의지와 분별력을 발휘해야 한다고 말한다. 그래서 나는 그의 말을 따르려 노력하는 중이다.

가끔 드는 생각인데 글을 조금이나마 쓸 수 있을 정도로만 몸이 건강해도 여러 상념들의 압박감을 덜고 편히 쉴 수 있을 것 같다.

그러나 막상 글을 쓰면 나는 무척 지치고 만다.

내 일에 대해 조언을 얻거나 의견을 나눌 사람이 없는 게 정말 아쉽다. 존은 내 건강이 많이 회복되면 사촌 헨리와 줄리아를 초대해 장기간 머물게 할 계획이지만, 당장은 그들을 불러 자극을 만드느니 차라리 내 베개에 폭죽을 넣는 편이 낫다고 말한다.

건강이 빨리 좋아졌으면 좋겠다.

하지만 지금은 그런 생각을 해서는 안 된다. 이 벽지는 자신이 어떠한 사악한 영향력을 가지고 있는지 아는 것 같다. 이 벽지에는 부러진 모가지가 축 늘어지고, 튀어나온 눈알 두 개가 거꾸로 빤히 쳐다보는 듯한 무늬가 반복되는 지점이 있다.

그 무늬가 뻔뻔하게도 끝없이 이어지고 있다는 사실에 너무 화가 난다. 무늬들은 위로, 아래로, 옆으로 기어 다닌다. 저 말도 안 되고, 깜박이지도 않는 눈알들이 도처에 있다. 한 군데는 두 폭이 맞지 않아 눈알 하나가 다른 눈알보다 약간 위에 있는 상태여서 눈알들이 일렬로 오르락내리락 한다.

저렇게 표정이 풍부한 무생물은 본 적이 없다. 우리는 눈이 얼마나 풍부한 표정을 담아내는지 잘 안다. 어렸을 때 나는 방에 누워 빈 벽과 단조로운 가구를 주시하곤 했고, 그럴 때면 아이들이 장난감 가게에서 느끼는 것보다 더 큰 재미와 공포를 느꼈다.

커다랗고 낡은 서랍장의 손잡이들이 친절하게 윙크를 던지던 게 떠오른다. 항상 강인한 친구 같던 의자도 하나 있었다.

어느 것이라도 너무 무섭게 보일 때는 그 의자에 올라앉으면 안전할 거라고 믿었다.

가구들을 아래층에서 모두 가지고 올라와야 했기 때문에 방안 가구들은 부조화 그 자체다. 이 방을 놀이방으로 썼을 때 육아 용품들을 모두 치워야만 했을 테니 놀랄 일도 아니다. 아이들이 만들어놓은 모습이 이 방처럼 끔찍한 곳을 본 적이 없다.

전에 말했듯이 벽지는 군데군데 찢겨 있으면서도 친형제보다 가까이 붙어 있다. 아이들이 벽지에 대한 증오심뿐 아니라 집요함도 함께 가지고 있었던 게 분명하다.

바닥은 흠집이 나 있고, 파이고, 갈라져 있으며, 회반죽 벽도 여기저기 벗겨져 있다. 이 방의 유일한 가구인 크고 육중한 침대도 몇 차례 전쟁을 겪은 듯한 몰골이다.

그러나 저 벽지만 빼면 다른 것은 조금도 신경 쓰이지 않는다.

존의 여동생이 오고 있다. 상냥하고 지극정성으로 나를 돌봐주는 여자! 그녀에게 글 쓰는 걸 들키면 안 된다.

그녀는 완벽하고 열성적인 살림꾼이다. 더 나은 직업은 바라지도 않는다. 분명 그녀는 글 쓰는 일이 나를 병들게 한다고 생각하고 있을 거다.

그녀가 외출하면 글을 쓸 수 있다. 그리고 창문으로 그녀가 멀어지는 것을 볼 수 있다.

그늘이 드리워진 구불구불한 아름다운 길이 보이는 창문이 하나 있고, 다른 창문으로는 멀리 전원 풍경이 보인다. 느릅나무들과, 비단 물결같이 펼쳐진 풀밭이 가득한 전원 풍경 역시 아름답다.

벽지 무늬 밑에 빛에 따라 달라지는 속무늬가 깔려 있다. 이 속 무늬는 특정 불빛에서만 보이고 그조차 선명하게 보이지 않아 나를 정말 짜증나게 한다.

색이 바래지 않은 벽지 부분을 적당량의 햇빛이 비출 때면 이상하고, 기분 나쁘고, 형체가 없는 어떤 형상이 보인다. 이 형상이 유치하고 뚜렷한 겉무늬 뒤를 살금살금 돌아다니는 것 같다.

시누이가 계단을 올라오고 있잖아!

독립기념일이 지나갔다. 사람들은 모두 떠났고 나는 완전히 진이 빠졌다. 존은 내가 사람들을 좀 만나도 좋겠다고 생각했고, 그래서 엄마와 넬리, 아이들을 불러 일주일간 함께 지냈다.

물론 나는 아무 일도 하지 않았다. 지금은 제니가 모든 걸 도맡아 하고 있다.

그런데도 피곤했다.

존은 내 건강이 빨리 좋아지지 않으면 가을에는 나를 위어 미첼(히스테리 증상을 휴식요법으로 치료했던 미국의 의사. 실제로 이 글의 작가인 샬롯 퍼킨스 길머은 산후우울증을 앓을 때 위어 미첼에게 치료를 받았다—옮긴이)에게 보내겠다고 한다.

그 사람한테 가는 건 정말 싫다. 내 친구 하나가 그에게 치료를 받은 적이 있는데, 친구 말에 따르면 그는 존이나 내 오빠와 다를 바가 없다고 했다. 더하면 더 했지!

게다가 그렇게 멀리 가는 것도 만만치 않은 일이다.

모든 것이 손 하나 갖다 댈 가치도 없는 일로 느껴진다. 그래서 짜증과 불평도 자주 치솟는다.

나는 아무것도 아닌 일에 운다. 거의 항상 운다.

물론 존이나 다른 사람이 있을 때는 그렇지 않지만 혼자 있으면 계속 운다.

요즘은 상당히 많은 시간을 혼자 보낸다. 존은 위중한 환자들 때문에 자주 읍내에 나가고 제니는 착해서 내가 원하면 날 혼자 있게 내버려둔다.

나는 정원이나 아름다운 길 위를 조금 걷고, 현관 장미 넝쿨 아래 앉아 있다가, 여기로 올라와 오랫동안 누워 있는다.

나는 벽지에도 불구하고 이 방이 점점 마음에 든다. 아니, 아마도 벽지 때문에 좋아지는 것 같다.

머릿속에서 벽지에 대한 생각이 떠나지 않는다.

나는 이 거대하고 못으로 고정된 듯 꿈쩍도 않는 침대에 누워 몇 시간이고 무늬를 따라간다. 곡예와 같은 활동일 거라는 생각이 든다. 말 그대로 밑바닥부터, 그러니까 사람 손이 닿은 적 없는 저쪽 모퉁이 아래부터 시작해서 의미 없는 무늬를 따라가면서 나는 끝까지 따라가 어떤 결론을 얻고야 말겠다는 다짐을 한 천 번은 하고 있다.

나는 디자인의 원리를 아주 조금은 알고 있다. 이 무늬는 내가 들어봤던 방사, 교체, 반복, 대칭, 또는 다른 어떠한 법칙도 따르지 않은 채 배열되어 있다.

물론 일정한 폭을 두고 무늬가 반복되고 있긴 하지만 그게 전부다.

한쪽에서 보면 각각의 폭이 혼자 서 있다. 저질 로마네스크 식으로 된 부푼 곡선들과 장식들이 마치 알코올 중독자가 금단 현상을 겪는 것처럼 제각각 우둔하게 열을 지어 어기적대며 오르락내리락한다.

그러나 다른 쪽에서 보면 무늬들이 대각선으로 연결되어 있다. 제멋대로 뻗어나가는 선들은 시각적으로 아찔할 만큼 비스듬한 물결 모양을 내달린다. 마치 물속에서 흐느적대는 엄청난 해초 떼가 쏜살같이 아오는 듯하다.

무늬 전체가 수평으로도 이동한다. 최소한 그렇게 보인다. 나는 그 방향으로 가는 규칙을 알아내려고 애쓰다 지쳐버리고 만다.

집주인이 벽지를 띠 모양으로 장식하려고 수평의 폭을 사용해서 무늬가 훨씬 혼란스럽다.

방 한쪽 끝에는 무늬가 거의 손상되지 않았다. 교차 광선이 희미해지고, 낮게 든 해가 직접적으로 이곳을 비추면 결국 어떤 방사무늬를 떠올리게 된다. 중심점을 둘러싸고 끊임없이 생겨난 괴기한 형상들이 정신없이 돌진해 곤두박질치며 떨어진다.

무늬를 계속 따라가다 보니 진이 빠진다. 낮잠이나 자야겠다.

이런 걸 왜 글로 쓰고 있는지 모르겠다.

별로 쓰고 싶지도 않은데…….

이럴 기운도 없는데…….

남편은 글을 쓰는 건 어리석은 짓이라고 생각할 거다. 그래도 내가 느끼고 생각하는 것을 어떤 방식으로든 말해야 한다. 말하고 나면 한 시름 놓을 수 있을 거다.

그러나 그를 통해 얻는 위안에 비해 힘이 너무 든다.

이제 나는 온 종일을 엄청나게 게으르게 보낸다. 누워 있는 시간도 그 어느 때보다 길어졌다.

존은 기력을 잃어서는 안 된다며 에일, 와인, 희귀 고기는 말할 것도 없고 대구 간유, 많은 양의 강장제 등을 먹게 한다.

다정한 존! 그는 나를 매우 사랑하며 내가 아픈 걸 무척 싫어한다. 어느 날인가 존과 진정으로 이성적인 대화를 해보려고 시도했다. 내가 사촌 엔리와 줄리아를 얼마나 만나고 싶어하는지, 그가 그들을 만날 수 있게 해주기를 얼마나 간절히 원하는지 존에게 내 마음을 전달하려고 했다.

그러나 그는 내가 그들에게 갈 수 조차 없을 것이며, 간다 하더라도 그곳에서 버티지 못할 거라고 말했다. 나는 말을 마치기도 전에 울음을 터뜨렸고 결국 내 주장을 제대로 펼치지 못했다.

논리적으로 생각하는 게 점점 더 힘들어진다. 그게 다 신경쇠약 때문이겠지.

다정한 존은 나를 안아서 위층으로 옮기고는 침대에 눕혔다.

그러고는 옆에 앉아 내 머리에 쥐가 날 지경이 될 때까지 책을 읽어주었다.

그는 내가 그의 사랑이자 평안이자 전부라고 말하고는 그러니 내가 그를 위해서라도 내 스스로를 돌보고 건강해야 한다고 말했다.

또한 이 상황에서 나를 구할 수 있는 사람은 나 자신뿐이라며 내 의지와 자제력을 동원해서 어리석은 공상에 빠지지 않게 해야 한다고 말했다.

그나마 내게 위안이 되는 한 가지는 건강하고 행복한 내 아기가 끔찍한 벽지로 도배된 이 육아실에 있을 필요가 없다는 것이다.

우리가 이 방을 쓰지 않았다면 저 사랑스런 아기가 써야 했을 지도 모른다. 정말 다행이다. 작고 사랑스러운 내 아기가 절대 이런 방에서 살게 할 수는 없다.

전에는 미처 생각하지 못했는데 이제는 존이 나를 이 방에 머물게 하는 게 너무 다행스럽다. 아기보다는 내가 이곳을 훨씬 잘 참아낼 수 있을 테니까.

물론 나는 다른 사람 앞에서는 더 이상 이런 얘기를 꺼내지 않지만―나는 현명하니까―여전히 벽지를 예의주시하고 있다.

나를 제외한 다른 사람들은 알지 못하는, 앞으로도 알 수 없는 무언가가 벽지 안에 있다.

겉무늬 밑에서 저 흐릿한 모양이 날마다 점차 뚜렷해지고 있다.

모양은 항상 같은데, 단지 그 수가 엄청나게 많아졌다.

그 모양은 여자가 허리를 굽혀 무늬 뒤에서 기어다니는 것 같은 형상이다. 정말 맘에 들지 않는다. 존이 나를 여기서 데리고 나가주기를 바랄 뿐이다.

존은 매우 현명하고 나를 많이 사랑하기 때문에 내 건강 상태에 대해 존에게 이야기하기가 너무 힘들다.

그러나 나는 지난밤에 대화를 시도했다.

태양과 마찬가지로 사방을 비추는 달이 밝게 떠 있는 밤이었다.

때때로 저 형상을 보는 게 너무 싫다. 너무 천천히 기어가고, 늘 이 창문이든 저 창문이든 창문 하나를 통해 기어나온다.

존은 잠들어 있었고, 나는 그를 깨우고 싶지 않았다. 그래서 나는 달빛이 물결치는 벽지를 비추는 모습을 가만히 지켜보았다. 오싹한 기분이 들었다.

뒤쪽의 희미한 형체가 탈출을 원하는 듯 무늬를 흔드는 것 같았다.

나는 조심스럽게 일어나 벽지가 정말 움직였는지 보고 느끼려고 다가갔다. 침대로 돌아왔을 때 존이 깨어 있었다.

그가 말했다. "귀염둥이, 무슨 일이지? 그렇게 돌아다니면 안돼요. 감기 들면 어쩌려고 그래."

그와 대화를 할 좋은 기회가 왔다고 생각한 나는 이곳에서 내 건강이 전혀 나아지지 않고 있으니 나를 다른 곳으로 데려가 달라고 그에게 말했다.

그가 말했다. "왜 그러는데? 임대 계약도 3주 뒷면 끝나는데 그 전에 나갈 방법이 어디 있겠소. 집수리도 아직 안 끝났고, 지금은 나도 이 마을을 떠날 수 없는 상황이야. 물론 당신한테 조금의 위험이라도 있다면 나갈 수도, 아니 당연히 나가겠지만 당신 상태가 좋아지고 있는걸. 당신이 아는지 모르겠지만 난 의사니까 알 수 있소. 당신 체중도 늘고, 혈색도 좋아지고, 식욕도 좋아졌어. 이제 마음이 훨씬 놓인다오."

"체중은 전혀 늘지 않았어요. 예전만큼도 안 나가는걸요. 식욕도 당신이 집에 있는 저녁에나 좋아지지 당신이 없는 아침에는 훨씬 안 좋아요."

그가 나를 끌어안으며 말했다. "아, 이것 참! 당신 원하는 대로 아픈 거군. 어쨌든 지금은 밤이니까 어서 잠자리에 들고 얘기는 아침에 하지."

내가 침울해 하며 물었다. "여기 정말 안 떠날 거예요?"

"당장 어떻게 떠나겠소? 3주만 있으면 돼. 그때 우리 며칠간 멋진 여행을 갑시다. 그 동안 제니가 우리 집을 정리해놓을 거요. 당신 정말 많이 건강해졌다니까."

"몸은 나아졌을지 모르지만......." 내가 말을 시작하려다 바로 입을 다물었다. 그가 똑바로 앉아서 근엄하고 책망하는 얼굴로 나를 바라보고 있어서 더 이상 말을 이을 수 없었다.

"여보, 정말 부탁이오. 나를 위해서, 우리 아이를 위해서, 그리고 당신 자신을 위해서 제발 한 순간이라도 그런 생각은 하지 말아줘. 다인처럼 예민한 기질에는 그런 생각이 가장 우험하고 정신을 빼놓는다고. 그런 생각은 말도 안 되는 거짓 상상일 뿐이야. 의사인 내 말을 그렇게 못 믿겠소?"

나는 당연히 더 이상 이 문제에 대해 말하지 못했고, 우리는 이내 잠을 청했다. 그는 내가 먼저 잠들었다고 생각했지만 그렇지 않다. 나는 누운 채로 겉무늬와 속무늬가 정말 함께 움직였는지 아니면 다로 움직였는지를 몇 시간이고 생각해보았다.

무늬는 햇빛이 비치는 낮 동안에는 연속성이 부족하고 규칙도 따르지 않는다. 이 점이 평범한 사람의 마음을 계속 괴롭힌다.

무늬는 고문 그 자체고, 색깔은 흉측하고 허황되며 사람을 열받게 하기 충분하다.

무늬에 대해 잘 알게 되었다는 생각을 하며 무늬를 잘 따라가고 있을라치면 무늬는 뒤로 재주를 넘어 원점에 와 있다. 따귀를 때리고, 두들겨 패서 땅에 쓰러뜨리고, 짓밟는 악몽과도 같다.

겉무늬는 곰팡이를 연상시키는 화려한 아라베스크 무늬다. 마디마디의 독버섯, 복잡하게 얽히고설켜 싹이 트고 자라나는 일련의 끝없는 독버섯들을 상상해보라. 그 모습과 비슷하다.

아니, 어쩔 때 보면 딱 그 모습이다.

이 벽지에는—나 말고는 아무도 눈치 채지 못하는—뚜렷한 특징이 하나 잇다. 바로 빛에 따라 바뀐다는 점이다.

동쪽 창문으로 해가 떠오르기 시작하면 나는 언제나 길게 직선으로 들어오는 첫 햇빛을 주시한다. 무늬가 너무 빨리 바뀌어 믿을 수 없을 정도다.

그래서 항상 무늬를 보고 있어야 한다.

달빛이 비칠 때면—달이 뜨면 밤새도록 달빛이 비친다—동일한 벽지인지 분간이 안 갈 정도다.

밤에는—석양, 촛불, 등불, 최악의 경우 달빛까지—어떤 종류의 빛이든지 무늬가 철창으로 바뀐다. 겉무늬가 철창이고, 그 뒤로 여자가 뚜렷하게 보인다. 뒤쪽에 보이는 흐릿한 속무늬가 무엇인지 오랫동안 알지 못했었는데 지금은 여자라는 걸 확신한다.

그녀는 낮 동안은 억눌린 채 조용하다. 나는 그녀를 잠자코 있게 하는 게 무늬라고 생각한다. 얼마나 불가사의한 일인가. 그 때문에 나는 몇 시간씩이고 잠자코 있다.

이제 누워 있는 시간이 그 어느 때보다 길다. 존은 내 건강에 좋다며 가능한 많이 자두라고 말한다.

실제로 그는 매 식사 후 한 시간씩 내가 침대에 누워 있도록 했다.

나는 잠을 자지 않으니까 이건 매우 나쁜 습관이 분명하다.

내가 깨어 있다는 사실을 그들에게 말하지 않으니 속임수만 는다. 이런!

실은 존이 조금씩 두려워지기 시작했다.

때때로 그가 아주 이상해 보인다. 제니 또한 알 수 없는 표정을 지을 때가 있다.

무슨 과학적 가설처럼 벽지 때문이 아닐까 하는 생각이 가끔 든다.

나는 그가 눈치 채지 못하게 남편을 주시했다. 그러다 가장 순수해 보이는 구실들을 대고 불쑥 방으로 들어갔고, 그가 벽지를 보고 있는 모습을 여러 차례 목격했다. 제니도 마찬가지다. 한번은 그녀가 벽지에 손을 대고 있는 걸 본 적도 있다.

제니는 내가 방에 들어온 것을 몰랐다. 나는 최대한 가장 절제된 태도로 조용한, 아주 조용한 목소리로 그녀에게 벽지에 손을 대고 뭘 하는 거냐고 물었다. 그러자 그녀는 물건을 훔치다 들킨 사람처럼 홱 돌아서서는 화난 얼굴로 왜 자기를 그렇게 놀라게 하냐고 따졌다.

그러고는 벽지에 닿는 것마다 얼룩이 묻으며, 나와 존의 모든 옷에 얼룩이 있는 걸 봤다고 말했다. 그녀는 존과 내가 좀더 조심해주길 바란다고 했다.

그럴싸하게 들리지 않는가? 하지만 나는 그녀가 실제로는 무늬를 관찰하고 있었다는 걸 안다. 나는 나를 뺀 그 누구도 무늬의 비밀을 알아내지 못하게 해야겠다고 다짐했다.

더 많이 예상하고, 고대하고, 관찰할 거리가 있으니 이제는 삶이 이전보다 훨씬 흥미롭다. 나는 예전보다 더 잘 먹고 더 차분해졌다.

내 건강이 개선되는 걸 본 존은 굉장히 기뻐한다. 지난번에 그는 내가 벽지를 싫어하는데도 불구하고 잘 지내는 것 같다고 말하면서 조금 웃기까지 했다.

나는 미소로 넘겼다. 상태가 호전된 게 다 벽지 때문이라고 그에게 말할 생각은 추호도 없었기 때문이다. 얘기해봤자 비웃을 테고 어쩌면 나를 데리고 이곳을 떠나려 할지도 몰랐다.

비밀을 밝혀내기 전까지는 떠나고 싶지 않다. 일주일 남았다. 그 정도면 충분한 시간이다.

정말 많이 건강해진 게 느껴진다. 어떤 상황이 전개되는지를 관찰하는 게 너무 재미있어서 밤에는 별로 잠을 자지 않는다. 대신 낮에 많이 잔다.

낮에는 피곤하고 어리벙벙하다.

벽지에는 항상 곰팡이가 새로 피고, 그 위를 누런 색이 온통 덮어버린다. 곰팡이들을 아무리 공들여 세어보려고 해도 그 수를 헤아릴 수가 없다.

벽지는 가장 요상한 누런 색으로, 내가 봤던 모든 누런 것들을 떠올리게 한다. 미나리아재비처럼 예쁜 노란 것 말고 나쁜 의미의 누리끼리한 것들 말이다.

저 벽지에는 다른 문제가 또 있다. 바로 냄새. 우리가 처음 이 방에 들어왔을 때 나는 바로 냄새를 알아챘지만, 통풍도 잘 되고 햇빛도 많이 들어와 냄새가 아주 심각하지는 않았다. 그러나 일주일간 안개 끼고 비 내리는 날씨가 계속된 뒤인 지금은 창문이 열려 있든 닫혀 있든 상관없이 냄새가 방에 그대로 있다.

온 집 안에서 냄새가 꿈틀거린다.

냄새가 식당을 맴돌고, 응접실에서 살금살금 돌아다니고, 복도에 숨고, 계단 위에 숨어 나를 기다린다.

내 머리카락 속까지 냄새가 스민다.

마차를 타러 가다가 냄새를 놀래주려고 갑자기 고개를 돌리면 이미 그곳에 냄새가 있다.

그것도 아주 독특한 냄새! 나는 냄새를 분석해서 무엇과 유사한지 알아내려고 애쓰며 몇 시간을 보내고 있다.

매우 미미한 냄새로 처음에는 그리 나쁘지 않지만, 내가 아는 그 어떤 냄새보다 가장 미묘하고 계속 지속되는 냄새다.

이런 축축한 날씨에는 냄새가 더 지독하다. 밤에 깨어나도 냄새가 뇌리에 박혀 있다.

처음에는 냄새 때문에 마음이 뒤숭숭했다. 냄새를 없애기 위해 집을 태워버리는 방법까지 고민했을 정도로. 하지만 이제는 냄새에 익숙하다. 내가 생각해낼 수 있는 거라고는 냄새가 벽지 색깔과 같다는 거다. 누런 냄새!

벽 아래쪽의 굽도리판자 가까이에 아주 괴상한 흔적이 있다. 그것은 사방을 빙 둘러 지나가는 줄무늬다. 침대를 제외한 모든 가구 뒤를 지나는 줄무늬는 길고 곧으며, 마치 거듭해서 문질러댄 것처럼 번져 있다.

이 줄무늬는 어떻게, 누구에 의해, 그리고 왜 생긴 건지 궁금하다. 빙글, 빙글, 빙글, 빙글, 빙글, 빙글, 어지럽다!

드디어 정말 뭔가를 알아냈다.

무늬가 바뀌는 것을 밤 사이 오래 관찰하다 마침내 알게 된 것이다.

겉무늬가 정말 움직인다! 그럴 수밖에 없다. 그 뒤의 여자가 겉무늬를 흔들어대고 있으니까!

어느 때는 저 뒤에 수많은 여자들이 있는 것 같다. 또 때로는 여자는 한 명뿐인데, 그녀가 이리저리 빠르게 기어다니면서 무늬를 흔들어대서 벽지 전체가 흔들리는 거라는 생각이 든다.

그녀는 매우 밝은 지점에서 움직이지 않다가, 아주 어두운 지점에서는 철창을 잡고 세게 흔들어댄다.

그녀는 항상 철창 사이로 나오려고 애쓴다. 그러나 무늬가 목을 조여버리기 때문에 아무도 그 무늬를 통과해 나올 수 없다. 그래서 무늬에 이렇게나 많은 머리들이 있는가 보다.

여자들이 무늬 사이로 나오면 무늬가 그들의 목을 매달고 거꾸로 매달아 눈을 허옇게 만들어버린다!

만약 이 머리들을 무언가로 가려놓거나 아예 치워버리면 훨씬 덜 흉측할 것이다.

여자는 낮에는 밖으로 나오는 것 같다.

내가 그렇게 생각하는 이유는 슬쩍 말해주자면 내가 그녀를 보았기 때문이다.

내 방의 어느 창문에서든 그녀의 모습을 볼 수 있다.

그 여자가 바로 벽지 속의 그녀라는 걸 알 수 있다. 그녀는 항상 기어다니는 데 반해 다른 대부분의 여자들은 낮에는 기어다니지 않기 때문이다.

나무 아래 기다란 길 위를 따라 기고 있는 그녀가 보인다. 마차가 오면 그녀는 블랙베리 넝쿨 아래로 숨는다.

낮에 기어다니다 들키면 몹시 창피할 테니 그녀의 행동을 조금도 탓할 수 없다.

나는 내가 낮에 기어다닐 때면 늘 방문을 잠근다. 밤에는 그러지 못하는 건 남편이 금세 눈치를 챌 것이기 때문이다.

요새 존이 너무 이상하다. 그래서 그의 신경을 건드리고 싶지 않다. 그가 다른 방을 썼으면 좋겠다. 게다가 밤에 나 말고 다른 사람이 여자를 밖으로 나오게 하는 걸 원치 않는다.

나는 종종 모든 창문에서 나오는 그녀를 동시에 볼 수는 없을까 궁금하다.

내가 아무리 빨리 돌아서도 한 번에 창문 하나에서 나오는 모습만 볼 수 있다.

항상 그녀를 보기는 하지만 내 회전 속도보다 그녀가 기는 속도가 더 빠른가 보다.

때때로 그녀가 세찬 바람 속의 구름 그림자만큼이나 빠르게 기어 탁 트인 시골길로 멀어지는 모습을 본다.

저 겉무늬만 속무늬에서 떼어낼 수 있다면! 나는 조금씩, 조금씩 시도해보려고 한다.

또 다른 재미난 사실을 알아냈지만 지금은 말하지 않겠다. 사람을 너무 믿는 건 좋지 않다.

벽지를 떼어낼 수 있는 시간이 이틀밖에 남지 않았다. 게다가 존이 눈치 채기 시작한 것 같다. 그의 눈빛이 마음에 걸린다.

그가 제니에게 나에 관해 여러 가지 전문적인 질문을 해대는 걸 들었다. 그녀는 중요한 보고할 거리들을 가지고 있었다.

그녀는 내가 낮에 많이 잔다고 말했다.

존은 내가 밤에는 아주 조용히 있으면서도 잠을 안 자는 걸 알고 있다.

그는 매우 다정하고 친절한 척하면서 나에게도 온갖 질문을 했다.

내가 그의 속을 모르는 것처럼.

석 달이나 이 벽지 아래서 잤으니 그가 저런 행동을 하는 것은 당연하다.

그저 흥미로울 뿐이다. 존과 제니가 은밀하게 벽지의 영향을 받은 것이 분명하다.

만세! 오늘이 마지막 날이지만 시간은 충분하다. 존은 저녁에 나가면 밤새 읍내에 머물 것이다.

제니가 나랑 함께 자고 싶다고 했다. 교활한 것! 나는 혼자 있어야 푹 쉴 수 있다고 그녀에게 말했다.

기발한 대답이었다. 왜냐하면 나는 혼자 있는 게 아니니까. 달이 밝자마자 저 안쓰러운 여자가 기기 시작했고 무늬를 흔들어댔다. 나는 일어나서 그녀를 돕기 위해 달려갔다.

내가 당기며 그녀는 흔들고 내가 흔들면 그녀는 당기고 하면서 아침이 밝기 전에 우리는 벽지를 아주 많이 벗겨냈다.

벗겨낸 벽지는 내 머리 높이까지 오는 너비에 방 둘레 절반에 해당하는 길이다.

태양이 떠오르자 저 끔찍한 무늬가 나를 비웃기 시작했고 나는 바로 오늘, 이 일을 마치리라고 선포했다.

우리는 내일이면 떠난다. 사람들이 물건을 원래대로 돌려놓으려고 모든 가구를 아래층으로 옮기고 있다.

제니는 놀란 눈으로 벽을 바라보았다. 나는 단지 이 사악한 벽지에 앙심이 있어서 그랬을 뿐이라고 그녀에게 쾌활하게 말했다.

그녀는 웃었고 자기가 해도 될 일이라며 내가 피곤해지면 안된다고 말했다.

드디어 속셈을 드러내는군!

그러나 이곳에는 내가 있다. 나를 빼고는 살아있는 그 누구도 벽지에 손을 대서는 안 된다.

그녀는 나를 방 밖으로 내보내려고 했다. 속이 너무 빤히 보인다. 나는 이제 방이 무척 조용하고, 텅 비어 있고, 깨끗하니까 다시 누워서 잠을 푹 자겠다고 말했다. 그리고 내가 깨면 부를 테니 저녁식사 때도 나를 깨우지 말라고 했다.

그래서 그녀는 가고 없다. 시중들도 갔고, 모든 게 가고 없다. 이곳에는 꿈쩍도 않는 거대한 침대틀, 그 위에 놓여 있는 캔버스천 매트리스밖에 없다.

우리는 오늘밤 아래층에서 잘 것이고 내일 배를 타고 집으로 돌아간다.

방이 텅 비어 있으니 꽤 좋다.

아이들이 얼마나 뜯어댔을까!

침대틀이 이로 갉힌 자국투성이다.

내 할 일을 해야만 한다.

나는 문을 잠그고 열쇠를 앞쪽 길가로 던져버렸다.

밖에 나가기 싫다. 존이 올 때까지 아무도 들어오지 않았으면.

그를 깜짝 놀라게 해주고 싶다.

제니조차 찾지 못했던 밧줄을 내가 이곳으로 가져다놨다. 그 여자가 나와서 탈출하려 할 때 그녀를 묶을 수 있게.

그러나 내가 닫고 설 게 없으면 높은 곳까지 손이 닿지 않는다는 걸 잊고 있었다.

침대가 꿈쩍도 안 하는군!

나는 침대를 들어서 밀려고 기운이 다 빠질 때까지 애썼다. 그러다 너무 화가 나서 침대 한쪽 모퉁이를 조금 물어뜯었다. 내 이만 아플 뿐이었다.

바닥에 서서 닿을 수 있는 높이까지 모든 벽지를 뜯어냈다. 벽지는 지독히도 찰싹 달라붙고 무늬는 그걸 즐기고 있다. 저 모든 목 졸린 머리들과 튀어나온 눈알들, 어기적거리며 자라는 곰팡이들이 조롱을 하며 소리를 질러댔다.

어떤 필사적인 일을 하게 될 만큼 나는 약이 올라. 창문 밖으로 뛰어내리는 게 훌륭한 방법이겠지만 철창이 너무 튼튼해 시도조차 할 수 없다.

게다가 그런 짓은 안 할 것이다. 물론 안 할 것이다. 그런 행동은 부적절하며 잘못 오해 받을 수 있다는 걸 잘 알기 때문이다.

창문 밖은 쳐다보기도 싫다. 너무나도 많은 여자들이 기어다니고 있다. 그것도 아주 빠른 속도로.

그녀들 모두가 나처럼 벽지에서 나온 건지 궁금하다.

나는 잘 감춰두었던 밧줄에 단단히 묶여 있다. 그러니 나를 저 길로 내보낼 수 없다.

밤이 오면 나는 무늬 뒤로 돌아가야만 할 텐데, 그건 무척 어려운 일이다.

이 큰 방으로 나와서 내 마음대로 기어다니니까 너무 즐겁다.

밖에 나가기 싫다. 제니가 나가라고 해도 나가지 않을 것이다.

밖에서는 땅 위를 기어야 하고 모든 것이 노란색이 아닌 초록색이기 때문이다.

그러나 여기서는 방바닥 위를 순조롭게 길 수 있다. 내 어깨는 벽 둘레에 난 기다란 줄무늬 높이에 딱 맞다. 그래서 길을 잃지 않을 수 있다.

존이 문가에 있잖아!

이봐, 아무 소용없다고. 문을 열 수 없을 거야!

그가 계속 내 이름을 부르며 문을 쾅쾅 두드린다.

이제는 도끼를 가져다달라고 소리치고 있다.

저 멋진 문을 부숴버리는 것은 안타까운 일이다.

"여보, 열쇠는 현관 계단 옆, 질경이 아래 있어요."

그러자 존은 잠시 잠잠해졌다.

그러고는 아주, 아주 낮은 목소리로 말했다. "여보, 문 좀 열어봐요!"

"그럴 수 없어요. 열쇠는 현관 옆, 질경이 아래 있어요."

나는 매우 부드럽게 천천히 몇 번 더 말해주었다. 내가 여러 차례 그 말을 반복했으므로 결국 그는 열쇠를 찾으러 갔다. 물론 그는 열쇠를 찾았고 방에 들어왔다. 그가 문 앞에서 흠칫 놀라며 멈춰 섰다.

그가 소리쳤다. "도대체 왜 이래? 맙소사! 뭘 하는 거요!"

나는 하던 대로 계속 기면서 어깨 너머로 그를 흘끗 보았다.

"제니와 당신이 방해했지만 드디어 이렇게 나왔어요. 벽지도 대부분 뜯어냈고요. 그러니 다시 절 집어넣지 못할 거예요!"

그런데 저 남자, 왜 기절하는 걸까? 어쨌든 존이 기절했다. 그것도 벽 옆, 내가 가야 할 길을 가로질러서. 그래서 나는 매번 그를 타고 넘으며 기어야 했다.

6. 애러비(Araby)

• 제임스 조이스(James Joyce)

노스 리치몬드 거리는 막다른 길이라서, 크리스천 형제들의 학교가 학생들을 자유롭게 하는 시간이 아닐 때는 고요한 거리였다. 사람이 살지 않는 이층집 한 채가 광장 터의 이웃들과 따로 떨어져서 막다른 길의 끝에 서 있었다. 거리의 다른 집들은 내부의 점잖은 살림을 의식하는 듯 갈색의 침착한 얼굴로 서로를 응시했다.

우리 집에 전에 세 들어 살던 사람은, 사제였는데 그는 뒤편 거실에서 죽었다. 오랫동안 방이 닫혀 있어서 곰팡이가 피는 냄새가 나는 공기가 방안에 온통 가득했고, 부엌 뒤쪽의 다용도실은 낡고 쓸모없는 종이들로 가득 차 있었다. 그것들 사이에서 나는 낱장들이 말려 올라가고 축축한 종이 표지의 책 몇 권을 찾아냈다. 월터 스콧의「대수도원장」, 그리고「독실한 전달자」와「비도크의 자서전」이었다.

나는 맨 마지막 것이 제일 좋았는데, 그것은 책장이 노란색이기 때문이었다. 집 뒤의 가꾸지 않은 뜰에는 한가운데에 사과나무 한 그루 그리고 관목 몇 그루가 흩어져 있었는데, 그 중 한 그루 밑에서 나는 죽은 세입자의 녹슨 자전거의 펌프를 찾아냈다.

그는 매우 자비로운 사제였다. 유언장에서 그는 자신의 모든 돈을 복지기관들에 물려주었고 자기 집의 가구는 여동생에게 남겨주었다.

낮이 짧은 겨울이 오면, 우리가 저녁을 다 먹기도 전에 황혼이 졌다. 우리가 거리에서 만날 즈음이면 집들은 우중충한 빛을 띠고 있었다. 우리 위에 열린 하늘은 변덕스러운 보랏빛이었고 그 하늘을 향해 거리의 가로등들은 각자의 희미한 등잔을 받들어 올렸다. 찬 공기가 우리를 파고들었고 우리는 몸이 후끈해질 때까지 놀았다.

우리들의 고함소리가 고요한 거리에 메아리쳤다. 우리들의 노는 경로는 허름한 오두막에 사는 거친 아이들에게 모진 곤욕을 치러야 하는, 집들 뒤의 검은 진흙 샛길로 해서, 난로 재 구덩이에서 악취가 올라오는 어둡고 질척거리는 정원 뒷문까지, 마부가 말갈기를 펴주고 빗질해주거나 쇠붙 달린 마구를 흔들어 음악소리를 내는 그 컴컴하고 냄새가 진한 마구간에까지 이르렀다. 우리가 거리로 돌아올 때면, 부엌 창문에서 나오는 불빛이 그 일대를 가득 채우고 있었다. 나의 아저씨가 골목길을 돌아오는 것이 보이면, 우리는 그가 안전하게 집안에 들어갈 때까지 그늘 속에 숨어 있었다. 아니면 망간의 누나가 현관 층층대로 나와 저녁 먹으러 들어오라고 남동생을 부를 때, 우리는 그늘에 숨어 그녀가 거리 여기저기로 자세히 찾아보는 모습을 살폈다. 우리는 기다리며 그녀가 그냥 거기 서 있는지 아니면 안으로 들어가는지를 보았다. 그리고 그녀가 계속 버티면, 우리는 포기하고 숨어 있던 그늘에서 나와 망간의 집 층층대로 걸어갔다. 그녀는 반쯤 열린 문에서 나오는 불빛에 몸의 윤곽을 드러낸 채 우리를 기다리고 있었다. 그녀의 남동생은 항상 누나를 한참 애태게 하고 나서야 말을 들었고, 나는 그녀를 쳐다보며 난간 곁에 서 있었다. 그녀의 몸이 움직이면서 그녀의 옷도 따라 흔들렸고, 그녀의 부드러운 머리타래가 이리저리 살랑거렸다.

매일 아침 나는 길 쪽의 응접실 마루에 누워 그녀의 집 문을 살폈다. 차일이 창틀에서 1인치 정도 남겨놓고 내려져 있어서 내가 보일 리는 없었다. 그녀가 현관 층층대로 나올 때면 나는 가슴이 뛰었다. 나는 현관으로 달려가서 책가방을 집어 들고 그녀 뒤를 따랐다. 나는 그녀의 갈색 모습을 내내 눈에서 놓지 않았고 그러다가 갈 길이 각자 갈라지는 지점이 가까워졌을 때 걸음을 빨리하여 그녀를 지나쳤다. 이런 일이 매일 아침마다 되풀이되었다. 나는 무심결에 주고받은 몇 마디 말고는 그녀에게 말을 걸어본 적이 없었다. 그렇지만 그녀의 이름은 나의 모든 어리석은 피를 한군데로 솟구쳐 쏠리게 만드는 것이었다.

분위기가 연애에 가장 적대적인 장소에서조차 그녀의 영상은 나를 따라다녔다. 토요일 저녁 아줌마가 장보러 갈 때는 내가 따라가서 꾸러미를 몇 개 날라줘야 했다. 노무자들의 욕설과, 즐비한 돼지 엉덩잇살을 지키며 서 있는 상점 사환아이의 새된 장광설과, 오도노반 로사(아일랜드의 급진주의적 독립운동가)에 관한 '모두 모여라' 어쩌고 하는 노래나 우리 조국의 수난을 다룬 가요를 부르는 길거리 가수들의 단조로운 코맹맹이 소리 한가운데서, 술 취한 사내와 물건 사라는 여인네들에게 떠밀리며, 우리는 그 번지르르한 거리를 지나갔다. 이러한 소음들이 내게는 삶에 대한 하나의 느낌으로 한데 모아졌다. 나는 내가 적의 무리 사이로 나의 성배를 안전히 모셔가고 있다고 상상했다. 그녀의 이름이 순간순간 나 자신도 이해 못할 낯선 기도와 예찬이 되어 내 입술로 솟아났다. 내 눈엔 종종 눈물이 가득 괴었고(이유는 알 수 없었다) 때때로 홍수가 내 심장으로부터 가슴으로 쏟아 부어지는 것 같았다. 나는 앞으로의 일을 거의 생각지 않았다. 나는 내가 그녀에게 도대체 말을 걸기는 걸 것인지 아닌지, 혹은 그녀에게 말을 건다 해도 어떻게 그녀에게 나의 혼란스런 연모의 정을 얘기해줄지를 몰랐다. 그러나 나의 몸은 하프와 같았고 그녀의 말과 몸짓은 그 줄을 퉁기는 손가락 같았다.

어느 날 저녁 나는 사제가 죽었던 뒤편 거실로 들어갔다. 어두컴컴하고 비 내리는 저녁이었고 집안은 아무 소리도 없이 고요했다. 부서진 창 하나를 통해서 빗줄기가 땅에 내리꽂히는 소리가 들렸다. 가느다랗게 끊임없이 내리는 바늘 같은 물줄기들이 흠뻑 젖은 화단에서 뛰놀고 있었다. 저 멀리 아물거리는 등잔이나 불 켜진 창 같은 것이 내 아래쪽에서 빛났다. 눈에 보이는 게 거의 없다는 것에 대해 나는 감사하는 마음이었다. 나의 모든 감각들은 스스로 베일에 가려지기를 갈망하는 것 같았다. 그리고 내가 이제 막 그 감각들로부터 빠져나오려 한다는 것을 느끼면서, 나는 양 손바닥을 부르르 떨 정도로 서로 꽉 맞잡았다. 몇 번씩이고 이렇게 중얼대면서 말이다. "오 사랑! 오 사랑이여!"

마침내 그녀가 내게 말을 걸었다. 그녀가 내게 첫마디를 건넸을 때 나는 너무 당황해서 어떻게 대답해야 할지를 몰랐다. 그녀는 애러비에 갈 거냐고 내게 물었다. 그렇다고 대답했는지 아니라고 했는지 나는 잊어버렸다. 굉장한 바자회일 거라 했다. 그녀는 거기 가보고 싶다고 말했다.

"그런데 왜 못 가요?" 내가 물었다.

말하는 동안 그녀는 손목에 낀 은팔찌를 뱅글뱅글 돌렸다. 그곳에 갈 수 없는 것은 바로 그 주에 그녀의 수녀원에서 피정이 있기 때문이라고 했다. 그녀의 남동생과 다른 두 사내아이가 자기들의 모자를 놓고 싸우고 있었고, 나는 난간에 혼자 있었다. 그녀는 머리를 내 쪽으로 숙인 채 난간의 쇠못 하나를 잡고 있었다. 우리 집 문 반대편 등잔에서 나오는 불빛이 그녀 목의 하얀 곡선을 드러내고, 그 위에 얹힌 그녀의 머리카락을 밝히고는, 아래로 내려가 난간 위의 손을 밝혔다. 불빛은 그녀의 옷 한쪽 편으로 내려와, 편안한 자세로 서 있는 그녀의 보일락 말락 하는 속치마의 새하얀 가장자리를 비춰주었다.

"넌 좋겠다." 그녀가 말했다.

"내가 가게 되면," 난 말했다. "뭘 사다 줄게요."

그날 저녁 이후 얼마나 숱하디 숱한 어리석음들이 자나 깨나 나의 생각을 휩쓸고 지나갔던가! 나는 그 중간에 끼어든 그 지루한 날들을 없애버리고 싶었다. 학교 공부는 짜증이 났다. 밤이면 침대에서, 낮이면 교실에서 그녀의 영상이 나와 책 사이에 나타나 책읽기를 방해했다. 애러비라는 단어의 음절은 내 영혼이 탐닉하던 그 침묵 속에서 내게로 불려나와 어떤 동양적인 마법을 내게 걸어놓았다.

나는 토요일 밤 바자회에 가는 것을 허락해달라고 했다. 숙모는 깜짝 놀랐고, 무슨 프리메이슨(중세의 숙련 석공조합의 비밀조합원)의 비밀결사가 아니었으면 좋겠다고 했다. 교실에서 나는 묻는 말에 별로 대답을 하지 않았다. 나는 선생님의 얼굴 표정이 온화함에서 험한 쪽으로 바뀌는 것을 보았다. 그는 내가 게을러지기 시작하는 게 아닌가 걱정했다.

나는 오락가락하는 나의 생각들을 추스를 수가 없었다. 나는 진지한 일상사를 거의 견딜 수 없을 지경이었고, 그것이 이제는 나와 내 욕망 사이를 가로막고 선 이상, 내게는 어린애 장난, 그것도 보기 싫고 단조로운 어린애 장난처럼 보였던 것이다.

토요일 아침 나는 아저씨한테 저녁에 바자회에 가고 싶다고 상기시켰다. 그는 거울 달린 옷걸이 앞에서 모자솔을 찾으며 법석을 떠는 중이었고, 그래서 짤막하게 대답했다.

"그래 애야, 안다."

그가 현관 마루에 있었으므로 앞 응접실로 가서 창가에 누울 수도 없었다. 나는 집안이 저기압인 것을 느끼며 학교를 향해 느릿느릿 걸어갔다. 공기가 무자비하게 구저분하고 추웠고 나는 벌써 불안한 느낌에 차 있었다.

저녁을 먹으러 집에 왔을 때 아저씨는 아직 귀가하지 않은 상태였다. 아직 일렀다. 나는 앉아서 얼마간 시계를 물끄러미 쳐다보다가 째깍째깍 소리가 짜증나기 시작할 때에 방에서 나왔다. 나는 계단을 올라가 집 윗부분을 차지했다. 높고, 차갑고, 텅 빈, 우울한 방들이 해방감을 주었고, 나는 노래를 부르며 이 방 저 방을 돌아다녔다. 앞 창문을 통해서 친구들이 저 아래 길가에서 노는 것이 보였다. 그들의 고함소리는 희미하고 불분명해진 상태로 내게 들려왔다. 나는 이마를 시원한 유리에 기대고 그녀가 사는 어두운 집을 건너다보았다. 아마 한 시간 가량 서 있었으리라. 내 상상에 의해 만들어진 그 갈색 옷을 입은 모습, 등잔불이 그 목덜미의 곡선을, 난간을 쥔 손을, 그리고 옷자락 아래 속치마 단을 살며시 비추는 그 모습만을 바라보면서.

다시 아래층으로 내려왔을 때 머서 부인이 난롯가에 앉아 있었다. 그녀는 나이 들고 수다스러운 여자였다. 전당포를 하던 남편과 사별했는데, 사용한 우표를 어떤 경건한 목적(우표수집상에 판 돈을 모금하여 국외의 가톨릭 선교사들에게 보내주는 것) 때문에 모으고 있었다. 나는 차 탁자에서의 가십거리를 견뎌야 했다. 저녁이 한 시간 넘게 미뤄졌는데도 아직 아저씨는 오지 않았다. 머서 부인이 가려고 일어났다. 더 기다리지 못해 미안하다고, 하지만 여덟시가 넘었고 늦게까지 나와 있기가 뭣하다고, 밤공기는 자기한테 나쁘다고 말했다. 그녀가 가고 나서 나는 주먹을 불끈 쥐고 방 안을 왔다 갔다 했다. 아줌마가 말했다.

"우리 주님의 이 밤을 위해 아무래도 바자회 가는 건 연기해야 되겠구나."

아홉시에 아저씨의 현관문 열쇠 소리가 들렸다. 그가 혼자서 뭐라고 하는 소리와 현관의 옷걸이가 그의 외투 무게를 받고 흔들흔들하는 소리가 들렸다. 나는 이러한 몸짓의 의미들을 해석할 수 있었다. 그가 한참 저녁을 먹고 있을 때 나는 바자회에 가게 돈을 좀 달라고 말했다. 그는 깜빡 잊어버리고 있었다.

"사람들이 잠자리에 들어 지금쯤은 한잠 자고 난 다음일 게다." 그가 말했다.

나는 웃지 않았다. 아줌마가 그에게 힘주어서 말했다.

"돈 줘서 그를 보내주지 그래요? 당신 때문에 벌써 한참 늦었잖아요."

아저씨가 깜빡 잊어서 정말 미안하다고 말했다. 그는 이런 속담을 신봉한다고 말했다. '일만 하고 놀지 않으면 애들은 멍청해진다.' 그는 어딜 갈 거냐고 내게 물었고, 내가 두 번째로 그에게 얘기를 했더니, 「아랍인이 자기 말에게 보내는 작별인사」라는 작품을 아느냐고 물었다. 내가 부엌에서 나온 것은 그가 그 작품의 첫 연을 아줌마한테 막 읊으려는 참이었다.

나는 2실링짜리 은화 하나를 손에 꽉 쥐고 버킹엄도로를 내려가 역으로 향했다. 물건 사는 사람들로 북적거리고 가스등 번쩍거리는 거리 풍경이 내 나들이 목적을 일깨워주었다. 나는 승객이 없는 열차 삼등칸에 몸을 실었다. 참을 수 없을 정도로 늑장을 부리던 끝에 열차가 천천히 역을 빠져나갔다. 열차는 황폐한 집들 사이로 또 반짝이는 강을 건너 기어갔다. 웨스트 랜드 로우역에서 한 무리의 사람들이 객차 문으로 몰려들었다. 역무원이 이 열차는 바자회로 가는 특별열차라면서 그들을 밀쳐냈다. 나는 그 텅 빈 객차 칸에 내내 혼자였다. 몇 분 안 되어 열차가 나무로 급조된 플랫폼에 도착했다. 나는 길 쪽으로 나갔고 불 켜진 시계판을 보고 역시 십분 전임을 알았다. 내 앞에는 커다란 빌딩이 그 마법적인 이름을 내보이며 서 있었다.

나는 입장료가 6펜스인 입구를 찾을 수가 없었고, 바자회 문을 닫을까봐 겁이 난 나머지 지쳐 보이는 표정의 남자에게 1실링을 내고는 회전문을 통해 잽싸게 들어갔다. 나는 홀 높이의 반쯤 되는 부분에 빙 둘러 회랑이 설치된 거대한 홀 안으로 들어섰다. 거의 모든 진열대가 닫혀 있었고 홀 대부분이 어둠에 덮여 있었다. 나는 흡사 예배 후 교회에 감도는 그런 정적을 느낄 수 있었다. 나는 주춤주춤 바자의 한가운데로 걸어 들어갔다. 아직 열려 있는 판매대 주변에 몇 되지 않은 사람들이 모여 있었다. 까페 샹땅이라는 단어가 색 전구로 씌어 있는 그 휘장 앞에서 두 사내가 쟁반 위의 돈을 세고 있었다. 나는 동전이 짤그락 떨어지는 소리에 귀를 기울였다.

나는 왜 거기까지 갔는지를 어렵사리 상기하고, 한 진열대로 가서 도자기 꽃병과 꽃무늬 찻잔 세트를 살펴보았다. 판매대 입구에서는 젊은 여자 한 명이 두 명의 젊은 신사와 얘기하며 키득거리고 있었다. 나는 그들의 영국식 억양을 알아차릴 수 있었고, 어렴풋이 그들의 대화를 들었다.

"아이, 난 그런 얘기 한 적 없는데요!"

"아, 그랬잖아!"

"아이, 아녜요. 정말!"

"이 아가씨가 그렇게 말하지 않았나?"

"맞아. 나도 들었는데 뭘."

"아이, 이런 …… 거짓말!"

젊은 여자는 나를 보자 다가와서 뭘 사려느냐고 물었다. 그녀의 목소리는 별로 물건을 팔려는 어조가 아니었다. 의무감에서 말을 건 것 같았다. 나는 판매대의 어두운 입구 양쪽에 동방의 보초처럼 서 있는 거대한 항아리들을 초라하게 쳐다보고 중얼거렸다.

"아뇨, 됐어요."

젊은 여자는 꽃병 하나의 위치를 바꾸어놓고는 두 사내에게로 되돌아갔다. 그들은 같은 얘기를 다시 하기 시작했다. 그 젊은 여자는 한두 번 어깨 너머로 나를 흘끗 쳐다보았다.

더 있어봤자 소용없다는 것을 알았지만, 나는 그녀의 물건을 정말로 살 생각이 있었던 것처럼 보이게 하려고 그녀의 진열대 앞에서 꾸물댔다. 그런 다음 천천히 몸을 돌려 바자회장의 한가운데로 걸어 나왔다. 나는 호주머니 속에서 1페니 동전 두 개를 6펜스짜리 동전 위에 떨어뜨렸다. 회랑의 한쪽 끝에서 불을 끈다는 소리가 들렸다. 홀 위쪽은 이제 완전히 깜깜했다.

그 어둠속을 응시하면서 나는 허영심에 내몰리고 조롱당한 짐승 같은 내 모습을 보았다. 그리고 나의 눈은 고뇌와 분노로 이글거렸다.

9. 나는 다림질을 하며 여기 서 있다(I Stand Here Ironing)

• 틸리 올슨(Tillie Olsen)

나는 다림질을 하며 여기 서 있다. 당신이 내게 요구한 것이 다리미를 따라 몸부림치며 앞뒤로 왔다 갔다 한다.

"시간 내어 학교에 좀 오셔서 따님에 대해 함께 이야기 나눴으면 합니다. 제가 그 애를 이해할 수 있도록 분명히 도와주실 수 있을 겁니다. 도움이 필요한 아이입니다. 저 또한 진심으로 아이를 돕고 싶습니다."

"도움이 필요한 아이" … 내가 간다 해도 무슨 소용이 있단 말인가? 내가 그 애의 엄마니까 열쇠를 쥐고 있을 거라고, 아니면 나를 어떻게든 열쇠로 이용할 수 있을 거라고 생각하는가? 아이는 19년을 살아왔다. 아이에게는 나의 바깥에, 나의 너머에 있는 삶이 있다.

그리고 내게 기억하고, 가려내고, 따져보고, 평가하고, 정리할 시간이 어디에 있단 말인가? 시작을 한다 해도 중단될 것이고 그러면 다시 처음부터 그러모아야 할 것이다. 아니면 내가 하거나 하지 않았던 그 모든 일들, 내가 했어야 했거나 어쩔 수 없었던 그 모든 일들이 나를 집어삼킬 것이다.

그 애는 예쁜 아기였다. 다섯 아이 중 처음이자 유일하게 아름답게 태어난 아기였다. 지금 그 애가 가진 사랑스러움이 얼마나 생경하고 어색한지 당신은 짐작도 못한다. 그 애가 못생겼다는 소리를 들었던 그 수많은 시간들을 당신은 모른다. 그 애가 어렸을 적 사진을 들여다보며 다른 이들의 눈에 자기가 얼마나 예뻐보였는지(앞으로 얼마나 예쁠까, 나는 아이에게 그렇게 말해주곤 했다), 지금은 얼마나 예뻐 보이는지 계속계속 이야기해달라고 하던 모습도 당신은 보지 못했다. 하지만 그때 아이를 바라봐주는 사람은 거의 없거나 존재하지 않았다. 나를 포함해서.

나는 아이에게 젖을 먹였다. 요즘은 젖을 먹이는 게 중요하다고들 말한다. 나는 아이들 모두에게 젖을 먹였지만, 초보 엄마다운 지독한 엄격함으로 그 애한테만큼은 당시 책에서 말하는 대로 했다. 아이 울음소리로 온몸이 덜덜 떨리고 가슴이 아플 정도로 부어올라도 나는 정해진 시간까지 기다렸다.

왜 나는 이 이야기부터 하는가? 나는 이 사실이 중요한지, 이 사실이 뭔가를 설명해주는지조차 모른다.

그 애는 예쁜 아기였다. 반짝이는 비눗방울 같은 소리를 냈다. 움직임을 사랑했고, 빛을 사랑했고, 색과 음악과 질감을 사랑했다. 위아래가 붙은 파란색 아기 옷을 입고 바닥에 누워서는 어찌나 황홀해하며 격하게 바닥을 쓸었는지 손과 발이 지저분해질 정도였다. 그 애는 내게 기적이었다 하지만 아이가 8개월이 되었을 때 나는 아래층에 사는 여자에게 낮 시간 동안 아이를 맡겨야만 했다. 그 여자에게 아이는 전혀 기적이 아니었다. 나는 일을 했거나 일을 찾아야만 했고, "우리와의 가난한 삶을 더 이상 견딜 수 없다"던(그가 마지막으로 남긴 쪽지에 쓰여 있었다) 에밀리의 아빠를 찾아야만 했다.

나는 열아홉 살이었다. 세상은 공황에 빠져 있었고, 공공사업 진흥국이 구호 정책을 펴기 전이었다. 전차에서 내리자마자 뛰기 시작해 계단을 달음질쳐 시큼한 냄새가 나는 곳으로 뛰어 올라갔다. 아이는 깨어 있거나 자다가 놀라서 깨어났다. 나를 보면 꺽꺽거리며 눈물을 와락 터뜨렸고 쉬이 진정하지 못했다. 아직도 그 울음소리가 귀에 선명하다.

얼마 후 밤에 할 수 있는 일을 구해 낮 시간에 아이와 함께 있을 수 있었고 상황은 전보다 나아졌다. 하지만 결국 다시 아이를 아이 아빠에게 맡기고 떠나야 했다.

아이를 다시 데려올 수 있을 만큼 돈을 벌 때까지는 오랜 시간이 걸렸다. 그때 아이가 수두에 걸렸고 나는 다시 기다려야 했다. 마침내 그 애가 돌아왔을 때 나는 아이를 거의 알아보지 못했다. 아이는 자기 아빠처럼 종종거리며 빠르게 걸었고 아빠를 닮아으며 말랐고 피부가 누랬고 얽은 자국을 더 눈에 띄게 하는 조잡한 빨간색 옷을 입고 있었다. 아기의 사랑스러움은 전부 사라지고 없었다.

그 애는 두 살이었다. 사람들은 유아원에 보내도 충분하다고 했다. 그때 나는 지금 내가 알고 있는 걸 알질 못했다.

긴 하루 끝의 피곤함과, 아이들을 위한 장소라고는 주차장밖에 없는 유아원 단체 생활이 주는 상처를.

하지만 내가 그걸 알았더라도 달라지는 건 없었을 것이다. 그 곳은 유일한 장소였다. 그것이 우리가 함께할 수 있는 유일한 방법, 내가 일자리를 잃지 않을 수 있는 유일한 방법이었다.

나는 알지 못하면서도 알았다. 아이의 선생님이 악마라는 걸 알았다. 그 선생이 구석에 웅크려 있는 작은 남자아이에게 "앨빈이 너를 때렸다고 안 나가는 거니? 그건 이유가 못 돼. 어서 나가, 이 겁쟁아"라고 거칠게 말하던 장면은 수년이 지난 지금도 내 기억 속에 단단히 남아 있다. 나는 에밀리가 그곳을 싫어하는 걸 알았다. 하지만 그 애는 다른 아이들처럼 아침마다 나를 움켜잡고 "가지 마 엄마"라고 애원하지 않았다.

아이는 언제나 우리가 집에 있어야 하는 이유를 댔다. 엄마, 아파 보여. 엄마, 나 아파. 엄마, 오늘 선생님이 아파서 안 온대. 엄마, 우리 거기 못 가. 지난밤에 불이 났대. 엄마, 오늘 휴일이래. 문 안 연대. 선생님이 그랬어.

하지만 대놓고 말을 안 듣거나 반항한 적은 한 번도 없었다. 그 애 동생들이 세 살, 네 살이었을 때를 떠올려본다. 폭발, 분노, 비난, 요구. 갑자기 마음이 좋지 않다. 다리미를 내려놓는다. 나의 무엇이 그 애에게 착해질 것을 요구했는가? 그 대가는, 그 선량함의 대가가 무엇이었는가?

한번은 뒷집에 사는 할아버지가 조심스레 말한 적이 있다. "에밀리를 바라볼 땐 좀 더 웃어줘야 해." 그 애를 바라보는 내 얼굴에 무엇이 있었는가? 나는 그 애를 사랑했다. 내 얼굴에는 사랑에서 나오는 그 모든 것들이 있었다.

나는 다른 사람들하고 있을 때만 할아버지의 말을 기억했다. 내가 사람들에게 보여준 얼굴은 걱정과 긴장, 염려가 아닌 기쁨의 얼굴이었다. 에밀리에겐 이미 너무 늦었다. 거의 항상 웃고 있는 동생들과는 달리 그 애는 잘 웃지 않는다. 아이의 얼굴은 무뚝뚝하고 침울하다. 하지만 자기가 원할 때는 어찌나 표정을 잘 바꾸는지. 당신은 분명 연기할 때의 아이 얼굴을 봤다. 그러니 무대 위에서 희극을 연기하며 관객을 웃게 할 수 있는 아이의 특별한 재능에 대해 말하는 거겠지. 관객은 박수를 치고 또 치며 아이를 보내려 하지 않는다.

희극은 어디에서 오는가? 내가 아이를 또다시 다른 곳으로 보낸 후 두 번째로 아이가 내게 돌아왔을 때 아이 안에는 희극이랄 게 전혀 없었다. 이번에는 아이에게 사랑을 배울 수 있는 새 아빠가 있었다. 아마 아이에겐 더 좋은 시간이었을 것이다.

우리가 그 애는 충분히 컸다고 되뇌며 아이를 홀로 남겨두고 떠난 밤들을 빼면.

"엄마, 다른 때 가면 안 돼요? 내일요." 아이는 물었다. "금방 돌아올 거죠? 약속할 거예요?"

우리가 돌아왔을 때 대문은 열려 있고 시계는 복도 바닥에 있었다. 아이는 똑똑히 깨어 있었다. "금방 온다고 했잖아요. 난 안 울었어요. 나는 세 번, 겨우 세 번밖에 전화 안 했어요. 그리고 아래층으로 뛰어 내려가서 문을 열어놨어요. 엄마가 더 빨리 들어올 수 있게요. 시계가 너무 시끄러웠어요. 그래서 던져버렸어요. 시계 소리가 무서웠어요."

아이는 내가 수전을 낳으러 병원에 간 날 밤에도 시계가 너무 시끄러웠다고 했다. 그때 그 애는 홍역 전에 찾아온 고열로 정신을 가누지 못했지만 내가 없었던 그 주 내내 정신을 온전히 차리고 있었고 우리가 집에 돌아온 다음 주에는 홍역 때문에 아기와 내 근처에 오지 못했다.

아이는 나아지지 않았다. 해골처럼 말라갔고, 먹으려 하지 않았고, 매일 밤 악몽을 꿨다. 그리고 나를 불렀다. 나는 피곤한 채로 일어나 졸려하며 대답했다. "괜찮아, 아가야. 다시 자. 그냥 꿈이야." 그래도 나를 계속 부르면 더 엄격한 목소리로 말했다. "이제 자, 에밀리. 아무도 널 해치지 않아." 두 번, 단 두 번, 그것도 수전 때문에 일어날 수밖에 없었을 때, 나는 에밀리의 곁에 있어주었다.

너무 늦어버린 지금에야 나는 (마치 아이가 내가 다른 애들에게 하듯 자기를 안아주고 달래주게 놔둘 것처럼) 아이가 끙끙거리거나 계속 뒤척이면 바로 자리에서 일어나 아이 곁으로 간다. "일어났니, 에밀리? 뭐라도 갖다 줄까?" 대답은 항상 같다. "아니, 괜찮아요. 다시 자요, 엄마."

병원에서 아이를 시골에 있는 요양원으로 보내라고 나를 설득했었다. 거기서는 "내가 주지 못하는 음식과 보살핌을 아이에게 제공해주고, 그러면 나는 수전에게 오롯이 집중할 수 있다"는 것이었다. 사람들은 여전히 아이들을 그곳에 보낸다. 신문 사회면에 실린 사진을 볼 때가 있다. 사진 속에서는 세련된 젊은 여성이 기금을 모으기 위해 행사를 계획하고 있거나 행사에서 춤을 추고 있거나 부활절 달걀을 색칠하고 있거나 아이들을 위해 크리스마스 양말에 선물을 넣고 있다.

하지만 아이들 사진은 없다. 그래서 나는 "따로 연락이 없으면" 부모가 찾아올 수 있는 (우리는 아이를 보낸 후 6주 동안 따로 연락을 받았다) 격주 일요일마다 여자애들이 여전히 그 거대한 붉은색 리본을 매고 피폐한 얼굴을 하고 있는지 알지 못한다.

음, 그곳은 멋진 곳이다. 푸른 잔디밭과 키 큰 나무들, 장식된 화단이 있다. 건물마다 붙어 있는 높은 발코니 위에 아이들이 서 있다. 여자애들은 붉은 리본에 하얀 치마를, 남자애들은 하얀 의복에 거대한 붉은색 타이를 하고 있다. 부모들은 발코니 아래에 서서 아이가 들을 수 있도록 위를 향해 소리를 지르고 아이들은 부모가 들을 수 있도록 아래를 향해 소리를 지르며 부모와 아이 사이에는 "신체 접촉으로 부모의 세균이 옮지 않도록" 보이지 않는 벽이 있다.

에밀리 곁에는 항상 에밀리의 손을 잡고 서 있는 자그마한 여자아이가 한 명 있었다. 그 아이의 부모는 한 번도 오지 않았다. 어느 날 가보니 그 아이는 없었다. "사람들이 걔를 로즈 코티지로 보냈어요." 에밀리가 소리를 질러 설명해주었다. "여기선 누구든 사랑하는 걸 싫어해요."

아이는 일주일에 한 번 편지를 썼다. 일곱 살짜리가 고심해서 쓴 글이었다. "저는 잘 지내요. 아기는 어때요. 내가 편지를 훌륭하게 잘 쓰면 별을 받을 수 이써요. 사랑해요." 하지만 별 같은 건 없었다. 우리는 이틀에 한 번씩 아이에게 편지를 썼다. 하지만 아이는 절대 편지를 손으로 만지거나 간직할 수 없었고, 오로지 들을 수만 있었다. 딱 한 번. "저희에게는 아이들이 개인 소지품을 보관할 수 있는 공간이 없습니다." 어느 일요일 서로 소리를 지르며 대화를 나누다 편지는 에밀리에게 매우 의미가 크며 에밀리는 자기 것을 간직하는 걸 너무나도 좋아하므로 아이가 편지와 카드를 보관할 수 있게 허락해달라고 애원하자 그들이 차분한 목소리로 내놓은 대답이었다.

방문할 때마다 에밀리는 더 약해졌다. 그 사람들은 우리에게 이렇게 말했다. "애가 먹질 않아요."

(이후 에밀리가 이런 말을 했다. 아침밥으로 안 익은 계란하고 덩어리진 옥수수죽을 줬어요. 난 입에 넣고 삼키진 않았어요. 맛있는 게 하나도 없었어요. 닭고기 줄 때를 빼면요.)

아이를 다시 집으로 데려오는 데 8개월이 걸렸다. 7파운드 줄었던 아이의 몸무게가 아주 조금 늘었다는 사실로 겨우 사회복지사를 설득할 수 있었다.

아이가 돌아오고 나서 나는 아이를 안아주고 사랑해주려고 애썼지만 아이의 몸은 뻣뻣했고 얼마 지나지 않아 아이는 나를 밀어냈다. 아이는 조금밖에 안 먹었다. 아이는 음식에, 그리고 내 생각엔 삶 자체에 구역질을 냈다. 아이의 몸은 민첩했고 명랑했고 스케이트를 타며 반짝거렸고 줄넘기를 하며 마치 공처럼 위아래로 팔짝팔짝 뛰었고 언덕을 날래게 오르기도 했다. 하지만 이것도 찰나일 뿐이었다.

그 애는 자기 외모가 걱정이었다. 마르고 머리칼이 어두운 색이었고 외국인 같았다. 당시 어린 여자애들은 아역 배우 셜리 템플(Shirley Temple)의 모형처럼 통통하고 금발이어야 했다. 아니 그래야 한다고 여겨졌다. 가끔 아이를 찾는 초인종 소리가 울리기도 했지만 집에 찾아와서 놀거나 친해 보이는 친구는 아무도 없었다. 아마도 우리가 이사를 너무 많이 다녀서일 것이다.

아이가 두 학기 동안 고통스러울 정도로 사랑했던 남자애가 한 명 있었다. 몇 달 후 아이는 내 지갑에서 동전을 훔쳐 그 애에게 사탕을 사줬다고 말했다. "걔는 감초 사탕을 제일 좋아해요. 그래서 매일 조금씩 갖다 줬어요. 그런데도 걔는 나보다 제니퍼를 더 좋아해요. 왜 그런 거예요, 엄마?" 답이 존재하지 않는 그런 질문이었다.

학교도 아이의 걱정거리였다. 말주변과 민첩함을 학습 능력으로 혼동하는 세계에서 아이는 말주변도 없고 민첩하지도 않았다. 과로로 짜증이 나 있는 선생님들에게 아이는 따라잡으려 노력하지만 결석을 너무 자주하는, 지나치게 성실한 "지진아"였다.

아프다는 아이의 말이 핑계일 때도 있었지만 나는 아이가 학교에 빠지도록 내버려뒀다. 엄격하게 그 애 동생들의 출석을 관리하는 지금의 내 모습과는 너무나도 다르다. 당시 나는 돈을 벌지 않았다. 아이를 또 한 명 낳았고, 나는 집에 있었다. 수전이 어느 정도 자란 후로는 가끔 수전도 학교에 가지 말라고 했다. 아이들 모두와 함께 있기 위해서였다.

에밀리는 천식이 있었다. 괴로워하는 아이의 거친 호흡은 이상하게도 평온한 소리가 되어 집안을 가득 채웠다. 나는 오래된 화장대 두 개와 그 애의 보물 상자를 침대 옆으로 가져다주었다. 그러면 아이는 상자에서 구슬과 귀걸이 한쪽, 병뚜껑과 조개껍질, 말린 꽃잎과 조약돌, 오래된 엽서와 오려둔 종이들 같은 온갖 종류의 잡동사니들을 골랐다. 그리고 수전과 함께 마을을 만들고 가구를 놓은 다음 작은 물건들이 그곳에 사는 사람인 것처럼 왕국 놀이를 했다.

하지만 그것도 에밀리와 수전이 평화롭게 지낼 때뿐이었다. 나는 둘 사이의 악의적 감정에서 물러서 있었다. 상처와 욕구 사이의 그 불균형 사이에서 나는 뭐라도 했어야 했다. 하지만 그 옛날 나는 너무 미숙했다.

다른 아이들도 서로 다툰다. 각각 한 명의 인간으로서 무언가를 필요로 하고, 요구하고, 상처를 주고, 원하는 걸 취한다. 하지만 에밀리와 수전 사이의, 아니 수전을 향한 에밀리의 분노는 마음속을 파고들며 좀먹었다. 둘의 관계는 겉으로는 너무 뻔해 보여도 사실은 뻔하지 않다. 둘째인 수전, 금발에 곱슬머리에 통통한 수전은 재빠르고 자기 생각을 잘 말하고 자신감이 있다. 외모나 행동의 모든 면에서 에밀리는 그렇지 않다. 수전은 에밀리가 소중하게 여기는 물건들을 건들지 않고는 못 참았다. 그렇게 에밀리의 물건을 잃어버리고 가끔은 어설프게 부서뜨리기도 했다. 수전은 친구들에게 농담도 하고 수수께끼도 내면서 박수를 받았지만 에밀리는 조용히 앉아 있었다(이후 에밀리가 내게 말했다. 그건 내가 지은 수수께끼였어요, 엄마. 내가 수전한테 말해준 거예요.) 수전은 에밀리보다 다섯 살 어렸지만 신체 발육 면에서는 에밀리와 일 년 정도밖에 차이가 나지 않았다.

나는 에밀리의 느린 발육이 기쁘다. 하지만 그건 에밀리와 또래 간의 차이를 더욱 벌려놓았고 에밀리는 괴로워했다. 그 애는 어린애들의 경쟁이라는 그 끔찍한 세계에 너무 취약했다. 멋을 부리고 과시하고 자신을 다른 사람과 끊임없이 비교하고 질투하는 세계 말이다. "저 적갈색 머리카락이 내 거였으면", "내 피부가 저랬으면..." 아이는 다른 사람과 다르게 생겼다는 이유로 스스로를 너무 많이 괴롭혔다. 너무 불안정했고, 말하기 전에 단어를 조심스럽게 골라야 했고, 끊임없이 신경을 썼다. 저 사람들은 나를 어떻게 생각할까? 무자비한 신체적 충동이 이 모든 걸 부풀리기 전이었는데도.

로니가 나를 찾는다. 오줌을 싼 아이의 기저귀를 갈아준다. 이제 아이가 이렇게 우는 일은 흔치 않다. 내 귀가 나의 것이 아닌 것처럼 항상 아이 울음소리에 시달리던 시기는 지나갔다. 나는 로니와 잠시 앉아 있다가 아이를 안아 들고 부드러운 한 줄기 빛이 흐르는 암회색 도시를 내다본다. "슈길리." 로니가 숨을 내쉬며 몸을 더 가까이 웅크린다. 아이를 다시 침대에 누여 재운다. 슈길리. 우스운 단어다. 에밀리에게서 시작된 우리 가족끼리의 단어. 아이가 만들어낸, 위안이라는 뜻의 단어.

에밀리는 이런저런 방식으로 자기 표시를 남긴다, 라고 소리 내어 말한다. 그리고 내 말에 깜짝 놀란다. 무슨 뜻이지? 내가 무엇을 그러모아서 설명하려 했던 거지? 나는 끔찍한 경제 성장 시대에 있었다. 전쟁의 시대였다. 기억이 잘 나지는 않는다. 나는 일을 하고 있었고, 에밀리의 동생이 넷이나 있었고, 에밀리를 위한 시간은 없었다. 그 애는 엄마가, 가정부가, 장 보는 사람이 되어 일을 도와야 했다. 그 애는 자기 표시를 남겨야만 했다. 도시락을 싸고, 머리를 빗기고, 코트와 신발을 찾고, 모두가 제시간에 학교나 탁아소에 가고, 아기를 유모차에 태우려고 애쓰는 위기의, 아니 거의 히스테리에 가까운 아침들. 그리고 언제나 어린애들이 무엇인가를 휘갈겨놓은 종이들, 수전이 보고 아무 데나 던져둔 책, 하지 않은 숙제가 있었다. 에밀리가 달려간 그 큰 학교에서 아이는 혼자였고 갈피를 못 잡았고 뒤떨어졌다. 수업 시간에는 준비 부족으로 힘들어했고 말을 더듬었고 자신이 없었다.

밤이 되어 아이들을 재우고 난 후에는 시간이 거의 없었다. 에밀리는 책들과 씨름했고 언제나 무언가를 먹었으며 (그 애가 우리 가족에게는 전설과도 같은 엄청난 식욕을 보인 시기가 이때다) 나는 다림질을 하거나 다음날 먹을 음식을 준비하거나 다른 나라로 파병된 빌에게 편지를 쓰거나 아기를 돌봤다. 가끔 에밀리는 나를 웃게 하기 위해, 아니면 본인의 절망으로 인해 학교에서 있었던 사건이나 사람 흉내를 내곤 했다.

한번은 내가 이렇게 말했던 것 같다. "이런 걸 학교 공연에서 해보면 어때?" 어느 날 아침 에밀리는 일터에 있는 내게 전화를 했다. 울고 있는 탓에 말을 거의 알아들을 수 없었다. "엄마, 나 해냈어요. 내가 차지했어요. 내게 1등을 줬어요. 사람들이 박수를 치고 또 치면서 나를 무대에서 떠나질 못하게 했어요."

순식간에 에밀리는 중요한 사람이 되었다. 그리고 그 전까지 익명성에 갇혀 있었던 것만큼이나 자기 특색에 갇혔다.

에밀리는 다른 고등학교, 심지어 대학교, 주 전체 행사에서까지 공연 요청을 받기 시작했다. 우리가 처음 공연을 보러 갔을 때 나는 공연을 시작하던 그 순간에만 그 애를 알아볼 수 있었다. 깡마르고 부끄러움이 많은 그 애는 숨이 막힐 정도로 커튼에 파묻혀 있었다. 하지만 그 다음에는, 저 사람이 에밀리라고? 그 장악력, 그 말주변, 갑작스럽게 터지는 웃음과 배꼽 빠지게 하는 연기, 그 마력, 그러고는 와자지껄 웃으며 발을 구르는 관객, 자기 삶에서 흔치 않은 이 귀중한 웃음을 떠나보내고 싶지 않은 마음들.

그 이후. 이런 재능을 가진 아이에겐 뭐라도 해줘야 한다. 하지만 돈도 없고 어떻게 해야 할지도 모르는데, 무엇을 할 수 있단 말인가? 우리는 모든 책임을 아이에게 넘겼다. 재능을 발휘되고 성장하기도 하지만 내면에서 휘몰아치다 막혀서 엉겨버리는 일도 잦다.

에밀리가 들어온다. 가볍고 우아한 발걸음으로 한 번에 두 칸씩 계단을 뛰어 올라온다. 오늘 밤 아이는 행복하다. 오늘 왜 전화가 걸려온 것인지는 몰라도 오늘 있었던 일 때문은 아니다.

"다림질 언제까지 할 거예요, 엄마? 화가 휘슬러는 자기 엄마가 흔들의자에 앉아 있는 모습을 그렸다는데, 아마 나는 다리미판 앞에 서 있는 엄마를 그릴까 봐요." 오늘은 에이미가 말이 많은 밤이다. 그 애는 접시에 얼굴을 박고 냉장고에서 꺼낸 음식을 먹으며 내게 시시콜콜한 일들을 이야기한다.

아이는 너무나도 사랑스럽다. 왜 당신은 내가 학교에 와야 한다고 생각하는가? 왜 걱정을 하는가? 아이는 길을 찾을 수 있을 것이다.

아이가 자러 2층으로 올라간다. "내일 아침에 나 깨우지 마세요." "하지만 중간고사 중인 줄 알았는데." "아, 그거요." 아이가 다시 내려와 내게 뽀뽀를 하며 대수롭지 않은 듯이 말한다. "핵전쟁 때문에 몇 년 안에 우리 모두 죽을 거예요. 그러니 중간고사 따위는 전혀 중요하지 않아요."

아이는 전에도 이 말을 한 적이 있다. 그 애는 정말로 그걸 믿는다. 하지만 나는 과거를 쭉 돌아보고 있었으므로, 한 명의 인간을 이루는 모든 것은 내게 너무나도 중요하고 의미가 크므로, 오늘밤은 아이의 농담을 참을 수가 없다.

나는 이 모든 걸 정리하지 않을 것이다. 가서 이렇게 말하지 않을 것이다. 그 애는 사람들이 많이 웃어주지 않는 아이였어요. 아이 아빠는 아이가 한 살도 되기 전에 우릴 떠났어요. 아이가 여섯 살이 될 때까지 일을 해야 했기 때문에 그동안 아이를 유아원에 보내거나 아이 아빠에게 맡겼어요. 몇 년 동안 아이는 자기가 싫어하는 곳에서 치료를 받았어요. 아이는 금발과 곱슬머리와 보조개를 선망하는 세상에서 머리칼이 어두웠고 말랐고 외국인 같아보였어요. 말주변을 높게 쳐주는 세상에서 느릿느릿했어요. 자신감이 넘치고 사랑스러운 아이가 아니라 불안해하는 아이였어요. 우리는 가난했고 맘 편히 자라날 수 있는 환경을 제공해주지 못했어요. 나는 어린 엄마였고, 집중하지 못하는 엄마였어요. 그 애의 동생들이 저를 끌어당기고 징징댔어요. 아이 여동생은 아이가 갖지 못한 모든 걸 가진 것처럼 보였어요. 아이에겐 제가 자기를 만지는 걸 원치 않았던 시기가 있었어요. 그 애는 자기 안에 너무 많은 걸 눌러 담았고, 그 애의 삶은 자기 안에 너무 많은 것을 눌러 담아야만 하는 그런 삶이었어요. 저는 너무 늦게 깨달았어요. 아이는 너무 많은 것을 감당하고 있기에 아마 의지가 강하지 못할 거예요. 그 애는 자기 시대의, 불경기의, 전쟁의, 두려움의 아이예요.

아이를 내버려두자. 아이 안에 있는 것이 꽃피지 못하도록. 하지만 그렇다고 얼마나 사라지겠는가? 그래도 삶에 필요한 것은 충분히 남아 있을 것이다. 그저 아이가 알게 끔 도와주기를. 아이가 알아야 할 이유를 만들어주기를. 너는 다리미판에 놓여 있는, 다리미 앞에 무력한 이 옷가지보다 더 강하다는 사실을.

11. 헛간 방화(Barn Burning)

• 윌리엄 포크너(William Faulkner)

치안재판이 열리고 있는 상점에서는 치즈 냄새가 풍기었다. 물건이 빼빽하게 들어찬 방 뒤 구석 작은 못 통에 웅크리고 앉아 있는 소년은 치즈 냄새니 그 밖에 다른 냄새가 나는 것을 알았다. 소년은 앉은 자리에서 땅딸막하고 단단한데다가 동적(動的)인 형태를 가진 통조림이 꽉 들어찬 열 지은 선반을 바라다보았다. 이 통조림 레이블을 보니 식욕이 일었다. 무슨 뜻인지 통 모르는 레이블의 글자를 본 때문이 아니라 새빨간 짐승의 그림이나 은빛 곡선을 이룬 생선 그림을 보았기 때문이다. 아무튼 치즈 냄새는 분명히 냄새 맡은 것이었고 밀봉한 고기 냄새는 또 다른 하나의 꾸준한 냄새에 섞이어 가끔가다 슬쩍 스쳐가는 바람을 타고 그의 뱃속까지 스며드는 듯했다. 또 하나의 냄새란 주로 절망과 비애, 말하자면 옛날부터의 강렬한 기질 때문에 으레 생기기 마련인 공포의 느낌인지도 모른다. 보안관이 앉아 있는 책상은 보이지 않고 그 책상 앞에 소년의 아버지와 그의 적(敵) (우리의 적! 하고 그는 바로 그 절망적인 느낌에서 생각했다. 우리의 적! 나의 적이며 아버지의 적이기도 한! 그는 나의 아버지야!) 이 서 있었다. 그러나 소년은 세 사람 중 두 사람이 이야기하는 소리는 들을 수 있었다. 그의 아버지는 아직 한 마디도 입을 열지 않았던 것이다.

"그런데 무슨 증거라도 있소. 해리스씨?"

"벌써 말씀 드렸습죠. 그놈의 돼지가 저의 밭에 들어 왔기에 그 놈을 잡아서 그에게 돌려보냈죠. 그는 돼지를 가두어둘 울이 없었다오. 그래 그에게 단단히 말해두고 앞으로 조심하라고 말했죠. 그 다음 번엔 그 돼지를 저의 돼지우리에다 넣어두었죠. 그가 돼지를 찾으러 왔더군요. 그래 돼지우리를 수리하리만큼 넉넉하게 철사줄을 주었던 것이죠. 그 다음 번엔 돼지를 잡아 가두어 보관해 놓고는 그의 집으로 말을 달려 가 보았더니, 글쎄 제가 준 철사줄은 그냥 틀에 감긴 채 뜰에 내버려지고 있더군요. 그래서 돼지보관 요금으로 일불을 지불하면 돼지를 도로 찾을 수 있다고 말했죠. 그날 저녁 어떤 흑인이 돈을 가지고 와서 돼지를 찾아갔었죠. 그는 낯선 흑인이었소. 그런데 그 흑인이 '나무와 말먹이풀은 한꺼번에 타버릴 거라구요.' 그날 밤 저의 외양간은 타버리고 말았죠. 외양간에 든 가축은 끌어냈습니다만 외양간은 깨끗이 잃고 말았죠."

"그 흑인은 지금 어디 있소? 그자를 잡아 두고 있소?"

"낯선 흑인이라 말하지 않았소. 지금 어찌 됐는지 통 알 길이 없죠."

"그러나 그건 증거가 못되오. 증거가 못되는 걸 모르겠소?"

"저기 저 소년을 이리 좀 데려오시오. 저 애는 압니다." 그 순간 소년은 그 사나이가 자기 형을 가리키고 한 말인 줄 알았으나 "아닙니다. 작은 애 말이요. 저 소년 말이요"라고 곧 해리스씨는 말했다. 나이에 비해 작은 편이고, 아버지처럼 작달막하고 억세게 생긴 그 소년은, 그의 작은 키에도 짧은데다 꿰매고 낡아빠진 바지를 입고 웅크리고 앉아 있었다. 빗질을 하지 않아 빳빳이 일어선 갈색의 머리칼에 폭풍우의 비바람처럼 거친 회색의 눈을 갖고 있었다. 그는 저 자신과 책상 있는 쪽 사이에 있는 사람들, 그리고 그 사람들이 짓고 있는 찌푸린 얼굴의 행렬을 바라보았다. 그 행렬 맨 끝에 안경을 쓰고 초라하게 칼라도 달지 않은 흰 머리칼의 사나이가 손짓을 하며 부르는 것을 보았다. 그가 바로 보안관이었다. 소년은 자기의 맨발 밑에 마루바닥이 있는 것 같이 느껴지진 않았다. 자기 쪽을 쳐다보는 무섭게 생긴 사람들의 압력을 뚜렷이 받아가며 걸음을 옮기는 듯했다. 어떤 심문을 받기 위해서가 아니라 이사를 하기 위해서 흑색 나들이옷을 걸친 말쑥한 그의 아버지는 그를 쳐다보지도 않았다. '아버지는 나더러 거짓말을 하라는 거야.' 미칠듯한 비애와 절망을 느끼며 그는 또 이렇게 생각했다. '그래 나는 거짓말을 잘 이어대야 해!'

"이름이 뭐지?" 하고 보안관이 물었다.

"커넬 사토리스 스노우프스에요." 라고 소년은 나직이 대답했다.

"이것 봐!" 하고 보안관은 말했다. "좀 더 큰소리로 말해 봐. 커넬 사토리스라고? 이 지방에서 커넬 사토리스라고 이름을 가진 사람이면 누구나 진실만을 말하지 않고는 배길 수 없다고 생각하는데 안 그런가?" 소년은 아무 말도 없었다. '적이야! 적!' 그는 생각했다. 잠시 동안 소년은 보안관의 얼굴이 좀 부드러워졌다는 것도 알 수 없었고, 또 보안관이 해리스라는 사나이에게 '이 소년을 심문해 볼까요?' 라고 말했을 때 그의 말소리가 좀 난처한 듯이 들리었다는 것도 알아차리지 못했다. 그러나 말소리는 들렸다. 그리고 그 후 얼마 동안 좁고 작은 상점 안은 쥐죽은 듯 조용하고 벅찬 숨소리만 들려올 뿐, 그것은 마치 그가 포도덩굴의 끝마디를 잡아쥐고 계곡 너머로 휠휠 날아가다 한창 높이에 이르자, 시간에 무게없이 일순간의 오래 끈 마비된 인력에 사로잡힌 것과 같았다.

"아니 그만둡시다." 라고 해리스는 폭발하듯 격하게 말했다. "제기랄 것! 그 놈을 이 고장에서 내쫓아버리세요!" 비로소 유동적인 세계인 시간이 다시 그의 발밑으로 닥쳐왔고, 따라서 치즈 냄새니 밀봉한 고기 냄새, 공포와 절망, 그리고 예부터의 피의 슬픔, 이런 따위를 통하여 말소리는 다시금 들려왔다.

"이 사건은 종말 짓겠소. 스노우프스씨, 당신에겐 유죄를 찾아낼 수 없으나 견책을 할 수 있소. 그것은 이 고장을 떠나 다신 돌아오지 말라는 것이요."

그때에 비로소 그의 부친이 입을 열었다. 그의 말소리는 별로 박력도 없어 쌀쌀하고 거칠고 밋밋했다. "그러지요. 나도 그 따위 사람들 틈에 끼어 이런 곳에서 살 생각은 없소이다." 그는 누구에게다 말하는 것도 아니었다. 그저 분명치 않게 비열한 말을 몇 마디 뇌까렸다.

"좋소!" 하고 보안관은 말했다. "그럼 짐마차를 준비하고 어둡기 전에 이 고장을 떠나가오. 공소사건(控訴事件)은 취하하겠소."

그의 부친은 되돌아섰다. 소년은 흑색 코트를 입고 뻣뻣이 걸어가는 아버지 뒤를 따라갔다. 억센 몸집의 부친은 30년 전에 말 한 필을 훔쳐 타고 도망가다가 남부연방(南部聯邦)의 헌병의 총탄에 맞아 발뒤꿈치를 다쳤기 때문에 약간 뻣뻣한 걸음걸이로 걷고 있었다. 그런데 소년의 형이 군중들 틈에서 나타났기 때문에 그는 두 사람 뒤를 따라갔다. 형은 아버지보다 키는 크지 않으나 뚱뚱한 편이었고 담배를 천천히 씹고 있었다. 소년이 두 줄로 늘어선 무서운 얼굴을 한 사나이들의 중간으로 해서 상점 밖으로 나와 초라한 복도를 지나 계단을 내려 오월의 가벼운 먼지를 덮어쓴 몇 마리의 개와 제법 굵직한 애들 사이로 지나갈 때 '방화자!' 하고 소곤거리는 소리가 들려왔다.

그는 다시 정신이 아찔해져서 뭐가 뭔지 분간할 수 없었다. 새빨간 몽롱 속에서 어떤 얼굴이 보였다. 달처럼 둥글고 만월보다 더 큰 얼굴이었다. 그 얼굴의 주인공은 소년의 몸집보다 한 배 반이나 더 큰 몸집이었다. 몽롱한 의식 속에서도 그는 그 얼굴 쪽으로 뛰어 들어갔다. 그의 머리가 땅에 부닥쳐도 아무런 쇼크나 타격도 느끼지 않았다. 그래서 기를 쓰고 다시 덤벼들었으나 이번에도 아무런 타격을 느끼지 않았으며 피도 맛보지 않았다. 죽자고 내빼는 다른 아이를 쫓기 위해 기를 쓰며 일어서서 그 뒤를 쫓았다. 그때 그의 부친이 그를 꽉 잡아 쥐고 뒤로 내제쳤다. "가서 짐마차에 올라 타!" 거칠고 쌀쌀한 음성이 그의 머리 위에서 들려왔다.

짐마차는 길 건너편 아카시나무와 뽕나무 수풀 속에서 대기하고 있었다. 나들이옷을 입은 덩치가 큰 그의 두 누이와 비단옷을 입고 넓적한 모자를 덮어쓴 어머니와 이모들은 벌써 짐마차에 올라타 소년의 기억에도 생생한 수십 점의 하찮은 이삿짐 유물들 사이에 제멋대로 걸터앉아 있었다. 이삿짐 유물이란 쭈그러진 난로, 부서진 침대, 의자, 그리고 진주층(眞珠層)이 들어박히기는 했으나, 기억에도 없는 어느 지난날의 2시 14분을 가리키다 선 채 가지 않고 있는 시계 따위였는데, 이것은 그의 어머니가 시집올 때 가져온 혼숫감이었다. 어머니는 울고 있었다. 허나 어머니는 소년을 보자 옷소매로 얼굴을 닦고는 짐마차에서 내리기 시작했다.

"올라가 있어요!" 하고 아버지가 말했다.

"저애 어디 다쳤나봐요. 물을 좀 얻어와서 얼굴을…."

"짐마차에 올라가 있으라니까." 라고 그의 아버지는 말했다. 뒷문으로 해서 그도 마차에 올라탔다. 아버지는 이미 형이 자리잡고 앉아 있는 운전 자리에 걸터앉아서 말라빠진 노새말을 껍질 벗긴 버들가지 회초리로 사납게 그러나 악을 쓰지 않고 두 번 갈겼다. 자학적인 것은 아니었다. 이것은 바로 후세의 그의 자손들이 자동차의 발동을 걸기 전에 제자리에서 몰았다 멈추었다 하면서 엔진을 못살게 구는 성질과 똑같은 것이었다. 짐마차는 움직이며 앞으로 나갔다. 심각한 얼굴로 바라보고 서 있는 마을 사람들과 더불어 상점은 점점 뒤로 멀어지고 큰길의 모퉁이를 돌자 상점은 보이지 않게 되었다. '영원히 안녕' 소년은 생각했다. '아마 그는 지금 만족하고 있으리라! 우리를 이렇게 보내버리고!' 혼잣말이라도 소리를 내지 않으려고 그만두었다. 어머니의 손이 그의 어깨에 와 닿았다.

"어디 다치지 않았니?" 어머니가 말했다.

"아뇨, 다치진 않았어요. 내버려두세요."

"상처가 말라붙기 전에 피를 좀 닦아낼 수 없겠니?"

"오늘밤에 닦겠어요. 제발 그냥 내버려두세요, 어머니!" 하고 그는 말했다.

짐마차는 계속 움직이고 있었다. 소년은 어디로 가는 것인지 모른다. 언제나 그렇듯이 하루고 이틀이고 혹은 사흘이고 이렇게 가기만 하면 반드시 아무데고 집이란 것이 있기 마련이니 아무도 목적지를 아는 사람이 없었고 물어보려고 하는 사람도 없었다. 혹시 그의 아버지만은 벌써 다른 농장에서 농사를 지을 수 있게 미리 마련해놓았을지도 모른다. 그는 다시 생각을 멈추지 않을 수 없었다. 그의 아버지는 노상 그랬다. 이익이 적어도 반반일 때에 그의 늑대와도 같은 결단성이니 용맹성에는 낯모르는 사람도 감동케 하는 무엇이 깃들고 있었다. 마치 낯모르는 사람들이 그의 잠재적인 탐욕적 격렬성에서 의지감이라기보다 오히려 그 자신의 행동의 정당성을 확신하고 있는 그의 격렬성이 그와 이해관계를 같이하는 모든 사람에게 유리하리라는 느낌을 받은 것처럼.

그날밤 그들은 참나무와 떡갈나무의 숲속, 샘이 흐르는 곳에서 야숙했다. 밤은 아직 추워 근처 울타리에서 뽑아온 가람대를 짧게 잘라 차가운 공기를 막고자 불을 피웠다. 작은 모닥불, 알뜰하면서도 인색한 불이었다. 꽁꽁 얼어붙은 추운 날씨에도 그의 아버지는 이런 불을 피우는 버릇이 있었다. 소년이 더 나이가 들었더라면 이런 점을 눈치채고, 왜 큰 불을 피우지 않는가 하고 이상히 여겼을 것이다. 전쟁터에서 볼 수 있는 황폐한 광경과 끔찍한 일들을 목격했을 뿐만 아니라 선천적으로 자기 소유가 아닌 물건이라면 닥치는 대로 처분해버리는 그런 성격을 이어받은 사람으로서 왜 눈에 띄는 대로 모조리 불태워버리지 않을까? 그리고나선 그는 한 발자국 더 나아가서 그것이 바로 그 이유라고 생각했을 것이다. 그 인색한 모닥불은 그의 아버지가 말 떼 지어 끌고 다니면서 모든 사람들의 눈을 피해 수풀 속으로만 들어가 살던 지난 사년 동안(그 말을 언제나 잡아온 말이라고 그는 말했다) 보낸 밤마다의 생명의 결실이었던 것이다. 소년이 좀 더 나이가 들었다면 참다운 동기를 알아냈을 것이리라. 그 불의 성분은 깊이 깃들어 있는 그의 아버지의 성격의 주요 성분을 말하는 것이다. 마치 강철의 성분이나 화약의 성분이 다른 사람들의 성격을 각각 나타내듯이 본래부터 지니고 있는 자기 성격의 자태를 보존하려는 하나의 방패인지도 모른다. 이것마저 없었다면 살아있다는 보람마저 없었을 것이며, 이로써 그는 존경을 받게 되는 것이고 또한 적절히 처리되는 것이다.

소년은 아직 이런 일까지는 생각이 미치지 못하였으나 이때까지 살아오는 동안에 그는 언제나 이와 똑같은 빈약한 불꽃만을 보아 왔던 것이다. 그는 모닥불 옆에서 저녁이랍시고 한 술 떠먹고나서는 쇠판에 기대어 졸고 있는데 아버지가 불러대는 것이었다. 그는 또 다시 뻣뻣하고 꼴불견인 절름발이 아버지의 뒷모습을 따라 언덕을 올라 다시 별빛 은은한 큰 길까지 와서 거기서 되돌아 서자 아버지의 큼직한 몸집과 얼굴은 보이지 않았으나 별을 배경으로 한 아버지의 시꺼먼 모습을 볼 수 있었다. 그 모습은 아버지를 위해서 만든 것이 아닌 프록 코트의 쇠로 만든 주름의 철판에서 오려낸 것처럼 까맣고 편편하고 핏기 없고 메마른 모습이었다. 그리고 그 음성은 양철소리처럼 거칠고 힘이 없었다.

"너 그놈들한테 이야기를 다 털어놓을 뻔했지, 특히 그자에게다 다 말해버릴 뻔했단 말이다." 소년은 대답하진 않았으나 그래도 꽤 세게 바로 상점 앞에서 두 마리의 노새를 후려갈긴 것처럼 말에 달라붙은 파리를 잡으려고 회초리로 내리갈기는 것과 꼭 같았다. 그의 말투에는 아무런 두려움도 노여움도 없었다. "너도 이젠 차차 어른이 돼가니 뭣 좀 알아야겠어. 너의 핏줄기를 따를 일을 좀 알아야겠단 말이다. 그렇잖으면 너를 받들어 줄 핏줄기를 갖지 못할 테니 말이다. 오늘 아침 거기 있던 놈들 중 그 어느 놈을 믿을 수 있다고 생각하나? 그놈들은 내가 속인 것을 알고 있기 때문에 나를 못살게 할 기회만 노리고 있는 걸 모르느냐, 응?" 20년 후에 와서 소년은 스스로 자기 자신에게 이렇게 말했으리라. "그 사람들은 진실과 정의를 바랐을 뿐이라고 내가 말했더라면 아버지는 나를 또 한 번 후려갈겼을 거야."라고. 그러나 소년은 아무 대꾸도 하지 않았다. 울고 있는 것도 아니고 그저 그 자리에 서 있기만 했다.

"대답해 봐." 그의 아버지가 말했다.

"그렇습니다." 소년은 나지막하게 대답했다. 그의 아버지는 돌아섰다.

"가서 자. 내일이면 그곳에 도착할 거야."

다음날 그들은 그곳에 도착했다. 오후에 들어서자 소년이 열 살이라는 나이를 먹는 동안에 늘 짐마차를 그 앞에 멈추게 하던 십여 채의 집과 별 차이가 없는, 페인트칠도 하지 않은 어떤 두 칸 방 집 앞에 짐마차를 멈추었다. 어머니와 아주머니는 지난 번 십 여 차례의 이사 때와 마찬가지로 짐마차에서 내려 짐을 부리기 시작하였다. 그런데도 두 누이와 아버지, 그리고 형은 그대로 자리에 눌러앉아 있었다.

"돼지우리 만도 못하구나, 얘." 하고 두 누이 중 하나가 말했다.

"천만에, 이만해도 훌륭하지. 너도 정을 붙이게 될걸. 자리에서 일어나 엄마와 함께 짐을 부리란 말이야."라고 아버지가 말했다. 두 누이는 값싼 리본을 펄럭이면서 커다란 몸짓으로 느릿느릿 내렸다. 그 중 한 누이는 엉망으로 흐트러진 마차 밑바닥에서 망가진 등잔을, 또 한 누이는 낡아빠진 빗자루를 끌어내렸다. 아버지는 말고삐를 큰 아들에게 넘겨주고 마차 바퀴로 해서 더듬더듬 내리기 시작했다. "짐을 다 부리거든 말을 외양간으로 가져다 두고 먹이를 줘." 이렇게 말한 다음 "날 좀 따라와." 하고 말하는 것이었다. 그는 처음엔 형을 보고 하는 소린 줄로 알았다.

"저요?" 소년이 되물었다.

"그래 너야."

"여보!" 그의 어머니가 말했다. 아버지는 걸음을 멈추고 돌아보았다. 숱이 많고 뻣뻣한 회색의 눈썹 아래엔 성미 급하게 쳐다보는 눈초리가 있었다.

"내일부터 앞으로 팔 개월 동안 여러 가지로 돌보아 줄 그 사람을 좀 만나볼까 해."

그들은 큰 길 쪽으로 도로 걸어 올라갔다. 일주일 전만 해도 아니 바로 어제 전만 해도 어디로 가느냐고 물어보기도 했겠건만 지금은 그렇잖았다. 어제 밤까지만 해도 아버지는 그를 때리곤 했으나 그 후 때린 이유를 설명하는 일은 전연 없었던 것이다. 마치 자기를 때리는 일, 그리고 소리소리 지르는 아버지의 고함소리는 여전히 쟁쟁하게 울려왔으나 그 뒤에 오는 적막은 자기가 아직 어리다고 하는 무서운 핸디캡 이외에는 아무것도 드러내지 않았으며, 그가 이 세상을 마음대로 날지 못할 만큼 무겁긴 하나 지상에 발을 단단히 디뎌 이에 저항하고 이의 여러 가지 사건의 방향을 바꾸게 하리만큼 무겁지 않은 그의 몇 해라는 가벼운 무게를 반향하고 있는 것 같았다.

얼마 안 가서 곧 참나무·이깔나무 그리고 여러 가지 꽃피는 나무들의 수풀과 관목들이 보였는데, 어쩐지 그 속에 집이 있음직하였으나 아직 그 집은 보이지 않았다. 그들은 인동초와 체로키 장미가 우거진 울타리를 지나 두 개의 벽돌기둥 사이로 흔들이면 열리는 대문까지 왔다. 그 순간 소년은 아버지 생각이고 공포고 절망이고 뭐고 잊어버리고 말았다. 여전히 걷고만 있는 그의 아버지 생각이 불시에 다시 일어났어도 공포와 절망은 되살아오지 않았다. 왜냐하면 여태까지 열두 번이나 이사를 했건만 농장이라야 얼마 안되고 밭도 적고 집도 작은 그런 메마른 고장에서만 살았을 뿐이지 이런 집은 통 구경한 일이 없었기 때문이었다. 새로 생긴 집은 재판소만큼이나 크군! 그는 물결처럼 파도치는 평화와 기쁨을 느끼면서 혼자 가만히 생각했다. 왜 자기가 이런 생각을 하게 되는지 소년은 아직 어려서 그 까닭을 말로 표현할 수는 없었지마는, 누구나 그(은근히 자기 아버지를 말한다)에게서 아무런 해도 받지 않을 거야. 이러한 평화와 기쁨이 그들 생활의 일부를 이루고 있는 사람들이라면 그의 손에서 벗어날 거야. 그가 뭐라 해도 그것은 윙윙대는 벌 — 약간 따끔하게 찌르고 나면 그것뿐인 벌 — 그런 정도에 지나지 않을 거야. 지금 이 집에 속하고 있는 외양간이니 곳간 그리고 마구간조차 그가 꾸며낼지 모르는 보잘 것 없는 불꽃쯤은 아랑곳하지 않는 이 매력적인 평화와 위엄…. 이 평화와 기쁨도 아버지의 뻣뻣하고 검은 뒷모습을 한 번도 크게 보이게 하지는 않았으며, 듬직하게 서 있는 기둥을 배경으로 하여 해가 만일 옆으로 비친다면 그림자도 던지지 않을 듯 얇다란 양철에서 아무렇게나 잘라낸 무슨 스미지 않는 성질을 전보다 더욱 많이 지니고 있어 이집 때문에 적어 보이지도 않는 그 뻣뻣하고 가련한 절름발이의 모습을 쳐다보자, 일순 조수가 밀려나가 듯 사라지고 말았다. 한참 바라보다가 소년은 아버지가 걷고 있는 방향이 조금도 옆으로 빗나가지 않는다는 것을 알았다. 차도에 서 있던 말이 금세 떨어뜨린 말똥 무더기를 조금만 발걸음을 옆으로 옮기면 얼마든지 피할 수 있는데도 그는 그냥 똑바로 밟고 지나가는 것이었다. 이 집 생각에 매혹되어 걷고 있는 동안 그는 자기 생각을 말로써 나타낼 수는 없었지만, 그러나 혹시 바랄 수도 있겠지 하는 기대가 그만 순식간에 사라지고 말았다. 부러워하거나 아깝게 여기는 그런 마음이 아니었고 더군다나 앞에서 쇳덩이같이 검은 코트를 입고 걸어가는 아버지의 탐욕적이며 질투적인 노여움 — 소년은 전연 모르는 — 따위의 마음은 추호도 없었다. '아버지도 그렇게 느낄 거야. 아버지를 그렇게 될 수밖에 없을는지 모르는 것과 좀 다르게 할지도 몰라.'

　그들은 주랑현관(柱廊玄關)을 지났다. 널판자로 된 마룻바닥까지 왔을 때 몸집을 움직이는 동작과는 전혀 어울리지도 않는, 또박또박 정확한 시계바늘의 소리와도 같은 아버지의 발걸음 소리를 들을 수 있었으며, 하얗게 칠한 현관 문 앞에 서 있는 아버지의 모습은 초라하게 보이지도 않았다. 심술궂고 욕심이 많은 듯 보이는 적은 몸집이기는 했으나 어떤 옷차림도 — 납작하고 넓적한 모자, 그전에도 검은 빛깔의 포프린 외출 코트였으나 이젠 하도 오래 입어서 번들번들 하여 마치 낡아빠진 집에 매달려 있는 파리의 껍질같이 푸릇푸릇한 윤이 나는 코트, 걷어 올린 너무 큰 소매, 꼬부라진 손톱처럼 쳐 올린 손 — 이런 것 때문에 그의 몸집이 대조적으로 초라하게 보이지는 않았다. 문이 지체 없이 활짝 열린 것으로 보아 분명히 흑인이 그들의 동정을 처음부터 살피고 있었음에 틀림없구나 하고 소년은 생각했다. 그 흑인은 흰 머리가 약간 섞이고 린넨 쟈켓을 입고 있었는데, 자기 몸으로 문을 가로막고 서서, "여보 백인! 여기 들어오려면 신발을 털고 닦으쇼. 소령(少領)님은 지금 댁에 계시지 않습니다." 라고 말했다.

　"비켜 서! 이놈의 검둥이." 그다지 흥분한 목소리는 아니었으나 그의 아버지는 이렇게 뇌까리면서 문을 박차고 흑인을 밀어제치면서 모자를 쓴 채 안으로 들어갔다. 소년은 문 입구 기둥에 묻은 신발자국에 눈이 갔다. 또 바닥에 깔아놓은 연한 빛깔의 양탄자 위엔 또박또박 걸어간 신발자국이 고스란히 나타나 있는 것도 보았다. 그 발자국은 소년이 남긴 발자국보다 두 배나 더 세게 꽉꽉 밟아놓은 듯했다. 어디선가 뒤에서 흑인이, "루라 아가씨! 루라 아가씨!" 하고 소리를 지르고 있었다. 날씬한 곡선을 그리는 양탄자를 깔아놓은 계단과 샹들리에에 달린 장식품의 화려한 광채, 그리고 금빛의 그림들이 발산하는 은은한 빛깔들 때문에 흐뭇한 마음의 격동을 일으킨 듯 어리둥절한 소년은 급히 서두르면서 달려오는 발자국 소리와 함께 어떤 여인이 나타난 것을 보았다. 생전 처음 보는 여인이었다. 목에는 레이스가 달린 회색의 반들반들한 가운을 걸치고, 허리엔 앞치마를 둘렀고, 옷소매는 뒤로 걷어 젖히고 손에 묻은 케이크 혹은 비스킷의 밀가루 반죽을 수건으로 닦아내면서 현관방에까지 나오고 있었다. 그 여인은 소년의 아버지를 거들떠보지도 않고 아주 의아스러운 듯 깜짝 놀란 표정으로 금빛 양탄자에 묻은 발자국을 내려다볼 뿐이었다.

　"들어오지 못하게 했습죠. 저 사람보고…." 흑인은 애원하는 듯이 말했다.

"제발 나가 주세요." 여인은 떨리는 목소리로 말했다. "드 스페인 소령은 지금 안 계십니다. 어서 나가주세요."

그의 아버지는 두 번 다시 말하지 않았다. 여인을 쳐다보기조차 하지 않았다. 그는 모자를 덮어쓴 채 양탄자 한복판에 뻣뻣이 서 있을 뿐 집 내부를 좀 유심히 살펴보려 할 때만 투명한 빛깔의 두 눈위로 철회색이 뒤섞인 텁수룩한 검은 눈썹이 바르르 떨릴 뿐이었다. 여전히 신중한 태도를 지닌 채 그는 몸을 돌렸다. 소년은 그의 아버지가 온전한 다리에다 중심을 두고 몸을 되돌리는 것을 지켜보았고, 질질 끄는 뻣뻣한 발이 반원형을 그리면서 점점 희미해지는 기다란 자국을 남기고 있는 것이 눈에 띄었다. 그의 아버지는 절대로 그 발자국을 바라보려 하지도 않는 듯한 번도 양탄자를 내려다보지도 않았다. 흑인은 문을 잡아 당겼다. 뒤에선 무슨 소린지 알아들을 수 없는 여인의 발작적인 울부짖음이 들리고 문이 쾅 하고 닫히었다. 아버지는 층층대 꼭대기에 잠시 멈추어 그 가장자리에다 장화를 깨끗이 문질렀다. 대문간까지 나오자 그는 다시 걸음을 멈추었다. 그는 뻣뻣한 발로 꼿꼿이 버티어 서서는 집 쪽을 돌아다보았다. "깨끗하고 하얗고, 그렇잖아?" 하고 말했다. "애쓴 보람이지, 흑인이 애쓴 거야. 희긴 한데 아직 주인에겐 흡족하지 않을 거야 아마. 그는 백인이 와서 좀 애를 써주었으면 하고 바라고 있을 걸!"

두 시간 후 소년은 집 뒤뜰에서 나무를 쪼개고 있었다. 집안에는 어머니와 아주머니, 그리고 두 누이(아니 두 누이는 아니고 어머니와 아주머니인 것을 알았다. 이렇게 거리가 떨어져 있고 또 사방 벽으로 둘러싸여 있어도 두 계집애들의 따분하고도 요란스런 말소리는 고칠 수 없는 게으른 타성을 발산하고 있었으니까 말이다)는 저녁을 준비하느라고 난롯불을 일으키고 있었다. 그때 말굽소리가 들려왔다. 린넨 옷을 입고 밤색 털의 날씬한 말을 탄 사람을 보았고, 역시 밤색의 살찐 마차용 말을 타고 뒤따르는 젊은 흑인의 앞자리에 둘둘 말아놓은 양탄자가 눈에 띄자 그가 누구인지 벌써 알아차렸던 것이다. 흥분한데다 노기를 띤 흑인의 얼굴 표정은 사라지고 그대로 말을 전속력으로 몰아 그의 아버지와 형이 기울어진 의자에 앉아 있는 집 모퉁이를 지나갔다. 그리고 조금 후 소년이 도끼를 내리칠까 말까 할 때 말굽소리가 다시 들리더니 그 밤색의 말이 뜰 밖으로 도로 달려 나가는 것을 보았다. 그의 아버지는 두 누이들 중의 한 누이의 이름을 불러대더니 얼마 안 있어 그 누이는 둘둘 말은 양탄자의 한쪽 끝을 잡아 쥐고 땅바닥을 질질 끌면서 부엌에서 뒷걸음치며 나타났는데 그 뒤에 다른 누이도 따라 나왔다.

"같이 나르지 않으려면 가서 물그릇이라도 준비해." 라고 한 누이가 먼저 말했다.

"요런 사티 년! 물그릇을 어쩌라고?" 하고 다음 누이가 소리쳤다. 그의 아버지는 비열한 언쟁을 혼내어 주려는 듯 문간에 나타났다. 이런 비열한 언쟁과는 정반대로, 부드럽고 얌전하여 하나 나무랄 데 없는 거룩한 엄마의 모습, 아무런 영문도 모르고 그저 그의 어깨너머로 불안하게 엿보고만 있던 어머니의 모습, 그것마저 욕설로 대해주려는 듯이.

"나두란 말이야 버쩍 처들고." 라고 그의 아버지는 말했다. 두 누이는 일부러 꾸물거리면서 마지못해 허리를 굽는 것이었다. 허리를 굽혀 보니 색이 바란 옷이 아주 크게 벌어지고 싸구려 리본이 펄럭이었다.

"내가 만일 프랑스로부터 쭉 오는 동안에 잘 보관해서 끔찍하게 여기는 그런 양탄자를 갖고 있다면 사람들이 드나들면서 발로 밟을 그런 장소에는 아예 깔아놓지 않을 텐데." 하고 처음 누이가 말했다. 그들은 둘이서 양탄자를 들어올렸다.

"여보 내가 할 테요." 하고 어머니가 말했다.

"당신도 가서 저녁이나 짓구려. 내가 돌볼 테니." 하고 아버지가 말했다.

장작을 쌓아 올려놓은 틈을 통하여 소년은 오후 내내 그들을 살펴보고 있었다. 양탄자를 물이 펄펄 끓고 있는 솥 옆 땅바닥에 쫙 펼쳐 놓아 있었다. 두 누이는 도무지 하기 싫은 일을 억지로 하는 듯 무기력한 모양을 지으며 양탄자 위에 허리를 굽히고 있었다. 아버지는 한 마디의 음성을 높이지 않고도 빈틈없이 엄격한 태도로 그들을 조리 있게 부려먹고 있었다. 소년은 집에서 만든 거친 잿물이 솥에서 끓고 있는 냄새를 맡을 수 있었다. 어머니는 문간에 와서 걱정스런 표정이라기보다 거의 절망적인 표정으로 그저 보고만 있었다. 아버지가 돌아서는 것이 보였다. 그래서 소년도 도끼질을 시작하는 척하면서 옆 눈으로 슬쩍 살펴보니 아버지는 납작한 돌조각을 땅에서 주워 자세히 들여다보더니 물 솥 쪽으로 되돌아서는 것이 보였다. "여보, 제발 그러지 마세요. 제발, 여보."

　이럭저럭 소년도 하던 일을 다 마쳤다. 날은 어두워졌다. 벌써 쏙독새 소리가 들려왔다. 오후의 식사에서 먹다 남은 찬 음식을 가족들이 나누어먹고 있으리라 생각되는 방안에서는 웬일인지 커피 냄새가 났다. 소년은 집안으로 들어갔다. 커피를 마시고 있는 것은 아마 화로에 불이 남아 있으니까 그러려니 하고 소년은 짐작했다. 화로 앞의 두 개의 의자 등 위에다 양탄자를 널어놓고 있었다. 아버지의 발자국은 없어졌다. 그러나 그 발자국이 있던 자리는 소인국(小人國)에서 사용하는 제초기로 군데군데 밀어놓은 것처럼 화암석이 타다 남은 모양 같은 것이 길쭉하고 희미하게 보였다.

　모두들 찬 음식을 먹고 있는 동안에도 양탄자는 거기 그대로 걸려 있었다. 식사 후 두 칸 방에서 제각기 제멋대로 흩어져 잠자리에 들었다. 어머니는 침대 — 물론 그의 아버지도 나중엔 그 침대에 눕지만 — 에로 갔다. 형은 다른 침대를 차지하고 그 자신은 아주머니 그리고 누이와 함께 마룻바닥에 깐 짚방석에 누웠다. 아버지는 아직 잠자리에 들어가지 않았다. 소년이 마지막 기억하고 있는 것은 양탄자 위에 엎드려 들여다보고 있는 거친 모자와 코트의 그림자였다. 사람의 윤곽을 나타내는 그 그림자가 소년을 들여다볼 때까지 그는 그대로 눈 뜬 채 있었던 것 같았다. 화롯불은 다 꺼져가고 있었다. 아버지는 뻣뻣한 발로 그를 흔들어 깨웠다. "말을 몰고 떠날 준비를 해."라고 아버지는 말했다.

　소년이 말을 끌고 돌아오니 아버지는 벌써 둘둘 말은 양탄자를 어깨에 둘러메고 문 안쪽 컴컴한데 서 있었다. "아버지 타지 않으실래요?" "그래 안 탄다. 이리 발을 내놔" 소년이 무릎을 꿇고 아버지 손에다 발을 올려놓으니 아버지는 그의 억세고 놀라 만한 힘으로 슬쩍 그를 들어 안장 업은 말 등에다 올려놓고(언제 어디서인지는 몰라도 소년은 언젠가 안장이라는 걸 가지고 있었던 일이 생각났다.) 그 앞자리에는 별로 힘들이지 않고 양탄자를 올려놓았다. 그으른 별빛을 받아가며 오후에 걸어서 그 길을 다시 걸어간 것이었다. 인동초가 우거진 먼지투성이의 길을 따라 올라가 대문을 지나고 캄캄한 터널처럼 뚫어진 차도를 지나 불도 켜 있지 않는 그 집으로 왔다. 말 위에 앉아 있던 소년은 탄 채 양탄자의 꺼칠꺼칠한 털이 그의 양쪽 무릎을 스쳐 끌어내려지고 보이지 않는 것을 느꼈다. "내가 좀 도와 드릴까요" 하고 소년은 가만가만히 말했다. 아버지로부터는 대답이 없었다. 나뭇조각과 같은, 시계의 똑딱 소리와도 같이 따각 거리는 소리를 내면서 그의 아버지는 서슬이 당당한, 뻣뻣한 걸음으로 텅 빈 주랑 현관을 걸어가는 것이 들렸다. 양탄자는 내던지지 않고(소년은 어둠속이지만 알 수 있었다.) 그의 아버지의 어깨에서 불룩 솟아나와 벽이니 마룻바닥의 모서리에 부딪힌 굉장히 요란한 소리를 냈다. 그러자 묵직하고 천천히 걸어오는 발자국 소리가 다시 들려왔다. 집안에선 누가 등불을 들고 내려오는 것이었다. 소년은 긴장한 가운데 숨을 죽이고 가만히 앉아 있었다. 숨소리가 좀 빨라졌을 뿐 아버지의 걸음소리는 조금도 빨라지지도 않고 계단을 내려오고 있었다. 비로소 아버지의 모습이 나타났다.

　"타실래요? 같이 타세요." 소년은 가만히 말했다. 집안에서 보이는 등불은 커졌다 작아졌다 하면서 껌벅거리고 있었다. '저 사람은 지금 층층대를 내려오고 있어' 소년은 그렇게 생각했다. 소년은 말을 승마대 옆까지 몰고 왔다. 아버지는 곧 그의 뒷자리에 올라타고 손에 쥔 말고삐를 반으로 접어 말 목덜미를 찰싹 때렸다. 그러나 말이 재빨리 뛰기 시작한 순간 아버지의 가늘고 억센 팔은 소년을 휘감고 말고삐를 뒤로 꽉 당겨 천천히 걸어가게 했다. 빨간 첫 햇빛이 비칠 때 그들은 집에 돌아와 보습을 이어둘 고리쇠를 달고 있었다. 이때 밤색의 말은 어느새 그들 집에 와 있었다. 말을 타고 온 사람은 칼라도 달지 않고 모자도 쓰지 않은 채 그 집에 있던 그 여인이 울부짖음과 꼭 같은 음성으로 떨며 말했다. 말 멍에를 고리에 다 맞추어 대느라고 허리를 구부리기 전에 그의 아버지는 슬쩍 한번 쳐다볼 뿐이었다. 그래서 말을 타고 있던 사나이는 웅크리고 있는 그의 등에다 대고 말을 계속 하는 것이었다.

　"이봐요 당신은 그 양탄자를 망쳐버렸다는 걸 알아야 해요. 여기 누가 없었소? 당신네 여자들 중 누가 그 양탄자를 망쳤어…"

그는 떨리는 음성으로 여기서 멈추었다. 소년은 그를 바라보고 그의 형은 입에 무얼 씹으면서 누구를 쳐다보는 것도 아니면서 노상 눈만 껌벅거리면서 외양간 문에 기대어 서 있었다.

"그것은 백불짜리라오. 그만한 돈이 있겠소? 앞으로도 그만한 돈은 어림도 없을 걸 당신은 20부셀의 곡식으로 변상해야 하오. 그러니 계약서에는 더 추가해 둘 테니 대리점에 와서 서명하란 말이요. 글쎄 그렇게 한들 드 스페인 부인의 노여움을 풀 수는 없지만 그래도 앞으론 집안에 들어오기 전에는 신발을 잘 털고 들어와야 한다는 것쯤은 단단히 가르친 셈이 되겠죠."

그런 다음 그 사나이는 가버렸다. 소년은 아버지를 쳐다보았다. 그는 여전히 잠자코만 있을 뿐 누굴 쳐다보지도 않았다. 그저 멍에에 달린 철봉을 바로 잡고 있었다.

"아버지" 하고 소년은 말했다. 아버지는 소년을 쳐다보았다 그 얼굴은 도무지 알수 없는 의심쩍은 표정이었고 검은 털의 눈썹 밑에선 회색빛 눈이 차갑게 번쩍이고 있었다. 소년은 와락 아버지 쪽으로 달려가 갑자기 딱 멈추어 섰다. "아버지 참 잘하셨어요. 다른 방법으로 일을 원만히 해결할 것을 그이가 바란다면 왜 좀 기다렸다가 어떻게 했으면 좋겠느냐고 아버지하고 의논하지 않았을까요. 20부셀도 주지 맙시다! 아무것도 주지 맙시다! 우린 추수를 거두면 감추어 둡시다! 내가 감시를 하고..." 소년은 이렇게 소리 질렀다.

"추수 재단기를 내가 말한 대로 저 광속에다 도로 넣어두었냐?"

"아뇨." 소년이 말했다.

"그럼 가서 넣어둬라."

이 일이 있었던 것은 수요일이었다. 그 주일의 나머지 며칠 동안 그는 착실히 일을 했다. 누가 하라 해서 하는 일도 아니고 누가 두 번 시켜서 하는 일도 아니었고 그저 힘닿는 데까지 아니 그 이상의 열성으로 일을 했던 것이다. 적어도 그가 한 일은 작은 꼬마 도끼를 갖고 나무를 쪼개는 일 따위는 그가 좋아하는 일이었다. 이런 점은 그의 어머니와는 좀 다르기는 했지만 아무튼 어머니로부터 물려받은 것이었다. 이 작은 꼬마 도끼는 그의 어머니와 아주머니가 벌어서 혹은 푼푼이 모아 크리스마스 때 그에게 선물로 사준 것이었다. 그는 어머니와 아주머니는 함께 (가끔가다 오후면 누이도 하나 끼는 수가 있었지만) 그의 아버지가 땅 주인과 맺은 계약의 일부인 소나 새끼 돼지의 우리를 만들어 세우기도 하였다. 어떤 날 오후 아버지가 말을 타고 어디 출타하고 없었기에 그는 농장으로 나가보았다. 그들은 꽤 큰 농장을 갖고 있었다. 그의 형은 보습을 똑바로 잡고 그는 말고삐를 쥐고 힘들여 일하는 말 옆을 따라가기도 하고 축축하게 발목에 느껴지는 검고 비옥한 땅을 밟아가면서 그는 생각했다. '아마 이렇게 밭을 가는 것은 그 목적은 그것 때문인지도 몰라. 양탄자의 값을 갚기에도 힘들게 보이는 20부셀의 곡식이지만 아버지가 이때까지 해오던 버릇을 영원히 버리게 한다면 그것도 아깝지 않겠지.' 이렇게 꿈같은 일을 곰곰이 생각하고 있자 그의 형은 정신 좀 차리고 말을 돌보라고 무섭게 꾸짖었다. '아마 아버지는 20부셀의 곡식도 추수하지 못할 거야. 아마 추수하고 갚을 것을 다 갚고 나면 하나도 남지 않을 거야. 추수·양탄자, 그리고 화재. 이런 순서로 말이 양쪽에 끌어당기는 그 중간에 끼어 어쩔 줄 모르고 있듯이 비애와 공포의 중간에서 헤매는 일도 영영 없어지겠지.'

이렇게 지나는 동안 토요일이 되었다. 소년이 마구를 달고 있던 말밑에서 치켜보니 검은 코트에다 모자를 쓴 아버지를 보았다. "그것 아니고 짐마차 고리쇠를 달란 말이야."라고 아버지는 말했다. 이 일을 마치고 난지 두 시간 후 소년은 아버지와 형이 앉아 있는 마차 뒷자리 밑바닥에 주저앉은 채 가노라니 마침내 마차는 마지막 모퉁이를 꺾었다. 담배 광고, 약 광고가 찢어진 대로 그냥 붙어 있으며 페인트칠도 하지 않은 낡아빠진 상점이 보였고 그 복도 앞에 밧줄로 매달아둔 몇 대의 짐마차와 말이 있었다. 그는 아버지와 형 뒤를 따라 널판자가 다 썩어빠진 층층대로 올라갔다. 그랬더니 조용히 지켜보는 얼굴들이 늘어서 그들 셋을 안으로 들어가게 했다. 소년은 안경을 쓰고 널판자 책상에 앉아 있는 사나이를 보았다. 그가 보안관이라는 것은 누가 일러주지 않아도 알 수 있었다. 소년은 날카롭고 의젓하고 두고 보자는 듯한 도전적인 눈초리로 칼라도 달고 넥타이도 맨 그 사나이를 쏘아 붙였다.

생전에 꼭 두 번 보았던 것이다. 말을 달려왔던 사람의 얼굴은 분노의 표정이 아니라 소년이 도저히 영문을 모른 깜짝 놀란 불신의 표정을 짓고 달려왔으며 자기의 한 소작인의 고소를 받아, 믿기 어려운 놀라운 형편에 놓여 있었는데 가까이 와서 그의 아버지에의 맞은편에 서자 소년은 보안관을 보고 소리 질렀다. "그는 그런 짓을 하지 않았습니다. 그는 불태우지 않고⋯."

"짐마차에 가 있어." 라고 그의 아버지는 말했다. "태웠다고? 아니 이 양탄자가 타기도 했단 말인가?" 하고 보안관이 말했다.

"여기 누구라도 이 양탄자가 탔다고 주장할 사람이 있소?" 아버지가 말했다.

"짐마차에 가 있으라니까." 그러나 소년은 가지 않고 지난번의 그 상점처럼 복잡한 구석으로 약간 물러섰다. 그러나 이번엔 앉지 않고 서 있는 사람들의 틈에 바싹 기대어 말소리를 엿듣고 있었다.

"이 양탄자를 망쳐버린 대가로 20부셸의 곡식을 요구한 것이 너무 지나치다고 생각하오?"

"그 사람이 양탄자를 가져와서 하는 말이 자국을 완전히 지워버리라고 하더군요. 그래서 자국을 없애고 다시 그에게 돌려보냈지요."

"그러나 발자국을 만들어 놓기 전과 꼭 같은 상태로 해서 양탄자를 돌려보낸 것은 아니지 않소?"

아버지는 대답이 없었다. 약 30초 동안은 한 마디도 빠뜨리지 않고 열심히 듣느라고 하였으나 간신히 들리는 숨소리와 한숨소리 이외에는 아무런 소리도 없었다.

"이 질문엔 대답 않기로 했는가요? 스노우프스씨?" 아버지는 여전히 대답이 없었다. "그럼 스노우프스씨, 당신에게 불리한 판결을 내리겠소. 드 스페인 소령의 양탄자를 망친 데 대한 책임을 지는 동시에 마땅히 벌을 받아야 할 줄 아오. 그렇지만 그것을 변상하기 위해서 20부셸의 곡식을 바쳐야 함은 당신과 같은 처지에 있는 사람으로선 좀 지나친 부담인 것 같소. 드 스페인 소령은 그 양탄자가 백 불의 값이 나간다고 하지만 10월에 추수를 거두어봐야 기껏 50센트 정도 밖에 되지 않을 거요. 만일 드 스페인 소령이 현금으로 사들인 그 물건에 대해 95불의 손실을 각오한다면 당신도 아직 번 돈은 아니지만 5불의 배상쯤은 각오해야 할 게 아니요? 그러니 드 스페인 소령에 대한 배상으로 그와의 계약에 적혀 있는 조건 외에 추수 때의 수확에서 10부셸의 곡식을 갚아줄 것을 본관은 결정하오. 이만 법정집회를 휴회하오."

시간은 그리 오래 걸리지 않았다. 아침나절이 막 시작될 무렵이었다. 바로 집으로 돌아가거나 다른 농가보다 일이 많이 밀렸으니 농장으로 되돌아가리라고 소년은 생각했다. 그러나 그와 아버지는 손으로 그의 형에게 따라오라고 손짓을 하면서 짐마차 뒤로 해서 돌아가는 것이었다. 길 건너편 대장간으로 건너갔다. 소년은 빠른 걸음으로 그 뒤를 쫓아가면서 색이 낡아빠진 모자 밑에서 거칠고도 태연해 보이는 아버지 얼굴을 쳐다보며 가만히 말을 건넸다. "10부셸도 주지 맙시다. 1부셸도 주지 맙시다. 우리는 저⋯." 이 말에 아버지는 소년을 내려다보았다. 그의 얼굴은 태연하게 보였고 회색빛으로 약간 희끗희끗한 눈썹은 쌀쌀한 두 눈 위에서 살짝 움직이는 듯했고 말소리는 유쾌하고도 거의 부드럽게 들렸다.

"그렇게 생각해? 그래 아무튼 10월까지 기다려 봐야지."

차바퀴의 살 한두 개를 갈아 끼우고 바퀴를 꽉 죄이는 일 따위는 그리 시간이 오래 걸리지 않았다. 차바퀴를 고치는 일은 그저 짐마차를 대장간 뒤 스프링 수선소에 끌고 가서 거기다 세워두기만 하면 다 되는 것이다. 말은 물통에다 이따금씩 코를 박고 소년은 축 늘어진 말고삐를 잡아 쥔 채 자리에 앉아 천장의 기울어진 대들보를 쳐다보기도 하고 천천히 내리 휘두르는 망치소리에 귀를 기울이기도 하고 이야기를 주고받으면서 똑바로 세워놓은 심게 나무 문 빗장 위의 까맣게 그을은 터널과 같은 작업장을 들여다보기도 했다. 소년이 기름투성이 짐마차를 수선소에서 몰고 나와 문 앞에 끌고 왔을 때까지 아버지는 여전히 그 자리에 앉아 있었다.

"말을 저 응달에다 끌고 가서 매두어라." 하고 그의 아버지가 말했다. 소년은 시키는 대로 해놓고 돌아왔다.

그와 아버지와 대장간 아저씨, 그리고 문 안쪽에 무릎을 꿇고 있는 또 한 사람하고 마주 앉아 농작물이니 가축에 대해서 이야기하고 있었다. 소년도 구린내 나는 먼지와 말굽 깎은 쓰레기 또는 녹슨 쇠붙이의 떨어진 쇳가루 등 너저분하게 깔린 자리에 웅크리고 앉아, 아버지가 전문적으로 말 매매상으로 활약하던 시절, 그러니까 그의 형을 낳기 전부터의 오랜 이야기를 천천히 늘어놓는 것을 들었다. 그런 다음 그 상점 바깥 쪽 벽에 붙어 있는 찢어진 작년 서커스 포스터 앞에 서서 빨갛게 색칠한 말, 희극배우의 멋진 포즈, 얇은 비단을 둘둘 감은 모습, 몸에 착 달라붙은 옷차림, 과장해서 그린 흘겨보는 눈매 등을 가만히 서서 황홀한 듯 바라보고 있으니 그의 아버지는 다가와서 말했다. "밥 먹을 시간이야."

그러나 집에서 식사하는 것은 아니다. 벽에 기대고 서 있는 형 옆에 웅크리고 앉아 있던 소년은 아버지가 상점에서 커다란 종이봉지를 안고 나와 치즈 조각을 끄집어내어 주머니칼로 조심조심 자르고, 같은 종이 봉지에서 비스킷도 끄집어내는 것을 보았다. 세 사람은 복도에 쪼그리고 앉아 말도 없이 천천히 먹고 있었다. 먹고 난 다음 그들은 다시 상점으로 들어가 이깔나무 양동이 냄새와 참나무 냄새를 풍기는 미지근한 물을 양철 그릇에 받쳐 떠 마셨다. 그리고도 그들은 집으로 돌아가지 않았다. 이번엔 말 매매소였다. 사람들이 주욱 기대서거나 걸터앉았거나 하는 높은 가로지른 울타리에 따라 말을 한 마리씩 끌어내다가 천천히 걷게도 하고 구보로 달리게도 하고 뛰기를 시키는 동안 말을 팔고 사고 하는 상담도 진행되는 것이다. 해는 이제 서산으로 기울어지기 시작했다. 그들 세 사람은 ― 형은 흐리멍덩한 눈을 뜨고 언제나 꼭 가지고 다니던 파이프를 물고, 아버지는 막연히 이따금씩 어떤 말에 대한 의견을 늘어놓으면서 이 광경을 바라보고 있는 것이었다.

그들이 집에 도착할 때는 해가 진 다음이었다. 등불 옆에서 저녁을 먹었다. 식사를 마친 다음 문간의 층층대에 앉아 소년은 울어대는 쏙독새와 개구리의 소리에 귀를 기울이며 깊어가는 밤을 물끄러미 바라다보고 있었다. 그때 그의 어머니의 음성이 들려왔다. "여보, 아니에요, 아니에요! 제발 그러지 마세요! 아!" 그는 일어서서 사방을 두리번거렸다. 책상 위 병 구멍에선 양초 끝이 간들간들 타고 있으며 그 불빛이 문을 통해 비쳐 나오는 것이 보였다. 그리고 모자와 코트는 여전히 걸친 채 무슨 보잘것없는 의식적인 폭행을 위하여 조심스럽게 옷차림 한 듯이 의젓하기도 하고 어색하기도 한 그의 아버지는 램프 등에 남아 있는 석유를 늘 따라 쓰던 5갤론짜리 석유통에 도로 쏟아 넣고 있었다. 그런데 그의 어머니는 그의 팔을 끌어당기고 있었다. 아버지는 램프 등을 다른 손으로 바꿔 쥐고는 사정없이 밀어내지는 않았으나 좀 세차게 어머니를 구석지에 떠밀어 붙였다. 어머니는 쓰러지지 않으려고 벽에다 대고 두 손을 내저었다. 입을 벌리고 으악 하고 소리 질렀다. 그 소리가 절망의 비명이라면 그 얼굴 표정도 절망 바로 그것이었다. 그러자 문간에 서 있는 소년을 보았다.

"외양간에 가서 짐마차에다 기름칠 하던 그 기름깡통을 갖고 오라." 라고 아버지는 말했다. 소년은 꼼짝 하지 않고 그 자리에 선채 말했다.

"무얼⋯뭘 하시려고⋯."

"잔말 말고 가서 기름통만 가져오란 말이야, 어서."

소년은 몸을 움직여 집 밖 마구간 쪽으로 달려갔다.

결코 그 자신이 좋아서 스스로 택한 것이 아닌 이 옛 습관, 이 옛 기질은 어쩔 수 없이 이 소년에게도 유전되었으며 그에게 유전되기 전에도 이미 오래 전부터 조상들의 혈관을 흐르고 있었던 것이다. (조상들은 난폭한 기질, 야만적인 기질, 탐내는 성질 중 어느 것 때문에 이런 기질이 점점 자라나게 된 것인가를 잘 알고 있었다.) 내 할대로 해보자! 소년은 생각했다. 뛰고 또 뛰어 뒤돌아보지도 않고 다시는 그의 생각을 보지 않으리라. 그러나 그것만은 할 수 없으리라. 이윽고 녹슨 깡통을 손에 잡아 쥐었다. 안에서 기름이 출렁거리는 대로 그냥 깡통을 들고 집으로 뛰어와 어머니가 흐느껴 우는 소리가 들리는 건넌방으로 뛰어 들어가 아버지에게 깡통을 내밀었다.

"껌둥이를 보내지 않으실래요? 요전번에도 껌둥이를 보냈었는데요!" 하고 소년은 소리쳤다.

그의 아버지는 이번엔 그를 갈기지는 않았으나 그 손은 갈길 때보다 더 날쌔게 소년에게로 날아왔다. 마음에 거리끼는 점이 있는 듯 걱정스런 얼굴을 지으며 책상 위에 깡통을 올려놓은 바로 그 손이 번개같이 날쌔게 소년에게로 날아가더니 소년의 셔츠 등을 꽉 움켜쥐었다. 깡통에서 떨어지기도 전에 벌써 아버지의 얼굴은 숨 가쁘고 무서움에 질린 잔인한 표정으로 소년을 내려다보고 있었다. 아버지는 책상에 기댄 채 소처럼 천천히 그리고 묘하게 입을 옆으로 움직이면서 무얼 씹고 있는 형을 보고 냉랭하고 힘없는 말로 몇 마디 속삭였다.

"깡통에 들어 있는 걸 큰 통에 모두 따라 넣고 먼저 가거라. 곧 뒤따라 갈 테니!"

"그놈을 침대 다리에다 붙들어 매어두는 게 좋겠어요." 하고 형이 말했다.

"내가 하라는 대로 만 해!" 하고 아버지가 말했다. 그때 소년의 셔츠는 쭈글쭈글 구겨지고 딱딱하고 앙상한 손은 견갑골(肩胛骨) 중간쯤에 대고 양쪽 발끝은 마루바닥에 닿을랑 말랑 하게 끌려가고 있었다. 그 방을 지나고 다음 방으로, 그 다음은 불이 다 꺼진 화로 저쪽 두 의자에 묵직한 넓적다리를 쩍 벌린 채 앉아 있는 두 누이들 앞을 지나 아주머니가 두 팔을 어머니 어깨에다 올려놓고 침대 위에 나란히 앉아 있는 곳까지 소년은 움직여 왔다.

"이놈을 잡고 있어요." 하고 아버지가 말했다. 아주머니가 깜짝 놀라 일어섰다. "당신 아니요, 여보, 레니, 이놈 좀 짚구려. 어디 짚을 수 있나 봐야지."라고 아버지는 말했다. 어머니는 소년의 팔목을 잡았다. "당신이 더 잘 잡을 거요. 놓쳐버리면 그놈이 무슨 짓을 할는지 알겠죠? 그놈 저기 저쪽으로 길거란 말이요." 그는 머리를 큰 길 쪽으로 내저었다.

"아아 그놈을 묶어두는 게 좋을까봐."

"제가 잡고 있겠어요." 하고 그의 어머니는 조용히 말했다.

"그럼 어디 잡아두나 보자." 이렇게 일러두고는 아버지는 사라지고 널판자를 걸어가는 탁탁하고 묵직한 발걸음소리도 마침내 사라지고 말았다. 그러자 소년은 몸부림치기 시작했다. 그의 어머니는 두 팔로 그를 꽉 붙들고 소년은 또 몸을 흔들며 어머니 팔에서 빠져나오려고 몸부림치고 있었다.

결국 그가 더 힘이 세다는 것은 알고 있었으나 어머니가 지칠 때까지 기다릴 시간이 없었다. "날 놓아줘! 난 엄마를 치고 싶지는 않아!" 하고 그는 소리쳤다.

"그 애 보내줍시다요." 하고 아주머니가 말했다. "만일 그 애가 가지 않으면 정말이지 나라도 갈 테에요."

"글쎄 놔 줄 순 없잖니? 앗! 사티야! 안 돼, 안 돼! 좀 도와주구려, 여보, 리지!" 그의 어머니는 소리 질렀다. 이제 소년이 빠져 나왔다. 아주머니가 그를 잡아 쥐기까지 했으나 이미 때는 늦었다. 소년이 휙 돌아서 달리기 시작하자 뒤에선 어머니가 무릎을 꿇고 앞으로 넘어지면서 가까이에 있던 누이에게 소리 질렀다. "저 애를 잡아, 넷트야! 저 애를 붙들어!" 그러자 그것도 이미 늦었다. 넷트 누이(두 누이는 같은 시에 난 쌍둥이였다. 그런데 둘 다 식구 중의 누구보다도 꼭 두 배나 되는 살과 몸집과 체중을 갖고 있는 감을 주었다)는 그런데도 의자에서 꼼짝할 생각도 않고 그저 얼굴만 돌린 채 그가 옆을 지나가는 데도 놀란 기색도 없이 굉장히 넓은 얼굴을 쳐들고 그를 올려다보았다. 그 꼴이 꼭 황소와 같은 표정이었다. 소년은 방을 빠져나와 집 밖으로 뛰어나갔다. 다시 별빛 총총한 한길을 지나 가벼운 먼지를 밟으며 인동초 우거진 속을 달라갔다. 달리는 발밑에서 무섭게 천천히 리본이 풀어졌다. 드디어 대문 있는 데까지 이르자 두근거리는 가슴과 허파를 안고 또 달렸다. 차도까지 오자 불이 빤히 켜져 있는 집을 향해 달려 불빛이 새어나오는 문에까지 당도했다. 노크도 하지 않고 박차고 들어갔으나 숨만 헐떡일 뿐 아무 말도 못했다. 소년은 린넨 자켓을 입은 흑인의 놀란 얼굴을 하고 있는 것을 알았다. 그 흑인이 언제 나타났는지도 몰랐다.

"드 스페인씨! 그는 지금…." 소년은 숨을 몰아쉬면서 말했다. 그때 백인이 하얀 문에서 나오더니 현관으로 내려오는 것이 보였다. "외양간이요! 외양간!" 하고 그는 소리쳤다.

"뭣이? 외양간이라고?" 백인이 말했다.

"예, 외양간이요!" 소년이 소리 질렀다.

"그놈 잡아라!" 백인이 고함쳤다.

그러나 이번에도 때는 이미 늦었다. 흑인이 그의 셔츠를 붙들긴 했으나 세탁을 여러 번 한 것이라 소매가 홀딱 떨어져 나갔다. 소년은 들어온 문으로 다시 뛰어나가 차도에 이르렀다. 그리고 백인이 비명을 지르고 있을 동안에도 노상 뛰고 있었다.

뒤에선 백인이 고함을 지르고 있었다. "내 말을 가져와! 내 말을!" 소년은 공원을 가로질러 담을 기어 넘어 큰 길로 빠져나갈 것을 문득 생각했으나 공원이 어디 있는지도 모르고 또 포도덩굴이 우거진 담이 얼마나 높은지도 모르기에 그렇게 할 생각을 버렸다. 그래서 그는 차도를 쭉 달려 내려갔다. 피가 들끓고 숨이 벅찼다. 앞이 보이지 않았으나 하여튼 큰길로 나갔다. 아무런 소리도 들리지 않았다. 뒤따라오는 말굽소리를 듣기도 전에 말은 거의 그의 뒤를 바싹 따르고 있었다. 그는 마치 격렬한 슬픔에 잠겨 위급한 순간을 당하면 틀림없이 날개 같은 것이 돋친다는 듯이, 가던 길을 그대로 달리고 있었다. 그러나 말이 요란하게 그의 머리 위를 지나가려는 찰나, 그는 몸을 옆으로 내던져 길옆 잡초 우거진 도랑에 나가떨어졌다. 일순 말과 말 탄 사람의 모습이 사라지기도 전에 무엇인지 갑자기 높이 얼룩진 조용한 초여름의 밤하늘을 배경으로 하여 격분한 옆모습이 스쳐 지나갔다. 소리도 없이 엄청나게 길게 솟아오르는 것이 있어 별빛마저 가리고 있었다. 소년은 일어나서 다시 큰길로 나와 달리기 시작했다. 때는 이미 늦은 줄 알면서도 그는 여전히 달리고 있었다. 총소리가 한 방 탕 울려오는 것을 듣고서도 그는 달렸다. 조금 있다 두 번째 총소리가 들려왔다. 소년은 제 자신 달리고 있지 않다는 생각을 미처 의식지도 못하고 멍하니 서서 "아버지! 아버지!" 하고 울음소리로 말했다. 그러자 자기도 모르게 또 뛰기 시작했다. 길가의 돌 같은 것에 걸려 넘어지고 쓰러지고 하면서도 일어서선 헐레벌떡 또 달렸다. 그러다 쓰러지면 또 일어나서 저 멀리 타오르는 불길을 어깨너머로 되돌아보며 달렸다. 어두워서 잘 뵈지 않는 나무들 사이를 헐떡거리며 달리면서도 그는 연방 "아버지! 아버지!" 하고 서글프게 우는 것이었다.

깊은 밤인데 그는 어느 언덕 위에 앉아 있었다. 밤이 얼마나 깊었는지 또 얼마나 멀리까지 왔는지조차 몰랐다. 이제는 뒤에서 타오르던 불길도 보이지 않았다. 소년은 지난 나흘 동안 어쨌든 내 집이라고 부른 그 집이 위치해 있는 방향에다 등을 대고, 그의 얼굴은 호흡이 제대로 회복되면 걸어 들어갈 캄캄한 숲 쪽을 향한 채 가만히 앉아 있었다. 차가운 밤하늘 아래, 몸은 자꾸 떨리기만 하여 그는 얇고 찢어진 셔츠로 몸을 감싸며 쪼그리고 앉았다. 비애와 절망의 느낌은 이젠 공포나 두려움은 결코 아니었으나 그저 슬픔과 절망에 지나지 않았다. '아버지, 우리 아버지!' 소년은 생각했다. "아버지는 용감했어!" 소년은 갑자기 울음을 터뜨리는 것이었다. 소리를 내어 울부짖는 것이었으나 큰 소리는 아니었고 속삭임에 지나지 않았다. "아버지는 용감했어! 싸움터에 나간 일이 있거든! 그래 사토리스 대령의 기병대였다든가!" 그의 아버지는 옛 유럽식 의미에서 한 졸병으로 군복도 입지 않고 싸움터에 나갔으며, 어느 누구에게나 혹은 어느 군대도 어느 깃발에도 권위나 충성을 인정하지 않고 그저 말브룩이 싸움터에 나간 것처럼 종군했다는 것도 모르면서. 그리고 전리품에 대해선 그것이 적군의 전리품인지 아군의 것인지 전연 상관하지 않았다는 사실을 소년은 모르고 있었다.

별들은 천천히 그 자리를 바꾸었다. 좀 있으면 동이 트고 해가 뜨겠지. 그리고 배도 고프고. 그러나 그것은 내일의 일이었다. 당장 그는 추워서 못살 지경이었다. 걸으면 추위는 좀 덜하겠지. 그의 호흡도 좀 가라앉고 하여 그는 일어서서 걷기로 하였다. 그러자 이미 동이 트고 밤은 지났기에 여태까지 자고 있었다는 것을 알았다. 쏙독새소리를 듣고도 곧 동이 튼다는 것을 알 수 있었다. 쏙독새는 저만큼 아래쪽에 있는 컴컴한 나무들 사이에 있었다. 그 소리는 높고 낮음이 가지각색으로 그칠 줄 몰랐고 그리하여 밤이 낮으로 옮겨가는 순간 다른 새들도 점점 가까이 모여들기 때문에 밤과 낮을 구별하는 경계선이 없었다. 소년은 일어났다. 몸이 빳빳했으나 걸으니까 그것도 좀 나아졌고 추위도 덜했다. 곧 해가 뜰 것이다 소년은 언덕을 내려갔다. 은빛과 같이 맑은 새소리가 끊임없이 지저귀고, 늦은 봄의 밤을 노래하는 소년의 벅차고 두근거리는 마음을 마냥 불러대는 어두컴컴한 숲속을 향하여 내려갔다. 소년은 뒤돌아보지도 않았다.

12. 제비뽑기(The Lottery)

• 셜리 잭슨(Shirley Jackson)

　6월 27일 아침은 날이 맑고 햇볕이 눈부시게 내리쬐었으며 완연한 여름날답게 싱그러운 온기로 가득했다. 꽃들은 흐드러지게 피어올랐고 풀들은 진초록으로 물들었다. 10시쯤 되자 우체국과 은행 사이의 광장에 마을 주민이 하나둘 모여들었다. 사람이 워낙 많아 제비를 뽑는 데 이틀이 걸리는 고장에서는 6월 26일에 시작하지만, 이 마을은 인구가 고작 삼백 명이라 제비뽑기에 두 시간도 채 걸리지 않았고 10시에 시작해도 주민들은 점심시간에 맞춰 집으로 돌아갈 수 있었다.

　당연하게도 아이들부터 모여들었다. 여름방학을 맞은 지 얼마 나지 않았기에 아이들 대부분은 아직 제 시간이 자유롭다는 사실을 거북해했다. 처음에는 조용히 모여 있던 아이들이 갑자기 떠들썩하게 장난을 쳤다. 아직도 교실과 선생님과 책과 꾸중이 화제중심이었다. 보비 마틴은 주머니를 이미 돌멩이로 가득 채웠다. 다른 아이들도 이내 따라하며 가장 매끄럽고 둥근 돌을 골랐다. 보비와 해리 존스와 디키 들라크루아(마을 주민들은 델라크로이라고 발음했다)는 광장 한쪽 모퉁이에 커다랗게 돌더미를 쌓고 다른 아이들이 빼앗지 못하도록 지키고 있었다. 여자아이들은 한쪽에 서서 자기들끼리 이야기를 나누며 어깨 너머로 남자아이를 흘깃거렸고, 아주 어린 꼬맹이들은 흙바닥에서 뒹굴거나 손위 형제자매의 손을 꼭 쥐고 있었다.

　이내 남자들이 모여들더니 자식들이 어디에 있는지 살피며 농사와 비와 트랙터와 세금 이야기를 나누고 있다. 광장 모퉁이의 돌더미에서 멀찍이 떨어져 선 그들은 조용히 농담을 주고 받으며 요란하게 웃기보다 미소만 지었다. 남자들이 도착하고 얼마 안 있어 여자들이 빛바랜 실내복과 스웨터 차림으로 들어섰다. 서로 인사한 그들은 짤막한 소문을 주고받고 남편에게로 합류했다. 남편 곁에 선 여자들이 네다섯 번은 소리쳐 부른 다음에야 아이들은 마지못해 다가왔다 보비 마틴은 붙잡으려는 엄마의 손을 휙 피해 돌무더기로 달려가며 깔깔 웃어댔다. 아버지가 날카롭게 부른 후에야 얼른 다가와 아버지와 큰형 사이에 자리를 잡았다.

　제비뽑기 의식이 시작되었다. 광장 무도회나 십 대 클럽이나 할로윈 파티와 마찬가지로 이 의식 역시 서머스 씨가 진행했다. 그는 지역사회를 위해 헌신할 시간과 기운이 넘쳤다. 얼굴이 동그랗고 쾌활한 성품인 그는 석탄회사를 운영했다. 마을 사람들이 그를 가엾이 여기는 건 그에게 자식이 없는데다 부인이 잔소리꾼이기 때문이었다. 그가 검은색 나무 상자를 들고 광장에 도착하자 주민들이 웅성거렸다. 그가 팔을 저으며 소리쳤다. "오늘 좀 늦었습니다. 여러분." 우체국장인 그레이브스 씨가 삼발이 의자를 들고 따라오고 있었다. 의자가 광장 중앙에 놓이자 서머스 씨가 그 위에 검은 상자를 올렸다. 마을주민들은 의자에서 적당히 거리를 둔 채 서 있었다. "누가 도와주지 않으시겠습니까?" 서머스 씨가 말하자 사람들이 망설였다. 이윽고 마틴 씨와 그의 장남인 백스터가 앞으로 나와 의자에서 흔들리지 않도록 상자를 붙잡았고 서머스 씨가 상자 속 종이를 휘휘 저어댔다.

　최초의 상자는 오래전 사라졌지만 그래도 지금 의자 위에 놓여있는 검은 상자는 마을에서 가장 나이가 많은 워너 영감이 태어나기 전부터 사용되던 것이었다. 서머스 씨는 새 상자를 만들자고 주민들에게 종종 이야기했지만 누구도 이 검은 상자로 대변되는 전통을 무너뜨리고 싶어 하지 않았다. 현재의 상자가 그전에 사용된 상자의 조각으로 만들어졌다는 이야기가 있었다. 최초로 이 마을에 정착한 사람들이 쓰던 상자 말이다. 제비뽑기가 끝나면 매년 서머스 씨가 새 상자 이야기를 꺼냈지만 번번이 그 안건은 아무 조치도 없이 흐지부지됐다. 검은 상자는 해마다 조금씩 낡아갔다. 한쪽 표면이 꽤 많이 떨어져 나가 원래의 나무색이 드러나는 바람에 이제는 완전한 검은색 상자도 아니었다. 거기다 군데군데 색이 바래고 얼룩이 져 있었다.

　마틴 씨와 그의 장남 백스터가 의자 위의 상자를 단단히 붙잡고 있는 동안, 서머스 씨가 손을 저어 종이를 빈틈없이 섞었다. 의식의 많은 부분이 잊히거나 폐기된 덕분에 서머스 씨는 몇 세대 동안 사용되었던 나무패를 종이로 바꾸는 데 성공할 수 있었다. 마을이 작을 때야 나무패가 유용했겠지만 이제는 인구가 삼백 명이나 되는데다 앞으로 더 늘 가능성이 크니 검은 상자에 다 담을 수 있도록 다른 재질로 패를 바꿔야 한다고 설득했던 것이다. 전날 밤 서머스 씨와 그레이브스 씨는 종이로 제비를 만들어 상자에 담은 뒤 서머스 씨의 석탄 회사금고에 넣고 자물쇠를 잠갔다. 그리고 오늘 아침 서머스 씨가 광장에 가져올 때에야 금고를 개방했다. 제비뽑기 날이 아닐 때 상자는 여기저기에 보관되었다. 어떤 해는 그레이브스 씨의 창고에, 어떤 해는 우체국 지하실에 때로는 마틴 씨의 식료품점 선반에 놓이기도 했다.

서머스 씨가 제비뽑기의 시작을 선언하기 전에 번잡한 여러 절차를 거쳐야 했다. 우선, 목록을 작성해야 했다. 집안의 대표자 목록, 집안에 속한 가족 목록, 각 가족의 구성원 목록. 또한 우체국장이 적절한 형식에 따라 서머스 씨가 제비뽑기의 공식 감독인으로서 취임하는 의식을 주재했다. 몇몇 사람이 기억하기로 예전에는 매년 의례적으로 감독인이 단조로운 성가를 일정 시간 암송하는 낭송회 같은 것이 있었다. 감독인이 말로 읊었는지 노래로 불렀는지 모르지만 몇몇은 서서 의식을 진행했다고 생각했고 몇몇 사람들 사이를 걸어 다니며 했으리라 믿었다. 의식의 이 부분은 한 해 또 한 해 시간이 흐르면서 차츰 사라졌다. 또 예전에는 상자에서 제비를 뽑을 사람을 호명하면서 감독인이 의례를 따져 경례를 했지만 역시 시간이 흐르며 달라져 이제는 상자로 다가오는 사람과 대화를 나누기만 하면 되었다. 서머스 씨는 감독인 역할을 훌륭히 수행해냈다. 깨끗한 하얀 셔츠와 청바지 차림에 한 손을 아무렇게나 검은 상자에 얹고서 그레이브스 씨와 마틴 부자와 쉴 새 없이 이야기를 나누는 모습은 그를 대단히 유능하고 중요한 인물처럼 보이게 했다.

서머스 씨가 마침내 이야기를 끝내고 주민들을 바라보았을 때 허친슨 부인이 어깨에 스웨터를 걸친 채 부리나케 광장으로 들어와 뒤쪽의 군중 사이에 끼어들었다. "오늘이 그날인지 까맣게 잊었지 뭐야." 그녀는 바로 옆의 들라크루아 부인에게 말한 뒤 같이 나직이 웃었다. 허친슨 부인은 말을 이었다. "남편이 장작을 하러 나갔나 보다 했어. 그런데 창밖을 내다보니 아이들이 안 보이잖아. 그제야 27일이라는 게 떠올라서 부랴부랴 뛰어왔지." 그녀는 앞치마에 두 손을 닦았다. 들라크루아 부인이 말했다. "그래도 늦지는 않았네. 이야기를 안 마쳤거든."

허친슨 부인은 군중 사이로 목을 길게 빼어 앞쪽의 남편과 아이들을 보았다. 그녀는 작별 인사로 들라크루아 부인의 팔을 두드리고는 사람들을 헤치고 나아갔다. 주민들은 기분 좋게 비켜주었다. 두세 사람이 광장 전체에 들리도록 큰 소리로 말했다. "허친슨 부인이 나가십니다." "빌, 자네 집사람이 그래도 늦지는 않았군." 서머스 씨는 허친슨 부인이 남편 곁에 이를 때까지 기다린 후 활기차게 말했다. "테시 없이 시작하려고 했습니다." 허친슨 부인은 빙그레 웃으며 대꾸했다. "그럼 싱크대에 쌓여 있는 접시를 깨끗이 치울걸 그랬나요, 조?" 부드러운 웃음소리가 사람들 사이로 퍼져가는 사이, 허친슨 부인이 지나온 틈새가 도로 메워졌.

"자, 이제 시작해 볼까요." 서머스씨가 엄숙하게 말했다. "어서 끝내고 일하러 돌아가야지요. 누구 빠진 사람 있습니까?"

"던바요." 몇몇 사람이 말했다. "던바요, 던바."

서머스 씨가 목록을 살피고는 말했다. "클라이드 던바, 그렇군요 다리가 부러졌다지요. 그럼 누가 대신 제비뽑기를 하나요?"

"제가요." 한 여자가 말하자 서머스 씨가 돌아보았다. "부인이 대신 하시는군요. 제비를 뽑을 만한 다 큰 아들은 없나요, 제이니?" 서머스 씨와 다른 주민들 모두 답을 알더라도 감독인이 공식적으로 묻는 것이 관례였다. 서머스 씨가 예의상 흥미를 보이는 태도로 정중하게 기다리자 던바 부인은 안타깝다는 어조로 대답했다. "호레이스는 이제 겨우 열여섯 살이에요. 올해는 제가 남편을 대신하는 편이 나을 듯합니다."

"좋습니다. 서머스 씨는 들고 있던 목록에 메모를 했다. 그리고 물었다. "왓슨 네는 아들이 올해 제비를 뽑나요?"

군중사이에서 꺽다리 소년이 손을 들었다. "여기 있습니다. 제가 어머니와 저를 대표해 제비를 뽑을 겁니다." 그가 초조하게 눈을 깜박이며 꾸벅 인사를 하자 군중 사이에서 몇 사람이 말했다. "훌륭한 아들이야. 잭" "이렇게 어엿한 아들이 있으니 자네 어머니는 얼마나 뿌듯하겠어."

서머스 씨가 말했다. "그럼, 모두 왔군요. 워너 영감님도 오셨나요?"

"여기 있네." 목소리가 들리자 서머스 씨는 고개를 끄덕여 인사했다.

목청을 가다듬은 서머스 씨가 목록을 보자 군중 사이에 불현듯 침묵이 내려앉았다. 서머스 씨가 소리쳤다. "모두 준비됐습니까? 자 이제 각 집안 대표를 부르겠습니다. 성이 불린 사람은 앞으로 나와 상자에서 제비를 뽑으세요. 모두 다 뽑을 때까지 종이를 펼치지 말고 손에 꼭 쥐고 계세요. 아시겠죠?"

무수히 반복된 일이라 사람들은 지시 사항을 대충 흘려들었다. 대부분은 고개도 돌리지 않고 조용히 서서 입술을 혀로 축였다. 서머스 씨가 손을 높이 올리고서 말했다. "애덤스." 군중 사이에서 빠져나온 한 남자가 앞으로 나왔다. "안녕하십니까. 스티브." 서머스 씨가 인사하자 애덤스 씨도 대꾸했다. "안녕하세요. 조." 그들은 초조하고 뻣뻣한 미소를 서로에게 보냈다. 애덤스 씨가 검은 상자로 팔을 뻗어 접힌 종이를 꺼냈다. 그리고 종이의 한쪽 모서리를 꽉 쥔채 돌아서서 서둘러 자리로 돌아갔다. 그는 가족에게서 야간 떨어져 서서 손을 내려다보지 않았다.

"앨런." 서머스 씨가 호명했다. "앤더슨. ……벤담."

"자고 나면 또 제비뽑기 날이 되는 것 같아요." 들라크루아 부인이 뒷줄에 있던 그레이브스 부인에게 말했다. "바로 지난주에 제비를 뽑은 것만 같은데."

"시간이 그렇게 쏜살같이 흐르다니." 그레이브스 부인이 대꾸했다.

"클라크. ……들라크루아"

"우리 차례네요." 들라크루아 부인은 남편이 앞으로 나가는 동안 숨을 죽였다.

"던바." 서머스 씨가 말하자 던바 부인이 침착하게 걸어갔다. 한 여자가 말했다. "잘 뽑아요 제이니." 다른 여자가 말했다. "저기 가는군."

"다음은 우리 차례예요." 그레이브스 부인은 남편이 상자 옆에서 걸어 나와 서머스 씨에게 진지하게 인사하고 제비를 뽑는 것을 주시했다. 이쯤 되자 군중 속 여기저기에서 남자들이 커다란 손에 접힌 종이쪽을 쥐고서는 초조하게 뒤집고 또 뒤집었다. 던바 부인은 제비를 꼭 쥔 채 두 아들과 함께 서 있었다.

"하버트, 허친슨."

"가요. 빌." 허친슨 부인이 말하자, 주위의 사람들이 웃음을 터뜨렸다.

"존스."

애덤스 씨는 바로 옆에 있는 워너 영감에게 말했다. "북쪽의 어느 마을에서는 더 이상 제비뽑기를 하지 말자고 논의하는 모양이더군요."

워너 영감이 코웃음을 쳤다. "어리석은 미치광이들, 요즘 젊은 놈들은 입만 열면 불평불만이라니까. 조만간 동굴에서 원시생활을 하자고, 더 이상 일하지 말자고 주장해 댈 거야. 어디 한번 그렇고 그렇게 살아보라고 해. '유월에 제비를 뽑아야 곡물이 금방 익는다'고 옛 어른들이 말씀하셨지. 제비뽑기를 안 하면 별꽃과 도토리로 끼니를 때우게 될 거야. 매년 해왔다고." 노인은 성마른 어조로 덧붙였다. "새파랗게 젊은 조 서머스가 모두와 농담을 해대는 꼴을 보는 것만으로도 속이 상하건만."

"어떤 곳에서는 이미 제비뽑기를 없앴다고 하더라고요." 애덤스 씨가 말했다.

"그래봐야 문제만 생겨." 워너 영감은 단호히 말했다. "요새 젊은 것들이란."

"마틴."

보비 마틴은 아버지가 앞으로 나아가는 모습을 바라보았다.

"오버다이크. ……퍼시."

"어서 마쳤으면 좋겠구나. 어서 마쳤으면 좋겠어." 던바 부인이 큰아들에게 말했다.

"거의 다 끝나가요." 아들이 대답했다.

"어서 아버지한테 달려가 알릴 준비해." 던바 부인이 말했다.

서머스 씨가 자기 이름을 부르더니 신중하게 앞으로 나와 상자에서 종이를 뽑았다. 그리고 소리쳤다. "워너."

"칠십칠 년간 제비뽑기에 참여했지." 워너 영감은 군중 사이로 나아가며 말했다. "일흔일곱 번째야."

"왓슨." 꺽다리 소년이 어색한 걸음으로 나아가자 누군가가 말했다. "긴장 풀어, 잭." 서머스 씨는 말했다. "천천히 하게, 젊은이."

"자니니."

숨죽인 듯한 긴 침묵이 이어졌다. 이윽고 서머스 씨가 제비를 공중에 쳐들고서 말했다. "펴봅시다, 여러분." 한동안은 누구도 움직이지 않았다. 그러더니 일제히 종이를 펼쳤다. 불현듯 여자들 모두가 동시에 떠들어댔다. "누구야?" "누구래?" "던바야?" "왓슨이야?" 그러더니 사람들이 말하기 시작했다. "허친슨이야. 빌이 뽑았어." "빌 허친슨이 걸렸어."

"아버지한테 어서 알리렴." 던바 부인이 큰아들에게 말했다.

사람들은 허친슨 가족이 어디에 있는지 둘러보았다. 빌 허친슨은 손에 든 종이를 가만히 응시하고 있었다. 별안간 테시 허친슨이 서머스 씨에게 소리쳤다. "그이를 재촉하는 바람에 제대로 못 뽑았잖아요. 내가 다 봤어요. 공평하지 않아요!"

"깨끗이 받아들여, 테시." 들라크루아 부인이 소리쳤다. 그레이브스 부인이 말했다. "우리 모두 똑같이 뽑았어."

"입 닥쳐, 테시." 빌 허친슨이 아내를 말렸다. 서머스 씨가 선언했다. "자, 여러분 지금까지 순조롭게 진행되긴 했지만 시간을 맞추려면 좀 서둘러야 합니다." 그는 다음 목록을 살폈다. "빌, 허친슨 집안을 대표해서 뽑았죠? 허친슨 집안에는 몇 가족이 속해 있지요?"

"돈과 에바가 있어요. 개네들도 제비를 뽑아야 해요!" 허친슨 부인이 소리쳤다.

서머스 씨는 상냥하게 대꾸했다. "여자는 남편 집안에 속한답니다, 테시. 잘 아시잖아요."

"이건 공평하지 않다고요." 테시가 말했다.

"아닙니다, 존. 제 딸은 당연히 사위 집안에 속하지요. 그래야 공평하죠. 개네들을 제외하고 우리 집안에는 한 가족뿐입니다." 빌 허친슨이 유감스럽다는 듯이 말했다.

"그럼 당첨된 집안은 당신 집안입니다." 서머스 씨는 설명하듯 말했다. "그리고 당첨된 가족 역시 당신 가족입니다. 그렇지요?" "네." 빌 허친슨이 대답했다.

"아이가 몇이나 되죠, 빌?" 서머스 씨가 공식적으로 물었다.

"셋입니다. 빌 주니어와 낸시, 그리고 꼬마 데이브, 그리고 테시와 제가 있죠."

"좋아요. 해리, 제비를 다 거둬들였습니까?"

서머스 씨의 질문에 그레이브스 씨는 고개를 끄덕이며 종이 더미를 들어 보였다. 서머스 씨가 지시했다. "상자에 넣어요. 빌의 제비도 받아 넣고요."

"처음부터 다시 해야 해요." 허친슨 부인은 되도록 차분하게 말하려고 애썼다. "단언하지만, 정말 공평하지 않았어요. 그이한테 선택할 시간을 충분히 주지 않았다고요. 여기 모두들 봤잖아요." 그레이브스 씨가 종이 다섯 장을 골라 상자에 넣고 나머지는 그대로 땅바닥에 버렸다. 종이들이 산들바람에 나풀나풀 날아올랐다.

"모두들, 제 말 좀 들어봐요." 허친슨 부인이 주변 사람들에게 말했다.

"준비됐나요, 빌?" 서머스 씨가 묻자 빌 허친슨이 아내와 아이들을 힐끗 보고는 고개를 끄덕였다.

"명심하세요. 제비를 뽑은 뒤 다른 사람이 다 뽑을 때까지 펼쳐보지 마세요. 해리, 꼬마 데이브를 좀 도와주겠어요?" 그레이브스씨가 손을 잡자 꼬맹이는 기꺼이 따라서 상자로 갔다. "종이 하나를 고르렴, 데이비." 서머스 씨가 말하자 데이비는 상자에 손을 넣고 깔깔 웃음을 터뜨렸다. "딱 한 장만 골라야 해, 데이비." 서머스 씨가 말했다. "해리, 제비를 대신 쥐고 있어요." 그레이브스 씨는 아이의 손을 잡아 꼭 쥔 주먹에서 접힌 종이를 빼내어 쥐었다. 꼬마 데이브는 옆에 서서 의아한 듯 그를 올려다보았다.

"다음은 낸시 차례란다." 서머스 씨가 말했다. 낸시는 열두 살이었다 그녀가 스커트를 흔들며 앞으로 걸어가 상자에서 제비를 우아하게 뽑는 동안 학교 친구들은 무겁게 숨을 쉬었다. "빌 주니어." 서머스 씨가 호명했다. 얼굴이 붉고 발이 지나치게 큰 빌리는 종이를 꺼내려다 상자를 넘어뜨릴 뻔했다. "테시." 서머스 씨가 부르자 그녀는 일순 주저하며 주위를 반항적으로 둘러보았다. 그러다 입술을 앙다물고 상자로 걸어갔다. 재빨리 제비를 뽑아 등 뒤로 가져갔다.

"빌." 서머스 씨가 부르자 빌 허친슨은 상자로 다가가 마지막 남은 종이를 찾느라 상자 안을 더듬거렸다.

군중은 조용했다. 소녀 하나가 속삭였다. "낸시가 아니면 좋겠어." 나직한 소리가 군중 전체에 들렸다.

"전에는 안 이랬는데, 옛 사람들은 이러지 않았어." 워너 영감이 다 들리도록 말했다.

"좋아요." 서머스 씨가 선언했다. "종이를 펴보세요. 해리, 꼬마 데이브 대신 펴주세요."

그레이브스 씨가 종이를 펼쳐 들어올렸다. 텅 빈 종이를 보고는 모두들 안도의 한숨을 내쉬었다. 낸시와 빌 주니어가 동시에 종이를 펼쳤다. 둘 다 활짝 웃고 커다란 웃음소리를 내며 제비를 머리 위로 쳐들고 군중을 향해 몸을 돌렸다.

"테시." 서머스 씨가 말했다. 그녀가 주저하자 서머스 씨는 빌 허친슨을 바라보았고 빌이 종이를 펼쳐 사람들한테 내보였다. 텅 비어 있었다.

"테시로군요." 하고 서머스 씨가 말하더니 목소리를 낮추었다.

"부인의 종이를 우리한테 보여줘요, 빌."

빌 허친슨은 아내에게 다가가 제비를 억지로 빼앗았다. 종이에 검은 점이 찍혀 있었다. 전날 밤 서머스 씨가 석탄 회사 사무실에서 굵은 색연필로 표시한 것이었다. 빌 허친슨이 종이를 들어 올리자 군중들이 술렁였다.

"좋아요, 여러분 빨리 끝내도록 합시다." 서머스 씨가 말했다. 의식의 대부분이 사라지고 최초의 검은 상자도 없어져버렸지만 마을 주민들은 돌을 사용해야 한다는 것만은 여전히 기억했다. 아이들이 미리 쌓아놓은 돌더미가 준비되어 있었다. 상자에서 나온 종잇조각들이 흩날리는 바닥에 돌들이 놓여 있었다. 들라크루아 부인은 두 손으로 들어야 할 만큼 커다란 돌을 고르고는 던바 부인을 돌아보며 말했다. "어서, 서둘러야 해."

던바 부인은 양손에 작은 돌멩이들을 쥔 채 쌔근대며 말했다. "나는 달릴 수가 없어요. 먼저 가세요. 좀 있다 따라갈게요."

아이들은 이미 돌을 챙겨두었다. 누군가 꼬마 데이비 허친슨에게 자갈 서너 개를 쥐어 주었다.

테시 허친슨은 이제 텅 빈 공간의 한가운데 서 있었다. 마을 주민들이 점점 다가오자 그녀는 두 손을 절망적으로 내밀며 말했다. "이건 공평하지 않아요." 돌멩이 하나가 그녀의 옆머리를 강타했다. 워너 영감이 재촉했다. "어서, 어서, 모두 다 던져야 해." 스티브 애덤스는 군중들 맨 앞에 있었고 바로 그 옆에 그레이브스 부인이 자리했다.

"이건 공평하지 않아요. 옳지 않다고요." 허친슨 부인이 비명을 지르고, 모두 그녀를 향해 돌을 던졌다.

15. 흔들 목마(The Rocking-Horse Winner)

• D. H. 로렌스(D. H. Lawrence)

한 여자가 있었다. 아주 아름다운 여자였다. 그녀는 모험심이 강했지만, 운만은 없었다. 그녀는 사랑 때문에 결혼했으나 그 사랑은 곧 재로 변하였다. 그녀는 예쁜 아이들을 낳았다. 하지만 그 아이들이 꼭 그녀에게 떠맡겨진 것 같았기에, 그녀는 그 아이들을 사랑할 수 없었다. 아이들은 항상 그녀를 차갑게 바라보았다. 마치 그녀에게서 어떤 잘못을 찾으려는 듯이. 그러면 그녀는 항상 그녀 안의 어떤 잘못을 숨겨야 할 것 같은 기분이 드는 것이었다. 그것이 어떤 잘못인지도 모르는 채로.

그녀의 자식들이 안길 때조차 그녀는 자신의 심장이 딱딱해지는 것을 느낄 수 있었다. 이것이 그녀를 죄책감으로 괴롭혔고, 그럴수록 그녀의 어린애들을 대하는 태도는 더욱 상냥하고 근심스러워졌다. 그녀가 그 애들을 마치 매우 사랑하기라도 하듯이. 오직 그녀 자신만이, 그녀의 심장은 이미 딱딱하게 죽어, 아무에게도 – 어떤 누구에게라도 – 사랑을 느끼지 못함을 알았다. 모든 사람이 그녀에 대해 말했다. "그녀는 정말 좋은 어머니야. 자기 자식들을 위하는 것 좀 봐." 오직 그녀 자신과 그녀의 자식들만이 그렇지 않다는 것을 알았다. 그들은 그 사실을 서로의 눈에서 읽었다.

한 소년과 두 소녀가 있었다. 그들은 아름다운 정원이 딸린 집에서 하인들과 함께 살았다. 이웃의 어떤 가족보다도 호사스러웠다.

그 세련된 집 안에서, 그들은 언제나 집 안이 걱정으로 가득 차 있음을 알았다. 돈이 충분치 않았다. 어머니는 작은 수입이 있었으나, 아버지의 수입은 그보다 더 작았다. 그들의 품위를 유지하기에 턱없이 작은 돈이었다. 아버지는 마을의 작은 사무실에 출근했다. 전망 좋은 직장이었지만 전망 같은 건 돈이 되지 않는 법이다. 돈 문제에 따른 갈등이 있었지만, 생활수준은 절대 내려가지 않았다.

결국 어머니가 말했다. "내가 어떻게든 해봐야겠어." 하지만 그녀는 무엇을 어떻게 해야 할 지 전혀 몰랐다. 지식도 없었고, 나름대로 이것저것 건드려보았으나 결국 신통한 일을 해내진 못했다. 실패가 그녀의 얼굴에 굵은 주름살을 새겨 놓았다. 아이들은 자랐고, 이제 학교에 가야 했다. 더 많은 돈이 필요했다. 더 많은 돈이 있어야만 했다. 잘 생기고, 세련된 취향을 가졌던 아버지는, 실질적으로 쓸모 있는 구석이라고는 한 면도 없었다. 그리고, 자신에 대한 대단한 확신에 찬 어머니도 그에 비해 나은 면이 없었다. 그리고 그녀의 취향은 남편보다 더 고급스런 것이었다.

그 집은 절대 말해지지 않는 한 단어에 사로잡힌 꼴이었다. "더 많은 돈이 필요해! 더 많은 돈이 있어야만 해!" 아이들은 그것을 언제나 듣고 있었지만, 절대로 크게 소리 내어 말하지 못했다. 그들은 크리스마스에 사치스러운 장난감이 가득 찬 선물을 받을 때도 그 소리를 들었다. 현대적이고 번쩍번쩍한 흔들목마 뒤에서도, 최신식 인형 집 뒤에서도, 그 목소리는 속삭이기 시작했다. "더 많은 돈이 필요해! 더 많은 돈이 있어야만 해!"

아직도 흔들리고 있는 흔들목마의 재갈 물린 나무 머리 뒤에서도, 온통 분홍색으로 차리고 유모차에 들어앉아 뽐내듯 웃고 있는 큰 인형 뒤에서도, 그 속삭임이 조용하게 흘러나오는 것을 들을 수 있었다. 그 인형은 심지어 그 소리 때문에 더 위풍당당하게 뽐내는 것처럼 보였다. 곰인형의 자리를 차지하고 있는 멍청한 강아지도 마찬가지였다. 그는 그 속삭임을 듣고 있어 특히 더 멍청해 보이는 것 같았다. "더 많은 돈이 필요해!" 아무도 그것을 소리 내 말하지 않았지만, 그 속삭임은 어디에서나 들려왔다. 사실, 우리도 언제나 숨을 쉬지만 "우리는 숨을 쉰다"라고 말하지는 않지 않은가?

"어머니."

폴이 어느 날 말했다. "우리는 왜 우리 차가 없나요? 왜 우리는 언제나 오스카 삼촌 차를 타거나 택시를 불러요?"

"그야 우리가 가난하니까 그렇지" 어머니가 대답했다.

"하지만 왜 우리가 그런데?"

"글쎄 – 내가 생각하기론," 그녀가 씁쓸하게 말했다. "너희 아버지가 운이 없으니까 그런 게지"

소년이 잠시 동안 조용히 생각에 잠겼다.

"운이란 것은 돈인가요?" 그가 주저하면서 물었다.

"아냐, 폴, 그런 건 아니지. 운이란 건 네게 돈을 벌어다 주는 거다."

"아!" 그가 애매하게 말했다. "오스카 삼촌이 언젠가 누구를 보고 더럽게도 운이 좋은 놈이라고 말한 적 있었죠. 그건 돈이에요?"

"아니, 더러운 이익이라면 돈이겠지. 하지만 이익이 운인 건 또 아니란다."

"아! 정말요? 그리고 아버지는 운이 없고?"

"정말 운이 없다고 밖엔 말할 수 없구나." 그녀가 씁쓸하게 말했다.

소년이 어머니의 눈을 의심스럽다는 듯이 쳐다보았다.

"왜죠?"

"모르지. 어떤 사람이 왜 운을 타고났는가, 혹은 아닌가는 사람의 힘으로 알 수 있는 게 아니란다."

"누구도? 절대로? 정말 누구도? 어머니?"

"글쎄, 어쩌면 신만은 아시겠지. 그렇지만 신께서는 말씀하시는 법이 없으니까."

"그렇지요. 그럼 어머니도 운이 없어요?

"그럴 수가 있겠니. 나는 이 운 없는 남자와 결혼했으니 말이다."

"아니, 어머니 스스로 말이에요."

"글쎄, 난 내 스스로 운이 좋을 거라고 생각했었지. 내가 결혼하기 전에… 하지만 지금 나는 네 아빠만큼이나 박복하다고 생각한다."

"왜?"

"글쎄 – 얘야, 신경쓰지 마라! 어쩌면 내가 원래 그냥 박복한가 보지!" 그녀가 말했다.

아이는 어머니가 그에게서 뭔가 숨기려고 한다는 듯이 그녀의 꽉 다물린 입을 쳐다보았다.

"그치만 어쨌든," 그가 말했다. "내게는 그 운이 있어요"

"글쎄 어쨌든," 그가 말했다. "나는 운을 타고났어요."

"왜?" 그의 어머니가 별안 웃으며 되물었다.

그는 어머니를 다시 쳐다보았다. 자신이 왜 그런 말을 했는지도 알 수 없단 투였다.

"어… 하느님이 말해줬어요." 그가 깨지듯 확언했다.

"아니, 정말 그랬으면 좋겠다, 얘야!" 그녀가 다시 웃으며 말했다. 하지만 이번엔 아까보다 더 씁쓸한 웃음이었다.

"정말 그랬다니까요!"

"훌륭해!" 어머니가 자기 남편의 말버릇을 흉내내어 말했다.

아이는 그녀가 자신의 말을 믿지 않는 것을 알았다. 아니, 어쩌면 신경조차 쓰지 않는 것일지도. 그는 그것 때문에 왠지 참을 수 없으리만큼 화가 났고, 어머니가 자기 말을 진지하게 들었으면 하는 생각이 커졌다.

그는 '운'이란 건 대체 뭘까 하고 멍하니 생각했다. 아이같이, 다른 사람은 안중에도 없이. 그는 '운'이라는 단어의 실마리를 잡고자 했다. 그는 운을 원했다. 그는 운을 원했다. 그는 운을 원했다. 두 누이가 놀이방에서 인형놀이를 할 때면, 그는 그의 흔들목마에 앉아 미친 듯 몸을 흔들었고, 여자아이들은 그 발작을 보며 겁에 질렸다. 목마의 거친 움직임 때문에 소년의 검은 머리카락은 이리 저리 흩날렸고, 그럴 때마다 그의 눈에서 알 수 없는 광채가 번뜩이곤 했다. 그런 때면 여자아이들은 감히 그에게 말을 걸 엄두도 내지 못하는 것이었다.

그가 그 광기에 찬 여행을 마치고 흔들목마에서 기어내가면, 그는 언제나 얼굴을 숙이고 그 머리를 빤히 쳐다보곤 했다 목마의 시뻘건 입은 살짝 벌려져 있었고, 부릅뜨인 눈은 유리처럼 빛났다.

"이제 지금!" 그는 투레질하는듯한 말 머리에 대고 낮은 목소리로 명령했다. "이제 나를 운에게 데려다 줘! 자 이제! 나를 데려다 줘!"

그는 오스카 삼촌이 사다 준 채찍으로 말의 목을 때렸다. 그는 자기가 명령만 한다면 그 말이 자신을 운에게로 데려다 줄 것을 알고 있었다. 그리고 그는 말에 다시 기어올라 그 광기 어린 질주를 다시 시작하는 것이었다. 그는 자신이 운에 가 닿기를 원했다. 그는 자신이 운에 가 닿을 것을 알고 있었다.

"그러다 말이 부서지고 말겠다! 폴!" 유모가 말했다.

"쟤는 항상 저런 식으로 목마를 타! 제발 그만 좀 뒀으면 좋겠어!" 그의 누나 조안이 말했다.

하지만 그는 침묵 속에서 그들을 노려볼 뿐이었다. 유모는 포기했다. 그는 원체 그를 다루지 못했다. 어쨌든, 폴은 유모가 다루기엔 너무 큰 애였으니까. 어느날 그의 어머니와 오스카 삼촌이 그가 미친듯이 말을 타는 모습을 보았다. 폴은 그들에게 말조차 걸지 않았다.

"안녕! 우리 어린 기수님! 우승마를 타고 있느냐?" 그의 삼촌이 말했다.

"너는 이제 흔들목마를 타기에는 좀 크지 않았니? 너는 이제 그렇게 어리지도 않은데." 그의 어머니가 말했다.

그러나 폴은 그들에게 반쯤 감긴 눈으로 푸른 시선을 한번 던졌을 뿐, 대답하려고 하지 않았다. 그의 어머니는 근심스러운 빛을 띠었다.

결국 그가 속도를 늦추더니 말에서 뛰어내렸다.

"가 닿았어요!" 그가 당당하게 선언했다. 다리를 벌리고 우뚝 서서 눈을 푸른 빛으로 불태우며.

"어디를 가 닿았단 말이지?" 어머니가 물었다.

"내가 가고 싶었던 곳에." 그가 불에 맞불이 부딪히듯 대답했다.

"말 한번 잘했다, 내 아들!" 삼촌이 말했다. "남자라면 목적에 도달할 때까지 멈추지 말아야 하는 법이지. 그 말의 이름은 뭐냐?"

"이름은 없어요." 소년이 말했다.

"없어도 괜찮은 거니?" 그의 삼촌이 물었다.

"글쎄, 다른 이름이 있긴 있어요. 지난주 이름은 산소비노였어요."

"산소비노라구, 응? 애스콧 경마에서 이긴 말 말이지. 그걸 어떻게 다 알았느냐?"

"얘는 바셋하고 언제나 경마 이야기만 해요!" 그의 누이 조안이 말했다.

삼촌은 그의 어린 조카가 경마에 취미가 있는 걸 알고 크게 기뻐했다. 바셋은 젊은 정원사로, 전쟁 중 왼발을 다쳤다가 그가 상사로 모시던 오스카 크래스웰의 소개로 이 집에 들어오게 되었는데, 경마에 관해서라면 뭐든 척척이었다. 그는 경마장에서 살다시피 했으며 소년은 그를 따라 살다시피 했다.

오스카 크래스웰은 곧 바셋이 애를 물들인 것을 알았다.

"폴 도련님은 저에게 와서 물어보시지요. 어쩔 땐 저보다 한수 더 위시랍니다." 바셋이 말했다. 거의 종교

이야기를 하는 것만큼이나 끔찍하게 진지한 얼굴이었다.

"그 애가 자기가 고른 경주마에 뭐를 걸던가?"

"글쎄요 – 일러바치고 싶지는 않습니다만 – 폴 도련님은 꽤 능란한 꾼이시랍니다. 썩 잘하시기도 하고요. 직접 한번 물어보시겠습니까? 그분은 경마를 정말로 좋아하십니다. 어쩌면 그분이 제가 고자질을 했다고 생각하실지 모르겠습니다. 한번 직접 물어보시지요, 괜찮으시다면요." 바셋은 교회당처럼 진지했다.

삼촌은 다시 조카에게 돌아가서 그를 드라이브에 데리고 나갔다.

"폴, 말해 봐. 너 경마에 무엇이든 걸어 본 적 있느냐?" 삼촌이 물었다.

소년은 그 잘생긴 남자를 빤히 쳐다보았다.

"왜요? 제가 말에 뭘 건다고 생각하세요?" 그가 대답을 슬쩍 피했다.

"아니! 절대 아니지! 난 그냥 네가 링컨 경마에 대해 뭐라도 충고를 해 줄 수 있을까 궁금해서 그런단다."

차가 삼촌의 집이 있는 햄프셔로 통하는 시골 교외를 달렸다.

"정말? 삼촌? 남자의 명예를 걸고?" 조카가 말했다.

"물론이지, 남자의 명예를 걸고!" 삼촌이 말했다.

"그럼 삼촌, 수선화야."

"수선화라니! 못 믿겠는걸! 우리 아들아, 미르자는 어떠냐?"

"난 딱 우승마만 알아요." 소년이 말했다. "우승마는 수선화야."

"수선화란 말이지?"

잠시 정적이 있었다. 수선화는 승률이 퍽 낮은 말이었다.

"삼촌!"

"그래, 우리 아들!"

"아무에게도 말하지 않을 거지요? 난 바셋이랑 약속한걸."

"망할 놈 같으니라구. 그 늙은 놈이, 대체 그놈이 또 뭐라고 그러디?"

"우린 파트너에요. 우린 처음부터 파트너였어요. 삼촌, 그가 나한테 5실링을 처음 빌려줬어. 나는 그걸 잃었어. 나랑 바셋은 우리 둘만 알기로 꼭꼭 약속했어. 남자의 명예야. 나는 삼촌이 빌려준 10실링으로 처음 따기 시작한 거에요. 그래서 난 삼촌은 운이 있는 사람이구나 하고 생각했어요. 이걸 아무한테도 이야기하지 않을 거죠, 그렇죠?"

소년은 반쯤 감긴 눈으로 그를 쳐다보았다. 뜨겁고 푸른 시선이었다. 삼촌이 한번 어렵게 웃었다.

"네 말이 맞다! 일급 비밀로 삼으마. 수선화라구? 너 대체 그 말에 얼마나 걸었느냐?"

"비상금 20파운드만 남겨 두고 전부 다." 소년이 말했다. "그건 꼭 숨겨놨어요."

삼촌은 그게 농담이라고 생각했다.

"비상금으로 20파운드나 남겨 두다니, 이 어린 공상가가. 그럼 건 것은 대체 얼마니?"

"삼백." 소년이 엄숙하게 말했다. "삼촌하고 나만 알아야 해요, 삼촌! 남자의 명예를 걸고 약속했죠?"

삼촌이 거칠게 으르렁거리듯 웃었다.

"물론 너와 나 뿐이지, 조그만 냇 굴드 양반!" 그가 웃으며 말했다. "그 삼백은 대체 어디서 난 삼백이지?"

"바셋이 내 대신 가지고 있어요. 우리는 파트너니까."

"그렇겠지. 그렇겠지. 바셋도 수선화에 걸었느냐?"

"어, 내 생각으론, 나처럼 전부 다 걸진 않았을 것 같아요. 아마도 한 150 정도…?"

"뭐, 150페니?" 삼촌이 웃었다.

"파운드로." 애가 말했다. 그는 놀란 듯이 삼촌을 쳐다보았다. "바셋은 나보다 더 많이 남겨뒀어요."

삼촌은 궁금함과 즐거움을 느꼈지만, 아무 말도 하지 않았다. 그는 아무에게도 이 일을 말할 생각은 없었지만, 어쨌든 이 조카를 링컨 경마에 데려가야겠다고 결정했다.

"자, 우리 아들." 그가 말했다. "난 벌써 미르자에 20을 걸었다. 그리고 네가 고르는 말에 5파운드 더 거마. 누굴 고르겠니?"

"수선화야, 삼촌."

"수선화 말고!"

"어쨌든 그게 내 돈이라면 난 수선화에 걸겠어요." 애가 말했다.

"좋아! 좋아! 네 마음대로 하자! 수선화에 나를 위해서 5파운드 걸고 널 위해서 5파운드 더 걸지!"

아이는 이전에는 한번도 실제 경마를 구경하러 간 적이 없었다. 경기를 보는 그의 눈빛은 푸른 불길 같았다. 그는 입을 꽉 다물고 경기만을 바라봤다. 그들 앞에 있는 프랑스인은 랭슬롯에 돈을 걸었다. 그는 흥분해서 팔을 함부로 휘두르며 "랭슬롯! 랭슬롯!"이라고 프랑스 악센트로 소리질렀다.

수선화가 첫번째로 들어왔다. 랭슬롯이 두번째였다. 미르자는 세번째로 들어왔다. 아이는 의기양양한 홍조를 띠고 눈을 빛냈다. 묘하게 침착한 태도였다. 그의 삼촌이 5파운드 몫의 배당금을 타 주었다. 4대 1의 확률이었다.

"자, 이제 어떻게 해야 하겠느냐!" 삼촌이 그 돈을 소년의 눈 앞에 대고 흔들며 소리질렀다.

"바셋이랑 이야기를 해 봐야 할 것 같아요." 소년이 말했다. "이제 내 돈은 1500파운드로 늘어났죠. 그리고 비상금 20파운드랑. 그리고 새로 번 이 20파운드랑."

삼촌은 잠시 동안 조카의 말을 곱씹고 있었다.

"잠깐 봐라!" 그가 말했다. "너, 설마 그 바셋이 가지고 있다는 그 1500파운드 이야기가 정말인 건 아니겠지."

"아니, 정말이에요. 하지만 삼촌하고 나만 알고 누구도 더 알면 안돼요. 삼촌, 신사의 명예를 걸고 약속했어요."

"신사의 명예를 걸고 약속했고 말고! 우리 아들. 하지만 난 바셋이란 놈하고 이야기 좀 해 봐야겠다."

"만약 삼촌이 우리 파트너가 되고 싶으면요, 바셋하고 나하고 말이에요, 아마 삼촌은 될 수 있을거에요. 삼촌이 신사의 명예를 걸고 약속해주기만 하면요. 이 일은 우리 사이에서만 알고 절대로 누구도 알면 안 돼요. 바셋이랑 나는 운이 좋아요. 그리고 삼촌도 틀림없이 운 좋은 사람이야. 왜냐하면 나는 삼촌이 나한테 준 10실링으로 따기 시작했으니까…"

오스카 삼촌은 오후에 바셋과 폴을 리치몬드 공원에 데려 가서 셋이서 이야기했다.

"그렇게 된 겁니다." 바셋이 말했다. "폴 도련님과 저는 경주가 있을 때마다 이야기를 하지요. 실낫기처럼 말입니다. 도련님은 언제나 제가 잃을지 아니면 딸지를 아시지요. 벌써 좋이 1년은 되었습니다. 제가 도련님을 위해 새벽의 여명에게 5실링 대신 걸어드렸지요. 그리고 잃었습니다. 그리고 운이 다시 돌아와서, 당신께서 폴 도련님께 주신 10실링을 싱할레스에 걸었지요. 그때부터 우린 꽤 꾸준히 따왔습니다. 폴 도련님, 뭔가 하실 말씀 있으십니까?"

"우리가 확실히 알고 있을 땐 아무 문제 없어요." 폴이 말했다. "만약에 확실히 모르겠다 싶으면, 그땐 져요."

"아, 하지만 우리는 퍽 조심하고 있습죠." 바셋이 말했다.

"하지만 네가 확신할 때는?" 오스카 삼촌이 미소지었다.

"폴 도련님 말입니다." 바셋이 비밀스럽게 말했다. 경건한 목소리었다. "꼭 천국에서 어떤 계시를 받으시는 것 같아요. 수선화 일처럼, 이번 링컨 경주의 수선화처럼 말입니다. 마치 알을 훔치기만큼이나 확실했어요."

"자네도 수선화에 뭔가 걸었나?" 오스카 크레스웰이 물었다.

"그렇습죠. 제 몫을 걸었습니다."

"그리고 내 조카도?"

바셋은 폴 쪽을 돌아보며 고집스럽게 침묵했다.

"난 거진 1200파운드를 땄어. 그렇지, 바셋? 난 벌써 삼촌에게 수선화에게 300 걸었다고 말씀드렸어."

"그렇습죠." 바셋이 끄덕이며 말했다.

"그 돈은 대체 어디다 뒀니?" 삼촌이 물었다.

"제가 보관하고 안전하게 자물쇠를 채워 놨습니다. 폴 도련님은 언제 어느 때라도 원하실 때 제게 말씀만 하시면 됩니다."

"뭐, 1500파운드를 말인가?"

"그리고 20파운드 더 있습죠. 아니, 40입니다만, 이번 경주에서 20파운드 더 따셨으니까요."

"대단하군!" 삼촌이 말했다.

"폴 도련님이 먼저 제게 파트너가 되자고 말하셨습죠. 제가 만약 어르신이라면 꼭 하겠습니다. 제가 낀 게 불편하지만 않으시다면 말씀입니다." 바셋이 말했다.

오스카 크레스웰은 잠시 생각에 잠겼다.

"일단 그 돈을 봐야겠네."

그들은 다시 차를 타고 집에 돌아갔다. 그리고 확실히 바셋은 1500파운드를 들고 돌아왔다. 20파운드는 경마 위원회의 조 글리에게 보증금 조로 맡겨두었다.

"보셨죠, 삼촌? 내가 확신하고 있을 때면 모든 게 다 괜찮아요. 그럼 우린 세게 나가요. 그렇지, 바셋?"

"그렇지요. 폴 도련님."

"우리가 확신할 때라고?" 삼촌이 웃으며 말했다.

"어, 그게요, 내가 완벽하게 확신할 때가 있어요. 수선화 때처럼." 소년이 말했다. "그리고 가끔은 그냥 이럴 것 같다는 생각만 들어요. 어쩔때는 그런 생각도 안 들 때도 있어요. 그렇지, 바셋? 그러면 우리는 조심해요. 왜냐면 그럴 때 우리는 거의 지니까."

"그렇겠지, 그렇겠지! 그리고 네가 수선화 때처럼 확신을 가질 때 말이다. 내 조카야, 대체 어떻게 그걸 아니?"

"어, 그게, 잘 모르겠어요." 소년이 어렵사리 말했다. "그냥 알아요. 삼촌. 그게 다에요."

"마치 천국에서 계시를 받으시는 것 같습죠!" 바셋이 반복했다.

"나도 그렇게 말할 수밖에 없을 것 같으이!" 삼촌이 말했다.

하지만 그도 파트너가 되었다.

그리고 레저 경마가 다가왔을 때, 폴은 라이블리 스파크라는 별로 승률 높지 않은 말이 우승할 것이라고 확신했다. 소년은 1000파운드를 걸었다. 바셋은 500을 걸었다. 오스카 크레스웰은 200을 걸었다. 라이블리 스파크가 첫번째로 들어왔다. 그리고 배당은 1대 10이었다. 폴은 1만 파운드를 벌었다.

"봤죠." 소년이 말했다. "난 벌써 확실히 알고 있었어요."

오스카 크레스웰조차도 2천 파운드를 벌었다.

"봐라, 애야." 그가 말했다. "난 왠지 점점 불안해지는구나."

"괜찮아요, 삼촌! 어쩌면 난 오랫동안 확신이 들지 않을지도 몰라요."

"하지만 넌 대체 이 돈을 어떻게 할 작정이냐?" 삼촌이 물었다.

"물론," 소년이 말했다. "먼저 엄마에게 드릴 거예요. 엄마는 자기가 운이 없대요. 아빠가 운이 없으니까. 그래서 난 생각했어요. 만약 내가 운이 좋다면, 내가 그 속삭임을 멈출 수 있을 거라고."

"뭐가 속삭임을 멈춘다는 거냐?"

"우리 집. 난 우리 집이 속삭이는 게 싫어요."

"아니, 대체 그 속삭인다는 게 뭐지?"

"왜 – 왜" – 갑자기 애가 안달을 부렸다. "왜? 왜인지 난 몰라요. 하지만 언제나 돈이 부족하단 건 알아요. 삼촌도 알죠?"

"알지. 애야. 물론 알고 있지."

"돈이 부족하면 집이 속삭여요. 사람들이 등 뒤에서 막 비웃을 때처럼. 너..너무 끔찍해요 그건! 난 그저 내가 만약 운이 좋다면…"

"네가 속삭임을 멈출 수 있을 거라고." 삼촌이 덧붙였다.

소년은 삼촌을 푸른 큰 눈으로 바라보았다. 차갑고, 어쩐지 불편한 불길이 눈에서 타오르고 있었다. 그는 아무 말도 하지 않았다.

"좋아, 그렇다면!" 삼촌이 말했다. "이제 어쩌지?"

"난 어머니가 내가 운이 좋다는 걸 몰랐으면 해요."

"왜 안 되지, 우리 아들?"

"어머니가 날 그만 두게 할 거예요."

"난 그 애가 그렇게 할 것 같지 않은걸."

"아!" – 그리고 소년이 기묘하게 몸을 떨었다 – "어머니가 알면 싫어요. 삼촌."

"좋다, 애야! 네 엄마한테 말하지 않고도 어떻게든 해나갈 수 있겠지."

사실 그들은 아주 잘 해 나갔다. 폴은 충고에 따라 5,000 파운드를 가족 변호사의 공증 하에 삼촌에게 넘겨주었다.

그 가족 변호사는 폴의 엄마에게 어느 친척이 그녀에게 5천 파운드를 남기고 죽었으며, 이제 돌아오는 생일마다 천 파운드씩, 5년 동안 5천 파운드를 받게 되리라고 알리는 역할을 맡았다.

"그러니, 그 애는 이제 5년 동안 생일 선물로 천 파운드씩 받게 되는 셈이지." 오스카 삼촌이 말했다.

"이것 때문에 그 애가 나중에 더 힘들어지지나 않게 되길 빌자꾸나"

폴의 어머니의 생일은 12월에 있었다. 집은 어떤 때보다도 더 심하게 "속삭였다." 그리고, 운을 차치하고서라도 폴은 그 소리를 견딜 수가 없었다. 그는 어머니가 천 파운드가 생긴 것을 알게 되면 어떤 일이 일어날까 하고 심히 걱정했다.

방문객은 없었다. 폴은 보모의 시중을 받으며 부모님과 함께 아침을 먹고 있었다. 그의 어머니는 요즘 매일같이 시내에 들렀다. 어머니는 자신이 모피나 다른 옷 종류를 그리는 데 썩 재주가 있단 걸 발견하고, 자기 친구인 어떤 호화 부티크의 "작가 선생님"의 스튜디오에서 몰래 일을 도와주고 있었다. 신문 광고용으로 쓸 모피나 실크, 반짝이로 몸을 휘감은 여자들을 그리는 일이었다. 이 작가 선생님은 1년에 몇천 파운드의 수입을 올렸다. 그러나 폴의 어머니는 고작 몇백 파운드를 벌었다. 그리고 그녀는 다시 불만족스러워하는 것이었다. 그녀는 무슨 일에서든지 제일이 되고 싶어했지만 성공하지 못했고, 지금은 부티크 광고나 그리고 있다.

생일날 아침에 그녀는 조반을 먹으려 내려왔다. 폴은 편지를 읽는 어머니의 얼굴을 관찰했다. 그는 그 편지가 변호사에게서 온 것인줄 알고 있었다. 그 편지를 읽는 어머니의 얼굴은 딱딱했고, 읽으면 읽을수록 더욱 표정이 없어져 갔다. 차갑고 단호한 표정이 그녀의 입매에 서렸다. 그녀는 그 편지를 다른 편지들 속에다가 갈무리하고 따로 아무 말도 하지 않았다.

"편지에 뭔가 좋은 일이라도 쓰여있어요, 어머니?" 폴이 말했다.

"그럭 저럭 나쁘진 않구나." 그녀의 목소리는 차갑고 굳어 있었다. 그녀는 더 아무 말도 하지 않고 시내로 내려갔다.

하지만 오후에 오스카 삼촌이 나타났다. 그는 폴의 어머니가 그 5천 파운드를 한번에 받을 수 없는지 변호사와 긴 상담을 했다고 했다. 그녀에게 빚이 있다는 것이었다.

"삼촌은 어떻게 생각해요?" 소년이 물었다.

"네 생각대로 하려무나, 애야."

"아, 그렇다면 그냥 어머니가 가지시라고 해요! 우린 또 다른 데에서 그만큼 벌 수 있잖아요." 소년이 말했다.

"경솔하구나. 손 안의 새 한 마리가 덤불 속의 새 두 마리보다 낫단다!" 오스카 삼촌이 말했다.

"하지만 난 그랜드 내셔널이 어떻게 될지 확실히 알아요. 아니면 링컨셔, 아니면 더비. 어쨌든 그 중 하나는 확실히 알아요." 폴이 말했다.

그러자 오스카 삼촌은 동의서에 사인했고, 폴의 어머니는 5천 파운드를 손에 넣었다. 그러자 무엇인가 대단히 기묘한 일이 벌어졌다. 갑자기 집의 목소리가 광기에 휩싸였다. 마치 봄밤을 맞아 우는 수천 개구리떼의 합창 같았다.

새 커튼과 가구들이 들어왔다. 폴에게 가정교사가 생겼다. 그는 정말로 가을학기부터 아버지의 모교이기도 했던 이튼 학교에 다니게 되었다. 한 겨울임에도 집 안에는 꽃이 있었고, 폴의 어머니의 사치도 꽃처럼 피어났다. 그리고 미모사 다발과 아몬드 꽃송이, 무지개색 쿠션 뒤편의 은밀한 곳에서, 집 안의 목소리는 정신을 잃고 쾌락에 차 신음했다.

"돈이 필요해! 오-오오, 돈이 더 있어야만 해! 오, 지금! 지-그-ㅁ! ㅈㅣ금-!-ㅁ! 돈이 더 있어야 해! 돈! 훨씬 더! 훨씬 더!"

그건 폴을 끔찍하게 괴롭혔다. 그는 과외 교사에게 라틴어와 희랍어를 배웠다. 그렇지만 그는 바셋과 있는 시간에 훨씬 더 집중적으로 투자했다. 그랜드 내셔널이 지나갔다. 그는 '알지' 못했다. 그리고 그는 100파운드를 잃었다. 여름이 코앞에 있었다. 그는 링컨 경마 때문에 괴로워했다. 그렇지만 링컨 경마도 그는 '알아내지' 못했다. 그는 50파운드를 잃었다. 그의 눈이 점점 커져갔다. 이상한 기운까지 감돌았다. 마치 그 안의 무엇이 폭발하기 직전이라는 듯이.

"이제 그만 해라! 애야! 너무 마음 쓰지 말아라!" 폴 삼촌이 권했다. 하지만 소년은 삼촌이 말하는 것을 듣고 있는 것 같지 않았다.

"난 더비 경마를 알아냈어요! 난 더비 경마를 알아요!" 아이가 저항했다. 그의 큰 푸른 눈이 광기를 내뿜었다.

그의 어머니가 그가 뭔가 이상하다는 것을 알아챘다.

"어딘가 해변으로 가서 정양하는 편이 좋겠다. 입학하기 전에 바닷가에 가 보고 싶지 않니? 아무래도 그게 좋겠구나." 그녀가 그를 근심스레 쳐다보면서 말했다. 그녀의 마음이 무거워졌다.

그러나 아이가 그의 열에 들뜬 푸른 눈을 들었다.

"더비 경마 이전엔 떠날 수 없어요, 어머니!" 그가 말했다. "그럴 수 없어요!"

"왜 안 된다는 거지?" 그녀의 목소리가 반대 탓에 무거워졌다. "왜 안 되지? 해변에서 있더라도, 만약 네가 더비에 그렇게 가고 싶다면 오스카 삼촌이 데려다 줄 거다. 꼭 집에서 기다릴 필요는 없어. 사실, 너는 너무 경마에 신경을 쓰는 것 같구나. 나쁜 징조야. 우리 집안은 도박벽이 있어. 그리고 넌 도박이라는 게 얼마나 무서운지 절대 모를 거다. 아무래도 바셋을 내보내야 할까 보다. 그리고 오스카에게 네게 경마 이야기는 꺼내지 말라고 말해야겠어. 네가 그렇게까지 집착하지 않겠다고 약속한다면 모르지만. 해변에 가서 머리를 식히렴. 그리고 다 잊어버려. 그렇게 안절부절하지 말고!"

"어머니가 가라고 하시면 어디든지 가 있을게요. 하지만 더비 경마 때까지만이라도 여기 있게 해 주세요." 소년이 말했다.

"어디든지라니 어디로? 그저 이 집 말고 어디든?"

"네." 소년이 그녀를 뚫어지게 쳐다보며 말했다.

"왜? 참 이상하구나. 왜 이렇게 이 집에 집착하니? 그것도 이렇게 갑자기. 네가 이 집을 그렇게 좋아하는지 전혀 몰랐다."

그는 그녀를 아무 말 없이 바라보았다. 그에겐 비밀 중의 비밀이 있었다. 바셋이나 오스카 삼촌에게조차 결코 말하지 않은 비밀이었다. 그러나 그의 어머니는 잠시 망설인 뒤 아무 것도 결정하지 않고 일어났다.

"좋아! 그렇다면 더비 경마가 열릴 때까지는 여기 있는 거다! 하지만 그렇게 안절부절해서 돌아다니지 않겠다고 약속하렴. 말이나, 네가 말한 대로라면 그 행사 같은 건 생각조차 하지 않겠다고 약속하는거야!"

"아! 절대로 안 할게요." 그가 가볍게 말했다. "그렇게 깊게 생각하지 않겠다고 약속할게요. 걱정하실 필요 없어요. 내가 어머니라면 절대 걱정하지 않을 거에요."

"네가 나라면, 그리고 내가 너라면 말이지." 그의 어머니가 말했다. "난 대체 우리가 어떻게 해야 할지 모르겠구나!"

"하지만 어머니는 걱정할 필요 없다는 걸 알잖아요. 어머니, 그렇죠?" 소년이 대답했다.

"글쎄, 그래서 기쁘다고 해야겠지." 그녀가 걱정스레 중얼거렸다.

"아, 괜찮아요, 그렇잖아요. 제 말은, 어머니는 당연히 걱정할 필요 없다는 걸 아실 거라고요."

"당연히라고? 한번 보자." 그녀가 말했다.

그의 비밀 중의 비밀은 그 이름 없는 목마에 있었다. 그가 유모와 보모에게서 놓인 뒤, 그는 그의 목마를 집 꼭대기에 있는 그가 쓰는 침실에 가져다 놓았다.

그의 어머니가 "너는 확실히 그 말을 타고 놀기에는 너무 컸어" 라고 하면, 그는 항상 "진짜 말을 타기 전까지는 이 말이라도 타고 놀겠어요" 라고 하는 것이었다.

"그 말이 네 친구라도 되느냐?" 그녀가 웃었다.

"아, 당연하죠! 이 애는 정말 착해요. 언제나 내 친구인걸요. 내가 그곳에 가 닿을 때면 말이에요." 폴이 말했다.

그래서 그 말은 때묻은 채로 소년의 방에 머물게 되었다.

더비 경마가 가까워졌고, 소년은 더더욱 긴장했다. 그는 속삭임을 간간이 들었다. 그는 점점 불안정해졌고, 그 눈은 점점 인간을 초월한 것 같은 빛을 띄었다. 그의 어머니는 갑자기 그에게서 불편한 기색이 없어진 것을 알았다. 종종 반시간 정도 그 애의 걱정이 머리에서 떠나지 않아 못 견디게 근심스러울 때가 있었다. 어쩔 때는 그가 무사히 있다는 걸 잘 알고 있음에도 한달음에 달려가서 아이를 확인해 보고 싶었다.

더비 경마 이틀 전, 그녀는 또 다시 자신의 아들에 대한 알 수 없는 근심이 그녀의 심장을 꽉 쥐어채는 것을 느꼈다. 그녀의 아들, 첫 아이에 대한 걱정 때문에 거의 말을 하기가 힘들 정도였다. 마침 그녀가 시내에 있는 큰 파티에 초대받아 나와 있을 때였다. 그녀는 그 감정에 맞서 싸웠다. 반복해서 아무 것도 아니라고 자신을 달랬지만,

그 육감은 너무나도 강했다. 그는 무도회장을 나와 전화가 있는 아래층까지 내려왔다. 보모는 한밤중에 걸려온 전화 때문에 깜짝 놀랐다.

"아이들에게 아무 일도 없나요, 윌못 양?"

"아, 당연하죠. 다들 잘 있습니다."

"폴은? 그 애도 잘 있지요?"

"아까 전에 잠자러 올라갔습니다. 잠깐 위층에 가서 보고 올까요?"

"아니요." 그녀가 마지못해 말했다. "아뇨, 그러실 것까지 없어요. 괜찮아요. 그냥 가만히 계세요. 우리도 금방 들어갈 테니까." 그녀는 애를 그런 식으로 귀찮게 굴고 싶지 않았다.

"알겠습니다." 보모가 말했다.

폴의 어머니와 아버지는 한시가 다 되어서야 집에 들어갔다. 집은 정적에 싸여 있었다. 폴의 어머니는 자신의 방에 들어가서 자신의 흰 모피 망토를 벗었다. 그녀는 자신의 하녀에게 기다리지 말고 편히 쉬라고 말했다. 그녀의 남편이 아랫층에서 위스키에 소다를 따르는 것이 들렸다.

그리고, 다시 그 이상한 불안이 그녀를 사로잡았다. 그녀는 아들의 방이 있는 위층으로 조심스레 올라가 복도를 따라 소리 없이 걸었다. 이상한 소리가 들렸나? 방금 그게 뭐였지?

그녀는 아들의 방문 밖에서 몸이 굳은 채 우뚝 서서, 그 이상한 소리를 들었다.

기괴하고, 무겁고, 작은 소리였다. 그녀의 심장이 멈췄다. 그것은 소리 없는 소리였지만,

힘차게 계속되는 소리였다. 뭔가 크고, 난폭한 움직임의…

저게 뭐지? 오 주여! 저게 뭐지? 그녀는 알려 했다. 그녀는 그 소리가 묘하게 낯익다고 생각했다. 그녀는 그 소리를 알고 있었다.

하지만 감히 방문을 열지 못했다. 그것이 뭔지 말할 수는 없었다. 그리고 그 소리가 되풀이될수록 – 그 소리는 점점 미쳐가는 것처럼 들렸다.

부드럽게, 공포에 잠긴 채 그녀가 방문 손잡이를 돌렸다.

방은 어두웠다. 그녀는 무엇인가가 창문가에서 미친 듯 앞뒤로 덜그럭거리는 것을 들었다.

그녀는 경악과 공포 속에서 그것을 보았다.

그녀가 불을 켰고, 불빛 속에서 아들의 모습을 보았다. 초록색 잠옷을 입고 광기서린 몸집으로 흔들목마를 앞뒤로 모는 모습을.

금발 머리의 그녀는, 연둣빛 비단옷과 크리스탈을 댄 찬란한 옷에 싸여, 문가에서 우두커니 서 있을 뿐이었다.

"폴!" 그녀가 울부짖었다. "대체 뭘 하고 있니?"

"말라바다!" 그가 고함쳤다. 괴기한 목소리였다. "말라바다!"

그의 눈이 낯선 이를 본다는 듯이 어머니를 힐끗 스쳤다. 무감각한 눈초리였다.

그가 흔들목마를 거칠게 몰아대었다. 그는 목마에서 떨어져 땅에 고꾸라졌고, 그녀는 별안 어머니로써의 억눌러진 모성애가 그녀에게 몰아닥치는 것을 느꼈다. 그녀는 달려가 그를 일으켜 세웠다.

하지만 그는 여전히 의식이 없고, 마치 정신이 열에 들뜬 것마냥 말하며 몸을 흔들었다. 어머니는 돌처럼 굳어 서 있을 뿐이었다.

"말라바! 말라바다! 바셋, 바셋, 난 알았어! 말라바야!"

아이는 그렇게 소리지르며 자신에게 그 계시를 준 목마에 기어올라가려 했다.

"말라바라는 게 대체 무슨 뜻이냐?" 얼음 심장의 어머니가 말했다.

"나도 모르겠소." 아버지도 돌처럼 뇌까렸다.

"대체 말라바라는 게 무슨 뜻이야?" 그녀가 오스카에게 물었다.

"더비 경마에서 뛰는 말 이름이다" 대답이 돌아왔다.

그리고, 오스카 크래스웰은 무심코 그 말을 바셋에게 흘렸다. 그리고 그는 말라바에게 천 파운드를 걸었다. 배당은 1대 14배였다.

사흘째 되는 날이 고비였다. 그들은 차도를 기다리고 있었다. 소년의 길고 굽이치는 머리카락이 베개 위에서 떨리고 있었다.

그는 자고 있는 것도 아니었지만 깨어 있는 것도 아니었다. 그의 눈은 마치 푸른 돌 같았다. 그의 어머니는 그의 옆에서 자신의 마음이 죽어 천천히 돌이 되어 굳는 것을 느끼고 있었다.

저녁에, 오스카 크레스웰은 오지 않았지만 바셋 편으로 메세지를 보냈다. 잠시, 아주 잠깐만이라도 들어갈 수 있겠느냐 것이었다.

그녀는 그 경우 없는 전언에 화가 났지만, 들어오기를 허락했다. 소년의 상태는 낫지 않고 있었다. 어쩌면 바셋이 들어와서 애가 정신을 차리게 될지도 몰랐다.

날카로운 눈초리와 짧은 콧수염을 한 정원사가 발끝으로 살금살금 걸어들어와 폴의 어머니에게 모자를 까닥이는 시늉을 하며 예를 차렸다. 그리고 침대가에 서서 반짝이는 작은 눈으로 몸을 떨며 죽어가는 아이를 내려보았다.

"폴 도련님!" 그가 속삭였다. "폴 도련님! 말라바가 1등으로 들어왔습니다. 깨끗한 압승이었지요. 저는 도련님께서 말씀하신대로 걸었습니다. 이미 7만 파운드 넘게 버셨었지요. 이제 가지신 총액은 8만 파운드가 넘습니다. 말라바가 우승했습니다. 폴 도련님!"

"말라바! 말라바! 내가 말라바라고 말했지 않아요, 어머니? 내가 말라바라고 했었지요? 어머니, 나야말로 운이 좋다고 생각지 않나요? 그렇죠? 어머니! 나는 말라바인걸 알았었어요. 그렇죠? 8만 파운드 그 이상! 나는 그걸 바로 운 자체라고 부르겠어요. 어머니는요? 어머니! 8만 파운드 그 이상! 난 알았어요. 나는 내가 안다는 걸 알았지 않나요? 말라바가 1등으로. 내가 만약 오랫동안, 충분히 오랫동안 내 말을 타고 달린다면, 바셋, 난 그때 네게 말하는 거야. 내가 원하는 만큼 높게 갈 수 있다고! 바셋, 얼마나 걸었어?"

"천 파운드 걸었습니다. 폴 도련님."

"어머니, 난 절대로 말하지 않았어요. 내가 만약 그 말을 달리면, 그리고 그곳에 닿게 되면, 나는 완벽하게 확신한다고 — 오, 완벽하게! 어머니, 내가 말 한 적 없나요? 내가 운이 좋다고!"

"아니. 말한 적 없어." 어머니가 말했다.

소년은 그 날 밤에 죽었다.

그리고 그가 죽어서 누워있을 때, 어머니는 그녀의 오빠가 그녀에게 말하는 것을 들었다.

"신이여, 헤스터. 너는 8만 파운드를 버는 편에 애처로운 악마 같은 네 아들을 잃었구나. 불쌍한, 애처로운 악마 같으니. 그는 승마를 알아냈던 그 최고의 순간에 삶에서 튕겨져 나가 버린 거야."

Chapter 03 Novels in the Exam

김수아 전공영어 | 영미문학 Reading for Literature II

1. Novels in the Teacher Certification Exam (2021~2014)

기입형

01 Read the excerpt from a novel and follow the directions. [2 points]   (21-A-4)

> It had seemed like a good idea at the time. Of course, Philip Danby had only been joking, but he had said it in a serious tone in order to humor those idiot New Age clients who actually seemed to believe in the stuff. "I want to come back as a(n) _____," he'd said, smiling facetiously into the candlelight at the Eskeridge dinner table. He had to hold his breath to keep from laughing as the others babbled about reincarnation. The women wanted to come back blonder and thinner, and the men wanted to be everything from Dallas Cowboys to *oak trees*. Oak trees? And he had to keep a straight face through it all, hoping these dodos would give the firm some business.
>
> The things he had to put up with to humor clients. His partner, Giles Eskeridge, seemed to have no difficulties in that quarter, however. Giles often said that rich and crazy went together, therefore, architects who wanted a lucrative business had to be prepared to put up with eccentrics. They also had to put up with long hours, obstinate building contractors, and capricious zoning boards. Perhaps that was why Danby had plumped for life as a cat next time. As he had explained to his dinner companions that night, "Cats are independent. They don't have to kowtow* to anybody; they sleep sixteen hours a day; and yet they get fed and sheltered and even loved—just for being their contrary little selves. It sounds like a good deal to me."
>
> • To be too eager to obey or be polite to someone in authority

Fill in the blank with the ONE most appropriate word from the excerpt.

02 Read the excerpt from a novel and follow the directions. **2 points**   (21-B-2)

> She went into the shop. It was warm and smelled deliciously. The woman was just going to put some more hot buns into the window.
>
> "If you please," said Sara, "have you lost fourpence—a silver fourpence?" And she held the forlorn little piece of money out to her.
>
> The woman looked at it and then at her—at her intense little face and draggled, once fine clothes.
>
> "Bless us, no," she answered. "Did you find it?"
>
> "Yes," said Sara. "In the gutter."
>
> "Keep it, then," said the woman. "It may have been there for a week, and goodness knows who lost it. You could never find out."
>
> "I know that," said Sara, "but I thought I would ask you."
>
> "Not many would," said the woman, looked puzzled [. . .] and good-natured all at once.
>
> "Do you want to buy something?" she added, as she saw Sara glance at the buns.
>
> "Four buns, if you please," said Sara. "Those at a penny each."
>
> The woman went to the window and put some in a paper bag.
>
> Sara noticed that she put in six.
>
> "I said four, if you please," she explained. "I have only fourpence."
>
> "I'll throw in two for makeweight," said the woman with her good-natured look. "I dare say you can eat them sometime. Aren't you hungry?"
>
> A mist rose before Sara's eyes.
>
> "Yes," she answered. "I am very hungry, and I am much obliged to you for your kindness; and"—she was going to add—"there is a child outside who is hungrier than I am." But just at that moment two or three customers came in at once, and each one seemed in a hurry, so she could only thank the woman again and go out.

Complete the commentary below by filling in the blank with the ONE most appropriate word from the excerpt.

> **Commentary**
>
> Reading this scene, the reader can sense that Sara feels _____ to share her buns with a hungry child outside the shop.

03 Read the passage and follow the directions. (19-A-7)

When I came to my castle, for so I think I call'd it even after this, I fled into it like one pursued; whether I went over by the ladder as first contriv'd, or went in at the hole in the rock, which I call'd a door I cannot remember; nor, nor could I remember the next morning, for never frighted hare fled to cover, or fox to earth, with more terror of mind than I to this retreat.

I slept none that night; the farther I was from the occasion of my fright, the greater my apprehensions were, which is something contrary to the nature of such things and especially to the usual practice of all creatures in fear: But I was so embarrass'd with my own frightful ideas of the thing, that I form'd nothing but dismal imaginations to my self, even tho' I was now a great way off of it. Sometimes I fancy'd it must be the devil; and reason joyn'd in with me upon this supposition: For how should any other thing in human shape come into the place? Where was the vessel that brought them? What marks was there of any other footsteps! And how was it possible a man should come there? But then to think that Satan should take human shape upon him in such a place where there could be no manner of occasion for it, but to leave the print of his foot behind him, and that even for no purpose too, for he could not be sure I should see it; this was an amusement the other way; I consider'd that the devil might have found out abundance of other ways to have terrify'd me than this of the single print of a foot. That as I liv'd quite on the other side of the island, he would never have been so simple to leave a mark in a place where 'twas ten thousand to one whether I should ever see it or not, and in the sand too, which the first surge of the sea upon a high wind would have defac'd entirely: All this seem'd inconsistent with the thing it self, and with all the notions we usually entertain of the subtility of the devil.

Complete the commentary by filling in the blank with ONE word from the passage.

Commentary

In this scene, instead of rejoicing at the possibility of rescue or of a companion, the narrator reacts with fear. His apprehension is intensified because where he expected to find a trail of _____, he only found one.

04 Read the passage and follow the directions. (2 points) (15-A-8)

We know nothing of David Swan until we find him, at the age of twenty, on the road to the city of Boston, where he will work at his uncle's grocery store. After journeying on foot from sunrise till nearly noon on a summer's day, his tiredness and the increasing heat force him to rest in the first convenient shade, and wait for a stage-coach. As if planted on purpose, there soon appeared a small growth of maple trees, with a delightful clearing in the middle beside a fresh bubbling spring. He kissed it with his thirsty lips, and then flung himself beside it, pillowing his head upon some shirts. The spring murmured drowsily beside him and a deep sleep fell upon David Swan.

While he lay sound asleep in the shade, other people were wide awake, and passed here and there along the sunny road by his bed. Some looked neither to the right nor to the left, and never knew he was there; some laughed to see how soundly he slept; and several, whose hearts were brimming with scorn, spoke aloud their criticism of David Swan. Soon, a wealthy merchant with no heir considered waking him to share his fortune, but walked away. A beautiful young woman, momentarily touched by his peacefulness, considered loving him, but continued on her way. Two dark and dangerous thieves considered taking his life for his wallet, but decided they did not have time. But disapproval, praise, amusement, scorn, and indifference, were all one, or rather all nothing, and had no influence on the sleeping David Swan.

He slept, but no longer so quietly as at first. Now he stirred as a noise of wheels came rattling louder and louder along the road, until it rushed into the sleepy mist of David's rest — and there was the stage-coach. He rose, with all his ideas about him. He knew not that the possibility of Wealth or Love or Death had recently stood beside him — all, in the brief hour since he lay down to sleep.

Sleeping or waking, we rarely hear the soft footsteps of the strange things that almost happen. Doesn't this argue that there is a superintending Providence that, while viewless and unexpected events throw themselves continually in our path, there should still exist enough regularity in mortal life for us to foresee at least some of the possibilities available to us?

Complete the commentary by filling in the blank with ONE word from the passage.

> **Commentary**
>
> The passage conveys that we are unaware of many events in our lives which could _____ our destiny. The occurrences are frequent but we do not notice them. Thus, we must wonder if it is better to know all of one's possibilities or if this knowledge is too much for an individual to comprehend.

05 Read the excerpt from a novel and follow the directions. [2 points] (14-A-15)

> "For some days I haunted the spot where these scenes had taken place; sometimes wishing to see you, sometimes resolved to quit the world and its miseries for ever. At length I wandered towards these mountains, and have ranged through their immense recesses, consumed by a burning passion which you alone can gratify. We may not part until you have promised to comply with my requisition. I am alone, and miserable; man will not associate with me; but one as deformed and horrible as myself would not deny herself to me. My companion must be of the same species, and have the same defects. This being you must create."
>
> The being finished speaking, and fixed his looks upon me in expectation of a reply. But I was bewildered, perplexed, and unable to arrange my ideas sufficiently to understand the full extent of his proposition. He continued —
>
> "You, my creator, must create a female for me, with whom I can live in the interchange of those sympathies necessary for my being. This you alone can do; and I demand it of you as a right which you must not refuse to concede."
>
> The latter part of his tale had kindled anew in me the anger that had died away while he narrated his peaceful life among the cottagers, and, as he said this, I could no longer suppress the rage that burned within me.
>
> "I do refuse it," I replied; "and no torture shall ever extort a consent from me. You may render me the most miserable of men, but you shall never make me base in my own eyes. Shall I create another like yourself, whose joint wickedness might desolate the world? Begone! I have answered you; you may torture me, but I will never consent."

Below is an analysis of the excerpt above. Fill in the blank with ONE word from the excerpt.

Setting	a mountainous area
Characters	a creator and a being
Point of view	first-person narration
Conflict	a serious disagreement about the creation of a female creature which, the narrator imagines, would _____ the future of human beings

서술형

01 Read the excerpt from a novel and follow the directions. **4 points** (20-B-5)

> My father is a failed documentary filmmaker. I say failed because he made only one film in his life. But for a short time in the late seventies, when I was growing up, he achieved what he would later refer to as moderate fame. The source of his moderate fame was a short documentary film about a group of Shoshone Indians living in southern Nevada. I doubt that anybody remembers the film now, but in the weeks and months that followed its release, my father received critical acclaim at several small film festivals, earned some grant money, and garnered enough [. . .] courage to continue making films for another ten years. To my knowledge, he never completed another film after that, but instead spent the next ten years of his life jumping around from one project to the next, shooting for several weeks or months, then eventually abandoning the current film for another that he believed had more _____.
>
> My mother and I were living in southern California, where she worked as a lawyer, and every few months my father would call from a different part of the country with news of his latest concept — it was always his best yet — and ask my mother to sell something of his, or cash a bond, or take out another mortgage on the house. And finally, when there was nothing left to sell, he began to simply ask her for loans. Technically my parents were separated by then, but my mother was still very much in love with him, never stopped loving him, and worse, she believed with an almost stubborn myopia in his talent. She wanted my father to succeed, perhaps even more than he did, and to this day I still think this was her greatest flaw.
>
> I can say now, twenty years later, that my father was never destined for the type of fame he once hoped to achieve. He was never meant to be a great filmmaker (few documentarians are), and he was never meant to receive even the lesser distinctions that so many of his contemporaries enjoyed. <u>The small amount of talent he did possess only seemed to serve as a source of frustration for him</u>, a constant reminder of some vague, unrealized potential. But at the time — this was in my early childhood — I believed fully in his potential, and though I missed him dearly, I never once faulted him for being away so often.

Fill in the blank with the ONE most appropriate word from the excerpt. Then, explain the underlined part in terms of the life-goal of the narrator's father.

02 Read the passage and follow the directions. 4 points (19-B-3)

(A) When about midway of a certain block the policeman suddenly slowed his walk. In the doorway of a darkened hardware store a man leaned, with an unlighted cigar in his mouth. As the policeman walked up to him the man spoke up quickly. "It's all right, officer," he said, reassuringly. "I'm just waiting for a friend. It's an appointment made twenty years ago. Sounds a little funny to you, doesn't it? Well, I'll explain if you'd like to make certain it's all straight. About that long ago there used to be a restaurant where this store stands — 'Big Joe' Brady's restaurant." "Until five years ago," said the policeman. "It was torn down then." The man in the doorway struck a match and lit his cigar. The light showed a pale, square-jawed face with keen eyes, and a little white scar near his right eyebrow. His scarfpin was a large diamond, oddly set.

(B) The policeman twirled his club and took a step or two. "I'll be on my way. Hope your friend comes around all right. Going to call time on him sharp?" "I should say not!" said the other. "I'll give him half an hour at least. If Jimmy is alive on earth he'll be here by that time. So long, officer." "Good night, sir," said the policeman, passing on along his beat, trying doors as he went.

(C) About twenty minutes he waited, and then a tall man in a long overcoat, with collar turned up to his ears, hurried across from the opposite side of the street. He went directly to the waiting man. "Is that you, Bob?" he asked, doubtfully. "Is that you, Jimmy Wells?" cried the man in the door. "Bless my heart!" exclaimed the new arrival, grasping both the other's hands with his own. "It's Bob, sure as fate. I was certain I'd find you here if you were still in existence. Well, well, well! — twenty years is a long time. The old restaurant's gone, Bob; I wish it had lasted, so we could have had another dinner there. How has the West treated you, old man?" "Bully; it has given me everything I asked it for. You've changed lots, Jimmy. I never thought you were so tall by two or three inches." "Oh, I grew a bit after I was twenty."

(D) At the corner stood a drug store, brilliant with electric lights. When they came into this glare each of them turned simultaneously to gaze upon the other's face. The man from the West stopped suddenly and released his arm. "You're not Jimmy Wells," he snapped. "Twenty years is a long time, but not long enough to change a man's nose from a Roman to a pug." "It sometimes changes a good man into a bad one," said the tall man. "You've been under arrest for ten minutes, 'Silky' Bob. Chicago thinks you may have dropped over our way and wires us she wants to have a chat with you. Going quietly, are you? That's sensible. Now, before we go to the station here's a note I was asked to hand you. You may read it here at the window. It's from Patrolman Wells." The man from the West unfolded the little piece of paper handed him. His hand was steady when he began to read, but it trembled a little by the time he had finished. The note was rather short. "Bob: I was at the appointed place on time. When you struck the match to light your cigar I saw it was the face of the man wanted in Chicago. Somehow I couldn't do it myself, so I went around and got a plain clothes man to do the job. JIMMY."

Situational irony occurs when expected outcomes do not happen, or when they are the opposite of what is expected. First, identify the section (A, B, C, D) where the irony is revealed. Then, regarding the underlined part, explain what he couldn't do and why he couldn't do it.

03 Read the passage and follow the directions. **4 points** (18–B–2)

> While Ashbury was still in New York, he had written a letter to his mother which filled two notebooks. He knew, of course, that his mother would not understand the letter at once. Her literal mind would require some time to discover the significance of it, but he thought she would be able to see that he forgave her for all she had done to him. For that matter, he supposed that she would realize what she had done to him only through the letter.
>
> If reading it would be painful to her, writing it had sometimes been unbearable to him — for in order to face her, he had had to face himself. "I came here to escape the slave's atmosphere of home," he had written, "to find freedom, to liberate my imagination, to take it like a hawk and set it 'whirling off into the widening gyre' (Yeats) and what did I find? It was not capable of flight. It was some bird you had domesticated, refusing to come out!" The next words were underscored twice. "I have no imagination. I have no talent. I can't create. I have nothing but the desire for these things. Why didn't you kill that too? Woman, why did you pinion me?"

Explain why Ashbury thinks that his mother might not immediately grasp the message he wants to get across through his letter. (Do NOT copy more than THREE consecutive words from the passage.) Then, complete the commentary below by filling in the blank with the ONE most appropriate word from the passage.

> Ashbury employs figurative language to represent his imagination as a(n) _____ _____ animal in contrast Yeats' wild hawk.

04 Read the passage and follow the directions. [4 points] (17-A-10)

> As time went by, Freddie Drummond found himself more frequently crossing the Slot and losing himself in South of Market . . .
>
> Somewhere in his make-up there was a strange twist or quirk. Perhaps it was a recoil from his environment and training, or from the tempered seed of his ancestors, who had been bookmen generation preceding generation; but at any rate, he found enjoyment in being down in the working-class world. In his own world he was "Cold-Storage," but down below he was "Big" Bill Totts, who could drink and smoke, and slang and fight, and be an all-around favorite. Everybody liked Bill, and more than one working girl made love to him. At first he had been merely a good actor, but as time went on, <u>simulation became second nature</u>. He no longer played a part, and he loved sausages, sausages and bacon, than which, in his own proper sphere, there was nothing more loathsome in the way of food.
>
> From doing the thing for the need's sake, he came to doing the thing for the thing's sake. He found himself regretting as the time drew near for him to go back to his lecture-room and his inhibition . . .

Explain what the underlined part means by including one example of "simulation" from the passage. Do NOT copy more than FOUR consecutive words from the passage.

Then, complete the commentary below with TWO consecutive words from the passage.

> Freddie, whose job is a college professor, experiences something unusual as he starts to mingle with people outside "his own proper sphere." Until then, Freddie used to do things for the _____, such as giving a lecture.

05 Read the passage and follow the directions. **4 points** (16−A−9)

> A little lamp with a white china shade stood upon the table and its light fell over a photograph which was enclosed in a frame of crumpled horn. It was Annie's photograph. Little Chandler looked at it, pausing at the thin tight lips. She wore the pale blue summer blouse which he had brought her home as a present one Saturday. It had cost him ten and eleven pence; but <u>what an agony of nervousness it had cost him!</u> How he had suffered that day, waiting at the shop door until the shop was empty, standing at the counter and trying to appear at his ease while the girl piled ladies' blouses before him, paying at the desk and forgetting to take up the odd penny of his change, being called back by the cashier, and finally, striving to hide his blushes as he left the shop by examining the parcel to see if it was securely tied. When he brought the blouse home Annie kissed him and said it was very pretty and stylish; but when she heard the price she threw the blouse on the table and said it was a regular swindle to charge ten and elevenpence for it. At first she wanted to take it back, but when she tried it on she was delighted with it, especially with the make of the sleeves, and kissed him and said he was very good to think of her.
>
> Hm! . . .
>
> He looked coldly into the eyes of the photograph and they answered coldly. Certainly they were pretty and the face itself was pretty. But he found something mean in it. Why was it so unconscious and ladylike? The composure of the eyes irritated him. They repelled him and defied him: there was no passion in them, no rapture. He thought of what Gallaher had said about rich Jewesses. Those dark Oriental eyes, he thought, how full they are of passion, of voluptuous longing! . . . Why had he married the eyes in the photograph?
>
> He caught himself up at the question and glanced nervously round the room. He found something mean in the pretty furniture which he had bought for his house on the hire system. Annie had chosen it herself and it reminded him of her. It too was prim and pretty. A dull resentment against his life awoke within him. Could he not escape from his little house? Was it too late for him to try to live bravely like Gallaher? Could he go to London? There was the furniture still to be paid for. If he could only write a book and get it published, that might open the way for him.

Explain what the underlined words mean. Then write ONE word from the passage that best describes the emotional state of the main character in his home.

06 Read the excerpt and follow the directions. [5 points] (15-A-3)

(A) There is a time in the life of every boy when he for the first time takes a backward view of life. Perhaps that is the moment when he crosses the line into manhood. George is walking through the street of his town. He is thinking of the future and of the figure he will cut in the world. Ambitions and regrets awake within him. Suddenly something happens; he stops under a tree and waits as for a voice calling his name. Ghosts of old things creep into his consciousness; the voices outside of himself whisper a message concerning the limitations of life. From being quite sure of himself and his future he becomes not at all sure.

(B) If he be an imaginative boy a door is torn open and for the first time he looks out upon the world, seeing, as though they marched in procession before him, the countless figures of men who before his time have come out of nothingness into the world, lived their lives and again disappeared into nothingness. The sadness of sophistication has come to the boy. With a little gasp he sees himself as merely <u>a leaf blown by the wind</u> through the streets of his village. He knows that in spite of all the stout talk of his fellows he must live and die in uncertainty, a thing blown by the winds, a thing destined like corn to wilt in the sun. He shivers and looks eagerly about. The eighteen years he has lived seem but a moment, a breathing space in the long march of humanity. Already he hears death calling. With all his heart he wants to come close to some other human, touch someone with his hands, be touched by the hand of another. If he prefers that the other be a woman, that is because he believes that a woman will be gentle, that she will understand. He wants, most of all, understanding.

A rite of passage is a transition associated with a crisis or a change of status for an individual. With this in mind, explain the figurative meaning of the underlined words in section (B). Support your explanation with TWO examples from section (A). Do NOT copy more than FIVE consecutive words from the excerpt.

Answer Keys for Chapter 03 — Novels in the Teacher Certification Exam

기입형

1. cat **2.** obliged **3.** footsteps **4.** influence **5.** desolate

서술형

1. The word is 'potential' The underlined part means that the narrator's father has small amount of talent for his life goal. To explain, his father's pursuit of a great documentary filmmaker only frustrated him. Since the moderately successful film twenty years ago, he could not make great ones despite all the family money and time poured in.

2. First, the irony is revealed in the section (D). Next, Jimmy as a policeman couldn't arrest Bob who was a criminal. It was because of their friendship. That is, Bob appeared in the appointed place as a friend to keep the promise with Jimmy despite the risk of being caught, so Jimmy kept the loyalty as a friend by letting others do the job as a policeman.

3. Ashbury thinks that his mother might not immediately grasp the message because it would take some time to understand his figurative expressions with her literal mind. The word for the blank is 'domesticated.'

4. The underlined part means that Freddie was assimilated to the working-class life as Bill Totts. For example, he came to love food such as sausages, which was regarded as loathsome in his upper-class life. Two consecutive words for the blank are "need's sake."

5. The underlined part means that he suffered a lot in the process of buying the blouse and delivering it to Annie. As a man, long hesitation before entering the shop, standing at the counter choosing one, being called back for the change and Annie's accusation were all the more hardships to him. The word to best describe the emotional state of the main character is "resentment."

6. The underlined words in section (B) figuratively describe the passive destiny of an adolescent boy. That is, he realizes that his life is a short moment destined to die in uncertainty. For example, in (A), George's wondering through the streets with ambitions and regrets implies his uncertainty in life. Also, on hearing a message on the limitations of life from the outside voices, his belief in certainty of life changes into uncertainty.

Chapter 04 Novels in the Mock-Exam by Task

1. Theme

01 Read the passage and follow the directions. **4 points**

> Mathilde suffered endlessly, <u>feeling herself born for every delicacy and luxury</u>. She suffered from the poorness of her house, from its mean walls, worn chairs, and ugly curtains. All these things, of which other women of her class would not even have been aware, tormented and insulted her. The sight of the little Breton girl who came to do the work in her little house aroused heart-broken regrets and hopeless dreams in her mind. She imagined silent antechambers, heavy with Oriental tapestries, lit by torches in lofty bronze sockets, with two tall footmen in knee-breeches sleeping in large arm-chairs, overcome by the heavy warmth of the stove. She imagined vast saloons hung with antique silks, exquisite pieces of furniture supporting priceless ornaments, and small, charming, perfumed rooms, created just for little parties of intimate friends, men who were famous and sought after, whose homage roused every other woman's envious longings.
>
> When she sat down for dinner at the round table covered with a three-days-old cloth, opposite her husband, who took the cover off the soup-tureen, exclaiming delightedly: "Aha! Scotch broth! What could be better?" she imagined delicate meals, gleaming silver, tapestries peopling the walls with folk of a past age and strange birds in faery forests; she imagined delicate food served in marvellous dishes, murmured gallantries, listened to with an inscrutable smile as one trifled with the rosy flesh of trout or wings of asparagus chicken.

Explain what the underlined part means by including one example of "every delicacy" from the passage. Do NOT copy more than FOUR consecutive words from the passage.

Then, complete the commentary below by filling in each blank with ONE word from the passage. If necessary, you can change the form.

> Mathilde is unhappy locked up in her house, just being there makes her (1) _____. She spends her time living in a dream world, in which she (2) _____ all the fabulous things she'd have if she were rich.

02 Read the passage and follow the directions. [4 points]

> Knowing that Mrs. Mallard was afflicted with a heart trouble, great care was taken to break to her as gently as possible the news of her husband's death. It was her sister Josephine who told her, in broken sentences. Her husband's friend Richards was there, too, near her. She did not hear the story as many women have heard the same, with a paralyzed inability to accept its significance. When the storm of grief had spent itself she went away to her room alone.
>
> There was something coming to her and she was waiting for it, fearfully. What was it? She did not know. She was beginning to recognize this thing that as approaching to possess her, and she was striving to beat it back with her will. When she abandoned herself a little whispered word escaped her slightly parted lips. She said it over and over under her breath: "free, free, free!" The vacant stare and the look of terror that had followed it went from her eyes. They stayed keen and bright.
>
> She knew that she would weep again when she saw the kind, tender hands folded in death. But she say beyond that bitter moment a long procession of years to come that would belong to her absolutely. "Free! Body and soul free!" she kept whispering.
>
> Josephine was kneeling before the closed door with her lips to the keyhole, imploring for admission. She arose at length and opened the door to her sister's importunities. She clasped her sister's waist, and together they descended the stairs. Richards stood waiting for them at the bottom.
>
> Some one was opening the front door with a latchkey. It was Brently Mallard who entered, a little travel-stined, composedly carrying his grip-sack and umbrella. He had been far from the scene of accident, and did not even know there had been one. He stood amazed at Josephine's piercing cry; at Richards' quick motion to screen him from the view of his wife.
>
> But Richards was too late. When the doctors came they said she had died of heart disease — of joy that kills.

Explain the meaning of the underlines words, "its significance," that Mrs. Mallard accepted. (Do NOT copy more than THREE consecutive words from the passage.) Then, complete the commentary below by filling in the blank with the ONE most appropriate word from the passage.

> _____ can be lethal. Surprising information doesn't just have the power to shock — it can actually kill someone. Ideas have to be communicated carefully, with preparation and delicacy.

03 Read the passage and follow the directions. 4 points

> But all this — the mysterious, far-reaching hairline trail, the absence of sun from the sky, the tremendous cold, and the strangeness and weirdness of it all — made no impression on the man. It was not because he was long used to it. He was a new-comer in the land, a *chechaquo*, and this was his first winter. The trouble with him was that he was without imagination. He was quick and alert in the things of life, but only in the things, and not in the significances. Fifty degrees below zero meant eighty odd degrees of frost. Such fact impressed him as being cold and uncomfortable, and that was all. It did not lead him to meditate upon his frailty as a creature of temperature, and upon man's frailty in general, able only to live within certain narrow limits of heat and cold; and from there on it did not lead him to the conjectural field of immortality and man's place in the universe. Fifty degrees below zero stood for a bite of frost that hurt and that must be guarded against by the use of mittens, ear-flaps, warm moccasins, and thick socks. Fifty degrees below zero was to him just precisely fifty degrees below zero. That there should be anything more to it than that was a thought that never entered his head.

Explain why lacking imagination is a problem with "the man." (Do NOT copy more than THREE consecutive words from the passage.) Then, complete the commentary below by filling in the blank with the ONE most appropriate word from the passage.

> The man's inability to appreciate the _____ of things makes him mistake the difference between fifty degrees below zero and some other degrees that he is familiar with, a difference that might affect him enormously.

04 Read the passage and follow the directions. **4 points**

> "Fortunato, as you are engaged, I am on my way to Luchesi. If any one has a critical turn, it is he. He will tell me" —
>
> "Luchesi cannot tell Amontillado from Sherry."
>
> "And yet some fools will have it that his taste is a match for your own."
>
> "Come let us go."
>
> "Whither?"
>
> "To your vaults."
>
> "My friend, no; I will not impose upon your good nature. I perceive you have an engagement. Luchesi" —
>
> "I have no engagement; come."
>
> "My friend, no. It is not the engagement, but the severe cold with which I perceive you are afflicted. The vaults are insufferably damp. They are encrusted with nitre."
>
> "Let us go, nevertheless. The cold is merely nothing. Amontillado! You have been imposed upon; and as for Luchesi, he cannot distinguish Sherry from Amontillado."
>
> Thus speaking, Fortunato possessed himself of my arm. Putting on a mask of black silk and drawing a roquelaire closely about my person, I suffered him to hurry me to my palazzo.
>
> There were no attendants at home; they had absconded to make merry in honour of the time. I had told them that I should not return until the morning and had given them explicit orders not to stir from the house. These orders were sufficient, I well knew, to insure their immediate disappearance, one and all, as soon as my back was turned.
>
> * palazzo: palace
> * Sherry, Amontillado: a type of wine

Explain the reasons that the narrator asserts in dissuading Fortunato from going with him. (Do NOT copy more than THREE consecutive words from the passage.) Then, complete the commentary below by filling in the blank with the ONE most appropriate word from the passage.

> The contrast between freedom and confinement is clear in this story. Fortunato is letting "I" know that he is free to go with "I" to check out the Amontillado. Ironically, this freedom becomes a/an _____ that confines him, even physically in the narrator's house.

05 Read the passage taken from the novel, An awakening, and follow the directions.　　　[4 points]

> (A) The excited young man, George Willard, unable to bear the weight of his own thoughts, began to move cautiously along the alleyway. A dog attacked him and had to be driven away with stones, and a man appeared at the door of one of the houses and swore at the dog. George went into a vacant lot and throwing back his head looked up at the sky. He felt unutterably big and remade by the simple experience through which he had been passing and in a kind of fervor of emotion put up his hands, thrusting them into the darkness above his head and muttering words. The desire to say words overcame him and he said words without meaning, rolling them over on his tongue and saying them because they were brave words, full of meaning. "Death," he muttered, "night, the sea, fear, loveliness."
>
> (B) George Willard came out of the vacant lot and stood again on the sidewalk facing the houses. He felt that all of the people in the little street must be brothers and sisters to him and he wished he had the courage to call them out of their houses and to shake their hands. "If there were only a woman here I would take hold of her hand and we would run until we were both tired out," he thought. "That would make me feel better." With the thought of a woman in his mind he walked out of the street and went toward the house where Belle Carpenter lived. He thought she would understand his mood and that he could achieve in her presence a position he had long been wanting to achieve. In the past when he had been with her, he had felt like one being used for some obscure purpose and had not enjoyed the feeling. Now he thought he had suddenly become too big to be used.

The title of this novel indicates that the protagonist feels or realizes something anew. Describe the realization of Protagonist George Willard in section (A) that best suggests the title. Then, explain the change that he experiences in section (B). Do NOT copy more than FIVE consecutive words from the passage.

2. Plot

01 Read the poem and follow the directions. `4 points`

> "Come on!" cried the old man, "this is a dull pace for the beginning of a journey. Take my staff, if you are so soon weary."
>
> "Friend," said the other, exchanging his slow pace. "Too far, too far!" he exclaimed, unconsciously resuming his walk. "My father never went into the woods on such an errand, nor his father before him. We have been a race of honest men and good Christians, since the days of the martyrs. And shall I be the first in my family, that ever took this path, and kept.
>
> "Such company, you would say," observed the elder person, interpreting his pause. "Well said, young man! I have been as well acquainted with your family as with ever a one among the Puritans; and that's no trifle to say. I helped your grandfather, the constable, when he lashed the Quaker woman so smartly through the streets of Salem. And it was I that brought your father a pitch-pine knot, kindled at my own hearth, to set fire to an Indian village, in King Philip's war. They were my good friends, both; and many a pleasant walk have we had along this path, and returned merrily after midnight. I would fain be friends with you, for their sake.

Describe the conflict between the two characters in the passage by completing the story map below.

Story Map	
SETTING	On a journey to the forest
CHARACTERS	the elderly man and the protagonist
CONFLICT	
The protagonist's claim	①
The old man's claim	②

02 Read the passage and follow the directions. [4 points]

> Nancy was talking loud when we crossed the ditch and stooped through the fence where she used to stoop through with the clothes on her head. Then we came to her house. She lit the lamp and closed the door and put the bar up. There was something about Nancy's house; something you could smell besides Nancy and the house. Jason smelled it, even. "I don't want to stay here," he said. Nancy stood by the door. She was looking at us, only it was like she had emptied her eyes, like she had quit using them.
>
> She came and sat in a chair before the hearth. She told a story. She talked like her eyes looked, like her eyes watching us and her voice talking to us did not belong to her. Like she was living somewhere else, waiting somewhere else. <u>She was outside the cabin</u>. Her voice was inside and the shape of her, the Nancy that could stoop under a barbed wire fence with a bundle of clothes balanced on her head as though without weight, like a balloon, was there. But that was all.
>
> "And so this here queen come walking up to the ditch, where that bad man was hiding. She say, 'If I can just get past this here ditch,' was what she say..."
>
> "What ditch?" Caddy said. "A ditch like that one out there? Why did a queen want to go into a ditch?"
>
> "To get to her house," Nancy said. She looked at us. "She had to cross the ditch to get into her house quick and bar the door."
>
> "Why did she want to go home and bar the door?" Caddy said.
>
> NANCY LOOKED at us. She quit talking. She looked at us.

Explain what the underlined part means by including one example from the passage. Do NOT copy more than FOUR consecutive words from the passage.

Then, complete the commentary below with the ONE most appropriate word from the passage.

> Nancy seems unable to cope with the reality of her plight and compelled to create another version of it, a/an _____ that obviously resembles the truth of what is going on. And she's left to express her fear to children who can't fully understand, as shown by Caddy's questions.

03 Read the passage and follow the directions. **4 points**

So we set in, like we done before with the duke, and tried to comfort HIM. But he said it warn't no use, nothing but to be dead and done with it all could do him any good; though he said it often made him feel easier and better for a while if people treated him according to his rights, and got down on one knee to speak to him, and always called him "Your Majesty," and waited on him first at meals, and didn't set down in his presence till he asked them. So Jim and me set to majestying him, and doing this and that and the other for him, and standing up till he told us we might set down. This done him heaps of good, and so he got cheerful and comfortable. But the duke kind of soured on him, and didn't look a bit satisfied with the way things was going; still, the king acted real friendly towards him, and said the duke's great-grandfather and all the other Dukes of Bilgewater was a good deal thought of by HIS father, and was allowed to come to the palace considerable; but the duke stayed huffy a good while, till by and by the king says:

" .... This ain't no bad thing that we've struck here — plenty grub and an easy life — come, give us your hand, duke, and let's all be friends."

The duke done it. It took away all the uncomfortableness that we felt over it, because it would had been a miserable business to have any unfriendliness on the raft; for what you want, above all things, on a raft, is for everybody to be satisfied.

It didn't take me long to make up my mind that these liars warn't no kings nor dukes at all, but just low-down humbugs and frauds. But I never said nothing, never let on; kept it to myself; it's the best way; then you don't have no quarrels, and don't get into no trouble. If they wanted us to call them kings and dukes, I hadn't no objections, 'long as it would keep peace in the family; and it warn't no use to tell Jim, so I didn't tell him. If I never learnt nothing else out of pap, I learnt that the best way to get along with his kind of people is to let them have their own way.

To complete the story map below, fill in the blank ① by describing the conflict between "the duke" and "the king" in the passage. Then, fill in the blank ② with the ONE most appropriate word from the passage.

Story Map

SETTING	On a journey on the raft along a river
CHARACTERS	I and Jim; the king and the duke
CONFLICT	The duke _____ ① _____ .
RESOLUTION	The king attempts at a reconciliation and the duke agrees. After the duke and the king decide to work together, the narrator is _____ ② _____ .

04 Read the passage and follow the directions. 4 points

> (A) Although it was so brilliantly fine—the blue sky powdered with gold and great spots of light like white wine splashed over the Jardins Publiques—Miss Brill was glad that she had decided on her fur. The air was motionless, but when you opened your mouth there was just a faint chill, like a chill from a glass of iced water before you sip, and now and again a leaf came drifting—from nowhere, from the sky. Miss Brill put up her hand and touched her fur. Dear little thing! It was nice to feel it again. She had taken it out of its box that afternoon, shaken out the moth-powder, given it a good brush, and rubbed the life back into the dim little eyes. "What has been happening to me?" said the sad little eyes.
>
> (B) On her way home she usually bought a slice of honey-cake at the baker's. It was her Sunday treat. Sometimes there was an almond in her slice, sometimes not. It made a great difference. If there was an almond it was like carrying home a tiny present—a surprise—something that might very well not have been there. She hurried on the almond Sundays and struck the match for the kettle in quite a dashing way.
>
> But to-day she passed the baker's by, climbed the stairs, went into the little dark room—her room like a cupboard—and sat down on the red eiderdown. She sat there for a long time. The box that the fur came out of was on the bed. She unclasped the necklet quickly; quickly, without looking, laid it inside. But when she put the lid on she thought she heard something crying.

Protagonist Miss Brill shows her emotional change from rapture in section (A) to pain in section (B). Identify the most appropriate TWO expressions indicating the settings that represent her emotion: one from section (A) and the other from section (B). Then explain what the underlined words mean.

3. Figures of Speech

01 Read the passage and follow the directions. `4 points`

> (A) Lengel sighs and begins to look very patient and old and gray. He's been a friend of my parents for years. "Sammy, you don't want to do this to your Mom and Dad," he tells me. It's true, I don't. But it seems to me that <u>once you begin a gesture it's fatal not to go through with it</u>. I fold the apron, "Sammy" stitched in red on the pocket, and put it on the counter, and drop the bow tie on top of it. The bow tie is theirs, if you've ever wondered. "You'll feel this for the rest of your life," Lengel says, and I know that's true, too, but remembering how he made that pretty girl blush makes me so scrunchy inside I punch the No Sale tab and the machine whirs "pee-pul" and the drawer splats out. One advantage to this scene taking place in summer, I can follow this up with a clean exit, there's no fumbling around getting your coat and galoshes, I just saunter into the electric eye in my white shirt that my mother ironed the night before, and the door heaves itself open, and outside the sunshine is skating around on the asphalt.
>
> (B) I look around for my girls, but they're gone, of course. There wasn't anybody but some young married screaming with her children about some candy they didn't get by the door of a powder-blue Falcon station wagon. Looking back in the big windows, over the bags of peat moss and aluminum lawn furniture stacked on the pavement, I could see Lengel in my place in the slot, checking the sheep through. His face was dark gray and his back stiff, as if he'd just had an injection of iron, and my stomach kind of fell as I felt how hard the world was going to be to me hereafter.

Growth and independence often go along with turmoil and sacrifice. With this in mind, explain the meaning of the underlined words. Support your explanation with TWO examples, one from section (A) and the other from section (B). Do NOT copy more than FIVE consecutive words from the excerpt.

02 Read the passage and follow the directions. 4 points

> That was when people had begun to feel really sorry for her. People in our town, remembering how old lady Wyatt, her great-aunt, had gone completely crazy at last, believed that the Griersons held themselves a little too high for what they really were. None of the young men were quite good enough for Miss Emily and such. We had long thought of them as a tableau, Miss Emily a slender figure in white in the background, her father a spraddled silhouette in the foreground, his back to her and clutching a horsewhip, the two of them framed by the back-flung front door. So when she got to be thirty and was still single, we were not pleased exactly, but vindicated; even with insanity in the family she wouldn't have turned down all of her chances if they had really materialized.
>
> When her father died, it got about that the house was all that was left to her; and in a way, people were glad. At last they could pity Miss Emily. Being left alone, and a pauper, she had become humanized. Now she too would know <u>the old thrill and the old despair of a penny more or less</u>.

Explain what the underlined words mean. Then write ONE word from the passage that best describes the emotional state of the narrators on the main character's marital status.

03 Read the passage and follow the directions. **4 points**

> Sarty and his father went back up the road. A week ago—or before last night, that is—he would have asked where they were going, but not now. His father had struck him before last night but never before had he paused afterward to explain why; it was as if the blow and the following calm, outrageous voice still rang, repercussed, divulging nothing to him save the terrible handicap of being young, the light weight of his few years, just heavy enough to prevent his soaring free of the world as it seemed to be ordered but not heavy enough to keep him footed solid in it, to resist it and try to change the course of its events.
>
> Presently he could see the grove of oaks and cedars and the other flowering trees and shrubs where the house would be, though not the house yet. They walked beside a fence massed with honeysuckle and Cherokee roses and came to a gate swinging open between two brick pillars, and now, beyond a sweep of drive, he saw the house for the first time and at that instant he forgot his father and the terror and despair both, and even when he remembered his father again (who had not stopped) the terror and despair did not return. Because, for all the twelve movings, they had sojourned until now in a poor country, a land of small farms and fields and houses, and he had never seen a house like this before. It's big as a courthouse he thought quietly, with a surge of peace and joy whose reason he could not have thought into words, being too young for that: They are safe from him. People whose lives are a part of this peace and dignity are beyond his touch, he no more to them than a buzzing wasp.

Explain literally what has been happening to Sarty and how his emotional state changes accordingly by including one reason for each emotional state from the passage. Then, complete the commentary below with the ONE most appropriate word from the passage.

> Sarty is just beginning to understand the way the world works. As such, he doesn't feel completely lost in the chaos of his father's world. Still, he lacks _____, figuratively speaking. As far as the world is concerned he has no authority to determine his own life.

Answer Keys for Chapter 04   Novels in the Mock-Exam by Task

1. Theme

01 The underlined part means that Mathilde had not accepted her poor situation and had illusions of being one of the rich who enjoy the delicacy and luxury of life. For example, she imagined she had delicate food served in silver dishes in a fancy room when she dined with her husband around the humble table. The word for (1) and (2) are 'suffer' and 'imagines', respectively.

Expressions & Vocabulary

faerie (←faery) n. [고어·시어] 요정의 나라(fairyland); 요정; 몽환경, 선경(仙境)
gallantry n. [명사] (남성이 여성에게 보이는) 정중한 관심
inscrutable a. (사람·표정이) 불가해한[헤아리기 어려운]
tapestry n. pl. -ies 태피스트리(여러 가지 색실로 그림을 짜 넣은 직물. 또는 그런 직물을 제작하는 기술)

Sua TOKS!

Task

Interpretation, Theme (17-A-10 유형)
Novel – *The Necklace* by Guy de Maupassant

Organization

Do NOT copy more than FOUR consecutive words from the passage.

1. Explaining what the underlined part means by including one example of "every delicacy"
 – The underlined part means that ~ . For example, ~ .

2. Completing the commentary below by filling in each blank with ONE word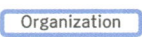
 – The word for (1) and (2) are '_____' and '_____', respectively.

Keywords

Mathilde **suffered** endlessly, feeling herself born for every delicacy and luxury. She **suffered** from the poorness of her house, from its mean walls, worn chairs, and ugly curtains. All these things, of which other women of her class would not even have been aware, **tormented and insulted** her. The sight of the little Breton girl who came to do the work in her little house aroused heart-broken **regrets** and **hopeless dreams** in her mind. She

imagined silent antechambers, heavy with Oriental tapestries, lit by torches in lofty bronze sockets, with two tall footmen in knee-breeches sleeping in large arm-chairs, overcome by the heavy warmth of the stove. She **imagined** vast saloons hung with antique silks, exquisite pieces of furniture supporting priceless ornaments, and small, charming, perfumed rooms, created just for little parties of intimate friends, men who were famous and sought after, whose homage roused every other woman's envious longings.

When she sat down for dinner at the round table covered with a three-days-old cloth, **opposite** her husband, who took the cover off the soup-tureen, exclaiming delightedly: "Aha! Scotch broth! What could be better?" she **imagined** delicate meals, gleaming silver, tapestries peopling the walls with folk of a past age and strange birds in faery forests; she **imagined** delicate food served in marvellous dishes, murmured gallantries, listened to with an inscrutable smile as one trifled with the rosy flesh of trout or wings of asparagus chicken.

Translation

자기가 온갖 좋은 것, 값진 것을 누리기 위해 태어났다고 생각하는 그녀에게 매일 매일의 구차스러운 살림이 고통의 연속일 뿐이었다. 초라한 집, 얼룩진 벽, 부서져 가는 의자, 누더기 같은 빨랫줄에 빨래가 널린 것까지 모두가 보기 싫고 괴로움의 씨앗이었다. 같은 계급의 다른 여자라면 그다지 마음 상하지 않을 그 모든 것이 그녀를 괴롭히고 부아를 돋구었다. 브르타뉴 태생 여자애를 하나 하녀로 두었지만 이 소녀를 볼 적마다 절망적인 안타까움과 미칠 것 같은 꿈이 떠올라 시달리곤 했다. 그녀가 항상 꿈에 그리는 것은 동양풍 벽걸이가 걸려 있는 조용한 거실에 청동으로 만든 촛대에 불이 켜진 그런 풍경이었다. 거기 짧은 바지를 입은 건장한 하인 둘이 의자에 파묻혀서 졸고 있다. 실내가 너무 따뜻해 깜박 졸고 있는 것이다. 고급 비단을 깐 넓은 객실도 그녀의 몽상에 떠올랐다. 진귀한 골동품들이 가득 찬 으리으리한 가구들…… 가까이 지내는 친구들은 모든 여자가 선망하는 유명인들이다. 그런 가까운 친구들과 오후 다섯 시에 모여 그윽한 향기로 가득 찬 멋진 살롱에서 고상한 대화를 나눈다.

저녁을 먹을 때, 사흘이나 빨지 않은 식탁보를 씌운 둥근 식탁에서 남편과 마주 앉는다. 남편은 스프 그릇 뚜껑을 열며 기쁜 듯이 "야, 이 스프 맛있겠는데! 이보다 맛있는 건 세상에 없을 거야!"하며 큰 소리로 말한다. 그럴 때면 으레 그녀는 으리으리한 만찬을 생각하지 않을 수 없다. 번쩍거리는 은 식기, 요정이 사는 숲 한가운데 이상한 새나 옛날 이야기의 인물이 수놓아진 벽걸이, 고급 그릇에 듬뿍 담아 내놓는 산해진미가 있다. 송어의 빨간 고기나 아스파라거스를 곁들인 닭요리의 부드러운 날개를 입에 넣으면서 속삭이는 사람이나 듣는 사람 모두 스핑크스처럼 신비한 미소를 띠고, 여성의 환심을 사려는 그런 대화를 나누는 것이다. 그녀는 그런 광경을 떠올리지 않고는 견딜 수 없었다.

> **Character Analysis of Mathilde**
>
> Mathilde spends her time living in a dream world, in which she imagines all the fabulous things she'd have if she were rich. The most detail we get in the otherwise sparse story comes in Maupassant's descriptions of the fancy stuff Mathilde wants. But being rich also means more than just nice stuff to her: it means having the glamour to attract men.

02 The meaning of the underlines words, "its significance," that Mrs. Mallard accepted is freedom of life. To explain, after hearing her husband's death, she feels that freedom possesses her. She expects that long years in her life after this bitter moment of grief would be all her possession, a complete freedom of her body and soul. The word is 'News.'

Expressions & Vocabulary

implore v. 애원[간청]하다
importunity n. 끈덕짐, 끈덕진 요구[간청]
composedly adv. 침착하게, 태연히, 평온하게

latchkey n. 현관[정문] 열쇠
clasp v. (꽉) 움켜쥐다[움켜잡다]
gripsack n. 손가방, 여행 가방

Sua TOKS!

Task

theme, interpretation (18-B-2)
Novel – *The Story of an Hour* by Kate chopin

Organization

1. **Explaining the meaning of the underlines words, "its significance," that Mrs. Mallard accepted.**
   (Do NOT copy more than THREE consecutive words from the passage.)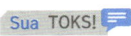

   – The meaning of the underlines words, "its significance," that Mrs. Mallard accepted is freedom of life. That is/To be specific/In other words, ~ .

   – The underlined words mean/indicate that ~ . That is/To be specific/In other words, ~ .

2. **Completing the commentary below with the ONE most appropriate word from the passage.**
   2points

   – The word is 'News.'

Knowing that Mrs. Mallard was afflicted with a heart trouble, great care was taken to break to her as gently as possible **the news** **of her husband's death.** It was her sister Josephine who told her, in broken sentences. Her husband's friend Richards was there, too, near her. She did not hear **the story** as many women have heard the same, with a paralyzed inability **to accept its significance**. When the storm of grief had spent itself she went away to her room alone.

There was something coming to her and she was waiting for it, fearfully. What was it? She did not know. **She was beginning to recognize this thing that as approaching to possess her**, and she was striving to beat it back with her will. When she abandoned herself a little whispered word escaped her slightly parted lips. **She said it over and over under her breath:** "free, free, free!" The vacant stare and the look of terror that had followed it went from her eyes. They stayed keen and bright.

She knew that she would weep again when she saw the kind, tender hands folded in death. **But she saw beyond that bitter moment a long procession of years to come that would belong to her absolutely. "Free! Body and soul free!"** **she kept whispering.**

Josephine was kneeling before the closed door with her lips to the keyhole, imploring for admission. She arose at length and opened the door to her sister's importunities. She clasped her sister's waist, and together they descended the stairs. Richards stood waiting for them at the bottom.

Someone was opening the front door with a latchkey. It was **Brently Mallard** who entered, a little travel-stined, composedly carrying his grip-sack and umbrella. He had been far from the scene of accident, and did not even know there had been one. He stood amazed at **Josephine's** piercing cry; **at Richards'** quick motion to screen him from the view of **his wife.**

But **Richards** was too late. When **the doctors** came they said **she had died of heart disease — of joy that kills.**

_____ can be lethal. Surprising information doesn't just have the power to shock — it can actually kill someone. Ideas have to be communicated carefully, with preparation and delicacy.

Translation

다들 아는 것처럼 Mallad 부인에겐 한 가지 심장병이 있어서 부군의 사망에 관한 소식을 드러내지 않고 전하는 데 온 신경을 쏟아야 했다. 부인에게 남편의 사망에 관한 소식을 전한 것은 바로 부인의 언니 조세핀이었다. 부군의 친구인 리차드 씨도 그 때 거기 있었다. 많은 여인들이 넋을 읽고 사고 소식을 받아들이지 못했지만 부인은 그렇지 않았다. 한 순간의 회오리 같은 깊은 슬픔이 가시자 부인은 그녀의 방으로 갔다.

무엇인지 그녀에게 다가오고 있었고, 두려움을 느끼면서도 그녀는, 그것을 맞아들이고 있었다. 뭘까? 그녀는 알 수 없었다. 갑자기 그녀의 가슴이 격렬하게 위아래로 요동쳤다. 지금 그것이 자신을 잠식하고 있다는 것을 인식하기 시작했다. 그래서 그녀의 의지력으로 그것을 물리치려 발버둥 쳤다. 스스로 물리칠 수 없다는 것을 알게 되자 나즈막히 속삭이는 소리가 얇게 벌어진 그녀의 입술 사이로 새어 나왔다. "자유다, 자유, 자유야" 공허한 눈빛, 그리고 뒤이어 나타났던 공포가 이젠 그녀의 눈에서 사라져 버렸다. 지금 그녀의 눈빛은 날카롭고 예리했다.

망자를 보게 되면 다시 울게 될 것이었다. 죽은 자의 몸 위로 핏기 없이 무기력하게 포개어진 두 손. 그러나 그렇게 쓰디 쓴 순간이 지난 후 그녀가 맞이하게 될 긴 시간은 오로지 그녀만의 것이라는 걸 알 수 있었다. "자유야! 몸도, 마음도 이젠... !" 그녀는 쉬지 않고 속삭였다.

조세핀은 문 앞에 꿇어앉아 열쇠구멍에 입술을 대고 문을 열어달라고 애걸했다. 언니의 끈질긴 독촉에 그녀는 곧게 일어서서는 문을 열었다. 언니의 허리를 감싸 안고 그 성스러운 계단을 내려왔다. 아래층에는 리차드가 기다리고 서 있었다.

누군가 밖에서 열쇠로 현관문을 열고 있었다. 안으로 들어선 사람은 바로 남편 Brently Mallad 이었다. 얼룩이 좀 묻긴 했지만 평소처럼 편하게 여행가방과 우산을 들고 있었다. 그는 사고와는 동떨어져 있는 것 같았다. 심지어는 사고가 있었는지 조차도 전혀 알지 못했다. 꼬집힌 듯 외치는 조세핀을 보고 그는 깜짝 놀란 채 서 있었다. 리차드가 재빨리 부인의 모습을 가리려 했다.

그러나 리차드는 너무 늦었다. 의사들이 왔을 때 그들은 부인이 심장질환으로 사망했다고 했다. ― 너무 지나친 기쁨도 사람을 죽음에 이르게 할 수 있다는 말이었다.

―――――――――― 은(는) 치명적이다. 놀랄만한 소식은 충격을 줄 뿐만 아니라 ― 실제로 누군가를 죽음으로 몰고 갈 수도 있다. 생각은, 준비하고 세심함을 가지고, 조심스럽게 전달되어야 한다.

Theme of Language and Communication

In "The Story of an Hour," how you tell someone what happened is almost more important than what actually happened. The biggest concern isn't whether someone lives or dies, **it's how you tell a person with a weak heart bad news without killing her.** In other words, **communication or news can be lethal. Surprising information** doesn't just have the power to shock — it can actually kill someone. In this case, **the surprise that a husband isn't dead after all is more deadly than a railroad accident. Ideas have to be communicated carefully, with preparation and delicacy. Otherwise, the listener may very well end up dead.**

Theme of Freedom and Confinement

At first, freedom seems like a terrible thing to Mrs. Mallard, who's restricted in lots of ways: through her marriage, by her bad heart, and even inside her home, which she doesn't leave during "The Story of an Hour." On the other hand, though, she has considerable freedoms as an upper-class, married lady. She can tell freedom's coming for her, and she dreads it. Once it arrives, though, it fills her with an overpowering joy. Yet, **she experiences this mental and emotional freedom while being confined to a room. As soon as she leaves that room, the freedom she'd only just barely begun to understand is taken away from her.**

03 His lacking imagination is a problem because it prevents him from realizing what the cold weather of fifty degrees below zero means to him. To be specific, he fails in thinking that he, as a mortal being, can not survive the extremely cold weather without preparing something to protect himself against that cold condition. The word for the blank is 'significances.'

Expressions & Vocabulary

conjectural a. 추측상의, 억측상의, 확정적이 아닌
moccasin n. 모카신(부드러운 가죽으로 만든 납작한 신, 원래 북미 원주민들이 신던 형태)
immortality n. 불멸

Sua TOKS!

Task

theme, interpretation (18-B-2)(17-A-10)
Novel – *To Build a Fire* by Jack London

Organization

1. **Explaining why lacking imagination is a problem with "the man."** 2points
   – His lacking imagination is a problem in that/because ~ . That is/To be specific, ~

2. **Completing the commentary below by filling in the blank with the ONE most appropriate word from the passage.** 2points
   – The word (for the blank) is '_____.'

Keywords

But all this — the mysterious, far-reaching hairline trail, the absence of sun from the sky, the tremendous cold, and the strangeness and weirdness of it all — made no impression on the man. It was not because he was long used to it. He was a new-comer in the land, a *chechaquo*, and this was his first winter. **The trouble with him was that he was without imagination. He was quick and alert in the things of life, but only in the things, and not in the significances.** Fifty degrees below zero meant eighty odd degrees of frost. Such fact impressed him as being cold and uncomfortable, **and that was all. It did not lead him to meditate upon his frailty as a creature of temperature, and upon man's frailty in general, able only to live within certain narrow limits of heat and cold; and from there on it did not lead him to the conjectural field of immortality and man's place in the universe. Fifty degrees below**

zero stood for a bite of frost that hurt and that must be guarded against by the use of mittens, ear-flaps, warm moccasins, and thick socks. **Fifty degrees below zero** was to him just precisely fifty degrees below zero. That there should be anything more to it than that was a thought that never entered his head.

The man's inability to appreciate the _____ of things makes him mistake the difference between fifty degrees below zero and some other degrees that he is familiar with, a difference that might affect him enormously.

Translation

끝없이 이어진 그 신비한 길, 해가 뜨지 않는 하늘, 무시무시한 추위, 그리고 이 일대의 엄청나게 신비하고 두려운 분위기가 그에겐 별로 대수롭지 않은, 일상적인 사물인 것이다. 이것은 그가 그런 환경에 오랜 동안 젖어 있었기 때문은 아니었다. 그는 이를테면 '체차크'였다. 그는 여기 와서 처음 겨울을 보내고 있었다. 문제는 그에게 생각을 하는 능력이 부족하다는 점이었다. 일상적인 삶에서 부딪히는 일에 대해서는 그도 재빠르고 예민하게 대처한다. 하지만 그런 일의 중요성(의미)에 대해서는 그렇지 못하다. 그에게는 영하 50도나 영하 80도나 그게 그것일 뿐, 특별히 다른 의미를 갖는 사건으로 느껴지지 않았다. 그저 좀 더 춥고 불쾌하고 불편한 사건일 뿐이다. 자신이 기온이라는 외부 조건에 의해 심각하게 제약을 받는 하나의 생물이라는 사실, 인간이라는 일정한 더위와 추위 사이의 아주 좁은 영역 안에서밖에 살 수 없는 무력한 존재라는 사실에 대해서는 생각할 능력이 없는 것이다. 하나의 생물로서 인간이라는 종류가 갖는 허약함이라는 것에 대해서 그가 뭔가 명상한다는 것은 있을 수 없는 일이었다. 불멸의 존재, 영속적인 것, 이 우주 속에서 인간의 위치가 갖는 의미… 이런 것들은 그의 머릿속에 없었다. 영하 50도가 되면 여기 사는 사람들은 심각한 동상의 위협에 대비해야 한다. 장갑, 귀 덮개, 발을 따뜻하게 하는 모카 신발, 두꺼운 양말 따위 몸을 지킬 수 있는 물건들을 반드시 준비해야 하는 것이다. 그러나 그에게는 영하 50도는 그저 영하 50도일 뿐이었다. 그 이상의 어떤 것이 그것과 관련돼 있다는 것에는 도무지 생각이 미치지 않았다.

그 남자는 일의 <u>중요성(의미)</u>를 인식하는 능력이 부족해서 영하 50도와 그가 익숙한 다른 온도와의 차이점을 알지 못하는 실수를 저질렀는데, 이것은 그에게 엄청나게 영향을 미칠지도 모를 차이이다.

Commentary

... the man doesn't appreciate the significance of things. Only here there's a connection between the man's lack of imagination and the fact that he might be foolishly endangering himself in the frozen Yukon. The man's inability to appreciate the significance of things makes him mistake the difference between fifty degrees below zero and seventy-five, a difference that might be enough to cost him his life.

Theme of Foolishness and Folly

In the third paragraph of "To Build a Fire," the narrator tells readers all about the "trouble" with the man, which is that he is "without imagination" (3). Now out in the cold Yukon, you probably don't think that having an imagination is going to help you much. But the timing of the narrator's comment suggests that this lack of imagination is a significant shortcoming that will lead the man to make foolish decisions. As readers, we must wonder what good it would do the man to think deeply about the vast wilderness around him. After all, the guy's not a writer. He just wants to go get some bacon! So why suggest he's foolish for not having imagination? This is a question to dear readers.

04 The narrator asserts with two reasons. One is that Fortunato has already been engaged so no time to go with him. The other is that he got a cold so the damp vault is not good for Fortunato's health. The word for the blank is 'engagement.'

Expressions & Vocabulary

engage v. (주의·관심을) 사로잡다[끌다], 약속하다, 〈시간 등을〉 채우다, 차지하다
engagement n. 개입, 종사, 관심, (회합 등의) 약속, 계약, 연결
have it that ~ ~라고 전하다, 말하다
whither adv. conj. (옛글투) 어디로; ~한 (곳)
vault n. 지하 납골당, (특히 은행의) 금고
impose upon v. ~을 이용하다(=take advantage of)
afflict v. (흔히 수동태로) (격히) 괴롭히다, 피해를 입히다
insufferable (←insufferably) a. 참을[견딜] 수 없는

damp a. (흔히 불쾌감을 줄 정도로) 축축한[눅눅한]
encrusted a. ~ (with/in sth) (얇고 딱딱한 막 같은 것이) 싸인[덮인/형성된]
nitre n. 질산칼륨, 칠레초석(硝石), 질소소다
possess oneself of v. …을 자기 것으로 만들다
roquelaure (roquelaire) n. 로클로르 (18세기의 무릎까지 오는 남자 외투)
abscond v. ~ (from sth) (허가 없이 떠날 수 없는 장소를) 무단이탈하다, 종적을 감추다

Task

interpretation, theme (17-A-10)(18-B-2)
Novel – *The Cask of Amontillado* by Edgar Allan Poe

Organization

1. **Explaining the reasons that the narrator asserts in dissuading Fortunato from going with him. Do NOT copy more than THREE consecutive words from the passage.** 2points
   - The narrator asserts with two reasons. One is that ~ . The other is that ~.

2. **Completing the commentary below by filling in the blank with the ONE most appropriate word from the passage.** 2points
   - The word (for the blank) is '_____.'

Keywords

"Fortunato, **as you are engaged,** I am on my way to Luchesi. If any one has a critical turn, it is he. He will tell me" —

"Luchesi cannot tell Amontillado from Sherry."

"And yet **some fools** will have it that his taste is a match for your own."

"Come let us go."

"Whither?"

"To your vaults."

"My friend, no; I will not impose upon your good nature. I perceive **you have an engagement.** Luchesi" —

"I have no engagement; come."

"My friend, no. It is not the engagement, but the severe cold with which I perceive you are afflicted. The vaults are insufferably damp. They are encrusted with nitre."

"Let us go, nevertheless. The cold is merely nothing. Amontillado! **You have been imposed upon; and as for Luchesi,** he cannot distinguish Sherry from Amontillado."

Thus speaking, Fortunato possessed himself of my arm. Putting on a mask of black silk and drawing a roquelaire closely about my person, I suffered him to hurry me **to my palazzo.**

There were no attendants at home; they had absconded to make merry in honour of the time. I had told them that I should not return until the morning and had given them explicit orders not to stir from **the house.** These orders were sufficient, I well knew, to insure their immediate disappearance, one and all, as soon as my back was turned.

The contrast between freedom and confinement is clear in this story. Fortunato is letting "I" know that he is free to go with "I" to check out the Amontillado. Ironically, this freedom becomes a/an _____ that confines him, even physically in the narrator's house.

Translation

"포르투나토, 자네는 일이 있나 보군. 그러면 나는 루체시한테 가봐야겠네. 그 사람은 가르쳐 줄 거야······"

"루체시 따위는 아몬틸라도와 셰리 주도 가려내지 못한단 말이야."

"그러나 감정하는 데는 그가 자네에게 지지 않을 거라고 말하는 명청이도 있단 말이야."

"자아, 가보자구."

"어디로?"

"자네 집 술 창고로."

"아니야, 친구. 자네한테 폐를 끼치다니 될 말인가. 자네는 약속이 있는가 본데. 루체시라면······"

"약속 같은 건 없네······ 자아, 가기로 하세."

"그렇지만 자네는 안되겠네. 약속 같은 건 없는지 모르지만, 내가 보기엔 악성 감기에 걸려 있는 듯한데. 술 창고 속은 습기가 차 있다네. 초석도 사방에 널려 있고."

"아랑곳할 것 없네. 가세. 감기 따위가 다 뭐야. 아몬틸라도라고! 자넨 속은 거야. 더욱이 루체시 따위 녀석은 셰리 주와 아몬틸라도를 구분하지 못하지."

이렇게 말하면서 포르투나토는 내 팔을 잡았다. 나는 까만 비단의 가면을 쓰고 외투로 몸을 꼭 감싸고는 그가 말한 대로 나의 저택으로 걸음을 재촉했다.

집에는 하인들이 없었다. 마음껏 기분에 들떠서 돌아다니느라고 모두 자취를 감춘 것이다. 나는 아침까지는 돌아오지 않을 테니 모두 다 집에서 나가서는 안 된다고 일러두었던 것이다. 이렇게 일러두면 그 작자들은 내가 밖으로 나가기가 무섭게 한 놈도 빠짐없이 즉시 뛰쳐나간다는 것은 의심할 나위도 없다는 것을 알고 있었다.

자유와 얽매임 사이의 대조가 이 이야기에서는 분명하다. 포르투나토는 "나"에게 자신은 "나"와 자유롭게 가서 아몬틸라도를 확인할 수 있다고 한다. 아이러니하게도, 이 자유는 그를 얽매는 <u>개입</u>이 되는데, 물리적으로 화자의 집에 얽매이게까지 된다.

Theme of Freedom and Confinement

- The contrast between freedom and confinement is extreme in "The Cask of Amontillado." For one character to be free, another must die. Most of the story takes place in a vast and incredibly foul smelling catacomb, or underground graveyard. Dead bodies (or at least bones) abound. Freedom becomes less and less of a possibility as the characters move into smaller and smaller crypts, each one more disgusting than the last. Such confinement makes both the readers and the characters appreciate the deliciousness of fresh air. Hopefully, it makes us, the readers, think more deeply about what makes us feel trapped, and what makes us feel free.

- ["I have no engagement;–come." (10)] Fortunato is letting Montresor know that he is "free" to go with him to check out the Amontillado. Ironically, this freedom is part of what traps him in the end.

05 In section (A), George Willard felt that he had become enlightened and matured through his simple experience of thoughts leading to muttering such meaningful words as 'Death.' In section (B), he has changed in his attitude toward Belle Carpenter. That is, now he believes that he has matured enough not to be used by her comparing to the unpleasant past when he was treated by her for a certain purpose.

Expressions & Vocabulary

fervor n. 열렬, 열정

unutterably adv. 발음할 수 없게, 형언할 수 없게

Sua TOKS!

Task

theme, interpretation (16-A-9) (07서-12)
Novel – 'An awakening' from *Winesburg, Ohio* by the Sherwood Anderson

Organization

The title of this novel indicates that the protagonist feels or realizes something anew.

1. **Describing the realization of Protagonist George Willard in section (A) that best suggests the title.** 2points

   – In section (A), George Willard felt/realized that ~ .

2. **Explain the change that he experiences in section (B).** Do NOT copy more than FIVE consecutive words from the passage. 2points

   – In section (B), he has changed in ~ . That is/To be specific/To explain, ~ .

Keywords

(A) The excited young man, George Willard, unable to bear **the weight of his own thoughts,** began to move cautiously along the alleyway. A dog attacked him and had to be driven away with stones, and a man appeared at the door of one of the houses and swore at the dog. George went into a vacant lot and throwing back his head looked up at the sky. **He felt unutterably big and remade by the simple experience through which he had been passing** and in a kind of fervor of emotion put up his hands, thrusting them into the darkness above his head and muttering words. **The desire to say words** overcame him and he said **words without meaning,** rolling them over on his tongue and saying them because they were **brave words, full of meaning.** "Death," he muttered, "night, the sea, fear, loveliness."

(B) George Willard came out of the vacant lot and stood again on the sidewalk facing the houses. He felt that all of the people in the little street must be brothers and sisters to him and he wished he had the courage to call them out of their houses and to shake their hands. "If there were only a woman here I would take hold of her hand and we would run until we were both tired out," he thought. "That would make me feel better." With the thought of a woman in his mind he walked out of the street and went toward the house where Belle Carpenter lived. He thought she would understand his mood and that he could achieve in her presence a position he had long been wanting to achieve. **In the past when he had been with her, he had felt like one being used for some obscure purpose and had not enjoyed the feeling. Now he thought he had suddenly become too big to be used.**

Translation

흥분한 젊은이 조지 윌러드는 **자신의 생각의 무게를 견딜 수 없어** 골목을 따라 조심스럽게 움직이기 시작했다. 개 한 마리가 그에게 달려드는 바람에 돌을 던져 쫓아버려야 했고 어느 집 문 앞에 남자가 나타나 개에게 욕설을 퍼부었다. 조지는 빈터로 가서 고개를 뒤로 젖혀 하늘을 올려다보았다. **그는 자신이 거쳐 가고 있는 그 단순한 경험으로 인해 다시 태어나고 말할 수 없이 성장한 것을 느꼈고** 일종의 격렬한 감정 속에서 두 손을 내밀어 머리 위 어둠 속으로 들어 올리며 중얼거렸다. 말들을 하고자 하는 욕망이 그를 엄습했고 그는 별다른 뜻 없이 그 말들을 했다. 그 **단어들 모두 의미로 가득 찬 용감한 말들**이었으므로 혀 위로 굴리면서 말했다. "**죽음.**" 그가 중얼거렸다. "**밤, 바다, 두려움, 사랑스러움.**"

조지 윌러드는 빈터에 나와 다시 집들을 마주 보며 보도 위에 섰다. 그는 그 작은 거리에 있는 모든 사람들이 자기의 형제이자 자매임이 틀림없다고 느꼈고 자기가 그들을 집 밖으로 불러내어 악수할 수 있는 용기를 가졌기를 바랐다. '여기 여자가 있었더라면 나는 그 여자의 손을 잡고 두 사람 모두 지쳐 떨어질 때까지 달릴 텐데.' 그는 생각했다. '그러면 내 기분이 더 좋아질 텐데.' 마음속에 여자 생각을 하면서 그는 거리에서 나와 벨 카펜터가 살고 있는 집으로 갔다. 그는 여자가 자기 기분을 이해할 것이며 여자 앞에서 자신이 오랫동안 원했던 지위를 얻을 수 있을 것이라고 생각했다. 그는 **전에는 여자와 함께 있으면 어떤 알지 못하는 목적에 자신이 이용당하는 것처럼 느꼈고 그 느낌을 즐길 수 없었다. 그는 이제 자신은 이용당하기에는 너무 자랐다고 생각했다.**

Theme of the false Epiphanies of Adolescence

"Awakening" is an ironic title for the story of Belle Carpenter — which is really the story of George Willard. The odd relationship between Belle and Ed Handby, who seems to be her true love despite his inability to do anything but bark orders at her, serves principally as a vehicle for Anderson to illuminate one of **the false epiphanies of adolescence.** Wandering through the darkened town, **George Willard believes himself to have become enlightened, to have taken a jump forward into adulthood. Everything suddenly appears different to him, and he feels that his inner self has matured.** But when he tries to convey this revelation to someone else — Belle — the result is dull boasting, for which Ed Handby quickly humiliates him. George realizes that his epiphany was empty, and his mood swings rapidly from exultation to sour depression. **He is a victim, like most adolescents, of the gap between his own illusions about himself and a world that often seems designed to shatter those illusions.**

Analytical Overview

Winesburg, Ohio, Sherwood Anderson's most famous book, is a peculiar work, part novel and part collection of short stories. Its twenty-four sections are interconnected accounts that focus on various inhabitants of Winesburg, a sleepy midwestern town, around the turn of the century. The book opens with a framing device of sorts: the prologue-like section entitled "The Book of the Grotesque," in which a nameless old writer has a bedtime vision of human beings who pursue various "truths" to so great an extent that they become "grotesque." These hallucinations prefigure the lives of the inhabitants of Winesburg (at least of those inhabitants in whose lives the reader is allowed to peer). From the would-be Old Testament patriarch Jesse Bentley, to the filthy, obese, misogynistic Wash Williams, the souls of Anderson's Winesburgers are all somehow deformed and most of these deformations spring from two linked sources — **alienation and loneliness.**

Synonyms

- 경험하다 (n)
  - experience — (지식과 기능을 쌓게 되는) 경험[경력]
  - involvement — 휩쓸리게 함, 연루, 연좌
  - participation — 관여, 참가, 참여, 분배, 공유
- (v)
  - undergo — (특히 변화·안 좋은 일 등을) 겪다[받다]
  - go through — ~을 겪다
  - face — 정면으로 대하다
  - encounter — 만나다, 부닥치다, 마주침, 마주치다
  - endure — 참다, 견디다, 인내하다, 지탱하다

2. Plot

01 ① His ancestors have never took the path, a bad behavior, so he hesitates to go on the journey to the forest.

② The protagonist's ancestors did wicked behaviors and took the path to the forest pleasantly in the past, and he is willing to help the protagonist in the same way.

Expressions & Vocabulary

martyr n. 순교자   hearth n. 난로 (바닥); 난로 부근
constable n. police constable, 치안경찰관

Sua TOKS!

Task

conflict (14-A-15)(11-40)

Novel – *Young Goodman Brown* by Nathaniel Hawthorne

Organization

1. Describing the conflict between two characters by completing the story map below.

Story Map	
SETTING	On a journey to the forest
CHARACTERS	the elderly man and the protagonist
CONFLICT	
The protagonist's claim	(state the claim directly)
The old man's claim	(state the claim directly)

> Keywords

"Come on!" cried the old man, "this is a dull pace for the beginning of a journey. Take my staff, if you are so soon weary."

"Friend," said the other, exchanging his slow pace. **"Too far, too far!"** he exclaimed, unconsciously resuming his walk. "**My father never went into the woods on such an errand, nor his father before him. We have been a race of honest men and good Christians, since the days of the martyrs. And shall I be the first in my family, that ever took this path, and kept.**

"Such company, you would say," observed the elder person, interpreting his pause. "Well said, young man! I have been as well acquainted with your family as with ever a one among the Puritans; and that's no trifle to say. **I helped your grandfather, the constable, when he lashed the Quaker woman so smartly through the streets of Salem. And it was I that brought your father a pitch-pine knot, kindled at my own hearth, to set fire to an Indian village, in King Philip's war.** They were my good friends, both; **and many a pleasant walk have we had along this path,** and returned merrily after midnight. I would fain be friends with you, for their sake.

Translation

"자!" 하고 노인이 소리쳤다, "이건 여행의 시작으로는 굼뜬 속도네. 자네가 그렇게 쉬 지치면, 내 지팡이를 가지게."

"동지," 하고 상대편이 천천히 걷다가 완전히 멈춰서면서 말했다, "너무 멀리! 너무 멀리 (왔어요)!" 하고 그는 무의식적으로 다시 걷기 시작하면서 소리쳤다. "나의 부친은 이런 용건으로 숲 속에 들어간 적이 없었고, 또 그 분에 앞서 그의 부친도 그런 적이 없었소. 우린 순교자들의 시절 이래로 정직한 사람이자 착한 기독교인들의 가계였고, 나는 우리 가문에서 첫 번째 사람일 거요, 이 길에 들어가 어울린"

"이러한 동료들이라고 자넨 말할 것이겠지," 하고 그 연장자는 그가 말을 멈춘 뜻을 해석하면서 평했다. "말 잘했네, 젊은이! 나는 청교도들 중의 어느 가족 못지않게 자네 가족과 아는 사이였고, 그건 말하기에 전혀 하찮은 일이 아닌데, 자네 할아버지가 세일럼의 온 거리에서 퀘이커 교도 여자를 매우 호되게 채찍질했을 때, 치안 담당관인 자네 할아버지를 도왔고, 킹 필립의 전란에서 인디언 부락에 방화하기 위해서 송진소나무 옹이를 나의 집 난로에서 불을 붙여 자네 아버지에게 가져다 준 사람은 바로 나였네. 그들은 둘 다 나의 좋은 친구들이었고, 이 오솔길을 따라서 우리는 많은 산보를 했었고, 자정이 지난 다음에 즐겁게 돌아왔지. 나는 그 분들을 위해서 기꺼이 자네와 친구가 되어 주겠네."

Themes

- **Young Goodman Brown's guilty conscience is evident in his wavering between whether to turn back home or join the perverted communion service in the forest.**
- Though Brown triumphs in resisting evil, he develops an inability to trust others.
- It is unclear whether Brown dreamed the entire incident in the woods or whether any part of it actually occurred.
- Goodman Brown uncovers evil in everyone he knows, but Hawthorne suggests that Brown is merely confirming his suspicions without sufficient proof and demonstrating his arrogance.
- Hawthorne critiques the Puritan belief in good and evil by portraying Brown as an absolutist. His wife Faith, on the other hand, manages to accept Brown despite his trip into the forest.

Summary

In "Young Goodman Brown," Brown walks into the forest to meet with the Devil. There, he stumbles upon a debauched Walpurgis Night celebration in which his wife participates. Appalled, Brown becomes suspicious of everyone and dies a hopeless man.

Young Goodman Brown goes into the forest to meet with a character who resembles both Brown and the Devil. He meets a pious member of the village on the way to meet this sinister character, and is surprised that someone so good would be undertaking the same errand. He discovers a witches' Sabbath where the minister, the deacon, and even his wife are in attendance. Brown calls out to his wife and the scene dissolves. He turns back and returns to the village. Brown is forever changed by the incident and suspicious of others. He dies a hopeless man.

Characters

- **Young Goodman Brown** is a pious, devoted member of the community until he becomes convinced that the outward goodness of those he knows is merely a sham.
- **Faith** is Goodman Brown's wife who represents goodness and devotion. Goodman comes to distrust her after he sees her at the witches' Sabbath.
- **The Devil** may represent the darker side of Goodman Brown's nature as well as the evil acts of his ancestors.
- **Goody Cloyse**, the Minister, and **Deacon Gookin** represent the hypocrisy that Goodman Brown sees in the village.

02 The underlined words indicate Nancy's mental state. That is, even though she is physically in the cabin with others, her mind is losing touch with reality. For example, ① she seemed to have emptied her eyes like quitting using them. (② when she was talking her eyes didn't look like belonging to her even though she was watching and talking to others in the cabin. ③ she seemed to be living and waiting somewhere else.) The word is 'story.'

Expressions & Vocabulary

ditch n. (들판도로가의) 배수로
hearth n. 난로 (바닥); 난로 부근[근처]

stoop v. (자세가) 구부정하다, 구부정하게 서다[걷다]

Sua TOKS!

Task

theme, interpretation (17-A-10)
Novel – *That Evening Sun* by William Faulkner

Organization

1. **Explaining what the underlined part means by including one example from the passage.** Do NOT copy more than FOUR consecutive words from the passage. 3points
    – The underlined words mean/indicate (NP). That is/To be specific/In other words, ~ .
    – The underlined words mean/indicate that ~ . That is/To be specific/In other words, ~ .
    – For example/instance, ~ .
        ① only it was like she had emptied her eyes, like she had quit using them.
        ② She talked like her eyes looked, like her eyes watching us and her voice talking to us did not belong to her.
        ③ Like she was living somewhere else, waiting somewhere else.

2. **Completing the commentary below with the ONE most appropriate word from the passage.** 1points
    – The word is '_____.'

Keywords

Nancy was talking loud when we crossed the ditch and stooped through the fence where she used to stoop through with the clothes on her head. Then we came to her house. She lit the lamp and closed the door and **put the bar up.** There was something about

Nancy's house; something you could smell besides Nancy and the house. Jason smelled it, even. "I don't want to stay here," he said. Nancy stood by the door. She was looking at us, **only it was like she had emptied her eyes, like she had quit using them.**

She came and sat in a chair before the hearth. She told a story. **She talked like her eyes looked, like her eyes watching us and her voice talking to us did not belong to her. Like she was living somewhere else, waiting somewhere else.** She was outside the cabin. Her voice was inside and the shape of her, the Nancy that could stoop under a barbed wire fence with a bundle of clothes balanced on her head as though without weight, like a balloon, was there. But that was all.

"And so this here queen come walking up to the ditch, where that bad man was hiding. She say, 'If I can just get past this here ditch,' was what she say…"

"What ditch?" Caddy said. "A ditch like that one out there? Why did a queen want to go into a ditch?"

"To get to her house," Nancy said. She looked at us. "She had to cross the ditch to get into her house quick and bar the door."

"Why did she want to go home and bar the door?" Caddy said.

NANCY LOOKED at us. She quit talking. She looked at us.

Nancy seems unable to cope with the reality of her plight and compelled to create another version of it, a/an _____ that obviously resembles the truth of what is going on. And she's left to express her fear to children who can't fully understand, as shown by Caddy's questions.

Translation

낸시는 도랑을 건널 때도 큰 소리로 얘기했고, 빨래 보따리를 머리에 이고 무릎걸음으로 지나곤 하던 울타리를 이번에도 무릎걸음으로 지날 때도 큰 소리로 떠들었다. 우리는 마침내 그녀의 집에 도착했다. 그녀는 등잔을 켜고, 뭔을 닫은 뒤, 빗장을 걸었다. 낸시의 집에는 뭔가가 있는 것 같았다. 낸시와 집에서 나는 냄새뿐 아니라 뭔가 다른 냄새도 났기 때문이다. 제이슨조차 그 냄새를 맡은 듯 이렇게 말했다. "난 여기 있고 싶지 않아." 낸시는 문가에 서 있었다. 그녀는 우리를 보고 있었지만, 두 눈은 텅 비어 있는 것 같았다. 그녀는 마치 눈을 더 이상 사용하지 않는 것 같았다.

그녀가 난로 앞에 놓인 의자에 앉았다. 그녀가 이야기를 하기 시작했다. 이야기를 하면서 우리를 바라보는 그녀의 두 눈과 이야기를 들려주는 그녀의 목소리는, 모두 그녀의 것이 아닌 것 같았다. 그녀는 다른 곳에 살고, 다른 어떤 곳을 기다리고 있는 것 같았다. 그녀는 오두막 밖에 있었다. 그녀의 목소리는 오두막 안에 있었지만, 그녀, 낸시라는 여자의 형상은 머리에 옷 보따리를 이고 균형을 잡으며 울타리

아래를 마치 풍선처럼 가볍게 지나가던 곳에 있었다.

"그래서 여왕은 나쁜 사람이 숨어 있는 도랑으로 올라가단다. 그러고는 말했지. 만약 내가 여기 이 도랑을 건널 수 있다면..."

"어떤 도랑이요?" 캐디가 물었다. "저기 바깥에 있는 도랑 같은 거요? 왜 여왕이 도랑을 건너려는 거예요?"

"집으로 가려고." 낸시는 그렇게 말하며 우리를 바라보았다. "빨리 자기 집으로 가서 빗장을 잠그려면 도랑을 건너야 하니까."

"뭣 때문에 집에 가서 빗장을 잠그려는 거예요?" 캐디가 물었다.

낸시는 우리를 보고 있었지만 더 이상 이야기는 하지 않았다. 그저 우리를 보고만 있었다.

낸시는 궁핍한 현실을 잘 이겨나가지 못하는 것 같고 확실히 현재 상황을 닮아있는 _____, 즉 현실의 또 다른 모습을 만들도록 내몰리었다. 그리고 캐디의 질문에서 나타나는 바와 같이, 그녀는 잘 이해하지도 못하는 어린 아이들에게 그녀의 공포감을 표현할 수밖에 없었다.

Summary

"That Evening Sun" is mainly a story about fear — fear rendered all the more terrible by Nancy's total isolation among others who cannot understand, share, or relieve it.

Nancy is a black woman who has been filling in as cook in the Compson household during the illness of their live-in servant Dilsey. She has an unreliable husband, and she has taken to prostitution to supplement her income. She has been knocked down and kicked in the face by a white client from whom she demanded payment, after which she, not he, has been jailed. While in jail she has made an attempt on her own life.

At the time of the story she is visibly pregnant, and Jesus, her husband, has gone off, first vowing vengeance against the father. Afraid that he will return and menace her, Nancy begs Mrs. Compson to let her sleep at the Compsons' house, but Mrs. Compson will not permit it; therefore, except for one evening when she sleeps in the Compson kitchen, Mr. Compson and the three children escort her home in the evening. Between the Compson house and her cabin is a ditch, which she views as the likely place for an ambush.

After Nancy's final day with the Compsons, when Mr. Compson will no longer accompany her, she cajoles the children, all under the age of ten, to accompany her. On their arrival at the cabin, she is so terrified that she uses every ploy she knows to delay the children's return, offering to tell them stories and make them popcorn, but her hospitality falls short of pleasing the children.

Finally Mr. Compson comes for the children and offers to take her to a relative's house, but she will not leave. When the Compsons depart Nancy is sitting, petrified, in her house and moaning. The author does not reveal whether her fears are groundless.

Theme of Versions of Reality

Reality in "That Evening Sun" is not a clear-cut matter. There's the reality of the white residents of Jefferson, and then there's the reality of the black residents. **There's the reality of Nancy, who fears her dangerous husband, and then there's the reality of the father who tells her not to worry about the man.** The world of children is juxtaposed with the world of adults, too. And none of these divisions are neat and precise — the realities spill over into one another.

The given passage conveys the seeming **unreality of Nancy,** the way she seems not allowed to be a full member of her society or the way she is so afraid of Jesus that her mind is losing touch with reality. The real Nancy, Quentin senses, is beyond them; the one the kids see in the cabin is simply the laborer, the shell of her true self. **The children perceive one version of Nancy, but the real version of her is elsewhere.**

03

(1) shows disgruntled attitude to the king while the king represent friendly attitude to the duke. To explain, while the king feels comfortable being treated well by others like a king, the duke is unsatisfied on this scene. Even when the king recounts the favors his ancestors had done to the duke's family, the duke remains so unhappy.

(2) satisfied.

Expressions & Vocabulary

huffy (특히 다른 사람의 말·행동 때문에) 발끈 성을 내며[홱 토라져서]

by and by 머지않아, 곧
humbug 사기, 협잡, 협잡꾼

Sua TOKS!

Task

theme, interpretation (17-A-10)
Novel – *The Adventure Of Huckleberry Finn* by Mark Twain

Organization

To complete the story map below, fill in the blank (1) by Then,

1. **Describing the conflict between "the duke" and "the king" in the passage.** 2points
   – The duke ~ while/but ~ the king

2. **Filling in the blank (2) with the ONE most appropriate word from the passage.** 2points
   – The word (for the blank) is '_____.'

Keywords

So we set in, like we done before with the duke, and tried to comfort HIM. But he said it warn't no use, nothing but to be dead and done with it all could do him any good; though he said **it often made him feel easier** and better for a while if **people treated him according to his rights,** and got down on one knee to speak to him, and always called him "Your Majesty," and waited on him first at meals, and didn't set down in his presence till he asked them. So Jim and me set to majestying him, and doing this and that and the other for him, and standing up till he told us we might set down. This done him heaps of good, and **so he got cheerful and comfortable. But the duke kind of soured on him, and didn't look a bit satisfied with the way things was going; still, the king acted real friendly towards him, and said the duke's great-grandfather and all the other Dukes of Bilgewater was** a good deal thought of by HIS father, and was allowed to come to the palace considerable; but the duke stayed huffy a good while, till by and by the king says:

" ……. **This ain't no bad thing that we've struck here** — **plenty grub and an easy life** — **come, give us your hand, duke, and let's all be friends.**"

The duke done it. It took away all the uncomfortableness that we felt over it, because **it would had been a miserable business to have any unfriendliness on the raft; for what you want, above all things, on a raft, is for everybody to be satisfied.**

It didn't take me long to make up my mind that these liars warn't no kings nor dukes at all, but just low-down humbugs and frauds. But I never said nothing, never let on; kept it to myself; **it's the best way; then you don't have no quarrels, and don't get into no trouble.** If they wanted us to call them kings and dukes, I hadn't no objections, **'long as it would keep peace in the family;** and it warn't no use to tell Jim, so I didn't tell him. If I never learnt nothing else out of pap, I learnt that the best way to get along with his kind of people is **to let them have their own way.**

Translation

그래서 우리는 공작의 경우와 마찬가지로, 이 노인도 위로해 주려고 했다 그러나 그는 그러한 짓을 해도 소용없다. 죽어서 이 모든 고생으로부터 모면되는 것만이 상팔자다. 하기야 사람들이 자기에게 그 신분에 상당한 대우를 해주고 자기에게 얘기를 걸 때에는 한쪽 무릎을 꿇고 반드시 '폐하'라고 부르며, 식사 시에는 우선 남보다 먼저 자기에게 시중을 들고, 자기 앞에선 앉으라고 할 때까지 있어 주면, 그래도 얼마 동안만은 마음이 가벼워지고, 기분이 명랑해지는 수가 가끔 있었다고 했다. 그래서 짐과 나는 그를 폐하 대우를 하기 시작했고, 이일 저일 그의 일을 보살펴 주었고, 그가 앉아도 좋다고 할 때까지 서 있었다. 그 효과가 대번에 나타나 그는 만면에 희색이 가득 차 기분이 좋은 것 같았다 그런데 공작은 왕에 대해서 못마땅한 얼굴을 하고는, 이 결과에 대해서 자못 불만스러운 얼굴이었다. 그러나 왕은 공작에 대해 아주 친하게 대했다 그리고 공작의 증조부도 브릿지워터 공작 일족 전부도 자기 선제께선 친하게 대해 주셨으며 궁중 출입을 허락했노라고 했다. 그러나 공작이 언제까지나 못마땅한 얼굴을 하고 있었으므로 마침내 왕은 이런 말을 했다.

"……우리가 여기 오게 된 것도 그리 나쁘진 않단 말이야. 먹을 것에 부족은 없고, 퍽 맘이 놓이고 말이야. 자, 공작이여, 악수하자고, 그리고 우리 모두 친하게 해나갑시다."

공작은 그렇게 했다. 이것으로 꺼림칙하던 마음이 모두 가시게 되어 우리는 어쨌든 마음이 놓였다 어떠한 불화도 뗏목 위에 있고 보면 여간 비참한 일이 아닐 테니까. 뗏목을 타고 무엇보다도 필요한 것은 전원이 만족한 마음을 갖는다는 것이다.

이 거짓말쟁이들이 왕도 공작도 아니고, 그저 천한 사기꾼이며 엉터리라고 하는 것을 알기에 나는 그다지 많은 시간이 걸리지 않았다. 그러나 나는 그 일을 한 마디도 입 밖에 내놓지 않았으며 얼굴에도 내색을 하지 않고 그저 자기 혼자의 가슴속에만 넣어두고 있었다. 그게 제일 좋은 방법이다. 그렇게 해두면 자연 싸움도 일어나지 않고, 귀찮은 일도 생기지 않으니까 말이다. 놈들이 자기들을 왕이니 공작이니 하고 우리들에게 그 호칭을 원한다면 그것이 가족의 평화를 유지하는 한 나는 반대하지는 않았다. 또 짐에게 얘기해도 아무 소용도 없는 일이고 해서 짐에게도 잠자코 있었다. 나는 아빠에게서 무엇 하나 배운 것이 없다고는 하더라도 이런 종류의 인간들과 함께 살아나가는 데 제일 좋은 방법은 놈들 마음대로 내버려둔다고 하는 이 일 하나만은 배운 것이었다.

배경	강을 따라 뗏목 여행 중
인물	나와 짐, 왕과 공작
갈등	공작은 _____①_____.
결말	왕은 화해를 시도하고 공작은 이에 동의한다. 공작과 왕이 함께 하기로 결정하자, 화자는 ___②___ .

Theme of Conflict between civilization and "natural life"

The primary theme of the novel is the conflict between civilization and "natural life." Huck represents natural life through his freedom of spirit, uncivilized ways, and desire to escape from civilization. He was raised without any rules or discipline and has a strong resistance to anything that might "sivilize" him. This conflict is introduced in the first chapter through the efforts of the Widow Douglas: she tries to force Huck to wear new clothes, give up smoking, and learn the Bible. Throughout the novel, Twain seems to suggest that the uncivilized way of life is more desirable and morally superior. Drawing on the ideas of Jean-Jacques Rousseau, Twain suggests that civilization corrupts, rather than improves, human beings.

Mississippi River

The majority of the plot takes place on the river or its banks. For Huck and Jim, the river represents freedom. On the raft, they are completely independent and determine their own courses of action. Jim looks forward to reaching the free states, and Huck is eager to escape his abusive, drunkard of a father and the "civilization" of Miss Watson. However, the towns along the river bank begin to exert influence upon them, and eventually Huck and Jim meet criminals, shipwrecks, dishonesty, and great danger. Finally, a fog forces them to miss the town of Cairo, at which point there were planning to head up the Ohio River, towards the free states, in a steamboat.

Synonyms

- **이야기하다 (v)**

	tell	말하다, 이야기하다
	recount	(격식) (특히 자기가 경험한 것에 대해) 이야기하다[말하다]
	recite	자세히 이야기하다
	narrate	이야기하다, 말하다, 서술하다
	describe	묘사하다, 기술하다, 말로 설명하다
	depict	그리다, 묘사하다
	repeat	되풀이하다, 반복하다; 다시 경험하다; 되풀이하여 말하다

- **불만족스러운 (a)**

	dissatisfied	~ (with sb/sth) 불만스러워 하는
	unsatisfied	만족하지 않은
	discontented	불만을 품은, 불만스러운, 불평스러운
	unhappy	불행한, 불운한, 비참한
	disgruntled	~ (at sb/sth) 불만스러워 하는, 언짢은
	displeased	화난
	unhappy	불행한, 불운한, 비참한
	disappointed	실망한, 기대가 어긋난; 실현되지 못한, 좌절된
	frustrated	실망한, 좌절한, 좌절감을 느낀; 욕구 불만의

04 One in section (A) is 'the blue sky powdered with gold and great spots of light like white wine' and the other one in section (B) is 'the little dark room — her room like a cupboard.' The underlined words mean Miss Brill's habitual behavior on Sundays. To explain, on Sundays she used to treat herself on the way back home by buying a slice of honey-cake, which she thought as a surprising gift to herself when an almond is laid on it.

Expressions & Vocabulary

dashing a. 멋진, 근사한
sip v. (음료를) 홀짝이다[거리다], 조금씩 마시다
unclasp v. …의 걸쇠를 벗기다

Sua TOKS!

Task

simile, emotion, setting, event (16-A-9)
Novel − *Miss Brill* by Katherine Mansfield

Organization

Protagonist Miss Brill shows her emotional change from rapture in section (A) to pain in section (B).

1. **Identifying the most appropriate TWO expressions indicating the settings that represent her emotion: one from section (A) and the other from section (B).** 2points
   − One in section (A) is '_____' and the other one in section (B) is '_____.'

2. **Explaining what the underlined words mean.** 2points
   − The underlined words mean (NP). That is/To be specific/In other words, ~ .
   − The underlined words mean that ~ . That is/To be specific/In other words, ~ .

Keywords

(A) Although it was so brilliantly fine — **the blue sky powdered with gold and great spots of light like white wine** splashed over the Jardins Publiques — Miss Brill was **glad** that she had decided on her fur. The air was motionless, but when you opened your mouth there was just a faint chill, **like a chill from a glass of iced water before you sip**, and now and again a leaf came drifting — from nowhere, from the sky. Miss Brill put up her hand and touched her fur. Dear little thing! It was **nice** to feel it again. She had taken it out of its box that afternoon, shaken out the moth-powder, given it a good brush, and rubbed the life back into the dim little eyes. "What has been happening to me?" said the sad little eyes.

(B) **On her way home she usually bought a slice of honey-cake at the baker's. It was her Sunday treat. Sometimes there was an almond in her slice, sometimes not. It made a great difference. If there was an almond it was like carrying home a tiny present — a surprise — something that might very well not have been there.** She hurried on the almond Sundays and struck the match for the kettle in quite a dashing way.

But to-day she passed the baker's by, climbed the stairs, went into **the little dark room — her room like a cupboard —** and sat down on the red eiderdown. She sat there for a long time. The box that the fur came out of was on the bed. She unclasped the necklet quickly; quickly, without looking, laid it inside. But when she put the lid on **she thought she heard something crying.**

Translation

(A) 날씨가 기가 막히게 좋았지만 — 공원에 마치 백포도주와 같은 근사한 황금빛 가루가 뿌려진 푸른 하늘 — 미스 브릴은 모피를 두른 것은 잘했다고 생각했다. 공기는 미동조차 없었다. 하지만 입을 열면 희미한 냉기가 있었다. 마치 홀짝 마시기 전 얼음물이 담긴 컵에서 느껴지는 그저 작은 냉기가 있었다. 이따금 어딘지 모르는 하늘에서 나뭇잎 하나가 떨어지고는 했다. 미스 브릴은 손을 들어 그녀의 모피를 만졌다. 나의 귀여운 것! 다시 만지니 기분이 좋다. 그녀는 그날 오후 박스에서 모피 목도리를 꺼내고 좀약 가루를 털어내고는 빗질을 잘하고 희미해진 작은 눈을 닦아서 생기를 불어넣었다. 저에게 무슨 일이 일어나고 있는거죠? (모피 목도리가 말하는 것) 작은 슬픈 눈들이 말했다.

(B) 미스 브릴은 집에 가는 길에 보통 빵집에 들러 허니케이크를 한 쪽 산다. 그게 일요일의 특식이었다. 케이크 조각에 어떤 날은 아몬드가 들어 있고 어떤 날은 없었다. 그건 아주 중대한 차이였다. 아몬드가 들어 있는 날은 작은 선물, 뜻하지 않은 깜짝 선물 같은 것을 집에 가지고 가는 것이었다. 그런 날에는 얼른 집으로 돌아가 서둘러 주전자에 물을 끓였다.

하지만 오늘은 빵집을 그냥 지나쳐 계단을 올라가 어두컴컴한 작은 방으로 들어갔다. 마치 벽장 같은 자기 방에 들어서서 붉은 솜털이불 위에 주저앉았다. 한참 그러고 있었다. 모피가 들어 있던 상자가 침대 위에 있었다. 미스 브릴은 목도리를 재빨리 풀었다. 얼른, 쳐다보지도 않고 상자 안에 넣었다. 뚜껑을 닫을 때 어떤 울음소리가 들린 것 같았다.

Summary

In "Miss Brill," Miss Brill works as an English tutor in Paris. Her only respite from her dull, dreary life is the weekly concert she attends in the park. However, it becomes clear at one of these concerts that she's the subject of ridicule. She returns to her shabby apartment.

- Miss Brill makes a living by reading to invalids and tutoring French children in English.
- She goes to a concert and sits in her "special seat," where she feels she can participate in the lives of people around her.
- Gradually, she realizes that these people are looking down on her, and she returns to her little room in a boarding house, ashamed and lonely.

Theme of Disconnect Between Fantasy and Reality

Miss Brill's construction of **an invented narrative for the park visitors** that take the form of a play being enacted for her sole benefit becomes **a metaphor for her entire life.** Everything is **an illusion and a fantasy** because she has become **disconnected from what is real. This alienation from reality** is in part **a defense mechanism to deal with her loneliness**, but it also serves as a link to her conscious **disengagement from pursuing a real life that involves real interaction with others.** Just as most people realize that it is impossible to actually interact with characters on a stage or screen, so **Miss Brill's construction of a fantasy life** fulfills the purpose of **allowing her the excuse for disengagement**; the people making up the cast of her interior plays are nothing more than phantoms on celluloid.

Theme of Alienation

Miss Brill is a **supremely alienated character**. She is alienated from the world around her. She is **alienated from the people in the park she sees**. She even seems to **suffer from self-alienation** as she does appear to be fully in touch with the reality of her own appearance or image that she presents to the world. Overriding all this concrete alienation is the pervasive philosophical conceptualization that **Miss Brill is alienated from God or fate or whatever deity or being is supreme in handing out the destinies to puny human beings.**

3. Figures of Speech

01 The meaning of the underlined words imply that the speaker decides to face all the hardships and responsibilities that ensue once he leave. For example, in section (A), Lengal warns him that he will feel the outcomes of his action while he lives. Sammy also worries about what obstacles would come "hereafter" in the end of section (B).

Expressions & Vocabulary

go through (일련의 행동·방법·절차를) 거치다, ~을 겪다
fatal a. 치명적인, 돌이킬 수 없는 (사태를 초래하는)
bow tie 보 타이, 나비 넥타이
scrunch v. (손 안에 넣고) 돌돌 구기다[뭉치다]
splat n. 철퍼덕(물기 있는 것이 무엇에 세게 부딪치는 소리)
fumble ~ (around) v. (무엇을 하거나 찾느라고 손으로) 더듬거리다

galoshes n. [보통 pl.] 오버슈즈(overshoes) (비 올 때 방수용으로 구두 위에 신는 덧신)
saunter v. 한가로이[느긋하게] 걷다
heave v. (아주 무거운 것을 잔뜩 힘주어) 들어올리다[끌어당기다/던지다]
peat n. 토탄(土炭)
moss n. 이끼
hereafter adv. 지금부터는, 금후(로는), 장차는

Task

interpretation, metaphor (18-B-2)
Novel — *A & P* by John Updike

Organization

Growth and independence often go along with turmoil and sacrifice. With this in mind,

1. **Explain the meaning of the underlined words.** 2points
   - The underlined words mean/refer to (NP)/that ~ .

2. **Supporting your explanation with TWO examples, one from section (A) and the other from section (B).** Do NOT copy more than FIVE consecutive words from the excerpt. 2points
   - For example/That is/To be specific/In other words, ~ .
   - In section (A), ~. In section (B)
   - Firstly, in section (A), ~ Also, ~ in section (B)
   - This is supported by the fact that ~ and that ~
   - "You'll feel this for the rest of your life," Lengel says. (warning)
     (this → result/responsibility/suffer)
   - as I[Sammy] felt how hard the world was going to be to me hereafter.

(worry/concern/confess)　(hard → difficulties/obstacles)
(feel → go through, for the rest of your life/heareafter → in life)

> **Keywords**

(A) Lengel sighs and begins to look very patient and old and gray. He's been a friend of my parents for years. "Sammy, **you don't want to do this to your Mom and Dad,**" he tells me. It's true, I don't. But it seems to me that <u>once you begin a gesture it's fatal not to go through with it.</u> **I fold the apron**, "Sammy" stitched in red on the pocket, and put it on the counter, and **drop the bow tie on top of it. The bow tie is theirs**, if you've ever wondered. **"You'll feel this for the rest of your life," Lengel says, and I know that's true, too,** but remembering how he made that pretty girl blush makes me so scrunchy inside I punch the No Sale tab and the machine whirs "pee-pul" and the drawer splats out. One advantage to this scene taking place in summer, I can follow this up with a clean exit, there's no fumbling around getting your coat and galoshes, I just saunter into the electric eye in my white shirt that my mother ironed the night before, and **the door heaves itself open, and outside the sunshine is skating around on the asphalt.**

(B) I look around for my girls, but they're gone, of course. There wasn't anybody but some young married screaming with her children about some candy they didn't get by the door of a powder-blue Falcon station wagon. Looking back in the big windows, over the bags of peat moss and aluminum lawn furniture stacked on the pavement, **I could see Lengel in my place in the slot,** checking the sheep through. His face was dark gray and his back stiff, as if he'd just had an injection of iron, and **my stomach kind of fell as I felt how hard the world was going to be to me hereafter.**

Translation

렌젤은 한숨을 쉬었고 이 상황을 인내하는 듯 보였지만 늙고 창백했다. 그는 몇 년 전부터 나의 부모님의 친구였다. "쌔미, 너희 부모님은 그만두는 짓 따윈 원치 않으실 텐데" 그가 나에게 말했다. 그래 사실이다. 그렇게 하길 원치 않으실 것이다. 그러나 나에게 있어 일단 행동을 시작한 이상은 겪어봐야 되지, 그렇지 않는다면 그것이 더 치명적인 일이었다. 나는 주머니가 있고 빨간색으로 된 앞치마를 접었다. 그리고는 카운터 위에 놓았다. 그리고 나비넥타이를 그 위에다 놓았다. 당신이 궁금할 수도 있는데, 나비넥타이는 그들의 것이었다. "너는 이제 남은 인생에서 이 사건이 얼마나 큰 타격을 주는 것인지 절실히 느낄 거다." 렌젤이 말했다. 나는 그것이 또한 사실임을 안다. 그러나 그가 그 귀여운 소녀들을 어떻게 붉히게 만들었는지를 생각하면 아직도 내 안에서 분노가 끓어오른다. 나는 "No Sale" 탭을 두드렸고 기계는 "피이-풀" 소리를 내었고 서랍은 철썩 튀어 나왔다. 이 일들이 여름에 일어났다는 사실에 대해 참 다행인 것은 코트와 덧신을 찾을 필요 없이 곧장 출구로 그들을 쫓아갈 수 있었다는 데에 있다. 나는 어제 밤에 어머니가 다려준 하얀 셔츠를 입고 자동문 센서를 향해 뛰어갔다. 문이 열려졌고 바깥에는 햇볕이 아스팔트 위를 스케이트 타는 듯 미끄러지며 비추고 있었다.

나는 나의 소녀들을 찾기 위해 둘러보았지만 그들은 가고 없었다. 거기에는 아무도 없었고 단지 젊은 유부녀와 함께 사탕으로 인해 울고 있는 그녀의 아이들만 있을 뿐이었다. 그들은 엷은 청색의 Falcon 역 짐마차의 문 옆에 있었다. 거대한 유리창을 뒤돌아보자, 포장도로 위에 쌓여 있는 토탄 이끼로 채워진 가방들과 알루미늄 잔디 관리 기구 너머로 렝젤이 양들이 지나가는 것을 체크하며 내가 담당했던 계산대에 서 있는 것이 보였다. 그의 얼굴은 어둡고 늙어보였고 그의 뒤는 마치 받침대를 꽂아놓은 것처럼 매우 뻣뻣해 보였으며, 그리고 험한 세상이 어떻게 장차 내게 닥쳐올런지 생각하자 배가 힘없이 덜컹 내려앉는 느낌을 받았다.

Summary

Sammy, a teenage clerk in an A & P grocery, is working the cash register on a hot summer day when three young women about his age enter barefoot and clad only in swimsuits, to purchase herring snacks.

Although they are dressed for the beach, Sammy allows the girls to continue shopping while he appraises them sexually. He imagines details about the girls based on their appearance alone, impressions that, to his surprise, are shaken when the leader of the trio, a gorgeous, classy-looking beauty he has dubbed "Queenie", speaks in a voice unlike that which he had created in his mind. Lengel, the old and prudish manager, feels the girls are not clothed appropriately for a grocery store, and admonishes them, telling them they must have their shoulders covered next time, which Sammy believes embarrasses them.

Offended by the manager's disregard for the three customers' dignity, Sammy ceremoniously removes his store apron and bow tie and resigns on the spot, despite the mention by the manager of the pain this would cause his parents. Sammy then leaves the store, seemingly in expectation of some display of affection or appreciation from the young women involved, only to find that they've already left, apparently oblivious to his presence.

Commentary

- John Updike's "A&P" is a story about **consequences.** Each character in the story **makes a choice that results in a negative consequence.** Queenie and the other girls, for instance, choose to enter the A&P wearing nothing but their bathing suits. **Sammy then decides to quit his job to defend their honor.** By quitting, Sammy is also attempting to defend the girls' principles and define his own. His act requires courage and daring.

- John Updike gives us a lusty 19-year old guy for a narrator and has him perform what Updike calls "**an act of feminist protest.**" Updike is talking about **Sammy quitting his job to show the girls in bathing suits that he respects their right to dress the way they like and still be treated with respect.** We can look at the girls' behavior as a feminist protest as well. By standing up for their right to wear bathing suits in public, **they inspire Sammy to his act.** We think the story suggests something powerful – **that men and women can work together to create more freedom for both genders.**

Synonyms

- **경험하다 (n)**
  - experience — (지식과 기능을 쌓게 되는) 경험[경력]
  - involvement — 휩쓸리게 함, 연루, 연좌
  - participation — 관여, 참가, 참여, 분배, 공유
- **(v)**
  - undergo — (특히 변화·안 좋은 일 등을) 겪다[받다]
  - go through — ~을 겪다
  - face — 정면으로 대하다
  - encounter — 만나다, 부닥치다, 마주침, 마주치다
  - endure — 참다, 견디다, 인내하다, 지탱하다

- **책임감 (n)**
  - responsibility — (to do sth) 책임(맡은 일), 책무
    책임감을 느끼다 feel responsible
    책임감을 기르다 develop a sense of responsibility
    책임감이 없다 lack responsibility
  - accountability — 책임, (교육) 성적 책임
  - importance — 중요성, 중요한 지위
  - role — 역할, 구실
  - culpable — (격식) 과실이 있는, 비난받을 만한

- **독립심 (n)**
  - independence — (개인의) 자립
  - autonomy — 자치, 자치권, 자치 국가, 자치 단체, 자율
  - self-reliance — 자기 의존, 독립독행
  - self-reliant — 자립[독립]적인
  - free — 자유로운

- **걱정하다 (v)**
  - worry — 걱정하다
  - be anxious — 걱정하다
  - be concerned — 우려를 나타내다

02 The underlined words describe common human feelings and experiences that people go through due to poverty. In other words, narrators expect Emily would have such a poor life like themselves contrary to the prior 'high' life since her father's death. The word to describe the emotional state of the narrators on the main character's marital status is "vindicated."

Expressions & Vocabulary

tableau n. 광경[장면](역사적인 장면 등을 여러 명의 배우가 정지된 행동으로 재현해 보여주는 것)
vindicate v. (특히 남들이 달리 생각할 때) …의 정당성을 입증하다
pauper n. (옛글투) 아주 가난한 사람, 극빈자

Sua TOKS!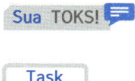

Task

Theme, Simile (16-A-9)

Novel – *A Rose for Emily* by William Faulkner

Organization

1. Explaining what the underlined words mean. **2points**
   - The underlined words mean that ~

2. Writing ONE word from the passage that best describes the emotional state of the narrators on the main character's marital status. **2points**
   - The word to describe the emotional state of the narrators on the main character's marital status is "_____."

Keywords

That was when people had begun to feel really sorry for her. People in our town, remembering how old lady Wyatt, her great-aunt, had gone completely crazy at last, believed that **the Griersons held themselves a little too high for what they really were**. None of the young men were quite good enough for Miss Emily and such. We had long thought of them as a tableau, Miss Emily a slender figure in white in the background, her father a spraddled silhouette in the foreground, his back to her and clutching a horsewhip, the two of them framed by the back-flung front door. So when she got to be thirty and was still single, **we were not pleased exactly, but vindicated**; even with insanity in the family she wouldn't have turned down all of her chances if they had really materialized.

When her father died, it got about that **the house was all that was left to her**; and in a way, people were glad. At last they could pity Miss Emily. **Being left alone, and a pauper, she had become humanized**. Now she too would know the old thrill and the old despair of a penny more or less.

Translation

읍 사람들이 정말로 그녀를 불쌍히 여기기 시작한 것은 바로 그 무렵이었다. 우리 읍에 사는 사람들은 그녀의 고모 할머니가 되는 와이어트 부인이 마침내 완전히 미쳐 버리고 만 것을 회상하고는 그리어슨 가(家) 사람들이 자기네 분수도 잊어버리고 지나치게 거만을 부린다고 믿었던 것이다. 마을 청년들 가운데는 어느 누구도 미스 에밀리의 배필로 알맞게 보이지 않았다. 우리는 오랫동안 이 일족을 한 폭의 활인화(活人畫) — 예전에, 배경을 적당하게 꾸미고 분장한 사람이 그림 속의 사람처럼 보이게 만든 구경거리 — 로 여기고 있었다. — 미스 에밀리는 흰옷차림의 날씬한 모습으로 뒤에 서고, 그녀의 부친은 그녀에게 등을 돌린 채 말채찍을 손에 쥐고 양다리를 버티고 선 실루엣의 모습으로 전면을 가리우고 있다 — 그들 두 사람 뒤에 활짝 열린 현관문이 사진틀의 구실을 하는 것이었다. 이리하여 에밀리의 나이가 서른이 되도록 독신으로 지낼 때 **우리들은 반드시 기분이 좋았다고 까지는 못해도 속으로 고소함을 금치 못했다**. 아무리 집안 혈통에 유전적으로 미친 사람이 있었다 하더라도, 정말 결혼할 기회가 나타나기만 했더라면 그 기회를 모조리 거절하지는 않았을 것이라고 생각되었기 때문이다.

에밀리의 부친이 죽었을 때 그녀가 이어받은 것은 집 한 채밖에 없었다는 소문이 나돌았다. 그리고 어느 의미에서 사람들은 좋아하였다. 이로써 미스 에밀리를 동정할 수 있으리라고 생각했기 때문이다. 거지꼴이나 다름없이 외톨이로 남게 됐으니 그녀도 인간미를 보이게 될 것이라고 생각했던 것이다. 이제는 그녀도 **돈이 한 푼이라도 더 많으냐 적으냐에 따라서 전율을 느끼기도 하고 절망에 빠지기도 하고 예부터의 인간의 속성**을 알게 되리라고 생각했기 때문이다.

Summary

Miss Emily Grierson was born into an aristocratic family. Isolated at an early age by her father, Emily is placed on a pedestal by the townspeople, who like to think of her as "a tradition, a duty," even though they find her haughty and scornful. Emily appears to have a mental breakdown following the death of her father. She initially refuses to acknowledge his death, then retreats into her house with a mysterious illness.

One day, Homer Barron and his crew of laborers come to town to build sidewalks. Emily takes an interest in Homer in spite of the disapproval of the townspeople, who argue that he is too low class for Emily. Emily buys some arsenic, but refuses to explain why. Years later, when Emily dies, the townspeople find a man's skeleton in her bed. It's strongly implied that this skeleton is Homer Barron.

Theme of Versions of Reality

By showing people with skewed versions of reality, "A Rose for Emily" asks us to take off our "rose-colored" glasses and look reality in the face. What we confront is the reality of America in the story, and the reality of the main character's complete isolation. Faulkner reveals how difficult it can be to see the past and the present clearly and honestly by depicting memory as flawed and subjective. This "difficulty" is part of why the main characters goes insane, or so it certainly appears. Luckily, there are healthy doses of compassion and forgiveness in the novel. When we start to feel that, we start to see things more clearly.

03 Literally Sarty walks the road together with his father until they find the big house. While they walk, Sarty is in terror and despair remembering the last night's struck by his father. However, when he sees the house he feels joy and peace expecting people in that huge house would be safe from his father. The word is 'weight.'

Expressions & Vocabulary

repercuss v. (transitive) To drive or beat back.   **wasp** n. 말벌
shrub n. 관목

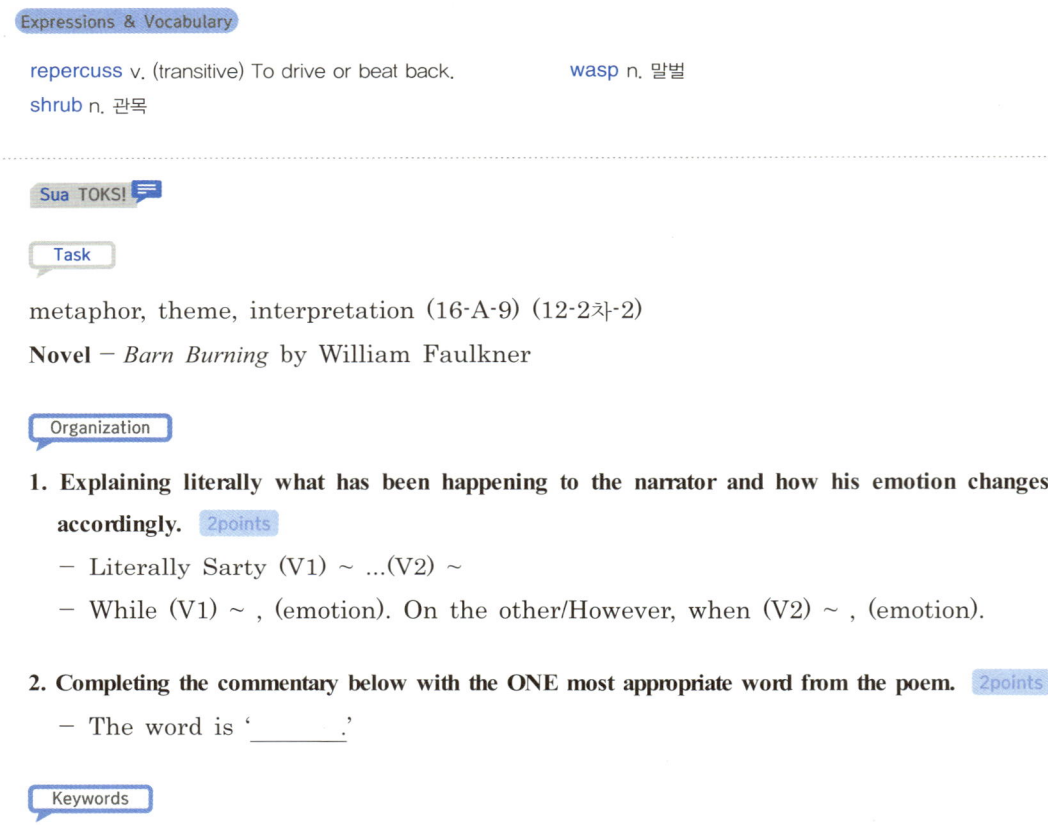

Sua TOKS!

Task

metaphor, theme, interpretation (16-A-9) (12-2차-2)
Novel – *Barn Burning* by William Faulkner

Organization

1. **Explaining literally what has been happening to the narrator and how his emotion changes accordingly.** 2points
   – Literally Sarty (V1) ~ …(V2) ~
   – While (V1) ~ , (emotion). On the other/However, when (V2) ~ , (emotion).

2. **Completing the commentary below with the ONE most appropriate word from the poem.** 2points
   – The word is '_____.'

Keywords

   Sarty and his father went back up the road. A week ago—or before last night, that is—he would have asked where they were going, but not now. His father had struck him before last night but never before had he paused afterward to explain why; it was as if the blow and the following calm, outrageous voice still rang, repercussed, divulging nothing to him save the **terrible handicap of being young,** the **light weight** of his few years, just **heavy enough to prevent his soaring** **free of the world as it seemed to be ordered** **but not heavy enough to keep him footed solid in it,** **to resist it and try to change the course of its events.**
   Presently he could see the grove of oaks and cedars and the other flowering trees and shrubs where the house would be, though not the house yet. They **walked beside a fence** massed with honeysuckle and Cherokee roses and **came to a gate** swinging open between two brick pillars, and now, beyond a sweep of drive, **he saw the house** for the first time

and at that instant he forgot his father and **the terror and despair** both, and even when he remembered his father again (who had not stopped) the terror and despair did not return. Because, for all the twelve movings, they had sojourned until now in a poor country, a land of small farms and fields and houses, and **he had never seen a house like this before.** It's big as a courthouse he thought quietly, **with a surge of peace and joy** whose reason he could not have thought into words, being too young for that: They are safe from him. People whose lives are a part of this peace and dignity are beyond his touch, he no more to them than a buzzing wasp.

Sarty is just beginning to understand the way **the world** works. As such, he doesn't feel completely lost in **the chaos of his father's world**. Still, he lacks _____ figuratively speaking. As far as the world is concerned he has no authority to determine his own life.

Translation

소년과 아버지는 길을 따라 올라갔다. 일주일 전이었다면 — 바로 어젯밤이었다 해도 — 소년은 어디로 가느냐고 물었겠지만 지금은 그럴 수 없었다. 아버지는 어젯밤 그를 때렸다. 아버지는 나중에라도 왜 때렸는지 설명해 주는 법이 없었다. 마치 폭풍 뒤에 고요가 찾아오듯 그것으로 끝이었다. 난폭한 소리가 여전히 소년의 귀에 메아리치고 있었지만, 그가 가진 것은 어리다는 치명적인 약점뿐이었다. 그의 몇 해 되지 않는 인생의 무게는 이 세계를 떠나 날아가고 싶은 그의 욕망을 저지할 만큼은 무거웠지만, 이 세계 안에 굳건히 두 발로 서서 저항하고 변화를 꾀하게 만들기엔 너무 가벼웠다.

참나무와 삼나무로 가득한 숲을 지나자, 얼마 후면 사람이 사는 집이 나타난다는 표시인 꽃나무와 관목들이 보였다. 소년과 아버지는 그곳을 지나 인동초와 금앵자 덩굴이 휘감긴 울타리를 따라 두 개의 벽돌 기둥 사이에 있는, 열린 대문까지 걸어갔다. 길게 뻗은 진입로 너머로 처음 저택을 본 순간, 그의 의식 속에 아버지도 두려움도 절망도 사라졌다. 그러다가 다시 아버지는 떠올랐지만(아버지는 계속 걸음을 멈추지 않았다), 공포와 절망은 되살아나지 않았다. 모두 열두 번이나 이사를 다니면서 머문 곳은 늘 조그만 농장과 들판과 집들이 있는 가난한 시골뿐이었기에, 지금 눈앞에 보이는 저택 같은 것은 본 적이 없었다. *법원만큼 크구나.* 그는 숨죽이며 생각했다. 어린 그가 말로는 다 표현할 수 없는 평화와 기쁨에 휩싸인 채. *여기 사는 사람들은 저 사람으로부터 안전하겠군. 저 사람은 이런 평화롭고 위엄 있는 곳에 사는 사람들은 감히 건드릴 수 없을 테니까. 저 사람은 그저 윙윙거리는 말벌에 지나지 않아.*

사티는 세상이 돌아가는 방식을 막 이해하기 시작하고 있다. 이와 같이, 그는 아버지의 세상의 혼돈 속에서 완전히 방황에 빠지지는 않는다. 여전히 그는, 비유적으로 말하자면, <u>무게감</u>이 부족하다. 세상에 관한한 그는 자신의 인생을 결정할 권한이 없다.

Theme of Youth

Since the hero of "Barn Burning" is Sarty Snopes, a ten-year-old boy, it's no surprise that youth is a major theme. The story gets lots of mileage out of the contrast between Sarty's youthful vision of the events and the disturbing adult life he is forced to lead. As a coming-of-age story, this one is rather unique. Though Sarty doesn't come of age in a literal sense (he doesn't turn eighteen), he willingly takes on a host of adult roles. This extends to a feeling of responsibility for his neighbors – and their barns. He can't sit back and watch needless destruction (i.e., barn burning) without trying to stop it. At times, Sarty seems so mature that it's easy to forget he's only a kid.

[…] the terrible handicap of being young, the light weight of his few years, just heavy enough to prevent him soaring free of the world […] but not heavy enough to keep him footed solid in it […]. (40)

In other words, Sarty is just beginning to understand the way the world works. As such, he doesn't feel completely lost in the chaos of his father's world. On the other hand he lacks weight. As far as the world is concerned he has no authority to determine his own life.

Synonyms

- 예상하다 (v)　　expect　　　　　예상[기대]하다
　　　　　　　　anticipate　　　　예기하다, 예상하다; 기대하다, 미리 걱정하다, 예상하다
　　　　　　　　predict　　　　　예언하다, 예측하다, 예보하다
　　　　　　　　suppose　　　　　(이미 알고 있는 지식에 의거하여) 생각하다, 추정[추측]하다
　　　　　　　　assume　　　　　(사실일 것으로) 추정[상정]하다

Reading for Literature II

PART 02

Reading for Dramas

- Chapter 01 Drama Analysis
- Chapter 02 Dramas to Read
- Chapter 03 Dramas in the Exam
- Chapter 04 Dramas in the Mock-Exam by Task

Chapter 01 Drama Analysis

When you read a play, you will notice features it shares with works of fiction — for instance, the use of language and symbols, the interaction among characters, and the development of a themes. In addition, you will notice features that distinguish it from fiction — for example, the presence of stage directions and the division of the play into acts and scenes.

The following guidelines, designed to help you explore works of dramatic literature, focus on issues that are examined in depth in chapters to come:

- *Trace the plays's **plot**.*
  What conflicts are present? Where does the rising action reach a climax? where does the falling action begin?

- *Analyze the play's characters.*
  Who are the central **characters**? What are their most distinctive traits? How do you learn about their personalities, backgrounds, appearances, and strengths and weaknesses?

- *Consider how the characters interact with one another.*
  Do the characters change and grow in response to the play's events, or do they remain essentially unchanged?

- *Examine the play's **language**.*
  How does **dialogue** reveal characters' emotions, conflicts, opinions, and motivation?

- *Look for **soliloquies** or **asides**.*
  What do they contribute to your knowledge of the play's characters and events?

- *Read the play's **stage directions**.*
  What do you learn from the descriptions of the characters, including their dress, gestures, and facial expressions? What information do you gain from studying the playwright's descriptions of the play's setting? Do the stage directions include information about lighting, props, music, or sound effects?

- *Consider the play's **staging***.

    Where and when does the action take place? What techniques are used to convey a sense of time and place to the audience?

- *Try to identify the play's **themes***.

    What main idea does the play communicate? What additional themes are explored?

- *Identify any **symbols** in the play*.

    How do these symbols help you to understand the play's theme?

01 Plot

Plot denotes the way events are arranged in a work of literature. Although the conventions of drama require that the plot of a play be presented somewhat differently from the plot of a short story, the same components of plot are present in both. Plot in a dramatic work, like plot in a short story, consists of conflicts that are revealed, intensified, and resolved through the characters' actions.

1. Plot Structure

A play typically begins with **exposition**, which presents characters and setting and introduces the basic situation in which the characters are involved. Then, during the **rising action**, complications develop, conflicts emerge, suspense builds, and crises occur. The rising action culminates in a **climax**, a point at which the plot's tension peaks. Finally, during the **falling action**, the intensity subsides, eventually winding down to a **resolution**, or **denouement**, in which all loose ends are tied up.

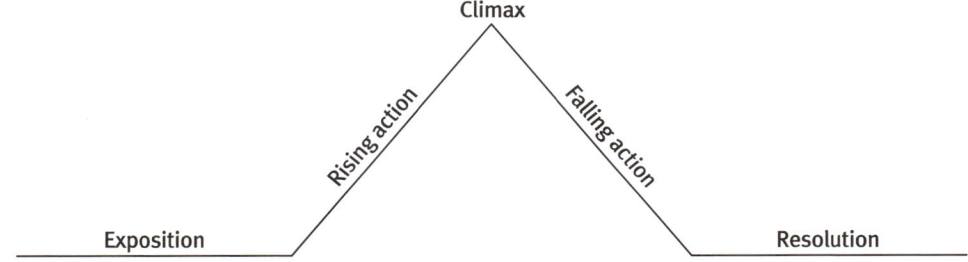

The familiar plot of a detective story follows this concept of plot: the exposition section includes the introduction of the detective and the explanation of the crime; the rising action develops as the investigation of the crime proceeds, with suspense increasing as the solution approaches; the high point of the action, the climax, comes with the revelation of the crime's solution; and the falling action presents the detective's explanation of the solution. The story concludes with a resolution that typically includes the capture of the criminal and the restoration of order.

The action of Susan Glaspell's one-act play *Trifles*[1], which in many ways resembles a detective story, can be diagrammed as follows:

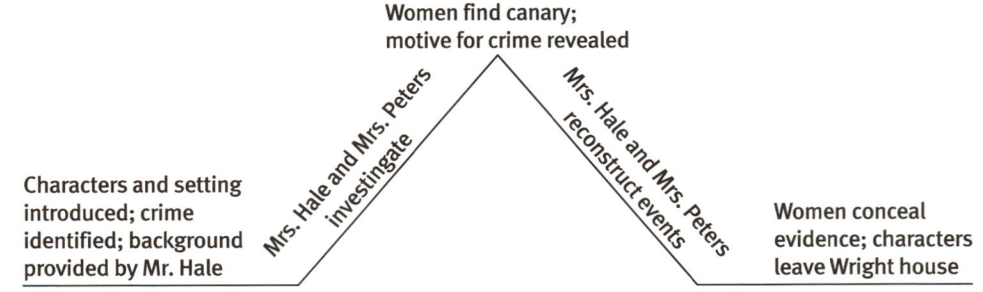

Of course, the plot of a complex dramatic work rarely conforms to the neat pattern represented by the plot pyramid. For example, a play can lack exposition entirely: because long stretches of exposition can be dull, a playwright may decide to arouse audience interest by moving directly into conflict, as Sophocles does in *Oedipus the King*. Similarly, because audience tend to lose interest after the play's climax is reached, a playwright may choose to dispense with extended falling action. Thus, after Hamlet's death, the play ends quite abruptly, with no real resolution.

2. Plot and Subplot

While the main plot is developing, a parallel plot, called a subplot, may be developing alongside it. This structural devide is common in the works of Shakespeare and in many other plays as well. The subplot's function may not immediately be clear, so at first it may seem to draw attention away from the main plot. Ultimately, however, the subplot reinforces elements of the primary plot. In Henrik Ibsen's *A Doll's House*[2], for example, the threat of Dr. Rank's impending death parallels the threat of Nora's approaching exposure; for both of them, time is running out.

3. Plot Development

In a dramatic work, plot unfolds through **action**: what characters say and do. Generally, a play does not include a narrator. Instead, dialogue, stage directions, and various staging techniques work together to move the play's action along.

Exchange of **dialogue** reveal what is happening — and, sometimes, indicate what happened in the past or suggest what will happen in the future. Characters can recount past events to other characters, announce an intention to take some action in the future, or summarize events that are occurring offstage. In such cases, dialogue takes the place of formal narrative.

On the printed page, **stage directions** efficiently move readers from one location and time period to another by specifying entrances and exits and identifying the play's structural divisions — acts and scenes — and their accompanying changes of setting.

Staging techniques can also advance a play's action. For example, a change in **lighting** can shift the focus to another part of the stage — and thus to another place and time. An adjustment of **scenery** or **props** — for instance, a breakfast table, complete with morning paper, replacing a bedtime setting — can indicate that the action has moved forward in time, as can a change of costumes. **Music** can also move a play's action along, predicting excitement of doom or a romantic interlude — or a particular character's entrance.

In Tennessee Williams' The *Glass Menagerie*[3], unusual staging devices — such as words projected on a screen that preview words to be spoken by a character and visual images on screen that predict scenes to follow — were designed to help keep the action moving. For example, a screen image of blue roses leads into a scene in which Laura tells her mother how Jim gave her the nickname "Blue Roses." Other staging techniques are also used to advance the plot. For example, toward the end of scene 5, stage directions announce, "*The Dance-Hall Music Changes To A Tango That Has A Minor and Somewhat Ominous Tone*"; a "music legend" repeated throughout the play serves as a signature in scenes focusing on Laura.

Occasionally, a play does have a formal narrator. In Thornton Wilder's play *Our Town* (1938), a character known as the Stage Manager functions as a narrator, not only describing the play's setting and introducing the characters to the audience but also soliciting questions from characters scattered around the audience, prompting characters, and interrupting dialogue. In *The Glass Menagerie*[3], the protagonist, Tom Wingfield, also serves as a narrator, summarizing what has happened and moving readers on to the next scene: "After the fiasco at Rubicam's Business College, the idea of getting a gentleman caller for Laura began to play a more important part in Mother's calculations" (scene 3)

(1) Flashbacks

Many plays — such as *The Glass Menagerie*[3] and Arthur Miller's *Death of a Salesman*[4] — include **flashbacks**, which depict events that occurred before the play's main action. Dialogue can also summarize events that occurred earlier, thereby overcoming the limitations set by the chronological action on stage. Thus, Mr. Hale in *Trifles*[1] tells the other characters how he discovered John Wright's murder, and Nora in *A Doll's House*[2] confides her secret past to her friend Kristine. As characters on stage are brought up to date, the audience is also given necessary information — facts that are essential to an understanding of the character's motivation. (In less realistic dramas, characters can interrupt the action to deliver long monologues or soliloquies that fill in background details — or even address the audience directly, as Tom does in *The Glass Menagerie*[3].)

(2) Foreshadowing

In addition to revealing past events, dialogue can foreshadow, or look ahead to, future action. In many cases, seemingly unimportant comments have significance that becomes clear as the play develops. For example, in act 3 of *A Doll's House*[2], Torvald Helmer says to Kristine, "An exit should always be effective, Mrs. Linde, but that's what I can't get Nora to grasp." At the end of the play, Nora's exit is not only effective but also memorable.

Elements of staging can also suggest events to come. In *The Glass Menagerie*[3], the ever-present photograph of the absent father — who, Tom tells the audience in scene 1, may be seen as a symbol of "the long delayed but always expected something that we live for" — foreshadows Tom's escape. Various bits of stage business — gestures or movements designed to attract the audience's attention — may also foreshadow future events. In *A Doll's House*[2], Nora's sneaking forbidden macaroons seems at first to suggest her fear of her husband, but her actions actually foreshadow her eventual defiance of his authority.

> **Points to Think about Plot**
>
> - What happens in the play?
> - What is the play's central conflict? How is it resolved? What other conflicts are present?
> - Is there the play's rising action? Or climax? Or falling action?
> - What crises can you identify?
> - How do characters' actions, dialogue, stage directions, and staging techniques advance the play's plot?
> - Does the play include a narrator?
> - Does the play include flashbacks? Foreshadowing?
> - Does the play's dialogue contain summaries of past events or references to events in the future?

02 Character

In Tennessee Williams' *The Glass Menagerie*[3], the protagonist, Tom Wingfield, functions as the play's narrator. Stepping out of his role as a character and speaking directly to the audience, he summarizes characters' actions, explains what motivates them, and discusses the significance of their behavior in the context of the play — commenting on his own character's actions as well. As narrator, Tom also presents useful background information about the characters. For instance, when he introduces his coworker, Jim, he prepares the audience for Jim's entrance and helps them to understand his subsequent actions:

> In high school Jim was a hero. He had tremendous Irish good nature and vitality with the scrubbed and polished look of white chinaware. He seemed to move in a continual spotlight. ⋯ But Jim apparently ran into more interference after his graduation. ⋯ His speed had definitely slowed. Six years after he left high school he was holding a job that wasn't much better than mine.
> (고교 시절에 짐이야말로 영웅이었습니다. 그는 아일랜드계 특유의 좋은 성품과 패기에 넘쳐 있었답니다. 잘

손질한 백색 도자기처럼 흰칠하게 잘생긴 용모였고요. 그는 가는 곳마다 스포트라이트를 받는 것 같았습니다. … 그러나 짐은 고교를 졸업하자 많은 장애에 부딪쳤습니다. … 그의 출세 속도는 거북이걸음이 되고 말았죠. 고등학교를 나온 지 6년 만에 직장을 구했지만 제 직업보다 별로 나을 게 없었습니다.)

Most plays, however, do not include narrators who present background. Instead, the audience learns about characters from their own words and from comments by other about them, as well as from the characters' actions and from the playwright's stage directions. Also, at a performance, the audience gains insight into characters from the way actions interpret them.

Characters in plays, like characters in novels and short stories, may be **round** or **flat**, **static**, or **dynamic**. Generally speaking, major characters are likely to be round, whereas minor characters are likely to be flat. Through the language and the actions of the characters, audiences learn whether the characters are multidimensional, skimpily developed, or perhaps merely **foils**, players whose main purpose is to shed light on more important characters. Audiences also learn about the emotions, attitudes, and values that help to shape the characters — their hopes and fears, their strengths and weaknesses. In addition, by comparing characters' early words and actions with later ones, audiences learn from the play whether or not characters grow and change emotionally.

1. Character's Words

(1) Monologue, soliloquy, dialogue

Characters' words reveal the most about their attitudes, feelings, beliefs, and values. Sometimes information is communicated (to other characters as well as to the audience) in a **monologue** — an extended speech by one character. This device is used throughout Margaret Edson's *Wit*[5]. A **soliloquy** — a monologue revealing a character's thoughts and feelings, directed at the audience and presumed not to be heard by other characters — can also convey information about a character. For example, Hamlet's well-known soliloquy that begins "To be or not to be" eloquently communicates his distraught mental state — his resentment of his mother and uncle, his confusion about what course of action to take, and his suicidal thoughts. Finally, **dialogue** — an exchange of words between two characters — can reveal misunderstanding or conflict between them, or it can show their agreement, mutual support, or similar beliefs.

In Henrik Ibsen's *A Doll's House*[2], dialogue reveals a good deal about the characters. Nora Helmer, the spoiled young wife, has broken the law and kept her crime secret from her husband. Through her words, we learn about her motivation, her values, her emotions, and her reactions to other characters and to her potentially dangerous situation. We learn, for instance, that she is flirtatious — "If your little squirrel begged you, with all her heart and soul ..." — and that she is childishly unrealistic about the consequences of her actions. When her husband, Torvald, asks what she would do if he was seriously injured, leaving her in debt, she says, "If anything so awful happened, then it just wouldn't matter if I had debts or not." When Torvald presses, "Well, but the people I'd borrowed from?" she dismisses them: "Them? Who cares about them! They're strangers." As the play progresses, Nora's lack of understanding of the power of the law becomes more and more significant as she struggles with her oral and ethical dilemma.

The inability of both Nora and Torvald to confront ugly truths is also revealed through their words. When, in act 1, Nora tells Krogstad, her blackmailer, that his revealing her secret could expose her to "the most horrible unpleasantness," he responds, "Only unpleasantness?" Yet later on, in act 3, Torvald echoes her language, fastidiously dismissing the horror with, "No, we're not going to dwell on anything unpleasant."

The ease with which Torvald is able to dismiss his dying friend Dr. Rank in act 3 ("He with his suffering and loneliness — like a dark cloud setting off our sunlit happiness. Well, maybe it's best this way.") foreshadows the lack of support he will give Nora immediately thereafter. Especially revealing is his use of *I* and *my* and *me*, which convey his self-centeredness:

Now you've wrecked all my happiness — ruined my whole future. Oh, it's awful to think of. I'm in a cheap little grafter's hands; he can do anything he wants with me, ask for anything, play with me like a puppet — and I can't breathe a word. I'll be swept down miserably into the depths on account of a featherbrained woman.

(나의 모든 행복을 당신은 깨뜨려 놓았어. —나의 전 장래를 파괴해 버렸단 말야. 오오, 생각만 해도 무서운 일을. 나는 이제 양심도 없는 자의 손아귀에 들어 있단 말이요. 그 자는 제가 하고 싶은 대로 나를 이끌 것이고, 가지고 싶은 건 다 빼앗아 갈게고, 마음대로 나를 써먹을 수 있게 되었어. 나는 잠자코 그대로 따라가야 된다는 말이야. 하나의 경솔한 여자 때문에 나는 원통하게 나락에 빠지고, 멸망하게 되었단 말이야!)

Just as Torvald's **words reveal** that he has not been changed by the play's events, Nora's words show that she has changed significantly. Her dialogue near the end of act 3 shows that she has become a responsible, determined woman — one who understand her situation and her options and is no longer blithely oblivious to her duties. When she says, "I've never felt more clearheaded and sure in my life," she is calm and decisive. When she says, "Our home's been nothing but a playpen. I've been your doll-wife here, just as at home I was Papa's doll-child," she reveals a new self-awareness. And, when she confronts her husband, she displays — perhaps for the first time in their relationship — complete honesty.

Sometimes what other characters say to (or about) a character can reveal more to an audience than the character's own words. For instance, in *A Doll's House*[2], when the dying Dr. Rank says, apparently without malice, "[Torvald] Helmer with his sensitivity has such a sharp distaste for anything ugly," the audience not only thinks ill of the man who is too "sensitive" to visit his sick friend but also questions his ability to withstand situations that may be emotionally or morally "ugly" as well.

When a character is offstage for much (or even all) of the action, the audience must rely on other characters' assessments of the **absent character**. In Susan Glaspell's *Trifles*[1], the play's focus is on an absent character, Minnie Wright, who is described solely through other characters' remarks. The evidence suggests that Mrs. Wright killed her husband, and only Mrs. Hale's and Mrs. Peter's comments about Mrs. Wright's dreary life can delineate her character and suggest a likely motive for the murder. Although Mrs. Wright never appears on stage, we learn essential information from the other women about her: that as a young girl she liked to sing and that more recently she was so distraught about the lack of beauty in her life that even her sewing revealed her distress. Similarly, the father in *The Glass Menagerie*[3], never appears (and therefore never speaks), but the play's other characters describe him as "A telephone man who — fell in love with long-distance!" — the absent husband and father who symbolizes abandonment and instability to Laura and Amanda and the possibility of freedom and escape to Tom.

Whether a character's words are in the form of a monologue, a soliloquy, or dialogue, and whether they reveal **information about the character** who is speaking or about someone else, such words were always revealing. Explicitly or implicitly, they convey a character's nature, attitudes, and relationships with other characters.

The language characters use can vary widely. A character may, for instance, use learned words, foreign words, elaborate figures of speech, irony or sarcasm, regionalisms, slang, jargon, clichés, or profanity. Words can also be used to indicate **tone** — for example, to express irony. Any of these uses of language may communicate vital information to the audience about a character's background, attitudes, and motivation. And, of course, a character's language may change as a play progresses, and this change too may be revealing.

(2) Tone

Tone reveals a character's mood or attitude. Tone can be flat or emotional, bitter or accepting, affectionate or aloof, anxious or calm. Contrasts in tone can indicate differences in outlook or emotional state between two characters; changes in tone from one point in a play to another can suggest corresponding changes within a character. At the end of *A Doll's House*[2], for instance, Nora is resigned to what she must do, and her language is appropriately controlled. Her husband, however, is desperate to change her mind, and his language reflects this desperation. The following exchanges from act 3 of the play illustrate their contrasting emotional states:

HELMER: But to part! To part from you! No, Nora, no — can't imagine it.
NORA: [*going out, right*] All the more reason why it has to be.
HELMER: Over! All over! Nora, won't you ever think about me?
NORA: I'm sure I'll think of you often, and about the children and the house here.
(헬머: 헤어진다! 당신과 헤어진다고! 안돼, 노라, 안돼... 그렇게 생각하는 것만도 견딜 수 없어.
노라: [오른편 방으로 들어간다.] 그렇다면 더더군다나 여기서 딱 잘라 단념하지 않으면 안돼요.
헬머: 끝! 이것으로 끝장이라니! 노라, 앞으로 당신은 내 생각을 전혀 하지도 않을 거요?
노라: 당신과 아이들, 그리고 이 집에 관해서는 아무래도 생각이 나겠지요.)

In earlier scenes between the two characters, Nora is emotional — at times, hysterical — and her husband is considerably more controlled. As the above exchange indicates, both Nora and Torvald Helmer change drastically during the course of the play.

(3) Irony

Irony, a contradiction or discrepancy between two different levels of meaning, can reveal a great deal about character. **Verbal irony** — a contradiction between what a character says and what he or she means — is very important in drama, where the verbal interplay between characters may carry the weight of the play. For example, when Nora and Dr. Rank discuss the latest news about his health in *A Doll's House*[2], there is deep irony in his use of the phrase "complete certainty." Although the phrase usually suggests reassuring news, here it is meant to suggest death, and both Nora and Dr. Rank understand this.

Dramatic irony depends on the audience's knowing something that a character has not yet realized, or on one character's knowing something that other characters do not know. In some cases, dramatic irony is created by an audience's awareness of historical background or events of which characters were unaware. Familiar with the story of Oedipus, for instance, the audience knows that the man who has caused all the problems in Thebes — the man Oedipus vows to find and take revenge on — is Oedipus himself. In other cases, dramatic irony emerges when the audience learns something — something the characters do not yet know or comprehend — from a play's unfolding action. The central irony in *A Doll's House*[2], for example, is that the family's "happy home" rests on a foundation of secrets, lies, and deception. Torvald does not know about the secrets, and Nora does not understand how they have poisoned her marriage. The audience, however, quickly becomes aware of the atmosphere of deceit — and aware of how it threatens the family's happiness.

Dramatic irony may also be conveyed through dialogue. Typically, dramatic irony is revealed when a character says something that gives the audience information that other characters, offstage at the time, do not know. In *A Doll's House*[2], the audience knows — because Nora has explained her situation to Kristine — that Nora spent the previous Christmas season hard at work, earning money to pay her secret debt. Torvald, however, remains unaware of her activities and believes her story that she was using the time to make holiday decorations, which the cat destroyed. This belief is consistent with his impression of Nora as an irresponsible child, yet the audience has quite a different impression of her. This discrepancy, one of many contradictions between the audience's view of Nora and Torvald's view of her, helps to create dramatic tension in the play.

Finally, **asides** (comments to the audience that other characters do not hear) can create dramatic irony by undercutting dialogue, providing ironic contrast between what the characters on stage know and what the audience knows. In Anton Chekhov's *The Brute*, for example, the audience knows that Mr. Smirnov is succumbing to Mrs. Popov's charms because he says, in an aside, "My God, what eyes she has! They're setting me on fire." Mrs. Popov, however, is not yet aware of his infatuation. The discrepancy between the audience's awareness and the character's adds to the play's humor.

2. Character's Actions

Through their actions, characters convey their values and attitudes to the audience. Actions also reveal aspects of a character's personality. When Laura Wingfield, a character in *The Glass Menagerie*[3], hides rather than face the "gentleman caller," audiences see how shy she is; when Nora in *A Doll's House*[2] plays hide-and-seek with her children, eats forbidden macaroons, and takes childish joy in Christmas, her immaturity is apparent.

Audiences also learn about characters from what they do not do. Thus, Nora's failure to remain in touch with her friend, Kristine, who has had a hard life, reveals her selfishness, and the failure of Mrs. Peters and Mrs. Hale in *Trifles*[1] to give their evidence to he sheriff indicates their support for Mrs. Wright and their understanding of what motivated her to take such drastic action.

Audiences also learn a good deal about characters by observing how they interact with other characters. In William Shakespeare's *Othello*, Iago is the embodiment of evil, and as the play's action unfolds, we discover his true nature. He reveals the secret marriage of Othello and Desdemona to her father; he schemes to arouse Othello's jealousy making him believe Desdemona has been unfaithful with his lieutenant, Cassio; he persuades Cassio to ask Desdemona to plead his case with Othello, knowing this act will further arouse Othello's suspicions; he encourages Othello to be suspicious of Desdemona's defense of Cassio; he plants Desdemona's handkerchief in Cassio's room; and, finally, he persuades Othello to kill Desdemona and then kills his own wife, Emilia, to prevent her from exposing his role in the intrigue. As the play progresses, then, Iago's dealings with others consistently reveal him to be evil and corrupt.

Points to Think about Character

- Does any character serve as a narrator? If so, what information does this narrator supply about the other characters? How reliable is the narrator?
- What do the major characters and minor characters contribute to the play?
- Does the play include monologue or soliloquies? What do these extended speeches reveal

about the characters?
- What is revealed about the characters through dialogue?
- What is revealed about the characters through their actions?

03 Staging

Staging refers to the physical elements of a play's production that determine how the play looks and sounds to an audience. It encompasses the **stage settings**, or sets — furnishings, scenery, props, and lighting — as well as the costumes, sound effects, and music that bring the play to life on the stage. In short, staging is everything that goes into making a written script a play.

1. Stage Directions

Usually a playwright presents instructions for the staging of a play in **stage directions** — notes that comment on the scenery, the movements of the performers, the lighting, and the placement of props. (In the absence of detailed stage directions, dialogue can provide information about staging.) Sometimes there stage directions are quite simple, leaving much to the imagination of the director.

When we read a play, we also read the playwright's italicized stage directions that contribute to the way the play looks and sounds to an audience. In addition to **commenting on staging**, stage directions may supply **physical details** about the characters, suggesting their age, appearance, movements, gestures, and facial expressions. These details may in turn convey additional information about characters: appearance may reveal social position or economic status, expressions may reveal attitudes, and so on. Stage directions may also indicate **the manner** in which a line of dialogue is to be delivered — *haltingly*, *confidently*, *hesitantly*, or *loudly*, for instance. The way a line is spoken may reveal a character to be excited, upset, angry, shy, or disappointed. Finally, stage directions may indicate **changes in characters** — for instance, a character whose speech is described as timid in early scenes may deliver lines emphatically and forcefully later on in the play.

Some stage directions provide a good deal of detail about character, others do little more than list characters' names. Arthur Miller is one playwright who often provides detailed information about character through stage directions. In *Death of a Salesman*[4], for instance, Miller's stage directions at the beginning of act I characterize Willy Loman immediately and specifically:

He is past sixty years of age, dressed quietly. Even as he crosses the stage to the doorway of the house, his exhaustion is apparent. He unlocks the door, comes into the kitchen, and thankfully lets his burden down, feeling the soreness of his palms. A word-sigh escapes his lips...

(환갑이 넘은 그는 옷차림이 수수하다. 무대를 지나 집 문앞으로 걸어오는 그는 몹시 고단해 보인다. 열쇠로 문을 열고 부엌으로 들어와 이제는 살았다는 듯이 가방을 내려놓고 아픈 손바닥을 만져본다. 무어라 중얼거리며 한숨짓는다...)

Subsequent stage directions indicate how lines are to be spoken. For example, in the play's opening lines, Willy's wife Linda calls out to him "*with some trepidation*"; Linda speaks "*very carefully, delicately*," and Willy speaks "*with casual irritation*." These instructions to readers (and actors) are meant to suggest the strained relationship between the two characters.

Points to Think about Stage Directions

- What information about staging is specified in the stage directions of the play?
- What information about staging is suggested by the play's dialogue?
- Do the stage directions provide information about how characters are supposed to look or behave?
- What costumes or props are specified? Do they plan an important part in the play? Do they have symbolic meaning?

---

04 Theme

Like a short story or a novel, a play is open to interpretation. Readers' reactions are influenced by the language of the text, and audiences' reactions are influenced by the performance on stage. Just as in fiction, every element of a play — its title, its conflicts, its dialogue, its characters, and its staging, for instance — can shed light on its theme.

1. Conflicts

The unfolding plot of a play — especially the **conflicts** that develop — can also reveal the play's themes. In Henrik Ibsen's *A Doll's House*[2], for example, at least three major conflicts are present: one between Nora and her husband Torvald, one between Nora and Krogstad (and old acquaintance), and one between Nora and society. Each of these conflicts sheds light on the themes of the play.

Through Nora's conflict with Torvald, Ibsen examines the constraints placed on women and men by marriage in the nineteenth century. Both Nora and Torvald are imprisoned within their respective roles: Nora must be passive and childlike, and Torvald must be proper and always in control. Nora, therefore, expects her husband to be noble and generous and, in a crisis, to sacrifice himself for her. When he fails to live up to her expectations, she is profoundly disillusioned.

Nora's conflict with Krogstad underscores Ibsen's criticisms of the class system in nineteenth-century Norway. At the beginning of the play, Nora finds it "immensely amusing: that we — that Torvald has so much power over ... people." Krogstad, a bank clerk who is in the employ of Torvald, visits Nora in act 1 to enlist her aid in saving his job. It is clear that she sees him as her social inferior. When Krogstad questions her about a woman with whom he has seen her, she replies, "What makes you think you can cross-examine me, Mr. Krogstad — you, one of my husband's employees?" Nora does not realize that she and Krogstad are, ironically, very much alike: both occupy subordinate positions and therefore have no power to determine their own destinies.

Finally, through Nora's conflict with society, Ibsen examines an important theme of his play: the destructive nature of the forces that subjugate women. Nineteenth-century society was male dominated. A married woman could not borrow money without her husband's signature, own real estate in her own name, or enter into contracts. In addition, all her assets — including inheritances and trust funds — automatically became the property of her husband at the time of marriage. As a result of her sheltered life, Nora at the beginning of the play is completely unaware of the consequences of her actions. Most readers share Dr. Rank's confusion when he asks Nora, "Why do you laugh at that?

Do you have any idea of what society is?" It is Nora's disillusionment at finding out that Torvald and the rest of society are not what she has been lead to believe they are that ultimately causes her to rebel. By walking out the door at the end of the play, Nora rejects not only her husband and her children (to whom she has no legal right once she leaves), but also society and its laws.

Those three conflicts underscore many of the themes that dominate. *A Doll's House*[2]. First, the conflicts show that marriage in the nineteenth century imprisons both men and women in narrow, constricting roles. They also show that middle-class Norwegian society is narrow, smug, and judgemental. (Krogstad is looked down upon for a crime years after he committed it, and Nora is looked down upon because she borrows money to save her husband's life.) Finally, the conflicts show that society does not offer individuals — especially women — the freedom to lead happy and fulfilling lives. Only when the social and economic conditions that govern society change, Ibsen suggests, can women and men live together in mutual esteem.

2. Dialogue

Dialogue can also give insight into a play's themes. Sometimes a character suggests — or even explicitly states — a theme. In act 3 of *A Doll's House*[2], for example, Nora's friend, Mrs. Linde, comes as close as any character to expressing the central concern of the play when she says, "Helmer's got to learn everything; this dreadful secret has to be aired; those two have to come to a full understanding; all these lies can't go on." As the play goes on to demonstrate, the lies that exist both in marriage and in society are obstacles to love and happiness.

One of the main theme of Arthur Miller's *Death of a Salesman*[4] — the questionable validity of the American Dream, given the nation's social, political, and economic realities — is suggested by the play's dialogue. As his son Biff points out, Willy Loman's stubborn belief in upward mobility and material success is based more on fantasy than on fact:

WILLY: [*With hatred, threateningly*.] The door of your life is wide open!

BIFF: Pop! I'm a dime a dozen, and so are you!

WILLY: [*Turning on him now in an uncontrolled outburst*.] I am not a dime a dozen! I am Willy Loman, and you are Biff Loman!

[*BIFF starts for WILLY, but is blocked by HAPPY. In his fury, BIFF seems on the verge of attacking his father.*]

BIFF: I am not a leader of men, Willy, and neither are you. You were never anything but a hard-working drummer who landed in the ash can like all the rest of them! I'm one dollar an hour, Willy! I tried seven states and couldn't raise it. A buck an hour! Do you gather my meaning? I'm not bringing home any prizes anymore, and you're going to stop waiting for me to bring them home!

(월리: [*증오에 차서 위협하며*] 네 인생의 문이 활짝 열려 있다니까!

비프: 아버지, 전 10센트 열두 개짜리 싸구려예요. 아버지도 그렇구요!

월리: [*더 참을 수 없다는 듯이 비프를 향해*] 난 그런 싸구려는 아니다. 난 월리 로먼이야.

[*비프는 월리에게 다가간다. 그러나 해피가 막는다. 격한 나머지 비프는 금시에라도 월리에게 덤벼들 기세이다.*]

비프: 우리 부자는 남을 지도할 자격이 없어요. 뼛골이 빠지도록 일이나 하는 도붓장수에 불과해요. 결국 어떻게 됐죠. 다른 외판원들이나 마찬가지로 쓰레기통 속에 처박혔단 말예요. 전 한 시간 한 달러짜리 인간예요. 일곱 주를 돌아다녔어도 그 값밖에 못 받는 인간이 되고 만 거예요. 아시겠죠? 그러니까, 내가 무슨 선물이라도 사들고 올 줄 아신다면 큰 착오예요. 애당초 단념하시는 게 낫죠.)

Though not explicitly stating the theme of the play, this exchange strongly suggests that Biff rejects the desperate optimism to which Willy clings.

3. Characters

Because a dramatic work focuses on a central character, or **protagonist**, the development of this character can shed light on a play's themes. Willy Loman in *Death of a Salesman*[4] is developed in great detail. At the beginning of the play, he feels trapped, exhausted, and estranged from his surroundings. As Willy gradually sinks from depression into despair, the action of the play shifts from the present to the past, showing the events that shaped his life. His attitudes, beliefs, dreams, and dashed hopes reveal him to be an embodiment of the major theme of the play — that an unquestioning belief in the American dream of success and upward mobility is unrealistic and possibly destructive.

Nora in *A Doll's House*[2] changes a great deal during the course of the play. At the beginning, she is more her husband's possession than an adult capable of shaping her own destiny. Nora's status becomes apparent in the first act when Torvald gently scolds his "little spendthrift" and refers to her as his "little lark" and his "squirrel." She is reduced to childish deceptions, such as hiding her macaroons when her husband enters the room. After Krogstad accuses her of committing forgery and threatens to expose her, she expects her husband to rise to the occasion and take the blame for her. When Torvald instead accuses her of being a hypocrite, a liar, and a criminal, Nora's neat little world come crashing down. As a result of this experience, Nora changes; no longer is she the submissive and obedient wife. Instead, she becomes assertive — even rebellious — ultimately telling Torvald that their marriage is a sham and that she can no longer stay with him. This abrupt shift in Nora's personality gives the audience a clear understanding of the major themes of the play.

Unlike Willy and Nora, Laura in Tennessee Williams' *The Glass Menagerie*[3] is a character who changes every little during the course of the play. Laura suffers from such pathological shyness that she is unable to attend typing class, let alone talk to a potential suitor. Although the "gentleman caller" draws Laura out of her shell for a short time, she soon withdraws again. Laura's inability to change reinforces the play's theme that contemporary society, with its emphasis on progress, has no place for people like Laura who live in private worlds "of glass animals and old, worn-out phonograph records."

4. Staging

Various physical elements, such as props and furnishings, may also convey the themes of a play. In *Death of a Salesman*[4], Biff's trophy, which is constantly in the audience's view, ironically underscores the futility of Willy's efforts to achieve success. Similarly, the miniature animals in *The Glass Menagerie*[3] reflect the fragility of Laura's character and the futility of her efforts to fit into the modern world. And, in *Trifles*[1], the depressing farm house, the broken birdcage, and the dead canary suggest Mrs. Wright's misery and the reason she murdered her husband.

Special lighting effects and music can also suggest a play's themes. Throughout *The Glass Menagerie*[3], for example, words and pictures are projected onto a section of the set between the front room and dining room walls. When Laura and her mother discuss a boy Laura knew, his picture is projected on the screen, showing him as a high school hero carrying a silver cup. In addition to the slides, Williams uses music — a recurring tune, dance music, and "Ave Maria" — to increase the emotional impact of certain scenes. He also uses shafts of light focused on selected areas or characters to create a dreamlike atmosphere for the play. Collectively, the slides, music and lighting reinforce the theme that those who retreat into the past inevitably become estranged from the present.

As you read, your values and beliefs influence your interpretation of a play's theme. For instance, your interest in the changing status of women could lead you to focus on the submissive, almost passive, role of Willy's wife, Linda, in *Death of a Salesman*[4]. As a result, you could conclude that the play shows how, in the post — World War II United States, women like Linda often sacrificed their own happiness for their husbands. Remember, however, that the play itself, not just your own feelings or assumptions about it, must support your interpretation.

Points to Think about Theme

- What is the central theme of the play?
- What other themes can you identify?
- What conflicts exist in the play? In what way do they shed light on the themes of the play?
- Do any characters' statements express or imply a theme of the play?

Chapter 02 Dramas to Read

01 Summary of Dramas To Read

01. ***Trifles** (1916) – Susan Glaspell
02. **A Doll's House** (1879) – Henrik Ibsen
03. ***The Glass Menagerie** (1945) – Tennessee Williams
04. ***Death of a Salesman** (1949) – Arthur Miller
05. ***The Zoo Story** (1958) – Edward Albee

• Dramas referenced in the teacher certification exam.

02 Analysis of Dramas To Read

1. *Trifles (1916)
• Susan Glaspell

Sheriff Henry Peters, local attorney George Henderson, and neighbor Lewis Hale enter the Wrights' farmhouse to investigate the murder of its previous owner, John. John's wife Minnie is suspected of the murder.

- Mrs. Hale and Mrs. Peters come along to collect some of Minnie's personal effects to bring to her in jail. The men search the house for evidence against Minnie, leaving the two women alone.
- Mrs. Hale and Mrs. Peters begin their own search in the kitchen, which the men overlooked. During their search, they find a broken birdcage and a dead canary wrapped in silk. It's suggested that John killed the bird and that this was what caused Minnie to snap.
- Mrs. Hale and Mrs. Peters sympathize with Minnie, realizing that her husband was abusive. They decide to hide the evidence from the men, who think of these things as mere "trifles."

Themes:

- In *Trifles*, the psychological divide between the men and women is visible throughout the play, as their different social roles and natures lead them to perceive radically different aspects of Minnie's life.
- The play considers the effects of isolation on men and women; while men seem mostly untroubled by the lack of a community, women suffer psychologically.
- By hiding the evidence, the women achieve justice for Minnie; justice can only be enacted when both men and women are part of the process.
- Women are women first and wives second; despite the fact that they call each other only by their husbands' last names, they ultimately identify and side with Minnie.

Characters:

- In *Trifles*, Lewis Hale, the neighbor who found John Wright dead, is reluctant to suggest Minnie had anything to do with the murder; he appears plainspoken and honorable.
- Mrs. Hale, wife of Lewis Hale, empathizes with Minnie and conceals the evidence of Minnie's crime as she remembers what her friend used to be like before she married Wright.
- George Henderson, left in charge of the investigation by Sheriff Peters, is the lawyer who

intends to prosecute Minnie; in his arrogance and haste, he misses vital details.
- Mr. Peters, sheriff of the rural community, arrested Minnie but leaves Henderson to head the investigation.
- Mrs. Peters, though she didn't know the younger Minnie, can relate to Minnie's loneliness and isolation as she recalls her own losses; she helps Mrs. Hale hide the evidence.

Dramatic Devices:

- In *De poetica* (c. 334-323 b.c.e.; Poetics, 1705), Aristotle's treatise on drama, he argued that a tragedy should consist of a single action, completed in one place and taking no longer than one day. *Trifles* follows these rules perfectly, taking place in a single room and far less time than one day. However, *Trifles* is more a social criticism than tragedy. Glaspell uses a variety of dramatic devices to critique her society. There are no formal scene breaks in *Trifles*. Instead, the entrances and exits of the male characters define the play. Each time the men leave, the women exchange private information; each time they enter, the men force or prevent crucial decisions. This action controls the pace of the play and symbolizes how men run women's lives, controlling and silencing them as John Wright silenced his wife.

- The many doubles in *Trifles* create a symbolic structure. Mr. Hale is accompanied by his wife; the sheriff is accompanied by his wife, Mrs. Peters. The county attorney is there because another pairing, Mr. and Mrs. Wright, was disrupted, indicating that the law must step in when the symbolic foundations of society breaks down. To underscore this point, the county attorney looks for a way to speak for Mrs. Wright, who refuses to speak for herself, and who is, indeed, completely absent from the play, making her invisibility to the social order literal. The final doubling is between Mrs. Wright and her bird. The bird symbolizes Mrs. Wright, a beautiful creature who loved to sing. When her husband killed it, it was as if she had been killed, and she killed him in turn.

- Glaspell adapts a technique from German expressionist drama, referring to the male characters primarily by their social roles. Yet, Glaspell gives this casting an ironic twist by giving the characters names that reveal who they really are. Mr. Hale is hale and hearty; Mr. Peters, whose name means "rock," is a sheriff, or a foundation of society. These names fit far less well for the women. Minnie Foster was out of place as a foster child, and the man she marries, John Wright, is anything but Mr. Right. Irony runs through the dialogue as well. During the play's climax, the women discuss how Mrs. Wright killed her husband, but the men assume the women are still discussing housework. This is the final example of the "trifles" that give the play its ironic title.

2. A Doll's House (1879)

• **Henrik Ibsen**

In *A Doll's House*, housewife Nora hides her financial problems from her husband Torvald. When Torvald learns of her deceit, he becomes angry. Disgusted by his selfishness, Nora leaves him to become an independent woman.

- In order to protect her secret, Nora tries to defend one of Torvald's employee who knows that she is misleading her husband. Torvald insists on firing the employee.
- Krogstad, the fired employee, sends a letter to Torvald detailing Nora's deceit. She tries to distract her husband to prevent him from reading the letter.
- Torvald eventually reads the letter and is angry at Nora, insisting that her deceit has harmed his reputation. He dismisses the fact that she borrowed the money to save his life.
- After learning that the money does not need to be repaid, Torvald forgives Nora, but she cannot forgive his self-centeredness and leaves the family.

Themes:

- Nora Helmer realizes that she has little agency in her marriage and leaves her family in order to establish a separate identity.
- While Nora and Torvald appear to be an ideal married couple, in reality their marriage is based on deception.
- Nora betrays Torvald by hiding her financial debt, and Torvald betrays Nora's trust with his inability to understand her.
- Nora matures from a childlike, dependent role into an independent woman who understands her own worth.
- Torvald's pride leads him to treat Nora like a possession instead of loving her as an equal.

Characters:

- Nora Helmer is Torvald's "doll wife" who hides her financial debt from her husband and ultimately leaves him after realizing that his love for her is superficial.
- Torvald Helmer is motivated by honor and pride to dismiss his wife after learning that she has taken out a substantial loan for his health.
- Nils Krogstad works for Torvald at the bank and blackmails Nora before ultimately returning the bond she had taken out.

- Christine Linde is a friend of Nora's who is widowed and in need of money. She decides to marry Krogstad.
- Dr. Rank is a family friend who falls in love with Nora. She refuses his help after learning of his infatuation and remains loyal to Torvald.

Form and Content:

- *A Doll's House*, a realistic three-act play, focuses on late nineteenth century life in a middle-class Scandinavian household, in which the wife is expected to be contentedly passive and the husband paternally protective. Nora Helmer, however, has subverted this model. At that time, a woman could not sign a legal contract alone; thus, when her beloved husband, Torvald, became ill, Nora secretly obtained a loan by forging her father's signature so that they could travel to a warmer climate. As the play opens, Torvald is about to become manager of the bank and Nora has almost repaid the loan through odd jobs and scrimping on the household expenses. Nora discloses her actions to her friend Kristine Linde and exults in her accomplishment.

- The structure of the play is linear; after the exposition, the action becomes complicated with the appearance of Nora's debtor, Nils Krogstad, a man disgraced by crimes that he committed to protect his family. Insecure in his position at the bank, he threatens to expose Nora's loan and forgery unless she pleads his case to Torvald. In her ignorance, Nora had not fully understood that forgery is a criminal act.

- The major conflict of the play, concerning honesty in marriage, arises from this situation. Nora cannot discuss the blackmail with her husband, since her role in their relationship is that of a charming child; thus, she must plead for Krogstad. Torvald, however, refuses to hear her plea, labeling Krogstad morally lost for the crimes that he committed and not fit to bring up his children. The parallel is not lost on Nora, who sends her children away from her at the end of the first act.

- Nora's fear increases when Torvald rejects her second plea and fires Krogstad. As Kristine helps with her costume for the Christmas party, Nora confesses that Krogstad has left a letter to Torvald in the mailbox revealing everything. She is convinced that now a wonderful thing will happen — that, when Torvald discovers her actions, he will assume the blame and that she then will commit suicide. As the second act ends, Nora dances a violent tarantella in an effort to distract Torvald from opening the mailbox.

- The final act begins with Kristine and Krogstad resuming a relationship formerly hindered by their economic circumstances. Although Krogstad now regrets his blackmail, Kristine decides that the letter should remain in the mailbox and that Torvald must discover the truth. Torvald reads the letter and immediately denounces Nora as a liar and a criminal, the destroyer of his future. When another letter arrives containing the promissory note, however, Torvald realizes that he is "safe." He forgives Nora, promising to "be conscience and will" to her thereafter. In the classic scene that follows, Nora speaks openly with her husband, the first such occasion in their entire married life, and admits her ignorance of herself and the world beyond. Declaring that she must leave Torvald and the children to find herself, she leaves and slams the door behind her.

3. *The Glass Menagerie (1945)   • Tennessee Williams

In *The Glass Menagerie*, Amanda Winfield lives with her children in a shabby St. Louis apartment. Amanda worries that her son Tom will abandon them just like her husband did. At the end of the play, that's exactly what Tom does.

- Uneducated and unskilled, Amanda depends entirely on Tom for the family's livelihood. She fears he will abandon her and Laura, just as her husband left them, a possibility made even more frightening since Laura is disabled.
- When Tom mentions Jim O'Connor, a young man he works with at the warehouse, Amanda insists he invite Jim to dinner. She thinks of Jim as Laura's "gentleman caller" and imagines a secure future for Laura as Jim's wife.
- When Jim comes to dinner, the shy, introverted Laura is terrified, as she had known and admired him in high school. Jim remembers Laura fondly. As they reminisce, Jim is attracted by Laura's gentleness and beauty and kisses her.
- Laura is shattered when Jim apologizes for the kiss, explaining that he is engaged. Her dreams for Laura's future destroyed, Amanda vents her fury at Tom. Tom leaves to pursue his own dreams but discovers he can't escape the past.

Themes:

- In *The Glass Menagerie*, the themes of illusions and impossible dreams offer an escape from reality, but they cannot be sustained.
- The past informs the present, and the possibility of escaping the past is only an illusion.
- Resolving the conflict between personal desires and responsibility to others exacts an emotional price that is difficult to bear.
- Overwhelming fear is more powerful than love in motivating human behavior.
- The twentieth century is fraught with turmoil, economic depression, and war.

Characters:

- In *The Glass Menagerie*, Amanda Wingfield lacks the education and skills to support herself and her family during the Depression. She is a former Southern belle who fell in love and married an irresponsible man who later abandoned her and their children,
- Amanda's fears drive her attempts to control Tom's and Laura's thinking and behavior. She nags them continually, creating conflict and tension in the household. Amanda escapes reality

in romantic memories of her youth.

- Tom Wingfield, his family's sole support, dreams of being a writer and living a life of adventure. Trapped in a job he despises and resentful of Amanda, he runs away and travels the world, but he is haunted by the memory of Laura.

- Disabled by fear and insecurity and unable to fulfill her mother's expectations, Laura Wingfield escapes life by collecting glass figurines and listening to old records. A brief romantic encounter with Jim O'Connor breaks her heart.

- Jim O'Connor confidently pursues unrealistic dreams of a future in radio. Carried away with the sound of his own voice, he engages Laura's fragile emotions and kisses her before revealing he is engaged to another girl.

Form and Content:

- According to Tennessee Williams, *The Glass Menagerie* is a "memory play." It is narrated from the perspective of the character Tom Wingfield. What Williams calls "personal lyricism" is employed in the play not so much to challenge the accountability of Tom's narrative as to display, from a character's point of view, the impact that illusion has on individuals. The play, for example, portrays a large group of characters whose obsession with the past complicates their connection to the present. Illusory worlds are created by these characters, either to cherish the not-so-accurate memory of an idealized past or to protect an already-tattered emotional integrity. It is typical of Williams, a self-proclaimed romantic dramatist, to create characters who prefer dwelling in a fantasy world. Yet, the playwright, aware of the inevitability of the conflict between illusion and reality, also leaves the audience with no doubt about his cynical and bitter attitude in dramatizing the sometimes self-deceptive but always debilitating nature of his characters' illusory world. Flashbacks are used effectively to underscore the struggle that characters must undergo when they do not know how to disentangle themselves from the past.

- The main plot of *The Glass Menagerie* centers on what happens to the Wingfield family on one unforgettable evening. A childhood illness has left Laura Wingfield crippled; one of her legs is slightly shorter than the other and is held in a brace. Self-consciousness and a lack of self-confidence have turned Laura into an extremely shy person. She prefers living in a dream world created through her fantasies and her collection of glass animals. Laura's mother, Amanda Wingfield, believes strongly in tradition. Her faith in the traditional Southern practice of having a "gentleman caller" has led her to make an arrangement for Laura to meet with one of Tom's coworkers at the warehouse.

- Jim O'Connor shows up one evening at the Wingfields' apartment as the "gentleman caller." He behaves like a gentleman, charming Amanda and strengthening her belief in this tradition. During the meeting, Jim's outward glamour and glibness temporarily rekindle hopes in Laura's closed heart. She tells him how much she admired him in high school and entrusts him with her favorite glass animal, the unicorn. When Jim clumsily breaks the unicorn's horn and tells her that they are not compatible with each other, Laura loses even more of her ever-dwindling confidence in herself and furthers her alienation from reality.
- At the end of the play, Laura is apparently thrown off her emotional balance and ready to retreat permanently into her fantasy world. Amanda, holding Tom responsible for the fiasco of Jim and Laura's meeting, blames him as the manufacturer of dreams and illusions. Tom, now fully aware of the detrimental effects of the conflicts between the past and the present and between illusion and reality, decides to leave the family and take on the challenge of shaping his own life.

4. *Death of a Salesman (1949)

• Arthur Miller

In *Death of a Salesman*, Willy Loman is an aging salesman who's fired from his job. When his son Biff admits that he couldn't get a loan to start his new business, Willy commits suicide so that Biff can use the insurance money to secure his future.

- Willy expresses disappointment with his son Biff, who's unable to find a job at the beginning of the play.
- A series of flashbacks reveals Willy's thoughts of suicide, which his sons dispel by promising to go into business together.
- Despite Willy's last wishes, his funeral is not well attended. The play ends tragically.

Themes:

- In *Death of a Salesman*, Willy struggles to reconcile his idea of himself with his failures. This theme of self-deception weaves through the play, building as Willy disappoints his family and fails to help his sons financially.
- The American Dream is one of the underlying themes in *Death of a Salesman*. Willy's desire to be financially and socially secure stem directly from his belief in the American Dream. In the end, the play suggests that the American Dream is unattainable.
- *Death of a Salesman* also addresses the theme of aging. Willy Loman is a middle-aged salesman with outdated ideas about himself and the world around him. He still believes that he can succeed in life, even though it's abundantly clear that his time has passed.

Characters:

- Willy Loman, an aging traveling salesman who laments not being able to help his sons achieve financial success.
- Biff Loman, Willy's eldest son, who fails to secure a loan to start his business.
- Happy Loman, Willy's youngest son.
- Uncle Ben, Willy's brother, who strikes it rich in the diamond mines and sparks Willy's feelings of inadequacy.

Analysis:

- *Death of a Salesman* takes place at Willy Loman's home in New York City. Development has boxed the small house in, making it feel cramped and confining. Willy often thinks of

his brother's adventures in distant lands, which suggests that Willy wants to escape his life.
- Material items such as tennis rackets and diamonds are symbols of wealth. Willy is jealous of his brother Ben's success in the diamond mining industry, and he feels like a failure because he can't provide for his family as well as Ben could. Ultimately, the diamonds are symbols of Willy's desire for and failure to achieve a better life.
- Willy puts pressure on himself to be a success. He measures a man's worth by his possessions and social status. He wants a big, ostentatious funeral, because he believes that will reflect how great a man he was. In the end, Willy Loman's funeral is small and disappointing, just like his life.

5. *The Zoo Story (1958)   • Edward Albee

The Zoo Story is a one-act play that explores themes of isolation, loneliness, miscommunication as anathematization, social disparity and dehumanization in a materialistic world.

- This play concerns two characters, Peter and Jerry, who meet on a park bench in New York City's Central Park. Peter is a wealthy publishing executive with a wife, two daughters, two cats, and two parakeets. Jerry is an isolated and disheartened man, desperate to have a meaningful conversation with another human being. He intrudes on Peter's peaceful state by interrogating him and forcing him to listen to stories about his life and the reason behind his visit to the zoo. The action is linear, unfolding in front of the audience in "real time". The elements of ironic humor and unrelenting dramatic suspense are brought to a climax when Jerry brings his victim down to his own savage level.

- Eventually, Peter has had enough of his strange companion and tries to leave. Jerry begins pushing Peter off the bench and challenges him to fight for his territory. Unexpectedly, Jerry pulls a knife on Peter, and then drops it as initiative for Peter to grab. When Peter holds the knife defensively, Jerry charges him and impales himself on the knife. Bleeding on the park bench, Jerry finishes his zoo story by bringing it into the immediate present: "Could I have planned all this. No... no, I couldn't have. But I think I did." Horrified, Peter runs away from Jerry, whose dying words, "Oh...my...God", are a combination of scornful mimicry and supplication.

Themes:

- The Zoo Story is an intensely harrowing expression of estrangement in American society. The lack of communication between Jerry and his landlady's vicious dog is merely an analogy for the hostility among living beings in a world in which alienation and lack of sympathy are deep-seated psychological conditions. The story of the dog leads to Jerry's zoo story, but the roundabout, digressionary mode of relation is emblematic of Edward Albee's style. This drama is one in which a lonely man on the verge of nervous breakdown desperately attempts to find at least one individual who will hear him out and come to an understanding of the existential plight that Jerry sees as a malaise in the world.

- You don't get any family members on stage in The Zoo Story, but family — or the absence of family — flutters about the edges of the play like one of Peter's pet parakeets. Peter has a typical family — wife, daughters, pets. Jerry has nothing except for some extra picture frames. Jerry seems to envy Peter his family — and Peter, maybe, envies Jerry because he doesn't have a family, or at least because he isn't boring the way people with normal families are considered boring. "Family" in the play means "normal": Peter is, Jerry isn't, and both sort of wish they could switch (though Peter's probably happy enough at the end of the play that he isn't Jerry, what with all the blood and everything).

Characters:

- Peter – Peter, an executive for a publishing house. An average-sized and nearsighted man in his early forties, Peter has Catholic tastes and dresses conservatively; he is an upper-class representative of the Eisenhower years. His family life is predictably normal: a good wife, two daughters, two cats, two parakeets, and a nice apartment in the East Seventies of Manhattan. His attitude reflects his status: He is naïve, complacent, passive, proper, and a bit bored. His intention on this afternoon was to read quietly in Central Park. A stranger, Jerry, interrupts him with talk and then aggression. Although Peter is slow to anger, Jerry's incessant prodding eventually drives him to pick up Jerry's knife. After Jerry impales himself, Peter exits the now-ending play with his previously established character destroyed by this chance and absurd encounter.

- Jerry – Jerry, an emotionally disturbed man in his late thirties. Anxious and angry about his bisexuality, poverty, and alienation, Jerry tries to make sense of his pain by walking from the New York Zoo looking for another human to confront. Finding Peter, he talks in a rambling yet intelligent way about the miseries of his life. His autobiography reveals his inability to relate to others, including the fellow residents of his rooming house on the upper West Side.

03 Dramas To Read

> 01. **Trifles** (1916) – Susan Glaspell
> 02. **A Doll's House** (1879) – Henrik Ibsen
> 03. **The Glass Menagerie** (1945) – Tennessee Williams
> 04. **Death of a Salesman** (1949) – Arthur Miller
> 05. **The Zoo Story** (1958) – Edward Albee

1. Trifles (1916) – full text of Trifles

• Susan Glaspell

SCENE. The kitchen in the now abandoned farmhouse of John Wright, a gloomy kitchen, and left without having been put in order — unwashed pans under the sink, a loaf of bread outside the bread-box, a dish-towel on the table — other signs of incompleted work. At the rear the outer door opens and the Sheriff comes in followed by the County Attorney and Hale. The Sheriff and Hale are in middle life, the County Attorney is a young man; all are much bundled up and go at once to the stove. They are followed by the two women — the Sheriff's wife first; she is a slight wiry woman, a thin nervous face. Mrs. Hale is larger and would ordinarily be called more comfortable looking, but she is disturbed now and looks fearfully about as she enters. The women have come in slowly, and stand close together near the door.

COUNTY ATTORNEY: [Rubbing his hands.] This feels good. Come up to the fire, ladies.

MRS. PETERS: [After taking a step forward.] I'm not — cold.

SHERIFF: [Unbuttoning his overcoat and stepping away from the stove as if to mark the beginning of official business.] Now, Mr. Hale, before we move things about, you explain to Mr. Henderson just what you saw when you came here yesterday morning.

COUNTY ATTORNEY: By the way, has anything been moved? Are things just as you left them yesterday?

SHERIFF: [Looking about.] It's just the same. When it dropped below zero last night I thought I'd better send Frank out this morning to make a fire for us — no use getting pneumonia with a big case on, but I told him not to touch anything except the stove — and you know Frank.

COUNTY ATTORNEY: Somebody should have been left here yesterday.

SHERIFF: Oh — yesterday. When I had to send Frank to Morris Center for that man who went crazy — I want you to know I had my hands full yesterday. I knew you could get back from Omaha by today and as long as I went over everything here myself —

COUNTY ATTORNEY: Well, Mr. Hale, tell just what happened when you came here yesterday morning.

HALE: Harry and I had started to town with a load of potatoes. We came along the road from my place and as I got here I said, "I'm going to see if I can't get John Wright to go in with me on a party telephone." I spoke to Wright about it once before and he put me off, saying folks talked too much anyway, and all he asked was peace and quiet — I guess you know about how much he talked himself, but I thought maybe if I went to the house and talked about it before his wife, though I said to Harry that I didn't know as what his wife wanted made much difference to John —

COUNTY ATTORNEY: Let's talk about that later, Mr. Hale. I do want to talk about that, but tell now just what happened when you got to the house.

HALE: I didn't hear or see anything; I knocked at the door, and still it was all quiet inside. I knew they must be up, it was past eight o'clock. So I knocked again, and I thought I heard somebody say, "Come in." I wasn't sure, I'm not sure yet, but I opened the door — this door [indicating the door by which the two women are still standing] and there in that rocker — [pointing to it] sat Mrs. Wright. [They all look at the rocker.

COUNTY ATTORNEY: What — was she doing?

HALE: She was rockin' back and forth. She had her apron in her hand and was kind of — pleating it.

COUNTY ATTORNEY: And how did she — look?

HALE: Well, she looked queer.

COUNTY ATTORNEY: How do you mean — queer?

HALE: Well, as if she didn't know what she was going to do next. And kind of done up.

COUNTY ATTORNEY: How did she seem to feel about your coming?

HALE: Why, I don't think she minded — one way or other. She didn't pay much attention. I said, "How do, Mrs. Wright, it's cold, ain't it?" And she said, "Is it?" — and went on kind of pleating at her apron. Well, I was surprised; she didn't ask me to come up to the stove, or to set down, but just sat there, not even looking at me, so I said, "I want to see John." And then she — laughed, I guess you would call it a laugh. I thought of Harry and the team outside, so I said a little sharp: "Can't I see John?" "No," she says, kind o' dull like. "Ain't he home?" says I. "Yes," says she, "he's home." "Then why can't I see him?" I asked her, out of patience. "'Cause he's dead," says she. "Dead?" says I. She just nodded her head, not getting a bit excited, but rockin' back and forth. "Why-where is he?" says I, not knowing what to say. She just pointed upstairs — like that [himself pointing to the room above]. I got up, with the idea of going up there. I walked from there to here — then I says, "Why, what did he die of?" "He died of a rope round his neck," says she, and just went on pleatin' at her apron. Well, I went out and called Harry. I thought I might — need help. We went upstairs and there he was lyin' —

COUNTY ATTORNEY: I think I'd rather have you go into that upstairs, where you can point it all out. Just go on now with the rest of the story.

HALE: Well, my first thought was to get that rope off. It looked ... [Stops, his face twitches] ... but Harry, he went up to him, and he said, "No, he's dead all right, and we'd better not touch anything." So we went back downstairs. She was still sitting that same way. "Has anybody been notified?" I asked. "No," says she, unconcerned. "Who did this, Mrs. Wright?" said Harry. He said it business-like — and she stopped pleatin' of her apron. "I don't know," she says. "You don't know?" says Harry. "No," says she. "Weren't you sleepin' in the bed with him?" says Harry. "Yes," says she, "but I was on the inside." "Somebody slipped a rope round his neck and strangled him and you didn't wake up?" says Harry. "I didn't wake up," she said after him. We must 'a looked as if we didn't see how that could be, for after a minute she said, "I sleep sound." Harry was going to ask her more questions but I said maybe we ought to let her tell her story first to the coroner, or the sheriff, so Harry went fast as he could to Rivers' place, where there's a telephone.

COUNTY ATTORNEY: And what did Mrs. Wright do when she knew that you had gone for the coroner?

HALE: She moved from that chair to this one over here [Pointing to a small chair in the corner] and just sat there with her hands held together and looking down. I got a feeling that I ought to make some conversation, so I said I had come in to see if John wanted to put in a telephone, and at that she started to laugh, and then she stopped and looked at me — scared. [The County Attorney, who has had his note book out, makes a note.] I dunno, maybe it wasn't scared. I wouldn't like to say it was. Soon Harry got back, and then Dr. Lloyd came, and you, Mr. Peters, and so I guess that's all I know that you don't.

COUNTY ATTORNEY: [Looking around.] I guess we'll go upstairs first — and then out to the barn and around there. [To the Sheriff.] You're convinced that there was nothing important here — nothing that would point to any motive.

SHERIFF: Nothing here but kitchen things. [The County Attorney, after again looking around the kitchen, opens the door of a cupboard closet. He gets up on a chair and looks on a shelf. Pulls his hand away, sticky.

COUNTY ATTORNEY: Here's a nice mess. [The women draw nearer.]

MRS. PETERS: [To the other woman.] Oh, her fruit; it did freeze. [To the Lawyer.] She worried about that when it turned so cold. She said the fire'd go out and her jars would break.

SHERIFF: Well, can you beat the women! Held for murder and worryin' about her preserves.

COUNTY ATTORNEY: I guess before we're through she may have something more serious than preserves to worry about.

HALE: Well, women are used to worrying over trifles. [The two women move a little closer together.

COUNTY ATTORNEY: [With the gallantry of a young politician.] And yet, for all their worries, what would we do without the ladies? [The women do not unbend. He goes to the sink, takes a dipperful of water from the pail and pouring it into a basin, washes his hands. Starts to wipe them on the roller-towel, turns it for a cleaner place.] Dirty towels! [Kicks his foot against the pans under the sink.] Not much of a housekeeper, would you say, ladies?

MRS. HALE: [Stiffly.] There's a great deal of work to be done on a farm.

COUNTY ATTORNEY: To be sure. And yet [With a little bow to her] I know there are some Dickson county farmhouses which do not have such roller towels. [He gives it a pull to expose its full length again.

MRS. HALE: Those towels get dirty awful quick. Men's hands aren't always as clean as they might be.

COUNTY ATTORNEY: Ah, loyal to your sex, I see. But you and Mrs. Wright were neighbors. I suppose you were friends, too.

MRS. HALE: [Shaking her head.] I've not seen much of her of late years. I've not been in this house — it's more than a year.

COUNTY ATTORNEY: And why was that? You didn't like her?

MRS. HALE: I liked her all well enough. Farmers' wives have their hands full, Mr. Henderson. And then —

COUNTY ATTORNEY: Yes —?

MRS. HALE: [Looking about.] It never seemed a very cheerful place.

COUNTY ATTORNEY: No — it's not cheerful. I shouldn't say she had the homemaking instinct.

MRS. HALE: Well, I don't know as Wright had, either.

COUNTY ATTORNEY: You mean that they didn't get on very well?

MRS. HALE: No, I don't mean anything. But I don't think a place'd be any cheerfuller for John Wright's being in it.

COUNTY ATTORNEY: I'd like to talk more of that a little later. I want to get the lay of things upstairs now. [He goes to the left, where three steps lead to a stair door.

SHERIFF: I Suppose anything Mrs. Peters does'll be all right. She was to take in some clothes for her, you know, and a few little things. We left in such a hurry yesterday.

COUNTY ATTORNEY: Yes, but I would like to see what you take, Mrs. Peters, and keep an eye out for anything that might be of use to us.

MRS. PETERS: Yes, Mr. Henderson. [The women listen to the men's steps on the stairs, then look about the kitchen.

MRS. HALE: I'd hate to have men coming into my kitchen, snooping around and criticising. [She arranges the pans under sink which the Lawyer had shoved out of place.

MRS. PETERS: Of course it's no more than their duty.

MRS. HALE: Duty's all right, but I guess that deputy sheriff that came out to make the fire might have got a little of this on. [Gives the roller towel a pull.] Wish I'd thought of that sooner. Seems mean to talk about her for not having things slicked up when she had to come away in such a hurry.

MRS. PETERS: [Who has gone to a small table in the left rear corner of the room, and lifted one end of a towel that covers a pan.] She had bread set. [Stands still.]

MRS. HALE: [Eyes fixed on a loaf of bread beside the breadbox, which is on a low shelf at the other side of the room. Moves slowly toward it.] She was going to put this in there. [Picks up loaf, then abruptly drops it. In a manner of returning to familiar things.] It's a shame about her fruit. I wonder if it's all gone. [Gets up on the chair and looks.] I think there's some here that's all right, Mrs. Peters. Yes — here; [Holding it toward the window] this is cherries, too. [Looking again.] I declare I believe that's the only one. [Gets down, bottle in her hand. Goes to the sink and wipes it off on the outside.] She'll feel awful bad after all her hard work in the hot weather. I remember the afternoon I put up my cherries last summer. [She puts the bottle on the big kitchen table, center of the room. With a sigh, is about to sit down in the rocking-chair. Before she is seated realizes what chair it is; with a slow look at it, steps back. The chair which she has touched rocks back and forth.]

MRS. PETERS: Well, I must get those things from the front room closet. [She goes to the door at the right, but after looking into the other room, steps back.] You coming with me, Mrs. Hale? You could help me carry them.

They go in the other room; reappear, Mrs. Peters carrying a dress and skirt, Mrs. Hale following with a pair of shoes.

MRS. PETERS: My, it's cold in there. [She puts the clothes on the big table, and hurries to the stove.]

MRS. HALE: [Examining the skirt.] Wright was close. I think maybe that's why she kept so much to herself. She didn't even belong to the Ladies Aid. I suppose she felt she couldn't do her part, and then you don't enjoy things when you feel shabby. She used to wear pretty clothes and be lively, when she was Minnie Foster, one of the town girls singing in the choir. But that — oh, that was thirty years ago. This all you was to take in?

MRS. PETERS: She said she wanted an apron. Funny thing to want, for there isn't much to get you dirty in jail, goodness knows. But I suppose just to make her feel more natural. She said they was in the top drawer in this cupboard. Yes, here. And then her little shawl that always hung behind the door. [Opens stair door and looks.] Yes, here it is. [Quickly shuts door leading upstairs.

MRS. HALE: [Abruptly moving toward her.] Mrs. Peters?

MRS. PETERS: Yes, Mrs. Hale?

MRS. HALE: Do you think she did it?

MRS. PETERS: [In a frightened voice.] Oh, I don't know.

MRS. HALE: Well, I don't think she did. Asking for an apron and her little shawl. Worrying about her fruit.

MRS. PETERS: [Starts to speak, glances up, where footsteps are heard in the room above. In a low voice.] Mr. Peters says it looks bad for her. Mr. Henderson is awful sarcastic in a speech and he'll make fun of her sayin' she didn't wake up.

MRS. HALE: Well, I guess John Wright didn't wake when they was slipping that rope under his neck.

MRS. PETERS: No, it's strange. It must have been done awful crafty and still. They say it was such a — funny way to kill a man, rigging it all up like that.

MRS. HALE: That's just what Mr. Hale said. There was a gun in the house. He says that's what he can't understand.

MRS. PETERS: Mr. Henderson said coming out that what was needed for the case was a motive; something to show anger, or — sudden feeling.

MRS. HALE: [Who is standing by the table.] Well, I don't see any signs of anger around here. [She puts her hand on the dish towel which lies on the table, stands looking down at table, one half of which is clean, the other half messy.] It's wiped to here. [Makes a move as if to finish work, then turns and looks at loaf of bread outside the breadbox. Drops towel. In that voice of coming back to familiar things.] Wonder how they are finding things upstairs. I hope she had it a little more red-up up there. You know, it seems kind of sneaking. Locking her up in town and then coming out here and trying to get her own house to turn against her!

MRS. PETERS: But Mrs. Hale, the law is the law.

MRS. HALE: I s'pose 'tis. [Unbuttoning her coat.] Better loosen up your things, Mrs. Peters. You won't feel them when you go out. [Mrs. Peters takes off her fur tippet, goes to hang it on hook at back of room, stands looking at the under part of the small corner table.

MRS. PETERS: She was piecing a quilt. [She brings the large serving basket and they look at the bright pieces.]

MRS. HALE: It's log-cabin pattern. Pretty, isn't it? I wonder if she was goin' to quilt it or just knot it? [Footsteps have been heard coming down the stairs. The Sheriff enters followed by Hale and the County Attorney.]

SHERIFF: They wonder if she was going to quilt it or just knot it! [The men laugh, the women look abashed.]

COUNTY ATTORNEY: [Rubbing his hands over the stove.] Frank's fire didn't do much up there, did it? Well, let's go out to the barn and get that cleared up. [The men go outside.

MRS. HALE: [Resentfully.] I don't know as there's anything so strange, our takin' up our time with little things while we're waiting for them to get the evidence. [She sits down at the big table smoothing out a block with decision.] I don't see as it's anything to laugh about.

MRS. PETERS: [Apologetically.] Of course they've got awful important things on their minds. [Pulls up a chair and joins Mrs. Hale at the table.]

MRS. HALE: [Examining another block.] Mrs. Peters, look at this one. Here, this is the one she was working on, and look at the sewing! All the rest of it has been so nice and even. And look at this! It's all over the place! Why, it looks as if she didn't know what she was about! [After she had said this they look at each other, then start to glance back at the door. After an instant Mrs. Hale has pulled at a knot and ripped the sewing.]

MRS. PETERS: Oh, what are you doing, Mrs. Hale?

MRS. HALE: [Mildly.] Just pulling out a stitch or two that's not sewed very good. [Threading a needle.] Bad sewing always made me fidgety.

MRS. PETERS: [Nervously.] I don't think we ought to touch things.

MRS. HALE: I'll just finish up this end. [Suddenly stopping and leaning forward.] Mrs. Peters?

MRS. PETERS: Yes, Mrs. Hale?

MRS. HALE: What do you suppose she was so nervous about?

MRS. PETERS: Oh — I don't know. I don't know as she was nervous. I sometimes sew awful queer when I'm just tired. [Mrs. Hale starts to say something, looks at Mrs. Peters, then goes on sewing.] Well I must get these things wrapped up. They may be through sooner than we think. [Putting apron and other things together.] I wonder where I can find a piece of paper, and string.

MRS. HALE: In that cupboard, maybe.

MRS. PETERS: [Looking in cupboard.] Why, here's a bird-cage. [Holds it up.] Did she have a bird, Mrs. Hale?

MRS. HALE: Why, I don't know whether she did or not — I've not been here for so long. There was a man around last year selling canaries cheap, but I don't know as she took one; maybe she did. She used to sing real pretty herself.

MRS. PETERS: [Glancing around.] Seems funny to think of a bird here. But she must have had one, or why would she have a cage? I wonder what happened to it.

MRS. HALE: I s'pose maybe the cat got it.

MRS. PETERS: No, she didn't have a cat. She's got that feeling some people have about cats — being afraid of them. My cat got in her room and she was real upset and asked me to take it out.

MRS. HALE: My sister Bessie was like that. Queer, ain't it?

MRS. PETERS: [Examining the cage.] Why, look at this door. It's broke. One hinge is pulled apart.

MRS. HALE: [Looking too.] Looks as if someone must have been rough with it.

MRS. PETERS: Why, yes. [She brings the cage forward and puts it on the table.]

MRS. HALE: I wish if they're going to find any evidence they'd be about it. I don't like this place.

MRS. PETERS: But I'm awful glad you came with me, Mrs. Hale. It would be lonesome for me sitting here alone.

MRS. HALE: It would, wouldn't it? [Dropping her sewing.] But I tell you what I do wish, Mrs. Peters. I wish I had come over sometimes when she was here. I — [Looking around the room] — wish I had.

MRS. PETERS: But of course you were awful busy, Mrs. Hale — your house and your children.

MRS. HALE: I could've come. I stayed away because it weren't cheerful — and that's why I ought to have come. I — I've never liked this place. Maybe because it's down in a hollow and you don't see the road. I dunno what it is, but it's a lonesome place and always was, I wish I had come over to see Minnie Foster sometimes. I can see now-[Shakes her head.]

MRS. PETERS: Well, you mustn't reproach yourself, Mrs. Hale. Somehow we just don't see how it is with other folks until — something comes up.

MRS. HALE: Not having children makes less work — but it makes a quiet house, and Wright out to work all day, and no company when he did come in. Did you know John Wright, Mrs. Peters?

MRS. PETERS: No; I've seen him in town. They say he was a good man.

MRS. HALE: Yes — good; he didn't drink, and kept his word as well as most, I guess, and paid his debts. But he was a hard man, Mrs. Peters. Just to pass the time of day with him — [Shivers.] Like a raw wind that gets to the bone. [Pauses, her eye falling on the cage.] I should think she would 'a wanted a bird. But what do you suppose went with it?

MRS. PETERS: I don't know, unless it got sick and died. [She reaches over and swings the broken door, swings it again, both women watch it.]

MRS. HALE: You weren't raised round here, were you? [Mrs. Peters shakes her head.] You didn't know — her?

MRS. PETERS: Not till they brought her yesterday.

MRS. HALE: She — come to think of it, she was kind of like a bird herself — real sweet and pretty, but kind of timid and — fluttery. How — she — did — change. [Silence; then as if struck by a happy thought and relieved to get back to every day things.] Tell you what, Mrs. Peters, why don't you take the quilt in with you? It might take up her mind.

MRS. PETERS: Why, I think that's a real nice idea, Mrs. Hale. There couldn't possibly be any objection to it, could there? Now, just what would I take? I wonder if her patches are in here — and her things. [They look in the sewing basket.]

MRS. HALE: Here's some red. I expect this has got sewing things in it. [Brings out a fancy box.] What a pretty box. Looks like something somebody would give you. Maybe her scissors are in here. [Opens box. Suddenly puts her hand to her nose.] Why — [Mrs. Peters bends nearer, then turns her face away.] There's something wrapped up in this piece of silk.

MRS. PETERS: Why, this isn't her scissors.

MRS. HALE: [Lifting the silk.] Oh, Mrs. Peters — its — [Mrs. Peters bends closer.]

MRS. PETERS: It's the bird.

MRS. HALE: [Jumping up.] But, Mrs. Peters — look at it! Its neck! Look at its neck! It's all — to the other side.

MRS. PETERS: Somebody — wrung — its — neck. [Their eyes meet. A look of growing comprehension, of horror. Steps are heard outside. Mrs. Hale slips box under quilt pieces, and sinks into her chair. Enter Sheriff and County Attorney. Mrs. Peters rises.]

COUNTY ATTORNEY: [As one turning from serious things to little pleasantries.] Well, ladies, have you decided whether she was going to quilt it or knot it?

MRS. PETERS: We think she was going to — knot it.

COUNTY ATTORNEY: Well, that's interesting, I'm sure. [Seeing the birdcage.] Has the bird flown?

MRS. HALE: [Putting more quilt pieces over the box.] We think the — cat got it.

COUNTY ATTORNEY: [Preoccupied.] Is there a cat? [Mrs. Hale glances in a quick covert way at Mrs. Peters.

MRS. PETERS: Well, not now. They're superstitious, you know. They leave.

COUNTY ATTORNEY: [To Sheriff Peters, continuing an interrupted conversation.] No sign at all of anyone having come from the outside. Their own rope. Now let's go up again and go over it piece by piece. [They start upstairs.] It would have to have been someone who knew just the —

Mrs. Peters sits down. The two women sit there not looking at one another, but as if peering into something and at the same time holding back. When they talk now it is in the manner of feeling their way over strange ground, as if afraid of what they are saying, but as if they can not help saying it.

MRS. HALE: She liked the bird. She was going to bury it in that pretty box.

MRS. PETERS: [In a whisper] When I was a girl — my kitten — there was a boy took a hatchet, and before my eyes — and before I could get there — [Covers her face an instant.] If they hadn't held me back I would have — [Catches herself, looks upstairs where steps are heard, falters weakly] — hurt him.

MRS. HALE: [With a slow look around her.] I wonder how it would seem never to have had any children around. [Pause.] No, Wright wouldn't like the bird — a thing that sang. She used to sing. He killed that, too.

MRS. PETERS: [Moving uneasily.] We don't know who killed the bird.

MRS. HALE: I knew John Wright.

MRS. PETERS: It was an awful thing was done in this house that night, Mrs. Hale. Killing a man while he slept, slipping a rope around his neck that choked the life out of him.

MRS. HALE: His neck. Choked the life out of him.

[Her hand goes out and rests on the bird-cage.]

MRS. PETERS: [With rising voice.] We don't know who killed him. We don't know.

MRS. HALE [Her own feeling not interrupted.] If there'd been years and years of nothing, then a bird to sing to you, it would be awful — still, after the bird was still.

MRS. PETERS: [Something within her speaking.] I know what stillness is. When we homesteaded in Dakota, and my first baby died — after he was two years old, and me with no other then —

MRS. HALE: [Moving.] How soon do you suppose they'll be through, looking for the evidence?

MRS. PETERS: I know what stillness is. [Pulling herself back.] The law has got to punish crime, Mrs. Hale.

MRS. HALE: [Not as if answering that.] I wish you'd seen Minnie Foster when she wore a white dress with blue ribbons and stood up there in the choir and sang. [A look around the room.] Oh, I wish I'd come over here once in a while! That was a crime! That was a crime! Who's going to punish that?

MRS. PETERS: [Looking upstairs.] We mustn't — take on.

MRS. HALE: I might have known she needed help! I know how things can be — for women, I tell you, it's queer, Mrs. Peters. We live close together and we live far apart. We all go through the same things — it's all just a different kind of the same thing. [Brushes her eyes, noticing the bottle of fruit, reaches out for it.] If I was you I wouldn't tell her her fruit was gone. Tell her it ain't. Tell her it's all right. Take this in to prove it to her. She — she may never know whether it was broke or not.

MRS. PETERS: [Takes the bottle, looks about for something to wrap it in; takes petticoat from the clothes brought from the other room, very nervously begins winding this around the bottle. In a false voice.] My, it's a good thing the men couldn't hear us. Wouldn't they just laugh! Getting all stirred up over a little thing like a-dead canary. As if that could have anything to do with — with — wouldn't they laugh!

[The men are heard coming down stairs.]

MRS. HALE: [Under her breath.] Maybe they would — maybe they wouldn't.

COUNTY ATTORNEY: No, Peters, it's all perfectly clear except a reason for doing it. But you know juries when it comes to women. If there was some definite thing. Something to show — something to make a story about — a thing that would connect up with this strange way of doing it —

[The women's eyes meet for an instant. Enter Hale from outer door.]

HALE: Well, I've got the team around. Pretty cold out there.

COUNTY ATTORNEY: I'm going stay here a while by myself. [To the Sheriff.] You can send Frank out for me, can't you? I want to go over everything. I'm not satisfied that we can't do better.

SHERIFF: Do you want to see what Mrs. Peters is going to take in? [The Lawyer goes to the table, picks up the apron, laughs.]

COUNTY ATTORNEY: Oh, I guess they're not very dangerous things the ladies have picked out. [Moves a few things about, disturbing the quilt pieces which cover the box. Steps back.] No, Mrs. Peters doesn't need supervising. For that matter, a sheriff's wife is married to the law. Ever think of it that way, Mrs. Peters?

MRS. PETERS: Not — just that way.

SHERIFF: [Chuckling.] Married to the law. [Moves toward the other room.] I just want you to come in here a minute, George. We ought to take a look at these windows.

COUNTY ATTORNEY: [Scoffingly.] Oh, windows!

SHERIFF: We'll be right out, Mr. Hale.

Hale goes outside. The Sheriff follows the County Attorney into the other room. Then Mrs. Hale rises, hands tight together, looking intensely at Mrs. Peters, whose eyes make a slow turn, finally meeting Mrs. Hale's. A moment Mrs. Hale holds her, then her own eyes point the way to where the box is concealed. Suddenly Mrs. Peters throws back quilt pieces and tries to put the box in the bag she is wearing. It is too big. She opens box, starts to take bird out, cannot touch it, goes to pieces, stands there helpless. Sound of a knob turning in the other room. Mrs. Hale snatches the box and puts it in the pocket of her big coat. Enter County Attorney and Sheriff.

COUNTY ATTORNEY: [Facetiously.] Well, Henry, at least we found out that she was not going to quilt it. She was going to — what is it you call it, ladies?

MRS. HALE: [Her hand against her pocket.] We call it — knot it, Mr. Henderson.

[CURTAIN]

2. A Doll's House (1879) – Part of Act II

• Henrik Ibsen

THE SAME SCENE. —THE Christmas Tree is in the corner by the piano, stripped of its ornaments and with burnt-down candle-ends on its dishevelled branches. NORA'S cloak and hat are lying on the sofa. She is alone in the room, walking about uneasily. She stops by the sofa and takes up her cloak.

NORA: [drops her cloak] Someone is coming now! [Goes to the door and listens.] No — it is no one. Of course, no one will come today, Christmas Day — nor tomorrow either. But, perhaps — [opens the door and looks out]. No, nothing in the letterbox; it is quite empty. [Comes forward.] What rubbish! of course he can't be in earnest about it. Such a thing couldn't happen; it is impossible — I have three little children.

[Enter the NURSE from the room on the left, carrying a big cardboard box.]

NURSE: At last I have found the box with the fancy dress.

NORA: Thanks; put it on the table.

NURSE: [doing so] But it is very much in want of mending.

NORA: I should like to tear it into a hundred thousand pieces.

NURSE: What an idea! It can easily be put in order — just a little patience.

NORA: Yes, I will go and get Mrs. Linde to come and help me with it.

NURSE: What, out again? In this horrible weather? You will catch cold, ma'am, and make yourself ill.

NORA: Well, worse than that might happen. How are the children?

NURSE: The poor little souls are playing with their Christmas presents, but —

NORA: Do they ask much for me?

NURSE: You see, they are so accustomed to have their mamma with them.

NORA: Yes, but, nurse, I shall not be able to be so much with them now as I was before.

NURSE: Oh well, young children easily get accustomed to anything.

NORA: Do you think so? Do you think they would forget their mother if she went away altogether?

NURSE: Good heavens! — went away altogether?

NORA: Nurse, I want you to tell me something I have often wondered about — how could you have the heart to put your own child out among strangers?

NURSE: I was obliged to, if I wanted to be little Nora's nurse.

NORA: Yes, but how could you be willing to do it?

NURSE: What, when I was going to get such a good place by it? A poor girl who has got into trouble should be glad to. Besides, that wicked man didn't do a single thing for me.

NORA: But I suppose your daughter has quite forgotten you.

NURSE: No, indeed she hasn't. She wrote to me when she was confirmed, and when she was married.

* * * * * *

NORA: [advancing towards him] Speak low — my husband is at home.

KROGSTAD: No matter about that.

NORA: What do you want of me?

KROGSTAD: An explanation of something.

NORA: Make haste then. What is it?

KROGSTAD: You know, I suppose, that I have got my dismissal.

NORA: I couldn't prevent it, Mr. Krogstad. I fought as hard as I could on your side, but it was no good.

KROGSTAD: Does your husband love you so little, then? He knows what I can expose you to, and yet he ventures —

NORA: How can you suppose that he has any knowledge of the sort?

KROGSTAD: I didn't suppose so at all. It would not be the least like our dear Torvald Helmer to show so much courage —

NORA: Mr. Krogstad, a little respect for my husband, please.

KROGSTAD: Certainly — all the respect he deserves. But since you have kept the matter so carefully to yourself, I make bold to suppose that you have a little clearer idea, than you had yesterday, of what it actually is that you have done?

NORA: More than you could ever teach me.

KROGSTAD: Yes, such a bad lawyer as I am.

NORA: What is it you want of me?

KROGSTAD: Only to see how you were, Mrs. Helmer. I have been thinking about you all day long. A mere cashier, a quill-driver, a — well, a man like me — even he has a little of what is called feeling, you know.

NORA: Show it, then; think of my little children.

KROGSTAD: Have you and your husband thought of mine? But never mind about that. I only wanted to tell you that you need not take this matter too seriously. In the first place there will be no accusation made on my part.

NORA: No, of course not; I was sure of that.

KROGSTAD: The whole thing can be arranged amicably; there is no reason why anyone should know anything about it. It will remain a secret between us three.

NORA: My husband must never get to know anything about it.

KROGSTAD: How will you be able to prevent it? Am I to understand that you can pay the balance that is owing?

NORA: No, not just at present.

KROGSTAD: Or perhaps that you have some expedient for raising the money soon?

NORA: No expedient that I mean to make use of.

KROGSTAD: Well, in any case, it would have been of no use to you now. If you stood there with ever so much money in your hand, I would never part with your bond.

NORA: Tell me what purpose you mean to put it to.

KROGSTAD: I shall only preserve it — keep it in my possession. No one who is not concerned in the matter shall have the slightest hint of it. So that if the thought of it has driven you to any desperate resolution —

NORA: It has.

KROGSTAD: If you had it in your mind to run away from your home —

NORA: I had.

KROGSTAD: Or even something worse —

NORA: How could you know that?

KROGSTAD: Give up the idea.

NORA: How did you know I had thought of that?

KROGSTAD: Most of us think of that at first. I did, too — but I hadn't the courage.

NORA: [faintly] No more had I.

KROGSTAD: [in a tone of relief] No, that's it, isn't it — you hadn't the courage either?

NORA: No, I haven't — I haven't.

KROGSTAD: Besides, it would have been a great piece of folly. Once the first storm at home is over —. I have a letter for your husband in my pocket.

NORA: Telling him everything?

KROGSTAD: In as lenient a manner as I possibly could.

NORA: [quickly] He mustn't get the letter. Tear it up. I will find some means of getting money.

KROGSTAD: Excuse me, Mrs. Helmer, but I think I told you just now —

NORA: I am not speaking of what I owe you. Tell me what sum you are asking my husband for, and I will get the money.

KROGSTAD: I am not asking your husband for a penny.

NORA: What do you want, then?

KROGSTAD: I will tell you. I want to rehabilitate myself, Mrs. Helmer; I want to get on; and in that your husband must help me. For the last year and a half I have not had a hand in anything dishonourable, amid all that time I have been struggling in most restricted circumstances. I was content to work my way up step by step. Now I am turned out, and I am not going to be satisfied with merely being taken into favour again. I want to get on, I tell you. I want to get into the Bank again, in a higher position. Your husband must make a place for me —

NORA: That he will never do!

KROGSTAD: He will; I know him; he dare not protest. And as soon as I am in there again with him, then you will see! Within a year I shall be the manager's right hand. It will be Nils Krogstad and not Torvald Helmer who manages the Bank.

NORA: That's a thing you will never see!

KROGSTAD: Do you mean that you will — ?

NORA: I have courage enough for it now.

KROGSTAD: Oh, you can't frighten me. A fine, spoilt lady like you —

NORA: You will see, you will see.

KROGSTAD: Under the ice, perhaps? Down into the cold, coal-black water? And then, in the spring, to float up to the surface, all horrible and unrecognisable, with your hair fallen out —

NORA: You can't frighten me.

KROGSTAD: Nor you me. People don't do such things, Mrs. Helmer. Besides, what use would it be? I should have him completely in my power all the same.

NORA: Afterwards? When I am no longer —

KROGSTAD: Have you forgotten that it is I who have the keeping of your reputation? [NORA stands speechlessly looking at him.] Well, now, I have warned you. Do not do anything foolish. When Helmer has had my letter, I shall expect a message from him. And be sure you remember that it is your husband himself who has forced me into such ways as this again. I will never forgive him for that. Goodbye, Mrs. Helmer. [Exit through the hall.]

NORA: [goes to the hall door, opens it slightly and listens.] He is going. He is not putting the letter in the box. Oh no, no! that's impossible! [Opens the door by degrees.] What is that? He is standing outside. He is not going downstairs. Is he hesitating? Can he — ? [A letter drops into the box; then KROGSTAD'S footsteps are heard, until they die away as he goes downstairs. NORA utters a stifled cry, and runs across the room to the table by the sofa. A short pause.]

NORA: In the letter-box. [Steals across to the hall door.] There it lies — Torvald, Torvald, there is no hope for us now!

[MRS. LINDE comes in from the room on the left, carrying the dress.]

MRS. LINDE: There, I can't see anything more to mend now. Would you like to try it on — ?

NORA: [in a hoarse whisper] Christine, come here.

MRS. LINDE: [throwing the dress down on the sofa] What is the matter with you? You look so agitated!

NORA: Come here. Do you see that letter? There, look — you can see it through the glass in the letter-box.

MRS. LINDE: Yes, I see it.

NORA: That letter is from Krogstad.

MRS. LINDE: Nora — it was Krogstad who lent you the money!

* * * * * *

NORA: [takes out of the box a tambourine and a long variegated shawl. She hastily drapes the shawl round her. Then she springs to the front of the stage and calls out] Now play for me! I am going to dance!

[HELMER plays and NORA dances. RANK stands by the piano behind HELMER, and looks on.]

HELMER: [as he plays] Slower, slower!

NORA: I can't do it any other way.

HELMER: Not so violently, Nora!

NORA: This is the way.

HELMER: [stops playing] No, no — that is not a bit right.

NORA: [laughing and swinging the tambourine] Didn't I tell you so?

RANK: Let me play for her.

HELMER: [getting up] Yes, do. I can correct her better then.

[RANK sits down at the piano and plays. NORA dances more and more wildly. HELMER has taken up a position beside the stove, and during her dance gives her frequent instructions. She does not seem to hear him; her hair comes down and falls over her shoulders; she pays no attention to it, but goes on dancing. Enter MRS. LINDE.]

MRS. LINDE: [standing as if spell-bound in the doorway] Oh! —

NORA: [as she dances] Such fun, Christine!

HELMER: My dear darling Nora, you are dancing as if your life depended on it.

NORA: So it does.

HELMER: Stop, Rank; this is sheer madness. Stop, I tell you! [RANK stops playing, and NORA suddenly stands still. HELMER goes up to her.] I could never have believed it. You have forgotten everything I taught you.

NORA: [throwing away the tambourine] There, you see.

HELMER: You will want a lot of coaching.

NORA: Yes, you see how much I need it. You must coach me up to the last minute. Promise me that, Torvald!

HELMER: You can depend on me.

NORA: You must not think of anything but me, either today or tomorrow; you mustn't open a single letter — not even open the letter-box —

HELMER: Ah, you are still afraid of that fellow —

NORA: Yes, indeed I am.

HELMER: Nora, I can tell from your looks that there is a letter from him lying there.

NORA: I don't know; I think there is; but you must not read anything of that kind now. Nothing horrid must come between us until this is all over.

RANK: [whispers to HELMER] You mustn't contradict her.

HELMER: [taking her in his arms] The child shall have her way. But tomorrow night, after you have danced —

NORA: Then you will be free. [The MAID appears in the doorway to the right.]

MAID: Dinner is served, ma'am.

NORA: We will have champagne, Helen.

MAID: Very good, ma'am. [Exit.]

HELMER: Hullo! — are we going to have a banquet?

NORA: Yes, a champagne banquet until the small hours. [Calls out.] And a few macaroons, Helen — lots, just for once!

HELMER: Come, come, don't be so wild and nervous. Be my own little skylark, as you used.

NORA: Yes, dear, I will. But go in now and you too, Doctor Rank. Christine, you must help me to do up my hair.

RANK: [whispers to HELMER as they go out] I suppose there is nothing — she is not expecting anything?

HELMER: Far from it, my dear fellow; it is simply nothing more than this childish nervousness I was telling you of. [They go into the right-hand room.]

3. The Glass Menagerie (1945) – Scene 1 • Tennessee Williams

The Wingfield apartment is in the rear of the building, one of those vast hive-like conglomerations of cellular living-units that flower as warty growths in overcrowded urban centres of lower-middle-class population and are symptomatic of the impulse of this largest and fundamentally enslaved section of American society to avoid fluidity and differentiation and to exist and function as one interfused mass of automatism.

The apartment faces an alley and is entered by a fire-escape, a structure whose name is a touch of accidental poetic truth, for all of these huge buildings are always burning with the slow and implacable fires of human desperation. The fire-escape is included in the set — that is, the landing of it and steps descending from it.

The scene is memory and is therefore non-realistic. Memory takes a lot of poetic licence. It omits some details; others are exaggerated, according to the emotional value of the articles it touches, for memory is seated predominantly in the heart. The interior is therefore rather dim and poetic.

At the rise of the curtain, the audience is faced with the dark, grim rear wall of the Wingfield tenement. This building, which runs parallel to the footlights, is flanked on both sides by dark, narrow alleys which run into murky canyons of tangled clothes-lines, garbage cans, and the sinister lattice-work of neighbouring fire-escapes. It is up and down these alleys that exterior entrances and exits are made, during the play. At the end of Tom's opening commentary, the dark tenement wall slowly reveals [by means of a transparency] the interior of the ground floor Wongfield apartment.

Downstage is the living-room, which also serves as a sleeping-room for Laura, the sofa is unfolding to make her bed. Upsatge, centre, and divided by a wide arch or second pro-scenium with transparent faded portières [or second curtain], is the dining-room. In an old fashioned what-not in the living-room are seen scores of transparent glass animals. A blown-up photograph of the father hangs on the wall of the living-room, facing the audience, to the left of the archway. It is the face of a very handsome young man in a doughboy's First World War cap. He is gallantly smiling, ineluctably smiling, as if to say, "I will be smiling forever."

The audience hears and sees the opening scene in the dining-room through both the transparent fourth wall of the building and the transparent gauze portières of the dining-room arch. It is during this revealing scene that the fourth wall slowly ascends out of sight. This transparent exterior wall is not brought down again until the very end of the play, during Tom's final speech.

The narrator is an undisguised convention of the play. He takes whatever licence with dramatic convention is convenient to his purpose.

TOM enters dressed as a merchant sailor from alley, stage left, and strolls across the front of the stage to the fire-escape. There he stops and lights a cigarette. He addresses the audience.

> TOM: Yes, I have tricks in my pocket, I have things up my sleeve. But I am the opposite of a stage magician. He gives you illusion that has the appearance of truth. I give you truth in the pleasant disguise of illusion.
> To begin with, I turn bark time. I reverse it to that quaint period, the thirties, when the huge middle class of America was matriculating in a school for the blind. Their eyes had failed them or they had failed their eyes, and so they were having their fingers pressed forcibly down on the fiery Braille alphabet of a dissolving economy.
> In Spain there was revolution. Here there was only shouting and confusion.
> In Spain there was Guernica. Here there were disturbances of labour, sometimes pretty violent, in otherwise peaceful cities such as Chicago, Cleveland, Saint Louis. ... This is the social background of the play.

> *MUSIC*

> The play is memory. Being a memory play, it is dimly lighted, it is sentimental, it is not realistic. In memory everything seems to happen to music. That explains the fiddle in the wings. I am the narrator of the play, and also a character in it. The other characters are my mother Amanda, my sister Laura and a gentleman caller who appears in the final scenes. He is the most realistic character in the play, being an emissary from a world of reality that we were somehow set apart from. But since I have a poet's weakness for symbols, I am using this character also as a symbol; he is the long-delayed but always expected something that we live for. There is a fifth character in the play who doesn't appear except in this larger-than-life-size photograph over the mantel. This is our father who left us a long time ago. He was a telephone man who fell in love with long distances; he gave up his job with the telephone company and skipped the light fantastic out of town. ... The last we heard of him was a picture postcard from Mazatlan, on the Pacific coast of Mexico, containing a message of two words — 'Hello — Good-bye!' and no address. I think the rest of the play will explain itself ...

AMANDA's voice becomes audible through the portières.

LEGEND ON SCREEN: 'Où SONT LES NEIGES'.

He divides the portieres and enters the upstage area.

AMANDA and LAURA are seated at a drop-leaf table. Eating is indicated by gestures without food or utensils. AMANDA faces the audience. TOM and LAURA are Seated is profile. The interior has lit up softly and through the scrim we see AMANDA and LAURA seated at the table in the upstage area

AMANDA: [calling] Tom? Yes, Mother.

AMANDA: We can't say grace until you come to the table!

TOM: Coming, Mother. [He bows slightly and withdraws, reappearing a few moments later in his place at the table.]

AMANDA: [to her son] Honey, don't push with your fingers. If you have to push with something, the thing to push with is a crust of bread. And chew !chew! Animals have sections in their stomachs which enable them to digest flood without mastication, but human beings are supposed to chew their food before they swallow it down. Eat food leisurely, son, and really enjoy it. A well-cooked meal has lots of delicate flavours that have to be held in the mouth for appreciation. So chew your food and give your salivary glands a chance to function !

TOM deliberately lays his imaginary fork down and his chair back from the table.

TOM: I haven't enjoyed one bite of this dinner because of your constant directions on how to eat it. It's you that makes me rush through meals with your hawk-like attention to every bite I take. Sickening — spoils my appetite — all this discussion of — animals' secretion — salivary glands — mastication!

AMANDA: [lightly] Temperament like a Metropolitan star ! [He rises and crosses downstage.] You're not excused from the table.

TOM: I'm getting a cigarette.

AMANDA: You smoke too much.

LAURA rises.

LAURA: I'll bring in the blancmangé.

He remains standing with his cigarette by the portières during the following.

AMANDA: [rising] No, sister, no, sister — you be the lady this time and I'll be the darkey

LAURA: I'm already up.

AMANDA: Resume your seat, little sister, I want you to stay fresh and pretty for gentleman callers!

LAURA: I'm not expecting any gentleman callers.

AMANDA: [crossing out to kitchenette. Airily] Sometimes they come when they are least expected! Why, I remember one Sunday afternoon in Blue Mountain — [Enters kitchenette.]

TOM: I know what's coming

LAURA: Yes. But let her tell it.

TOM: Again?

LAURA: She loves to tell it.

AMANDA returns with bowl of dessert.

AMANDA: One Sunday afternoon in Blue Mountain, your mother received seventeen! gentlemen callers! Why, sometimes there weren't chairs enough to accommodate them all. We had to send the nigger over to bring in folding chairs from the parish house.

TOM: [remaining at portières] How did you entertain those gentleman callers?

AMANDA: I understood the art of conversation!

TOM: I bet you could talk.

AMANDA: Girls in those days knew how to talk, I can tell you.

TOM: Yes?

IMAGE: AMANDA AS A GIRL ON A PORCH GREETING CALLERS.

AMANDA: They knew how to entertain their gentlemen callers. It wasn't enough for a girl to be possessed of a pretty face and a graceful figure although I wasn't alighted in either respect. She also needed to have a nimble wit and a tongue to meet all occasions.

TOM: What did you talk about?

AMANDA: Things of importance going on in the world! Never anything coarse or common or vulgar. [She addresses Tom as though he were seated in the vacant chair at the table though he remains by portieres. He plays this scene as though he held the book.] My callers were gentleman — all! Among my callers were some of the most prominent young planters of the Mississippi Delta — planters and sons of planters!

Tom motions for music and a spot of light on AMANDA. Her eyes lift, her face glows, her voice becomes rich and elegiac.

SCREEN LEGEND: 'Où SONT Les NEIGES'

There was young Champ Laughlin who later became vice-president of the Delta Planters Bank. Hadley Stevenson who was drowned in Moon Lake and left his widow one hundred and fifty thousand in Government bonds. There were the Cutrere brothers, Wesley and Bates. Bates was one of my bright particular beaux! He got in a quarrel with that wild Wainwright boy. They shot it out on the floor of Moon Lake Casino. Bates was shot through the stomach. Died in the ambulance on his way to Memphis. His widow was also well provided for, came into eight or ten thousand acres, that's all. She married him on the rebound — never loved her — carried my picture on him the night he died! And there was that boy that every girl in the Delta had set her cap for! That brilliant, brilliant young Fitzhugh boy from Greene County!

TOM: What did he leave his widow?

AMANDA: He never married! Gracious, you talk as though all of my old admirers had turned up their toes to the daisies!

TOM: Isn't this the first you've mentioned that still survives?

AMANDA: That Fitzhugh boy went North and made a fortune — came to be known as the Wolf of Wall Street! He had the Midas touch, whatever he touched turned to gold! And I could have been Mrs Duncan J. Fitzhugh, mind you! But — I picked your father!

LAURA: [rising] Mother, let me clear the table.

AMANDA: No, dear, you go in front and study your typewriter chart. Or practise your shorthand a little. Stay fresh and pretty! It's almost time for our gentlemen callers to start arriving. [She flounces girlishly toward the kitchenette.] How many do you suppose we're going to entertain this afternoon?

Tom throws down the paper and jumps up with a groan.

LAURA: [alone in the dining-room] I don't believe we're going to receive any, Mother.

AMANDA [reappearing, airily] What? Not one — not one? You must be joking!

[*LAURA nervously echoes her laugh. She slips in a fugitive manner through the half-open portières and draws them in gently behind her. A shaft of very clear light is thrown on her face against the faded tapestry of the curtains.*] [MUSIC: 'THE GLASS MENAGERIE' UNDER FAINTLY.][Lightly.] Not one gentleman caller? It can't be true! There must be a flood, there must have been a tornado!

LAURA: It isn't a flood, it's not a tornado, Mother. I'm just not popular like you were in Blue Mountain. ... [Tom utters another groan. LAURA glances at him with a faint, apologetic smile. Her voice catching a little.] Mother's afraid I'm going to be an old maid.

THE SCENE DIMS OUT WITH 'GLASS MENAGERIE' Music.

4. Death of a Salesman (1949) – Part of Act II   • Arthur Miller

WILLY: [With hatred, threateningly.] The door of your life is wide open!

BIFF: Pop! I'm a dime a dozen, and so are you!

WILLY: [Turning on him now in an uncontrolled outburst.] I am not a dime a dozen! I am Willy Loman, and you are Biff Loman!

[BIFF starts for WILLY, but is blocked by HAPPY. In his fury, BIFF seems on the verge of attacking his father.]

BIFF: I am not a leader of men, Willy, and neither are you. You were never anything but a hard-working drummer who landed in the ash can like all the rest of them! I'm one dollar an hour, Willy! I tried seven states and couldn't raise it. A buck an hour! Do you gather my meaning? I'm not bringing home any prizes anymore, and you're going to stop waiting for me to bring them home!

WILLY: [Directly to BIFF.] You vengeful, spiteful mut!

[BIFF breaks from HAPPY. WILLY, in fright, starts up the stairs. BIFF grabs him.]

BIFF: [At the peak of his fury.] Pop, I'm nothing! I'm nothing, Pop. Can't you understand that? There's no spite in it anymore. I'm just what I am, that's all.

[BIFF's fury has spent itself, and he breaks down, sobbing, holding on to WILLY, who dumbly fumbles for BIFF's face.]

WILLY: [Astonished.] What're you doing? What're you doing? [To LINDA.] Why is he crying?

BIFF: [Crying, broken.] Will you let me go, for Christ's sake? Will you take that phony dream and burn it before something happens? [*Struggling to contain himself, he pulls away and moves to the stairs.*] I'll go in the morning. Put him — put him to bed. [*Exhausted, BIFF moves up the stairs to his room.*]

WILLY: [After a long pause, astonished, elevated.] Isn't that — isn't that remarkable? Biff — he likes me!

LINDA: He loves you, Willy!

HAPPY: [Deeply moved.] Always did, Pop.

WILLY: Oh, Biff! [Staring wildly.] He cried! Cried to me. [He is choking with his love, and now cries out his promise.] That boy — that boy is going to be magnificent!

[*BEN appears in the light just outside the kitchen.*]

BEN: Yes, outstanding, with twenty thousand behind him.

LINDA: [*Sensing the racing of his mind, fearfully, carefully.*] Now come to bed, Willy. It's all settled now.

WILLY: [*Finding it difficult not to rush out of the house.*] Yes, we'll sleep. Come on. Go to sleep, Hap.

BEN: And it does take a great kind of man to crack the jungle.

[*In accents of dread, BEN's idyllic music starts up.*]

HAPPY: [*His arm around LINDA.*] I'm getting married, Pop, don't forget it. I'm changing everything. I'm gonna run that department before the year is up. You'll see, Mom. [*He kisses her.*]

BEN: The jungle is dark but full of diamonds, Willy.

[*WILLY turns, moves, listening to BEN.*]

LINDA: Be good. You're both good boys, just act that way, that's all.

HAPPY: 'Night, Pop. [*He goes upstairs.*]

LINDA: [*To WILLY.*] Come, dear.

BEN: [*With greater force.*] One must go in to fetch a diamond out.

WILLY: [*To LINDA, as he moves slowly along the edge of the kitchen, toward the door.*] I just want to get settled down, Linda. Let me sit alone for a little.

LINDA: [*Almost uttering her fear.*] I want you upstairs.

WILLY: [*Taking her in his arms.*] In a few minutes, Linda. I couldn't sleep right now. Go on, you look awful tired. [*He kisses her.*]

BEN: Not like an appointment at all. A diamond is rough and hard to the touch.

WILLY: Go on now. I'll be right up.

LINDA: I think this is the only way, Willy.

WILLY: Sure, it's the best thing.

BEN: Best thing!

WILLY: The only way. Everything is gonna be — go on, kid, get to bed. You look so tired.

LINDA: Come right up.

WILLY: Two minutes.

[*LINDA goes into the living-room, then reappears in her bedroom. WILLY moves just outside the kitchen door.*]

WILLY: Loves me. [Wonderingly.] Always loved me. Isn't that a remarkable thing? Ben, he'll worship me for it!

BEN: [With promise.] It's dark there, but full of diamonds.

WILLY: Can you imagine that magnificence with twenty thousand dollars in his pocket?

LINDA: [Calling from her room.] Willy! Come up!

WILLY: [Calling into the kitchen.] Yes! Yes. Coming! It's very smart, you realize that, don't you, sweetheart? Even Ben sees it. I gotta go, baby. 'Bye!' Bye! [Going over to BEN, almost dancing.] Imagine? When the mail comes he'll be ahead of Bernard again!

BEN: A perfect proposition all around.

WILLY: Did you see how he cried to me? Oh, if I could kiss him, Ben!

BEN: Time, William, time!

WILLY: Oh, Ben, I always knew one way or another we were gonna make it, Biff and I!

BEN: [Looking at his watch.] The boat. We'll be late. [He moves slowly off into the darkness.]

WILLY: [Elegiacally, turning to the house.] Now when you kick off, boy, I want a seventy-yard boot, and get right down the field under the ball, and when you hit, hit low and hit hard, because it's important, boy. [He swings around and faces the audience.] There's all kinds of important people in the stands, and the first thing you know... [Suddenly realizing he is alone.] Ben! Ben, where do I...? [He makes a sudden movement of search.] Ben, how do I...?

LINDA: [Calling.] Willy, you coming up?

WILLY: [Uttering a gasp of fear, whirling about as if to quiet her.] Sh! [He turns around as if to find his way; sounds, faces, voices, seem to be swarming in upon him and he flicks at them, crying.] Sh! Sh! [Suddenly music, faint and high, stops him. It rises in intensity, almost to an unbearable scream. He goes up and down on his toes, and rushes off around the house.] Shhh!

LINDA: Willy?

[*There is no answer. LINDA waits. BIFF gets up off his bed. He is still in his clothes. HAPPY sits up. BIFF stands listening.*]

LINDA: [With real fear.] Willy, answer me! Willy!

[*There is the sound of a car starting and moving away at full speed.*]

LINDA: No!

BIFF: [Rushing down the stairs.] Pop!

[*As the car speeds off, the music crashes down in a frenzy of sound, which becomes the soft pulsation of a single cello string. BIFF slowly returns to his bedroom. He and HAPPY gravely don their jackets. LINDA slowly walks out of her room. The music has developed into a dead march. The leaves of day are appearing over everything. CHARLEY and BERNARD, somberly dressed, appear and knock on the kitchen door. BIFF and HAPPY slowly descend the stairs to the kitchen as CHARLEY and BERNARD enter. All stop a moment when LINDA, in clothes of mourning, bearing a little bunch of roses, comes through the draped doorway into the kitchen. She goes to CHARLEY and takes his arm. Now all move toward the audience, through the wall-line of the kitchen. At the limit of the apron, LINDA lays down the flowers, kneels, and sits back on her heels. All stare down at the grave.*]

5. The Zoo Story (1958) – the first half of the full text
• Edward Albee

Characters:

PETER: A man in his early forties, neither fat nor gaunt, neither handsome nor homely He wears tweeds, smokes a pipe, carries horn-rimmed glasses. Although he is moving into middle age, his dress and his manner would suggest a man younger.

JERRY: A man in his late thirties, not poorly dressed, but carelessly. What was once a trim and lightly muscled body has begun to go to fat; and while he is no longer handsome, it is evident that he once was. His fall from physical grace should not suggest debauchery; he has, to come closest to it, a great weariness.

THE SCENE:

It is Central Park; a Sunday afternoon in summer; the present. There are two park benches, one towards either side of the stage; they both face, the audience. Behind them : foliage, trees, sky.

[At the beginning PETER is seated on one of the benches. As the curtain rises, PETER is seated on the bench stage-right. He is reading a book. He stops reading, cleans his glasses, goes back to reading. JERRY enters.]

JERRY: I've been to the zoo. [PETER doesn't notice.] I said, I've been to the zoo. MISTER, I'VE BEEN TO THE ZOO!

PETER: Hm? ... What? ... I'm sorry, were you talking to me?

JERRY: I went to the zoo, and then I walked until I came here. Have I been walking north?

PETER: [puzzled] North? Why ... I ... I think so. Let me see.

JERRY: [pointing past the audience] Is that Fifth avenue?

PETER: Why ya; yes, it is.

JERRY: And what is that cross street there; that one, to the right?

PETER: That? Oh, that's Seventy-fourth Street.

JERRY: And the zoo is around Sixty-5fth Street; so, I've been walking north.

PETER: [anxious to get back to his reading] Yes; it would seem so.

JERRY: Good old north.

PETER: [lightly, by reflex] Ha, ha.

JERRY: [after a slight pause] But not due north.

PETER: I ... well, no, not due north; but, we ... call it north. It's northerly.

JERRY: [watches as PETER, anxious to dismiss him, prepares his pipe] Well, boy, you're not going to get lung cancer, are you?

PETER: [looks up, a little annoyed, then smiles] No, sir. Not from this.

JERRY: No, sir. What you'll probably get is cancer of the mouth, and then you'll have to wear one of those things Freud wore after they took one whole side of his jaw away, What do they call those things?

PETER: [uncomfortable] A prosthesis?

JERRY: The very thing! A prosthesis. You're an educated man, aren't you? Are you a doctor?

PETER: Oh, no; no. I read about it somewhere: Time magazine, I think. [He turns to his book.]

JERRY: Well, Time magazine isn't for blockheads.

PETER: No, I suppose not.

JERRY: [after a pause] Boy, I'm glad that's Fifth Avenue there.

PETER: [vaguely] Yes.

JERRY: I don't like the west side of the park much.

PETER: Oh? [Then, slightly wary, but interested] Why?

JERRY: [offhand] I don't know.

PETER: Oh. [He returns to his book.]

JERRY: [stands for a few seconds, looking at PETER, who finally looks up again, puzzled] Do you mind if we talk?

PETER: [obviously minding] Why ... no, no.

JERRY: Yes you do; you do.

PETER: [puts his book down, his pipe out and away, smiling] No, I really; I don't mind.

JERRY: Yes you do.

PETER: [finally decided] No; I don't mind at all, really.

JERRY: It's ... it's a nice day.

PETER: [stares unnecessarily at the sky] Yes. Yes, it is; lovely.

JERRY: I've been to the zoo.

PETER: Yes, I think you said so ... didn't you?

JERRY: you'll read about it in the papers tomorrow, if you don't see it on your TV tonight.

You have TV, haven't you?

PETER: Why yes, we have two; one for the children.

JERRY: You're married!

PETER: [with pleased emphasis] Why, certainly.

JERRY: It isn't a law, for God's sake.

PETER: No ... no, of course not.

JERRY: And you have a wife.

PETER: [bewildered by the seeming lack of communication] Yes!

JERRY: And you have children.

PETER: Yes; two.

JERRY: Boys?

PETER: No, girls ... both girls.

JERRY: But you wanted boys.

PETER: Well ... naturally, every man wants a son, but ...

JERRY: [lightly mocking] But that's the way the cookie crumbles?

PETER: [annoyed] I wasn't going to say that.

JERRY: And you're not going to have any more kids, are you?

PETER: [a bit distantly] No. No more. [Then back, and irksome] Why did you say that? How would you know about that?

JERRY: The way you cross your legs, perhaps; something in the voice. Or maybe I'm just guessing. Is it your wife?

PETER: [furious] That's none of your business! [A silence.] Do you understand? [JERRY nods. PETER is quiet now.] Well, you're right. We'll have no more children.

JERRY: [softly] That is the way the cookie crumbles.

PETER: [forgiving] Yes ... I guess so.

JERRY: Well, now; what else?

PETER: What were you saying about the zoo ... that I'd read about it, or see ...?

JERRY: I'll tell you about it, soon. Do you mind if I ask you questions?

PETER: Oh, not really.

JERRY: I'll tell you why I do it; I don't talk to many people except to say like: give me a beer, or where's the john, or what time does the feature go on, or keep your hands to yourself, buddy. You know — things like that.

PETER: I must say I don't ...

JERRY: But every once in a while I like to talk to somebody, really talk; like to get to know somebody, know all about him.

PETER: [lightly laughing, still a little uncomfortable] And am I the guinea pig for today?

JERRY: On a sun-drenched Sunday afternoon like this? Who better than a nice married man with two daughters and ... uh ... a dog? [PETER shakes his head.] No? Two dogs. [PETER shakes his head again. Hm. No dogs? [PETER shakes his head, sadly.] Oh, that's a shame. But you look like an animal man. CATS? [PETER nods his head, ruefully.] Cats! But, that can't be your idea. No, sir. Your wife and daughters? [PETER nods his head.] Is there anything else I should know?

PETER: [he has clear his throat] There are ... there are two parakeets. One ... uh ... one for each of my daughters.

JERRY: Birds.

PETER: My daughters keep them in a cage in their bedroom.

JERRY: Do they carry disease? The birds.

PETER: I don't believe so.

JERRY: That's too bad. If they did you could set them loose in the house and the cats could eat them and die, maybe. [PETER look blank for a moment, then laughs.] And what else ? What do you do to support your enormous household?

PETER: I ... uh ... I have an executive position with a ... a small publishing house. We ... uh ... we publish text books.

JERRY: That sounds nice; very nice. What do you make?

PETER: [still cheerful] Now look here!

JERRY: Oh, come on.

PETER: Well, I make around eighteen thousand a year, but: don't carry more than forty dollars at any one time ... in case you're a ... a holdup man ... ha, ha, ha.

JERRY: [ignoring the above] Where do you live? [PETER is reluctant.] Oh, look; I'm not going to rob you, and I'm not going to kidnap your parakeets, your cats, or your daughters.

PETER: [too loud] I live between Lexington and Third Avenue, on Seventy-fourth Street.

JERRY: That wasn't so hard, was it?

PETER: I didn't mean to seem ... ah ... it's that you don't really carry on a conversation; you just ask questions. And I'm ... I'm normally ... uh ... reticent. Why do you just stand there?

JERRY: I'll start walking around in a little while, and eventually I'll sit down. [Recalling.] Wait until you see the expression on his face.

PETER: What? Whose face? Look here; is this Something about the zoo?

JERRY: [distantly] The what?

PETER: The zoo; the zoo. Something about the zoo.

JERRY: The zoo?

PETER: You've mentioned it several times.

JERRY [still distant, but returning abruptly]: The zoo? Oh, yes; the zoo. I was there before I came here. I told you that. Say, what's the dividing line between upper-middle-middle-class and lower-upper-middle-class?

PETER: My dear fellow, I ...

JERRY: Don't my dear fellow me.

PETER: [unhappily] Was I patronizing? I believe I was; I'm sorry. But, you see, your question about the classes bewildered me.

JERRY: And when you're bewildered you become patronizing?

PETER: I ... I don't express myself too well, sometimes. [He attempts a joke on himself.] I'm in publishing, not writing.

JERRY: [amused, but not at the humour] So be it. The truth is: I was being patronizing.

PETER: Oh, now; you needn't say that.

[It is at this point that JERRY may begin to mow about the stage with slowly increasing determination and authority, but pacing himself, so that the long speech about the dog comes at the high point of the arc.]

JERRY: All right. Who are your favourite writers? Baudelaire and J.P. Marquand?

PETER: [wary] Well, I like a great many writers; I have a considerable ... catholicity of taste, if I may say so. Those two men are fine, each in his way. [Warming up] Baudelaire, of course ... uh ... is by far the finer of the two, but Marquand has a place ... in our ... uh ... national ...

JERRY: Skip it.

PETER: I ... sorry.

JERRY: Do you know what I did before I went to the zoo today? I walked all the way up Fifth Avenue from Washington Square; all the way.

PETER: Oh; you live in the Village! [This seems to enlighten Peter.]

JERRY: No, I don't. I took the subway down to the Village so I could walk all the way up Fifth Avenue to the zoo. It's one of those things a person has to do; sometimes a person has to go a very long distance out of his way to come back a short distance correctly.

PETER: [almost pounting] Oh, I thought you lived in the Village.

JERRY: What were you trying to do? Make sense out of things? Bring order? The old pigeonhole bit? Well, that's easy; I'll tell you. I live in a four-storey brownstone rooming-house on the upper West Side between Columbus Avenue and Central Park West. I live on the top floor; rear; west. It's a laughably small room, and one of my walls is made of beaverboard; this beaverboard separates my room from another laughably small room, so I assume that the two rooms were once one room, a small room, but not necessarily laughable. The room beyond my beaver board wall is occupied by a coloured queen who always keeps his door open; well, not always but always when he's plucking his eyebrows, which he does with Buddhist concentration. This coloured queen has rotten teeth, which is rare, and he has a Japanese kimono, which is also pretty rare; and he wears this kimono to and from the john in the hall, which is pretty frequent. I mean, he goes to the john a lot. He never bothers me, and never brings anyone up to his room. All he does is pluck his eyebrows, wear his kimono and go to the john. Now, the two front rooms on my floor are a little larger, I guess; but they're pretty small, too. There's a Puerto Rican family in one of them, a husband, a wife, and some kids; I don't know how many. These people entertain a lot. And in the other front room, there's somebody living there, but I don't know who it is. I've never seen who it is. Never. Never ever.

PETER: [embarrassed] Why ... why do you live there?

JERRY: [From a distance again] I don't know.

PETER: It doesn't sound a very nice place ... where you live.

JERRY: Well, no; it isn't an apartment in the East Seventies. But, then again, I don't have one wife, two daughters, two cats and two parakeets. What I do have, I have toilet articles, a few clothes, a hot plate that I'm not supposed to have, a can opener, one that works with a key, you know: a Knife, two forks, and two spoons, one small, one large; three plates, a cup, a saucer, a drinking glass, two picture frames, both empty, eight or nine books, a pack of pornographic playing cards, regular deck, an old Western Union typewriter that prints nothing but capital letters, and a small strong-box without a lock which has in it ... what? Rocks! Some rocks ... sea rounded rocks I picked up on the beach when I was a kid. Under which ... weighed down ... are some letters ... please letters ... please why don't you do this, and please when will you do that letters. And when letters, too. When will you write? When will you come? When? These letters are from more recent years.

PETER: [stares glumly at his shoes, then] About those two Empty picture frames ...?

JERRY: I don't see why they need any explanation at all. Isn't it clear? I don't have pictures of anyone to put in them.

PETER: Your parents ... perhaps ... a girl friend ...

JERRY: You're a very sweet man, and you're possessed of a truly enviable innocence. But good old Mom and good old Pop are dead ... you know? ... I'm broken up about it, too ... I mean really. BUT. That particular vaudeville act is playing the cloud circuit now, so I don't see how I can look at them, all neat and framed. Besides, or, rather, to be pointed about it, good old Mom walked out on good old Pop when I was ten and a half years old; she embarked on an adulterous turn of our southern states ... a journey of a year's duration ... and her most constant companion ... among others, among many others ... was a Mr Barleycorn. At least, that's what good old Pop told me after he went down ... came back ... brought her body north. We'd received the news between Christmas and New Year's, you see, that good old Mom had parted with the ghost in some dump in Alabama. And, without the ghost ... she was less welcome. I mean, what was she? A stiff ... a northern stiff. At any rate, good old Pop celebrated the New Year for an even two weeks and then slapped into the front of a somewhat moving city omnibus, which sort of cleaned things out family-wise. Well no; then there was Mom's sister, who was given neither to sin nor the consolations of the bottle. I moved in on her, and my memory of her is slight excepting I remember still that she did all things dourly: sleeping, eating, working, praying. She dropped dead on the stairs to her apartment, my apartment then, too, on the afternoon of my high school graduation. A terribly middle-European joke, if you ask me.

PETER: Oh, my; oh, my.

04 Translated Dramas To Read

01. 사소한 것들(Trifles)
02. 인형의 집(A Doll's House)
03. 유리동물원(The Glass Menagerie)
04. 세일즈맨의 죽음(Death of a Salesman)
05. 동물원 이야기(The Zoo Story)

Interpretation of the original — 원문해석

1. 사소한 것들(Trifles) – 대본 전문

• 수전 글래스펠(Susan Glaspell)

등장인물

지방검사	조지 헨더슨
보안관	보안관 헨리 피터즈
피터즈 부인	보안관 헨리 피터즈의 부인
헤일	이웃 농부
헤일 부인	루이스 헤일의 부인
존 라이트	살해된 남자
라이트 부인	살해된 남자의 부인

장 면: 현재는 내버려진 존 라이트의 침침하고 정리되지 않은 채 내버려둔 부엌. 설거지가 안 된 채 그대로 놓여진 싱크대 안의 냄비들, 빵 상자 밖으로 나동그라져 있는 빵 덩어리, 그리고 식탁 위의 행주는 집안일을 채 마치지 못한 듯한 인상을 준다. 무대 뒤편에서 외부로 통하는 문이 열리고 보안관이 들어오며 지방 검사와 헤일이 그의 뒤를 따른다. 보안관과 헤일은 중년의 남성들이며 지방 변호사는 청년이다. 이들 모두는 무리를 지어 스토브 주위로 모여든다. 여기에 두 명의 여자가 차례로 들어온다. 보안관의 부인이 먼저 등장하는데 그녀는 호리호리하고 깐깐해 보이는 여인으로 신경과민성의 야윈 얼굴이다. 다음에 등장하는 헤일 부인은 평소에는 편안한 모습의 보다 넉넉한 몸집을 하고 있지만 지금은 불안한 눈초리로 무언가 두려워하는 인상이다. 이 여인들은 천천히 들어와 문 옆에 가까이 모여 선다.

지방검사 [손을 비비며] 따뜻해서 좋군요. 불 가까이로 오시죠, 부인들.

피터즈 부인 [한 발짝 다가선 후] 전… 안 추워요.

보안관 [외투의 단추를 끄르면서 마치 공무집행을 시작할 것을 알리기라도 하듯 스토브에서 멀어진다.] 자, 헤일 씨. 물건들에 손을 대기 전에 어제 아침 여기에 오셨을 때 목격했던 걸 헨더슨 검사께 설명해 드려야 할 것 같습니다.

지방검사 자 우선 말입니다, 무언가 달라진 거라도 있습니까? 어제 이곳을 떠나셨을 때 그대로인가요?

보안관 [주위를 훑어보며] 그대로예요. 어젯밤 기온이 영하로 떨어졌을 때 프랭크를 시켜 오늘 아침 불을 좀 피워놓게 하는 게 나을 거라는 생각이 들었어요. 이런 큰일에 폐렴에 걸려서는 안 되잖아요, 하지만 그에게 난로 외에는 아무 것도 건드리지 말라고 일렀지요. 프랭크가 어떤 사람이라는 건 검사님도 잘 아시겠지요.

지방검사 어제 누군가 여기 남아 있어야 했습니다.

보안관 아… 어제라. 전 어제 어떤 미친놈 때문에 프랭크를 모리스 센터로 보내야 했습니다. 아실지는 모르겠지만, 전 어제 숨 돌릴 틈도 없었어요. 오늘쯤 검사님께서 오실 줄 알고 있었거든요. 제가 조사해 본 바로는…

지방검사 저, 헤일 씨. 어제 아침 여기에 오셨을 때 어떤 일이 있었는지 정확히 말씀해 주세요.

헤일	해리와 난 감자를 싣고 읍내로 나가고 있었다우. 집에서 길을 따라 오다가 여기에 도착했는데 그때 난 해리에게 이렇게 말했지, "전화선을 같이 쓰는 거에 대해 존 라이트 씨가 어떻게 생각하는 지 알아봐야겠어." 라고 말이야. 전에도 존 라이트 씨에게 얘기 한 적이 있었는데 그 쪽에선 거절을 했었거든. 사람들이 말이 많다고 하면서 자기는 조용히 살고 싶다나? 그 사람 말 없기로 유명한 건 누구다 다 알지. 하지만 내가 직접 그 집에 찾아가서 안사람 있는 데서 말하면 뭔가 달라질 거라 생각했지. 물론 안사람이 원한다고 해도 존이 싫어한다면 어쩔 수 없는 거라고 해리한테도 말했지만서도…
지방검사	그건 나중에 얘기하기로 하죠, 헤일 씨. 물론 저도 그 이야길 듣고는 싶습니다만, 지금은 헤일 씨께서 이 집에 오셨을 때 어떤 일이 있었는지 만 말씀해 주세요.
헤일	들을 것도 본 것도 없다우. 문을 두드려도 집안에서는 아무런 인기척도 없더구만. 그 때가 여덟 시가 지났을 때라 틀림없이 다들 일어났을 터였는데 말이야. 그래서 내 다시 문을 두드렸지. 그때 안에서 "들어오세요" 하는 소리가 들린 것 같았어. 확실하지는 않지만. 지금도 내가 정말 그 말을 들은 건지 확실하지는 않지만, 아무튼 난 문을 열어보았다우… 이 문이야. [여전히 서 있는 두 여인 옆의 문을 가리키며] 그리고 저 흔들의자에 [흔들의자를 가리키며] 라이트 부인이 앉아 있었구. [그들은 모두 흔들의자를 바라본다.]
지방검사	그녀는… 뭘 하고 있었나요?
헤일	의자를 앞뒤로 흔들고 있었어. 손에는 앞치마가 들려 있었는데… 뭐라 그럴까… 주름을 잡고 있었던 거 같더군.
지방검사	그러면 안색이… 어떻던가요?
헤일	글쎄, 이상해 보였어.
지방검사	이상하다니… 무슨 뜻이지요?
헤일	그러니까, 무슨 일을 해야 할지 모르는 사람 같더군. 뭐라 그럴까, 지쳐 보인다고 할까… 뭐 그런 거 말이야.
지방검사	헤일 씨를 보고 어떻게 느끼는 거 같던가요?
헤일	글쎄, 이렇다 저렇다 별로 신경 쓰는 것 같지는 않았어. 별 관심이 없더라구. 내가 "안녕하세요, 라이트 부인, 추운 날씨네요, 안 그래요?" 하고 말하니까 "그래요?" 하더군. 그러면서 뭐라 그럴까… 계속 앞치마 주름을 잡고 있었어. 사실, 좀 놀라긴 했지. 난로가로 오라든지 아니면 좀 앉아 있으라는지 일언반구 말이 없더라니까. 그저 저기에 앉아서 시선 한 번 주지 않더란 말이야. 그래서 다시 말을 걸었지. "존을 좀 보러 왔는데요" 라고 말이야. 그러니까… 웃더군. 웃었다고 하는 게 맞을 거야. 난 밖에 있는 해리 일행이 생각났어. 그래서 좀 더 분명하게 "존을 좀 볼 수 없을까요?" 라고 말했더니만 뭐라 그럴까 흥미 없다는 듯이 "안 돼요" 하더란 말이야. 그래서 다시 "존 집에 없어요?" 라고 물었더니, "아뇨, 있어요." 하잖아? "그럼 왜 볼 수 없다는 거지요?" 라고 화딱지가 나는 걸 참으며 물었더니 글쎄 "죽었으니까요" 이러는 거야. "죽었다구요?" 라고 물었더니, 부인은 그저 고개만 끄덕일 뿐 별로 동요하는 기색 하나 없이 의자만 앞뒤로 흔들고 있지 뭐야. 무슨 말을 꺼낼지 몰라서 그냥 "그럼… 지금 어디 있는데요?" 라고 물었지. 그러니까 이층을 가리키기만 하더라구… 이렇게. [위층의 방을 가리킨다.] 난 그리로 가볼 양으로 일어섰지. 난 어쩔 줄 몰라 망설이다가… 물었어, "저, 어떻게 죽었나요?" 그랬더니 "목매달아 죽었어요" 라고 하면서 연신 앞치마 줄만 잡고 있는 거야. 난 당장 밖으로 나와 해리를 불렀어. 뭔가… 도움이 필요할 거라

지방검사	는 생각이 들었거든. 이층에 올라가 보았더니 존이… 누워있더라구.
지방검사	그 부분은 이층에 올라가서 하나하나 집어가며 자세히 말씀해 주세요. 지금은 그 나머지 이야기를 들어보도록 하지요.
헤일	글쎄요, 우선 그 줄을 끌어야겠다는 생각이 들었어. 그건… [이야기를 멈춘다. 그의 얼굴이 일그러진다.] … 하지만 존에게 다가가 보더니 이렇게 말하는 거야, "이런, 죽었어. 건드리지 않는 게 좋은 거 같아." 그래 우린 아래층으로 내려왔지. 라이트 부인은 여전히 앉아서 줄을 잡고 있더구만. "누구에게라도 알렸나요?" 라고 물었어. 그러니까 "아니요" 라며 관심 없다는 듯이 대답하더만. 해리가 "누가 이런 짓을 했나요, 라이트 부인?" 이라고 뭐라 그럴까, 다소 사무적으로 물었더니, 부인은 앞치마 주름 잡는 걸 멈추는 거야. 그러더니 이렇게 말했어. "저도 몰라요." "모른다구요?" 라고 해리가 다시 물으니깐 "몰라요" 라고 대답하는 거야. 해리가 "존하고 함께 주무시지 않았나요?" 라고 물었더니 "그래요, 하지만 전 안쪽에서 잤어요" 라고 하더구만. "누군가 줄로 존의 목을 졸라 죽였는데도 부인은 깨지 않았다구요?" 라는 해리의 질문에 막 바로 "전 깨지 않았다니까요" 라고 말하는 거야. 어떻게 그런 일이 있을 수 있는 지 도무지 이해할 수 없다는 표정을 짓고 있자 얼마 있다가 부인이 입을 열었어, "전 깊이 잠들어요." 해리는 좀 더 물어보려 했지만 난 우선 검시관이나 보안관에게 먼저 알리는 게 낫겠다고 일렀지. 그래서 해리가 전화가 있는 리버스로 서둘러 달려간 거라우.
지방검사	그럼 검시관에게 갔다는 걸 알고 나서 라이트 부인은 어떻게 행동하시던가요?
헤일	부인은 의자에서 일어나 [구석에 있는 작은 의자를 가리키며] 이쪽으로 건너왔어. 그러더니 두 손을 가지런히 모으고 앉아 바닥만 내려다보는 거야. 뭔가 말을 좀 꺼내야 할 것 같아서 난 부인에게 존이 전화를 놓을 생각이 있는가 알아보러 왔다고 말했지. 그랬더니 막 웃기 시작하는 거야. 그러더니 갑자기 웃음을 멈추고는 날 쳐다보지 않겠어?… 겁에 질린 표정이었어. [노트를 펼쳐놓고 있던 지방 변호사는 무엇인가를 적는다] 모르겠소이다. 그게 무서워했던 표정인지. 그렇게 말하긴 좀 그렇네. 하여간 조금 있으니까 해리가 돌아왔고 로이드 의사 선생하고 그 쪽하고 피터즈 씨가 도착했던 거라오. 이 정도가 내가 아는 전부요.
지방검사	[주위를 살펴보며] 일단 이층에 올라가봐야겠어요. 그리고 나서 헛간에 나가 그 쪽 주변을 좀 살펴봐야 할 것 같군요. [보안관에게] 여기엔 특별히 단서가 될 만한 어떤 동기가 될 만한 건 없는 게 확실합니까?
보안관	여긴 세간 살이 뿐인데요.

부엌 주위를 한 번 더 둘러본 후 지방 변호사는 찬장 문을 열어본다. 그는 의자 위에 올라가 찬장 선반을 들여다본다. 그는 끈적해진 손을 빼낸다.

지방검사	진창이군요. [두 여인 가까이 다가온다.]
피터즈 부인	[다른 여인에게] 아, 과일 통조림이네. 몽땅 얼어버렸군요. [변호사에게] 라이트 부인은 이 과일들이 얼어버릴까 걱정을 했어요. 난롯불이 꺼지면 통조림 병이 깨질 거라고 하던데.
보안관	세상에, 여편네들은 못 말린다니까! 살인이 났는데 통조림이나 걱정하고 있으니.
지방검사	아마 우리 일이 끝나기 전에 통조림 보관하는 거 보다 더 심각한 일이 그녀에게 닥칠 지도 모릅니다.
헤일	하긴 뭐, 여자들이란 원래가 사소한 일에 연연하기 마련이지요. [두 여인은 서로에게 좀더 가까

	이 다가간다.]
지방검사	[젊은 정치인다운 품위를 보이며] 하지만 아무리 여인네들이 사소한 것에 목숨을 던진다 해도, 여자 없이 우리가 어떻게 살아가겠어요? [두 여인은 걱정을 풀지 않는다. 그는 싱크대로 다가가 들통에서 물그릇을 떠 싱크대에 붓고 손을 씻는다. 두루마리 타월을 집어 좀 더 깨끗한 면으로 돌려 손을 닦기 시작한다.] 수건 한번 더럽군! [싱크대 아래에 있는 냄비들을 발로 툭툭 차 본다.] 집안 살림이 엉망입니다. 안 그래요, 부인들?
헤일 부인	[딱딱한 말투로] 농가에는 할 일이 많답니다.
지방검사	물론이지요. [그녀에게 살짝 고개를 숙이면서] 하지만 말입니다, 이곳 딕슨 지방의 농가에서 이런 두루마리 타월을 쓰는 집은 본 적이 없거든요. [그는 두루마리 타월을 펼쳐 전체 면을 보여준다.]
헤일 부인	두루마리 타월은 금세 더러워지지요. 남정네들 손이야 항상 더러우니까요.
지방검사	같은 여자라고 편을 드시는군요. 아, 부인과 라이트 부인은 이웃이었으니까 서로 친구 사이겠군요.
헤일 부인	[머리를 좌우로 흔든다.] 지난 몇 년 동안은 서로 본 적이 없어요. 이 집에 발을 들여놓은 지도 오래 됐구요… 일 년도 넘었어요.
지방검사	그건 왜지요? 라이트 부인을 좋아하지 않았나요?
헤일 부인	그건 아니었어요. 농부의 아낙네들이란 손을 놀릴 틈이 없답니다, 헨더슨 씨. 게다가…
지방검사	게다가… 뭐죠?
헤일 부인	[주위를 둘러보며] 이 집은 즐거워 보인 적이 없었어요.
지방검사	네. 그렇긴 하군요. 집안을 꾸리는 솜씨는 없나 봅니다.
헤일 부인	글쎄요. 라이트 씨의 솜씨는 얼마나 있었는지 모르겠네요.
지방검사	부부 사이가 좋지 않았다는 말씀인가요?
헤일 부인	아뇨, 그런 뜻은 아니에요. 하지만 존 라이트 씨가 집안에 있다고 해서 더 즐거워질 집이라고는 생각지 않아요.
지방검사	그 얘기는 나중에 더 듣도록 하지요. 지금은 이층의 상황이 어떤지를 좀 알아봐야겠습니다. [그는 위층 문으로 향하는 세 단짜리 계단이 있는 왼편으로 다가간다.]
보안관	제 아내가 물건에 손대는 건 괜찮겠지요. 아시다시피, 라이트 부인의 옷가지를 챙겨주러 왔거든요. 어제 너무 서둘러 가느라고 아무 것도 못 가져갔답니다.
지방검사	네, 그렇게 하세요. 하지만 피터즈 부인께서 가져가는 물건들은 꼭 보여주셔야겠습니다. 혹시 우리에게 단서가 될 만한 것이 있는지 보아야 하니까요.
피터즈 부인	네, 헨더슨 검사님. [두 여인은 계단으로 오르는 남자들의 발소리를 듣고 나서는 부엌을 둘러본다]
헤일 부인	난 남정네들이 부엌에 들어와 기웃거리며 불평이나 늘어놓는 건 질색이에요. [그녀는 검사가 발로 차서 흐트러진 싱크대 아래의 냄비들을 정돈한다.]
피터즈 부인	그래도 이건 저 사람들의 임무잖아요.
헤일 부인	임무라면야 어쩔 수 없겠지요. 하지만 난롯불을 지피러 왔다던 그 보안관 보좌라던가 하는 그 사람이 이걸 이 모양으로 해 놓았을 거예요. [두루마리 타월을 펼친다.] 좀 더 미리 알았더라

피터즈 부인	면 좋았을 뻔했어요. 급하게 불려가야 하는 바람에 집안을 제대로 치우지 못한 걸 가지고 살림살이가 어쩌구 하는 건 치사해요.
피터즈 부인	[방 왼편 구석의 작은 탁자로 가서 냄비를 덮어둔 수건 한쪽 끝을 쳐든다.] 상 차릴 준비를 했었군요. [여전히 서있다.]
헤일 부인	[방 반대편 하단 선반에 놓여 진 빵 상자 밖으로 나와 있는 빵 덩어리에 시선을 고정한다. 빵 쪽으로 천천히 다가간다.] 이걸 거기에 놓을 참이었나 봐요. [빵을 집더니 이내 떨어뜨린다. 친숙한 일상의 이야기로 돌아오면서] 아까 그 과일 통조림은 정말 아까워요. 모두 상했을까 모르겠네. [의자 위로 올라서 찬장을 들여다본다.] 괜찮은 것도 몇 개 있는 거 같아요. 그래... 피터즈 부인... 이걸 보세요. [창 쪽으로 들어 보인다.] 앵두에요. [다시 들여다본다.] 멀쩡한 건 이거 하나 뿐인 거 같아요. [손에 병을 들고 내려온다. 싱크대로 가서 병 표면을 닦아낸다.] 더운 날씨에 이걸 하느라 얼마나 고생했을 텐데. 정말 마음이 상할 거예요. 작년 여름 오후에 앵두 잼을 만들던 때가 생각나네요. [그녀는 방 중앙에 있는 커다란 탁자 위에 그 병을 놓는다. 한숨을 내쉬며 흔들의자에 앉으려 한다. 앉기 전에 이 의자가 어떤 의자인지를 깨닫는다. 천천히 들여다보며 이 의자에서 물러선다. 그녀가 건드렸던 흔들의자가 앞뒤로 흔들거린다.]
피터즈 부인	자, 이제 앞 방 옷장에서 가져갈 물건들을 챙겨와야겠어요. [그녀는 오른편에 있는 문으로 다가간다. 그러나 그 방을 들여다보고 나선 뒷걸음친다.] 같이 가시죠, 헤일 부인? 이것들을 꺼내야겠어요. 좀 도와주세요.

그들은 그 방으로 들어간다. 피터즈 부인은 드레스와 치마를 들고 헤일 부인은 구두 한 켤레를 들고 등장한다.

피터즈 부인	아휴, 저 방은 정말 춥네요. [그녀는 커다란 탁자 위에 옷가지들을 올려놓고는 난로 쪽으로 급히 다가간다.]
헤일 부인	[치마를 자세히 살펴보며] 라이트 부인은 정말 인색했지요. 제 생각엔 그녀가 그토록 교제를 피해왔던 이유가 아마도 이것 때문이지 않았나 싶어요. 그녀는 부녀회에도 속하지 않았잖아요. 자신이 할 일이 없다고 느꼈을 거예요. 생각해 봐요, 자신이 초라해지면 즐길 기분이 나겠어요? 미니 포스터라는 처녀 때 이름으로 성가대에서 노래했던 때 말이에요, 예쁜 옷을 입고 다니면서 얼마나 활달했었어요? 그런데 아... 그게 벌써 삼십년 전 이야기군요. 이게 가져갈 전부인가요?
피터즈 부인	앞치마를 갖다 달라고 했어요. 그런 걸 갖다 달라니 이상도 하지요. 감옥에서 먼지 묻힐 일도 없을 텐데. 도무지 알다가도 모르겠단 말이에요. 하지만 뭐 평소처럼 자연스런 기분을 내기 위해서 그럴 수도 있겠지요. 찬장 꼭대기 서랍에 있다고 했는데. 아, 여기 있네요. 그리고 문 뒤에 항상 걸려 있는 작은 숄도 갖다 달라고 했어요. [계단 문을 열고 들여다본다.] 네, 여기 있어요. [위층으로 향하는 문을 재빨리 닫는다.]
헤일 부인	[갑자기 그녀에게 다가가며] 피터즈 부인?
피터즈 부인	왜요, 헤일 부인?
헤일 부인	라이트 부인 소행일까요?
피터즈 부인	[놀란 목소리로] 어머, 저도 몰라요.
헤일 부인	글쎄 전 그녀가 했다고는 생각지 않아요. 앞치마와 작은 숄을 갖다 달라고 했다... 그리고 통조림 걱정이나 하는 여자가 말이에요.
피터즈 부인	[뭔가 말하려고 하나 위층에서 발소리가 나자 위를 올려다본다. 목소리를 낮추어] 우리 양반

	말로는 라이트 부인에게 불리할 거 같대요. 헨더슨 검사 말하는 것 좀 보세요, 얼마나 비꼬는 투지. 잠에서 깨지 않았다는 점을 내세울 거라구요, 그 양반.
헤일 부인	그거야, 존 라이트 씨도 살인범이 자기 목을 조르는 데도 깨지 않았는걸요.
피터즈 부인	그래요, 참 이상해요. 정말 교묘하게 해치웠던 게 분명해요. 사람들이 그러는데, 그렇게 감쪽같이 해치우는 방법치곤 아주 희한한 방법이라던데요.
헤일 부인	우리 집 양반도 똑같은 말을 했어요. 이 집에는 총도 한 자루 있었대요. 정말 이해할 수 없는 점이라는 거예요.
피터즈 부인	헨더슨 검사 말로는 이 사건에서 찾아내야 할 것은 동기라는군요. 분노를 유발하거나 혹은 돌발적인 감정 같은 걸 보여주는 그런 거 말이에요.
헤일 부인	[탁자 옆에 서 있다가] 글쎄요, 여기엔 화가 났다거나 하는 흔적은 볼 수 없는걸요. [그녀는 절반은 치워졌고 절반은 너저분한 탁자 위에 놓여 진 행주에 손을 가져간다.] 이쪽은 깨끗이 닦여 있어요. [마저 닦으려는 모양새를 취하려는 순간 시선을 돌려 상자 바깥에 나와 있는 빵 덩어리를 쳐다본다. 행주를 놓는다. 일상적인 이야기를 하려는 듯한 목소리로] 위층에서는 어떻게들 하고 있는지 궁금하군요. 좀 말끔하게 치워놓았으면 좋을 텐데요. 아시겠지만, 저 사람들 하는 짓이 참으로 맹랑해요. 집 주인은 읍내 감옥에 가둬놓고 여기에 찾아와서는 죄목을 찾으려고 주인도 없는 집을 이렇게 뒤지다니!
피터즈 부인	하지만 헤일 부인, 법은 법이니까요.
헤일 부인	그 말도 맞는 말이네요. [코트의 단추를 끄르며] 옷을 좀 벗지 그래요, 피터즈 부인. 그러면 밖에 나갈 때 덜 추울 거예요. [피터즈 부인 목도리를 풀어서 걸어두려고 방 뒤쪽으로 가더니 제자리에 서서 작은 모퉁이용 탁자의 하단 부를 바라본다.]
피터즈 부인	라이트 부인은 누비이불을 꿰매고 있었던 모양이에요. [그녀가 커다란 바느질 바구니를 집어 들자 그들은 밝은 빛깔의 헝겊 조각들을 들여다본다.]
헤일 부인	이건 통나무집 패턴이에요. 예쁘지 않아요? 조각이불을 누비려고 한 건지 아니면 그냥 아무 생각 없이 꿰매고 있었던 건지 모르겠군요. [계단을 내려오는 발소리가 들린다. 보안관이 들어오고 뒤이어 헤일과 지방 검사가 따라온다.]
보안관	저 부인들께선 라이트 부인이 조각이불을 누비려고 한 건지 아니면 그냥 꿰매고 있었던 건지 그게 궁금하신 모양이군요. [남자들이 소리 내어 웃자 두 여인은 얼굴이 빨개진다.]
지방검사	[난로 위에 손을 비비며] 프랭크가 지핀 불이 위층까지는 효과가 없더군요. 그렇지요? 자, 이제 헛간으로 가서 수습을 좀 해 봅시다. [남자들 밖으로 나간다.]
헤일 부인	[분개하며] 이상할 게 어디 있다고 그러는지 모르겠어요. 남정네들이 증거를 찾는답시고 있는 동안 우린 이렇게 자질구레한 일로 시간을 허비하고 있는 꼴이라니 말이에요. [그녀는 큰 탁자 옆에 앉아 결심한 듯 누비조각 헝겊 한 쪽을 만져본다.] 뭐가 그리도 우스운지 원...
피터즈 부인	[사과하는 투로] 물론 심중에 뭔가 엄청나게 중요한 것을 생각하고 있겠지요. [의자를 끌어와 헤일 부인이 앉아있는 탁자에 앉는다]
헤일 부인	[다른 헝겊 조각을 살펴보면서] 피터즈 부인, 이것 좀 보세요. 여기, 라이트 부인이 꿰매고 있던 부분이에요. 바느질 솜씨 좀 보세요! 다른 부분은 전부 촘촘하고 고르게 짜여 졌어요. 그런데 여길 좀 봐요! 여기 붕 떴어요! 세상에, 마치 딴 생각을 하고 있었던 거 같아요! [이 말이 끝나자

그들은 서로를 바라보더니, 문 쪽을 돌아보기 시작한다. 잠시 후에 헤일 부인이 매듭을 당겨 바느질 땀을 뜯어낸다.]

피터즈 부인 뭐 하는 거예요 지금, 헤일 부인?

헤일 부인 [부드럽게] 그냥… 이상 한 곳 한 두 바늘 푸는 것 뿐예요. [바늘에 실을 끼우며] 서툰 바느질을 보면 마음이 편치 않거든요.

피터즈 부인 [안절부절 하여] 괜히 건드렸다가 무슨 봉변을 당하려구요.

헤일 부인 이쪽 끝만 마무리 지을 건데요 뭐. [갑자기 행동을 멈추고 자세히 들여다보며] 피터즈 부인?

피터즈 부인 왜요, 헤일 부인?

헤일 부인 라이트 부인은 왜 그토록 신경이 예민했을까요?

피터즈 부인 글쎄. 잘 모르겠어요. 왜 그렇게 신경이 예민했는지는 모르지만, 저도 피곤하면 종종 괴상망측하게 바느질을 하거든요. [헤일 부인 무언가 말을 하려다가 피터즈 부인을 바라보고는 이내 계속 바느질을 하기 시작한다.] 아무래도 이것들을 도로 싸둬야겠어요. 저이들 일이 생각보다 빨리 끝날 지도 모르니까요. [앞치마와 다른 물건들을 한데 모은다.] 어디 종이하고 끈이 없을까요?

헤일 부인 찬장에 있을지 모르겠네요.

피터즈 부인 [찬장을 들여다보며] 세상에, 이 안에 새장이 있어요. [새장을 쳐든다.] 라이트 부인이 새를 길렀던가요, 헤일 부인?

헤일 부인 글쎄요. 그건 잘 모르겠어요. 여기 와본 지가 꽤 오래 됐거든요. 작년에 카나리아를 싼값에 팔러 돌아다니던 장사가 하나 있긴 했었는데, 그때 샀는지 어땠는지는 모르겠네요. 아마 그때 샀겠지요 뭐. 부인도 노래 하나는 정말 예쁘게 불렀었지요.

피터즈 부인 [주위를 훑어보며] 여기에 새가 있었다니 묘하네요. 분명 새를 길렀던 거예요, 그렇지 않고서야 새장이 여기 있을 턱이 없지 않아요? 그런데 새는 어떻게 되었을까.

헤일 부인 고양이가 채갔겠지요 뭐.

피터즈 부인 천만예요, 라이트 부인에겐 고양이가 없었어요. 부인은 고양이를 무서워했어요. 거 있잖아요, 고양이만 보면 벌벌 떠는 사람들 말이에요. 일전에 우리 집 고양이가 그녀의 방에 들어간 적이 있었는데 글쎄 버럭 화를 내더니 저보고 어서 가져가라고 성화였다니까요.

헤일 부인 내 동생 베시도 그랬지요. 참으로 이상하지요?

피터즈 부인 [새장을 훑어보며] 어머, 이 새장 문 좀 보세요. 망가졌어요. 경첩 한쪽이 떨어져나갔어요.

헤일 부인 [그녀 역시 새장을 바라본다.] 누군가 함부로 다루었던 거 같아요.

피터즈 부인 정말, 그렇군요. [그녀는 새장을 들고 나와 탁자 위에 놓는다.]

헤일 부인 어서 찾고 있는 증거라도 찾았으면 하네요. 빨리 이곳을 나가고 싶어요.

피터즈 부인 헤일 부인이 같이 와 주셔서 얼마나 다행인지 몰라요. 여기에 혼자 있었더라면 정말 외로웠을 거예요.

헤일 부인 정말 그랬겠어요. [바느질감을 내려놓으며] 헌데 제가 아쉬워했던 점을 말씀드리고 싶네요, 피터즈 부인. 전 라이트 부인이 이곳에 있을 때 가끔씩 둘러보고 싶어 했답니다… [방안을 둘러보며]… 와서 좀 들여다보았더라면 좋았을 것을.

피터즈 부인 하지만 집안 일이 오죽 바쁘셨겠어요, 헤일 부인… 집안일이니 아이들 뒤치다꺼리니…

헤일 부인	그래도 와볼 수도 있었어요. 이 집에 원체 음울해서 일부러 멀리 한 거지요. 그래서 그러지 못했던 것이 더욱 아쉬워요. 난… 난 이 곳을 결코 좋아하지 않았어요. 아마 골짜기 깊숙이 파묻혀 있었기 때문이었겠지요. 여기서는 거리도 보이지 않으니까요. 딱 집어서 말하기는 힘들지만, 아무튼 이곳은 우울한 곳이에요. 언제나 그랬어요. 가끔은 와봤어야 하는 건데. 이제야 알 것 같아요… [머리를 흔든다.]
피터즈 부인	아유, 그렇게 자신을 책망할 필요 없어요, 헤일 부인. 무슨 일이 터져야 깨닫는 법이잖우.
헤일 부인	아이들이 없으면 일은 줄지요. 그 대신 집은 쓸쓸해진답니다. 남편은 하루 종일 일하러 나가고 집에 돌아오면 아내와 이야기도 나누지 않았지요. 존 라이트 씨를 아셨던가요, 피터즈 부인?
피터즈 부인	몰랐어요. 한번 읍내에서 본 적은 있지만. 사람들이 그러는데 좋은 분이라고 하더만요.
헤일 부인	그래요. 좋은 사람이지요. 술도 안마시고 약속도 잘 지키는 사람이었어요. 빚도 꼬박꼬박 갚곤 했지요. 하지만 냉정한 사람이었답니다, 피터즈 부인. 그 사람과 하루만 지내보면 알지요… [치를 떤다.] 마치 뼈 속으로 바람이 으슬으슬 스미는 느낌이랄까. [잠시 멈춘다. 그녀의 눈이 새장에 멈춘다.] 아마 라이트 부인은 새를 기르고 싶었던 게 틀림없어요. 하지만 그 새는 어찌 되었을까요?
피터즈 부인	모르겠어요, 병들어 죽었을 거라는 것 외에는. [그녀는 부서진 새장 문을 여닫아본다. 두 여인은 이것을 바라본다.]
헤일 부인	피터즈 부인은 이 고장 출신이 아니신가 봐요? [피터즈, 부인은 머리를 좌우로 젓는다.] 그럼… 미니 포스터를 모르겠네요?
피터즈 부인	어제 남정네들이 데리고 왔을 때 처음으로 뵌 셈이지요.
헤일 부인	생각해보면… 그녀는… 마치 한 마리 새와 같았어요… 정말 예쁘고 귀여운… 하지만 겁 많고… 재잘대는 새 말이에요. 그런 그녀가 어떻게… 그렇게… 변했을까요. [침묵. 잠시 행복한 생각에 빠져 있는 듯 하더니 갑자기 일상으로 돌아온다.] 그런데 피터즈 부인, 이 누비조각도 함께 갖다 주지 그러세요? 그러면 라이트 부인도 여기다 마음을 붙일 수 있을 것 같은데.
피터즈 부인	세상에, 그거 정말 좋은 생각이에요, 헤일 부인. 그렇게 해도 누구 하나 반대할 사람은 없겠지요? 그럼, 어떤 걸 가져갈까요? 부인이 쓰던 헝겊 조각이 좀 있나 모르겠네요. [그들은 바느질 바구니를 바라본다.]
헤일 부인	여기 빨간 헝겊 조각이 있어요. 이 안에 반짇고리가 들어 있을 거 같아요. [화려하고 예쁜 상자를 꺼낸다.] 정말 예쁜 상자군요. 선물을 해도 좋을 듯 한 상자예요. 라이트 부인의 가위도 들어 있을 지 몰라요. [상자를 연다. 갑자기 손으로 코를 막는다.] 아휴… [피터즈 부인 허리를 구부려 가까이 다가가더니 고개를 돌린다.] 여기 무언가가 비단 헝겊에 싸여져 있어요.
피터즈 부인	세상에, 가위가 아녜요.
헤일 부인	[비단 헝겊을 걷어내며] 오, 피터즈 부인… 이건… [피터즈 부인 더욱 가까이 다가가 바라본다.]
피터즈 부인	새예요.
헤일 부인	[놀라 일어서며] 이럴 수가, 피터즈 부인… 이걸 좀 봐요! 모가지예요! 새 모가지라구요! 완전히… 완전히 뒤틀렸어요!
피터즈 부인	누군가… 목을… 부러뜨렸군요.

그들의 시선이 마주친다. 무언가 이해가 간다는 공포심에 휩싸인 표정이다. 바깥에서 발자국 소리가 들려온다.

헤일 부인은 누비 조각들 아래로 상자를 떠밀어 놓고는 의자에 주저앉는다. 보안관과 지방 검사가 들어온다. 피터즈 부인이 일어선다.

지방검사 [무언가 심각한 것을 생각하고 있다가 가벼운 농담으로 기분을 전환하는 듯이] 자, 부인들, 라이트 부인께서 누비려고 했는지 꿰매려고 했는지 결정들은 보셨는지요?

피터즈 부인 우리 생각에는… 꿰매려고 했던 것… 같군요.

지방검사 아, 거 참 흥미롭군요. [새장을 바라보며] 새는 날아갔나요?

헤일 부인 [상자 위에 헝겊 조각을 몇 장 더 덮으며] 고양이…가 채간 모양이에요.

지방검사 [생각에 열중하여] 거기에 고양이가 있다구요? [헤일 부인은 은밀한 시선을 재빨리 피터즈 부인에게 보낸다.]

피터즈 부인 아뇨, 지금은 없어요. 아시다시피, 고양이들은 영물이잖아요. 금새 나가버리지요.

지방검사 [보안관 피터즈와 중단되었던 대화를 계속 이어가며] 바깥에서 침입한 흔적은 볼 수 없습니다. 밧줄도 이집 거구요. 다시 이층에 올라가서 하나씩 차근차근 맞추어 봅시다. [그들은 이 층으로 올라간다.] 아마도 누군가 이 집 사람들의 소행일…

피터즈 부인 앉는다. 두 여인은 서로 바라보지 않은 채 앉아있으나 마치 무언가를 응시하는 동시에 이를 숨기고 있는 듯하다. 그들은 이제 말하는 것을 두려워하면서도 말하지 않고는 안 되는 것처럼 이야기한다.

헤일 부인 라이트 부인은 새를 좋아했어요. 부인은 저 죽은 새를 저 예쁜 상자에 묻으려 했던 거예요.

피터즈 부인 [속삭이듯] 제가 어렸을 때… 제겐 고양이가 한 마리 있었어요… 어느 남자애가 손도끼를 가져 왔지요. 그리고는 내 보는 앞에서… 내가 채 다가가 막기도 전에… [잠시 두 손에 얼굴을 파묻는다.] 날 말리지만 않았어도 난… [말하려다 멈추고 발자국 소리가 들리는 위층을 올려다보고는 약하게 더듬거린다.]… 그 자식을 가만두지 않았을 거예요.

헤일 부인 [주위를 찬찬히 바라보면서] 주위에 애가 없다는 것이 어떤 건지 모르겠어요. [잠시 멈춘다.] 그래요, 라이트 씨는 새를 좋아할 리가 없어요… 그 새가 노래하는 것을 좋아하지 않았던 거예요. 아내는 노래를 좋아했겠지요. 그는 그녀의 노래까지 죽여 버렸던 거예요.

피터스 부인 [불안하게 움직이면서] 누가 그 새를 죽였는지는 모르잖아요.

헤일 부인 난 존 라이트를 잘 알아요.

피터즈 부인 그날 밤 정말 끔찍한 일이 이 집에서 일어났던 거예요, 헤일 부인. 자고 있는 남자의 목에 밧줄을 감아 숨통을 조여 죽였던 거예요.

헤일 부인 남편의 목을. 그래요, 졸라 죽인 거지요. [그녀는 손을 뻗어 새장 위에 얹는다.]

피터즈 부인 [언성이 높아지며] 우린 누가 그를 죽였는지 몰라요. 우린 모른다구요.

헤일 부인 [감정을 지소하면서] 몇 년 동안이고 아무 일도 없다가, 당신을 위해 노래하는 새 한 마리가 생겼는데… 그 새가 죽어버린다면 정말 끔찍하리만큼 적막할 거예요.

피터즈 부인 [말속에 뼈가 있는 듯] 적막이 어떤 건지 알아요. 우리는 다코타 주의 한 농가에서 살았었지요. 그 때 우리 첫 아기가 죽었어요… 두 살 때였지요. 그 때 제겐 아무도 없었어요… 아무도…

헤일 부인 [움직이며] 저 사람들 증거 찾는 일이 언제나 끝날 것 같아요?

피터즈 부인 난 적막이 어떤 건지 알아요. [감정을 가다듬으면서] 법은 범죄를 처벌해야 합니다, 헤일 부인.

헤일 부인 [그 말에 대답하는 것 같지 않은 듯] 부인께서 미니 포스터를 보았더라면 얼마나 좋았을까요.

	파란 리본이 달린 하얀 드레스를 입고 성가대와 함께 무대에 서서 노래를 부르던 미니 포스터를 말이에요. [방안을 둘러본다.] 아, 가끔씩 이곳을 들려보았어야 했는데! 전 죄를 지었어요! 전 죄를 지었다구요! 그 죄를 누가 벌한단 말인가요?
피터즈 부인	[위층을 올려다보며] 우리가 책임을 지고 애태워야 할 일은 아니에요.
헤일 부인	그녀가 도움을 필요로 했다는 것을 알았어야 했어요! 이런 일이 여자에게 어떤 것인지. 전 알아요. 참으로 이상하지요. 피터즈 부인. 우린 참으로 가깝게 살면서도 그토록 멀리 떨어져 살고 있어요. 우린 모두 똑같은 처지에 있는 거예요. 단지 종류만 다를 뿐, 똑같은 삶을 살아가고 있어요. [눈을 닦다가 과일 잼 병을 발견하고는 이를 잡으려고 손을 뻗는다.] 제가 피터즈 부인이라면 과일 잼이 상했다는 말은 하지 않을 거예요. 괜찮다고 해 주세요. 다 멀쩡하다고 전하세요. 이 병을 가지고 가서 증명해 보이세요. 그녀는… 병이 깨졌는지 어쩐지 전혀 모를 거예요.
피터즈 부인	[병을 집어 들고는 그것을 쌀 만한 것을 찾는다. 다른 방에서 가지고 온 옷가지에서 속옷을 꺼내 들고 매우 초조하게 병을 말기 시작한다. 가장된 목소리로] 정말이지, 저 남자들이 우리 이야기를 듣지 못하는 게 얼마나 다행인지 모르겠어요. 우릴 보면 비웃겠지요. 그까짓 죽은 카나리아 한 마리 가지고 저렇게 법석이냐며 흥을 보겠지요. 무슨 중요한 일이냐 되느냐는 듯이 말이에요. 막 비웃겠지요! [남자들이 내려오는 소리가 들린다.]
헤일 부인	[숨을 죽이며] 그럴 수도… 그러지 않을 수도 있어요.
지방검사	아니오, 피터즈 씨. 살인의 동기만 빼고는 모든 것이 분명합니다. 하지만 피고가 여자인 경우 배심원들이 어떻게 나올 지는 잘 아시지 않습니까. 무언가… 확실하게 이야기를 짜 맞춰 줄 수 있는… 이런 이상한 수법을 모두 명쾌하게 밝혀줄 수 있는 증거가 있으면 좋겠어요. [두 여인의 눈이 순간 마주친다. 헤일 씨가 바깥문에서 들어온다.]
헤일	저, 일행이 바깥에 기다리고 있다우. 날씨 한번 춥군 그래.
지방검사	전 잠시 여기에 좀 남아 있어야겠습니다. [보안관에게] 가서 프랭크를 불러주시겠습니까? 모든 걸 다시 한 번 검토해 봐야 하겠습니다. 이 이상 진전이 없다는 것이 영 내키지 않는군요.
보안관	제 집사람이 가져갈 물건들을 좀 보시겠습니까? [지방검사는 탁자로 다가가 앞치마를 집어 들고는 웃는다.]
지방검사	아, 부인들께서 가져갈 물건들은 그다지 위험한 것으로 보이지는 않습니다. [상자를 덮고 있는 헝겊 조각 몇 개를 들추어보고는 물러선다.] 피터즈 부인을 감독할 필요는 없군요. 사실, 보안관의 아내는 법과 결혼한 셈이지요. 그렇게 생각하지 않으십니까, 피터즈 부인?
피터즈 부인	아뇨, 그렇게 생각해 본 적은 없어요.
보안관	[낄낄대면서] 법과 결혼을 한다. [다른 방으로 간다.] 전 이 방에 잠깐 들어가 보아야겠습니다. 이 창문들을 좀 살펴보아야 할 것 같군요.
지방검사	[경멸투로] 아, 창문이라!
보안관	우리도 곧 나갈 겁니다, 헤일 씨.

헤일 밖으로 나간다. 보안관은 지방 검사를 따라 그 방으로 들어간다. 그러자 헤일 부인이 자신의 두 손을 꼭 모아 쥐고 피터즈 부인을 바라보며 일어선다. 피터즈 부인의 눈이 천천히 돌아가던 끝에 헤일 부인의 눈과 마주친다. 잠시 헤일 부인은 피터즈 부인의 손을 잡고 나서 상자가 숨겨진 장소로 시선을 옮긴다. 갑자기 피터즈 부인이 헝겊 조각들을 집어낸 뒤 그 상자를 그녀가 메고 있던 가방에 집어넣으려 한다. 그러나 상자가 너무

크다. 그녀는 상자를 열어 새를 꺼내기 시작하지만 손이 닿질 않자 어찌할 바 모른 채 서 있다. 다른 방에서 문고리 돌리는 소리가 들린다. 헤일 부인은 그 상자를 낚아채서는 그녀의 큼직한 외투 주머니에 넣는다. 지방검사와 보안관이 들어온다.

지방검사   [익살맞게] 자, 헨리, 최소한 우리는 이 집 안주인께서 누비려고 한 것은 아니었다는 걸 알아냈군요. 그녀는, 뭐라고 했었지요, 숙녀 분들?

헤일 부인   [손으로 그녀의 주머니를 가리면서] 그건… 꿰맨다고 하지요, 헨더슨 검사님.

2. 인형의 집(A Doll's House) — 제2막 중 일부

• 헨릭 입센(Henrik Ibsen)

등장인물

헬머 ·· 변호사
노라 ·· 헬머의 아내
랑크 의사(醫師) ······················· 헬머 부부와 친한 사이
린데 부인 ······························ 노라의 친구
크로그스타 ·································· 변호사
보모(안네 마리) ····················· 헬머 집 보모
헬레네 ····································· 헬머 집 가정부
엠미, 봅, 이바르 ······················ 헬머 부부의 아이들

같은 방. 피아노 옆 구석에는 크리스마스 트리가 뜯겨지고 흐트러져, 타다 남은 양초와 함께 서 있다. 소파 위에는 노라의 외투가 놓여 있다. 혼자서 이리저리 초조하게 걸어 다닌다. 드디어 소파 곁에 서서 망토를 집는다.

노라 [망토를 밑으로 떨어뜨린다] 누가 오는구나! [문께로 가서 귀를 기울인다] 아니, 아무도 아니군. 물론 오늘은 아무도 안 오겠지. 크리스마스 주 첫날인데 — 그리고 내일도 역시 — 그렇지만 혹시 — [문을 열고 밖을 내다본다] 아니야, 편지통에도 아무것도 없고. 텅 비었는데. [전면으로 다가온다] 오오, 그까짓! 그자가 물론 진정으로 하지는 않을 거야. 그런 일을 할 수야 있을라고. 있을 수 없는 일이야. 내게는 아이들이 셋이나 있는데.

보모가 큰 종이 상자를 가지고 왼편 방에서 나온다.

보모 이 가장 무도회 옷상자를 겨우 찾았어요.
노라 수고했어요. 탁자 위에 놓아요.
보모 [그렇게 한다] 그런데 아주 몹시 꾸겨져 있어요.
노라 아아, 그런 것 천 갈래 만 갈래로 찢어 버리고만 싶어!
보모 어머나, 간단히 수리할 수 있어요. — 조금만 참으시면.
노라 응, 린데 부인한테 가겠어요. 그분이 도와주실 거야.
보모 또 나가세요? 날씨가 사나운데요. 감기 드시겠어요. 몸에 해로우세요.
노라 아아, 그까짓 괜찮아요. 아이들은 무얼 하고 있지요?
보모 가엾게 크리스마스 선물들을 가지고 놀고 있어요. 그런데 —.
노라 때때로 엄마 말 묻던가요?
보모 엄마와 같이 있어 보아 놔서.
노라 그래, 그렇지만 안네 마리, 앞으로는 전과 같이 애들을 돌볼 수 없게 돼요.
보모 어리니까 곧 익숙해지겠지요.
노라 그렇게 생각해요? 엄마가 아주 없어져도 애들은 엄마를 잊어버릴 것 같아요?

보모	그런 말씀을 — 아주 없어지다니요!
노라	보모, 말 좀 해주어요. — 나 때때로 생각해 보았지만 — 자기 아이를 남에게 넘겨주고 어떤 생각이 났을까 하고 말예요.
보모	그건 그럴 수밖에 없었잖아요. 어린 노라의 유모가 되기 위해서 말이에요.
노라	그래, 그렇지만 그럴 결심이 생기다니 말에요.
보모	좋은 자리를 얻을 수 있는데그럴 수밖에요! 가난한데다가 불행 속에 빠져 있는 계집애로서는 그것도 반가운 일 아니겠어요? 그 나쁜 작자가 저를 위해서 뭐 해준 일이 있었어야지요.
노라	그럼 따님은 어머니 생각을 모두 다 잊어버렸겠네요.
보모	아뇨, 그 애는 그렇지는 않아요. 그 애가 견진(堅振)을 받을 때하고 시집을 갔을 때는 두 번 다 편지를 했던데요.

** ****

노라	[그를 향해서] 조용히 말씀하세요. 주인이 계시니까요.
크로그스타	거 뭐 계시면 어때요.
노라	용건은 무엇이에요?
크로그스타	뭐 좀 말씀드릴 일이 있어서요.
노라	그럼 빨리 말씀하세요. 무엇인데요?
크로그스타	제가 면직 통지서를 받았다는 것은 아마 아시겠지요.
노라	크로그스타 씨, 제 힘으로는 막을 도리가 없었어요. 그 일을 위해서 최대한의 노력을 했어요. 보람은 없었지만.
크로그스타	주인께서는 부인을 그 정도밖에 사랑하지 않으시나요? 제가 부인께 어떠한 보복을 할지 그 사람도 알고 있을 텐데. 감히 그런 —.
노라	제가 그이에게 이야기한 줄 알고 계신가요?
크로그스타	아니지요. 저도 역시 그러리라고는 조금도 생각지 않았지요. 그 선량한 토르발트 헬머가 그만한 용기를 가진 사람이라고는 생각되지 않았으니까요.
노라	크로그스타 씨! 저의 주인에게 대한 예의를 지켜 주세요.
크로그스타	네, 그분에게 백 배 경례하지요! 그런데 부인께서는 그 일을 그분에게 알리기를 무척 두려워하시니 말씀이지, 부인께서 하신 일이 어떤 일이었던가 지금은 어제보다 다소 더 잘 알고 계신 줄로 생각했는데요?
노라	당신의 설명을 들을 필요가 없을 정도로 잘 알고 있어요.
크로그스타	물론 저 같은 악덕 법률가는 —.
노라	용건은 무엇이지요?
크로그스타	부인께 문안이나 드리러 왔지요. 하루 종일 부인을 생각하고 있었답니다. 저 같은 돈장수에 엉터리 변호사에 — 또 — 어쨌든 이런 놈이라도 역시 그 인정이란 것, 조금은 가지고 있답니다.
노라	그럼 그것을 표시하세요. 저의 어린것들을 생각해서요.

크로그스타	주인께서는 저의 아이들을 생각해 주셨던가요? 그러나 어쨌든 그 얘긴 그만두십시다. 부인께 단 한 가지 말하고 싶은 것은, 부인은 그 일을 그렇게 심각하게 생각하실 필요는 없다는 것입니다. 당분간은 제 편에서 이 일로 소송을 제기하지는 않을 것이니까요.
노라	아아, 그러시겠지요? 저도 그러실 줄 알고 있었어요.
크로그스타	이런 일은 잘 해결될 수도 있는 것입니다. 남들 앞에 드러내야 할 필요도 없는 일이에요. 우리들 세 사람 사이의 문제니까요.
노라	저의 주인에게는 이 일을 알릴 수 없어요.
크로그스타	그것을 어떻게 막으시렵니까? 잔금을 치르실 수 있다는 말씀인가요?
노라	아녜요, 당장 치를 수는 없어요.
크로그스타	그러시다면 또 다른 무슨 길이라도 있습니까? 말하자면 며칠 사이에라도 그 돈을 마련하신다든다 —.
노라	무슨 방도가 있는 것은 아녜요.
크로그스타	무슨 방도가 있다고 해도 소용없을 걸요. 부인께서 만일 지금 수중에 현금을 가지고 계신다 치더라도, 제 손에 있는 차용 증서를 받아 가시지 못하실 걸요?
노라	그럼 — 대체 당신은 그것으로 무엇을 하자는 거예요?
크로그스타	그저 가지고 있자는 — 말하자면 제 손아귀에 쥐고 있자는 거지요. 관계없는 사람에게 알리지는 않겠습니다. 그래, 만일 부인께서 어떤 절망적인 생각에서 —.
노라	그럴 테에요.
크로그스타	혹은 주인과 아이들을 버리고 나가실 생각을 하신다면 —.
노라	그래요, 그럴 테에요.
크로그스타	혹은 그보다 더 불행한 일을 생각하고 계신다면 —.
노라	알아서 어쩌자는 거지요?
크로그스타	그런 생각은 다 버리세요.
노라	제게 무슨 생각을 하든지 알아서 어쩌자는 거죠?
크로그스타	처음에는 대개 누구든지 그런 생각을 하지요. 저도 그랬어요. 다만 용기가 없어서 —.
노라	[힘없이] 저도 마찬가지에요.
크로그스타	[안심이 되어서] 그렇고말고요. 부인께서는 그런 용기가 없으십니다. — 부인께서는 말입니다.
노라	용기가 없어요, 용기가 없어요.
크로그스타	그건 또한 여간한 바보짓이 아니죠? 가정의 풍파란 그저 한 차례 지나가면 그만이니까요. — 그런데 저는 지금 댁의 주인에게 드릴 편지 한 통을 주머니에 넣고 왔는데 —.
노라	그럼 그 속에 모든 것이 다 써 있다니요?
크로그스타	될 수 있는 대로 부드럽게 썼습니다만 —.
노라	[빨리] 그이한테 그 편지가 가서는 안 돼요! 찢어 버리세요! 돈은 마련하겠어요.
크로그스타	미안합니다. 헬머 부인. 그 이야기는 아까 말씀드렸다고 생각하는데요 —.
노라	제가 빚진 돈 이야기를 한 것이 아니에요. 당신이 저의 주인에게 요구하는 액수를 말씀하세요. 마련해 드리겠어요.
크로그스타	댁의 주인에게 돈을 요구한 일은 없는데요?

노라	그럼 뭐예요?
크로그스타	말씀 드리겠습니다. 저는 다시 본 지위로 돌아가고 싶다는 겁니다. 헬머 부인, 저는 다시 머리를 들고 싶습니다. 그러기 위해서 댁의 주인의 조력이 필요한 것입니다. 일 년 반 동안 저는 조금도 불명예스런 일은 저질러 오지 않았어요. 그동안 저는 악전고투하면서 처신을 잘 해왔던 것이에요. 저는 한발 한발 전진할 수 있었다는 것이 만족스러웠습니다. 그러다가 이번에 쫓겨나고 말았습니다. 그래 이제는 저를 동정해서 다시 채용해 준다고 하는 것으로 저는 만족할 수 없습니다. 저는 머리를 들고 싶다는 말씀입니다. ― 다시 은행에 들어가고 싶습니다. ― 댁의 주인께서 자리를 마련해 주셔야겠어요.
노라	그이는 결코 그러시지 않을걸요.
크로그스타	압니다. 저는 그분을 잘 알고 있어요. 감히 이러쿵저러쿵 말하지 못할 겁니다. 그래서 일단 그분과 같이 은행에 있게 되면, 보세요! 일 년이 다 못 되어서 저는 은행장의 바른 팔이 됩니다. 토르발트 헬머가 아닌 닐스 크로그스타가 주식 은행을 지배하게 될 것입니다.
노라	절대로 그렇게 되지는 않을 걸요!
크로그스타	그럼 혹시 부인께서는 ―?
노라	물론이지요. 이제는 저도 그럴 용기는 가지고 있어요.
크로그스타	허어, 무섭지가 않은데요. 부인같이 가냘프고 고생 모르고 자란 분이 ―.
노라	곧 알게 될 거예요. 곧 알게 돼요.
크로그스타	얼음 밑으로 뛰어드신다는 말씀인가요? 컴컴하고 찬 물속에 말씀이지요? 그래 봄이 되어 기슭으로 떠나와서, 누구인지 분간도 못할 정도로 흉하게 되고, 머리털은 다 빠지고 ―.
노라	무섭지 않아요.
크로그스타	저 역시 무섭지 않군요. 사람치고 누가 그런 짓 하겠습니까? 헬머 부인, 또 그런들 무슨 소용이 있습니까? 어쨌든 그것은 제가 호주머니 속에 간직하고 있는데 말입니다.
노라	그렇게 돼도 말예요? 제가 이 세상에 없는데도?
크로그스타	그런다 해도 부인의 명예는 제 손에 달려 있다는 것을 부인은 잊고 계신데요.
노라	[말없이 그를 바라본다]
크로그스타	자아, 이만하면 부인도 아셨지요. 경솔한 행동은 마셔야 합니다. 헬머가 이 편지를 받는 순간, 무슨 회답이 있을 것으로 저는 고대하고 있겠습니다. 저를 이런 길로 인도한 것은 바로 댁의 주인이라는 것을 생각해 보세요. 저는 절대로 그를 용서 못 하겠어요. 그럼 안녕히, 헬머 부인. [문쪽으로 퇴장]
노라	[문께로 가서 문을 약간 열고 귀를 기울인다] 나가는군, 편지는 넣지 않고. 안 될걸, 안 돼. 그럴 수는 없을 거야! [문을 조금씩 더 연다] 웬일일까? 서 있는데. 층계를 내려가지 않는데? 망설이고 있는 것일까? 혹시나 ―? [편지 한 통이 편지통 속에 떨어진다. 조금 있다 크로그스타의 구두 소리가 층계에서 사라진다]
노라	[억눌린 듯한 소리를 지르면서, 소파 곁에 있는 탁자께로 달려간다. 잠깐 사이] 편지통 속에! [두려워하면서 현관 방문께로 간다] 저기 들어 있어. ― 토르발트, 토르발트. ― 이제 우리는 끝장이에요.
린데 부인	[의상을 들고 왼편 방에서 나온다] 자, 노라, 이만하면 다 되었어. 한번 입어 보아야 할 ― 걸?

노라	[쉰 목소리로 조용히] 크리스티네, 이리로 잠깐만.
린데 부인	[의상을 소파 위에 던진다] 어디 편찮아? 안색이 아주 안 좋은데?
노라	좀 와봐. 저 편지가 보이지? 저기, 저봐 — 편지통에 유리 속에.
린데 부인	응 응. 나도 보여.
노라	그게 크로그스타 편지야.
린데 부인	노라 — 돈을 꾸어 준 사람은 크로그스타였구먼!

** ****

노라	[상자 속에서 탬버린과 울긋불긋한 빛깔의 쇼올 하나를 꺼낸다. 이것을 얼른 등에 걸치더니 펄쩍 뛰어서 무대 전면에 서서 소리를 지른다] 그럼 시작해 줘요! 춤을 출 테니까요. [헬머는 반주를 하고 노라는 춤을 춘다. 랑크는 헬머 뒤에 피아노에 기대서서 구경한다]
헬머	[치면서] 더 느리게, — 좀더 느리게.
노라	이 정도밖에 안 돼요.
헬머	너무 빨라요, 노라!
노라	바로 이 정도라야 해요.
헬머	[멈춘다] 안 돼, 안 돼. 그러면 안 돼.
노라	[웃고는 탬버린을 흔든다] 그러기에 제가 말한 것 아녜요?
랑크	내가 한번 반주를 치지.
헬머	[일어선다] 그래, 해봐. 그래 주면 나는 코치하기가 수월하지. [랑크, 피아노 앞에 앉아 친다. 노라가 점점 난폭하게 춤을 추는 동안 몇 번이나 말로 코치를 한다. 노라에게는 귀에 들어가지 않는 것 같다. 머리칼이 풀려서 어깨 위에 늘어진다. 노라, 그것에 상관없이 춤을 계속한다.]
린데 부인	[어이가 없어 말도 나오지 않는 것같이 문 앞에 멈춰 선다] 어머나 —!
노라	[춤을 추면서] 재미있지? 크리스티네!
헬머	그런데 우리 귀여운 노라, 마치 생사를 걸고 춤을 추는 것 같군.
노라	사실이 그런걸요?
헬머	랑크, 그만! 이건 정말 미친 짓이야! 그만하라니까. [랑크, 손을 멈추고, 따라서 노라도 우뚝 선다. 노라를 향하여 간다] 정말 이럴 수가 있어. 내가 전에 가르쳐 주던 것을 모조리 다 잊어버렸군 그래.
노라	[탬버린을 앞으로 내던진다] 그러기에 한 말이에요.
헬머	이제 그럼 아주 근본적으로 연습해야 되겠어.
노라	그래요, 연습할 필요가 있다는 것은 보셔서 알았지요? 당신 끝까지 저하고 같이 연습해야 돼요. 약속하시지요? 토르발트.
헬머	그 점은 안심해도 좋아.
노라	오늘도 내일도 저밖엔 딴 생각하시면 안 돼요. 편지 한장 들어 보셔도 안 되고 — 또 편지통도 말예요.
헬머	아하하, 아직도 그자가 두려운 게로군.

노라	그래요. 그 점도 있어요.
헬머	노라, 당신 얼굴을 보니, 그자한테서 이미 편지가 와 있는 모양이군?
노라	저는 모르겠어요. 그럴 것도 같아요. 그렇지만 지금 그런 것 읽어서는 안 돼요. 모든 것이 끝나기 전에는 불쾌한 것은 하나도 우리들 사이에 끼어들어 와서는 안 돼요.
랑크	[조용한 말로 헬머에게] 부인 말대로 하는 게 좋겠네.
헬머	우리 애기 고집을 세워 주지! 그렇지만 내일 저녁에 춤이 끝나면 ―.
노라	그때는 당신 마음대로 하세요.
헬레네	[바른쪽 문에 서서] 마님, 식사 준비가 되었어요.
노라	샴페인을 할 테니까, 헬레네야.
헬레네	알았습니다. 마나님. [퇴장]
헬머	저런, 저런, ― 그럼 아주 진짜 연회군.
노라	그럼요. 샴페인 연회고 밤을 새워요. [밖을 향해서 소리친다] 그리고 마카롱도 몇 개 가져와요. ― 이번 한번이니까.
헬머	[노라의 손을 붙잡는다] 글쎄, 그렇게 흥분해서 떠들지 말고, 전과 같이 우리 귀엽고 작은 종달새로 돌아가요.
노라	아아, 네 그러세요. 벌써 그렇게 된 걸요. 자, 그럼 들어가세요. 또 선생님도. 그리고 크리스티네, 내 머리 좀 보아 줘야겠어.
랑크	[가면서 낮은 목소리로] 정말 아무 일도 아니겠지? ― 내 말은, 무슨 일이라도 있지 않았는가 하는 말야.
헬머	천만에, 랑크, 내가 이야기하던 바로 그 어린애 같은 걱정뿐이야. [이들은 바른쪽으로 걸어가 퇴장]

3. 유리동물원(The Glass Menagerie) – 제1막 1장

• 테네시 윌리엄즈(Tennessee Williams)

등장인물

아만다 윙필드 ··· 어머니
로라 윙필드 ··· 아만다의 딸
톰 윙필드 ··· 아만다의 아들
짐 오코너 ··· 젊은 신사 방문객

윙필드 가의 셋방은 아파트 건물의 뒤쪽에 자리 잡고 있다. 이 건물은 하층 중산계급의 주민들이 모여 사는 인구과잉의 도시지에 사마귀처럼 돋아난, 마치 세포 같은 주거단위가 벌집처럼 밀집되어 있는 거대한 빌딩 중 하나다. 그리고 이 하층 중산계급은 미국사회에서는 최대의, 기본적으로 노예화된 계층을 형성하고 유동과 분화를 피하며 무의식적, 자동적으로 행동하는 집단에 끼여 존재하고 기능하고자 하는 충동을 가지고 있다.

윙필드 가가 빌리고 있는 이 셋집은 뒷골목에 연해 있으며 화재용 비상계단이 통로로 되어 있다. 화재용 비상계단이라는 말은 우연히도 일말의 시적 진실을 담고 있다. 왜냐하면 이 거대한 빌딩들은 모두가 인간의 절망이라는 불꽃을 완만하면서도 무자비하게 불태우고 있기 때문이다. 이 비상계단은 무대장치의 일부로서, 비상계단의 층계참과 거기서부터 내려오는 계단이 마련되어 있다.

이 장면은 추억이며, 따라서 비현실적이다. 추억은 시적인 비약을 많이 한다. 추억은 접촉하는 문제의 정서적 가치에 따라 어떤 세부사항이 생략되기도 하고 어떤 것이 과장되기도 한다. 왜냐하면 추억은 마음속에 최우선적으로 자리잡고 있기 때문이다. 따라서 실내는 조명이 어렴풋하며 시정(詩情)이 감돈다.

막이 오르면 관객들의 앞쪽에 윙필드 가가 빌리고 있는 뒷방의 어둡고 음침한 외벽이 나타난다. 이 아파트 건물의 양측은 모두 어둡고 좁은 골목들이다. 이 골목들은 뒤엉킨 빨랫줄과 쓰레기통, 그리고 이웃집 화재용 비상계단들이 보기 흉한 격자무늬 꼴을 이루고 있는, 음산한 빌딩의 계곡이다. 연극중 등장인물은 양쪽 골목길을 통해서 건물로 들어갔다 나왔다 하게 된다. 톰의 개막 해설이 끝날 무렵 검은 빌딩의 외벽은 차츰 투명해서 1층에 자리잡은 윙필드 가의 실내가 보이게 된다.

무대 전면은 거실인데 소파를 펼치며 로라의 침대가 되어 그녀의 침실로도 이용된다. 거실의 바로 후면에 커다란 아치가 있는데 투명하고 바랜 커튼이 달린 제2의 프로시니어(무대막)로 구획되어 있어 식당으로 쓰인다. 거실의 장식선반에 수십 개의, 투명한 유리로 만든 동물들이 보인다. 아치의 왼쪽 거실 벽에는 부친의 확대사진이 객석을 향해 걸려 있다. 그것은 제1차 세계대전 때의 미국 보병 모자를 쓴 무척 잘생긴 청년의 얼굴이다. 그는 상냥하게 미소를 짓고 있는데, 마치 '나는 영원히 미소를 짓겠다'고 말하는 듯, 웃지 않을 수 없다는 그런 미소다.

관객들은 건물 외벽의 투명한 제4의 벽과 식당 아치의 투명한 얇은 커튼 두 개를 통해서 식당에서 벌어지는 개막장면을 보고 듣는다. 서두를 보여주는 이 장면이 계속되는 동안 제4의 벽이 서서히 상승해서 시야로부터 사라진다. 이 투명한 외벽은 다시 내려오지 않으며, 연극의 맨 마지막에 가서 톰이 최후의 연설을 하고 있는 동안에야 비로소 내려온다.

해설자가 이 연극의 줄거리를 설명하는 것은 당연한 관례로 되어 있다. 그는 자신의 목적에 맞추기 위해서 종래의 어떠한 연극적인 약속도 무시할 수 있다.

톰은 상선 선원 같은 옷을 입고 등장하여 화재용 비상계단으로 천천히 간다.

거기서 그는 걸음을 멈추고 담배에 불을 붙인다. 그는 관객들에게 말한다.

톰 그렇습니다. 저는 호주머니 속에 요술을 잔뜩 갖고 있습니다. 옷소매 안에도 감춰둔 것이 있습니다. 그렇지만 저는 무대 마술사와는 전혀 다릅니다. 마술사는 여러분에게 진실의 모습을 띤 환상을 보여줍니다만, 저는 환상이라는 즐거운 가면을 통해 여러분께 진실을 보여드리고자 합니다.
　이 이야기를 시작하기 위해 우선 시계 바늘을 뒤로 돌리겠습니다. 저 1930년대라는 별스러웠던 시대로 거슬러 올라갑니다. 그때의 미국사회는 방대한 중산층이 연달아 맹인학교에 입학하고 있었습니다. 왜냐고요, 눈이 그들을 저버린 것인지 그들이 눈을 저버린 것인지, 하여튼 모두 손끝에 힘을 주며 경제가 붕괴해가는 꼴을 타는 듯한 붉은 점자를 짚듯 한자 한자 더듬고 있었으니까요.
　스페인에서는 내란이 있었습니다. 이곳 미국에서는 고함소리와 혼란이 있었다 뿐이죠. 스페인의 게르니카에선 무참한 폭격이 있었습니다. 그리고 이곳 미국에서는 그저 노동분쟁이 있었을 정도죠. 때로는 꽤나 시끌시끌했지만요. 그런 일만 없었다면 시카고, 클리블랜드, 세인트루이스 등의 도시가 모두 태평스런 판국이었죠… 이것이 이 연극의 사회적 배경입니다.

음악이 흐른다.

　이 연극은 추억을 찾아가는 겁니다. 추억의 연극이기 때문에 조명은 어슴푸레하고 감상적이지 결코 현실적이 아닙니다. 추억 속에서는 모든 것이 음악에 맞추어 일어나는 것처럼 보이죠. 무대의 양쪽에서 바이올린 소리가 들려오는 것도 바로 그 때문입니다.
　저는 이 연극의 해설자이자 등장인물입니다. 다른 등장인물로는 저의 모친인 아만다, 누이 로라, 그리고 이 극의 후반에 가서 등장하는 젊은 신사 방문객이 한 사람 있는데 그는 이 연극에서 가장 현실적인 인물이고 우리와는 거리가 멀어진 현실의 세계로부터 파견된 사자(使者)라고나 할까요? 저는 그저 상징이라고 하면 깜박 죽는 시인의 기질을 갖고 있기 때문에 역시 이 연극에서 이 인물을 하나의 상징으로 삼고 있습니다. 즉 그는 우리의 삶 속에서 좀체 나타나지 않지만 언젠가는 나타나리라는 희망을 갖게 하는 존재이기도 합니다.
　이 연극에는 또 한 사람 제5의 인물이 있지만 실물보다 더 큰 사진으로 벽난로 위에 걸려 있을 뿐입니다. 바로 저의 부친인데, 오래 전에 우릴 버리고 집을 나갔죠. 아버지는 전화국 직원이었습니다. 장거리 전화에 홀린 건지 결국은 직장을 그만두고 마음 가는 대로 바람처럼 훌쩍 이 거리를 떠나버렸습니다…
　우리가 아버지한테서 마지막 소식을 들은 건 멕시코 태평양 연안에 있는 마자틀란이라는 곳에서 보낸 그림엽서였습니다. 딱 두 마디의 인사말이 들어있더군요. '잘 있느냐? 잘 있거라!' 물론 주소도 써 있지 않았고요.
　나머지 얘기는 연극이 진행되면 자연히 아시게 될 겁니다…

커튼을 통해 아만다의 목소리가 들려온다.

스크린의 명제 – '그저 꿈만 같구나.'

톰은 커튼을 헤치며 식당으로 들어간다. 아만다와 로라가 식탁(옆에 판을 달아 접어 내렸다, 펴서 올렸다 하며 크기를 조절할 수 있는 식탁)에 앉아 있다. 음식이나 식사도구는 없지만 마임동작으로 식사중임을 나타낸다. 아만다는 정면으로 객석을 향해 있다. 톰과 로라는 옆얼굴을 객석에 보이고 있다. 실내등이 은은하게 켜져 있고 얇은 커튼을 통해 아만다와 로라가 무대 후면 쪽의 식탁에 앉아 있는 것이 보인다.

아만다	[부른다] 톰?
톰	왜요, 어머니.
아만다	네가 와야 감사 기도를 올리지!
톰	곧 가요, 어머니. [톰은 관객들에게 가볍게 인사하고 물러갔다가 잠시 후 다시 나타나 식탁의 자기 자리에 앉는다.]
아만다	[아들에게] 애야, 그게 뭐냐, 손가락으로. 쑤셔넣을 게 따로 있지, 그러려거든 빵부스러기를 써라. 꼭꼭 씹어 먹어! 동물은 음식을 씹지 않고 먹어도 위의 분비물이 알아서 소화시켜 주지만, 사람은 달라. 음식을 잘 씹어서 넘기도록 돼 있어. 음식은 서둘지 말고 맛을 즐겨야 한다. 요리는 입 안에서 충분히 맛을 즐겨야 하는 법이다. 음식을 꼭꼭 씹어 침구멍도 제구실을 할 기회를 줘야지!

톰은 천천히 가상(假想)의 포크를 내려놓고는 의자를 식탁에서 뒤로 뺀다.

톰	참, 어머니도. 밥 먹는 걸 이렇게 먹어라 저렇게 먹어라 일일이 참견하시니 오늘 저녁식사는 한 숟갈도 제대로 먹지 못했어요. 내가 음식을 서둘러 먹도록 만든 건 바로 어머니예요. 음식을 먹을 때마다 어떻게 먹나 하고 잔뜩 쨰려보고 있으니 말입니다. 동물의 분비액이 어떻다느니 침구멍이 어떻다느니 꼭꼭 씹어 먹어야 된다느니, 어머니 잔소리에 신물이 나서 이젠 입맛이 싹 가셨다고요!
아만다	[가볍게 받아들이며] 원 자식도, 무슨 놈의 성미가 그렇담. 꼭 메트로폴리탄 오페라단의 주역가수 같구나! [톰은 의자에서 일어나 거실 쪽으로 걸어간다.] 식사가 끝나지 않았는데 왜 자릴 뜨냐?
톰	담배 좀 가져오려고요.
아만다	넌 담배를 너무 많이 피워!

로라가 자리에서 일어난다.

로라	후식 가져올게요.

톰은 다음 대사가 진행되는 동안 담배를 손에 든 채 커튼 옆에 그대로 서 있다.

아만다	[자리에서 일어서며] 안돼 안돼 — 이번 심부름은 내 차지다. 아가씨는 가만히 앉아 있기나 해.
로라	어차피 일어선걸요.
아만다	애야, 어서 앉으라니까, 넌 신선하고 예뻐 보여야지, 신사 방문객을 위해서!
로라	앉으며] 기다린다고 누가 와주나?
아만다	[부엌으로 나가며, 명랑하게] 글쎄, 손님들은 기다리지도 않는데 불쑥 찾아오는 수가 있단다!

	그러고 보니 어느 일요일 오후가 생각나는구나. 블루 마운틴에서 말이다. — [아만다가 부엌으로 들어간다.]
톰	그 다음 이야긴 안 들어도 뻔해!
로라	그래, 하지만 말씀하시도록 해 드려.
톰	그 넋두리를 또?
로라	엄만 그 얘기 하시는게 큰 재민걸.

아만다가 디저트 그릇을 들고 돌아온다.

아만다	블루 마운틴에서 살던 땐데, 어느 일요일 오후였지 — 이 엄만 무려 열일곱 명이나 되는 신사분들을 한꺼번에 맞았단 말이다! 그러니 그 신사분들을 모실 의자가 모자랄 지경이었지 뭐냐, 그래서 흑인 하인들을 교회로 보내어 접는 의자를 가져오게 해야만 했었지.
톰	[커튼 옆에 서서] 그 신사분들을 어떻게 접대했어요?
아만다	이래봬도 엄만 기찬 화술을 가졌거든!
톰	어련하셨겠습니까!
아만다	그 때 처녀들은 너나 할 것 없이 화법이 몸에 배어 있었단다.
톰	그래요?

스크린의 영상 — 현관에서 방문객들을 맞이하는 소녀 시대의 아만다.

아만다	그땐 손님 대접하는 법을 누구나 알고 있었단다. 당시는 아가씨들도 예쁜 얼굴이나 우아한 몸맵시만으로는 어림도 없었거든. 물론 난 그 점에서 얕잡아 보이진 않았지만, 재빠른 기지에다가 어떤 경우에라도 대응할 수 있는 말솜씨까지 있어야 했다고.
톰	그래서 무슨 얘길 했어요?
아만다	세상만사 중요한 건 모두지! 물론 천하고 시시하고 야비한 일은 빼고 말이다. [톰이 커튼 옆에 서 있는데도 아만다는 마치 톰이 식탁의 빈 의자에 앉아 있는 것처럼 이야기를 건다. 톰은 마치 대본을 낭독하고 있는 것처럼 이 장면을 연기한다.] 나를 찾아온 사람들은 하나같이 — 신사였어! 그 가운데는 미시시피 델타에서 손꼽히는 젊은 농장주도 있었지 — 농장주와 그 자제들도!

이 신호를 보내자 음악이 시작되고 아만다에게 스포트라이트가 비친다. 아만다는 눈을 크게 뜨고 얼굴은 상기되어 낭랑한 음성에 애수를 띠고 말한다.

스크린의 명제 — '옛일이 그저 꿈만 같구나.'

그 사람들 가운데 챔프 래플린이라는 젊은이가 있었지. 후에 델타 농민은행의 부총재가 된 사람이야. 그리고 하들리 스티븐슨이란 친구는, 문 호반(湖畔)에 빠져 죽었지만, 글쎄 미망인에게 정부공채로 15만 달러를 유산으로 남겼다지 뭐냐. 또 큐트리어 형제도 끼여 있었다. 웨슬리와 베이츠라는 이름이었어. 베이츠는 나를 열렬히 사랑했던 남자들 가운데 한 사람이었단다! 베이츠는 웨인라이트 가의 난폭한 녀석과 싸움이 붙었어. 그들은 문 호반의 카지노에서 총질을 벌였다고. 베이츠는 복부에 총을 맞았지. 구급차에 실려 멤피스로 가다가 죽었어. 베이츠의 미망인도 제법 넉넉한 유산을 물려받았단다. 8천 에이커라든가, 아니, 1만 에이커라든가

	하는 땅을 물려받았으니까. 그만하면 호박이 넝쿨째 굴러들어온 거지 뭐냐. 그 여자가 베이츠와 결혼할 수 있었던 건 베이츠가 나에게 딱지를 맞고 홧김에 결혼했기 때문이란다. — 베이츠는 그 여자를 결코 사랑하지 않았거든 — 죽던 날 밤에도 내 사진을 품고 있었다지 뭐니! 어디 그뿐이냐, 델타 지방의 처녀들이 침을 삼키던 청년이 있었단다! 그린 군의 피츠휴 가의 아주 똑똑하고 잘생긴 도련님이었어!
톰	그 친군 미망인에게 유산을 얼마나 남겼죠?
아만다	아무하고도 결혼하지 않았어! 나참 기가 막혀서. 넌 마치 지난날 나를 사모했던 사람들은 모두 죽어버린 것처럼 애길 하는구나!
톰	아직 살아있다고 말한 사람은 그가 처음 아닌가요?
아만다	그 피츠휴 가의 청년은 북부로 가서 큰 재산을 모았어 — 월가의 늑대로 알려지게 되었으니까! 요술망치라도 갖고 있나봐. 그저 그 망치로 두드리기만 하면 모든 게 황금으로 변했으니 말이다! 그래서 말인데, 난 던컨 J. 피츠휴 부인이 될 뻔했단다! — 끝내는 너희 아버지를 고르고 말았지만!
로라	[일어서며] 식탁은 내가 치울래.
아만다	아니다. 넌 저리 가서 타이프라이터 교본이나 공부하려무나. 아니면 속기연습을 좀 하든지. 발랄하고 예뻐 보여야 해! — 신사분들이 찾아올 시간이 됐어. [그녀는 가벼운 걸음걸이로 부엌으로 뛰어간다.] 오늘 오후엔 손님을 몇 분이나 접대할 것 같으냐?

톰은 신문을 집어 던지고 볼멘소리를 내며 벌떡 일어선다.

로라	[식당에 홀로 남아] 아무도 올 것 같지 않은걸요, 엄마.
아만다	[다시 나타나며, 명랑하게] 뭐라고? 손님이 안 올 거라고? 농담이겠지! [로라는 모친의 웃음에 마지못해 따라 웃는다. 그녀는 도망치듯 반쯤 열린 커튼 사이로 빠져나가 커튼을 다시 여민다. 퇴색한 커튼을 배경으로 하고 있는 그녀의 얼굴에 한줄기 밝은 조명이 비친다.] [음악 — '유리동물원'이 가냘프게 들린다.] [경쾌하게] 한 사람도 안 온다고? 그럴 린 없어! 홍수가 났거나 폭풍이라도 분다면 모르겠지만!
로라	홍수 때문도 폭풍 때문도 아녜요. 난 블루 마운틴 시절의 엄마만큼 인기가 없기 때문이야… [톰은 또다시 볼멘소리를 낸다. 로라는 희미하고 미안한 듯한 미소를 지으며 그를 바라본다. 그녀는 목소리를 낮추고] 엄만 내가 노처녀 될까봐 두려운 모양이지.

'유리동물원' 주제 음악과 함께 이 장면은 서서히 어두워지며 끝난다.

4. 세일즈맨의 죽음(Death of a Salesman) – 제2막 중 일부

• 아서 밀러(Arthur Miller)

등장인물

윌리 로먼	늙은 외판원(外販員)
린다	그의 아내
비프	큰 아들
해피	아들
버나드	이웃집 아들
여자	윌리의 정부
찰리	버나드의 아버지, 윌리의 친구
백부(伯父) 벤	윌리의 형
하워드 와그너	젊은 사장
제니	찰리의 비서
스탠리	식당 보이
미스 포사이드	거리의 여자
레타	거리의 여자

윌리   [증오에 차서 위협하며] 네 인생의 문이 활짝 열려 있다니까!

비프   아버지, 전 10센트 열두 개짜리 싸구려예요. 아버지도 그렇구요.

윌리   [더 참을 수 없다는 듯이 비프를 향해] 난 그런 싸구려는 아니다. 난 윌리 로먼이야.

[비프는 윌리에게 다가간다. 그러나 해피가 막는다. 격한 나머지 비프는 금시에라도 윌리에게 덤벼들 기세이다.]

비프   우리 부자는 남을 지도할 자격이 없어요. 뼛골이 빠지도록 일이나 하는 도붓장수에 불과해요. 결국 어떻게 됐죠. 다른 외판원들이나 마찬가지로 쓰레기통 속에 처박혔단 말예요. 전 한 시간 한 달러짜리 인간예요. 일곱 주를 돌아다녔어도 그 값밖에 못 받는 인간이 되고 만 거예요. 아시겠죠? 그러니까, 내가 무슨 선물이라도 사들고 올 줄 아신다면 큰 착오예요. 애당초 단념하시는 게 낫죠.

윌리   [비프에게 맞대고] 에이, 천하에 불효자식 같으니!

[비프, 해피를 뿌리친다. 윌리, 겁을 내며 계단으로 올라가려고 한다. 비프, 그를 붙잡는다.]

비프   [성이 머리끝까지 치밀어] 아버지, 난 쓰레기라니까요. 아버진 그걸 모르세요? 원망이구 뭐구가 어디 있어요? 난 요 모양 밖에 안 되는 인간이라니까요.

[비프의 분노는 제물에 힘이 빠진다. 비프는 풀이 죽어 울며 윌리에게 안긴다. 윌리는 말없이 비프의 얼굴을 더듬는다.]

윌리   [놀라서] 왜 이러니? 왜 이래 글쎄? [린다에게] 애가 왜 울까?

비프	[기진해서 울며] 제발 절 가도록 내버려 두세요. 그리구 그 허황된 꿈을 태워 버리세요. 이러다간 무슨 일이 일어나구야 말 거예요. [자제하려고 애쓰며 뿌리치고 계단쪽으로 간다.] 전 아침에 떠나겠어요. — 아버질 주무시게 해 드리세요.

[비프는 지쳐서 계단을 올라가 자기 방으로 간다.]

윌리	[한참 만에 놀랍고 기분이 좋아서] 희한하지 않소! 그 녀석이 그래도 — 날 위하는구료!
린다	그렇다니까요!
해피	[매우 감동되어] 언제고 그랬어요.
윌리	응, 비프가! [흥분하여 눈을 크게 뜨고] 그놈이 울었어! 애비한테 안겨 울었다니까! [부성애에 벅차 목이 메며 소망을 외친다] 그놈은, 그놈은, 훌륭하게 될 거야!

[벤이 주방 바로 밖의 조명 속에 나타난다.]

벤	아, 출중하지. 이만 삼천 달러가 따르니까.
린다	[질주하는 남편의 마음속을 눈치 채고 공포에 사로잡혀 조심스럽게] 여보, 그만 잡시다. 인제 다 끝나지 않았수!
윌리	[집에서 뛰쳐나가지 않고서는 못 견디게 되어] 그래 잡시다. 해피야, 너도 자거라.
벤	정글을 정복하는 데는 큰 인물이라야지.

[공포의 음조 속에서 벤의 목가적인 음악이 시작된다.]

해피	[한 팔로 린다를 안고] 아버지, 저 결혼하겠어요. 저도 인젠 달라질 거예요. 이 해가 가기 전에 제가 일하는 과의 과장이 될 테니까요. 두고 보세요. [린다에게 키스한다]
벤	정글은 어둡지만 다이아몬드로 가득 찼어.

[윌리, 몸을 돌려 벤의 말을 들으며 움직인다.]

린다	잘 해. 너희들 형제는 다 착하니까. 그대로만 하면 된다.
해피	아버지, 안녕히 주무세요. [이층으로 간다]
린다	[윌리에게] 여보, 잡시다.
벤	[더욱 힘을 주어] 다이아몬드를 가지고 나오려면 우선 들어가야지.
윌리	[주방 끝으로 천천히 걸어 문 쪽으로 가며 린다에게] 난 좀 앉아 쉬고 싶소. 잠깐 혼자 있게 해 주오.
린다	[거의 공포를 나타내는 음성으로] 어서 올라갑시다.
윌리	[두 팔로 린다를 안고] 금방 올라가리다. 지금은 잠이 올 것 같지 않소. 먼저 자요. 아주 고단해 보이는구료. [키스한다]
벤	만나는 약속과는 다르지. 다이아몬드는 만지면 거칠고 딱딱해.
윌리	어서 올라가요, 내 금방 올라가리다.

린다	이게 유일한 방법 같우.
윌리	암, 제일 좋은 방법이지.
벤	좋은 방법이라구!
윌리	유일한 방법야. 그 다음엔 만사가 다 — 어서 자요. 피곤해 뵌다니까.
린다	금방 올라오슈.
윌리	이 분만.

[린다, 거실로 들어간다. 이윽고 침실에 다시 나타난다. 윌리, 주방문 바로 밖으로 움직인다.]

윌리	날 위한다. [신기해서] 언제나 날 생각했다고. 신기한 일이 아닙니까? 그놈이 날 숭배하게 될 거라니까요.
벤	[틀림없다는 듯이] 거긴 어둡지만, 다이아몬드로 가득찼어.
윌리	생각해 보세요. 얼마나 굉장합니까? 이만 달러가 그놈 주머니로 들어갈 텐데요.
린다	[방에서 부른다] 여보! 올라와요!
윌리	[주방 안으로 대고] 그래, 지금 가리다. 역시 당신도 눈치를 챘지, 안 그래? 형님도 그건 아시거든. 난 가야 하오. 그럼, 잘 있소! [사뭇 춤추듯이 벤에게 가서] 생각해 보세요. 인제 비프에게 편지만 오면 그놈이 다시 버나드를 앞선다니까요.
벤	어느 모로 보든지 완전한 계획이야.
윌리	그놈이 저한테 안겨서 우는 걸 보셨죠? 키스라도 해 줄 걸 그랬어요.
벤	시간이다, 시간야!
윌리	결국 비프하구 저하고는 해결할 수 있다는 걸 알구 있었으니까요.
벤	[시계를 보며] 뱃시간. 늦겠는걸. [천천히 움직여서 어둠 속으로 사라진다]
윌리	[집을 향하여 애조를 띄우고] 비프야, 볼을 찰 땐 칠십 야드는 차야 된다. 그리군 볼이 떠가는 밑으로 돌진하는 거야. 그리구 야구할 때는 나지막하게 세게 쳐야 돼. 그게 중요하다니까. [그는 획 돌아서 객석을 향한다] 스탠드엔 굉장한 사람들이 와 있으니까 첫째로 알아둬야 할 일은 … [갑자기 혼자 있는 것을 알고] 형님, 형님, 전 어디로 … [갑자기 찾는 동작을 한다] 형님, 어떻게 …?
린다	[부른다] 여보, 올라오슈.
윌리	[린다에게 조용히 하라는 듯이 획 몸을 돌려 공포로 헐떡거리며] 쉿! [길을 찾으려는 듯이 돌아선다. 잡음, 얼굴들, 목소리들이 그를 덮치는 것 같다. 그는 이런 것들을 물리치려는 듯이 외친다] 쉿! 쉿! [갑자기 약하고 높은 음악이 그를 멈추게 한다. 음악은 점점 커지고 참을 수 없을 정도의 외침이 된다. 그는 발끝으로 왔다갔다 하다가 집을 돌아 급히 사라진다] 쉬잇!
린다	여보?

[대답이 없다. 린다, 기다린다. 비프, 침대에서 일어나 나온다. 그는 아직 양복을 입은 채로 있다. 해피, 일어나 앉는다. 비프는 들으면서 서 있다.]

| 린다 | [정말 공포에 사로잡혀] 여보, 대답해요! 여보! |

[자동차 떠나는 소리와 전속력으로 질주하는 소리가 들린다.]

린다   안 돼!

비프   *[계단을 뛰어 내려오며]* 아버지!

[자동차가 질주해 사라지자 음악은 광적인 소리로 깨지다가 작아지면서 첼로의 한 줄이 부드럽게 진동한다. 비프, 천천히 침실로 돌아간다. 비프와 해피, 상장(喪章)이 붙은 저고리를 입는다. 린다, 천천히 방에서 나온다. 음악은 장송 행진곡으로 바뀐다. 낮의 나뭇잎들이 모든 것 위에 나타난다. 찰리와 버나드, 정중한 옷차림으로 주방문에 나타나 노크한다. 비프와 해피, 천천히 계단을 내려와서 주방으로 가는데, 찰리와 버나드도 등장. 상복을 입은 린다가 조그만 장미꽃 다발을 들고, 휘장을 친 문을 나와 주방으로 들어오자 일동은 잠시 동작을 멈춘다. 린다, 찰리에게 가서 그의 팔을 잡는다. 이윽고 주방 벽선을 통하여 그들은 객석 쪽으로 나온다. 맨 앞무대 끝까지 오자 린다는 꽃을 내려놓고 무릎을 꿇고 두 발로 괸다. 그들 무덤을 내려다본다.]

5. 동물원 이야기(The Zoo Story) – 대본 전문 중 앞부분 반

• 에드워드 엘비(Edward Albee)

등장인물

피터 …… 40세를 갓 넘은 남자. 뚱뚱하지도 않고 메마르지도 않았으며, 잘생긴 쪽도 아니요 그렇다고 해서 못생긴 얼굴도 아니다. 스코치 나사 옷을 걸치고 파이프를 피우며 뿔로 테두리를 한 안경을 갖고 다닌다. 중년에 접어들었지만 옷차림과 태도는 그를 퍽 젊게 보여준다.

제리 …… 30세가 훨씬 넘은 남자. 초라한 것이 아니라 되는대로 걸친 옷차림. 옛날엔 산뜻하고 경쾌하게 근육적인 몸매가 살이 찌기 시작했는데, 더 이상 멋쟁이로 뵈지 않았지만 한때는 괜찮았다는 것이 분명하다. 육체적인 멋이 없어졌다고 해서 방탕을 일삼아 왔다는 말은 아니다. 좀 더 비슷하게 말해 그는 몹시 피곤을 느끼고 있다.

장 면: "센트럴 파크"(중앙공원) 여름철 어떤 일요일 – 오후. 현대무대 양측에 공원 벤치가 두 개 있다. 두 개 모두 관객을 향한다. 이 벤치 후면은 숲, 나무들, 하늘이 보인다. 시초에는 "피터"가 한쪽 벤치에 앉아있다

무대지시: [막이 오르자 "피터"가 무대 우측 벤치에 앉아있는 모습, 책을 읽고 있다. 독서를 중지하고 안경을 닦고서는 다시 읽는다. "제리"가 등장한다.]

제리	동물원에 갔다 왔어요. [피터는 눈치채지 못한다] 동물원에 갔다 왔다니까요. 여보, 동물원에 갔다 왔단 말이요
피터	응? — 뭐요? — 미안하오, 나한테 얘기했오?
제리	동물원에 갔었죠. 그리고선 걸어서 여기까지 왔지요. 내가 북쪽으로 걷고 있었던가요?
피터	[얼떨떨해서] 북쪽? 글쎄 — 응 그런 것 같군요. 어디 봅시다.
제리	[관객 뒤를 가리키며] 저것이 제5번가입니까?
피터	아 그럼, 그럼 맞았어요.
제리	그리구 저 네거리는 뭐죠? 왼쪽 바로 저거요.
피터	아 저거요? 아 그건 74번로.
제리	그럼 동물원은 65번로 근처니까. 그래 난 북쪽을 행해 걷고 있었군.
피터	[무척 그의 독서로 되돌아가고 싶어] 그래요, 그런 것 같군요.
제리	낯익은 좋은 북쪽이야.
피터	[반사적으로 가볍게] 하하.
제리	[잠시 쉬었다가] 그렇지만 정통 북쪽은 아니지.
피터	글쎄 — 정통 북쪽은 아니고 — 우린 북쪽이라 하죠. 북쪽 방향이죠.
제리	[자기를 보내고 저 마음 쓰는 피터가 파이프를 피울 차비를 하는 것을 바라보며] 근대 이 양반 가슴에 암이 생길려는 건 아닐 테죠?
피터	[약간 당황해서 위를 보며 이어 미소를 짓고] 천만에요. 이걸 피운다고 해서 그럴 리야.

제리	아니지, 아마 입에 암이 생길걸요. 그렇게 되면 "프로이트"가 한쪽 턱을 전부 뜯어 버렸을 때 덮었던 그 물건을 써야할 걸. 그걸 뭐라고 하죠?
피터	[불안하게] 보철 마스크 말이요?
제리	바로 그거지, 보철 마스크. 박식한 분이야. 그렇죠? 의사이신가요?
피터	오 아뇨. 어디서 읽었지. 타임 잡지에서 보았죠. [자기 책을 본다]
제리	그렇지, 타임지는 바보들이 볼 책은 아니야.
피터	네, 그럴 겁니다.
제리	[잠시 후] 참 저기가 5번가라니 잘됐어.
피터	[희미하게] 그래요.
제리	난 공원 서쪽은 싫단 말이야.
피터	그래요? [이어 약간 귀찮으면서도 관심이 있어] 왜요?
제리	[당장] 모르겠어.
피터	오 [다시 책으로 되돌아간다]
제리	[잠깐 일어서서 피터를 본다. 피터는 마침내 얼굴을 다시 올리고 당황해 한다] 좀 얘기해도 괜찮소?
피터	[분명 귀찮으면서도] 아뇨. 천만에, 천만에.
제리	귀찮군요. 그렇죠?
피터	[책은 도로 놓고 파이프를 입에서 꺼내놓고 미소를 지으며] 아뇨, 참말입니다. 괜찮아요.
제리	분명 귀찮을 거야.
피터	[마침내 단호하게] 아뇨, 참말이지 괜찮습니다.
제리	참… 좋은 날씨군요.
피터	[불필요한 하늘을 물끄러미 쳐다보며] 그래요, 그래. 참 좋군요.
제리	동물원에 갔다 왔죠.
피터	그래요, 그렇게 얘기했었던 같은데 — 안했어요?
제리	오늘밤 텔레비전에서는 못 볼지 모르겠지만 내일 아침 신문에 보도될 겁니다. 텔레비전을 가지고 계신가요?
피터	아 그렇죠. 두 개 있습니다. 하나는 애들을 위해서요.
제리	결혼했군요.
피터	[흡족히 여겨 강조해서] 아 물론이죠.
제리	원, 그런 그게 법은 아닐 텐데.
피터	아니죠… 물론 법은 없지.
제리	부인도 있겠군요?
피터	[말이 거의 안 통함에 당황해서] 그래요.
제리	애들도 있겠구.
피터	네, 둘 있죠.

제리	사내아이?
피터	아뇨 계집애 — 둘 다 계집애지.
제리	그렇지만 사내를 원했겠지.
피터	글쎄 — 물론 모든 사람이 사내애를 원하지만 —
제리	[가볍게 희롱조로] 세상일이 그렇게 돼먹지가 않았단 말이죠?
피터	[귀찮다는 듯] 내가 그런 말을 하려던 것은 아니요.
제리	더 이상 애를 낳을 생각은 없겠군요. 그렇죠?
피터	[좀 냉담하게] 아니지, 더 이상 필요 없지. [다시 되돌아와 갑갑하게] 왜 그런 말을 하죠? 그런 걸 어떻게 알죠?
제리	글쎄 당신이 다리를 모아 앉는 태도라든가 당신의 음성에서 알 수 있죠. 혹은 맹랑하게 추측을 하고 있었는지도 모르고. 당신 부인이 원하던가요?
피터	[화가 치밀어] 그건 당신이 관여할 문제가 아니요. [침묵] 알겠어요? [제리는 머리를 끄덕인다. 피터는 진정된다] 글쎄 당신이 맞았어. 애가 더 이상 필요 없소.
제리	[부드럽게] 세상일이 그렇게 돼먹지 않으니까
피터	[용서하여] 그래요… 그럴 겁니다.
제리	자 그럼 또 무슨 말을?
피터	동물원에 대해서 하던 말… 내가 그걸 신문에서 읽느니 어디서 본다니 하던 —
제리	차차 얘기하지요. 좀 물어보아도 괜찮아요?
피터	아, 괜찮습니다.
제리	내 묻는 이유를 얘기하겠습니다. 전 많은 사람들한테 얘기를 안 합니다. 그저 맥주를 주게, 변소가 어디죠? 또는 그 프로그램이 몇 시에 시작되죠? 혹은 이 친구 손을 얌전히 두게 따위의 말 이외는 안 하거든요. 그저 이러한 정도의 말 뿐이죠.
피터	난 도저히 그게 —
제리	그렇지만 가끔 난 누구한테 진짜 얘기를 하고 싶을 때가 있어요. 어떤 사람을 사귀고 그분에 대해서 모든 것을 알고 싶고.
피터	[가볍게 웃으며 그렇지만 약간 불안해서] 그래서 오늘은 내가 당신의 미끼가 됐다는 말이군?
제리	이렇게 햇볕에 흠뻑 젖은 일요일 오후에 말이죠? 선량한 기혼자요 딸이 둘에 — 응 개도 있는 남자하고 얘기하는 것 보다 더 좋은 기회가 어디 있겠소? [피터는 머리를 흔든다] 아닌가요? 개가 두 마리 [피터는 다시 머리를 흔든다] 흠 개가 없군요 [피터는 슬프게 머리를 흔든다] 오 그것 안됐군. 그렇지만 당신은 동물적인 인간으로 뵈는데 고양이는요? [피터는 애처롭게 머리를 끄덕인다] 고양이라… 그렇지만 당신이 좋아한 것은 아닐 게라, 아니구 말구. 부인과 딸들이 원했겠군? [피터는 머리를 끄덕인다] 내가 더 알아야 할 사항은 없을까요?
피터	[목청을 가다듬어야 한다] 또… 잉꼬새가 두 마리 있지. 딸 하나에… 한 마리씩.
제리	새들이라.
피터	딸들이 우리에 넣어서 침실에 놓고 있지.
제리	병이 없는가요? 새들 말입니다.

피터	그렇지 않을걸요.
제리	그거 안됐군. 병이 있다면 새를 집안에 풀어 놓아주면 고양이라는 놈이 그걸 먹고 죽는 꼴을 볼 텐데. [피터는 잠시 멍청하게 보인다. 이어 웃는다] 그 외에 또 무엇이 있지? 그 큼직한 가족을 먹이기 위해 무슨 일을 하시죠?
피터	난... 흠... 난 조그만 출판사의... 지배인 직을 갖고 있소. 우린... 저... 교과서를 출판하는 거요.
제리	재미있겠는데, 참 좋군요. 얼마나 벌죠?
피터	[아직 유쾌해서] 자 이러지 마슈.
제리	자, 얼마지요?
피터	글쎄 일 년에 한 8천불 법니다. 그렇지만 한번에 40불 이상은 안 가지고 다니죠... 당신이... 노상강도 일런지는 몰라도... 하하하.
제리	[이 말은 묵살하고] 어디서 살죠? [피터는 언짢아한다.] 자 보세요. 난 주머니를 털지도 않을 것이므로 잉꼬새, 고양이, 또 당신의 딸들을 가로챌 생각은 없어요.
피터	[너무나 큰 소리로] 난 렉싱턴과 3번가 사이 74통로에서 사오.
제리	그리 살림이 힘들진 않겠죠, 그렇죠?
피터	어찌... 당신은... 글쎄... 대화를 잘 이끌어갈 줄 모르는군요. 그저 질문만 하는군. 난... 보통은 — 침묵을 지키는 성미인데 왜 거기에서 있기만 하오?
제리	좀 근처를 걸어 다니기 시작하겠어요. 그러다 어차피 앉게 되겠죠. [회상을 하며] 그 사람 얼굴에 나타난 표정을 볼 때까지 기다려요.
피터	뭐요? 누구의 얼굴? 이것 좀 봐요. 동물원에 무슨 일이 있는가요?
제리	[마음은 먼데 있으며] 뭐요?
피터	동물원, 동물원 말이요. 동물원에 대한 말이요
제리	동물원?
피터	벌써 대여섯 번 얘기 하고서도
제리	[아직도 마음은 먼데 있다 갑자기 제정신으로 돌아오며] 동물원이요? 아, 그렇지, 동물원. 여기에 오기 전에 거기 있었지. 내가 얘기했어. 근데 상류적 중류식 중류계급하고 하류적 상류식 중류계급 사이를 뭐라고 부릅니까?
피터	자, 노형. 나는...
제리	날 노형이라고 하지 마시오.
피터	[맥이 빠져] 내가 너무 선심을 썼는가? 그랬던 것 같아 미안하오. 그렇지만 이것 봐요. 그 계급에 대한 질문은 나를 당황하게 했단 말이요.
제리	그래, 당신은 당황하면 선심을 쓰게 되오?
피터	난... 가끔 내 자신을 옳게 표현 못하거든. [자기 자신에게 농담을 걸고자 한다.] 난 출판업 하지 저술을 하는 것이 아니니까
제리	[흥미가 있지만 농담을 할 기분은 아니다] 그럴 거라. 지금 선심을 받고 있다는 것이 사실이군.
피터	아, 이런. 그런 말 할 필요가 없소. [이쯤 되면 제리는 점차 증가되는 결단성과 권위를 갖고 무대의 여기저기를 걷기 시작한다. 그러나 개에 대한 긴 얘기가 멋있게 터져 나오기 위해 스스

로의 걸음거리에 장단을 맞춘다]

제리 좋죠. 당신이 좋아하는 작가가 누구죠? 보들레르하고 J.P. 마퀀드요?

피터 [신중하게] 글쎄, 참 많은 작가들을 좋아하죠. 난 비교적 — 이렇게 말해서 좋을지 모르겠지만... 보편적인 취미를 가지고 있습니다. 그 두 작가는 자기들 나름으로 훌륭하죠 [흥분을 하며] 보들레르는 물론... 응... 둘 중에선 훨씬 낫지. 그렇지만 마퀀드도... 우리... 응... 국가적인... 응... 지위를...

제리 그건 생략해 버리지.

피터 그거... 미안하오.

제리 오늘 내가 동물원에 가기 전에 뭣을 했는지 알아요? 워싱턴 스퀘어에서부터 5번가까지를 줄곧 걸었어요.

피터 오, 그럼 "그리니치 빌리지"에서 사는군요. [피터를 퍽 즐겁게 하는 상 싶다.]

제리 아뇨. 그렇잖아도 난 그리니치 빌리지까지 지하철을 탔어요. 그래야 5번가를 거쳐 동물원까지 걸을 수 있거든. 사람이 해야 할 일들 중의 하나지. 가끔 사람이란 짧은 거리를 옳게 되돌아오기 위해 퍽 긴 거리를 가야 하거든.

피터 [거의 암상부리며] 아, 난 당신이 그리니치 빌리지에 사는 줄 알았군.

제리 뭣 때문에 그러시죠? 그런 사실에서 무슨 의미를 찾아내려고요? 질서를 찾게요? 그 낡아빠진 논리를 추려낼려고, 글쎄 그건 쉬운 일이지. 내 얘기하지. "콜럼버스" 가와 "센트럴 파크" 중간에 있는 위쪽 "웨스트 사이드"의 4층 갈색 돌로 지은 하숙집에서 삽니다. 난 서쪽을 향한 뒤에 있는 꼭대기 층에서 살죠. 우스꽝스럽게 생긴 조그만 방인데 내 벽 한쪽은 마분지로 만들었어요. 이 마분지벽을 사이에 두고 저쪽에 또 하나의 우스꽝스런 방이 있는데 아마 옛날엔 이 두 방이 하나였었나 봐. 적기는 하지만 구태여 우스꽝스럽게 생기지는 않은 방이 있을 거란 말이야. 내 마분지벽 저쪽 방은 한 흑인이 빌려 쓰고 있는데, 이 친구는 늘 방문을 열어두거든. 늘은 아니지만, 하여튼 눈썹을 잡아 뜯을 때는 말이야. 불교도식의 정신통일법으로 눈썹을 잡아 뜯고 있는데 이 흑인은 보기 드물 정도의 썩은 이빨을 갖고 있지. 또한 보기 드물 정도로 일본식 옷을 걸치고 있는 이 친구는 이 옷을 홀에 있는 뒷간에 오고 갈 때 입고 다녀. 참 뒷간에 자주 드나들지, 부리나케 드나든단 말이요. 나에게 폐를 끼친 적이 없고 자기 방에 아무도 끌어들이지 않아. 그저 늘 눈썹이나 뜯고 일본 옷을 걸치고 뒷간에나 갈 뿐이고. 그리구 내가 사는 층에 있는 앞방들은 좀 큰 것 같아. 그렇지만 아직도 적은 폭이지. 한 방엔 푸에르토리코인의 가족들이 살고 있는데 남편, 아내, 그리고 애들이 몇 명 살지. 몇 명이 사는지는 모르지만 참 재미있게 놀더군. 또 하나의 방에도 누가 살고 있지만 누군지 모르겠어. 본적이 없거든. 한 번도, 여태껏 한 번도 말이야.

피터 [어색하게] 왜... 왜 거기서 살지요?

제리 [다시 마음은 먼데로 간다] 모르겠소.

피터 그리 좋은 곳 같지는 않은데... 당신이 사는 데가 말이요.

제리 아니지. "이스트" 70번가에 있는 좋은 하숙집은 못 되지. 그리구 또한 아내도 하나 없고 딸 둘, 고양이 두 마리, 잉꼬새 두 마리도 없어. 내가 가지고 있는 것이라고는 뒷간에서 쓰는 물건, 옷이 두 서너 벌, 요리용 철판, 이건 내가 갖고 있을 필요가 없지만, 그리구 아시겠지만 병마개도 딸 수 있는 깡통 따는 쇠 나이프, 포크가 두 개, 하나는 크고 또 하나는 작은 스푼이 둘,

	접시가 셋, 컵 하나, 받침접시, 유리컵, 그림이 없는 사진틀이 두 개, 여덟아홉 권의 책들, 보통 사이즈인 춘화가 그려 있는 트럼프, 치면 대문자 밖에 안 나오는 낡아빠진 웨스턴 유니온 사에서 나온 타이프라이터, 열쇠가 없는 탄탄한 상자... 그 속에 뭣이 들어 있더라...? 바윗돌? 바윗돌이? 몇 개... 내가 어렸을 때 해변가에서 주워 모은 파도에 둥글게 된 바윗돌들. 그 돌 밑엔... 눌려있는 편지들... 제발 제발식의 편지... 제발 왜 그 일을 안 해요. 제발 뭣 때문에 그런 짓을 했는가 말이요 식의 제발편지. 또 언제식의 편지도 있구. 언제 소식 전하겠어요? 언제 오겠어요? 이런 언제식 편지, 이런 것들은 비교적 최근에 온 편지들이지.
피터	[무뚝뚝하게 자기 신만 보고 있다] 그 그림이 없는 두 개의 틀 말인데...
제리	거기에 무슨 설명이 필요 있을라구? 인젠 알겠소? 그 틀에 넣을 사진이 없으니 말이요.
피터	양친이라든가... 글쎄 여자 친구라든가의 그림은 있을 텐데...
제리	당신은 퍽 착하군요. 또한 참말로 부러울 정도로 순진하고. 그렇지만 착하고 정다운 어머니와 착하고 정다운 아버지는 죽었어요... 알겠어요? — 마음이 그것 때문에 쓰라렸지... 참말이요. 그렇지만 말이요. 이 특별한 한 쌍은 지금 구름 위에서 희극을 벌이고 있는 판이지. 그러니 내가 어떻게 그림들을 깨끗하게 짜가지고 양친의 사진을 모셔볼 수 있담? 뿐인가요. 하기야 꼬집어 말하자면 그 착하고 정다운 어머니는 내가 열 살 반 때 착하고 정다운 아버지를 차버리고 도망쳤어. 어머니는 우리나라 남쪽의 각주를 전전하며 바람잡이 여행을 시작했지... 한 일년 동안을 줄곧... 가장 오래 사귄 동반자는... 다른 남자들 중에서 말이요... 수많은 다른 남자들 중에서는... "발리콘" 씨였어. 최소한 이것이 내 착하고 정다운 아버지가 남쪽으로 내려갔다 어머니의 몸뚱이를 끌고 되돌아 왔을 때 나한테 한 얘기였어. 어머니가 "앨라배마" 주에서 맥없이 자기 혼하고 이별했다는 소식을 들은 것은 크리스마스와 정초 사이 때의 일이었어. 혼이 없이 돌아오니 — 덜 환영받을 수밖에. 근데 어머니가 어떤 여자였던가 말이야? 바보지... 북쪽의 바보. 하여간 착하고 정다운 아버지는 이 일로 해서 2주일 동안이나 정초를 축하했단 말이야. 그러더니 시내 합승 비슷한 차를 타고 정면으로 충돌해 버렸어. 이리해서 내 가족은 깨끗이 사라진 셈이 됐어 그런데 아니지, 어머니의 여동생이 있었어. 죄도 짓지 않았고 술병 속에서 위안을 얻으려고 하지 않은 여자였어. 난 이 여자 신세를 졌는데 기억에 남는 건 이 여자는 모든 일을 시무룩하게 했다는 것뿐이야. 잠이나 자고 먹고 일하고 기도나 하고. 내가 고등학교를 졸업하는 날 오후에 자기 하숙집, 아니 그땐 내 하숙집이었는데, 하숙집 층계에서 떨어져 죽어 버렸어. 기가 막힌 중부 유럽식의 장난 같은 사실이지.
피터	아이 참, 아이 참.

Chapter 03 Dramas in the Exam

김수아 전공영어 | 영미문학 Reading for Literature II

1. Dramas in the Teacher Certification Exam (2021~2014)

기입형

01 Read the excerpt from a play and follow the directions. [2 points]　　(19-A-6)

> PARRITT: What do they do for a living?
> LARRY: As little as possible. Once in a while one of them makes a successful touch somewhere, and some of them get a few dollars a month from connections at home who pay it on condition they never come back. For the rest, they live on free lunch and their old friend, Harry Hope, who doesn't give a damn what anyone does or doesn't do, as long as he likes you.
> PARRITT: It must be a tough life.
> LARRY: It's not. Don't waste your pity. They wouldn't thank you for it. They manage to get drunk, by hook or crook, and keep their pipe dreams, and that's all they ask of life. I've never known more contented men. It isn't often that men attain the true goal of their heart's desire. The same applies to Harry himself and his two cronies at the far table. He's so satisfied with life he's never set foot out of this place since his wife died twenty years ago. He has no need of the outside world at all. This place has a fine trade from the Market people across the street and the waterfront workers, so in spite of Harry's thirst and his generous heart, he comes out even. He never worries in hard times because there's always old friends from the days when he was a jitney Tammany politician, and a friendly brewery to tide him over. Don't ask me what his two pals work at because they don't. Except at being his lifetime guests.

Complete the commentary below by filling in the blank with the TWO most appropriate consecutive words from the passage.

Commentary

The different types of characters mentioned in Larry and Parritt's conversation in Harry Hope's bar dwell on _____. They sentimentally reminisce about their glory days while loafing around doing nothing. It is self-delusion rather than self-knowledge that sustains them.

02 Read the passage and follow the directions. [2 points] (18-A-6)

A king. He waits. A musician enters.

King   : Ah. Didn't see you come in. You're a ... .
Composer : Bachweist, your Majesty.
King   : And what can you do for me?
Composer : I can make you immortal.
King   : Already been taken care of.
Composer : I can delight you.
King   : Kings don't delight, Bachweist, children delight.
Composer : I can carry you away on gossamer wings of melody.
King   : Bachweist, you better kneel down. [Bachweist does.] I'm not interested in your talent, man, it's peripheral to the real business of governing, or even living for that matter. Oh, it's useful with women, but my position is a stronger attraction than that. Only other musicians could possibly be interested in music in any meaningful way. And critics, of course, as a way of making a reputation. No, Bachweist, what I want from you is the following: a few ceremonial pieces on demand, hummable, naturally. A printable paragraph on my respect for and understanding of art. Some good groveling to make clear my position, and a resolute and articulated belief that you haven't been censored in anyway. Satire might sometime be a problem, Bachweist, but that's beyond the province of serious music, in any case.

Complete the commentary below by filling in the blank with the TWO most appropriate consecutive words from the passage.

The king is not satisfied with the composer's replies as to the possible services that he can offer. What is interesting, though, is the way the king clarifies his dissatisfaction. He has the composer "groveling" not just figuratively but also literally by commanding the composer to _____, a command that makes clear his "position."

03 Read the passage and write TWO consecutive words from the passage that show what Steve thinks psychoanalysis does. **2 points**   (16–A–4)

> HENRIETTA: It's like this, Mabel. You want something. You think you can't have it. You think it's wrong. So you try to think you don't want it. Your mind protects you — avoids pain — by refusing to think the forbidden thing. But it's there just the same. It stays there shut up in your unconscious mind, and it festers.
>
> STEVE: Sort of an ingrowing mental toenail.
>
> HENRIETTA: Precisely. The forbidden impulse is there full of energy which has simply got to do something. It breaks into your consciousness in disguise, masks itself in dreams, makes all sorts of trouble. In extreme cases it drives you insane.
>
> MABEL [*with a gesture of horror*]: Oh!
>
> HENRIETTA [*reassuring*]: But psychoanalysis has found out how to save us from that. It brings into consciousness the suppressed desire that was making all the trouble. Psychoanalysis is simply the latest scientific method of preventing and curing insanity.
>
> STEVE [*from his table*]: It is also the latest scientific method of separating families.
>
> HENRIETTA [*mildly*]: Families that ought to be separated.
>
> STEVE: The Dwights, for instance. You must have met them, Mabel, when you were here before. Helen was living, apparently, in peace and happiness with good old Joe. Well — she went to this psychoanalyzer — she was "psyched," and biff! — bang! — home she comes with an unsuppressed desire to leave her husband. [*He starts work, drawing lines on a drawing board with a T-square.*]
>
> MABEL: How terrible! Yes, I remember Helen Dwight. But — but did she have such a desire?
>
> STEVE: First she'd known of it.
>
> MABEL: And she *left* him?
>
> HENRIETTA [*cooly*]: Yes, she did.
>
> MABEL: Wasn't he good to her?
>
> HENRIETTA: Why, yes, good enough.
>
> MABEL: Wasn't he kind to her?
>
> HENRIETTA: Oh, yes — kind to her.
>
> MABEL: And she left her good, kind husband — !

HENRIETTA: Oh, Mabel! "Left her good, kind husband!" How naive — forgive me, dear, but how bourgeois you are! She came to know herself. And she had the courage!

MABEL: I may be very naive and — bourgeois — but I don't see the good of a new science that breaks up homes.

[STEVE *applauds*.]

04 Read the excerpt from a play and follow the directions. [2 points] (15–A–9)

[PETER reacts scoffingly.]

Jerry: Yes, Peter; friend. That's the only word for it. I was heart-shatteringly et cetera to confront my doggy friend again. I came in the door and advanced, unafraid, to the center of the entrance hall. The beast was there . . . looking at me. And, you know, he looked better for his scrape with the nevermind. I stopped; I looked at him; he looked at me. I think . . . I think we stayed a long time that way . . . still, stone-statue . . . just looking at one another. I looked more into his face than he looked into mine. I mean, I can concentrate longer at looking into a dog's face than a dog can concentrate at looking into mine, or into anybody else's face, for that matter. But during that twenty seconds or two hours that we looked into each other's face, we made contact. Now, here is what I had wanted to happen: I loved the dog now, and I wanted him to love me. I had tried to love, and I had tried to kill, and both had been unsuccessful by themselves. I hoped . . . and I don't really know why I expected the dog to understand anything, much less my motivations . . . I hoped that the dog would understand. [PETER *seems to be hypnotized.*] It's just . . . it's just that . . . [JERRY *is abnormally tense, now.*] . . . it's just that if you can't deal with people, you have to make a start somewhere. WITH ANIMALS! [*Much faster now, and like a conspirator*] Don't you see? A person has to have some way of dealing with SOMETHING. If not with people . . . SOMETHING. . . . A dog. It seemed like a perfectly sensible idea. Man is a dog's best friend, remember. So: the dog and I looked at each other. I longer than the dog. And what I saw then has been the same ever since. Whenever the dog and I see each other we both stop where we are. The dog and I have attained a compromise; more of a bargain, really. We neither love nor hurt because we do not try to reach each other. And, *was* trying to feed the dog an act of love? And, perhaps, was the dog's attempt to bite me not an act of love? If we can so misunderstand, well then, why have we invented the word love in the first place?

[*There is silence.* JERRY *moves to Peter's bench and sits down beside him. This is the first time Jerry has sat down during the play.*]

The Story of Jerry and the Dog: the end.

[PETER *is silent.*]

Complete the commentary by filling in the blank with TWO consecutive words from the excerpt. Change the word form(s) if necessary.

Commentary

Jerry is desperate to have a meaningful conversation with Peter who lives in ignorance of the world outside his settled life. Jerry starts to with an animal first _____ in order to deal with Peter.

서술형

01 Read the excerpt from a play and follow the directions. `4 points`   (21-B-3)

> [MRS. DRUDGE's *approach to* FELICITY *makes* FELICITY *jump to her feet* [. . .] *She goes to the radio while* MAGNUS *declines his biscuit, and* MRS. DRUDGE *leaves.*]
>
> RADIO : We interrupt our programme for a special police message. The search for the dangerous madman who is on the loose in Essex has now narrowed to the immediate vicinity of Muldoon Manor. Police are hampered by the deadly swamps and the fog, but believe that the madman spent last night in a deserted cottage on the cliffs. The public is advised to stick together and make sure none of their number is missing. That is the end of the police message.
>
> [FELICITY *turns off the radio nervously. Pause.*]
>
> CYNTHIA: Where's Simon?
>
> FELICITY: Who?
>
> CYNTHIA: Simon. Have you seen him?
>
> FELICITY: No.
>
> CYNTHIA: Have you, Magnus?
>
> MAGNUS: No.
>
> CYNTHIA: Oh.
>
> FELICITY: Yes, there's something foreboding in the air, it is as if one of *us*—
>
> CYNTHIA: Oh, Felicity, the house is locked up tight—no one can get in—and the police are practically on the doorstep.
>
> FELICITY: I don't know—it's just a feeling.
>
> CYNTHIA: It's only the fog.
>
> MAGNUS: Hound will never get through on a day like this.
>
> CYNTHIA: [*shouting at him*] Fog!
>
> FELICITY: He means the Inspector.
>
> CYNTHIA: Is he bringing a dog?
>
> FELICITY: Not that I know of.

MAGNUS: —never get through the swamps. Yes, I'm afraid the madman can show his hand in safety now.

　　　　　[*A mournful baying hooting is heard in the distance, scary.*]

CYNTHIA: What's that?!

FELICITY: [*tensely*] It sounded like the cry of a gigantic hound!

MAGNUS: Poor devil!

CYNTHIA: Ssssh!

　　　　　[*They listen. The sound is repeated, nearer.*]

FELICITY: There it is again!

CYNTHIA: It's coming this way—it's right outside the house!

　　　　　[MRS. DRUDGE *enters.*]

MRS. DRUDGE : Inspector Hound!

CYNTHIA : A police dog?

　　　　　[*Enter* INSPECTOR HOUND. *On his feet are his swamp boots. These are two inflatable—and inflated—pontoons with flat bottoms about two feet across. He carries a foghorn.*]

HOUND : Lady Muldoon?

Complete the commentary below by filling in the blank with the ONE most appropriate word from the excerpt. Then, identify what Cynthia and Felicity think the underlined part is, respectively.

Commentary

As the residents of Muldoon Manor hear the special police message about a dangerous madman possibly lurking nearby, a sense of _____ that their safety may be at risk arises.

02. Read the excerpt from a play and follow the directions. **4 points** (20–B–11)

The sappers* have already mapped most of the area. YOLLAND's official task, which OWEN is now doing, is to take [. . .] —every hill, stream, rock, even every patch of ground which possessed its own distinctive Irish name —and Anglicize it, either by changing it into its approximate English sound or by translating it into English words. [. . .] OWEN's official function as translator is to pronounce each name in Irish and then provide the English translation.

OWEN: Now. Where have we got to? Yes — the point where that stream enters the sea — that tiny little beach there. George!

YOLLAND: Yes. I'm listening. What do you call it? Say the Irish name again?

OWEN: Bun na hAbhann.

YOLLAND: Again.

OWEN: Bun na hAbhann.

YOLLAND: Bun na hAbhann.

OWEN: That's terrible, George.

YOLLAND: I know. I'm sorry. Say it again.

OWEN: Bun na hAbhann.

YOLLAND: Bun na hAbhann.

OWEN: That's better. Bun is the Irish word for bottom. And Abha means river. So it's literally the mouth of the river.

YOLLAND: Let's leave it alone. There's no English equivalent for a sound like that.

OWEN: What is it called in the church registry?

[*Only now does* YOLLAND *open his eyes.*]

YOLLAND: Let's see . . . Banowen.

OWEN: That's wrong. [Consults text.] The list of freeholders calls it Owenmore — that's completely wrong: [. . .] And in the grand jury lists it's called — God! — Binhone! — wherever they got that. I suppose we could Anglicize it to Bunowen; but somehow that's neither fish nor flesh.

[YOLLAND *closes his eyes again.*]

YOLLAND: I give up.

OWEN: [*At map.*] Back to first principles. What are we trying to do?

YOLLAND: Good question.

OWEN: We are trying to denominate and at the same time describe that tiny area of soggy, rocky, sandy ground where that little stream enters the sea, an area known locally as Bun na hAbhann . . . Burnfoot! What about Burnfoot!

YOLLAND: [*Indifferently*.] Good, Roland. Burnfoot's good.

OWEN: George, my name isn't . . .

YOLLAND: B-u-r-n-f-o-o-t?

OWEN: I suppose so. What do you think?

YOLLAND: Yes.

OWEN: Are you happy with that?

YOLLAND: Yes.

OWEN: Burnfoot it is then. [He makes the entry into the Name-Book.] [. . .]

YOLLAND: You're becoming very skilled at this.

OWEN: We're not moving fast enough.

YOLLAND: [*Opens eyes again*.] Lancey lectured me again last night.

OWEN: When does he finish here?

YOLLAND: The sappers are pulling out at the end of the week. The trouble is, the maps they've completed can't be printed without these names. So London screams at Lancey and Lancey screams at me. But I wasn't intimidated. [. . .] 'I'm sorry, sir,' I said, 'But certain tasks demand their own tempo. You cannot rename a whole country overnight.' Your Irish air has made me bold.

* Soldiers whose job involves digging, building, and map-making

Complete the commentary below by filling in the blank with the ONE most appropriate word from the excerpt. Then, regarding the underlined part, explain what Owen thinks of the word "Bunowen."

Commentary

Yolland has been commissioned to remap Ireland with Anglicized place-names. For some reason, however, he shows little concern about finishing the mission on time. He even ignores his superior officer Lancey's order to increase his _____ .

03 Read the passage and follow the directions. 4 points   (17-A-11)

> *(Sitting weakly in the wheelchair, Vivian recites a poem and continues with a monologue.)*
>
> **Vivian:**
>
> This is my playes last scene, here heavens appoint
> My pilgrimages last mile; and my race
> Idly, yet quickly runne, hath this last pace,
> My spans last inch, my minutes last point,
> And gluttonous death will instantly unjoynt
> My body, 'and soule
>
> John Donne. 1609.
>
> I have always particularly liked that poem. In the abstract. Now I find the image of "my minute's last point" a little too, shall we say, *pointed*.
>
> I don't mean to complain, but I am becoming very sick. Very, very sick. Ultimately sick, as it were.
>
> In everything I have done, I have been steadfast, resolute — some would say in the extreme. Now, as you can see, I am distinguishing myself in illness.
>
> I have survived eight treatments of Hexamethophosphacil and Vinplatin at the *full* dose, ladies and gentlemen. I have broken the record. I have become something of a celebrity. Jason Posner is simply delighted. I think he foresees celebrity status for himself upon the appearance of the medical journal article he will no doubt write about *me*.
>
> But I flatter myself. The article will not be about me. It will be about my ovaries, which, despite his best intentions, are now crawling with cancer.
>
> What we have come to think of as *me* is, in fact, just the specimen jar, just the dust jacket, just the white piece of paper that bears the little black marks.

Based on the passage, explain what makes Vivian feel personal about John Donne's poem cited in her monologue. Then, based on the passage, identify Jason Posner's occupation.

Answer Keys for Chapter 03: Dramas in the Teacher Certification Exam

기입형

1. pipe dreams
2. kneel down
3. separating families
4. make contact

서술형

1. First, the word is 'foreboding.' Second, Cynthia thinks 'hound' as a dog that the Inspector will be bringing while Felicity thinks it as the Inspector, Hound.

2. The word is 'tempo.' Owen thinks the word "Bunowen" is not a appropriate translation. To explain, 'Bunowen' is a mixture of words that do not make sense altogether in either Irish or English like 'Owenmore' and 'Binhone.' So, Owen comes up with another word like "Burnfoot" by conjoining two complete and meaningful English words.

3. Vivian feels personal about John Donne's poem because the metaphors of death in the poem represent what she feels now. In the poem, metaphors such as "my playes last scene" and "My pilgrimages last mile" imply the speaker's upcoming death. Likewise, she reflects on her own condition as "ultimately sick" to death. Jason Posner's occupation is a doctor.

Chapter 04 Dramas in the Mock-Exam by Task

김수아 전공영어 | 영미문학 Reading for Literature II

1. Theme

01 Read the passage and follow the directions. `2 points`

> PROCTOR: I have three children—how may I teach them to walk like men in the world, and I sold my friends?
>
> DANFORTH: You have not sold your friends—
>
> PROCTOR: Beguile me not! I blacken all of them when this is nailed to the church the very day they hang for silence!
>
> DANFORTH: Mr. Proctor, I must have good and legal proof that you—
>
> PROCTOR: You are the high court, your word is good enough! Tell them I confessed myself; say Proctor broke his knees and wept like a woman; say what you will, but my name cannot—
>
> DANFORTH, *with suspicion*: It is the same, is it not? If I report it or you sign to it?
>
> PROCTOR, *he knows it is insane*: No, it is not the same! What others say and what I sign to is not the same!
>
> DANFORTH: Why? Do you mean to deny this confession when you are free?
>
> PROCTOR: I mean to deny nothing!
>
> DANFORTH: Then explain to me, Mr. Proctor, why you will not let—
>
> PROCTOR, *with a cry of his whole soul*: Because it is my name! Because I cannot have another in my life! Because I lie and sign myself to lies! Because I am not worth the dust on the feet of them that hang! How may I live without my name? I have given you my soul; leave me my name!
>
> DANFORTH, *pointing at the confession in Proctor's hand*: Is that document a lie? If it is a lie I will not accept it! What say you? I will not deal in lies, Mister! (*Proctor is motionless.*) You will give me your honest confession in my hand, or I cannot keep you from the rope. *Proctor does not reply.* Which way do you go, Mister?

Complete the commentary below with the ONE most appropriate word from the passage.

> **Commentary**
>
> Danforth's notion of justice is patently absurd. He realizes that Proctor's _____ is a lie—but without it, he cannot spare Proctor's life. Justice is hung by its own faulty legal reasoning.

02 Read the passage and follow the directions. [2 points]

> VLADIMIR: Let's wait till we know exactly how we stand.
> ESTRAGON: On the other hand it might be better to strike the iron before it freezes.
> VLADIMIR: I'm curious to hear what he has to offer. Then we'll take it or leave it.
> ESTRAGON: What exactly did we ask him for?
> VLADIMIR: Were you not there?
> ESTRAGON: I can't have been listening.
> VLADIMIR: Oh . . . Nothing very definite.
> ESTRAGON: A kind of prayer.
> VLADIMIR: Precisely.
> ESTRAGON: A vague supplication.
> VLADIMIR: Exactly.
> ESTRAGON: And what did he reply?
> VLADIMIR: That he'd see.
> ESTRAGON: That he couldn't promise anything.
> VLADIMIR: That he'd have to think it over.
> ESTRAGON: In the quiet of his home.
> VLADIMIR: Consult his family.
> ESTRAGON: His friends.
> VLADIMIR: His agents.
> ESTRAGON: His correspondents.
> VLADIMIR: His books.
> ESTRAGON: His bank account.
> VLADIMIR: Before taking a decision.
> ESTRAGON: It's the normal thing.

Complete the commentary by filling in the blank with the ONE most appropriate word from the passage. Change the form if necessary.

Commentary

The characters fail to realize that the very act of _____ is a choice; instead, they view it as a mandatory part of their daily routine. Even when these men manage to make a conscious decision, they can't translate that mental choice into a physical act.

03 Read the poem and follow the directions. **2 points**

> LENA: Son—how come you talk so much 'bout money?
>
> WALTER: (With immense passion) Because it is life, Mama!
>
> LENA: (Quietly) Oh—(Very quietly) So now it's life. Money is life. Once upon a time freedom used to be life—now it's money. I guess the world really do change …
>
> WALTER No—it was always money, Mama. We just didn't know about it.
>
> LENA: No … something has changed. (She looks at him) You something new, boy. In my time we was worried about not being lynched and getting to the North if we could and how to stay alive and still have a pinch of dignity too … Now here come you and Beneatha—talking 'bout things we ain't never even thought about hardly, me and your daddy. You ain't satisfied or proud of nothing we done. I mean that you had a home; that we kept you out of trouble till you was grown; that you don't have to ride to work on the back of nobody's streetcar—You my children—but how different we done become.
>
> WALTER: (A long beat. He pats her hand and gets up) You just don't understand, Mama, you just don't understand.

Complete the commentary below by filling in the blank with the ONE most appropriate word from the passage.

> Lena feels disconnected with her son because he is not so much more easily _____ than she is. From her perspective, he has a lot to be thankful for.

04 Read the passage and follow the directions. [2 points]

> JAMIE TYRONE: [His voice flutters.] I suppose I can't forgive mother—yet. It meant so much. I'd begun to hope, if she'd beaten the game, I could, too. [He begins to sob, and the horrible part of his weeping is that it appears sober, not the maudlin tears of drunkenness.]
>
> JAMIE TYRONE: [trying to control his sobs] I've known about her so much longer than you. Never forget the first time I got wise. Caught her in the act with a hypo. Christ, I'd never dreamed before that any women but whores took *dope! [He pauses.] And then this stuff of you getting consumption. It's got me licked. We've been more than brothers. You're the only pal I've ever had. I love your guts. I'd do anything for you.
>
> EDMUND TYRONE: [reaches out and pats his arm] I know that, Jamie.
>
> JAMIE TYRONE: No one is prouder you've started to make good, [drunkenly assertive] Why shouldn't I be proud? Hell, it's purely selfish. You reflect credit on me. I've had more to do with bringing you up than anyone I wised you up about women, so you'd never be a fall guy, or make any mistakes you didn't want to make! And who steered you on to reading poetry first? Swinburne, 26 for example? I did! And because I once wanted to write, I planted it in your mind that someday you'd write! Hell, you're more than my brother. I made you! You're my Frankenstein! [He has risen to a note of drunken arrogance, EDMUND is grinning with amusement now.]
>
> JAMIE TYRONE: All right, I'm your Frankenstein. So let's have a drink. [He laughs.] You crazy nut!
>
> • Dope is a drug, usually an illegal drug such as marijuana or cocaine.

Based on the passage, explain what makes Jamie thinks Edmund is his 'Frankenstein.' DO NOT copy more than FIVE consecutive words from the passage. Then, complete the commentary below by filling in the blank with the ONE most appropriate word from the passage.

> This passage gives us an angle on Jamie's suffering. In addition to finding out that Jamie thinks he has an addiction he wants to beat, we see that he was really counting on his _____ as a role model.

2. Plot

01 Read the passage and follow the directions. `2 points`

> Keller: (deeply touched) She cried hard?
>
> Chris: I could hear her right through the floor of my room.
>
> Keller: (after slight pause) What was she doing out here at that hour? (Chris silent. With an undertone of anger showing) She's dreaming about him again. She's walking around at night.
>
> Chris: I guess she is.
>
> Keller: She's getting just like after he died. (slight pause) What's the meaning of that?
>
> Chris: I don't know the meaning of it. (slight pause) But I know one thing, Dad. We've made a terrible mistake with Mother.
>
> Keller: What?
>
> Chris: Being dishonest with her. That kind of thing always pays off, and now it's paying off.
>
> Keller: What do you mean, dishonest?
>
> Chris: You know Larry's not coming back and I know it. Why do we allow her to go on thinking that we believe with her?
>
> Keller: What do you want to do, argue with her?
>
> Chris: I don't want to argue with her, but it's time she realized that nobody believes Larry is alive any more. (Keller simply moves away, thinking, looking at the ground) Why shouldn't she dream of him, walk the nights waiting for him? Do we say straight out that we have no hope any more?
>
> Keller: (frightened at the thought) You can't say that to her.
>
> Chris: We've got to say it to her.
>
> Keller: How're you going to prove it? Can you prove it?
>
> Chris: For God's sake, three years! Nobody comes back after three years. It's insane.

Complete the commentary below by filling in the blank with ONE most appropriate word from the passage.

We select things to focus on in life, but we also need to deny certain things in order to live well. All characters in the excerpt are in this state of self-deception: Mother denies Larry's death; Keller and Chris accept it but they willfully ignore the truth by being _____ to mother so that the family can continue to function in acceptable ways.

02 Read the passage and follow the directions. [2 points]

Eddie: (sitting at the table) What's all that about? Where's she goin'?

Beatrice: She's got a job.

Eddie: What job? She's gonna finish school.

Catherine: Listen a minute, it's wonderful.

Eddie: It's not wonderful. You'll never get nowheres unless you finish school. You can't take no job. Why didn't you ask me before you take a job?

Beatrice: She's askin' you now, she didn't take nothin' yet.

Eddie: What about all the stuff you wouldn't learn this year, though?

Catherine: There's nothin' more to learn, Eddie, I just gotta practice from now on. I know all the symbols and I know the keyboard. I'll just get faster, that's all. And when I'm workin' I'll keep gettin' better and better, you see?

Beatrice: Work is the best practice anyway.

Eddie: That ain't what I wanted, though.

Catherine: Why! It's a great big company.

Beatrice: She'll do great in the office, Eddie.

Eddie: I know, but that ain't what I had in mind.

Beatrice: (with sympathy but insistent force) Well, I don't understand when it ends. First it was gonna be when she graduated high school, so she graduated high school. Then it was gonna be when she learned stenographer, so she learned stenographer. So what're we gonna wait for now? I mean it, Eddie, sometimes I don't understand you; they picked her out of the whole class, it's an honor for her.

Complete the table below by filling in the blank with the TWO most appropriate consecutive words from the passage.

Setting	In the living room of Eddie's apartment
Character Relationship	Eddie is Catherine's uncle and Beatrice is Eddie's wife.
Conflict	Catherine wants to work, while Eddie wants her to _____ .

Answer Keys for Chapter 04 — Dramas in the Mock-Exam by Task

1. Theme

01 confession

Expressions & Vocabulary

beguile v. 구슬리다, (마음을) 끌다, 이끌다
absurd a. 불합리한, 모순된, 어리석은, 어처구니없는
patently adv. 명백히, 틀림없이

Sua TOKS!

Task

Theme, interpretation (15-A-9)

Drama – *The Crucible* by Arthur Miller

Organization-Keywords

PROCTOR: I have three children—how may I teach them to walk like men in the world, and I sold my friends?

DANFORTH: You have not sold your friends—

PROCTOR: Beguile me not! I blacken all of them when this is nailed to the church the very day they hang for silence!

DANFORTH: Mr. Proctor, I must have good and legal proof that you—

PROCTOR: You are the high court, your word is good enough! Tell them I **confessed** myself; say Proctor broke his knees and wept like a woman; say what you will, but my name cannot—

DANFORTH, *with suspicion*: It is the same, is it not? If I report it or you **sign to it**?

PROCTOR, *he knows it is insane*: No, it is not the same! What others say and **what I sign to** is not the same!

DANFORTH: Why? Do you mean to deny **this confession** when you are free?

PROCTOR: I mean to deny nothing!

DANFORTH: Then explain to me, Mr. Proctor, why you will not let—

PROCTOR, *with a cry of his whole soul*: Because it is my name! Because I cannot have another in my life! Because I **lie and sign myself to lies**! Because I am not worth the dust on the feet of them that hang! How may I **live without my name**? I have given you my soul; leave me my name!

DANFORTH, *pointing at the confession in Proctor's hand*: Is that document **a lie**? If it is a lie I will not accept it! What say you? I will not deal in lies, Mister! (*Proctor is motionless.*) You will give me your **honest confession** in my hand, or I cannot keep you from the rope. *Proctor does not reply.* Which way do you go, Mister?

Commentary

Danforth's notion of justice is patently absurd. He realizes that Proctor's **confession** is a **lie** — but without his **confession**, he cannot **spare Proctor's life**. Justice is hung by its own faulty legal reasoning.

Translation

프록터: 내게는 세 아이가 있습니다. 내가 내 친구들을 팔고 나서, 어떻게 아이들더러 사람답게 세상을 살아가라고 가르칠 수 있겠습니까?

댄포스: 당신이 친구들을 파는 것은 아니오.

프록터: 날 속이지 마시오! 내 친구들이 침묵의 대가로 교수형을 당하는 바로 그날 내 자백서가 교회 문에 못질되면 난 그들 모두를 더럽히는 것입니다!

댄포스: 프록터, 난 올바른 합법적 증거가 있어야만 하오. 당신이 ㅡ

프록터: 부지사님께서는 최고 재판관이십니다. 부지사님의 말이면 충분합니다! 그들에게 내가 자백했다고 말하십시오. 프록터가 무릎을 꿇고서 여자처럼 울었다고 전하십시오. 무엇이든 원하시는 대로 말하십시오. 그러나 내 이름만은 결코 ㅡ

댄포스(*의심스러워하며*): 그건 같은 것이오. 그렇지 않소? 내가 보고를 하거나 당신이 서명을 하거나.

프록터(*그는 이게 미친 짓이라는 걸 안다.*): 아뇨, 그건 같지 않습니다! 남들이 말하는 것과 내가 서명하는 것은 같지 않습니다!

댄포스: 어째서? 석방된 후에는 이 고백을 부인하겠다는 뜻이오?

프록터: 아무것도 부인하지 않습니다!

댄포스: 그렇다면, 내게 설명을 해 보시오. 프록터, 왜 당신이 거부하는지 ㅡ

프록터(*온 영혼을 다하여 외친다.*): 그것이 내 이름이기 때문입니다! 내 평생 또 다른 이름은 가질 수 없기 때문입니다! 나는 교수형을 당한 이들의 발바닥 먼지만큼도 가치가 없기 때문입니다! 내 이름이 없이 어떻게 살아갈 수가 있겠습니까? 난 당신에게 내 영혼을 주었습니다. 내 이름만은 나에게 남겨 주십시오!

댄포스(*프록터 손에 들린 자백서를 가리키면서*): 그 서류는 거짓말이오? 만약 거짓말이라면 난 그것을 받아들일 수 없소! 뭐라고 말하겠소? 나는 거짓말에는 관여하지 않겠소! 프록터! (*프록터, 꼼짝*

않고 있다.) 그대의 정직한 자백서를 내 손에 넘겨주지 않으면 나는 그대가 교수형에 처해지는 걸 막을 수 없소. (*프록터, 대답하지 않는다.*) 어느 쪽을 택하겠소, 프록터?

Commentary

댄포스가 가진 정의의 개념은 분명히 부조리하다. 그는 프록터의 고백이 거짓말이라는 것을 깨달았다. 그러나 그의 그 고백 없이는 프록터의 생명을 살릴 수가 없다. 정의는 스스로의 잘못된 법적 논리에 빠진 것이다.

Summary

- In Salem, Massachusetts in 1692, Puritan minister Reverend Parris finds a group of girls dancing naked in the forest. Among them are his niece Abigail and daughter Better, who faints upon being discovered by her father. Knowing that they've sinned, the girls claim they were bewitched.

- Given the severity of the claims, a special court is founded to investigate the accusations of witchcraft. Judges are sent from Boston to assist the residents of small town Salem. During the trials, the girls scream and faint whenever one of the supposed witches takes the stand.

- Over a hundred of Salem's citizens are found to be witches. One of them, Elizabeth Proctor, proclaims her innocence to her husband, John. Her accuser, Abigail, was once an employee and was dismissed after Elizabeth discovered that John and Abigail were having an affair.

- Realizing that Abigail has incited this witch hunt to target her enemies, John fights to save his wife. He admits his adultery, only to be accused of devil worship when Abigail denies the affair. John and Elizabeth are convicted of communing with the devil. The pregnant Elizabeth is spared, but John is hanged.

Themes

Hysteria costs innocent lives in The Crucible. Arthur Miller based the play on the historical Salem witch trials and drew inspiration from the second Red Scare, a period in United States history when Senator Joseph McCarthy falsely accused many citizens of having communist ties. Miller depicts how mass hysteria can destroy entire communities for no real reason.

In Miller's play, persecution becomes a tool to distract society from its real problems. By accusing others of witchcraft, Abigail and her friends shift blame for their own wrongdoing. This would not be necessary if they lived in a society where an institutionalized belief system such as Puritanism didn't repress its citizens, forcing them to lie when caught breaking the rules.

The Crucible is essentially a play about society: its pressures, its weaknesses, its tendency to ostracize and demonize those who aren't part of the status quo. Witch hunts like those in Salem prey on fear and ignorance, ultimately destroying societies from within by turning people against each other.

Characters

John Proctor, an innocent man accused of witchcraft by his former lover Abigail.

Elizabeth Proctor, John's wife, who is convicted of witchcraft but spared by the court when it's found that she's pregnant.

Abigail Williams, Reverend Parris' niece, who accuses John and Elizabeth of witchcraft as revenge for being fired.

Mary Warren, one of Abigail's friends, who tries to tell the truth.

Reverend Parris, who finds the group of girls dancing naked in the forest.

Tituba, a slave found dancing with the girls.

02 waiting

Expressions & Vocabulary

supplication n. 탄원, 애원

Sua TOKS!

Task

Theme, interpretation (15-A-9)

Drama – *Waiting for Godot* by Samuel Beckett

Organization-Keywords

VLADIMIR: **Let's wait till we know exactly how we stand.**

ESTRAGON: On the other hand **it might be better to strike the iron before it freezes.**

VLADIMIR: I'm curious to hear what he has to offer. Then **we'll take it or leave it.**

ESTRAGON: What exactly did we ask him for?

VLADIMIR: Were you not there?

ESTRAGON: I can't have been listening.

VLADIMIR: Oh . . . Nothing very definite.

ESTRAGON: A kind of prayer.

VLADIMIR: Precisely.

ESTRAGON: A **vague supplication**.

VLADIMIR: Exactly.

ESTRAGON: And what did he reply?

VLADIMIR: That he'd see.

ESTRAGON: That **he couldn't promise anything.**

VLADIMIR: That **he'd have to think it over.**

ESTRAGON: In the quiet of his home.

VLADIMIR: Consult his family.

ESTRAGON: His friends.

VLADIMIR: His agents.

ESTRAGON: His correspondents.

VLADIMIR: His books.

ESTRAGON: His bank account.

VLADIMIR: Before **taking a decision**.

ESTRAGON: **It's the normal thing.**

Commentary

The characters fail to realize that the very act of waiting is a choice; instead, they view it as a mandatory part of their daily routine. Even when these men manage to make a conscious decision, they can't translate that mental choice into a physical act.

Translation

블라디미르: 우리의 처지를 정확하게 알 수 있을 때까지 **기다리자구**.

에스트라공: 그 반대로 **쇠는 식기 전에 두드리는 게 좋다**는 말도 있잖아.

블라디미르: 그분이 뭐라고 할지 무척 기다려지는걸. 그때 가서 그분 말대로 **할 수도 있고 안할 수도 있는 거니까.**

에스트라공: 그 사람한테 요청했던 게 뭐였지?

블라디미르: 자네 그 자리에 없었나?

에스트라공: 나는 들을 수가 없었거든.

블라디미르: 아 ... 뭐 별것도 아니었어.

에스트라공: 일종의 기도였겠지.

블라디미르: 맞았어.

에스트라공: **막연한 애원**이랄까.

블라디미르: 바로 그거야.

에스트라공: 헌데 그는 뭐라고 대꾸하던가?

블라디미르: 두고보자더군.

에스트라공: 그러니까 **이렇다 할 약속은 없었구먼**.

블라디미르: 그분 역시 숙고해 봐야 한다니까.

에스트라공: 조용히 자기 집에 앉아서.

블라디미르: 자기 가족들과도 의논하고.

에스트라공: 친구들한테 자문도 구해야지.

블라디미르: 대리인들 말도 들어봐야지.

에스트라공: 특파원들과도 상의해야겠고.

블라디미르: 책도 떠들어봐야 될 테고.

에스트라공: 적금통장 사정도 고려해야지.

블라디미르: 그리고 나서 **결정을 내려야겠지**.

에스트라공: **보통 그렇게들 하니까.**

Commentary

등장인물들은 <u>기다리는</u> 바로 그 행동이 선택이라는 것을 깨닫지 못한다. 대신에 이들은 이것을 일상에서 의무적으로 해야 하는 것이라고 본다. 이 남자들이 겨우 의식적인 결정을 하지만, 그 정신적 선택을 실제적인 행동으로 바꾸지는 못한다.

Theme of Choices

Waiting for Godot consists of two men unable to act, move, or think in any significant way while they kill time waiting for a mysterious man, Godot. **The characters fail to realize that this very act of waiting is a choice; instead, they view it as a mandatory part of their daily routine.** Even when these men manage to make a conscious decision, they can't translate that mental choice into a physical act. They often "decide" to leave the stage, only to find that they are unable to move. Such inaction leads to stagnancy and repetition in the seemingly endless cycle of their lives.

03 satisfied

Expressions & Vocabulary

pinch n. 자밤(엄지와 검지의 두 손가락 끝으로 한 번 집을 만한 분량)

Sua TOKS!

Task

conflict, interpretation (18-A-6)

Drama − *A Raisin in the Sun* by Lorraine Hansberry

Keywords

LENA: Son─how come you talk so much 'bout money?

WALTER: (With immense passion) Because it is life, **Mama!**

LENA: (Quietly) Oh─(Very quietly) So now it's life. Money is life. Once upon a time freedom used to be life─now it's money. I guess the world really do change …

WALTER: No─it was always money, Mama. We just didn't know about it.

LENA: No … **something has changed.** (She looks at him) You something new, boy. **In my time** we was worried about not being lynched and getting to the North if we could and how to stay alive and still have a pinch of dignity too … **Now here** come you and Beneatha
─talking 'bout **things we ain't never even thought about hardly, me and your daddy. You ain't satisfied or proud of nothing we done.** I mean that you had a home; that we kept you out of trouble till you was grown; that you don't have to ride to work on the back of nobody's streetcar─You my children─but how different we done become.

WALTER: (A long beat. He pats her hand and gets up) **You just don't understand, Mama, you just don't understand.**

> **Lena** feels disconnected with her son because he is not so much more easily satisfied than she is. **From her perspective**, he has a lot to be thankful for.

Translation

레나: 애야 — 돈에 대해서 그토록 많이 말할 수 있지?

월터: (대단한 정열로) 그것이 인생이기 때문이에요, 어머니!

레나: (조용하게) 오 — (매우 조용하게) 이제 그게 인생이라. 돈이 삶이라. 옛날에는 자유가 삶이었단다 — 이젠 돈이야. 세상이 정말 바뀌고 있는 모양이구나…

월터: 아녜요 — 항상 돈이었어요, 어머니. 우리가 그저 모르고 있었을 뿐이죠.

레나: 아냐 … 뭔가 바뀌었어. 그녀가 그를 바라본다. 넌 뭔가 새롭구나, 애야.. 우리 시절에는 할 수만 있다면 린치를 당하지 않고 북부에 가는 것에 대해 걱정했었고 아직도 존엄성은 쥐꼬리만큼 밖에 안 되지… 이제 여기서 너와 베니사는 네 아빠나 나는 생각해본 적도 없던 것들을 이야기하고 있어. 넌 우리가 한 일에 만족하지도 자랑스러워하지도 않는구나. 내 말은 넌 가정이 있고; 네가 자랄 때까지 어려움에서 널 지켜주었어; 일터로 가려고 전차 뒤컨에 탈 필요도 없지 — 넌 내 자식이야 — 하지만 우린 달라졌구나.

월터: (긴 휴지. 그가 어머니의 손을 두드리고 일어난다) 어머니가 단지 이해하지 못하실 뿐이에요, 이해 못한다구요.

<1막 2장 中>

레나는 아들이 그녀만큼 쉽게 만족을 느끼지 않아서 그와 단절감을 느낀다. 그녀의 관점에서 볼 때, 그는 감사할 것이 많다.

Summary

The Youngers are a poor African American family living in the South Side of Chicago in the 1950s. Lena Younger, the matriarch of the family, receives a $10,000 insurance check when her husband dies. She wants to use the money to buy a house, but her son Walter has other ideas. Walter wants to invest the $10,000 in a liquor store. His sister, meanwhile, wants to use the money for medical school. Lena uses some of the money as a down payment on a new house, then entrusts the rest to Walter, reminding him of his sister's right to some of the insurance money. Walter loses the money entrusted to him. He makes a deal with the Clybourne Park Improvement Association, which intends to buy back Lena's new house in order to keep their neighborhood white. In the end, Walter refuses to sell the house, and the Youngers prepare to move to their new home.

Themes

A Raisin in the Sun is a play about the difficulty of following one's dreams. Its title is drawn from Langston Hughes' poem "Harlem," which famously asks, "What happens to a dream deferred?"

Generational tensions and ideological conflicts abound in this play. Lena's selfless desire to provide for her family stands in stark contrast to her children's more selfish concerns. Walter's cynicism conflicts with Lena's belief in hard work.

Race and racism are prominent themes in the play, as the family has to fight racial injustice in order to get ahead in life. When Lena puts a down payment on a house in a primarily white part of town, the neighborhood association tries to buy the house back in order to keep the Youngers out.

04 Jamie thinks Edmund is his 'Frankenstein' because he thinks he contributed most to Edmund's growth/success. In other words, he believes that he taught Edmund about women not to make a mistake, about reading poetry for the first time, and about writing. The word is 'mother.'

Expressions & Vocabulary

hypo n. 피하 주사기, 피하 주사   consumption n. (구식) 폐결핵 (유의어 tuberculosis)

Sua TOKS!

Task

Theme, interpretation (17-A-11)

Drama – *Long Day's Journey Into Night* by Eugene O'Neil

Organization

1. Explaining what makes Jamie thinks Edmund is his 'Frankenstein.' 3points

- Jamie thinks Edmund is his 'Frankenstein' because ~
- This is because ~
- That is/In other words/To be specific, ~

2. Completing the commentary with the ONE word. 1points

- The word is '_____.'

Keywords

JAMIE TYRONE: [His voice flutters.] I suppose I can't forgive **mother**— yet. **It meant so much.** I'd begun to hope, **if she'd beaten the game, I could, too.** [He begins to sob, and the horrible part of his weeping is that i**t appears sober,** not the maudlin tears of **drunkenness**.]

JAMIE TYRONE: [trying to control his sobs] **I've known about her so much longer than you.** Never forget the first time I got wise. Caught her in **the act with a hypo.** Christ, I'd never dreamed before that any women but whores took *dope! [He pauses.] And then this stuff of you getting **consumption**. It's got me licked. **We've been more than brothers. You're the only pal I've ever had. I love your guts. I'd do anything for you.**

EDMUND TYRONE: [reaches out and pats his arm] I know that, Jamie.

JAMIE TYRONE: **No one is prouder you've started to make good**, [drunkenly assertive] Why shouldn't I be proud? Hell, it's purely selfish. You reflect credit on me. **I've had more** to do with bringing you up than anyone. I wised you up about women, so you'd never be a fall guy, or make any mistakes you didn't want to make! And who steered you on to reading poetry first? Swinburne, for example? I did! And because I once wanted to write, I planted it in your mind that someday you'd write! Hell, you're more than my brother. I made you! You're my Frankenstein! [He has risen to a note of drunken arrogance, EDMUND is grinning with amusement now.]

JAMIE TYRONE: All right, I'm your Frankenstein. So let's have a drink. [He laughs.] You crazy nut!

This passage gives us an angle on **Jamie's suffering**. In addition to finding out that Jamie thinks he has **an addiction he wants to beat**, we see that he was really counting on his mother as **a role model**.

Translation

제이미: (소리가 떨린다) 그러니까 아직 어머니를 용서할 기분이 안 돼. 나한테는 중대한 일이거든. 어머니가 이번에 이겨 내신다면 나도 이겨 낼 수 있다고 희망을 갖기 시작했어. (제이미, 흐느끼기 시작한다. 주정뱅이의 가식이 아닌 진짜 눈물인 것이다)

제이미: (눈을 깜박거려 눈물을 억제하고) 너보다는 내가 어머니를 잘 알아. 처음 눈치 챈 때를 잊어버릴 수가 없어. 피하 주사 놓으시는 현장을 봤거든. 창부 아닌 여자가 마약을 쓰다니 그 때까진 생각조차 해 본 일이 없어. (사이) 그런데 이번엔 네가 폐병이란 말이야. 난들 뭐가 그리 신이 나겠니. 우린 형제 이상으로 친하거든. 내 상대는 너밖에 없어. 난 네 용기가 좋아. 너를 위해서라면 무엇이든 할 생각이다.

에드먼드: (손을 내밀어 형의 팔을 가볍게 친다) 나도 알아요.

제이미: (혼란해져서-또다시 취기가 나타난다) 네 출발이 성공적이었다는 것은 누구보다도 내가 자랑하고 있어. (취중에 자기 말이 옳다는 듯이) 자랑해서 나쁠 게 뭐 있니? 아주 이기적인 얘기지. 네 덕택으로 나까지 신용이 붙었으니 말이다. 네 교육에 대해서는 누구보다도 내 힘이 크거든. 여자한테 걸려들지 않도록, 본의 아닌 실수를 하지 않도록 말이야. 여자에 대한 지식을 준 것도 내가 아니냐. 시 읽는 법을 가르쳐 준 건 누구냐? 처음에 스윈버언을 읽지 않았니? 바로 나란 말이야. 나도 시를 쓰고 싶었기 때문에 언제고 네가 쓸 수 있도록 가르친 거야. 넌 그냥 동생이 아니라니까. 넌 내가 만든 사람이야. 넌 나의 프랑켄쉬타인이야. (취기 가운데 점점 오만한 태도가 불어난다. 에드먼드는 아까부터 재미있다는 듯이 싱글싱글 웃고 있다)

에드먼드: 좋아요. 난 형님의 프랑켄쉬타인이야. 그러니 한 잔 합시다. (소리 내어 웃는다) 형도 돌았어!

이 지문은 우리가 제이미의 고통을 볼 수 있게 해준다. 제이미가 이겨내고 싶어 하는 중독이 있다는 것과 더불어, 그가 역할 모델로서 실제로 엄마를 의지했음을 알 수 있다.

Summary

This play portrays **a family in a ferociously negative light as the parents and two sons express accusations, blame, and resentments** — qualities which are often paired with pathetic and self-defeating attempts at affection, encouragement, tenderness, and yearnings for things to be otherwise. The pain of this family is made worse by their depth of self-understanding and self-analysis, combined with a brutal honesty, as they see it, and an ability to boldly express themselves. The story deals with the mother's addiction to morphine, the family's addiction to whiskey, the father's miserliness, the older brother's licentiousness, and younger brother's illness.

Theme of Family

The Tyrone family has **no strong parent figure to take responsibility** for the care of its members. Without supportive parents, **the children are left to look after themselves and their parents, and they're simply not cut out for the responsibility.**

Psychologists might say none of the Tyrones has **a good support network.** The father acts childishly most of the time, and the eldest son, at least, doesn't look up to him. This son, Jamie, is the character who requires the least caretaking, but that's really because both he and his parents think he's a lost cause. The younger son Edmund, meanwhile, is the sickly baby of the family. He's clearly the parents' favorite and can't seem to put his adult life in order. If you're looking for helpless characters, though, his mother gives Edmund a run for his money – she has to be coddled and protected from herself and the family's anger.

There's a weird vacuum, then, at the top of this family, with no respected leader and **lots of people who demand help and care.** The failure to take familial responsibility is a real problem in Long Day's Journey, **as none of the characters has anyone they feel they can turn to in times of need.**

Commentary

JAMIE I suppose I can't forgive her — yet. It meant so much. I'd begun to hope, if she'd beaten the game, I could, too. (4.1.92)

This passage gives us an angle on Jamie's suffering that we really didn't have before. In addition to finding out that Jamie thinks he has an addiction he wants to beat, we also discover that **he was really counting on his mother as a role model, and she let him down.** It's interesting to see Jamie admit that he hadn't completely forsaken his family and the idea that **his mother**

could be an inspiration to him. Now, though, it seems like all hope is lost.

JAMIE You reflect credit on me. I've had more to do with bringing you up than anyone […] Hell, you're more than my brother. I made you! You're my Frankenstein! (4.1.198)

After this passage, Jamie lists all the ways in which he helped Edmund growing up, and then on the next page, he lists all the ways in which he tried to **stunt Edmund's growth to make himself look better.** Whatever **Jamie** was planning to do, the fact of the matter is that he really was **a parental figure to Edmund,** since Mary was usually on morphine and James was rarely around. Most importantly, though, **Jamie was saddled with a role he clearly wasn't prepared for. The cycle of poor parenting,** which may have begun even before Mary and James's parents, goes on.

Synonyms

- 기여하다 (v)
  - contribute ~ (sth) to sth 기여하다, 이바지하다, ~(…의) 한 원인이 되다
  - provide ~ sth (for sb) 제공[공급]하다, 주다
  - attribute ~ sth to sth (~을 …의) 결과로[덕분으로] 보다
  - ascribe 〈원인·동기·기원 등을〉 …에 돌리다
  - donate (특히 자선단체에) 기부[기증]하다
  - (a) ascribable …에 돌릴 수 있는, …에 기인하는, …의 탓인 ((to))

- 생각하다 (v)
  - think 생각하다
  - ponder 숙고하다, 곰곰이[깊이] 생각하다
  - perceive 지각(知覺)하다, 감지(感知)하다, 인지[인식]하다, 눈치채다, 알아차리다
  - consider 고려하다, …으로 보다, 간주하다, 여기다
  - believe (…이라고) 생각하다, 여기다(suppose, think)
  - view …이라고 생각하다[간주하다], 판단하다; 고찰하다, 고려하다
  - regard …을 …으로 여기다
  - see 생각하다, 간주하다
  - rate …로 여기다, …이라고 생각하다
  - judge …이라고 판단하다, …이라고 생각하다
  - deem (…로) 여기다[생각하다]

2. Plot

01 dishonest

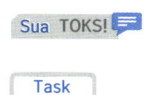

Conflict, Interpretation (18-A-6)(15-A-9)

Drama – *All My Sons* by Arthur Miller

Keller: (deeply touched) She cried hard?

Chris: I could hear her right through the floor of my room.

Keller: (after slight pause) What was she doing out here at that hour? (Chris silent. With an undertone of anger showing) She's dreaming about him again. She's walking around at night.

Chris: I guess she is.

Keller: She's getting just like **after he died.** (slight pause) What's the meaning of that?

Chris: I don't know the meaning of it. (slight pause) But I know one **thing, Dad. We've made a terrible mistake with Mother.**

Keller: What?

Chris: **Being dishonest with her.** That kind of thing always pays off, and now it's paying off.

Keller: **What do you mean, dishonest?**

Chris: You know Larry's not coming back and I know it. Why do we allow her to go on thinking that we believe with her?

Keller: What do you want to do, argue with her?

Chris: I don't want to argue with her, **but it's time she realized that nobody believes Larry is alive any more.** (Keller simply moves away, thinking, looking at the ground) Why shouldn't she dream of him, walk the nights waiting for him? **Do we say straight out that we have no hope any more?**

Keller: (frightened at the thought) You can't say that to her.

Chris: We've got to say it to her.

Keller: How're you going to prove it? Can you prove it?

Chris: For God's sake, three years! Nobody comes back after three years. It's insane.

We select things to focus on in life, but we also need to deny certain things in order to live well. All characters in the excerpt are in this state of self-deception. Mother denies Larry's death. Keller and Chris accept it but they willfully ignore the truth by being <u>dishonest</u> to mother so that the family can continue to function in acceptable ways.

Translation

[켈러] (몹시 마음이 상해서) 몹시 울던?

[크리스] 마루를 거쳐서 우리 방까지 들렸어요.

[켈러] (잠시 있다가) 아니 캄캄한 새벽에 여기서 무얼 했을까? (크리스도 대답이 없다) 약간 화가 난 듯한 음성으로 또 그 애 꿈을 꾸었나 보구나. 그래서 밤에는 그러고 돌아다니지.

[크리스] 그런가봐요.

[켈러] 그 애가 죽고 나서부터는 그 모양이란다. (잠간 쉬더니) 어쩌겠다는 거냐 그래?

[크리스] 저도 잘 모르죠. (잠시 말이 없다가) 그렇지만 저 한가진 알고 있어요. 아버지와 제가 어머니한테 큰 잘못을 저지르고 있어요.

[켈러] 뭐라고?

[크리스] 말하자면 정직하지 못하다는 거죠. 이런 일이란 언제나 청산이 되기 마련이니까요. 지금은 바로 그 청산이 되고 있는거죠.

[켈러] 정직하지 못하다니 그게 무슨 말이냐?

[크리스] 아버지도 아시겠지만 래리는 돌아오지 않아요. 전 그걸 알고 있어요. 그런데 왜 어머니에게 우리도 그 애가 돌아오리라고 믿고 있는 듯이 하고 있느냐는 겁니다.

[켈러] 그럼 네가 할려고 하는 것이 뭐냐? 아주 네 어머니하고 따질 셈이냐?

[크리스] 아-뇨. 그렇지만 이제는 어머니한테도 래리가 살아있다고 생각하는 사람은 아무도 없다는 걸 알려드려야 할 것 같아요. (켈러는 사색에 잠기어 땅바닥을 보며 몸을 돌린다) 어째서 어머니는 밤마다 그 애의 꿈을 꾸면서 기다려야 하느냐 말이예요? 아주 이젠 희망이 없다고 얘기를 해드릴까요?

[켈러] (놀라서) 아-니, 그런 말은 못한다.

[크리스] 그렇지만 이젠 해야되요.

[켈러] 그래 무슨 증거를 대겠니? 증거가 있니?

[크리스] 그렇지만 3년을 기다렸지 않아요? 3년이나 기다려서 안 오는 사람이 올 리가 만무예요. 그건 정신이상자나 생각할 일이예요.

우리는 인생에서 집중할 것들을 선택하지만, 우리는 또한 잘 살기 위해 어떤 것들은 거부하기도 한다. 위에 나오는 모든 인물들은 이런 자기기만 상태에 있다. 엄마는 래리의 죽음을 받아들이기를 거부한다. 켈러와 크리스는 그것을 받아들이지만 고의적으로 그 진실을 무시하고 엄마에게 정직하지 못함으로써 이 가족은 수용 가능한 방식으로 계속 유지될 수 있는 것이다.

Theme of Denial and Self-Deception

How do we deceive ourselves and others? We select things to focus on in life, but do we also need to deny certain things in order to live well? What toll does denial take on the psyche, the family, and society? Two main facts about the Keller family history must be confronted. One is Larry's death, and the other is Keller's responsibility for the shipment of defective parts. Mother denies the first while accepting the second, and Keller accepts the first while denying the second. The result is that both characters live in a state of self-deception, willfully ignoring one of the truths so that the family can continue to function in acceptable ways.

02   finish school

Expressions & Vocabulary

stenographer n. (특히 美) 속기사(速記士)

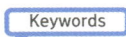

conflict, interpretation (18-A-6)(09-40)

Drama – *A View from the Bridge* by Arthur Miller

Keywords

Eddie: (sitting at the table) What's all that about? Where's she goin'?

Beatrice: She's **got a job.**

Eddie: What job? She's gonna **finish school.**

Catherine: Listen a minute, it's wonderful.

Eddie: It's not wonderful. You'll never get nowheres unless you finish school. You can't take no job. Why didn't you ask me before you **take a job?**

Beatrice: She's askin' you now, she didn't take nothin' yet.

Eddie: What about all the stuff you wouldn't learn this year, though?

Catherine: There's nothin' more to learn, Eddie, I just gotta practice from now on. I know all the symbols and I know the keyboard. I'll just get faster, that's all. And when I'm workin' I'll keep gettin' better and better, you see?

Beatrice: Work is the best practice anyway.

Eddie: That ain't what I wanted, though.

Catherine: Why! It's a great big company.

Beatrice: She'll do great in the office, Eddie.

Eddie: I know, **but that ain't what I had in mind.**

Beatrice: (with sympathy but insistent force) Well, I don't understand when it ends. First it was gonna be when she graduated high school, so she graduated high school. Then it was gonna be when she learned stenographer, so she learned stenographer. So what're we gonna wait for now? I mean it, Eddie, sometimes I don't understand you; they picked her out of the whole class, it's an honor for her.

배경	에디 아파트 거실
인물관계	에디는 캐서린의 외삼촌이고 베아트리체는 아내이다.
갈등	캐서린은 일하기를 원하고, 반면 에디는 그녀가 <u>학교를 마치기</u>를 원한다.

Translation

에디: (테이블에 앉으며) 대체 무슨 일이야? 그녀가 어디를 간다구?

베아트리체: **직장**을 얻었어요.

에디: 직장이라구? **학교를 마쳐야지.**

캐서린: 잠깐만, 이건 잘된 일이에요.

에디: 잘된 일이 아니야. **학교를 마치기 전에는 어디도 못 간다.** 직장에 갈 수 없어. 직장을 택하기 전에 왜 먼저 나한테 물어보지 않았지?

베아트리체: 지금 물어보고 있잖아요. 지금은 아무 **직장**도 택하지 않았어요.

에디: 올해 **배워야 할 것들**을 다 못 배우는 것은 어쩔테냐, 그러면?

캐서린: 더 배울 것은 없어요, 에디 삼촌. 지금부터 그냥 연습하면 되는 거예요. 모든 기호랑 자판을 다 알아요. 앞으로는 더 빨라지면 돼요, 그게 다예요. 게다가 일하고 있으면 점점 더 능숙해져요, 아시겠어요?

베아트리체: 어쨌든 **일**하는 게 가장 좋은 연습이지요.

에디: 그래도 그건 **내가 원하던 게 아니야.**

캐서린: 왜요! 아주 좋은 큰 **회사**예요.

베아트리체: 캐서린은 **직장**에서 잘 할거예요, 에디.

에디: 알아. 그렇지만 **내가 생각했던 게 아니라구.**

베아트리체: (동정하는 마음이 있지만 강하게 주장하며) 그런데 이게 언제 끝날지 난 모르겠네요. 처음엔 캐서린이 고등학교를 졸업하면 끝나겠지 했었는데, 그래서 고등학교를 졸업했어요. 그다음에는 속기를 배우면 끝나겠지 했었는데, 그렇게 속기를 다 배웠어요. 그런데도 지금 뭐를 더 기다려야 하는 거지요? 진심이에요, 에디, 어떤 때는 정말 당신을 이해하지 못하겠어요. 전 학급에서 캐서린이 선발됐어요. 캐서린에게는 영광스러운 일이에요.

Theme of Hopes and Dreams

Everything looks bright and sunny at the beginning of A View from the Bridge. A man's life's work is about to finally pay off. A young girl is about to embark on a new career. Two immigrants have come to live the American Dream. But, this is a tragedy. So, by the end of the play, most every beautiful thing they hoped for has been systematically destroyed.

> **Commentary**
>
> In Arthur Miller's A View From the Bridge, **Eddie's death** is made all the more tragic because it stems from his inability to understand – let alone articulate – his feelings.
>
> - **The play depicts the downfall and death of a decent man due to a fatal flaw**. While Eddie's incestuous desire for Catherine is the impetus of his downfall and the threat of **Rodolpho the catalyst, what ultimately causes his destruction is his inherent inability to understand or express what he feels.**
>
> - As a result Eddie suffers confusion and inner turmoil that lead to extreme overprotection of his niece, an intense hatred of Rodolpho, and problems within his own marital life.
>
> - All of these problems stem from **Eddie's inability to understand or express his feelings, and eventually they culminate in his death.**

Reading for Literature II

PART
03

Literary Terms

Chapter 01 — **Literary Terms**

Chapter 01 Literary Terms

01. Allegory

Allegory is a form of narrative that conveys a message or doctrine by using people, places, or things to stand for abstract ideas.

02. Alliteration

Repetition of consonant sounds in consecutive or neighboring words.

03. Allusion

An allusion is a brief reference to a person, place, or event (fictional or actual) that readers are expected to recognize. Like symbols and allegories, allusions enrich a work by introducing associations from another context.

04. Apostrophe

A poem's speaker addresses an absent person or thing — for example, a historical or literary figure or even an inanimate object or an abstract concept.

05. Asides

Comments to the audience in plays that other characters do not hear.

06. Assonance

Repetition of vowel sounds at the ends of words.

07. Blank verse

Unrhymed poetry with each line written in a set pattern of five stressed and five unstressed syllables called iambic pentameter.

08. Carpe diem theme

The belief that life is brief, so we must seize the day.

09. Connotation

Emotional associations that define your response. What a word suggests.

10. Consonance

Repetition of consonant sounds at the ends of words.

11. Couplet

A two-line stanza with rhyming lines of similar length and meter is called a couplet.

12. Denotations

What a word signifies without emotional associations, judgements, or opinions.

13. Dramatic Irony

Dramatic irony occurs when a narrator (or character) perceives less than readers do — when the main character see less than readers do.

14. Extended simile or metaphor

A single simile or metaphor is developed throughout a poem.

15. Figures of speech

Expressions that use words to achieve effects beyond the power of ordinary language.

16. Flashbacks

A flashback moves out of sequence to examine an event or situation that occurred before the time in which the story's action takes place. Flashbacks in dramas depict events that occurred before the play's main action. Dialogue can also summarize events that occurred earlier, thereby overcoming the limitations set by the chronological action on stage.

17. Foot

A group of syllables with a fixed pattern of stressed and unstressed syllables.

18. Foreshadowing

Dialogues in dramas can foreshadow, or look ahead to, future action. In many cases, seemingly unimportant comments have significance that becomes clear as the play develops.

19. Formal diction

It is characterized by a learned vocabulary and grammatically correct forms. In general, formal diction does not include colloquialisms, such as contractions and shortened word forms (*phone* for *telephone*).

20. Heroic Couplet

Heroic couplet, first used by Chaucer and especially popular throughout the eighteenth century, consists of two rhymed lines of iambic pentameter, with a weak pause after the first line and a strong pause after the second.

21. Hyperbole

Intentional exaggeration — saying more than is actually meant.

22. Imagery

Words or phrases that describe the sense; Language that evokes a physical sensation produced by one or more of the five senses — sight, hearing, taste, touch, smell.

23. Informal diction

It is the language closest to everyday conversation. It includes colloquialisms — contractions, shortened word forms, and the like — and may also include slang, regional expressions, and even nonstandard words.

24. Irony

A contradiction or discrepancy between two different levels of meaning.

25. Metaphor

An imaginative comparison between two unlike items that do not use *like* or *as* — that is, when it says "a *is* b" rather than "a *is like* b" — it is a metaphor.)

26. Meter

The recurrence of regular units of stressed and unstressed syllables. A stress (or accent) occurs when one syllable is emphasized more than another, unstressed, syllable.

27. Metonymy

The substitution of the name of one thing for the name of another thing that most readers associate with the first — for example, using hired gun to mean "paid assassin" or suits to mean "business executives."

28. Monologue

An extended speech by one character.

29. Onomatopoeia

It occurs when the sound of a word echoes its meaning, as it does in common words such as *bang, crash,* and *hiss*.

30. Open form

An open form poem may make occasional use of rhyme and meter but has no easily identifiable pattern or design: no conventional stanzaic divisions, no consistent metrical pattern or line length, no repeated rhyme scheme.

31. Oxymoron

An oxymoron puts together two seemingly contradictory words or phrases that actually end up making a whole lot of sense. For example, in "The jumbo shrimp she brought to the party was terribly good," "terribly good" means 'very good,' not 'terrible.'

A form of paradox where two contradictory terms are combined in one phrase.
Examples: cold fire, honest thief

32. Paradox

A statement that appears to be absurd, untrue, or contradictory, but may actually be true.
Example: From "Death, Be Not Proud, Though Some Have Called Thee"
"One short sleep past, we wake eternally, And death shall be no more; death, thou shalt die."
(John Donne)

33. Personification

A special kind of comparison, closely related to metaphor, that gives life or human characteristics to inanimate objects or abstract ideas.

34. Petrarchan sonnet

The Petrarchan sonnet, popularized in the fourteenth century by the Italian poet Francesco Petrarch, also consists of fourteen lines of iambic pentameter, but these lines are divided into an eight-line unit called an octave and a six-line unit (composed of two tercets) called a sestet. The rhyme scheme of the octave is *abba abba;* the rhyme scheme of the sestet is *cde cde.*

35. Plot

Plot is more than "what happens"; it is how what happens is revealed, the way in which a story's events are arranged. Plot is shaped by causal connections — historical, social, and personal — by the interaction between characters, and by the juxtaposition of events.

36. Shakespearean sonnet

The English or Shakespearean sonnet, which consists of fourteen lines divided into three quatrains and a concluding couplet, is written in **iambic pentameter** and follows the rhyme scheme *abab cdcd efef gg.*

37. Simile

A comparison between two unlike items that uses *like* or *as.*

38. Situational Irony

Situational irony occurs when what happens is at odds with what readers are led to expect — when the situation itself contradicts readers' expectations.

39. Soliloquies

A monologue revealing a character's thoughts and feelings, directed at the audience and presumed not to be heard by other characters.

40. Spencerian sonnet

A sonnet form composed of three quatrains and a couplet in **iambic pentameter** with the rhyme scheme *abab bcbc cdcd ee.*

41. Stage directions

Notes that comment on the scenery, the movements of the performers, the lighting, and the placement of props in dramas.

42. Stanza

A group of two or more lines with the same metrical pattern — and often with a regular rhyme scheme as well — separated by blank space from other such groups of lines. Stanzas in poetry are like paragraphs in prose: they group related ideas into units.

43. Symbol

A symbol is an idea or image that suggests something else and transcends its literal, or denotative, meaning in a complex way. Symbol is using an object or action that means something more than its literal meaning. A symbol enables the poet to enrich a poem by giving it additional layers of meaning often recognized by its prominence or repetition.

44. Synecdoche

A specific kind of metonymy. The substitution of a part for the whole. For example, using bread — as in "Give us this day our daily bread" — to mean "food".

Or the substitution of the whole for a part. For example, saying "You can take the boy out of Brooklyn, but you can't take Brooklyn [meaning its distinctive traits] out of the boy".

45. Tone

The tone of a poem conveys the speaker's attitude toward his or her subject or audience. Tone in novels and dramas reveals a character's mood or attitude. Tone can be flat or emotional, bitter or accepting, affectionate or aloof, anxious or calm.

46. Understatement

The opposite to hyperbole — saying less than it meant.

47. Verbal Irony

A contradiction between what a narrator (or speaker or character) says and what he or she means. Verbal irony occurs when the narrator says one thing but actually means another. When verbal irony is particularly biting, it is called **sarcasm**.

김수아 영미문학 Reading for Literature II

ISBN 979-11-91391-24-4

- 발행일 · 2021년 2月 19日 초판 1쇄
- 발행인 · 이용중
- 저 자 · 김수아
- 발행처 · 도서출판 배움
- 주 소 · 서울시 영등포구 영등포로 400 신성빌딩 2층 (신길동)
- 주문 및 배본처 · Tel : 02) 813-5334 Fax : 02) 814-5334

저자와의
협의하에
인지생략

본서의 無斷轉載·複製를 禁함. 본서의 무단 전재·복제행위는 저작권법 제136조에 의거 5년 이하의 징역 또는 5,000만 원 이하의 벌금에 처하거나 이를 병과할 수 있습니다. 파본은 구입처에서 교환하시기 바랍니다.

정가 27,000 원